Introduction to

Early Childhood Education

Second Canadian Edition

Eva Essa
University of Nevada (Reno)

Rosemary Young
Brock University

Lori Lehne
Brock University

 I(T)P Nelson

an International Thomson Publishing company

Toronto • Albany • Bonn • Boston • Cincinnati • Detroit • London • Madrid • Melbourne
• Mexico City • New York • Pacific Grove • Paris • San Francisco • Singapore • Tokyo • Washington

I(T)P™
International Thomson Publishing
The ITP logo is a trademark under licence

Published in 1998 by
I(T)P Nelson
A division of Thomson Canada Limited
1120 Birchmount Road
Scarborough, Ontario M1K 5G4

Cover photo: Ken Fisher / Tony Stone Images

Canadian Cataloguing in Publication Data
Essa, Eva
   Introduction to early childhood education

2nd Canadian ed.
Previous ed. written by Rosemary Young.
Includes bibliographical references and index.
ISBN 0-17-607348-5

1. Early childhood education—Canada. I. Lehne, Lori. II. Young, Rosemary Elaine. Introduction to early childhood education. III. Title.

LB1139.3.C3Y685 1998   372.21'0971   C98–930104-4

Publisher and Team Leader   Michael Young
Executive Editor   Charlotte Forbes
Project Editor   Evan Turner
Senior Production Editor   Bob Kohlmeier
Production Coordinator   Brad Horning
Cover Design and Interior Design   Suzanne Peden
Composition   Bookman Typesetting Co.
                                          and Daryn DeWalt

Printed and bound in Canada
  2 3 4 (WC) 01 00

To the child in each of us

Brief Contents

Contents

Chapter 7   Appropriate Practices in Early Childhood Education   265

List of Exhibits

Preface

Welcome.

Of all the career choices available to you, you chose early childhood education. In doing so you have made a personal and professional commitment to the lives of children.

Of all the choices available to *us,* we have chosen you as the caregiver for our children. In doing so we have made a personal and professional investment in the lives of our children.

You depend on us to understand and support you in your efforts. We trust you to nurture our children by listening to them, hugging them, reassuring them, and encouraging them each and every day as they grow and develop and learn.

Together with "our" children we are embarking on a journey that will evolve into a relationship that forms a lifelong bond of caring.

As we enter a new century that holds in store for us changes we cannot even imagine, let us never underestimate our impact and always remember the simplest of truths.

Rationale for Change

Change is necessary and welcome yet daunting. What is daunting about it is not usually *what* is changed so much as how and why it is changed. Will it benefit everyone? Has it simplified and enriched our situation? Are supports in place to enhance the transition? We kept such questions in mind while we revised this text. The only reason one should change, we felt, is that one has grown, learned, and conferred with others for the purpose of improving and building on what one has accomplished already.

This second Canadian edition of *Introduction to Early Childhood Education* has, at first glance, changed dramatically from its predecessor. Its design is friendlier and more open. In terms of the text itself, the book is restructured more than anything else. Little information has been removed relative to the amount added. The first (and very rough) draft of this edition was greatly enhanced and tightened, as we took into account the concerns and suggestions of many people across the country. Now there are fewer chapters. The sections are shorter, more distinct. We made better use of charts, and conveyed much information in concise point form. The theory was simplified. Terminology was updated. Additional information was incorporated. Our approach became more nurturing, child-centred, and collaborative.

Our goal was to provide a text that is an excellent comprehensive resource to be enjoyed and utilized by students and teachers alike. One step we took to make the book more user-friendly was to reduce the number of chapters to 12 from 18.

Most early childhood education courses are 12 to 14 weeks in duration. Students told us that to give them one topic and one chapter per week would make the material more manageable.

The tone of the book is, we hope, positive, inviting, nurturing, empowering, and inclusive.

The first chapter, unnumbered, is titled Orientation. We walk you through a day in a child care centre and introduce you to the ideas and terms you first encounter. The Reggio Emilia approach is featured here as a program model. This chapter is brand-new to this edition. It reaches out, invites the reader in, and says, "Welcome. This is what child care is about."

Chapter 1, The Early Childhood Educator. At this point students are new to the field. Before they can focus on the field, on the children, or on the children's families, they must focus on themselves. Once centred—that is, once they fully understand what it is they do and are as early childhood educators—they can look outward to see how they can affect and be affected by others.

Professional organizations are included to encourage students to join them as soon as possible. Also included are early childhood education training programs from across the country, to provide students with some notion of the national scope of the field.

Issues are included here, not to hinder but to motivate. Students are bright. They know and need to know up front the issues that face them so they can begin immediately to make choices and decisions that will make a difference.

The information in this chapter is primarily from the original Chapters 6 and 18, with new information on careers, core knowledge, and other topics.

Chapter 2, Childhood. Before diving into what a 2-, 3-, or 4-year-old is, students must understand that the concept of childhood is a recent phenomenon. Students must also realize that our ideas about children come from identifiable sources.

This chapter begins with a chronological historical overview. It includes influential people, all from the original Chapter 2 and adding Loris Malaguzzi for Reggio Emilia. It also highlights five theories and eight theorists and has added Vygotsky, Bandura, and Gardner. We summarize this information in a handy new time line.

We provide an overview of children from birth to school age (from the original Chapter 5) and add a developmental chart on children 2–5 years as a new resource. We end with a thorough discussion of inclusion and diversity—themes woven throughout this text.

Chapter 3, Families. Children are a part of families. To understand children we must view them within this context. Chapter 3 leaves much of the original Chapter 5 intact but adds to the idea of communication and partnerships and uses headings to improve organization.

Chapter 4, The Field of Early Childhood Education. Once the student is comfortable with the definitions and roles that describe them and those they work with, they need to look at the field overall. Why is there a need for early childhood education? We answer that question and define programs, terminology, and the human resource positions. We expand on the original Chapters 1 and 6.

Chapter 5, Quality in Early Childhood Education. We felt it imperative to devote a chapter to quality but not without first providing the student with a fundamental working knowledge of the program. We review specific program models—Montessori, High Scope/Cognitively Oriented Curriculum, Open Education, and Reggio Emilia—across eight program components. With knowledge of program and quality features, students can research, evaluate, and compare these and other models in terms of their ability meet the needs of teachers, children, families, and communities. Students may then choose to focus on one of these for a field practicum. Head Start and Distar qualities are covered in terms of how they affect the overall development of children.

Also provided here is a summary of the legislation that governs provincial child care regulations such as group size, ratios, and training.

Now that the students are familiar with the people, basic principles, terminology, quality factors, and program models, they are ready to study the program and methodology in greater detail. Chapters 6–10 provide this depth.

Chapter 6, Play and Guidance: A Framework for Emotional Guidance. Try to find the connection among these three domains: the car, the school, the doctor's office. Children play there every day; inevitably, adults are called on to guide them. The interface between play and guidance is a child–adult interaction. These interactions with children help shape their emotional development. Hence, a teacher has an enormous responsibility and powerful impact on children moment to moment. This chapter discusses the role of early childhood educators as nurturer, empowerer, and mentor as they create an atmosphere of trust that supports development.

Emotional development, not covered in the preceding edition, is explained here. Play is reviewed (from Chapter 6 of the previous edition) and the discussion is expanded. Guidance is greatly expanded from the original Chapter 16. Guiding routines from the original Chapter 15 are covered in the new Chapter 7.

Chapter 7, Appropriate Practices. In the original Chapters 15 and 9 (Physical Environment) and in many other sections of the book, the term "developmentally appropriate" was used in some of the headings (e g , Developmentally Appropriate Schedules, Developmentally Appropriate Equipment, and so on). We amalgamated these sections into one chapter that covers all aspects of the framework of the day and points out the things that make these routines, physical features, etc., developmentally appropriate.

Chapter 8, Curriculum. What happens within each area of the program? This chapter defines curriculum and planning in terms of components of the curriculum—observation, assessment, setting standards and learning outcomes, and evaluation—within the context of accountability. Most information is drawn from original Chapters 7 and 8, but we've expanded on it and reorganized it.

Chapter 9, Curriculum and Development. Perhaps the most changed chapter in the text, Chapter 9 combines five of the original chapters (10–14).

Those original chapters were short, however, and for the most part they reiterated theoretical information found in other chapters. As well, they were reported to be too long for introductory courses and too short for curriculum courses. The purpose of the new chapter, then, is to define each developmental domain and to suggest strategies for supporting this development throughout the curriculum.

Chapter 10, Helping Children Cope with Stress. This chapter remains similar to its original counterpart (Chapter 17). It is unique to our text and, we feel, of critical importance. An added feature—How Teachers Can Help Children Cope with Stress—contains excellent suggestions.

The last chapter, like the first, is unnumbered. It is titled Progression and it outlines early childhood education in each province (with material from Chapter 4 in the earlier edition) and concludes with The Future of Early Childhood Education (from Chapter 18 in the earlier). We moved provincial overviews to the last chapter because the student will by then have a solid grasp of the field, terminology, curriculum knowledge, and perhaps some experience. The students will be able to analyze the differences in the field of early childhood education across Canada in terms of historical, theoretical, and political (i.e., regulations, legislation, associations, governing bodies) implications. They can investigate their own province as an informed party, formulate appropriate questions, and appreciate their role in their province's future.

This chapter also presents a number of Canadian initiatives—research and projects in early childhood education that are currently being conducted around the province and that will affect the development of our field. We feel that the excellent work of early childhood educators in our country deserves recognition. If you know that such initiatives exist, you, as a future early childhood educator, are more likely to become involved in them.

Features of Each Chapter

The chapters have a number of features in common:

1. A brief introduction opens each chapter. (No student learning outcomes are presented; their omission means that individual instructors from a variety of courses and settings can choose their own focus for presenting the material in the chapter.)

2. A Canadian Professional Speaks Out is a box written by a person (or persons) with a vested interest in early childhood education on a topic pertinent to the chapter. Children write about children in Chapter 2, Childhood, for instance, and parents write from their own perspective in Chapter 3, Families.

3. Partnerships is a box that highlights topics and issues that directly affect relationships between the partners in early childhood education: families, children, teachers, and community. It offers ideas to enhance working together.

4. A Closer Look is a box that investigates in greater depth a topic or idea mentioned in the chapter. It offers further resources, suggestions, and practical tips.

5. Exhibits, such as charts, help organize and simplify information. We have rearranged information from the preceding edition into charts that visually integrate the information and present it in a concise, at-your-fingertips, ready-to-use format.

6. Key Terms is an end-of-chapter list that compiles the terms you'll find in bold type in that chapter. These terms are then defined in the Glossary, which appears near the end of the book.

7. The Key Points, another end-of-chapter feature, do not simply reiterate facts from the chapter but encapsulates its key underlying message. By the last chapter these points can serve as a Framework for Practice.

From a Grateful Author

My deepest gratitude and respect go to Eva Essa for writing the first and second U.S. editions of *Introduction to Early Childhood Education*. Her second edition, recently published, served as an excellent resource for this second Canadian edition.

My heartfelt thanks go to my mentor and friend Rosemary Young, who planned the first Canadian edition of this text, who provided me with the opportunity to write this second edition, and who provided the ongoing support and advice necessary to finish it.

I used the first Canadian edition each year as I taught early childhood education at Brock University, Sheridan College, and Niagara College, so I knew it well from a practitioner's point of view. From colleagues and students I received tremendously helpful feedback on the text and many suggestions for revision.

I graduated from Humber College in 1980 with my ECE, D.H., and, though I have earned degrees since then, I feel this experience to have been my most influential. I have worked with people 0 years to 60-plus years as students, colleagues, and parents. I have worked in integrated and segregated settings. I have worked as a developmental teacher/therapist, as a resource teacher, and as a home visitor. I have held supervisory positions, executive positions with associations such as CEC, and have planned conferences. I have presented locally, provincially, nationally, and internationally on early childhood education. I have been a business operator and a consultant to the publishing industry on materials, resources, and training in early childhood education. I have participated in research and pilot projects.

I share this with you simply so you can see the many perspectives I write from. All these experiences, and the people they involved, have deepened my understanding and commitment to early childhood education.

My joy is in working with students of all ages. Each day, they reveal to me new challenges, new solutions, and a perseverance, joy, and dedication that teaches, strengthens, motivates, and warms me to my very core.

Further Acknowledgments

When I agreed to take on this project I had no inkling of the magnitude of the task. But I did know I would have the help of many trusted and respected people. As I laughed, worked, cried, and enjoyed my way through this exceptional endeavour I continued to develop as a person and as a professional. Finding a new angle or discovering a new idea or creating an original phrase were all very powerful experiences. But sharing them with others was even more so:

- My husband—my absolute love, best friend, and hero, who continues to have that uncanny ability to melt me and to make me smile (sometimes in spite of myself), and to enable me to see so many things in such novel, beautiful, and balanced ways.

- My family and friends—for always asking me the right questions at the right time (even if I thought then it was the wrong time), and for providing hugs, hints, and time—commodities that were truly necessary and welcome.

- Kathryn Smithyman—who made all my words look great and who adds new meaning to team effort.

- Corrine Pritoula—for her exhaustive research efforts and her patience. You were always there for me, Cor.

- Connie Stokes—whom I love so completely and unconditionally. Thanks for proofreading, etc., etc., etc., in the eleventh hour.

- Brock University Child Care staff and families—for their photogenic smiles, and Karen James, for capturing the moment.

- My friends at Brock.

- The features contributors—who add a fresh and integral flavour to the text, and those contributors from the first edition whom we were unable to include in the second edition due to space restrictions and other logistical reasons.

- The agencies and persons who granted permission to reprint copyrighted material—their information was invaluable for providing scope and balance to the text.

- The ITP Nelson staff, in particular Evan Turner, Charlotte Forbes, and Bob Kohlmeier—their coordinated efforts produced this wonderful finished product.

- The reviewers—whose thoroughness made my job so much easier: Ingrid Crowther, Loyalist College; Joan Kunderman, Red River Community College; Kathryn Lockwood, Humber College; Lois Rennie, Capilano College; and Heather Sloan, Niagara College. They provided many practical recommendations.

- Finally, the four very special little ones: Angel boy, Danie, Logie, and Toto (formerly Squeaky!)—whom I love beyond all measure, who bring to my life a constant, indescribable happiness, and for whom I would do anything.

In all of their wisdom—as I sat solemnly on the porch immersed in thought and muttering to myself, "What have I done?" as I contemplated the breadth and depth of this project—they surrounded me in their arms and offered me cookies, proclaiming, "These always help." And they did.

"I am a teacher, therefore I am a learner."

LORI (MONTEITH) LEHNE

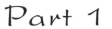

Part 1

The Premise

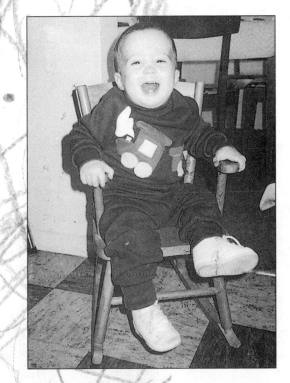

Welcome to our centre. In Part 1 we introduce you to the system of Early Childhood Education (ECE), beginning with an orientation to a typical day in the life of children, parents, and teachers in child care.

- Orientation: "Principles of Early Childhood Education" is our introductory chapter. It takes you on a tour of a quality program. During your visit to the centre, many new terms and concepts are introduced that will set the tone for your journey. These provide the threads that are woven throughout this text to create the tapestry that is early childhood education.

Principles of Early Childhood Education

This chapter is meant to orient you to early childhood education in general by providing you with a warm, positive feeling and a solid understanding of the threads that weave the fabric of early childhood education. Join us as we tour a high-quality, inviting, and nurturing early childhood program.

When you enter the Children's Centre, you notice that children's creativity is evident everywhere. There is a sense of warmth, compassion, and sincerity. There is a sense of family and fairness. You see it. You hear it. You feel it.

Introduction to the Tour

Welcome to the Children's Centre. I will be your guide today as you observe our class. We have 16 children in a **mixed age or family grouping,** ages 3 to 6, and 3 **early childhood educators.** Our centre is fully **inclusive.** We acknowledge, respect, and embrace **diversity.**

The principles of early childhood education are not something you do. They are a way of being—an approach or stance to something. They are principles you live by at school, home, work, and play. They guide how you initiate, interact, problem solve, respond, and live. They determine how you approach life, not just your job. Here we recognize **childhood** yet respect personhood.

Creativity is valued here. We view **learning** as a **model of communication.** It is an **interaction** through which we build **relationships** that are positive and **empowering.** This **collaboration** creates a sense of **ownership, respect, responsibility, trust,** and **accountability** among all **partners.** These partners include children, teachers, parents, and the community. They comprise a **team** that belongs to a **system** that is inter- and intradependent.

Our **mission statement advocates** that our primary **role** is to **nurture** children. Our **philosophy** reflects the principles of the **Reggio Emilia** approach, but our **program** is **eclectic.** It uses good ideas from many people and places to foster and encourage **wholistic, play-based, appropriate practices; positive guidance;** and **healthy development.** These, in turn, promote **autonomy.** We have posted the basic principles of Reggio Emilia on our bulletin board here, and there are copies if you would like one (see Partnerships).

We believe there needs to be a **rationale** for our actions, based on **historical, theoretical,** and **empirical** information, that lends **credibility** to our **profession.** We have adopted an **entrepreneurial spirit** that embraces the premise of **reflective practice** and **lifelong learning.** By always examining the **5WH questions**—who, what, where, when, why, and how—we continually gain new insight and understanding into, and direction for, ourselves, others, and the components of our **quality program.**

Let's observe the **curriculum** now and experience these ideas in practice.

Basic Principles of the Reggio Emilia Approach

This approach combines the ideas of progressive education from Dewey and the Constructivist approaches of Piaget; but it is clearly Vygotskian in nature. Knowledge is gained through positive social interaction or scaffolding. Varga (1997) summarizes the Vygotskian concept—it sees learning as leading development not as development leading learning. Developmentally appropriate programming (DAP) attempts to match developmental abilities or to elicit specific learning behaviours (Varga, 1997, p. 135). In contrast, a Vygotskian child care curriculum respects self-determination and meaning making through interaction. It does not predetermine developmental goals and objectives and attempt to foster their outcome. Instead, it observes the learning that is occurring and builds upon it. Development is continual and lifelong, as long as the individual has opportunities to engage in activities of meaning making (Varga, 1997, p. 135).

The following summary is adapted from J. Hendrick, 1997:

Image of the Child
- The child is valued as competent.

Children's Relationships and Interactions within a System
- The child is seen in relation to all others.
- Relationships are interconnected and reciprocal.
- School is a system made up of these relationships.

Three Subjects of Education: Children, Parents, Teachers
- All have rights.
- The well-being of one is connected to the well-being of the others.

The Role of Parents
- Parents' participation is expected and supported.

The Role of Space
- The setting is inviting and beautiful in that it conveys the close relationship of the children and teachers.
- It fosters communication, interaction, and relationships.
- It fosters discovery, problem solving, and choices.
- It is personal and family-oriented.
- It is full of children's work.

The Value of Relationships and Interaction of Children in Small Groups
- Children learn through peer exchange, negotiation, and dynamic communication.

The Role of Time and Importance of Continuity
- Children stay with the same teacher and peer group for three years (0–3, 3–6).
- There is a general schedule that is flexible—attends to children's sense of time and personal rhythms.
- A "full day provides sufficient time for being together among friends in a good environment and getting things done with satisfaction" (p. 19).

Teachers as Partners
- Observation and listening are important.
- Teachers have the role of researching and learning with the children and colleagues through questioning and dialogue.
- Learning is spiral, not linear.
- Ideas emerge *then* plans and preparations are made.

Cooperation and Collaboration as the Backbone of the System
- Teachers work in pairs at the same level as one another.
- Teachers view themselves as researchers gathering information.
- There is continual documentation, observation, and discussion.
- The system is interconnected and integrated through peer support, meetings, and discussions on all issues.

The Interdependence of Cooperation and Organization
- *Everything* is discussed and organized.
- All hold the conviction that by working together they can offer the best experience for children.

The Many Languages of Children: Atelierista (Art Teacher) and Atelier (Studio)
- The art teacher works as part of a team with the teacher *not* just in studio but as part of the whole school to create the warm, beautiful, inviting team atmosphere.
- Art is not a separate subject but an inseparable, integral part of the cognitive/symbolic expression involved in the process of learning.

The Power of Documentation
- Videos, photographs, art media, and audio recordings are used for archival purposes and to document the process of learning, to evaluate children's experiences

and interactions, to facilitate communication, and to display to the world a love of children and learning.

The Emergent Curriculum

- Curriculum is not established in advance.

- Staff make general goals and hypotheses.

- Staff have a set of guiding principles that work regardless of the subject or project decided upon. Therefore, themes do not dictate curriculum; curriculum (the children!) decide on the theme.

- Staff observe children; document, compare, interpret, and discuss observations; dialogue with the children, and determine a detailed plan of action.

Projects

- They may start from a chance event, an interest, or a discussion.

- They support learning by doing.

- They are evolutionary.

- They can last a few days or months.

- Questions, hypotheses, team collaboration, preparation, and documentation occur from conception to completion.

Conclusion

Loris Malaguzzi (1993), originating founder of the Reggio schools, asks educators to reflect on three rights:

1. Children have the right to realize and expand their potential while receiving support from adults who value their capacity to socialize and to give and receive affection and trust, and who sustain the children's own constructive strategies of thought and action (rather than simply transmit knowledge and skills).

2. Parents have the right to participate actively and of free will in the experiences of growth, care, and learning of their children.

3. Teachers have the right to contribute to the content, objectives, and practice of education through a network of collaboration open to professional growth, training, and research

The respect of these rights will make it possible for child, parent, and teacher to construct their knowledge together along the path of learning. As they enjoy the process of discovering and working together, they create a school that is alive, welcoming, and authentic.

Adapted from Joanne Hendrick, 1997. *First Steps Towards Teaching the Reggio Way*
(Upper Saddle River, NJ: Prentice Hall).

The Tour

The early arrivers are already at the centre. Today, Teacher Kathy, who also works in the other classrooms, is in charge of the early morning shift which includes children from all the classes. This early time is relatively low-key, and children can choose from several easy-to-clean-up and safe activities, for instance, story reading. As well, one teacher is outside in the playground as it is available to those that need to expend energy on arrival. Jane, the lead teacher for the group, will arrive by 8:30 a.m. today and will spend some time preparing activities that were planned. Richard and Yvonne, the other two teachers, will get to the centre by 9:00 a.m. Through a team approach, parents and teachers have decided that rotating shifts, duties, and classrooms works best for everyone. Observe, listen, question, record, participate, and enjoy!

Teacher Jane stays near the door and greets arriving children and their parents. Nicholas's father briefly tells Jane about his son's fall over the weekend, when he cut his lip. After a kiss from Nicholas, the father is off to work.

Nicholas goes into the room and spots Joel in the reading area with Zachary and Amanda.

"My tooth went into my lip," Nicholas tells Joel. "See!"

Joel checks out Nicholas's lip.

"I fell and hurt my knee," Joel tells Nicholas.

"I hurt my knee too … and my arm … and my head … and my bottom … and my booboo!" Nicholas adds. The two of them laugh uproariously.

"My dad is bringing a snake today," Zachary tells them. Nicholas and Joel stop their conversation for a moment to look at Zachary then continue to discuss their various wounds.

All of the children are here now. Notice that several additional activities are now available to the children, like painting at the easel. Children can select and design their own activities, and you will see children finding things to do with friends or alone.

Jillian and Christine head for the dramatic play area. Jillian pulls a skirt on over her clothes then joins Christine to look for shoes to go with her outfit.

"OK, we'll go shopping. I have to get some food and some new dresses and some other stuff," she announces.

Within a few minutes, the two girls are dressed and ready to go shopping. Christine sees a blanket over the dolls in the cradle and spreads it out on the floor.

"We'll have a picnic first," she tells Jillian. The two of them fill a basket with plastic foods from the dramatic play cupboard and set out their picnic.

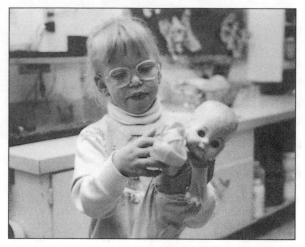

In the meantime, Alex has turned on the computer and is playing "Facemaker." He has been creating an insect man for the past week. Nicholas joins Alex and sits in the second computer chair, first watching, then participating.

"Put that nose on it," Nicholas suggests. "Boy, it looks funny." They laugh as they try different features and body parts. Shila walks by and watches quietly for a few minutes.

Sheena wanders about the room, then walks by Jillian and Christine's picnic. She sees the cradle and the uncovered dolls in it. She checks them out then picks up one of the dolls, rocking the baby in her arms. She walks to the mirror where she shows the baby to itself. "Look, look," she tells it.

Then she decides to undress the doll. "Take it off," Sheena says, pulling off the doll's shirt. She spends several minutes of great concentration working on this task. Teacher Yvonne holds the doll to help Sheena get its shirt off. Once the shirt is off the doll, Sheena works equally hard to get it back on.

Other children come and go from the picnic on their way to other activities.

"Could we have a real picnic, Teacher Yvonne?" asks Jillian.

"What a wonderful idea! Let's think about it today and we'll discuss it in circle tomorrow—beginning with everything you know about picnics and questions you have about picnics," answers Yvonne.

*The team's **goal** for Sheena is to help her improve her small muscle skills. Her **self-selected, natural activity** provides good practice. Notice that the dramatic play centre is not themed but houses a cupboard with many props and kits so that the children can accommodate many types of play and themes as they arise through play and discussion. Also notice the snack at the far table. The teachers consider the snack a morning activity option. Some of the children who arrive at the centre early are ready for a snack because it has been hours since their breakfast. Others want something a little later. To accommodate the children's varying schedules, the teachers provide a smorgasbord snack, available until 10:00 each morning. The snack is usually a "fix-it-yourself" affair.*

Jillian and Christine stay dressed up for eating their snack. Several children move to the snack table after washing their hands. Christopher spreads cream cheese on a celery stick then, with great concentration, tops it with a handful of raisins. He then places some raisins in a celery stick and watches them fall out. He discusses with Teacher Jane how the raisins stick to the cream cheese but not to the plain celery.

"It sticks because it's sticky!" exclaims Christopher, as he licks his gluey fingers then crunches down on his snack. During the next hour, children come and go to the snack table, making and eating "ants-on-a-log" (celery with cream cheese and raisins) and drinking milk. Periodically, Teacher Jane asks children who have not yet had a snack if they would like one.

Patrick tells her, "I'm not hungry yet. Maybe later."

It's almost 10:00. At this time, the children and teachers straighten the room and then participate in a short circle activity. This gets the children together for the first time of the day and helps the teachers focus on the current project. For the past two weeks, the children have been learning about insects. The interest in insects arose through the children's encounters on a nature walk. As a group, they discussed what they knew and what they would like to learn and devised several projects for the upcoming days.

Teacher Jane asks the children, "What can you tell me about caterpillars?" and later "What would you like to know about caterpillars?" She then tells the children a flannel board story "The Little Green Caterpillar," incorporating information given to her by the children.

"One day the little green caterpillar was looking for something to eat," Jane begins. She goes on to relate the caterpillar's search for a meal and its encounter with other insects. At the end, she asks the children some questions about the story and helps them recount its sequence. She leaves the story out for the children to explore.

Before the story, Teacher Jane checked for **prior knowledge**—*what did the children already know*—*and, therefore, she could determine and adjust the story to eliminate, reinforce, or add facts. She also knows that* **story structure**—*beginning, middle, end*— *is an important concept for* **emergent literacy** *and daily living.*

At this time, some of the children choose to get their coats. One teacher is available to help the children with zippers and buttons as needed. Marusha, like most of the children, has no problem getting dressed. Often the older children help the younger ones. Outside the children move to climbers, tricycles, swings, slides, and other equipment. Some children have brought magnifying glasses, paper, pen-

cils, and a book on ants to investigate some of the ideas that arose yesterday.

"All right, Jillian and Alex, you go first," prompts Teacher Richard. "Trade places."

The two children run under the parachute while the rest of the group lifts and lowers the parachute.

"Tako and Shila, now you two trade places," says Teacher Richard. Soon most of the children have had a chance to run under the parachute, and the giggling has intensified.

Angela has been watching this activity from the side.

"You can hold it right here," Patrick tells Angela. She takes hold of the edge of the parachute between Patrick and Marusha. Soon Angela is laughing and running under the parachute too. Teacher Richard then asks for suggestions about other ways to use the parachute. Discussion and experimentation ensue. Some children stay while others find different activities or quiet places on the playground.

The outdoor playground is available as a release all morning with children coming and going to this extended classroom learning centre.

Children come inside, hang up their coats, and reconvene on the rug. Teacher Jane has told the group that they have a special guest today—Zachary's father, a biologist who works with animals. Zachary's father tells the children about the beetles he has brought in a plastic box and then introduces the boa constrictor, which he pulls out of a sack. The children watch with reserved fascination as the boa emerges. It wiggles around, coiling and stretching, moving from the middle to the edges of the circle. Laughter erupts each time the snake nears any of the children.

"Does he sleep with Zachary?" Shila wants to know.

"Will he bite?" asks Christine.

"Only if you're a rat," Zachary's father tells her. "He likes to eat rats."

"I'm not a rat!" exclaims Vincent.

"No rats here. I guess he won't bite anyone."

"Why does he stick out his tongue?" Patrick asks.

"Does he bite with his tongue?" Joel chimes in.

"He smells with his tongue. See, he is smelling all of us."

More laughter erupts as the children watch the boa wiggle around the circle, tongue flipping in and out. The snake moves toward Alex, who squeals in delight as it comes near him. B.J., however, moves behind Teacher Yvonne, who reassures him quietly. Zachary pets the snake frequently. Later the teachers take the snake and let it crawl around them. Teacher Yvonne tells the children that she had a pet snake when she was a little girl.

After 15 minutes, Zachary's father and the snake leave. The beetles, however, will stay with the class for the day. Jane discusses with the children which activities are now available. She discusses their plans for the afternoon, and the children move toward various learning centres.

At the woodworking table, Christine puts on a pair of goggles, takes out a block of Styrofoam, a hammer, and nails, and starts to bang away. Jillian watches for a few moments then gets goggles and a hammer as well. Teacher Jane gives Jillian a piece of Styrofoam, into which she quickly hammers half a dozen nails.

The children often use Styrofoam when woodworking is set up as an indoor activity, although they can use wood as well when they are outside. The Styrofoam is quieter and safer in the enclosed space, and it also allows some of the younger children to experience success as they learn to use the woodworking tools. If wood is necessary for a project, the project can be done outside or in the project room.

Other children move to other activities. Tako and Sheena spend some time at the sand table Creature World. The moist sand holds a variety of plastic creatures as well as sticks, pine cones, and other sensory materials. This was the children's idea, and they gathered the materials they needed.

"I got a green spider," Tako says, as he digs in the sand.

Shila moves to the easel, puts a plastic apron over her head, and affixes a sheet of paper to the easel with clothespins. She works with great concentration on her painting, first using separate colours, then mixing them on the picture.

"Black and red. Hey, a lady bug!" she exclaims.

"Shall I write those words on your picture?" inquires Richard.

"Yes, and write 'She is eating' too," directs Shila. Richard writes the words and reads them aloud. Shila knows what she has asked to be written and can remember it. So she reads all the words. "I can read," she proudly announces.

In the block area, several children are joined by Richard. At first, Joel, Zachary, Chris, and Vincent build an enclosure with the large, hollow blocks. Tako spends

a few minutes rolling cars down a ramp-shaped block. By the time he joins the other boys, the block construction has become a house.

"Get a roof," Zachary says. Joel finds two flat pieces of cardboard, which he lays over the top and borrows a blanket from the dramatic play centre.

"See our house!" someone calls out. Several children crawl under the roof, and they have to lie flat to be enclosed inside their house. They take turns getting into it and repairing it each time the roof slips off.

"This is our boat. Let's go fishing. Hop in the boat." Vincent has turned the house into a boat now. Christopher, Tako, and Zachary hop in with Vincent.

"How's the fire doing in there, Zach?" Joel asks, apparently making the boating trip a camping trip as well.

"OK. Are you hungry now?" Zachary asks.

"Yeah," Joel answers.

Angela walks past the block area and starts to get in the boat. One of the boys pulls her out. "You can't get in here. This is our boat!"

Angela starts to cry, saying, "No! No!"

Teacher Yvonne comes over as Angela says, "He hurt me."

"She was getting in our boat," another boy says.

Yvonne spends a few moments helping Angela and the boys explore with one another how they feel and possible solutions to this dilemma.

In the project room, children are busy creating and planning their garden project which they want to build at the back of the playground.

You'll notice a write-up about our garden project that we printed in our newsletter under the heading A Closer Look.

THE GARDEN PROJECT

The children in the class became intrigued when a landscaping firm began to work across the street from their school. Sensing the children's interest in this activity, one of the teachers contacted the head of the company and asked whether they could observe and ask questions. The class walked across the street each day to watch and note the progress. They witnessed the transformation of a lot, which had contained a small, scraggly lawn surrounded by beds of weeds, into an attractive garden. The surface was cleared, earth was moved to create mounds and hills, shrubs and flowers were planted, decorative rocks were added, and a small birdbath was placed in one corner. The two men who worked on this project enjoyed the children's interest and answered their questions.

A week later, when the new garden was in place, several children asked the teachers whether they could also make such a garden. "Of course," they answered, and asked how they would go about it. A lively discussion ensued about where to plant their garden. The question of what to put in the garden was also explored. The children wanted lots of plants, rocks, and a statue just like the one Joel described from his neighbour's garden.

They considered what tools they would need to make the garden. Because they decided that they could not use "big tools" such as a bulldozer, they chose shovels and rakes. Where to get the plants was another question. Patrick thought that it would be hard to get bushes like the ones planted across the street. Shila reminded everyone that they could plant seeds like they did on their windowsill earlier in the year. Nicholas thought they could dig up things from other gardens and transplant them in their garden. The children decided that they would each ask their parents to help them find one plant for the garden.

The next day they began their work. Teachers, with the help of some of the parents, provided a variety of tools. The children dug, raked, watered, and moved earth in buckets from one area to another. As they encountered problems (e.g., a big rock just below the surface that they could not move) they tried different approaches and talked about how to deal with the problems. Having watched the project across the street, the children realized that they would have to prepare the soil before putting in the plants. Some of the plants came to school on the first day, but these were left in the classroom and watered carefully until the garden was ready. Within a few days, plants and seeds were put into the earth, and the children decorated their garden with rocks and pine cones.

The children also made pictures and wrote stories about their garden. Marusha wanted to make a picture as big as the garden was going to be, and soon several children joined her in making a mural containing flowers, trees, birds, butterflies, insects, the sun, and children working and playing. Teachers provided books and catalogues about gardens and plants in the reading area, which the children used to learn about and get new ideas for their own garden. With help, the children read seed packages and gardening books for descriptions of the plants they were putting into their garden. Teachers helped them develop a chart where they can mark the sizes of their plants now and measure and mark how large the plants will grow in future. For three weeks, the children have been engrossed in learning about gardening through observation, first-hand experience, and direct problem solving.

A little before noon, all of the teachers move around the classroom and remind groups of children that it will be time to clean up soon, and discuss steps with those who are not at final stages of their projects. A few minutes later, Teacher Jane rings a bell, the usual sign, and announces clean-up time.

"I need a couple of people to help put the top on the Creature World," Teacher Jane says. Alex, along with Zachary, Joel, and Nicholas, help the teacher place the wooden cover on the sand table.

When they are finished, Zachary says, "Hey, Tako, me and Nicholas and Alex, we put the top up. We have muscles!"

The children gather on the rug. They sing "Head, Shoulders, Knees, and Toes," touching the various named body parts as they sing. After singing the song at a reasonable tempo, they repeat it quickly, with fast movements, fast words, and giggles.

"Today we're going to play a bug game. This will be our bug house here," says Teacher Jane, indicating the centre of the circle. "I want you to think of a bug and move how you think that bug might move. And, if you think that bug makes a sound, I want you to make that sound. But don't tell us what the bug is. We'll try to guess. Who can think of a bug they'd like to be?"

"I know one," Jillian says. She moves around the circle, buzzing and flapping her arms.

"A bee! She's a bee!"

Vincent is an ant, Amanda is a fly, and Shila, crawling very quietly and slowly with hands tucked under her face, is a caterpillar.

Nicholas hops around the circle, saying, "Boing, boing, boing, boing."

"Is he a bunny?" asks B.J.

"Bunnies do hop. Are you a bunny?" asks Jane.

"I'm not a bunny. I'm a grasshopper!" explains Nicholas.

"Grasshoppers are bugs and they are good jumpers. I've never heard a grasshopper say 'Boing,' but if I did, I think it might sound just like that!" Jane tells him. Everyone laughs.

All of the children who wanted to be an insect have had a turn.

"We need some grasshoppers to wash their hands," suggests Jane. Children have come and gone to the washroom throughout the morning at their own discretion. Now they all need to wash their hands before lunch. Soon, going a few at a time, some jumping, some walking, all of the children are ready for lunch.

Richard and Sheena have brought a cart with the children's lunch from the kitchen into the room. The teachers join them in eating lunch. Lunch is served family style in bowls.

"Please pass the potatoes," asks Angela.

"No more peas, thank you," states B.J.

"More milk, please, to wash down my bread!" exclaims teacher Richard. Tako pours him a glass from the small pitcher.

Children finish lunch at different paces. After putting their dishes on the cart, some stop by the kitchen to thank the cook, Mrs. Evan, for a wonderful lunch.

The children move to the reading area to get a book, which they can look at quietly. Zachary and Joel are still eating. One of the other children, looking behind her as she walks, bumps into Zachary as she moves past him, spilling some of the milk he is drinking. Zachary bursts into tears. Joel, sitting next to him, reaches over and gives him a comforting hug.

"It's OK. It's OK," he tells Zachary, as he pats his back. Zachary calms down, rubbing his eyes.

Teacher Jane approaches Zachary, saying, "It's almost nap time, Zachary. We've had a really exciting morning, with your dad and the snake visiting, haven't we?" Zachary produces a weak smile, and he and Joel finish their lunches.

You may ask why Jane did not deal with the milk-spilling accident. I suspect Jane realizes that Zachary, who is usually very even-tempered, is just overtired at this point, so she's not adding to the over-stimulation but is simply trying to distract and calm him. Besides, Joel was doing an excellent job!

Teacher Yvonne is by the nap cots in the sleep room. She waits for the children who will be sleeping. When they arrive, they'll find their cot and blanket in their usual space, determined by the group at the beginning of the year.

In the early afternoon, some of the children sleep, but a number of the older ones do not take daily naps anymore. They will go to one of the other classrooms for quiet activities.

By 1:00 p.m., the nappers have gone to the bathroom, taken off their shoes, and snuggled down for their naps. The lights are dimmed, and soft music is

playing on the CD player. Some fall asleep quickly, others wiggle around for a while. Yvonne rubs Vincent's and Amanda's backs to help them sleep.

Children begin waking up about 2:30 p.m., some slowly, some with a burst of renewed energy, ready for snack and afternoon activities. It takes about a half hour before everyone is up.

"Hello, sleepy head. Can you remember where you put your shoes before nap?" Teacher Yvonne asks Angela with a smile. Angela smiles and shrugs. After a few minutes of looking, the shoes are found amid the dress-up shoes in the dramatic play area.

"Let's put these back on," suggests Yvonne. Angela pulls off her right sock while Yvonne puts on her left shoe. Yvonne smiles. In a few minutes, Angela's shoes and socks are back on both feet.

Amanda is one of the last children to wake from her nap. "I don't feel good," she tells Teacher Richard, rubbing her eyes.

Richard feels her forehead and tells Teacher Jane, "She feels like she might have a fever." A check with the thermometer confirms that Amanda does have a temperature.

We have an arrangement for children who do not feel well. While we try to reach one of their parents to discuss what to do, the children stay in the office with a staff member. We keep a cot and a few quiet toys in the office for such occasions.

Some of the group has now had a snack, and some are ready to go outside. Others have picked up projects where they left off.

"Look at me! Look at me!" calls Joel, sitting on a swing and swinging up high.

"Wow!" Teacher Jane says. "You're really swinging high. You've worked hard at learning to pump!"

The tricycles are all taken by this time, although Sheena indicates that she wants to ride one, too.

"There are no tricycles right now, Sheena," Teacher Yvonne says. "But I see that Marusha has an empty seat on the back of hers."

"Marusha, could I ride with you?"

Marusha pulls to the side and waits for Sheena to get into the passenger seat. Marusha pedals hard to pull the extra weight. Vincent, who had been digging in the sand, watches Marusha struggling with the tricycle, then lays down his shovel and gets behind Sheena to push. They gather speed and take several turns around the cement path.

"Can I ride now?" Vincent asks.

"OK. I'll push," suggests Marusha. Sheena stays in the passenger seat while Marusha and Vincent trade places.

The children go back inside around 4:00. A few parents have begun to pick up their children. In the room, children can choose quiet activities, finish projects, read, create, or find a quiet space and converse.

The beetles that Zachary's father had brought that morning are on the science table along with a book, paper labelled "My Observations," and pencils.

Christopher and Vincent check them out.

"I want the beetle to come out," Christopher says, poking his finger in the sand.

"You know, the beetles burrow in the sand. That's what they like to do," Teacher Richard tells them. "There is some beetle food on top of the sand. Maybe they'll come up where we can see them when they get hungry."

"Hey, there's one!" Vincent says, as one of the beetles emerges from the sand. The two boys continue to watch.

Christopher gets pencil crayons from the writing centre, brings them back, and begins to draw. "One, two, three …," he counts.

"How fast and far do they move?" asks Vincent. Teacher Richard suggests they time one and then get a ruler from the math centre to measure the distance. Christopher wants to write it down. They begin discussing how to find the beetles' mass.

Jillian and Christine move to the game shelf. Christine takes out the counting flowers and Jillian finds dominoes, both teacher-made materials. "One, two, three, four …" Christine accurately matches the 10 flowers and pots, placing the flowers with numerals on top of the flower pots with the corresponding number of dots.

Jillian, meanwhile, lays out a domino with two dots on one side and four on the other. She looks over the remaining dominoes and finds one with four dots, which she lays next to the other four-dotted piece. She continues building a chain of matching dominoes.

Alex wanders to their table and picks up the flower pot with two dots from Christine's game.

"That's two," he tells Christine, then moves off elsewhere.

Gradually all of the parents come to pick up their children, some stopping for a few moments to chat with the teacher, others rushing off. A little after 5:30 p.m., the last child has left and another day has ended.

The teachers have met at various stages in the day to compare notes and observations and clarify roles and responsibilities for tomorrow. As well, they were making plans for attending a conference on the weekend.

The Summary

Now you have had the chance to experience a day in the lives of a group of preschoolers and their teachers. A lot is going on, but all those activities don't just happen by accident. Careful planning and preparation are required. This planning and preparation includes the children since the program is based on the belief that

children should have ownership of decisions that affect them. By empowering children, we show that we respect and value their personhood and potential. Let's now consider what you observed.

Much of what you saw reflects our school's philosophy and mission statement. For instance, we aim to provide a high-quality program by maintaining an appropriate ratio of adults to children (one adult for every 8 children in this class) and a reasonable group size of no more than 16 children. That number of children works well within the size of this classroom. In addition, we have a multi-aged group of children. Did you notice on several occasions that older children helped or provided a model for the younger ones? For instance, Patrick was aware of Angela as she stood on the sidelines of the parachute activity and made a point of inviting her to join in.

We also include several children with diverse needs in this class. These needs include developmental, familial, cultural, and financial needs. This concept of inclusion and diversity has had many benefits for all the children and is a thread we weave throughout the text.

The teachers are another very important component in our program. We are fortunate to have such well-qualified teachers as Jane, Yvonne, and Richard. They strive constantly to develop as a team and provide a high-quality program for the children by applying their understanding of child development and early childhood education principles, and by maintaining a thorough knowledge of the profession—its roots and issues—through active involvement and continual professional development (see A Canadian Professional Speaks Out). They also work as a team with the parents of the children through frequent interactions. The teachers work together with many people—one another, parents, children, administrators, and those from other community disciplines such as health and social services. Through collaborative consultation, decisions about programs and children are made. This is a systems approach that considers communication and relationships as the major factors in establishing a positive, wholistic, integrated curriculum.

I'm glad that you have become more fully aware of the work of early childhood educators. Their job is complex and rewarding. They

implement planned activities and discussion times, such as those that occur during the large group times. They take advantage of the many learning opportunities that present themselves throughout the day: you saw this happening, for instance, during the discussion of stickiness between Teacher Jane and Christopher at the snack table.

The teachers also contribute to the socialization of the children and to the guidance of their behaviour. Teacher Yvonne helped Angela express her feelings when she was not allowed to join the block activity when the boys in the block area told her that she was not a member of their boat trip. Teachers also nurture children throughout the day. Teacher Jane helped Zachary cope when the day seemed to have reached the point of over-stimulation; Teacher Richard soothed Amanda when she woke up feeling sick.

The job of early childhood educators is challenging and important because they are such influential figures in the lives of young children. We will discuss your role as an early childhood educator and as a member of a profession. We also will look at how teachers guide children as they play and learn and examine how this interaction shapes a child's emotional development. We consider the primary role of the early childhood educator as a nurturer who promotes an inviting atmosphere of trust, security, and respect. Notice this is achieved through a firm but fair, calm, gentle, and patient mix of actions and words.

Teachers value the image of the child as a competent individual. We do, however, devote an entire chapter to helping children cope with stress as it is so prevalent in their lives today.

Teachers are change agents—people who facilitate dialogue and cooperation through flexibility, creativity, ingenuity, and inter- and intrapersonal skills. (Intrapersonal skils are those that one develops within oneself—i.e., for self-improvement.)

Let's talk now about what the children at the centre did. As you noted, they had a busy day. They always have many options because we operate on the assumption that the children select and create activities that are meaningful and important to them. Remember the concentration and wholehearted involvement of the children in some of the activities? You noticed how focused Sheena was on dressing and undressing the doll, how attentive Alex and Nicholas were at the computer, and how interested Christopher and Vincent were as they examined the beetles.

The teachers do not push the children into these activities; rather they prepare an environment that supports flexibility and contains appropriate materials, opportunities, and activities that the children self-select and through which they learn. Each child gains something uniquely important to him/her from the different materials, experiences, and activities. Teachers consistently monitor and adjust to children's growth and development. The teachers aim to provide development of the whole child in all areas by guiding, supporting, and encouraging children's natural interests. You saw how confident children were in working together or independently, in asking for help, and in making suggestions. They feel an integral part of their environment and program. We will reinforce these points in various chapters as we talk about the history of early childhood education, which provides a rationale for what we do and considers children and their unique character. We examine curriculum and how it promotes emotional, creative, physical, cognitive, language, and social development.

One of the unseen elements that you observed today is the schedule. This schedule is a framework, which provides a sense of consistency and security for the children. It has been refined and changed over time to suit this particular group of children. For instance, at the beginning of the year snack was at 10:00 a.m., and everyone participated at one time; now it is scheduled more flexibly to accommodate the children's needs. The schedule also represents a balance among the various components that you had the chance to observe: between indoor and outdoor times, between active and quiet periods, and between teacher-led and child-initiated activities. It also involves more free flow to allow for individual differences. It includes times for rest, food, and self-care and considers transitions between activities. Remember how smoothly clean-up time operated? These components reflect appropriate practices that are discussed together with guidance principles for these routines.

What you observed represents not only a consistent daily schedule, but also careful curriculum planning. Some of today's activities are unique for this day, others are available regularly, and projects that evolve, such as the garden,

can last from days to weeks to months. Because the class has been working on their bug interests, a number of planned activities are also aimed at supporting the topic. The visit of Zachary's father with the snake and beetles, the flannel board story, the "guess what bug I am" activity, and the Creature World at the sand table began as ideas and were planned out to augment the children's interests. Novelty of materials and experiences, and a breadth and depth of resources, such as books, also supplement the children's opportunities to build on and create new ideas. Curriculum planning, however, does not happen in a vacuum. It also involves setting goals and objectives, both for the group and for individuals, including children, parents, and teachers.

For instance, teachers have worked with Sheena on improving language and movement skills through her natural play, based on testing, documentation, discussion and observation of, *and with* Sheena, her parents, and community professionals.

Teachers and programs must demonstrate accountability for what they do. Teachers need to observe, document, dialogue, assess, plan, implement, and evaluate together with children, parents, and the community. Through reflective practice, they modify their program.

Another element involved in what you observed today is the environment. The teachers give careful consideration to providing a safe, cheerful, responsive learning environment. You noticed how the room is divided into learning areas or centres. These provide a sense of order, define purpose, and facilitate cleaning up. Within the learning centres, located where the children can reach them, are a wide variety of age-appropriate materials. These materials are carefully selected to encourage children to explore, manipulate, try out, master, create, and learn in many different ways—an atmosphere that any person would hope to work, live, and play in!

A CANADIAN PROFESSIONAL SPEAKS OUT
Care and Well-Being of Children

The Canadian Association for Young Children (CAYC) is Canada's oldest national association focusing specifically on the well-being of young children. Its roots go back to 1952, when the Ontario Council for Childhood Education was formed. It was officially recognized by the granting of a federal charter in 1974 and renamed the Canadian Association for Young Children. Three principles—addressing national issues, focusing on Canadian research, and recognizing outstanding accomplishments—may have changed slightly over time, but they still form the basis for the association's existence.

Diverse and Global Membership

The fact that CAYC is concerned specifically with the care and education of children, birth through age 9, at home, in preschool settings and at school, has attracted members from every province, the territories, and around the world. Members include parents, teachers, caregivers, administrators, students and all those wishing to share ideas and participate in activities related to the education and welfare of young children.

Credibility

A board of directors governs CAYC. Its constitution assures that there is representation from each of the provinces and territories, which makes up the provincial directorship.

Canadian Issues

CAYC strives to provide a Canadian voice on critical issues related to the quality of life of all young children and their families. One of the ways in which this is achieved is by influencing the direction and quality of policies and programs that affect a child's healthy development. Since children are unable to advocate for quality programming, professionals need to do it on their behalf. Advocacy can take many forms. It can be letters to government and/or education officials, a response to issues in the news, a telephone call to a school board member, or a brochure introducing the public to current education theories.

Professional Development

Meetings:
Since its inception, CAYC has provided opportunities for its members to come together and discuss issues, concerns, and ideas about working with young children.

Conferences:
CAYC has become known for its high-quality national conferences which are held every two years and are complemented by smaller regional conferences in alternate years.

Training:
Provincial branches of CAYC host ongoing special training events to provide professional development for members. In order to make CAYC training events accessible to students and other members with diverse needs, many local associations offer discounts.

Publications:
Canadian Children is the Association's current, semiannual, refereed journal. *Canadian Children* exists to meet the needs of Canadian primary teachers and early childhood educators by featuring practical, research-based articles that will improve teaching and learning and serve as a bridge between the distinct, but allied, fields of primary and early childhood education. A CAYC Web site is also planned.

Research and Projects:
In recent years, CAYC nationally has introduced theme action projects to address issues that affect the quality of life of young children and their families. The literacy project "Literacy and the Young Family" consisted of a video entitled *Loving Books* featuring David Booth, a well-known Canadian educator. Brenda Clark, an outstanding Canadian writer and illustrator of the well-loved Franklin series, consented to the use of her character on the T-shirt. "Literacy and the Young Family" was successful in communicating the message that reading to young children is very important to their total development.

Another theme action project has been the development and distribution of a position statement. CAYC launched its position statement on play entitled "Young Children Have a Right to Play" in 1996. There is an ongoing concern among Canadian professionals that, in some settings, in some parts of the country, children's play is not being valued, and this position statement urges all Canadians to become advocates for play. These brochures are being used effectively in parent meetings, workshop presentations, postsecondary classrooms, and education awareness campaigns.

Provincially, many associations have taken initiatives to improve the lives of children in their area. The following examples demonstrate the diversity of that involvement:

• CAYC British Columbia requested that the board send a letter of support to the premier congratulating his government on the establishment of a single ministry for the welfare of children, while CAYC members in Alberta represented the association in a joint meeting of like-minded groups.

- CAYC Saskatchewan developed and continues to administer the CAYC Friends of Children Award which recognizes Canadian professionals.
- A Workshop Series for Young Parents dealing with the importance of reading "with" young children emerged in Manitoba's high schools and medical clinics thanks to the dedication of the province's CAYC members.
- CAYC Ontario has established Special Projects for Needy Provinces with profits from its national conference.
- Montreal's Children's Library benefits from regular donations from CAYC Quebec.
- CAYC Nova Scotia recently participated in a Child Awareness Rally, and CAYC members in Newfoundland are developing an alliance with a group whose focus is to eliminate or decrease child poverty in the province.

These illustrations clearly demonstrate the impact an association like CAYC can have locally and nationally when resources are pooled.

Partnerships

In 1995, CAYC's National Conference was held in partnership with the National Council for Teachers of Mathematics, and many members believe this to be the catalyst for future joint ventures. Creating liaisons, exchanging information, and coordinating efforts is vital to our field and the children we serve.

Vision

CAYC has a very optimistic vision for the future. Any contribution that enhances the quality of life for Canada's young children is both beneficial and rewarding.

CAYC recognizes outstanding contributions to the well-being of children and supports those who have affected young children's lives in a very positive way. The importance of having highly skilled and well-trained people to lead our children into the next millennium cannot be overestimated. There are many challenges ahead and we must face them together—all of us who are charged with the care and education of Canada's most wonderful resource, our children.

Maxine Mercer, President
Canadian Association for Young Children

The Conclusion

Part 1, "The Premise," has served as an orientation to introduce key terms and concepts that guide early childhood education. These will be explored throughout the text. The following parts strive to introduce you to the who, what, where, when, why, and how of early childhood education.

Part 2 introduces you to "The Partners" that comprise the early childhood education team—the early childhood educator, the children, and their families.

Part 3 focuses on "The Profession" and explains terminology, programs, and people in the field of early childhood education and the factors that affect the quality of these programs.

Part 4 is called "The Pedagogy," which examines educational practices—what and how we do things in early childhood education as early childhood educators. It looks at why play, guidance, and emotional development go hand in hand. It outlines what is included in appropriate practices, and summarizes how curriculum enhances development. We also look at how to help children cope with stress.

Part 5 is called "The Promise" and it presents both the roots of early childhood education in Canada and the needs of early childhood education for the future.

Key Terms

accountability
advocates
appropriate practices
autonomy
childhood
collaboration
creativity
credibility
curriculum
diversity
early childhood educators
eclectic
emergent literacy
empirical
empowering
entrepreneurial spirit
5WH questions
goal

healthy development
historical
inclusive
interaction
learning
lifelong learning
mission statement
mixed age or family grouping
model of communication
nurture
ownership
partners
philosophy
play-based
positive guidance
prior knowledge
profession
program

quality program
rationale
reflective practice
Reggio Emilia
relationships
respect
responsibility
role

self-selected, natural activity
story structure
system
team
theoretical
trust
wholistic

Part 2

The Partners

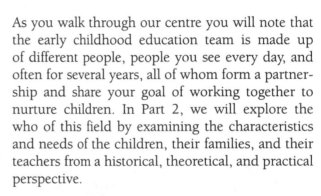

As you walk through our centre you will note that the early childhood education team is made up of different people, people you see every day, and often for several years, all of whom form a partnership and share your goal of working together to nurture children. In Part 2, we will explore the who of this field by examining the characteristics and needs of the children, their families, and their teachers from a historical, theoretical, and practical perspective.

- Chapter 1, "The Early Childhood Educator," highlights the different roles and the responsibilities, qualities, and knowledge you must possess on entering the field.

- Chapter 2, "Childhood," first examines the history of childhood and theories about how children learn and develop. It then looks at characteristics of young children today—the things they have in common and the things that make each child unique.

- Chapter 3, "Families," turns your attention to parents and other family members. They are the ones with whom early childhood educators share the responsibility for raising young children.

Chapter 1

The Early Childhood Educator

This chapter is about you and your entrance into a field that is virtually in its infancy. What does it take to be both a nurturer and a teacher? Most early childhood educators find they have to be a jack-of-all-trades. One day you are a fundraiser and an expert on caring for the frogs someone brought to the centre, and the next day the job requires a specialist on diaper rash and someone to fill in for the cook who went home sick. Two days later you're a carpenter, fixing the outdoor shed, and a professional, attending a conference on children with special needs. The list of roles and tasks that a teacher is expected

to assume is probably infinite, and no text or course can begin to anticipate what you may be called upon to do.

This chapter will focus on you not only as a teacher, but as an individual, as a caregiver, and as a member of a profession. Teachers in early childhood education programs must integrate knowledge about the development of children, the importance of families, creating a healthy and stimulating environment, about child-centred curriculum planning, and about appropriate and nurturing guidance to provide the best possible care and education for young children. And early childhood educators are people, too—with lives and needs and joys and sorrows. All people need to care for and be cared about. Recognizing your own strengths and needs together with those of others will help you to become a happy, healthy, and successful teacher.

The Early Childhood Educator

Before beginning a discussion of early childhood educators, it is important to clarify terminology. No universally accepted categories and titles define those who work with young children, although several have been proposed. Often labels

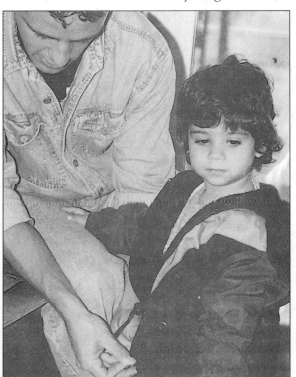

conjure up stereotypes and do not reflect different educational and experiential backgrounds found in the field (Phillips & Whitebook, 1986).

In keeping with our Canadian profession, we will use the term early childhood educator. Other terms, particularly **teacher, caregiver,** and **child care worker** will also be used. Traditionally, a caregiver has meant someone who cares for the physical and emotional needs of the child, whereas a teacher serves an educational function. "However, this distinction is not a particularly clear one, for the line between education and nurture in the early years is not a distinct one" (Spodek & Saracho, 1982, p. 401).

Certainly the early childhood teacher cares for and the caregiver teaches young children. Which teacher has not tied shoelaces, wiped noses, or dried tears? And which caregiver has not helped children learn how to zip a coat, assemble a puzzle, or share the tricycle? Teaching and caregiving functions are related to the point where a distinction is impossible to make (Willer, 1990).

Almy (1975) summarized it this way:

The early childhood educator role may be seen as that of "double specialist" in a variety of ways: In teaching young children and in assessing their development and learning; in working with children and in working with adults; in thinking concretely (maintaining insight into the child's thought) and thinking formally, in practice as well as in theory. (p. 28)

Qualities of the Early Childhood Educator

If asked what qualities a good teacher of young children should have, most of us would come up with an intuitive list of characteristics. Research, however, is not particularly clear-cut in showing a consistent relationship between teacher effectiveness and personal qualities. This is partly due to problems in the methodology of such research, inconsistency in what is being measured, difficulty in distinguishing between teaching style and teaching techniques, and even lack of agreement about what constitutes good teaching (Feeney & Chun, 1985; Katz, 1984a). Certainly, those who care for children need qualities beyond liking babies.

Some clues about what makes a good teacher of young children can be gleaned from early childhood educators and researchers based on their experience and insight. Almy et al. (1984) and Balaban (1992) list several qualities, some of which are included in the following list:

- patience
- warmth
- nurturance
- energy
- maturity
- openness to new ideas
- ability to move between concrete and abstract thinking

- ability to anticipate and plan
- ability to provide an interesting environment
- ability to elicit language
- ability to problem solve
- playfulness

Good teachers are able to:

- protect
- listen
- observe
- comfort
- cope

- facilitate social interactions
- guide parent–child separation
- care for the whole family
- smooth "jangled feelings"

You would certainly want to add many of your own characteristics to this list. Here are a few to think about:

- gentleness
- respectfulness
- intrinsic motivation
- optimism
- sincerity
- inquisitiveness
- humour
- openness

- fairness
- sensitivity
- ability to communicate
- reliability
- reflectiveness
- resourcefulness
- empathy
- ability to advocate

Your qualities are not something you have but something that make you who you are. It would be difficult to separate personal and professional qualities because you bring these with you in and out of every aspect of your life. What is important to note is that a good teacher is able to identify his/her qualities, strengths, and

needs as well as those of others. Knowing your **learning style** and that of others you interact with will help you to understand, adjust, and contribute to a positive, healthy interaction. You should be able to assess, implement, evaluate, and accommodate for differing learning styles on an ongoing basis in relationship to their effect on your self and others including children, families, colleagues, and communities in which you work. According to Adler (1993) the best teachers are those who "are able to systematically reflect on their own teaching" (p. 160) or, in other words, engage in reflective practice. Flexibility is second nature to good teachers. But there really is no simple or single definition of a good teacher of young children. In a summary of six in-depth interviews that searched for a definition of the "good preschool teacher," Ayers (1989) concludes that there is a "kaleidoscope of possibility, for there are endless good preschool teachers" (p. 141).

What does distinguish teachers, according to Katz (1984b), is their professionalism, the way they use their knowledge and standards of performance. Teachers possess advanced knowledge in child development and early childhood education that they apply when they have to make judgments and decisions on a moment-by-moment basis. At the same time, they also share with other professionals a commitment to maintaining the high standards set by the profession through its organizations.

The ideal early childhood professional is well paid and knowledgeable and demonstrates high-quality performance, which results in better outcomes for children (Willer & Bredekamp, 1993, p. 64).

Professionalism

This book stresses the importance of the early childhood years, early childhood education, and your role as an early childhood educator. To fully realize that importance, however, you must see yourself as a member of a profession. A profession is different from a job by virtue of certain characteristics. These include:

- a core knowledge base involving philosophical and theoretical principles,
- standards of practice that stem from that knowledge base (Katz, 1988; Vander Ven, 1986),
- a defined code of ethics, and
- specialized training founded on that knowledge base.

Those who have written at great length about early childhood professionalism, recognizing that there are many inconsistencies and problems to be faced, do not always agree to what extent the field meets the criteria of a profession. Increasing dialogue through conferences and written works has helped to sharpen the focus on relevant issues, for instance, low pay and shortage of qualified early childhood

teachers, as well as on strategies for combatting these. Nonetheless, the expanding concern about professionalism, evident at both national and local levels, should propel early childhood education toward its goals, which include a better definition and greater focus.

Although, in many ways, the early childhood field has moved toward professionalization, there is concern that professional status is not universally acknowledged by those who work in the field or by the public at large (Dresden & Myers, 1989; Radomski, 1986; Silin, 1985). The *Caring for a Living* (CCDCF, 1992) study found that 7 out of 10 early childhood educators had postsecondary degrees or diplomas, as opposed to 4 out of 10 workers in the general Canadian workforce. However, the salaries of the teachers were well below the average wage for Canadian industrial workers. In fact, the report indicated that someone working in a warehouse, a position that generally requires less skill, education, and responsibility, earned 58 percent more than the average teacher in a non-school-based early childhood program! *Caring for a Living* reported that teachers in the Northwest Territories did very well in a relative sense, but Gillian Moir from Arctic College cautions us about interpreting that finding in A Canadian Professional Speaks Out, in the Progression chapter at the end of this book.

Most of the Canadian teachers surveyed (84 percent) felt that their profession was not valued by the general public. "It's a bit of a Catch-22: for not only are staff paid poorly, they believe the value of the work they perform is neither acknowledged nor appreciated. And until they are paid higher wages, these perceptions are unlikely to change" (CCDCF, 1992, p. 1). Changes in salary levels and the public perception of the profession are definitely needed, and students entering the profession are most likely to effect these changes.

Students embarking on a career in early childhood education are in a unique position to develop from the start a sense of professionalism that is furthered by every course they take, every day they spend with children, and every conference they attend. Their competence and recognition of the importance of their role will enhance not only their work with children and families, but also their contributions to the early childhood profession. Early childhood education teachers who have a clear concept of who they are, what they do, and the importance of their role are quite effective in educating the public. Now let's look again at those four aspects of professionalism—core knowledge, standards of practice, ethics, and training.

Core Knowledge Base of the Early Childhood Education Profession

As in any profession, such as law or medicine, there is a **core knowledge base** from which early childhood educators draw. This helps define us as professionals within our field and evaluate our effectiveness. It gives us a framework within which to work and serves as a springboard for improvement.

Adapted from guidelines established by The National Association for the Education of Young Children (Willer & Bredekamp, 1993, p. 64) and supported by the Canadian Association of Young Children, the following outlines the exclusive knowledge base and competencies unique to the early childhood education program. An early childhood educator must:

- *understand child development* and demonstrate the implication of this knowledge in practice;
- *provide an environment that is safe, healthy, and nurturing* and is trustworthy, consistent and secure for all;
- *observe and assess children's behaviour* in order to plan, individualize, and evaluate children's learning, teaching practices, and curriculum;
- *plan, implement, and evaluate developmentally appropriate curriculum* to enhance all areas of children's learning and development including physical, intellectual, creative, language, emotional, and social;
- *guide* children by establishing and facilitating supportive relationships by *utilizing developmentally appropriate techniques;*
- *foster* and maintain *positive and productive relationships* (children, family, centre, community, profession);

- *support the development* of individual children, recognizing that children are best understood in the *context of family, culture, and society;* and
- *model* an understanding of the early childhood education profession by making a *commitment to professionalism.*

A person never stops the process of becoming a professional because she/he is always adding to her/his core knowledge base and skill level. Ongoing **professional development** is a part of lifelong learning and of personal and professional growth and development.

Developing Your Philosophy

It would be difficult to work with young children in an appropriate way without a belief system that dictates how you interact with people. This boundary has a profound effect upon everyone involved.

A philosophy is a statement of beliefs and is reflective of your value system. Philosophy is often based on a theory that can be guided by research.

Organizations often have a mission statement. This is a statement of what the organization both believes and hopes to accomplish. It is the organization's commitment based on a belief about its cause. This determines the way the organization conducts business. Hence, your philosophy, mission statement, beliefs, or goals determine your actions as well. They also hold you accountable to your intentions and imply a plan of action. The Reggio Emilia model (discussed in Chapter 5) is the most recent example in our field of a comprehensive and inclusionary approach to child care as it involves the entire community in the development of a system of "early childhood services based on a common value system and pedagogical philosophy" (Pence & Mass, 1994, p. 173).

Experience affects your philosophy. Though the basic premise, or foundation, of your philosophy may never change, your philosophy grows more comprehensive with experience and knowledge. Examples of philosophical statements might include common ideas or beliefs about children such as "I believe all children can learn" or "I believe all children have the right to **inclusive education**" or "I believe all children learn through play." You can also see by now that people hold different belief systems that will conflict with your own. Think of the opposite statements of those just given. What if educational policymakers believed children with special needs could not learn? What if a parent in your program believed children should not play? Their beliefs determine their actions just as your beliefs determine your actions.

That is why having evidence that supports your beliefs is important. Being able to explain, state why, or give a rationale for what you believe helps others understand your actions. Hence, a parent night focusing on the importance of play or a policy stating why your program is inclusive of all children will help people accept what, why, and how you do things. Communicating your philosophy is very important.

One way of communicating is through actions. We've all heard the saying that actions speak louder than words. A belief statement can be transformed into an action statement and into actions. For instance, a teacher might say, "I believe all children should be treated with respect," but her action of pulling a child up by the arm or yelling at the child does not support what she says. Your actions must also reflect your beliefs. In other words, you must practise what you preach.

So how do you go about developing your philosophy? You probably already have a good philosophical base. Write it out in "I believe …" statements. Write an action statement of "I will" for each belief statement. For each statement you make, find research that supports it. As you learn and gain more experience throughout your career, continue to refine your philosophy. You must always have a reason for what you do and be able to explain it to others. Just as your philosophy shapes you, so you shape it. It will reflect your growth and development as an early childhood educator and guide your practice. It will help you keep sight of why you entered this wonderful field in the beginning. Remember, in the spirit of childhood, never stop asking why!

Standards of Practice—Rights, Roles, and Responsibilities

As a member of a profession, and as a person, there are certain rights, justices, and privileges that you should expect. Similarly, as a professional, there are many roles or functions that you are expected to perform. In each of these roles, in the profession as a whole, and as a person, these parts you play and these rights offered to you imply certain responsibilities—duties, skills, and actions—that you are obligated and committed to carry out in a manner for which you are held accountable. When expectations are met, credibility—your honour and that of your profession—is established and upheld.

Rights of an Early Childhood Educator

As an early childhood educator, you have the right to:

- belong to a professional organization that advocates on behalf of its members, promotes the profession, conducts business in a positive, supportive, effective, responsible, and ethical manner, and collects, develops, and disseminates current information about the field to its members;

- access ongoing training and development that will directly impact on your effectiveness in working appropriately with children;

- have a written job description, a policies and procedures manual, training, a contract, and an ongoing evaluation process that includes field work and a plan to support and activate the recommendations and expectations as outlined in the evaluation;

- receive pay that is commensurate with your degree of education and training, expected knowledge base, nature of job responsibility, and community expectations;
- be recognized as a valued, respected, and credible partner in a reciprocal and mutually beneficial system of government; and
- belong to a work environment that is safe, nurturing, and healthy; that encourages, promotes, and supports the development of relationships, communication, and professional development; that recognizes and respects the needs, diversity, confidentiality, and privacy of its staff—in tandem with human rights and labour regulations; and that encourages freedom of speech in the assumption of democratic practice.

Roles of an Early Childhood Educator

As an early childhood educator, you are expected to be:

- a professional
- a member
- a nurturer
- a caregiver
- a teacher
- an advocate
- an employee
- a colleague
- a liaison
- a partner
- a learner
- an individual with specific strengths and needs in the context of your own family, culture, and society

Responsibilities of an Early Childhood Educator

Your responsibility is ultimately to understand and implement the core knowledge base previously discussed. This is a serious task with powerful consequences that affect the lives of many people. Your responsibilities are linked to each of your roles since each of your partners (i.e., children, families, colleagues) also have rights that must be recognized, respected, and addressed. By now you can see the importance and interrelatedness of a **systems approach** in the workplace and how impossible it would be to acknowledge only isolated elements of a system. Issues of philosophy and practice must be considered when viewing a system. A system has many parts that must work both dependently and independently to keep the system working. Thus a system is dynamic or fluid—it is always moving, changing, and adjusting—and needs components that are both flexible and adhesive to keep it malleable yet in tact. Communication is the substance that bonds the elements and the people of our profession.

Ethics

One of the hallmarks of a profession is its recognition of and adherence to a **code of ethics.** Such a code embodies guidelines for behaviour, facilitates decision making, and provides the backing of like-minded professionals when the practi-

tioner takes a "risky but courageous stand in the face of an ethical dilemma" (Katz, 1988, p. 77). In recent years, a number of provincial organizations have developed codes of ethics governing the profession. For example, the British Columbia code of ethics, developed by the Early Childhood Educators of British Columbia (ECEBC) is shown in Exhibit 1.1.

Some of the larger and older provinces, such as Ontario, have developed their own code of ethics (e.g., Association for Early Childhood Educators, Ontario). Smaller or newer provinces/associations have adopted codes of ethics from other provinces. The Saskatchewan Child Care Association (SCCA) is less than 10 years old and so has, for now, adopted British Columbia's code. This reflects a dedication to professionalism for such a young organization. Since codes consume a great deal of time and resources to develop, the SCCA wanted to ensure it had a code of ethics clearly outlined from the beginning. This helped to establish its credibility as an agency for its members and as a spokesperson for the field and the children in its care.

Codes of ethics recognize that many of the day-to-day decisions made by those who work with young children are of a moral and ethical nature. Early childhood educators, for instance, may find themselves in situations with conflicting values in which it is not clear whether the rights of the child, the parents, the school, other children in the program, or the teachers are most important (Feeney, 1988). A code of ethics provides common principles for dealing with such dilemmas, principles based on the value of childhood as a unique stage of life, on knowledge of child development, on appreciation of the importance of family and cultural ties, on respect for the dignity and value of children and adults, and on helping individuals reach their potential through trusting, positive relationships.

Because children are particularly vulnerable, those who work with them have an important responsibility that is supported and defined by a code of ethics (Feeney & Kipnis, 1985). As you enter the early childhood education profession, it is important to learn about the code of ethics followed in your area. If you are in a jurisdiction that does not yet have a code, you should familiarize yourself with one or more from other jurisdictions and perhaps help the professional association in your province or territory to develop one.

EXHIBIT 1.1: THE CODE OF ETHICS OF EARLY CHILDHOOD EDUCATORS OF BRITISH COLUMBIA (ECEBC)

Early childhood educators work with one of society's most vulnerable groups—young children. The quality of interactions between young children and their caregivers has a significant, enduring impact on the children's lives. The intimacy of the relationship and the potential that exists to do harm call for a commitment on the part of early childhood educators to the highest standards of ethical practice.

While individual children are the focus of the work done by early childhood educators, ethical practice extends beyond the child–educator relationship. Early childhood educators care for and educate young children while recognizing and supporting the nurturing and socializing responsibilities of the children's families. Early childhood educators accept their ethical obligations to the children and families they serve as both represent our society's future.

ECEBC recognizes its responsibility to promote ethical practices and attitudes on the part of early childhood educators. The following principles, explanations, and standards of practice have been developed to help early childhood educators monitor their professional practice. They are intended to both guide educators and protect the children and families with whom they work. Professionalism creates additional ethical obligations to colleagues and to the profession.

This code articulates the principles and standards of practice endorsed by ECEBC. Members of ECEBC undertake as a condition of membership in the association to incorporate them into their practice. ECEBC advocates the voluntary acceptance of these principles and standards by all early childhood educators, both members and non-members.

Structure

Eight ethical principles are presented. These principles are intended to guide early childhood educators in deciding what conduct is right and correct. Educators may use the principles to help them make decisions when they encounter ethical problems in the course of their work. Each principle is followed by an explanation and a list of standards of practice that represent an application of the principle in an early childhood setting.

Derivation

These ethical principles were agreed upon by ECEBC after reviewing the literature on the topic of ethics, examining and evaluating the codes of ethics of various professions, and consulting a number of experts in the field of professional ethics. These principles reflect the core values of early childhood education practice which are addressed in the codes of ethics of professional organizations in other jurisdictions.

All eight principles are reflected in the ethical practice of early childhood educators. However, there will be circumstances in which the ethical principles will conflict and educators will face the dilemma of having to choose between conflicting principles. In these difficult situations, it is recommended that the early childhood educators carefully think through the consequences of giving each of the conflicting principles primacy. By evaluating the consequences, it may become clear which principle ought to be given more weight.

ECEBC recognizes that the resolution of ethical dilemmas can be difficult. Educators are encouraged, if time permits, to consult with colleagues and obtain different perspectives on the problem. If this consultation does not clarify the best course of action, educators are encouraged to consult with the ECEBC Ethics Committee for guidance. Although the final decision will be made by the individual educator facing the ethical dilemma, consultation with others indicates a commitment to ethical practice.

Principles

- Early childhood educators promote health and well-being of all children.
- Early childhood educators use developmentally appropriate practices when working with children.
- Early childhood educators demonstrate caring for all children in all aspects of their practice.
- Early childhood educators work in partnership with parents, supporting them in meeting their responsibilities to their children.
- Early childhood educators work in partnership with colleagues and other service providers in the community to support the well-being of families.
- Early childhood educators work in ways that enhance human dignity.
- Early childhood educators pursue, on an ongoing basis, the knowledge, skills, and self-awareness needed to be professionally competent.
- Early childhood educators demonstrate integrity in all of their professional relationships.

Early Childhood Educators of British Columbia (ECEBC) wish to gratefully acknowledge the Child Care Initiatives Fund (CCIF) for supporting this project. The research and code development were conducted by Frances Ricks, Ph.D., and Sandra Griffin, M.A., from the School of Child and Youth Care at the University of Victoria, Victoria, British Columbia.

Source: Early Childhood Educators British Columbia. Reprinted with permission.

Training and Regulation in Early Childhood Education

Many individuals contribute toward providing a good early childhood education program, or system, through their levels and types of expertise. Such expertise

stems from different types of training. In addition, a variety of regulations and quality controls apply to early childhood programs and the personnel who staff them. The range of training options and requirements varies greatly across the country, as do the regulations governing early childhood programs.

Academic Teacher Training Programs

Because you are reading this text, you are most likely involved in an academic early childhood education program whose aim is to prepare qualified teachers and directors of programs for young children through a combination of course work and practicum experiences. Such programs exist at the college level and at the university and postgraduate levels. In more advanced programs, greater depth and more theoretical and research knowledge become increasingly important. You'll note in Exhibit 1.2 that availability and legislation of teacher training is as recent as 1989 and dates back only 40 years. Exhibit 1.3 lists all the ECE programs in Canada. You are entering a field of exciting growth, change, and recognition that has taken centuries to evolve and only decades to explode. In A Canadian Professional Speaks Out, Tara Lee Raycraft, an early childhood education student at Algonquin College in Ottawa, talks about why and how she entered the field, concerns of her peers, and hopes for the future.

EXHIBIT 1.2: EARLY CHILDHOOD EDUCATION TRAINING AND AVAILABILITY

Province or Territory	When Was Teacher Training Required?	When Was Teacher Training Available?
British Columbia	1955	1995
Alberta	1995	1970
Saskatchewan	1989	1981
Manitoba	1982	Late 1960s
Ontario	1960	AECEO programs 1960; college programs 1967
Quebec	1989	1960s
New Brunswick	—	Early 1980s
Prince Edward Island	1986	1987
Nova Scotia	1989	Early 1970s
Newfoundland	1989	Short-lived programs 1970s; widely available programs 1986
Yukon	—	1989
Northwest Territories	—	1988

— = No requirements in place in 1997

The founding dates of the few Canadian university-based programs (e.g., Institute for Child Study 1926), founded during the era of the child study movement are not included here.

Source: Young (1993b).

Early Childhood Administration
- Centennial College of Applied Arts & Technology, Scarborough, ON
- Grant MacEwan Community College, Edmonton, AB
- Seneca College of Applied Arts & Technology, North York, ON

Early Childhood Assistant
- Centennial College of Applied Arts & Technology, Scarborough, ON
- Sheridan College, Oakville, ON

Early Childhood Care Education
- Heritage College (CEGEP), Hull, QC

Early Childhood Development
- Alberta Vocational College (Lac La Biche, AB)
- Alberta Vocational College (Lesser Slave Lake, AB)
- Gardner College, Camrose, AB
- Grande Prairie Regional College, Grande Prairie, AB
- Grant MacEwan Community College, Edmonton, AB
- Keyano College, Fort McMurray, AB
- Lakeland College, Vermilion, AB
- Medicine Hat College, Medicine Hat, AB
- Red Deer College, Red Deer, AB
- Woodland Institute, Prince Albert, SK
- Yukon College, Whitehorse, YT

Early Childhood Development Certificate
- Kelsey Institute, Saskatoon, SK

Early Childhood Education
- Algonquin College of Applied Arts & Technology, Nepean, ON
- Assiniboine Community College, Brandon, MB
- Cambrian College of Applied Arts & Technology, Sudbury, ON
- Camosun College, Victoria, BC
- Canadore College of Applied Arts & Technology, North Bay, ON
- Centennial College of Applied Arts & Technology, Scarborough, ON
- Central Newfoundland Regional College, Grand Falls, NF
- Champlain Regional College, Sherbrooke, QC
- College of New Caledonia, Prince George, BC
- College of the North Atlantic, St. John's, NF (formerly Cabot College)

- Concordia University/Université Concordia, Montreal, QC
- Conestoga College of Applied Arts & Technology, Kitchener, ON
- Confederation College of Applied Arts & Technology, Thunder Bay, ON
- Douglas College, New Westminister, BC
- Durham College of Applied Arts & Technology, Oshawa, ON
- East Kootenay Community College, Cranbrook, BC
- Fanshawe College of Applied Arts & Technology, London, ON
- George Brown College of Applied Arts & Technology, Toronto, ON
- Georgian College of Applied Arts & Technology, Barrie, ON
- Holland College, Charlottetown, PEI
- Humber College of Applied Arts & Technology, Etobicoke, ON
- Keewatin Community College, The Pas, MB
- Kwantlen University College, Surrey, BC
- Lambton College of Applied Arts & Technology, Sarnia, ON
- Langara College, Vancouver, BC
- Lethbridge Community College, Lethbridge, AB
- Loyalist College of Applied Arts & Technology, Belleville, ON
- McGill University, Montreal, QC
- Medicine Hat College, Medicine Hat, AB
- Mohawk College of Applied Arts & Technology, Hamilton, ON
- Mount Saint Vincent University, Halifax, NS
- Niagara College of Applied Arts & Technology, Welland, ON
- Northern College of Applied Arts & Technology, South Porcupine, ON
- Northern Lights College, Dawson Creek, BC
- Nunavut Arctic College, Iqaluit, NWT
- Okanagan University College, Kelowna, BC
- Red River Community College, Winnipeg, MB
- Ryerson Polytechnic University, Toronto, ON
- St. Clair College of Applied Arts & Technology, Windsor, ON
- Saint Lawrence College Saint-Laurent, Brockville, ON
- Sault College of Applied Arts & Technology, Sault Ste. Marie, ON
- Selkirk College, Castlegar, BC
- Seneca College of Applied Arts & Technology, North York, ON
- Sheridan College, Oakville, ON
- Sir Sandford Fleming College, Peterborough, ON
- University College of the Cariboo, Kamloops, BC
- University College of the Fraser Valley, Abbotsford, BC
- University Colleges, Vancouver, BC

- University of Alberta, Edmonton, AB
- University of British Columbia, Vancouver, BC
- University of Calgary, Calgary, AB
- University of Toronto, Toronto, ON
- Vanier College (CEGEP), St. Laurent, QC
- Westviking College of Applied Arts, Technology & Continuing Education, Stephenville, NF
- York University, North York, ON
- Yukon College, Whitehorse, YT

Early Childhood Education (Advanced Studies in Special Needs)

- Humber College of Applied Arts & Technology, Etobicoke, ON

Early Childhood Education (Advanced Studies Post-Diploma)

- Humber College of Applied Arts & Technology, Etobicoke, ON

Early Childhood Education (Basic)

- North Island College, Courtenay, BC

Early Childhood Education (Early Childhood Education)

- Humber College of Applied Arts & Technology, Etobicoke, ON

Early Childhood Education (E.C.E. Certificate)

- University College of the Fraser Valley, Abbotsford, BC

Early Childhood Education (Infants & Toddlers)

- North Island College, Courtenay, BC
- Okanagan University College, Kelowna, BC

Early Childhood Education (Intensive)

- Algonquin College of Applied Arts & Technology, Nepean, ON

Early Childhood Education (Post Basic Certificate)

- College of New Caledonia, Prince George, BC

Early Childhood Education (Prior Learning Assessment)

- Red River Community College, Winnipeg, MB

Early Childhood Education (Psychology)

- University of Western Ontario, London, ON

Early Childhood Education (Resource Teacher)

- Georgian College of Applied Arts & Technology, Barrie, ON
- Niagara College of Applied Arts & Technology, Welland, ON

- St. Clair College of Applied Arts & Technology, Windsor, ON
- Seneca College of Applied Arts & Technology, North York, ON

Early Childhood Education (Special Needs)
- North Island College, Courtenay, BC

Early Childhood Education (Special Needs Diploma)
- University College of the Fraser Valley, Abbotsford, BC

Early Childhood Education Administration
- Confederation College of Applied Arts & Technology, Thunder Bay, ON
- Durham College of Applied Arts & Technology, Oshawa, ON

Early Childhood Education and Care
- Malaspina University College, Nanaimo, BC

Early Childhood Education and Development
- Mount Royal College, Calgary, AB

Early Childhood Education Assistant Level I
- Centennial College of Applied Arts & Technology, Scarborough, ON

Early Childhood Education Diploma
- Algonquin College of Applied Arts & Technology, Nepean, ON
- Kelsey Institute, Saskatoon, SK

Early Childhood Education Level I
- Vancouver Community College, Vancouver, BC

Early Childhood Education Level II
- East Kootenay Community College, Cranbrook, BC

Early Childhood Education Resource Teacher
- Conestoga College of Applied Arts & Technology, Kitchener, ON
- Lambton College of Applied Arts & Technology, Sarnia, ON
- Saint Lawrence College Saint-Laurent, Brockville, ON

Early Childhood Education Supervision and Administration
- Sheridan College, Oakville, ON

Early Childhood Music Education (Advanced)
- Ryerson Polytechnic University, Toronto, ON

Early Childhood Resource Teacher Certificate
- Algonquin College of Applied Arts & Technology, Nepean, ON

Early Childhood Studies

- Nova Scotia Community College (Cumberland), Springhill, NS

Early Elementary Education

- Nova Scotia Teachers College, Truro, NS

It is interesting to note that Canadians working with young children are relatively well educated. In 1991, the Canadian Day Care Advocacy Association and the Canadian Child Day Care Federation (CCDCF) jointly sponsored *Caring for a Living* (CCDCF, 1992), a study of the wages and working conditions of teachers working in licensed child care centres across the country. The report found that over 84 percent of administrative directors have diplomas and degrees, while about 87 percent of the teacher supervisors do. Over 70 percent of the senior teachers have diplomas or degrees. Assistant teachers are also well qualified—about 40 percent of them have a diploma or degree. The situation is comparable in the United States where two-thirds of teachers and more than one-half of assistant teachers have taken at least some early childhood or child development course work (Whitebook, Howes, & Phillips, 1989). Many colleges and universities across Canada have reciprocal agreements. These may be called "fast tracking," "**equivalency**," or "direct entry." These allow students with child studies degrees to enter the second year of a college's early childhood education program or a student with an early childhood education diploma to enter the second year of a child studies degree program. Some professional organizations also grant equivalency—a diploma equivalent to an early childhood education diploma and recognized by that province's Ministry governing early childhood education college programs—to individuals who have a unique combination of experience and education (e.g., someone trained in another country). With such a diverse and highly trained group of individuals working in the early childhood field, you would expect the profession to be viewed with considerable respect. However, early childhood teachers do not feel their work is held in high regard by the Canadian public, and they are trying to better this situation through their professional endeavours.

Careers in Early Childhood Education

In 1997, Human Resources Development Canada (HRDC) was in the process of compiling statistics from the 1992 National Graduate Survey. The sector study on

A CANADIAN PROFESSIONAL SPEAKS OUT
Student's Survival Guide to Success

1. Be Prepared: Work hard and do more than expected.
2. Be Organized: Use a monthly, weekly, and daily calendar. Record all due dates and exams immediately upon notification.
3. Manage Your Time: Don't leave projects and research until the last minute. This will just cause unneeded stress.
4. Keep an Open Mind: Never assume anything!
5. Be Spontaneous: Not everything that you learn in a textbook will work. Find your way. Investigate, initiate, and respond.
6. Clarify: If unsure, ASK!
7. Communicate: Be aware of your language, both verbal and non-verbal. Keep an open line of communication between peers, teachers, children, and yourself.
8. Be Aware: Model appropriate behaviour and follow through on your commitments.
9. Be Professional: Retain a style of maturity. Treat everyday interaction as though you were on the job.
10. Be Accountable: Your actions will have an impact on others. Be accountable for any consequences that may occur.
11. Daydream: Take 20 minutes a day to clear your mind of everything that stresses you. LESS STRESS = GREATER PRODUCTIVITY!
12. Keep Focused: It will be a very trying and tiring year, so find something to keep your mind on task (i.e., hang a graduation picture above your desk).
13. Exercise: This will help reduce anxiety and stress.
14. Sleep: Not always applicable, I know, but you're only harming yourself.
15. Socialize: This is a great release from school—just don't overdo it!
16. Eat Healthy Foods: You must feed your brain in order for it to run efficiently.
17. Take Your Vitamins.

And remember, the only detour of an early burnout is to lead a balanced lifestyle. Stay fit, both physically and mentally, get plenty of rest, eat healthy, and socialize.

MENTAL/EMOTIONAL WELL-BEING
↗   ↘
SOCIAL WELL-BEING ← PHYSICAL WELL-BEING

Tara Lee Raycraft, Algonquin College, Ottawa

child care hopes to present information on the number of early childhood education graduates and employment patterns. How many graduates are working in the field? Where are they working? In what setting are they working?

Typically we think of anyone trained in early childhood education as working in a child care centre. However, there are many other jobs available to early childhood education personnel. These are outlined in Chapter 4, "The Field of Early Childhood Education," under the heading Human Resources in Early Childhood Education. They include directors, teachers, assistants, resource teachers, home visitors, therapy assistants, and early intervention specialists. People with these positions work in varied settings such as assisting a classroom teacher in elementary school; working with children with special needs in a classroom, treatment centre, hospital playroom, recreation program, or other settings; working in the home with children with special needs; working through agencies in such areas as infant stimulation programs (often run by public health departments or hospitals), associations for community living, or children's aid; running play groups or drop-in centres (e.g., at the YMCA or YWCA or in a shopping mall); assessing children and programs in early childhood (e.g., for the province-, region-, town-, or city-governing body); and teaching early childhood education at the college level. They may also work in incidental fields like publishing children's books, textbooks, or teachers' manuals; developing early childhood education material (i.e., resources, toys, curriculums), marketing and sales; or working in any industry that might deal effectively and appropriately with the care and interaction of children (i.e., the media, computers, conferences).

Also watch for more agreements with boards of education to have early childhood educators in partnerships with teachers in kindergarten classrooms. Finally, for any entrepreneur, opening up your own school, designing your own materials, or promoting your own methods is possible if you investigate your province's and city's legislation, professional organizations, training programs, and business opportunities and incentives.

Regardless of the setting in which you work, you must strive to make it welcoming and supportive. In A Closer Look, this concept of invitational education is examined.

Teachers' Developmental Stages

Just as children are considered to progress through developmental stages of growth and development in many domains, so do teachers progress through stages

A Closer Look

INVITING SUCCESS IN EARLY CHILDHOOD EDUCATION

Of the many things young children learn, perhaps the most important is the picture they develop of who they are and how they fit into the world. This highly personal portrayal of existence and possibilities is called the self-concept. We see it as key in the development of each child's intellectual, psychological, social, moral, and physical potential. Children who believe in their personal worth and possibilities are more likely to engage in and sustain activities and relationships that call forth a greater realization of their potential. A vital question then for educators of young children is, "What can we do to promote the development of a positive self-concept?"

We believe that we do not have direct access to another's self-concept. Rather, because an individual's self-concept is personally constructed through the messages received, interpreted, acted upon, and evaluated, our role as educators is to be message designers and implementers. Thus, if we take self-concept to be the core of future development, our educational responsibility is to construct and extend signal systems that invite children to see themselves as valuable, able, and responsible learners who can behave accordingly. We call such an approach to child development **invitational education** and feel that it offers a systematic and morally defensible approach for working in early childhood education.

Invitational education is a perceptually based self-concept approach to teaching, learning, and caring that is centred on the following five principles:

1. People are able, valuable, and responsible and should be treated accordingly.
2. Education should be a cooperative activity.
3. Process is the product in the making.
4. People possess untapped positive potential in all areas of human endeavour.
5. Potential can best be realized by places, policies, processes, and programs specifically designed to invite development, and by people who are intentionally inviting with themselves and others personally and professionally.

Educators using these principles as an operating stance work together to make their centre or school "The Most Inviting Place in Town." Focusing on the development of caring interpersonal practices, nurturing environments, person-centred policies, and engaging programs, invitational educators aim to create an institutional culture that enables all involved to more fully relate, assert, invest, and cope. To assist educators in developing and sustaining inviting environments, several books have been written, International Alliance for Invitational Education (with a Canadian centre) has been formed, and a rating scale for early childhood education constructed.

—John M. Novak and Pamela Rogers, Brock University, St. Catharines

as they grow professionally gaining knowledge, training, skills, and experience. Katz (1977) concludes that teachers undergo a series of stages, each with unique developmental tasks and training needs. It is helpful to realize that others begin their teaching experiences with similar feelings of inadequacy or anxiety and that these evolve into more advanced stages as competence develops.

- *Stage 1: Survival*—Beginning teachers' main concern through the first year or so of teaching is usually focused on whether they will survive. The realization of the great responsibility they have for the group of children, as well as the discrepancy between the success they expect and the reality of the classroom, result in anxiety and feelings of inadequacy. In general, they are acquiring information about what children are like and what can be expected of them. At this stage, the teachers' main need is for support, encouragement, and guidance, provided on-site as required.

- *Stage 2: Consolidation*—Having recognized that they can indeed survive, teachers begin to focus on specific tasks. As they consolidate the information gained from their first year or two, they move their attention more specifically to problem children or to situations that deviate from the general norm. Their needs at this time are for continued on-site training that supports exploration of alternatives to deal with problem situations.

- *Stage 3: Renewal*—By now, teachers in their third or fourth year begin to seek some new approaches and ideas as they tire of the way they have been doing things for the past several years. The search for renewal can be met through meetings with colleagues, professional organizations and conferences, professional books and journals, and visits to other programs.

- *Stage 4: Maturity*—This final stage is reached by different teachers at different points and represents a coming to terms with themselves and their profession. Now they ask deeper and more abstract questions, looking at the broader implications of their work in the context of the larger society. Their experience makes these questions more meaningful. Mature teachers need opportunities to read widely, interact with others, and participate in seminars and other forums where such questions are addressed by others searching for similar insights.

Teacher Satisfaction and Evaluation

Canadian early childhood teachers, on average, find great job satisfaction in their profession, which compensates for some of the dilemmas facing the field. In *Caring for a Living,* it was noted that "the nature of the work and the opportunity to make a difference in the lives of children is the silver lining" (CCDCF, 1992, p. 1) in early childhood education. The opportunity to contribute to and observe the development of their young charges provides a great source of pleasure to early childhood educators. In addition, they find other aspects of the job gratifying. Satisfaction with co-workers is very high—8.6 out of 10 for over 7000 Canadian teachers. Undoubtedly, those of you who are planning to enter this profession will be happy to know it brings such rewards to its members.

Satisfaction is, however, combined with many other factors. Is the pay satisfactory? Do I have a voice? Can I see progress? Do I feel respected? Am I making a difference? Am I growing as a professional? Self-evaluation is critical to personal and professional development. As well, credible professions will be accountable to their mandate by ensuring that both their program and their teachers are evaluated on a regular basis. This evaluation should be done in the spirit of learning and for the purposes of improvement for the benefit of all parties concerned—teachers, children, parents, colleagues, and the community. Results of evaluations need to be shared and discussed and written action plans agreed upon and maintained by all those involved. Often professional organizations such as provincial early childhood education ones have an accreditation process for teachers.

Self-improvement is important. But recognizing that self-nurturing is vital is more difficult for those who tend to spend their career giving. As we mentioned earlier, self-care is as much a responsibility as it is a right. Caring for your needs means you are far more effective in caring for others. Being aware, being open, and being communicative—asking, listening, sharing, watching—show you are capable of both teaching and learning.

Professional Organizations

One sign of a profession is the existence of organizations to which members belong and of professional journals that members read. Such organizations and their literature provide members with support and a sense of common interest and

purpose. In Canada, early childhood educators have several pertinent organizations and journals at the national level; many more are found at the provincial and territorial levels. In addition, numerous organizations focus on more specialized groups, for instance, those involved in for-profit child care, Montessori, church-sponsored programs, home-based care, early childhood special education, and others. We will briefly discuss the major national organizations, as well as one influential American organization. The 1992 Canadian National Child Care Study (CNCCS), *Canadian Child Care in Context: Perspectives from the Provinces and Territories* (Pence, 1992), contains an extensive list of the professional organizations in each Canadian jurisdiction. Some of these are summarized in the following list.

Canada

1. *The Canadian Child Care Federation (CCCF)* (formerly the Canadian Child Day Care Federation) or *Fédération Canadienne des services de garde à l'enfance (FCSGE)* has a recent history. Although the idea for a national organization was formulated in 1983, it was not until 1987 that the CCDCF received federal funding and opened an office in Ottawa. The federation aims to improve the quality of child care in Canada by providing services to those in the field. It supports provincial and territorial organizations, and aims to provide information and services to professionals in the field. National conferences, regional workshops, a quarterly magazine (*Interaction*), information sheets, and a speakers' bureau are among the services the federation offers.

The CCDCF also developed the national statement on the quality of child care. In addition, the federation is addressing issues related to the training and education of people entering the field. In the fall of 1992, the CCDCF received federal funding for a three-year research project that aims to make Canadian resources widely available and to develop resources on topics where they do not exist. In 1993, the CCDCF changed its name to the Canadian Child Care Federation (CCCF). CCCF publishes a research journal entitled *Visions* and a quarterly bilingual magazine entitled *Interactions*.

2. *The Child Care Advocacy Association of Canada (CCAAC)* (formerly Canadian Day Care Advocacy Association), founded in 1983, aims to make high-quality, affordable, non-profit child care accessible to all Canadians who need it. It is funded by the Secretary of State and run by a non-profit volunteer board.

3. *The Canadian Association for Young Children (CAYC)* includes a diverse range of members concerned with the overall development and care of children up to nine years of age. It also mandates working toward quality practices and programs, providing professional growth and development, providing information on children, and coordinating efforts of all groups whose focus is children. The CAYC publishes *Canadian Children* semiannually.

4. *Canadian Council for Exceptional Children (CCEC)*. The council advocates for the needs of children who face challenges in many areas of learning and development. It has an extensive network of provincial and local chapters, publications including journals (*Exceptional Children*), magazines (*Teaching Exceptional Children*), newsletters, and resource materials. It has numerous subdivisions, one of which is called the Division for Early Childhood (DEC). Its provincial, national, and international (U.S.) membership attend annual conferences which are an excellent forum for professional development.

5. Although not an association, the *Child Care Resource and Research Unit* at the University of Toronto is an excellent source of information regarding Canadian research, statistics, legislation, projects, and issues surrounding child care in Canada.

United States

The National Association for the Education of Young Children (NAEYC), the largest early childhood education organization, is a powerful voice for children, families, and teachers in the United States. Its goals are (a) to improve professional practice and working conditions, and (b) to increase public understanding of and support for high quality in early childhood education (Smith, 1990). The association has a growing membership (77 000 in 1991) that represents a diverse group of individuals. In addition, NAEYC holds an annual conference that is attended by more than 20 000 early childhood education professionals yearly. The NAEYC also has an extensive series of publications that are invaluable to professionals in the field, including the bimonthly journal *Young Children*, and more than 80 books and other resources. At present, our Canadian organizations are not as well developed as the NAEYC and do not yet have a comparable range of publications. Canadians frequently turn to the NAEYC for additional resources they require.

As a student entering the early childhood profession, you should consider becoming a member of a professional organization. Most of the organizations have a student membership option, which costs considerably less than the regular membership. By becoming a member, you can keep abreast of new developments, have the opportunity to meet and participate in a support network with others in the same field, and attend workshops and conferences at the local, provincial, and national level. In fact, you may even be eligible for the CCCF's travel subsidy which would help you attend its national conference. (If you attend the conference, you can suggest to the instructor who assigned this text that you will do a conference report and/or seminar in place of another course assignment.) The contacts you make as a student can be very helpful when you are seeking a position in the field; professionals hiring in the field typically prefer to hire someone they know has been active in their association rather than a total stranger. If you need additional information about the organizations in your community and province, ask your instructor or professionals you know to elaborate on the available associations. We have included a partial list of provincial associations in Exhibit 1.4 The Canadian Child Care Federation (Ottawa, Ontario) retains an extensive, updated list of associations and addresses.

Issues Facing Teachers in Early Childhood Education

Early childhood education is, in many ways, a field of contradictions and extremes. Those who try to define it often find themselves in a dilemma, not clear on what to include and what to exclude. Where does a program fit that barely meets provincial minimum standards, and what about the program that genuinely strives for excellence in meeting the needs of its children and families? Are the kindergarten teacher, the child care provider, the preschool teacher, and the home care provider included? Are the preschool teacher who holds a master's degree in early childhood education and the high-school graduate who works in a child care centre equal in the same field? Can the child care provider who earns minimum wage and no benefits for the 8 hours a day spent caring for children 50 weeks of the year be lumped together with the kindergarten teacher who earns a public-school salary, often greater than $50 000, for 10 months of teaching?

EXHIBIT 1.4: CANADIAN PROVINCIAL/TERRITORIAL ASSOCIATIONS OF EARLY CHILDHOOD EDUCATION

1. Newfoundland	Association of Early Childhood Education of Newfoundland and Labrador
2. Nova Scotia	Association of Early Childhood Educators
3. Prince Edward Island	Early Childhood Development Association of P.E.I.
4. New Brunswick	Early Childhood Coalition Petite Enfance
5. Quebec	Association of Early Childhood Educators of Quebec
6. Ontario	Association of Early Childhood Educators of Ontario
	Ontario Coalition for Better Child Care
7. Manitoba	Manitoba Child Care Association
8. Saskatchewan	Saskatchewan Child Care Association Inc.
Alberta	Alberta Association for Young Children
	Early Childhood Professional Association of Alberta
9. British Columbia	Early Childhood Educators of B.C.
10. Northwest Territories	N.W.T. Child Care Association
11. Yukon Territory	Yukon Child Care Association
12. International	World Organization for Early Childhood Education Canada (OMEP), Laval University Quebec, Quebec G1K 7P4

How can the teacher job description that calls for someone who likes children be compared with the one that requires a degree in early childhood education or child development? How can the lack of teacher training requirements in three Canadian jurisdictions be acceptable in light of educators' insistence that those who work with young children need specific training? In fact, is there a good

reason to justify why some of you are enrolled in an academic program while others with no academic training may equally qualify for a position?

These questions and others are at the heart of the dilemma facing the early childhood profession. We will review some specific issues and look at some possible ways of addressing them. Although we will divide some of these issues into categories, such as teacher shortage and low pay, these concerns are all interrelated.

The purpose of presenting these issues in this chapter is aimed not at discouraging you but at enlightening and motivating you. If you enter the field knowing the risks, issues, and challenges that face you, then you also enter the profession prepared to face and meet these problems head on.

We end this section by discussing the positive impact of empowerment and activism and by outlining five key recommendations for resolving these issues. You should also note that these issues can also be found in other fields and professions and are not necessarily exclusive to early childhood education.

A Historical Perspective— Issues of Feminism and Equality

It might be helpful to look at a few historical issues in the field of early childhood education to gain a perspective on its current status. Early childhood education today is inextricably linked to the role and status of women in North America. Between the mid-18th and mid-19th centuries, "womanhood was redefined, its image re-created and reimagined, its social function reviewed, its links to child rearing and socialization forged, and its authority over the moral and cultural development of the nation rationalized" (Finkelstein, 1988, p. 12). When, in the latter half of the 19th century, the kindergarten became firmly established as a Canadian institution, women had found their niche in an environment that was not quite domestic, yet not quite public either.

The early 20th-century pioneers of the early childhood education movement, while building a scientific basis for child study, continued to see women as the guardians of the young, with a specialized role in upholding moral and cultural standards—a noble role that was held above concerns for economic and material comforts. Unfortunately, this legacy of selflessness has followed early childhood educators to the end of this century. While giving them a sense of the importance of their work, this ultimately resulted in the devaluing of the profession and the view of women as equal counterparts in the workforce. The placing of women in a low-paying, low-status social structure (Finkelstein, 1988) and their acceptance of this placement led to their inadvertent acceptance of the inequities accompanying this placement. As you will see later, low pay is inevitably tied to poor quality care which inevitably leads to a bad reputation. If care is our product, and our product is poor, we create a public image of mistrust and a lack of faith in our abilities. This also means we do not attract investors (i.e., government funding), clients (parents), or overall public support. Furthermore, because low pay traditionally attracted only women to the field, this negative perception directly affected the perception of women in general. By organizing ourselves professionally and through lobbying for **pay equity**, we have begun to elevate our field to a viable and respectable position.

Teacher Shortage

Over the past several years, increasing attention has been focused on the shortage of qualified early childhood educators. This shortage is partly caused by the high demand for child care as increasing numbers of mothers with children enter the workforce. In fact, Employment and Immigration Canada (1992) projections for the 1990s suggest that there will be approximately a 23 percent growth rate in the demand for preschool teachers. Yet, particularly in areas where there is low unemployment and a high cost of living, early childhood educators are scarce. In addition, a decreasing number of people are entering the workforce as the "baby bust" generation—those born during the 1970s when the national birth rate declined—reaches maturity (Galinsky, 1989).

Teacher shortage can be tied to the high rate of turnover among early childhood educators. According to *Caring for a Living* (Canadian Child Day Care, 1992), a Canadian survey of early childhood teachers found the national teacher turnover rate to be 26 percent. It ranges from a low of 16 percent in P.E.I. to a high of 84 percent in the Yukon. Although the data are not yet available, it is likely that the turnover rate varies with the type of facility. According to the National Child Care Staffing Study in the United States (Whitebook, Howes, & Phillips, 1989), the 1988 U.S. turnover rate was 41 percent ranging from a 74 percent annual staff change in chain, for-profit centres to a 30 percent rate in non-profit programs. Unless these high turnover rates can be halted, the teacher-shortage problem is likely to continue. However, there is little doubt that the turnover rate must be viewed along with information on salaries as well.

Teacher shortage can be viewed as positive for those of you in training. To keep you actively involved in the field, we all must understand and continue to address quality of care and salaries as it affects teacher turnover rates and creates a shortage.

Teacher Turnover and Low Pay

You have already entered this field knowing that salaries are lower than they should be in your chosen profession and for females in general. Our goal here is to inform you early on why this is so. You can then begin making career-path choices within the field of early childhood education: investigating programs, sending away for information, asking questions, focusing some of your assignments on these issues, lobbying for change, and ultimately having an impact on your field from day one. Students can be a very powerful and visible force to the public and the politicians.

High teacher turnover rates will continue to be a problem in early childhood programs in both Canada and the United States as long as wages remain low. Certainly high turnover rates are not characteristic of kindergarten and primary-level programs where the rate of pay is much higher—in fact, some teachers' federations are offering incentives for early retirement in an attempt to persuade aging teachers to leave the lucrative profession and create positions for young graduates in the teaching profession.

The staffing shortage in non-school-based early childhood programs would undoubtedly be much less of a problem if early childhood teachers were paid adequate salaries and if they received appropriate recognition and status. For most teachers of young children, however, monetary rewards are not equal to their professional training and value. Although there is wide variation in pay, early childhood teachers are generally paid poorly. *Caring for a Living* (Canadian Child Day Care, 1992) reported that the average salary for a senior teacher in Canada was $18 498 per annum, while assistants received an annual salary of $15 337. Administrative directors averaged $25 804 per year, while teacher supervisors earned $20 498. However, there was considerable variation in salaries across the provinces and territories. The average wage was as low as $5.57 per hour in Newfoundland (which was below Ontario's minimum wage of $6.35 per hour) and $6.23 in Alberta, and as high as $17.81 for an administrative director in the Northwest Territories. Only about 20 percent of the Canadian teachers surveyed were unionized, but these unionized workers had salaries that were 33 percent higher than those of teachers working in non-unionized settings. (In 1993 [Child Care Resource, 1993], the Canadian Union of Public Employees [CUPE] attempted a provincial unionization drive for Saskatchewan, but to date the province remains largely non-unionized. Manitoba, however, is provincially unionized with solid backing from provincial bodies dedicated to quality child care standards.)

Teachers in municipal non-profit centres generally earned substantially more than teachers in private non-profit and profit-making centres. For example, in Alberta, municipal teachers earned 26 percent more than teachers in non-profit centres and 63 percent more than teachers in profit-making centres.

The low wages of Canadian early childhood educators still remain somewhat discouraging given that over two-thirds of the teachers surveyed had postsecondary-level diplomas or degrees. In contrast, only 41 percent of the national labour force has a comparable education. Historically, the profession has been dominated by females, and historically, predominantly female occupations are associated with low pay and low status. Thus, this problem of low pay does not belong exclusively to our profession or our field. Moreover, over the years, females also have been less likely to protest their wages. However, this is definitely changing. In April 1993, for example, the Confédération des syndicats nationaux (CSN) organized a walkout of all unionized child care teachers in Quebec to support demands for a wage increase of $3.50 per hour (Childcare Resource Unit, 1993).

Benefits are another issue of concern. Generally, teachers of early childhood programs sponsored by larger institutions, such as municipalities, hospitals, school boards, or universities, benefit from the policies of their sponsoring agencies. In a similar way, teachers of employer-sponsored child care programs also often receive their company's benefits package. However, benefits are rare in smaller centres, especially profit-making ones. Canadian teachers' responses to *Caring for a Living* suggest that the high turnover rate in non-school-based early childhood programs is related to low wages. In the United States, Whitebook et al. (1989) found an inverse relationship between rate of pay and percentage of turnover. Those at the lower end of the pay scale changed jobs at twice the rate of those at the higher end. At the same time, however, they found that there was less turnover among teachers with early childhood training. In fact, the Canadian turnover rates are exceptionally high in the Yukon and the Northwest Territories (84 percent and 65 percent, respectively), where there are no training requirements. They are also high in Alberta (42 percent), which implemented its teacher training requirements in 1995. Staff consistency is a critical factor in quality care (see Chapter 5).

High staff turnover takes its toll in several ways. The National Child Care Staffing Study (Whitebook et al., 1989) found that in centres with a high turnover rate, children spent less time in social activities with peers and tended more to wander aimlessly. Very young children such as toddlers have been found to be very susceptible to turnover, exhibiting withdrawal and aggressiveness two years later (Howes & Hamilton, 1993). In addition, separation from parents becomes more critical when caregivers change frequently (Galinsky, 1989). Teachers also suffer when their co-workers change frequently because they have to assume the additional burden of orienting and training new staff (Whitebook, 1986). A follow-up study (Whitebook, Phillips, & Howes, 1993) made similar observations four years later. It did confirm that the rate of teacher turnover is affected by quality, salaries, and type of program (i.e., for-profit or non-profit).

Low pay fuels a vicious cycle. Poor pay causes qualified teachers to seek work elsewhere; as a result, jobs are often filled by unqualified staff. They, in turn, reinforce the low status in which early childhood education is held and negate the need for higher pay (Katz, 1984a). In a recent call for an "all-out effort to improve compensation and status," Marcy Whitebook (1986), director of the U.S. Child Care Employee Project under which the National Child Care Staffing Study was carried out, warned that child care "could become a less and less attractive career choice despite the many inherently gratifying aspects of working with young children. The most likely and scariest prospect is that the pressure will build at a faster pace to lower standards for child care personnel—some of which are already frighteningly inadequate—in order to fill teaching vacancies" (p. 11). Kyle (1992a) expressed similar concerns about teacher shortages in Ontario:

> There is also some concern that the [Ministry's] development of an options paper "to provide alternatives for determining equivalency" may result in the watering down of present training requirements in order to allow more semi-trained or untrained staff to work in child care centres (p. 444).

Semi-trained and untrained teachers might well solve the teacher shortage problem, and possibly reduce child care fees, but at what cost? While professionals with training command higher salaries, they also bring considerably more to their programs and enhance the quality of care young children receive.

Low Wages and Affordable Child Care

The low wages of early childhood educators are inextricably related to the issue of affordable child care. Teachers' wages (and benefits if they receive them) constitute the largest expenditure in early childhood programs. However, that allocation varies considerably from one jurisdiction to another. In Newfoundland, for example, only 49 percent of a centre's budget is used for salaries, while that figure jumps to 78 percent and 80 percent for Manitoba and the Northwest Territories, respectively. (The average for Canadian programs is 69 percent.)

Of course, the fee parents pay for a program is directly affected by how much is allocated to salaries. The higher the teachers' cheques are, the greater the cost of the program. Teacher–child ratios and group size regulations have a similar impact on budgets and fees. The more children per adult, the lower the cost because fewer adults have to be hired. On the other hand, high child–adult ratios are associated with higher levels of teacher stress and decreased responsiveness to children (Phillips & Howes, 1987; Whitebook, Howes, Darrah, & Friedman, 1982).

Yet the answer is not simply a matter of raising the cost of child care charged to parents. Although some families can afford to pay higher rates to ensure high-quality care offered by well-trained and well-paid professionals, many others cannot. Experts contend that the cost parents pay for child care includes a hidden subsidy—the low wages teachers receive (Willer, 1990). Many professionals advocate aggressive lobbying for public support of child care. Some advocates maintain that only when teachers collectively insist on higher wages and benefits will there be sufficient economic impetus to force a solution to the problem.

Since any additional costs would have to be borne by parents, parents will become more interested in the problem, unless they find public funds. If they cannot afford child care, parents will become involved in the political process of vying for funds. According to Morin (1989):

> Our advocacy efforts have been directed primarily toward increasing the supply of affordable care for parents, not to increasing compensation for employees. Common practice is to shield parents from the true cost of child care by having employees work at compensation levels that subsidize the cost to parents (p. 19).

Burnout Syndrome

Teacher burnout is another issue in the field, and it too is linked with teacher shortages, high turnover rates, low salaries, and the stress that arises as a consequence. Burnout is complex, resulting from multiple causes. It is characterized by job dissatisfaction, stress, loss of energy, irritability, and a feeling of being exploited. The **burnout syndrome** has been described as a feeling of exhaustion that results from too many demands on one's energy and resources (Mattingly, 1977).

Many factors contribute to burnout. Some of these, cited in the initial research findings (Whitebook et al., 1982), include long working hours, unpaid overtime, time spent outside working hours in curriculum planning or parent functions, expectations for maintenance duties, lack of breaks, the constant intensity of working closely with children, high child–adult ratios, and lack of power in the decision-making process.

Although burn-out is a final outcome for some of those who work in early childhood programs, most find great job satisfaction, which balances some of the negative aspects. *Caring for a Living* (Canadian Child Day Care, 1992) found Canadian teachers find their involvement with and their positive influence on young children very satisfying. They also enjoy the collegiality that accompanies their positions; over 85 percent of those surveyed are very happy with their colleagues. The opportunity for reflection and self-development, satisfying staff relations, job flexibility, autonomy, and staff interdependence have also been reported as positives in U.S. studies (Whitebook et al., 1982, 1989).

Men in Early Childhood Education

A somewhat different issue concerns the role of men in early childhood education. A 1992 study of Canadian early childhood teachers found that 98 percent of them were females; in the United States between 95 and 97 percent of practitioners are females (Seifert, 1988; Whitebook et al., 1989). There have been and continue to be male teachers who have a high commitment to the education and well-being of young children. For some children who grow up in single-parent homes without a father figure, a male teacher can fill a particularly special role.

Yet men leave the field of early childhood education at an even greater rate than women do. Some male teachers who changed careers reported that they were subject to subtle prejudicial attitudes from parents, female co-workers, and administrators. They were considered inferior to women because they had never been mothers. Suspicion that was initially based on vague sex stereotypes was intensified during the 1980s by several highly publicized cases of sexual abuse involving male teachers in child care settings (Robinson, 1988). Similarly, the 1993 abuse trial of four male police officers, one unrelated woman, and a family (father, mother, and son) who operated an unlicensed child care facility in Martensville, Saskatchewan, again raised public suspicions about men in child care (and about child care in general). While these are exceptional cases, they nonetheless have a deterrent effect on some men considering the child care field.

It is more likely that economic reasons prevent more men from entering the field of early childhood education or cause them to leave the field more readily if they do spend some time as preschool teachers. Robinson (1988) found that 85 percent of his sample of male early childhood teachers were married with at least one child and were the major wage-earners in their families. Low pay compelled them to look elsewhere for work. In part, men leave the field or do not enter it because they have more and better-paying career choices than women, not because of the nature of the job (Seifert, 1988). The absence of a substantial number of men in the field is undoubtedly another contributing factor to low salaries, though it has been argued that "recruiting more men would enhance the professional self-image of early childhood education" (Seifert, 1988, p. 114). We must remember that recruiting men in the absence of increasing salaries is ineffective. Low wages continue to be the pivotal factor affecting professionalism.

Empowerment and Activism

We have raised several issues that face the early childhood profession. It is heartening that increasingly more effort is being devoted to solving these issues. Articulate public statements, relevant publications, thoughtful research, and energetic political advocacy and lobbying are making an impact. There is no question that the needs of young children and families, the importance of high quality in child care, and the needs of early childhood teachers are becoming highly visible public matters.

Changes in the current realities of early childhood education can be brought about through joint political action and the empowerment of teachers (Dresden & Myers, 1989). Training for advocacy is being incorporated into some higher-education programs, so students learn how policies are made, how the political system operates, and how they can affect it (Lombardi, 1986). You may well be taking a course that covers advocacy as part of your program of study, something that probably would not have been part of the curriculum 15 or 20 years ago.

What is clear is the resolve of professionals and organizations to push for change. Interest in and support for quality child care comes from many sectors both within and outside of the field of early childhood education, including parents, teachers, administrators, resource and referral agencies, related service providers, professional organizations, teacher trainers and educators, researchers, civic and religious groups, business and labour organizations, volunteer service organizations, philanthropic organizations and foundations, and civic leaders. A coalition including members of such constituency groups can be a powerful force in beginning to address issues (Lombardi, 1990). However, the ultimate responsibility for enhancing the prestige—and the salaries—of early childhood educators lies with the members of the profession. As one of the reviewers of this text noted, some early childhood professionals "are quite apathetic and want other groups to plead their cause." In order to effect real change, professionals must be willing to commit their own time to lobbying efforts, and then other groups—parents, for example—may join them. In Partnerships, we examine the parents' role in supporting early childhood education.

The United States National Child Care Staffing Study (Whitebook et al., 1989) ends with five major recommendations for change and suggestions for achieving these. These recommendations are as relevant to the Canadian context as they are to that of the United States.

1. *Increase salaries.* To reach this goal, some of the recommendations are to establish salary levels that are competitive with jobs requiring comparable training and education, earmark government funds for salary enhancement, raise the minimum wage, and invest more public and private funds in child care to help low- and middle-income families.

2. *Promote education and training.* This goal can be reached by establishing a career ladder, as well as stipend programs to cover early childhood training costs.

3. *Adopt standards that will lead to higher-quality programs.* Such standards should establish national criteria for child–adult ratios, staff training, education, and compensation, and they should be required of recipients of any public funds.

4. *Develop industry-wide standards.* To increase the quality of early childhood programs, recommendations include a minimum allocation of a centre's budget for teaching-staff expenditures, a benefits package for all teaching staff, inclusion of time for curriculum preparation and staff meetings, and encouragement of staff to join a professional organization.

5. *Promote public education.* To educate the public about the importance of well-trained and adequately paid teachers, it is recommended that administrators, educators, professional organizations, and referral agencies participate in a concerted effort to promote this issue and its importance.

As you complete your course, remember that you can make a difference to the field of early childhood education and enhance its status in Canada. Just as you can be a powerful influence on the development of the young children in your program, you can have a major impact on the development of the field in the 21st century.

PARTNERSHIPS
Parent Support for Early Childhood Educators

The teacher–parent relationship is a reciprocal process. While teachers provide many services for parents, parents can also be extremely effective advocates for the early childhood education profession. One of the more effective lobbying efforts to promote increased funding allocation for early childhood programs in Quebec was the appearance of a large group of parents who spoke about the importance of that funding to their lives. The legislators found the taxpayers who came to promote this funding quite convincing.

Parental support, however, does not begin in the political arena. First and most important, parents must have a sound appreciation of early childhood educators and a clear understanding of the issues they face. Such understanding is promoted by a high-quality program in which teachers act professionally and are articulate about their field. When parents recognize that the quality of education and care their children receive is inextricably tied to improving the status and working conditions of their children's teachers, they will be better able to help bring about changes.

Key Terms

burnout syndrome
caregiver
child care worker
code of ethics
core knowledge base
inclusive education

invitational education
learning style
pay equity
professional development
systems approach
teacher

Key Points

- You must recognize your own strengths and needs and how these relate with others' to create positive, healthy relationships.

- Early childhood educators are nurturing caregivers as well as teachers.

- Professionalism is based on four criteria: core knowledge base, standards of practice which include rights, roles, and responsibilities, a code of ethics and training, and regulation in early childhood education.

- Teachers progress through developmental stages.

- Early childhood educators contribute to and observe children's development while also making appropriate evaluations that hold them accountable to their professional responsibilities.

- By knowing the risks, issues, and challenges that face them professionally, early childhood educators are motivated and prepared to enter the profession equipped with a solution-oriented attitude.

- Traditional roles assigned to women in the past have helped create decreased value and poor wages in the child care profession.

- Low wages often create high staff turnover, which has a negative impact on both teachers and children.

- To effect real change in the child care profession, you must advocate for change and lobby together with other groups that share your mandate.

Chapter 2

Childhood

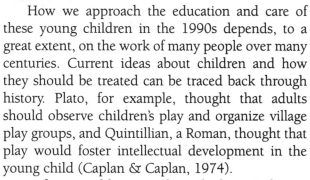

At the heart of early childhood education are young children. All the topics we will discuss in the following chapters are aimed at gaining a better understanding of children and how we, together with their families, can best meet their needs. Although our focus will be on children, it is important to keep in mind that children must never be seen in isolation, but rather as part of a family system that provides context and identity through its lifestyle, culture, heritage, and traditions.

How we approach the education and care of these young children in the 1990s depends, to a great extent, on the work of many people over many centuries. Current ideas about children and how they should be treated can be traced back through history. Plato, for example, thought that adults should observe children's play and organize village play groups, and Quintillian, a Roman, thought that play would foster intellectual development in the young child (Caplan & Caplan, 1974).

Defining and learning about the historical roots of childhood, our views of children, and how children learn is important for several reasons. First, it is valuable to know that our current practices are based on a blend of ideas and traditions that have evolved over centuries. At times, ideas become unfashionable, but they often re-emerge in a slightly altered way. Understanding these cycles of change will make it easier for you to accept and explain the

ongoing changes in early childhood education that you will experience as a professional, a parent, and/or an interested observer. Second, if you are a professional in the field, you will find that your knowledge of the history of early childhood can be a source of support, pride, and inspiration. Many of the early educators and thinkers in the field were driven to improve the quality of young children's lives, and they persisted in their efforts even when they paid a personal toll. Finally, knowing about children and about the theories that explain how they learn and why you do things in a certain way can be empowering. If you are questioned about your practices, you can confidently explain the theoretical basis and developmental appropriateness of how children learn and develop and why you do what you do with the children in your care.

Exhibit 2.1 shows the timeline linking history, influential people and events in early childhood.

When Is Early Childhood?

If you were to ask several individuals to define the term **early childhood,** it is likely that you would receive a different answer from each person. In fact, even early childhood educators have difficulty using terms consistently. Some of this uncertainty stems from the fact that the definition of early childhood has widened over the past 30 years, as has the range of early childhood programs (Doxey, 1990). In this text, the term "early childhood" refers to the period from birth to age 8, and most current works would agree with this definition.

History of Childhood

Ancient Greece—Children as Non-Persons

The idea that children are different from adults, and that there is a distinct period of life known as childhood, did not always exist. Without the concept of children or childhood to guide practices of the time, children often endured treatments and conditions that were unacceptable by today's standard. The second part of this chapter outlines the similarities and differences in children's development as we know them today. We placed that material later because it made little sense to present it without knowing how our current ideas of children came to be. Following is an outline of the history of the evolution of childhood.

EXHIBIT 2.1: TIMELINE: HISTORY OF EARLY CHILDHOOD EDUCATION

Year	Views of Children/Events	Period	People Theory Type	Main Points	National/ International Events
Ancient Greece	Plato and Aristotle differentiate childhood and adulthood. Children are seen as innocent and pure, however, abandonment, child slavery, and infanticide persist. Fall of Roman Empire: – concept of childhood lost – children seen as unruly mini-adults—tortured, beaten – by age 6, considered "adult" —worked, married, etc.				
1300–1400s		Renaissance: childhood is a waiting period			
1500s	Views of children as property, evil, sinful, mini-adults persist but people begin to see school as a way of turning them around. Religious exploitation and severe punishment are the norm.	Reformation: child seen as evil, sinful	Martin Luther (1483–1546) 1524—Writes a letter to cities of Germany	Universal public education for all	
1600s	Concepts and methods persist, but childhood at least is seen as separate and school is seen as important.	Colonial Period Enlightenment	John Amos Comenius (1592–1670) 1658—Writes *Orbus Pictus*, the first picture book 1667—Writes *The Great Didactic* John Locke (1632–1704)	Maturationist – Universal education – Active learning – Learning materials – Maturational view—child unfolds according to inner timetable, parental involvement Behaviourist – Child born as blank slate (*tabula rasa*)	

Year	Views of Children/Events	Period	People Theory Type	Main Points	National/ International Events
1700s	Although childhood is viewed as a distinct period in life, children are still seen as property and slaves and work 16-hour days in factories.	Industrial Revolution	Jean Jacques Rousseau (1712–1778) 1762—Writes *Emile*	– Experience important – Education should be pleasant, not rote drills – Use of sense is important Interactionist – Children innately pure and noble – Learn through experimentation – Child-centred learning – Uniqueness of childhood – Nature as an important teacher in the classroom	War of 1812 Confederation, 1867
1800s	– With industry, education becomes important again – Children begin to attend school regularly – Childhood is begun to be seen as a separate, unique period – Nursery schools, play groups appear – Public kindergarten, Toronto, 1873 – Victoria Day Care, 1896		Johann Pestalozzi (1746–1827) 1801—Writes *How Gertrude Teaches Her Children* Robert Owen (1771–1858) in 1816 set up British Infant School in cotton mills in New Lanark, England Friedrich Froebel (1782–1852) in 1827 writes *Education of Man*, in 1837 establishes the first kindergarten in Blankenberg, Germany.	Interactionist – Home education – Parent involvement – Discover learning through concrete experience and observation Compensatory Education – Counteract effects of poverty – Believed in child's natural curiosity – Value of experience – Concept of play as learning – Owen banned corporal punishment of children Father of Kindergarten – Saw childhood as separate stage – Play was the way to learn – Environment should accommodate child's natural abilities – Use of specific materials	

(continued)

Year	Views of Children/Events	Period	People Theory Type	Main Points	National/International Events
1900s	Margaret McMillan's Open-Air Nursery in Deptford, England, 1911. City Crèche Vancouver, 1910.	Child study and Age of Technology	Maria Montessori (1870–1952) 1907—opens Casa dei Bambini (Children's House) in Italy 1967—her book *The Absorbent Mind* translated into English John Dewey (1859–1952) 1896—starts Lido School at University of Chicago with a play-based, child-centred curriculum 1900—Writes *My Pedagogic Creed* 1911—writes *Democracy and Education*	Interactionist – Children learn through self-direction or auto-education. – Environment must be child-sized and prepared – Children are like sponges but have biologically sensitive periods for learning. – Special materials	World War I
1920	Kilpatrick's *The Montessori System Examined*, 1914. Isaac's Malting House School. University of Toronto's Institute for Child Study, 1926.		Sigmund Freud (1856–1939) 1906—Publishes *Three Essays of the Theory of Sexuality* John Broadus Watson (1878–1958) father of behaviourism 1952—Writes *Behaviourism* Arnold Gesell (1880–1961) 1911—Begins child development study at Yale University 1928—Publishes *Infancy and Human Growth*	Psychoanalytical – Importance of environment on emotional development – Concept of ages and stages Behaviourism – Believed development was environmentally determined and was observable, measurable, and changeable Maturational – Concept of developmental domains – Developmental norms, milestones – Checklist of skills that appear in all children at certain ages	
1930	B.C. licenses child care in 1937. Parent Cooperative Nursery Schools in Toronto.		Mildred Parten develops categories of play, 1932	Progressive Education – Activity leads to knowledge. – Play and education connected – Democracy and justice for children in schools	The Great Depression

Year	Views of Children/Events	Period	People Theory Type	Main Points	National/ International Events
1940			Benjamin Spock in 1946 writes *Common Sense Book of Baby and Child Care*	Interactionist – Importance of play – "Let kids be kids" – Brings ideas of field to parents and general public – A new generation to be raised on "Dr. Spock"	World War II
1950	Bowlby's *Maternal Care and Mental Health*, 1951. Berlyne's translation of Piaget's *Psychology of Intelligence*, 1950. 11 percent of Canadian women work in 1951. D.O. Hebb's research on early experience, McGill University.		Jean Piaget (1896–1980) 1952—his work, *The Origin of Intelligence in Children*, published in English Katherine H. Read writes one of the first texts on ECE, *The Nursery School*, 1950 Erik Erikson (1902–1994) 1950—Publishes his *Personality in the Making* Burrhus Frederick Skinner (1904–1990) 1958—Publishes *The Technology of Teaching*	Cognitive Developmental Theory (Constructivist, Interactionist) – Children develop in ages and stages. – Environment and heredity interplay. – Children construct knowledge through doing. Psychosocial Theory – Eight ages/stages of childhood that could be harmed/enhanced by environment Behaviourism – All behaviours are learned. – Concept of behaviour modification and accelerated teaching	*Sputnik*, 1957 Civil rights movement
1960	Hunt's *Intelligence and Experience*, 1961. Bloom's *Stability and Change in Human Characteristics*, 1964. Brunswick-Cornwallis Head Start Preschool, 1962. Perry Preschool Project (Cognitively Oriented Curriculum), 1962.		Benjamin Bloom J. McVicker Hunt Carl Bereiter Siegfried Engelmann David Weikhart Sara Smilansky		Educational upheaval

(continued)

Year	Views of Children/Events	Period	People Theory Type	Main Points	National/International Events
1970			Albert Bandura (1925–) 1977—Wrote *Social Learning Theory*	Social Learning Theory – Children can also affect environment just as it affects them. Therefore, children are active participants in their learning. – Children learn through observation, imitation, and modelling (e.g., TV).	Vietnam War
			Lev Vygotsky (1896–1934) – In 1978 his *Mind in Society* is translated into English	Sociohistoric Theory – Development dependent on social interaction – Teacher's role is to guide, model, question, explain – Children need bridge of interaction to give meaning to their constructions	
1980	44 percent of Canadian women work in 1975. *Lasting Effects of Early Education: Report from the Consortium for Longitudinal Studies*, 1982. First Canadian National Day Care Conference, 1982. Canadian Childcare Advocacy Association, 1983. Mary Wright's *Compensatory Education in the Preschool: The University of Western Ontario Preschool Project*, 1983. Manitoba pioneers salary enhancement grants for child care teachers in 1986.		David Elkind (1931–) 1988—Writes *The Hurried Child: Growing Up Too Fast Too Soon*	– Warns that childhood is again disappearing	
			Howard Gardner (1943–) 1983—Writes *Frames of Mind*	Multiple Intelligence Theory – Children are unique, distinct from one another as well as from adults – Identified seven intelligences/ways of knowing	
			Loris Malaguzzi (1920–1994) Lilian Katz	Reggio Emilia – 100 Languages of Children tours North America	

Year	Views of Children/Events	Period	People Theory Type	Main Points	National/International Events
	Bredekamp's NAEYC's *Developmentally Appropriate Practice in Early Childhood Education Programs Serving Children from Birth through Age 8* (DAP in ECE), 1987. Canadian Child Care Federation, 1987. Lero, Pence, Goelman, and Brockman launch National Child Care Survey and Canadian National Child Care Study in 1988. All Canadian jurisdictions have child care legislation with enactment of legislation in N.W.T. in 1988.				
1990	*Caring for a Living*, 1991. Pence's *Canadian Child Care in Context: Perspectives from the Provinces and Territories*, 1992. Unionization drives for child care teachers in Saskatchewan and Yukon, 1993. 70 percent of Canadian women work in 1993. CAP ceases in 1996. Census, 1996. Statistics available 1997–1998. HRDC—Child Care Visions Projects, 1997. National Longitudinal Study on Children and Youth due in late 1997. Bredekamp revises NAEYC's DAP in ECE		Donna Lero Alan Pence Hillel Goelman Lois Brockman		Berlin Wall comes down U.S.S.R. dissolves Operation Desert Storm Bosnia conflict

Interest in the care, education, and development of young children goes back thousands of years. Our Western tradition is traced to ancient Greece, where the writings of philosophers such as Plato and Aristotle reflected a keen sensitivity to the needs of children and the importance of appropriate education in shaping their character (deMause, 1974; Greenleaf, 1978). These educated Greeks saw human development as a transformation from the imperfect state of childhood to the ideal of adulthood, and the Greek tradition included education for girls as well as for boys (Sameroff, 1983). Unfortunately, however, this sensitivity to the needs of young children was not shared by most, and infanticide, torture, murder, and abuse were common in this era (deMause, 1974). Children of the wealthy were rarely cared for by their own parents, but rather by hired wet nurses and teachers. Children of the poor were sent to be apprentices, servants, and slaves at an early age. No purpose or use was seen for children, and it was believed that they had no thoughts or feelings.

Medieval Times—No Distinct Stage Known as Childhood

By the Middle Ages (5th to 13th century), any concept of childhood seemed to have been lost. Children became little more than property and were put to work, for instance, in the fields or tending animals, just as soon as they were big enough.

Renaissance—Childhood as a Waiting Period

The Renaissance (13th century) led to slight improvements in the child's lot in life, but the period from birth to 7 years was still viewed as an unfortunate waiting period for entry into the adult world.

Reformation—Childhood as Sinful and Evil

The 15th to 17th century saw little improvement: the Puritans' children in the Old and New Worlds were born "ignorant and sinful" (Borstelmann, 1983, p. 15). Puritan parents, as well as the Quakers, often resorted to restraint, harsh discipline, and the rod to ensure their children became holy.

Enlightenment—Childhood as Separate but Not Sacred

The Enlightenment was to bring welcome changes. John Locke, the child of strict Puritans, and Jean Jacques Rousseau, a product of Geneva's strict Calvinism, became children of the Enlightenment and emphasized the importance of the early years. Since their time, there have been slow but steady improvements in views about young children and early childhood education.

Industrial Revolution—Children as a Labour Force

By the 18th century, though children were recognized in their own right, the need for increased production in factories overshadowed children's rights. Children were commissioned to work in the factories 16 hours a day from the age of 6.

Childhood Rescue Mission

Significant changes in attitudes about children began to take shape in the 19th century. As the uniqueness of childhood became recognized, and the negative or positive impact adults could have upon it, a greater importance began to be placed on the education of the young and kindergarten programs became part of the educational system in some locations by the middle of the century. In fact, one of the first public **kindergartens** in North America was established in Toronto in 1873 by Dr. J.L. Hughes (Young, 1981). Hester Howe, a school principal, became concerned that the school children had to bring their preschool-aged siblings to school with them as their mothers were working. Hughes suggested opening a crèche for these preschool children, and in 1892, the crèche, which is now Victoria Day Care Services in Toronto, was opened.

Age of Technology—Childhood Is Unique from Adulthood

The 20th century, while a relatively short period in time, represents a very active time for the field of child development, child care, and education. For one thing, education for all children came to be increasingly accepted, and this reinforced the idea that childhood was a separate period in life. Education in North America, in the eyes of such progressive educators as John Dewey, was a training ground for democracy and justice. Philosophers, theorists, and scientists proclaimed the early years as critical in a person's overall development.

Scientific methods of observation led to the **child study movement,** out of which grew many university preschool laboratory programs designed to facilitate the careful study of young children. For example, the University of Toronto's Institute for Child Study was opened in 1926, and St. George's Nursery School was an integral part of the institute (Young, 1981). Important programs were developed throughout this century (as a means of social reform) with the idea of rescuing the children of poverty through compensatory education programs, such as Head Start, begun in the 1960s.

Finally, another change that has profoundly affected early childhood education this century is the steadily increasing need for child care due to recent changes in the economy, family life, and the workforce. For instance, during World War II, many women were required to work and needed arrangements for care of their young children (Braun & Edwards, 1972; Carter, 1987; Greenberg, 1987; Siegel & White, 1982; Stapleford, 1976; Weber, 1984). Child care centres were established in Canada and the United States. These changes have led to the rapid growth of the field during the past 30 years.

Views of Children

Traditionally, the way people view young children has been determined by the intellectual, social, religious, and economic context of each period. Because children are vulnerable and dependent, their image and treatment tends to be shaped by the needs of the times. When needs have changed, influential thinkers and writers have shaken the very foundation of thought about children. The concept of the child as evil or sinful perpetuated corporal punishment. The view of children as property led them to slavery and child labour. The view of children as mini-adults negated any concept of childhood or the privileges we afford it. Our view of children as our hope for the future, as human beings with rights, and as learners with immense potential underpins the policies and practices of today.

The current view of children is based to a greater extent on theory and research rather than on the religious or political ideas that, in part, determined the image of children in the past. Even today, although we recognize and acknowledge the uniqueness and importance of childhood at least in the developed world, by providing children with special environments and promoting education as a social and personal necessity, many would maintain we still do not place a high enough value on the care of the very young. Children in all countries remain at risk where images of the child as sinful, property, or mini-adults persist. Child labour is not a thing of the past. Well-organized protests in India in 1993, for example, highlighted the plight of child carpet-makers who "are not fed properly, seldom paid, and often beaten if they make mistakes while weaving" (Kids Freed, 1993, p. C10) (and brought to the attention of Canada by the resolve of an elementary school child). Similar problems are common in many areas of Africa, Central America, and Asia. Closer to home, over one million children of migrant farm workers are thought to be working illegally in the United States (Morrison, 1991). Caning or the rod remain popular in countries such as the Phillipines. Saskatchewan removed corporal punishment of children in schools as recently as 1997, and it is still on the books of many jurisdictions. Obviously, many children are still waiting to benefit from the more benign view of childhood that has evolved over the centuries.

Influential People in the History of Childhood

Many individuals have contributed to our current view of young children and their care and education. We will touch on the works of only a few of them in this text. When the opportunity arises, you'll find that reading original works by these

and others provides a sense of awe, inspiration, and insight. Some developed their ideas because of their direct work with children, often the poor and underprivileged; others' theories emerged out of political and philosophical concerns about the problems of society and how reforms could be brought about.

The Renaissance and Reformation periods led to profound changes in thinking about education and young children. Philosophers, writers, and church leaders of this time generated many new ideas that have influenced thinking in the field of early childhood education. These views range from the child as a growing plant to be nurtured, a blank slate to be written upon, industrious, intrinsically motivated, unique from adults, individually different, and innately predisposed to play. These views determine our treatment and education of children. Consider again your beliefs about children and the impact of your and others' beliefs upon them.

Martin Luther (1483–1546)

The name Luther is usually associated with the Protestant Reformation, but Luther also wrote extensively about education. During his time, education had been restricted to the sons of the wealthy, who were tutored in the Latin language.

Who's who? People in the field of early childhood education are (clockwise from top): Jean Jacques Rousseau, Johann Pestalozzi, Friedrich Froebel, Maria Montessori, Lev Vygotsky, Erik Erikson, Jean Piaget, and B.F. Skinner.

david kiphuth

Luther believed that education should be accessible to all, and to further that aim, he recommended that teaching should be done in one's native language. He thought that the way to salvation was through reading the Bible, and he translated it into German so that it would be readily available for German families.

John Amos Comenius (1592–1670)

Comenius, like Luther, was involved with the church. He was a bishop in Moravia, later Czechoslovakia, and an advocate of universal education. Perhaps more than any of his predecessors, Comenius understood and stressed the importance of the early years. In *The Great Didactic* (1967), he wrote:

> It is the nature of everything that comes into being, that while tender it is easily bent and formed, but that, when it has grown hard, it is not easy to alter.... A young plant can be planted, transplanted, pruned, and bent this way or that. When it has become a tree, these processes are impossible. (p. 58)

Comenius also emphasized the value of active learning, hands-on experiences, and the involvement of parents in their children's education, especially before the children were 6 years of age. His 1658 publication *Orbis Pictus* (The World of Pictures) is viewed as the first picture book for children, and it reflects his commitment to providing tangible learning materials that are appealing to the senses. Comenius, like Montessori and Piaget centuries later, maintained that a child's development followed an internal timetable, and that teachers needed to work with that natural order. He was perhaps the first critic of "hothousing" in arguing that education would succeed only "if the mind be duly prepared to receive it … [and] if the pupil be not overburdened by too many subjects" (Comenius, 1967, p. 127).

John Locke (1632–1704)

John Locke was an English physician and philosopher who spent time in exile in Holland because of his opposition to the throne. Locke proposed that children were born as *tabulae rasae* (blank slates), and that experience would determine what the infant became. Locke maintained that education should be pleasant for the young child rather than devoted to rote drills and learning. He also encouraged parents to abandon harsh discipline procedures as well as restrictive practices like swaddling babies in fabric and constraining their physical activity.

Jean Jacques Rousseau (1712–1778) *Respected children.*

Rousseau was not an early childhood educator, but his ideas have certainly influenced the field. As a philosopher writing in the context of the corrupt French society of his time, Rousseau developed the idea that society actually hindered human beings from developing according to their nature. Society, with its hierarchy of the few who were rich and powerful, imposed only misery on the masses, a state that is not natural. Rousseau, in fact, considered anything natural and primitive to be good. Thus, he argued, if children could develop without the artificial trappings of civilization, they would be able to achieve their true potential of being moral and good.

According to Rousseau, young children are innately pure and noble, but they need to be protected from the evil influences of society. In a protected rural environment, they learn from what is concrete and natural through trial and error and experimentation. Rousseau recognized that children's mode of thinking and learning is different from that of adults and considered good education to be based on the stage of development of the child, not on adult-imposed criteria. He believed that a child-centred, uncorrupted education would eventually result in adults who were moral and interested in the common good of society.

Rousseau never worked with children—in fact, he actually abandoned all of his own children to foundling homes—but he wrote extensively about his philosophy in his novels and essays. Today we agree with Rousseau that children have a unique nature that needs to be nurtured and protected in an appropriate environment. Although his highly idealistic view of childhood and human nature was never fully adopted by his followers, Rousseau, nonetheless, had a great influence on later early childhood educators, as we shall soon see (Braun & Edwards, 1972; Carter, 1987; Grimsley, 1976; Weber, 1984).

Johann Pestalozzi (1746–1827)

Pestalozzi, a native of Switzerland, was deeply influenced by Rousseau's educational ideas. He felt that all people, even the poorest, had the right to an education as a way of helping them develop their moral and intellectual potential. He believed in education according to nature and considered that learning for young children is intricately tied to concrete experiences and observation. Unlike Rousseau, however, he stressed the important role of the mother in children's earliest years.

Also unlike Rousseau, Pestalozzi actually worked with children, developing educational methods that are still used today. For instance, he stressed the importance of recognizing individual differences among children and the relevance of children's self-activity, rather than rote, as the basis of learning. One of the schools he established became world famous, drawing visitors and students from all over Europe. He is considered to be the first to actually teach young children of preschool age, marking the beginning of the kindergarten movement (Braun & Edwards, 1972; Ulich, 1967; Weber, 1984).

Robert Owen (1771–1858)

Robert Owen, a disciple of Pestalozzi, was a British industrialist, philosopher, philanthropist, and social reformer (Pence, 1990; Weber, 1971). When he began to manage a textile mill in New Lanark, Scotland, he became concerned about the plight of young children who typically began to work in the mill at 6 years of age. Owen disliked the image of dark, satanic mills, which Dickens so aptly painted, and wanted life in New Lanark to be better both for children and their parents. Owen quickly changed the minimum age for employment to 10 years, improved housing, opened a low-cost company store, and set up schools for children and their parents.

In 1816, Owen's **infant school** was opened for the young children in New Lanark, who attended once they could walk. Owen had visited Pestalozzi and had read his works as well as Rousseau's, but he adopted Locke's view of the child as a *tabula rasa*. Singing, dancing, outdoor experiences, and play were major components of his program; Owen wanted learning to stem from the child's natural curiosity rather than from rigid lessons. Corporal punishment was not permitted, and there was no fixed schedule. Rousseau's emphasis on learning from nature was evident in Owen's program, which highlighted learning from gardens, animals, woods, and orchards.

Friedrich Froebel (1782–1852) *Invented Kindergarten*

Friedrich Froebel, a German, was one of the visitors at Pestalozzi's school, observing it with some mixed feelings. He greatly admired Pestalozzi's skills but was concerned about his inability to articulate his methods. Froebel, however, was better able to put into words his educational principles. Like his predecessors, Rousseau and Pestalozzi, Froebel believed in the interrelatedness of nature and the child's developing mind. He also advocated that education should harmonize with the child's inner development, recognizing that children are in different stages at various ages. He saw childhood as a separate stage that was not just a transition to adulthood but a stage with great intrinsic value in its own right.

Froebel also stressed the important role of play in young children's development—play was a pure and natural mode of learning through which children achieve harmony (Braun & Edwards, 1972; Carter, 1987; Ulich, 1947, 1967; Weber, 1984). Froebel developed a carefully programmed curriculum and specific materials. Froebel's view of children differed from Locke's *tabula rasa* notion. While Locke emphasized the importance of *nurture* or the environment, Froebel leaned toward the *nature* or maturational side of this centuries-old controversy. Like plants, children arrived in the world with some predetermined traits that the teacher in the garden for children should help to unfold. However, just as a seed of corn could not grow into a rose even with the best gardener, so the teacher could not fundamentally alter the child's inborn characteristics.

Froebel was the educator who invented the kindergarten for children from ages 3 to 7. His first kindergarten was in Bad Blankenberg, Germany, in 1837. Toronto has the distinction of having the first public kindergarten in Canada (1883), and Ontario, in 1887, was the first government system to give grants to Froebel's kindergarten as part of the public school system.

The word "kindergarten" reveals Froebel's thought. The children are individual plants tended and cultivated by a kindergartner (gardener) in the social setting, called a **garden of children.** The **Froebel gifts,** which are toys consisting of solid geometrical shapes, tablets, lines, and points, allow children to objectively build their inner world as well as to imitate the outer environment in which they live and move every day. These planned plays are pleasant as well as informative and creative for the children who are in the process of becoming. In becoming, children are educated to be thinkers. Children so educated will become the leaders who take us into the 21st century.

John Dewey (1859–1952)

John Dewey, the father of **progressive education,** led the American attack on traditional forms of public schooling. In the late 1800s, schools in the United States were very teacher-centred and subject-centred, and the curriculum, rather than the individual child's needs, determined what happened on any day. Harsh punishment and rote learning were the norm, and students were passive receptacles to be filled with knowledge by the teacher.

Dewey studied under G. Stanley Hall, who had introduced child study and, ultimately, developmental psychology to North America (Cairns, 1983). Clearly, public education was not geared toward the child in Dewey and Hall's time, and they both warned parents and teachers about the negative consequences of traditional instruction (Borstelmann, 1983; Dewey, 1897, 1900, 1902). Dewey advocated that educators should use the child's interests and that education should emphasize active learning through real experiences; activity would lead to knowledge. He ran a model early childhood program at the University of Chicago, and demonstrated in his work a **child-centred approach** rather than a subject-centred approach.

The principles of progressive education influenced a number of developments in early childhood education. For example, the Open Education model in Britain and some areas of Canada grew out of Dewey's work (Weber, 1971). The nursery school movement, with its emphasis on play and parent education, also can be traced to Dewey (Fein & Clarke-Stewart, 1973). Dewey's work also had an impact on the popularity of the programs of other educators, including Froebel and Maria Montessori (Hunt, 1968).

Margaret McMillan (1860–1931)

Margaret McMillan and her sister Rachel were born in the United States (McMillan, 1919, 1930) but moved to Britain when they were children (Braun & Edwards, 1972; Gardner, 1949; Weber, 1971). Margaret became a social activist, and in the late 19th century, as a member of a school board, she became an outspoken advocate for poor children in the schools. Many children had significant medical and social problems that festered in urban slums, and although 80 percent of newborns were healthy at birth, only 20 percent of them were still healthy when they entered school at age 5. Margaret, with Rachel's assistance, set up a medical clinic in Deptford, a London slum, in 1902, and it soon expanded to include an open-air camp. In 1911, the McMillans opened their play-oriented, open-air nursery school. In addition to teaching self-care and hygiene, the McMillans experimented with open-air sheds. The shed was a shelter in a garden playground, and the children could wander freely from the indoors to the outdoors. Creativity was highly valued, and clay, drawing, block play, and movement were an integral part of their play-based program.

Rachel died in 1917, but Margaret worked in nursery education until her death in 1931. Chiefly because of Margaret's ongoing advocacy, the British government agreed to fund nursery schools for 3- to 5-year-olds in 1918, but the war and the economic devastation it brought slowed their spread until the 1930s. Margaret's work also influenced developments in North America, and most of the nursery schools founded in the 1920s and 1930s were modelled after the open-air nurseries. Of course, the term "nursery school" also comes from the McMillans, and their program remains one of the first models for compensatory education programs (Gardner, 1949; McMillan, 1919, 1930; Weber, 1971).

Maria Montessori (1870–1952)

A true feminist of her time, Maria Montessori was the first woman to become a medical doctor in Italy. Her psychiatric interest led her to work with children with cognitive disabilities, who, in her era, were placed in psychiatric institutions. Montessori thought their problems were often educational rather than medical, and she proved her point when a number of these institutionalized children easily passed regular school exams after she had worked with them. In 1907, the city of Rome asked Montessori to take charge of a children's day nursery that was attached to a housing tenement for the poor. The housing authorities wanted someone who would keep the children off the stairs and prevent them from dirtying the newly painted walls. But Montessori found in this *casa dei bambini* **(children's house)** the opportunity to explore her teaching methods with normal children.

Montessori's methods, which we will highlight in Chapter 5, were based on the principle that young children learn in a way that is fundamentally different from how adults learn. She was particularly impressed with the great capacity of children to learn so much during the first few years of life. She called this capacity the **absorbent mind,** similar to a sponge soaking up liquid. She believed that if children's absorbent minds were exposed to appropriate learning experiences in the developmental stages, their minds would grow. This is especially true during **sensitive periods,** times when children are most receptive to absorbing specific learning.

Montessori's curriculum takes advantage of these sensitive periods by making appropriate experiences available to children at times when they are most ready to learn from them. She used the term **prepared environment** to describe this match of the right materials to children's stages of development.

Much of Montessori's philosophy, approach, and tools, particularly her **self-correcting materials** and strong sense of respect for children, have had an enduring impact on early childhood education. Whether by design in contemporary

Montessori schools or by common acceptance in other programs, Montessori's influence is still strongly felt today (Braun & Edwards, 1972; Carter, 1987; Chattin-McNichols, 1992; Elkind, 1983; Gettman, 1987; Simons & Simons, 1986).

Loris Malaguzzi (1920–1994) Reggio Program

Born in Correggio, a province of Reggio Emilia, Italy, Loris Malaguzzi was the driving force behind the establishment of the schools in the town of Reggio Emilia in Italy. While teaching, Malaguzzi specialized in psychology at the Centre for National Research in Rome. He became an advocate for the innovative Reggio schools, recognizing their uniqueness and potential. The schools' philosophy and methods are quickly gaining notoriety and support worldwide.

Malaguzzi devised a complete system of education with a basis in the principles of Dewey, Piaget, and Vygotsky in which the school's first priority is in presenting and upholding its **image of the child** as an active and vital participant in constructing his/her own knowledge. The municipality of Reggio Emilia took a systems approach to education with relationships, interactions, and collaboration being at the centre. Children, parents, and teachers were equal partners in learning. Visual arts and an aesthetically pleasing environment provided the framework for learning through a teacher called an *atelierista* and a workshop called an *atelier.* An **emergent curriculum,** which evolves through continuous dialogue and documentation, frames learning as children devise and engage in **projects.**

Shortly before his death in 1994, as worldwide attention to Reggio grew, Malaguzzi was very concerned with protecting the purpose of the schools. Two organizations were formed. These are called Reggio Children and Friends of Reggio Children. These, together with the International Reggio Exchange, are affiliated with the Merrill-Palmer Institute at Wayne State University in Detroit, Michigan. The Reggio program is outlined in Part 1 and highlighted in Chapter 5.

The people of Reggio Emilia, Italy, wanted their schools to be different. They had a "universal aspiration … that their children first of all had to be taken seriously and believed in" (Malaguzzi, 1993, p. 51). They felt that all members of the community should gain great joy from learning and sharing. The first school was established in 1963 based on schools started by the people in the 1940s.

More Influential People

The "baby" doctors have written extensively on child development and child care, particularly for parents. Dr. Benjamin Spock was the forerunner of this when he wrote *The Common Sense Book of Baby and Child Care* in 1946. Generations have been raised on Dr. Spock. Since then, Dr. Burton White, Dr. Berry Brazelton, Frank and Theresa Caplan (*The First 12 Months of Life,* 1995), and Penelope Leach (*Your Baby and Child,* 1997) have published excellent child development books for parents.

Stanley Greenspan and Nancy Thorndike Greenspan published *First Feelings: Milestones in the Emotional Development of Your Baby and Child* in 1985. In 1988,

David Elkind wrote *The Hurried Child: Growing Up Too Fast, Too Soon,* warning that childhood was again in danger of disappearing. He recognized that our views of children had begun again to mirror views from former eras, including the view of children as mini-adults, as we dressed, employed, punished, and pushed our children to accelerate at extreme paces. These authors have since published many books and articles on child care and have proven to be excellent resources.

Theories of Child Development: How Children Learn

Although many of the predecessors of early childhood education developed a theoretical or philosophical viewpoint about how children develop, it was not until this century that such ideas were founded on a more systematic basis through observations and research. The **human development theory** is a way of describing what happens as individuals move from infancy through adulthood, identifying significant events commonly experienced by all people, and explaining why changes occur as they do. Such theories look at how people believe, learn, and change in their physical, cognitive or intellectual, social, emotional, language, and creative development. Each of these areas is called a **developmental domain.** It is useful to have a grasp of different theories as you develop your own professional identity and beliefs. This gives you not only a way of assessing your personal values but also offers some alternative views about how children develop and should be treated (Thomas 1990a). We will give an overview of just a few of the most influential developmental theorists whose ideas have contributed, directly or indirectly, to the field of early childhood education today.

Some theorists, such as behaviourists, believed that environment is the most important factor in development and that most behaviour, knowledge, and skills are learned and therefore can be taught, observed, influenced, or changed gradually and continuously. Others believed that behaviour, knowledge, and skills are innate or genetic, that they unfold in predictable stages, in sequence, at predictable ages in all people and, hence, environment has little impact.

You might have, or have had, debates about concepts such as **nature versus nurture,** heredity versus environment, maturation versus experience, or innate versus learned. These concepts reflect one side or the other of the issue of whether our learning and behaviour are shaped by inborn characteristics and a biological clock or outside forces. Current developmentalists lean toward the idea that learning occurs when there is an interaction between your inborn disposition and the environment. As well, theorists, philosophers, and teachers take on eclectic views by combining parts of each theory and practice into their own personal package. Below we highlight five theories on how children develop—constructivist, psychosocial, behavioural, sociohistoric, and motivational. Separate courses on development consider these ideas and theorists, as well as others, in detail, and they are invaluable for those planning a career in early childhood education. The program models that follow (opposite the "What?" subheading in the Theory blocks below) are considered in more depth in Chapter 5.

Constructivist Theory

Who?	**Jean Piaget**
When?	Born: August 9, 1896 Died: September 17, 1980
Where?	Born: Neuchatel, Switzerland Died: Geneva, Switzerland
What?	**Constructivist Theory** Intelligence is adaptation to the environment. Thinking is qualitatively different at each stage: infants and toddlers learn through movement and the senses; preschoolers use symbols to organize ideas; school-agers acquire logical structures of thought. Application: High/Scope (Cognitively Oriented Curriculum), Reggio Emilia, Bank Street Programs
What was he like?	Precocious, with his first publication at 10, and Ph.D. by 22; constantly searching for answers; always ingenious and inventive in his approach. Perhaps because his mother was in poor mental health, he developed an interest in psychoanalysis. This soon turned into his life-long fascination with normal development, especially with regard to the thinking of children. Much of his theory was developed by careful observation of his own three children.

One of the most influential forces in early childhood education today is Jean Piaget. Piaget's **cognitive developmental theory** presents a complex picture of how children's intelligence and thinking abilities emerge. Piaget's theory, in particular, is often called **constructivist theory** because of his belief that knowledge is not something that is poured into the child's head from the outside but rather something that the child must construct for himself by actively interacting with and manipulating the environment. Hence learning must occur by doing, as in a hands-on approach. Piaget believed there were different types of knowledge that helped make up intelligence. He identified three types: **logico-mathematical, physical,** and **social knowledge.**

1. *Physical knowledge* involves learning about objects in the environment and their properties such as colour, size, mass, or shape. **Discrimination,** the ability to distinguish between different features, is the basic cognitive task involved in this type of knowledge.

2. *Logico-mathematical knowledge* concerns the relationship among objects as well as their relationships in time and space. This type of knowledge allows children to organize their environment to make sense of it.

3. *Social knowledge* is conveyed by people and defined by culture. It involves the many social rules, morals, and values children must learn to function in society (Charlesworth & Lind, 1990; Forman & Kuschner, 1977; Kamii & DeClark, 1985; Saunders & Bingham-Newman, 1984).

Piaget did not suggest specific educational applications of his work, but educators have transformed his theory, more than any other, into actual models.

Piaget conducted most of his research by interviewing children and asking them questions, probing and engaging them in conversation. He was fascinated with children's explanations of natural phenomena. He devoted a great deal of time to observing his own three children.

Piaget, a biologist by training, thought human cognitive development was similar to how all organisms function physiologically, by adapting to and organizing the environment around them. A common example illustrates human biological adaptation to the physical environment. If the temperature becomes too warm or too cold, we sweat or shiver to adapt. In a way similar to this physiological adaptation, we also adapt mentally to changes in the environment. At the same time that we adapt, we mentally organize what we perceive in our environment so that it makes sense to us.

Piaget called the cognitive structures into which we adapt and organize our environment **schemata** (schema is the singular form). Schemata are concepts or mental representations of experiences that we constantly create, refine, and reorganize. You can visualize schemata as an index card file. Babies are born with only a few index cards, but, with experience, they create new cards and dividers as their store of information becomes more complex.

In a cognitive sense, **adaptation** is involved any time new information or a new experience occurs. The person must adapt to incorporate any new information or experience into the schema. When something new presents itself, however, the existing mental structure is upset or put into **disequilibrium** because this new information or experience does not exactly fit into the old structures. To return to balance, or **equilibrium,** adaptation takes place through the complementary processes of assimilation and accommodation. **Assimilation** occurs when a person tries to make the new information or experience fit into an existing concept or schema. **Accommodation** takes place when the schema is modified or a new concept is formed to incorporate the new information or experience. In other words, you modify and rearrange the new information on the old index card or you make a new index card for the new information. Then you have to rearrange the entire index file. Thus you have incorporated (assimilated) the new information, made room for it (accommodated), and reorganized the box. **Organization** is a process that is complementary to adaptation. While adaptation allows for new information and experiences to be incorporated into existing mental structures, organization defines how such information and experiences are related to each other.

As a **stage theorist**, Piaget conceived of qualitatively different characteristics and accomplishments in cognitive ability during the four stages of development shown in Exhibit 2.2. Each stage is built on and incorporates the accomplishments of the previous one. Children can progress through the stages at different rates but generally follow the same order. We can revert back to the thinking style of previous stages depending on the situation we are in. Piaget, himself, said he only operated in abstract thought a fraction of the time. Note that Piaget acknowledged the importance of experience as well as maturational factors, in contrast to other theorists who undermined the role of experience. As we've mentioned, he is known as a **constructivist** or **interactionist** since he believed we are predisposed to construct knowledge but must do so by interacting with the environment.

EXHIBIT 2.2 PIAGET'S PERIODS OF COGNITIVE DEVELOPMENT

Stage 1: Sensorimotor Period (0–2 Years)

The first period is characterized by motor behaviour through which schemata are formed. The child does not yet represent events mentally but relies on coordination of senses and movement, on **object permanence** development (infants' gradual recognition in their first year that objects continue to exist even when they are out of view), on learning to differentiate means from ends, and on beginning to understand the relationship of objects in space in order to learn about the environment.

Stage 2: Preoperational Period (2–7 Years)

Language and other forms of **representation** develop during this period, and thinking is based on personal perceptions and, therefore, may not appear logical. Children's internal mental representations, which allow them to think of objects even if these are not physically present, are the major accomplishment of this period. Children have an egocentric view of the world in terms of their own perspective. Early classification, seriation, and role playing begin.

Stage 3: Concrete Operations Period (7–11 Years)

The child has internalized some physical tasks or operations, no longer depends only on what is visible, and can apply **logical thinking** to solving problems. The child is now able to reverse operations (e.g., $5 - 3 = 2$; $3 + 2 = 5$). The child can also practise **conservation**—recognize that an object does not change in amount even if its physical appearance changes (e.g., a ball of clay stretched into a snake).

Stage 4: Formal Operations Period (11–15 Years)

The final period, rare even in adults, is characterized by sophisticated, **abstract thinking** and logical reasoning abilities applied to physical as well as social and moral problems.

Howard Gardner (1943–)

Howard Gardner, a professor of education at Harvard Graduate School, expanded on Piaget's idea of three intelligences by proposing seven intelligences when he wrote *Frames of Mind: The Theory of Multiple Intelligence* (1983). Unlike Piaget, who believed there to be a predetermined set of mental abilities that make up one measurable IQ, Gardner believes the seven intelligences to be a set of competencies quite distinct from one another. A person is born with a stronger predisposition to one of the intelligences and then constructs knowledge within this framework for learning.

Exhibit 2.3 lists the seven intelligences and how they relate to each type of learner and how each type learns best. This is significant to you as a teacher in understanding not just the children with whom you work but also the parents and colleagues with whom you come into contact. Also note that Gardner is an interactionist since he recognizes the influence the environment has on the intellectual learning construct with which you are born. His theory is relevant because it addresses ideas of individuality, emotional development, culture, potential, self-direction, and creative thinking.

Psychosocial Theory

Who?	**Erik Erikson**
When?	Born: June 15, 1902 Died: May 12, 1994
Where?	Born: Frankfurt, Germany Died: Harwich, Massachusetts
What?	**Psychosocial Theory** Identifies needs of children at different ages/stages, beginning with a need for trust for infants, autonomy for toddlers, initiative for preschoolers, and industry for school-aged children; highlights the importance of social interactions in development. Application: Bank Street model
What was he like?	Described as thoughtful, energetic, magnetic; a scholarly thinker and prolific writer. At 18, Erikson wandered

EXHIBIT 2.3: GARDNER'S SEVEN INTELLIGENCES

Type	Likes To	Is Good At	Learns Best By	Individuals
Linguistic Learner "The Word Player"	read, write, tell stories	memorizing names, places, dates, and trivia	saying, hearing, and seeing words	Margaret Atwood Martin Luther King
Logical/ Mathematical Learner "The Questioner"	do experiments, figure things out, work with numbers, ask questions, explore patterns and relationships	math, reasoning, logic, problem solving	categorizing, classifying, working with abstract patterns/ relationships	Albert Einstein Stephen Hawking
Spatial Learner "The Visualizer"	draw, build, design, and create things, daydream, look at pictures/ slides, watch movies, play with machines	imagining things, sensing changes, mazes/puzzles, reading maps and charts	visualizing, dreaming, using the mind's eye, working with colours/pictures	Bobby Fischer Emily Carr
Musical Learner "The Music Lover"	sing, hum tunes, listen to music, play an instrument, respond to music	picking up sounds, remembering melodies, noticing pitches/rhythms, keeping time	rhythm, melody, music	Mozart
Bodily/Kinesthetic Learner "The Mover"	move around, touch and talk, use body language	physical activities (sports/dance/ acting), crafts	touching, moving, interacting with space, processing knowledge through bodily sensations	Wayne Gretzky Karen Kain
Interpersonal Learner "The Socializer"	have lots of friends, talk to people, join groups	understanding people, leading others, organizing, communicating, manipulating, mediating conflicts	sharing, com- paring, relating, cooperating, interviewing	Mohandas Gandhi Mother Teresa
Intrapersonal Learner "The Individual"	work alone, pursue own interests	understanding self, focusing inward on feelings/dreams following instincts, pursuing interests/goals, being original	working alone, individualized projects, self- paced instruction, having own space	psychotherapists and counsellors urged to develop this "knowledge of self" to guide others

Sources: Chart from "Different Child, Different Style" by Kathy Faggella and Janet Horowitz, in *Instructor*, September 1990, p. 52. Copyright 1990 by Scholastic. Reprinted by permission. Names from W.G. McCaughey (1997), *Multiple Intelligences: An Introduction to the Work of Howard Gardner*. A Workshop for Adult Learners, Brock University, St. Catharines, Ont.

through Europe as an artist and stumbled on a job as a teacher in a progressive school in Vienna run by Anna Freud. This proved to be the turning point: his introduction there to Sigmund Freud's work led to his lifelong involvement with **psychoanalytic theory.** Later his writings were likened to works of art, paintings of word pictures with intricate detail and attention.

Erik Erikson was one of Sigmund Freud's followers. He modified and refined Freud's stages of development with **psychosocial theory** in a way that is much more acceptable to us today. Like Freud, Erikson saw each stage defined by conflict, but he viewed such conflict as healthy, resulting in opportunities for personal growth. Each stage and its attendant conflict are centred not just on the person alone but also on his or her relationships with others. Although Freud's five stages ended with adolescence, Erikson's theory includes eight stages that span infancy through adulthood. Erikson believed these stages, which are summarized in Exhibit 2.4, occur in all human beings in the described sequence at the time in life when their emergence is most critical.

EXHIBIT 2.4 ERIKSON'S DEVELOPMENTAL SEQUENCES

Erikson's Psychological Stages	Developmental Task	Positive Influences
Trust vs. mistrust (0–18 months)	Developing trust in the world (negative outcome is suspicion)	Warm and caring caregivers, especially the primary ones
Autonomy vs. shame and doubt (18 months–3 years)	Developing a positive sense of autonomy (negative outcome is shame, doubt, and low self-confidence)	Allowing the child to be independent and to explore
Initiative vs. guilt (3–5 years)	Developing a positive view of one's own actions and wishes (negative outcome is guilt over own actions)	Allowing the child to form own ideas, plans, and desires; having supportive parents and caregivers
Industry vs. inferiority (6 years–puberty)	Developing confidence in one's own accomplishments (negative outcome is sense of inadequacy)	Parents, teachers, and caregivers who support child's efforts and do not constantly compare child to others
Identify vs. identity diffusion (adolescent years)	Developing a sense of identity (negative outcome is role confusion and aimlessness)	

Erikson's Psychological Stages	Developmental Task	Positive Influences
Intimacy vs. isolation (early adulthood)	Development of close, rewarding relationships (negative outcome is flight from close ones)	
Generativity vs. stagnation (middle age)	Developing responsibilities to help others, including children (negative outcome is being self-absorbed)	
Integrity vs. despair (old age)	Developing a sense of satisfaction with one's life (negative outcome is a sense of bitterness and failure)	

The first four stages are particularly important to early childhood education because they describe significant tasks that occur in the young child's life. Stages occur at critical times in development but never completely disappear. Thus trust is still important beyond infancy; children continue to struggle with the balance between autonomy and dependency; and initiative and industry are relevant even beyond the early years, though in a more mature form. Erikson emphasized the importance of play in meeting the tasks of autonomy and initiative during the preschool years. Erikson's stages highlight some of the important issues for young children and the balance we must provide to help them achieve healthy development (Erikson, 1963; Maier, 1965, 1990; Tribe, 1982; Weber, 1984).

Sigmund Freud (1856–1939)

As mentioned, Erikson was a disciple of Sigmund Freud and his daughter Anna Freud. Freud's theory was psychoanalytical in nature, and he was the first theorist to emphasize the importance of the early years on later personality development. Freud was also revolutionary in proposing that there were particular ages and stages to a person's development. Neo-Freudians have modified many of Freud's views while maintaining these fundamental premises. Perhaps the most well-known mainstream concept coming from Freud is that of "ego."

Behavioural Theory

Who? B(urrhus) F(rederick) Skinner

When? Born: March 20, 1904
Died: August 18, 1990

Where?	Born: Susquehanna, Pennsylvania
	Died: Cambridge, Massachusetts
What?	**Behavioural Theory**
	Environment is important in shaping all aspects of behaviour. Consistent positive consequences (positive reinforcement) ensure that behaviour will be repeated; behaviour modification is an application of behaviourism.
	Application: Bereiter-Engelmann program (DISTAR)
What was he like?	Ambitious, goal-driven, persistent; seen as the Darth Vader of psychology by some, as a brilliant innovator by others. Fred Skinner experienced a calm and nurturing childhood. Perhaps his later theory was shaped by childhood experiences since his Grandmother Burrhus reinforced good behaviour with pie, candy, and letting him win at dominoes.

B.F. Skinner was the most famous follower of the father of behavioural theory, or **behaviourism**, J.B. Watson. Skinner both popularized and extended behaviourism so that it was the dominant force in psychology until at least the 1980s. Skinner's writings and those of his many followers have had a widespread influence on all aspects of education, including the early childhood years. The application of his theoretical and experimental work can be seen in **behaviour modification,** which operates on the underlying principle that behaviour can be learned, changed, or modified by manipulating the environment, which includes both physical and social components. Behaviourists centred their study on exact science because behaviours can be defined and are observable and measurable.

Skinner emphasized that almost all behaviours are learned through experience and can be increased or decreased in frequency as a function of what follows them. In other words, if something pleasant or enjoyable consistently happens after the child engages in a specific behaviour (the teacher smiles when Jeremy helps to put away the blocks), he is likely to repeat that behaviour.

Skinner used the term **reinforcement**, popularized by Edward Thorndike (1874–1949), to describe the immediate consequence following behaviour that is most likely to strengthen that behaviour. Reinforcement can be either positive or negative: **positive reinforcement** means providing something pleasant following the behaviour, while **negative reinforcement** means removing something unpleasant following the behaviour. Whether consciously using the behavioural approach or not, early childhood educators frequently use positive reinforcement because of its powerful effect on children's behaviour. For example, teachers of young children are most likely to use **social reinforcers**—for instance, a smile, a hug, attention, or involvement—when they see a child engaging in a behaviour they consider desirable. **Tangible reinforcers** like stickers are overused and misused as positive reinforcement because teachers forget that children are naturally or intrinsically motivated to please and that they feel an internal warmth or gratification when they please or succeed. Stickers can actually have a negative effect because they draw children's attention away from their own inner judgment, self-praise and evaluation, and self-directed and self-controlled activity.

Reinforcement is a very effective way of controlling behaviour because you are adding something pleasant (e.g., hug) or removing something unpleasant (e.g., a source of pain) both of which have positive consequences for the child.

Punishment, on the other hand, is an unpleasant or aversive consequence that immediately follows a behaviour. According to Skinner (and almost all early childhood professionals), punishment is not a very effective way of controlling behaviour because it means adding something unpleasant (e.g., a spanking) or removing something pleasant (e.g., a hug), both of which have severe negative consequences for the child.

Since teachers in many programs frequently use a number of behavioural techniques even if they do not strictly adhere to behaviour theory, it is important that they understand the consequences of their own behaviour on the children with whom they work (Braun & Edwards, 1972; Bushell, 1982; Neisworth & Buggey, 1993; Peters, Neisworth, & Yawkey, 1985; Sameroff, 1983; Skinner, 1969, 1974; Weber, 1984).

Albert Bandura (1925–)

Albert Bandura wrote *Social Learning Theory* in 1977. Bandura's work was significant because it noted that children affect the environment as much as the environment affects them. In this sense, behavioural theorists could view children as active, rather than passive, participants in the knowledge they construct. Bandura's experiments revealed that children learn vicariously, that is, they can learn simply by watching, without any direct instruction. They also imitate and model what they have observed. This was significant as it was applied to children and viewing television—especially violence on television. However, factors such as identification with the role model, memory skills, opportunities to practise, ability to replicate the behaviour, attention skills, desire to imitate, and guidance from valued others can influence children's choices of behaviours to model. Hence, television can also be a positive influence on children depending on what is watched, how much is watched, and with whom children watch.

Sociohistoric Theory

Who?	**Lev Vygotsky**
When?	Born: November 5, 1896
	Died: June 11, 1934
Where?	Born: Orsha, Russia
	Died: Moscow, Russia

What?	**Sociohistoric Theory**
	Believed social and historic forces shape intellectual ability: we are the product of our times. Thus, his cognitive theory reflects the Marxist-Leninist philosophy of Russia during his lifetime. Language is a primary tool for conveying society's values.
	Application: Reggio Emilia Programs
What was he like?	An intense yet very social person with the capacity to inspire others; deeply interested in a variety of fields and topics, many of which he mastered. His childhood friends called him "little professor" because of his academic pursuits; at age 15 he organized stimulating intellectual discussions for his peers. His ability to structure the environment so others could learn contributed to the formulation of his ideas about the **zone of proximal development (ZPD).**

All of the previously discussed theorists have focused primarily on the child in explaining how development occurs, although the importance of others, especially the family, is certainly not ignored. Other theorists have given much greater prominence to the importance of the cultural and historical context within which a child is socialized. The Russian psychologist Lev Vygotsky, originator of the **sociohistoric theory,** highly stressed the importance of the social environment to human development. Vygotsky's ideas have gained greater prominence in recent years, several decades after his death, and have spurred considerable interest in cross-cultural studies of child development and child-rearing practices. Vygotsky proposed that social interaction, especially dialogue, between children and adults is the mechanism through which specific cultural values, customs, and beliefs are transmitted from generation to generation.

Vygotsky was particularly intrigued by the question of how young children develop complex thinking. He concluded that the same mechanism through which culture is transmitted—social interaction—is the way in which increasingly more complex thinking develops, as part of learning about culture. Children gain knowledge and skills through shared experiences between themselves and adults or older peers. Furthermore, the dialogues that accompany these experiences gradually become a part of children's thinking. Thus, Vygotsky conceived of cognitive development as dependent on, not independent of, **social mediation.** This view contrasts with Piaget's, which conceives of the child as gradually becoming more social and less self-focused. In Vygotsky's view, the child is socially dependent at the beginning of his cognitive life, and becomes increasingly independent in his thinking through many experiences in which adults or older peers help.

The child acquires new skills and information within what Vygotsky termed the zone of proximal development. This is the level at which a child finds a task too difficult to complete alone but can accomplish with the assistance and support of an adult or older peer. Infants are frequently guided by adults in tasks they have not yet mastered. Many games adults play with infants encourage the infants to increasingly greater participation; many infant motor skills are preceded by periods in which the baby sits, stands, or walks with adult assistance. Similarly, toddlers accomplish many tasks with the **guided assistance** of adults. Toddlers' one- or two-word sentences, for example, are often extended by adults into a more complete format, which models as well as provides the structure for more elaborate dialogue. Preschoolers also learn many tasks through guided assistance and **scaffolding,** which, as at earlier and later ages, are adjusted to a child's skill level and gradually withdrawn as the child masters the task. The teacher who tells a child who is struggling to fit a puzzle piece into the frame "See what happens if you turn the piece around" is working within the zone of proximal development.

Vygotsky's ideas have acquired new relevance in early childhood education. The focus on finding the appropriate zone of proximal development for each child has validated the long-held concern with individualization in early childhood programs. Vygotsky's theory also suggests that, in addition to providing a stimulating environment in which young children are active explorers and participants, early educators need to promote discovery by modelling, explaining, and providing suggestions to suit each child's zone of proximal development (Gallimore & Tharp, 1990; Seifert, 1993; Wertsch, 1985).

Maturational Theory

Who?	**Arnold Gesell**
When?	Born: June 21, 1880 Died: May 29, 1961
Where?	Born: Alma, Wisconsin Died: New Haven, Connecticut
What?	**Maturational Theory** Believed that development and intelligence are determined at birth and that specific skills occur at predictable stages in a particular order. Believed children unfold according to this biological timetable when they are ready. Hence, environment has little influence over early growth and development. Application: Open Model
What was he like?	Single-minded (i.e., unswayed); shy—shunned publicity; hard worker with strong work ethic and high standards; high achiever with an early start; wide interest range yet focused; wrote over 400 publications; child-centred—personable and warm; devoted to humanity; married Beatrice Chandler in 1909 and had a son and daughter.

Gesell, like John Dewey, was a student of G. Stanley Hall, and has had a major influence on early childhood education as well as developmental psychology in the 20th century (Cairns, 1983). Gesell initially worked in the field of education and then returned to school in the middle of his career to pursue a degree in medicine at Yale. In 1911, after completing his M.D., he founded the Gesell Institute, a child study institute that still exists at Yale, where he worked until his death. Unlike Dewey, Gesell (and Montessori) accepted Hall's view that development is predetermined and that intelligence is fixed (Hunt, 1968). However, by Gesell's time, that notion had been altered somewhat, and Gesell used the term **maturation** to describe how children unfold in predetermined patterns.

Gesell studied the regularities in children's development for over 40 years, often with the assistance of his colleagues, Francis Ilg and Louise Bates Ames. They observed large numbers of children and studied their motor and language development, as well as their adaptive behaviours and personal-social skills. They recorded their observations of each child and averaged them for each age group so that they could present an overview of the typical child at different age levels. In 1928, Gesell published *Infancy and Human Growth,* a report on growth in infants, and by the time of his death he had studied children through to 16 years of age. The overviews of infants and children at different ages, outlined later in this chapter, follow Gesell's approach, and are referred to as **norms.** Gesell found the norms to be so orderly that, in the same year Watson wrote his polemic on early stimulation, Gesell wrote about "the inevitableness and surety of maturation" (Gesell, 1928, p. 378).

The growth of the nursery school movement in the 1920s was partly the result of Gesell's emphasis on the importance of the early years as "biologically the most important period in the development of the individual" (Gesell, 1923, p. 3). Moreover, Gesell's child study institute and the University of Iowa's Child Welfare Research Station and their laboratory schools became models for other institutes that were established in Canada and the United States in the 1920s and 1930s. As previously noted, the Institute for Child Study, founded in 1926, was the first Canadian centre, but child study was soon a focus in a number of centres across the country—in Montreal, Saskatoon, and Winnipeg, for example (Northway, 1973). Advanced degrees in the study of early childhood became available at these institutes, and many of the professionals who have shaped the field in Canada as well as the United States were trained in these facilities (Northway, 1973).

Other lasting contributions of Gesell include the perhaps archaic but persistent notion of **school readiness.** With his belief that maturation is predictable and orderly, Gesell discouraged parents and teachers from interfering with a child's development in most areas—but emphasized that this did not imply that guidance and discipline were not necessary. According to him, only social development was subject to environmental influences, and as a consequence, most early childhood programs from the 1920s until the 1960s emphasized social growth and did not tamper with or try to stimulate growth in the other spheres of development. If a child did not seem ready for a program (e.g., kindergarten), the child was kept home for an additional year of unfolding, rather than given stimulation to encourage development in the areas where there was a lag.

Research and the Rediscovery of the Early Childhood Years

A number of important advances in psychological knowledge, which are critical for our understanding of the early childhood years, occurred more recently. Psychological understandings reflect the political and educational pressures of their time. Perhaps the most important psychological advance was the replacement of the maturational view of development with the interactionist view, which said that development is determined by both environmental and genetic factors. J. McVicker Hunt, in his 1961 book, *Intelligence and Experience,* systematically presented evidence from studies showing the relationship between experience and

development in humans and animals. (Much of the research Hunt discussed had been completed at Canadian universities, especially at McGill where Donald Hebb and his students studied the effects of early experience on the neural development and behaviour of animals.) Hunt concluded that "the assumption that intelligence is fixed and that its development is predetermined by the genes [was] no longer tenable" (Hunt, 1961, p. 342).

The early childhood years were identified as the period when intelligence was most susceptible to the effects of experience. Benjamin Bloom reviewed a number of longitudinal studies of intelligence in his 1964 text, *Stability and Change in Human Characteristics,* and concluded that "marked changes in the environment in the early years can produce greater changes in intelligence than will equally marked changes in the environment at later periods of development" (Bloom, 1964, pp. 88–89). The work of Bloom and Hunt clearly had different implications for early childhood educators than did Gesell's maturational theory.

Another advance in the psychological knowledge of children was North America's belated discovery of Piaget's extensive investigations into the origins of intelligence in the young child. An eminent Canadian psychologist with a behaviourist background, Dr. Daniel Berlyne, from the University of Toronto, can be credited with helping North America to discover Piaget (Rowland & McGuire, 1968). Piaget's work had been ignored in North America for two reasons: (1) his clinical method was unorthodox in the heyday of behaviourism, and (2) "the lack of adequate translations into English of his elegant but difficult French" (Rowland & McGuire, 1968, p. 145) meant that his works were unavailable to the English-speaking world. Berlyne was among the first to recognize the severity of this problem and act upon it.

In 1950, Berlyne, in collaboration with M. Piercy, translated Piaget's *Psychology of Intelligence* into English. In that book, Piaget outlined his theory of mental development. After spending time with Piaget in Geneva, Berlyne continued to disseminate Piaget's thinking in North America and to integrate it into his own work. The post-*Sputnik* discovery of Piaget forced psychologists like Burton White and educators to realize that "if we pay little attention to the events occurring in the first years of life, much of the story may be over by the time we begin to 'educate' the child, even if we start as early as age 3, let alone age 6" (White, 1968, p 145).

A third factor that influenced North Americans' view of the young child in the 1960s was, in Ira Gordon's somewhat satirical words, the "rediscovery in sociology that language learning begins in the home" (Gordon, 1967, p. 20). The theoretical work of Basil Bernstein in England indicated that social class had a profound effect on the type of language and the cognitive style ultimately developed. Bernstein's work emphasized the significance of language learning in the early years and spawned considerable North American research in this area (e.g., Hess & Shipman, 1965a, 1965b, 1968).

The rediscovery of infancy and early childhood created a new series of challenges, at least for politicians, educators, psychologists, and sociologists if not for society at large. Gordon (1967) summarized the challenge:

> Our old norms are shaken.... Our present theory of the child as competent, as active, as individual ... requires that we intervene, that we do something during this period.... We cannot sit idly by and let [the child] flower, because he [or she] will not. We have to find and define the optimum environment and then we have to convince our public that it needs to provide it. (p. 20)

Chapters 5 to 9 delve into these ideas to greater extents. Partnerships looks at parental values concerning cognitive development—the domain that theorists, parents, and teachers alike strive to understand.

PARTNERSHIPS
Parental Values Concerning Cognitive Development

As it is with all areas of the early childhood curriculum, it is very important to share with parents a clear statement of the school's philosophy about how to support and further children's cognitive development. Parents should be aware, for instance, that the program is built on the conviction that children learn best through concrete, hands-on activities; that children are able to select meaningful activities on their own; and that play and learning go together. Conversely, such a philosophy means that the program's teachers do not engage in abstract and developmentally inappropriate practices that require children to sit quietly and inactively.

Today's parents are bombarded by pressures to succeed, which includes having successful children as well. Thus many well-intentioned parents feel a need to see evidence that their children are indeed learning in their early childhood program. For instance, parents may say to you, "But Marcia does nothing but play all day. When will she learn something?" or "Ron starts kindergarten next year. Shouldn't he be learning to read?" or "I'm thinking of enrolling Betsy in the school where my neighbour's son goes. He comes home with worksheets every day and Betsy only brings home paintings." How do you respond in a way that respects parental concerns but maintains the integrity of your program?

Conveying to parents your philosophy of how children learn best involves frequent explanation and supporting information. First, it requires that you, as the teacher, be secure in your understanding of how young children learn and acquire concepts; this will enable you to address parents' questions and concerns. It is also important to make information from experts, which supports your approach, available to parents. This might be done through a parent library, which includes such books as *Playtime Learning Games for Young Children* by Alice Honig. In addition, you can distribute reprints of well-written articles to each family, prominently post short quotes on the parent bulletin board, invite an appropriate speaker to a parent meeting, or plan parent discussion groups with a knowledgeable facilitator. Share with them the information you have from your provincial ECE association. Let parents know about *Developmentally Appropriate Practice in Early Childhood Programs Serving Children from Birth through Age 8* by Sue Bredekamp (1987; 1997), which supports your approach. In other words, let them know that your work with the children is founded on and backed by research and theory.

One teacher dealt creatively with the questions some parents posed about what their children were learning. She videotaped the children one day during a half-hour of self-selected activities. Then, during a parent meeting, she followed the showing of the videotape by discussing how the children engaged in problem solving and concept formation through their activities. The parents were amazed at how much learning was going on.

Although it is important to convey your approach and philosophy to parents, it is also vital to recognize that parents are the most important elements in their children's lives. When parents share anecdotes and experiences with you, convey the value you place on the importance of their role as their child's primary teacher and mentor. Recognize parents' expertise and invite them to share it with all of the children. Also inform parents of special community events or exhibits that they might want to attend or visit with their children.

Current Consensus on How Children Learn

- The period of most rapid developmental growth is in the early childhood years (birth to 8 years).
- The issue is no longer where the child is cared for—in a home or centre setting—but whether the quality of that care is poor or good. Development can be negatively affected by a low-quality environment or enriched by a high-quality environment, whether these be home or school environments (we will define and discuss quality further in Chapter 5).
- Many factors *interact* to influence a child's development—heredity, experience, environment, opportunity, nutrition, pre- and post-natal care, economy, culture, beliefs, perceptions, and child care practices.

Children

Recognizing Similarities

Now that we have determined that there is a childhood period and have examined particular views in the past about what a child is and how a child might learn and develop, let us look at children as we know them now. Generally, children are wonderfully engaging and winning, in part because of the freshness with which

they approach all experiences. Most children possess a sense of trust that the world and the people in it are friendly and kind, and they will tackle that world with joy and enthusiasm. The amount of information that children learn in the first few years of life is unparallelled in later learning. At no other time in life will there be such zest and liveliness toward acquiring skills and knowledge.

Our task in working with young children is to provide an environment in which this enthusiasm is nurtured and sustained rather than subdued or even destroyed. Preschoolers are eager to learn, but such eagerness can be battered down if they are frequently overwhelmed by developmentally inappropriate experiences. This awesome responsibility on the shoulders of early childhood educators can be met through careful and sensitive study and understanding of the characteristics and needs of young children.

Typically we look at children's growth across **developmental domains.** These domains include the physical, intellectual or cognitive, creative, language, emotional, and social realms. As stated earlier, we know that children are predisposed to develop certain skills in somewhat of a sequence, that children develop at different rates, and that the environment can influence development. Understanding the themes of development, the principles of development, and the impacts on development adds to your development as an excellent early childhood educator.

Age-Related Similarities among Children

Although each child is unique, all children nonetheless have much in common. All children share the need for nurturing and trustworthy adults, for stability and security, for increasing autonomy, and for a sense of competence and self-worth. Similarly, there are common attributes and skills that characterize children at different ages during the preschool years. In the course of normal development, children reach developmental milestones in a fairly predictable manner and within a

reasonable time range (Allen & Marotz, 1994). For that reason, you can make checklists or normative tables that describe the typical features of children at different ages within each developmental domain. Arnold Gessell, in fact, spent his life developing normative tables. More recently, Allen and Marotz (1994) published a book, with profiles of typical children from birth to 8 years, that you may wish to consult. The Toronto Board of Education's *Observing Children,* which looks at the typical child from 2 to 13 years, also is a valuable resource. Using this resource, Exhibit 2.5 shows the development of children 2 to 5 years. The NAEYC 1997 edition of DAP in ECE Birth to Age 8 also contains developmental milestones (Bredekamp, 1997).

Note that milestones are different from theories about how children learn. Milestones are a list of observable skills (e.g., walking). A theorist's job is to propose how the child reached these milestones (remember our discussion on genetics versus environment).

While a comprehensive summary of developmental norms is beyond the scope of this text, a brief overview of some developmental characteristics of children in the early childhood period is appropriate. Keep in mind that knowing what to expect of children is different than pushing children to reach milestones before they are ready. Hence, part of your job is knowing the individual children— where they've been, where they are, where they need to go, and how to appropriately guide them as they make their way there. This text emphasizes programs for children between 2 and 5 years of age but also provides an overview of infant and toddler programs as well as primary-school programs. However, students interested in working with infants, toddlers, and primary-school children will need to seek additional resources that discuss in more depth the development of children of these ages and programs for them. Following is a simplified compilation of what children tend to be like at these ages. Again, how they came to be this way is a different story.

Infants (Birth to 12 Months)   Early childhood programs for infants under 1 year were rare until the 1960s when a number of research-oriented programs were established to determine the effect of high-quality programs on infant development (Fein & Fox, 1988). While there still is considerable controversy about some of the findings, the weight of the evidence suggests that high-quality programs are beneficial even in the first year of life, especially for those from disadvantaged homes. There are excellent materials available for those who want to become caregivers in programs that serve the very young (Maxim, 1989; Morrison, 1988), including *Every Child Is Special* by R. Shimoni, J. Baxter, and J. Kugelmass (1992), a Canadian text on the topic.

The first year of life is characterized by constant change and many significant firsts (Fogel, 1991). Infants grow very rapidly and develop many physical skills in a short period of time. They learn to control their heads, and they begin to smile, roll over, and sit and then to crawl and creep. At birth, babies' movements are mostly reflexive and they are unable to manipulate objects. But by the time babies reach their first birthday, their caregivers are kept busy childproofing the environment by placing dangerous objects out of reach and watching as independence in eating finger foods and drinking from a cup begin to emerge. In fact, the first year is quite challenging for caregivers as their charges have developmental needs that alter almost from one day to the next.

Differences in temperament become evident early in the first year of life (Thomas, Chess, & Birch, 1968). Some infants are active and regular, while others are much quieter, and still others have an unpredictable schedule. Infants also differ on the approach–withdrawal dimension. Some approach new people, foods, and experiences with enthusiasm, while others tend to withdraw from or be upset by novelty. Some are very adaptable and responsive. Others may scream at any schedule disruption but sleep through a parade. In a group setting in particular, you will notice that some infants seem to fuss and cry much of the time, while others seem happy most of the time. These inborn characteristics demand that those caring for infants learn about the temperaments of those in their care and adapt their behaviours to meet the individuals' needs. Thomas et al. (1968) and Chess & Thomas (1987) referred to this as a "goodness of fit" between the child's and the caregiver's temperaments. Recognizing differences in our temperaments helps us adjust to make the fit a positive interaction in all of our relationships. A regular baby may adapt to a schedule that has some consistency, but the irregular baby will need a highly flexible schedule. A more active baby will respond to a program that offers a wide range of activities, but the tranquil, quiet baby will not try all of the activities.

Mainstream magazines such as *Life* and *Time* often carry well-researched articles on child development that should be shared with parents. For instance, in an excellent article in *Life* called "The Amazing Minds of Infants" (1993), Lisa Grunwald with Jeff Goldberg reported the latest evidence from top researchers—and so well that the piece featured even in the 1997 *Annual Editions in Early Childhood Education* (Paciorek & Munro, 1997). This evidence shows that babies can recognize emotions and can imitate within their first few weeks of life. Their memory is developing rapidly, as is their language. Predisposition to cognitive abilities such as math and physics has been seen in infants as young as 5 months.

One-Year-Old Children (1 to 2 Years)   While the first year of life is characterized by many rapid changes, the second year of life has its own excitement. Usually, children begin to take their first toddling steps between 12 and 15 months of age. Moreover, language begins to emerge and develop rapidly during this time; the use of speech is a characteristic that makes humans unique. The fact that these two major human traits develop *without direct teaching* often makes people take these accomplishments for granted, but it would be difficult to find a youngster who was not delighted with these new skills. Suddenly, with hands free, a child can explore the world with extra zeal. Having some language skills, a child can communicate pleasure and displeasure more easily. Of course, discussing whether walking and talking are learned behaviours or biological traits would make an interesting class debate!

In the second year, the child is quite egocentric and relates to adults better than to children. Early in the second year, children are usually willing to agree to adult requests and to receive adult assistance, but as they approach their second birthday, refusals to cooperate and a strong desire to "do it myself" become more frequent. It is important to remember, no matter how hurried we become, that the child's need and desire to master a task alone must be honoured if we hope to foster self-esteem and a developing sense of autonomy.

Usually one sees the beginnings of pretend play during the second year, and it becomes more complex as the child's abilities to communicate with others and to understand their requests improve. Storybooks become of greater interest, and the child's attention span slowly increases, even if it remains very short by adult standards. Most play is action-oriented, and a sense of ownership—often expressed by a loud "Mine!"—becomes apparent. Building with blocks, scribbling, and matching objects interest the child in the second year, and most activities are approached with vigour and delight.

Two-Year-Old Children It is true that 2-year-olds, with their limited self-control, may well express their growing independence and self-assertiveness by grabbing a desired toy from a peer or by throwing a tantrum. Tantrums, in fact, are common among 2-year-olds, and reflect, in part, their limited verbal skills, which often do not allow them to express what they want. Two-year-olds are also inept at delaying gratification; they do not have the ability to wait for something they want "right now" (Allen & Marotz, 1994; Ames, Gillespie, Haines, & Ilg, 1980; Bredekamp, 1987). Moreover, they are just beginning to acquire some social skills, and tend to play side-by-side with peers rather than interact with them.

While these trying characteristics are typical of 2-year-olds, this transitional stage is inspirational to behold. Curiosity is boundless in 2-year-olds, and the world is their oyster to explore, savour, and enjoy. Two-year-olds undertake many activities for the sheer pleasure rather than to reach a goal. Running is enjoyed in itself rather than as a means of getting somewhere fast; painting means involvement in a sensory process rather than an interest in producing a picture. Activities are also undertaken with enormous enthusiasm. Two-year-olds wholeheartedly throw themselves into activities, whether painting, squishing play dough, pouring sand and water, or reading books. They particularly enjoy sensory experiences, using touch, taste, and smell, as well as sight and sound. Two-year-olds are notorious for their desire to repeat, using newfound skills over and over again. This desire is normal and should be encouraged for it builds competence and allows children to fully assimilate skills before moving on to new ones.

During this year, most children increasingly gain body control: they are more self-assured about walking, their running no longer has a baby stagger, and their newfound finger control allows them to put together simple puzzles or paint with a brush. At the same time, they experience tremendous language growth. Their growing vocabulary, sentence length, and grammatical forms open up all sorts of possibilities because of this increased communicative competence. Self-help skills are also improving, including the achievement of toilet training for the majority of children during this year. Just as important as learning motor, language, and self-help skills is the process of gaining independence through this mastery.

Teachers of 2-year-olds need to provide a supportive, consistent, and safe environment in which rapidly growing skills can be practised and mastered. Frequent and enthusiastic praise conveys that adults value the acquisition of skills.

Gentle guidance acknowledges children's growing sense of self while helping them develop self-control in relation to others (Bredekamp, 1987).

Three-Year-Old Children   Three-year-olds have truly left babyhood behind, not only in appearance—with the loss of baby fat—but also in added skills. Increased balance and control are evident in large motor, fine motor, and self-help areas. Three-year-olds like to use their new skills by being helpful and wanting to please adults. Their added competence does not mean, however, that they won't occasionally have accidents or revert to earlier behaviours when upset. Overall, however, their characteristic way of responding to school experiences is with enthusiasm and enjoyment.

By age 3, children's speech is intelligible most of the time and consists of longer sentences. Language becomes much more of a social and cognitive tool. Three-year-olds engage in more extensive conversations, talking *with* and not just *to* people, and they delight in answering questions as well as asking them. In fact, 3-year-old children are usually bursting with questions, constantly asking why, what for, and where about everything imaginable. Three-year-olds can ask questions on topics not covered in encyclopedias, *The Guinness Book of Records,* or *The Farmers' Almanac!* Vocabulary continues to increase dramatically, and grammar becomes more accurate.

This greater language facility helps increase peer interaction among this age group. Three-year-olds are much more socially aware than younger children, and their make-believe play, which they began in the previous year by imitating simple personal and home routines, at times includes several children. Short-lived friendships begin to form, and children will play *with* one another as well as *near* one another. Social problem-solving skills are just beginning to emerge. With guidance, 3-year-olds may share and take turns, but they still find such behaviours difficult (Allen & Marotz, 1994; Ames, Gillespie, Haines, & Ilg, 1980).

Teachers of 3-year-olds need to respect the growing skills and competencies of their charges without forgetting just how recently they acquired them. It is important to maintain patience and good humour, remembering that the enthusiasm with which 3-year-olds use these skills is not always matched by accuracy and speed. Because 3-year-olds enjoy helping as well as practising self-help skills, such behaviours should be promoted and valued. The emerging social skills of 3-year-olds should be encouraged in an atmosphere where social exploration is safe and where playing alone or not giving up a favourite toy is also acceptable (Bredekamp, 1987).

Four-Year-Old Children   Four-year-olds have achieved a maturity and competence in motor and language development that leads them to assume a general air of security and confidence, sometimes bordering on cockiness. "It is a time of constantly testing limits in order to practice self-confidence and firm up a growing need for independence" (Allen & Marotz, 1989, p. 87).

Four-year-olds seem to be in perpetual motion, throwing themselves whole-heartedly into activities. They have mastered the basics of movement and now eagerly embellish on these. Climbing, pedalling, pumping on a swing, jumping over and off objects, and easily avoiding obstacles when running are routine, and all contribute to greater flexibility and exploration in play. Showing off new physical stunts—or trying to—is a favourite pastime. Improved muscle coordination is also evident in more controlled use of the fingers, such as in buttoning, drawing, and cutting with scissors. In addition, many self-care activities have become routines rather than the challenges they were at earlier ages.

If increased competence leads to noticeable embellishments in motor activities, this is even more evident in the language area. By age 4, most children's language usage has become remarkably sophisticated and skilled. This accomplishment seems to invite new uses for language beyond communication. Four-year-olds love to play with language, using it to brag, engage in bathroom talk, swear, tell tall tales, and make up silly rhymes. And, if you can imagine, 4-year-olds are even more persistent than 3-year-olds in asking questions.

For 4-year-olds, peers have become very important. Play is a social activity more often than not, although 4-year-olds enjoy solitary activities at times as well. Taking turns and sharing become much easier because 4-year-olds begin to understand the benefits of cooperation. Their imaginative variations of movement and language skills extend into group play, which is usually highly creative, ingenious, and touched by their sense of humour.

Teachers of 4-year-olds need to provide an environment in which children have many opportunities for interactions with one another, with adults, and with a wide selection of appropriate and stimulating materials. Because of their heightened social involvements, this age group needs consistent, positive guidance to help develop emerging social skills, for instance, in sharing, resolving conflicts, and negotiating (Allen & Marotz, 1994; Ames, Gillespie, Haines, & Ilg, 1980; Bredekamp, 1987).

Five-Year-Old Children Five-year-olds are much more self-contained and controlled; they have replaced some of their earlier exuberant behaviours with a calmer, more mature approach. They are competent and reliable, taking responsibility seriously. They seem to be able to judge their own abilities more accurately than at earlier ages, and they respond accordingly.

Five-year-olds' motor activities seem more poised, their movements more restrained and precise than ever before. There is also greater interest in fine motor activities as children have gained many skills in accurate cutting, gluing, drawing, and beginning writing. This interest is spurred by the new desire to make something rather than merely to paint, cut, or manipulate the play dough for the sheer enjoyment of these activities. The self-reliance of 5-year-olds extends to assuming considerable responsibility for self-care as well.

Language has also reached a height of maturity for this age group, exhibited through a vocabulary that contains thousands of words, complex and compound

EXHIBIT 2.5: APPROXIMATE DEVELOPMENT OF CHILDREN 2 TO 5 YEARS OF AGE

Physical Growth	Language/Intellectual Growth	Social/Emotional Growth
Rate of Growth • Period of rapid growth in all areas—turmoil at beginning and end of phase. • Girls more advanced physically from birth. **Body Growth** • Gradually loses baby fat (appears more streamlined and stable). • Body proportions begin to change—torso and limbs lengthen. • Wrist bones soft and not fully developed in number. • Muscles not yet firmly attached to skeleton. • Little strength, unaware of own limitations. • Large muscles continue to develop and become more coordinated. • Small muscles less developed—muscles in extremities develop last. **Organic Growth** • Brain development—right/left dominance not established. • Sensory development uneven (e.g., vision may be more or less developed than hearing). • Eyes not fully developed in size—naturally far-sighted. **Coordination and Control of Movement** • Steadiness of growth allows muscular coordination to keep pace—body	**Language** *Listening:* • Understands objective language of adults better than language of peers. • Comprehends simple instructions. • Listens for general rather than specific detail. *Speaking:* • Uses language to maintain self, to direct, to report, to imagine, to reason, to predict, to project. • Shows great spurt in language usage and structure. • Shows great range in language skill (e.g., expression, speed, volume, clarity of speech). • Asks many fact-finding questions. • Uses subjective language—meaning is clear to child but not always to listener. • Needs a listener yet does not consider listener's needs (egocentric). • Intuitively seeking the structure of language. • Manipulates language—creates and experiments with words. • Experiments with word order and negative forms (e.g., "Why I can't go?"). • Reveals rule-seeking through errors with plurals, past tense (e.g., "mouses"). • Over-generalizes and applies regular rules to irregular verbs and nouns (e.g., "I comed").	**Behaviour/Self Image** Periods of rapid growth at beginning and end of phase are times of unrest and disequilibrium accompanied by the following: • unpredictable behaviour—ranging from withdrawl to aggression; • inner urge to prove own will—"Let me do it my way"; • desire to develop personal autonomy—to stand on own feet; • prone to tantrums—non-verbal rebellion; • impulsive—struggles for control; • showing signs of tension (e.g., blinking, biting nails, sweeping tongue). Period of slower growth mid-phase is a time of relative calm and stability accompanied by: • more control of impulses; • more cooperation and sensitivity to moods and feelings of others; • sustained interest in an activity; Child is egocentric and unaware of perspective of others. Child: • enjoys regularity and personal ritual; • seeks success, new experiences; • desires some measure of independence;

Physical Growth	Language/Intellectual Growth	Social/Emotional Growth
movements become smoother and more controlled—capable of sudden starts and stops and changes in pace and direction. ■ Full arm movement until wrist, finger bones, and muscles develop. ■ Arm movement—sweeps away from and back to body—later circular, up and down, and sideways movements occur. ■ Hand gradually bends independently from shoulder and elbow, allowing more precise reaching, selecting, and holding. ■ Ability to run, hop, skip, climb, balance, push, pull, ride a tricycle develops. ■ Grasp becomes more precise. **Energy—Concentration, Motivation** ■ Enthusiastic. ■ High energy level. ■ Tires easily. ■ Changes activity frequently. ■ Easily distracted, yet capable of periods of intense concentration.	■ Reveals process of classifying and reclassifying to organize perception of world (e.g., child calls all animals dogs). Later learns significant differences and becomes more specific. *Reading:* ■ Watches adults read—pretends to read (begins to learn book skills). ■ Many aware that meaning can be sought through pictures and print. ■ Seeks meaning from symbols in the environment (e.g., signs, advertisements). ■ Some may begin to read. *Writing:* ■ Many children aware that meaning can be conveyed through pictures, symbols, print. **Intellectual Growth** ■ Learn by manipulating and changing things—trial and error technique gradually replaced as memory develops. ■ Action often precedes thought—thought not always analyzed. ■ Perceives from one point of view—child's own. ■ Judges on basis of appearance rather than logic. –Some may show intuitive awareness of conservation (e.g., selects correct size of clothes for doll, but does not generalize and transfer this ability to other situations).	■ is adventuresome—hates confinement; ■ is vulnerable; ■ is interested in realizing immediate goals. **Relationships to Adults** ■ Needs praise, acceptance, support, encouragement. ■ Follows adult suggestions quite readily until late in phase. ■ Needs reasonable limits and external controls. ■ Conforms to avoid consequences—accepts adult's way as "the way." **Relationships to Peers** ■ Needs and enjoys social contact to develop own idea of self. ■ Develops autonomy through play—regards other children as play objects. ■ Individualistic—finds it difficult to share and take turns. ■ May play alone, or beside but not with others (parallel play) until late in phase. ■ Frequently frustated with attempts to socialize but holds no grudges.

Physical Growth	Language/Intellectual Growth	Social/Emotional Growth
	• Classifies experiences and later learns to apply them to new situations (essential to learning routines). • Begins to make comparisons of two objects (e.g., big, little). • Begins to put objects in order. • Makes simple causal relationships by association when actively involved (e.g., "You press a button to turn on the T.V."). • Has limited ability to understand, compare, and use terminology related to quantity (e.g., child who selects sand play may know which container holds more but may confuse names when describing them. • May show intuitive feeling for symmetry, scale, and order without realizing it. • Time is understood as now and is measured by daily events—past, present, and future terminology presents difficulty (e.g., next week means not now). • Does not understand time constancy (necessary before clocks and calendars become meaningful). • Regards inanimate objects as live. • Distinguishes and describes differences according to a particular quality (e.g., "The little block is the baby"). • Memory is largely associative and linked with a particular experience and action (e.g., child pretends when playing in the blocks).	

Source: Norris, Doreen and Joyce Boucher, 1980. *Observing Children*. Board of Education for the City of Toronto. Reprinted with permission.

sentence structures, variety and accuracy in grammatical forms, and good articulation. Language increasingly reflects interest in and contact with a broadening world outside the child's intimate family, school, and neighbourhood experiences. The social sphere of 5-year-olds revolves around special friendships, which take on more importance. By age 5, children are quite adept at sharing toys, taking turns, and playing cooperatively. Their group play is usually quite elaborate and imaginative, and it can take up long periods of time (Allen & Marotz, 1994; Ames et al., 1980).

Teachers of 5-year-olds, after providing a stimulating learning environment and setting reasonable limits, can expect this age group to take on considerable responsibility for maintaining and regulating a smoothly functioning program. Five-year-olds need to be given many opportunities to explore their world in depth and assimilate what they learn through multiple experiences. One way in which children can discuss, plan, and carry out ideas stimulated by their experiences is through group projects (Katz, 1989).

Primary or School-Aged Children   Children from 6 through 8 years of age usually are in grades 1, 2, or 3. These grades are known as the primary grades in most provinces, and attendance at a formal school or an approved alternative is no longer an option at this stage in a child's life. Unfortunately, the years from birth to 5 seem to receive more attention from the early childhood field, despite the fact that primary-grade children still share many of the developmental needs evident in the earlier years.

The pressure-cooker, skill-oriented primary programs that have become more common in recent years fail to recognize the need of children aged 6 to 8 to play and to experience success. Moreover, such programs do not reflect an understanding of the developmental unevenness that typifies children of this age. Just because Jimmy's gross motor skills are at a 7-year-old level, it does not follow that his fine motor and language skills are at the same level. The situation can be even worse for those primary-grade children who have late birthdays relative to the majority of children in their class. Too often, subject- and skill-oriented teachers forget that some children in the class may be almost a year younger than others. At this stage in development, a year is a very long time, and it is unreasonable to assume that children who vary in age by almost a year should be achieving at the same level. Susie may be working at a beginning grade 1 level in reading while Mario is at a late grade 1 level; even though Susie may seem behind to the teacher, the fact that Susie is one year minus a day younger than Mario needs to be considered. The fact is that both Susie and Mario may be working at an *age-appropriate* level.

Certainly, physical growth has slowed down in 6- to 8-year-olds, relative to preschoolers, but basic skills still need to be refined, and children of these ages need active play on a regular basis. Primary-level children are boisterous and enjoy rough-housing, even though there is a risk of injury. Balancing stunts, including riding a two-wheeler and acrobatics, are challenges that are tackled with enthusiasm, but fatigue and hunger may follow.

Peer pressure and a need to be accepted become more marked during these years, and play has a highly social quality. While the 6-year-old has best friends for short periods of time, friendships become more enduring and more important for the 7- and 8-year-olds. However, 6-, 7-, and 8-year-olds have rigid gender-role stereotypes, are quite discriminatory, and rarely form close friendships with a member of the opposite sex. Nonetheless, they begin to test behaviours, things, and ideas with friends that they will later have to test in the wider world. The peer group will slowly increase in importance up to the adolescent years, when it will become a more important reference group than the family.

Simple competitive sports become a possibility during the primary years, but they are not without friction. Impatience, a lack of persistence, and complaints are not infrequent, but sensitivity and cooperation also increase during these years. As children approach 7 and 8 years of age, they become less egocentric, and logical thinking processes begin to emerge. A sense of morality also starts to develop along with an increasing understanding of rules.

Children in the primary grades like to chatter, but they talk *with* people rather than *to* them. Vocabulary growth is slower than it was during the preschool years, but it still increases steadily. The mechanical aspects of speech are not fully mature, and irregularities should not be a concern. However, the ability to appreciate the subtleties and the humour of language increases rapidly during this period as many parents and teachers know. Riddles, puns, and knock knock jokes are shared with delight.

Reading and writing usually begin—and are sometimes mastered—during this period, but reversals of letters and numbers are common. Mathematical concepts proliferate, and sequencing skills and storytelling abilities improve dramatically. Planning, sorting, classifying, and collecting are enjoyed, as are real gadgets like radios and cameras. Attitudes toward school as well as toward themselves are being formed at this time, so teachers and parents must ensure that primary-level children experience success on a regular basis. In A Canadian Professional Speaks Out we asked the little pros about being a child and about teachers.

Need for Self-Esteem

One thing shared by all children is the need to feel good about themselves. Young children are beginning to form a **self-concept**, perceptions and feelings about themselves gathered largely from how the important people in their world respond to them. One aspect of self-concept is **self-esteem**, children's evaluation of their worth in positive or negative terms (Greenspan & Greenspan, 1986; Essa & Rogers, 1992; Marshall, 1989; Samuels, 1977). Such evaluation can tell children that they are competent, worthwhile, and effective or, on the other hand, that they are incapable, unlikable, and powerless. It is particularly noteworthy that children who feel good about themselves seem to be more friendly and helpful toward peers (Marshall, 1989).

A CANADIAN PROFESSIONAL SPEAKS OUT
Little Pros on Childhood

This is not an official study! This is dialogue accumulated casually over time as we interacted with a diverse range of children from various settings, age groups, and locations. What were their ideas about kids? Grownups? Families? Schools? Teachers? Depending on the age of the child, we might have posed the questions in very different ways. What is a child? or What does a child do? or Tell me about children! Here's a sampling of the most typical answers from children between the ages of 2 and 12.

Topic	Children	Adults	Families	Schools	Teachers
Age 2	– throw things – me – kids – play – toys	– Mom – Dad – not you! – big	– Mom	– fun – (named items such as blocks)	– fun – (gave teachers' names)
Age 3	– a kid is a kid – plays – likes schools	– go to work – make supper – play with me	– for hugs	– for bigger kids to learn – read	– tell kids to do work – read
Age 4	– little kids – plays	– talk – cook – do dishes – get us in trouble	– kiss – hug – love their kids	– where you learn	– tell you what you have to do in school – preschool is fun because teachers love you
Age 5	– little kids – they play on their bikes	– they work – they cook – they play with you – read stories	– there's a mom and dad – sisters – brothers – live in a house – they go away together	– they have centres like blocks – computers – it's fun – learn to read in grade 1	– they are nice – they teach you

Topic	Children	Adults	Families	Schools	Teachers
Age 6	– a littler child – go to school – me!	– a big child – work, cook – parents	– whole bunch of people – 2 grownups and kids – get money for food – group of people love each other	– a place to learn math – learn subjects – for learning – you make friends – people teach you – have desks – fun	– someone who teaches kids so they can learn stuff – they are smart – they are nice – teachers should never yell!
Age 7	– a child – play – fight – eat – talk	– they chit-chat – take care of us – tell you to eat healthy food – work – watch out for us	– people who care for you – if you didn't have a family you would have no one who loved you – they protect you – they help you get better – help you when you get hurt	– you learn stuff from other people – learn to read, spell, do math – see friends	– they teach you – they work – they try to help – a few yell; most are nice, though
Age 8	– somebody 1 to 12 years old – have friends – play a lot – go to each other's house	– they can't get into trouble – cook – get money – work	– a lot of people – they love each other like a lot! – you can fight with your brothers and sisters but you love them	– sometimes boring – get taught – has subjects	– they teach you – they correct you – they want you to learn and improve – help you solve problems

Topic	Children	Adults	Families	Schools	Teachers
Age 9	– a little person – plays – bigger ones do work	– reads paper – older – work to get money to have a home for kids – tell you what you can and can't do	– live together – they love each other – do stuff together	– to learn – friends – sometimes hard	– a good teacher is nice – they teach new things – they really want you to learn, so they help a lot
Age 10	– play – little – watch TV – they have to go to school	– tell you what to do – make good food – they work – they help you	– people – do stuff together – they usually like each other even if they fight	– boring – you have to work hard – your friends are there – to make you learn	– a person who helps you – some are strict by yelling – some are good by caring
Age 11	– person between ages 3 and 16 – do homework – go to school	– old people – take care of kids – have jobs – get money	– people that are related to you – people who take care of you	– for teaching and learning – boring (only sometimes!) – should be fun but more fun sometimes	– they invented school – they discipline you – help you – a good teacher doesn't yell—please don't yell at us and we will smile and listen

A healthy self-concept is vital to all areas of a child's development. Although readiness in the natural progression of development is triggered internally and furthered by appropriate external stimuli, successful mastery of new learning also depends on a child's feelings of competence and ability to meet new challenges. **Perceived competence** reflects the child's belief in his or her ability to succeed at a given task (Marshall, 1989). Successful experiences result in self-confidence, which, in turn, boosts self-esteem. Thus, many appropriate yet challenging experiences help the child feel successful, confident, and capable (Essa & Rogers, 1992).

The child needs to feel competent and able to face challenges, as well as have a sense of **personal control**—the feeling of having the power to make things happen or stop things from happening. When children generally feel that what happens to them is completely out of their hands, particularly if what happens is not always in their best interest, they cannot develop this sense of control and will tend to see themselves as helpless and ineffective. All children need opportunities to make appropriate choices and exercise autonomy to begin to develop the perception that they have control, which also contributes to their emerging sense of responsibility for their own actions (Marshall, 1989).

The early years are crucial in the development of self-concept, since it forms and stabilizes early in life and becomes increasingly resistant to change (Samuels, 1977). Above all, children's positive concepts of themselves reflect healthy parent–child relationships that are founded on love, trust, and consistency. Then, when early childhood teachers enter young children's lives, they also contribute to the formation of that concept.

At the same time, if a child comes to school with a history of abuse or neglect, the teacher's contribution of offsetting positive experiences can help nurture self-esteem. Teachers strengthen children's positive self-esteem if they are sensitive to each child as an individual and to the needs of children for affection, nurturing, caring, and feelings of competence. Thus, teachers who understand children, know their characteristics, respond to them, and know how to challenge them in a supportive manner contribute to this positive sense of self. In essence, everything the early childhood teacher does has an impact on the children's self-concepts.

Need for Play

Another thing that children have in common is the need for play, which serves as a means of learning about and making sense of the world (Rubin, Fein, & Vandenberg, 1983). But more than that, play is essential to all aspects of children's development. "It is an activity which is concerned with the whole of his being, not with just one small part of him, and to deny him the right to play is to deny him the right to live and grow" (Cass, 1973, p. 11). Play promotes mastery as children practise skills; it furthers cognitive development as thinking abilities are stretched; it involves language, encouraging new uses; it involves physical activity; it helps children work through emotions; its inventive nature makes it creative; it is often a socializing event; beyond all that, however, it provides a way for children to assimilate and integrate their life experiences. In no way is play a trivial pursuit, but rather it is a serious undertaking necessary to healthy development for all children (Almy, Monighan, Scales, & Van Hoorn, 1984).

Although the different types of play will be discussed in more detail in Chapter 6, it is worth noting at this point that, with age, children develop increasing social and cognitive skills that influence their play. If you are aware that play changes with age, it helps you to have appropriate expectations for young children in an early childhood program and to engage in their play. For instance, a 10-month-old engages in simple games like "Peek-a-boo," whereas several 5-year-olds may collaborate to build a rocketship in the block centre. As a teacher, you are more likely to initiate play sequences with infants and toddlers. With older children, however, you probably will not initiate many play sequences; rather you would structure the environment to facilitate the child's play. Children between 3 and 5 years, for example, need sizable blocks of time to engage in self-selected play, both indoors and outdoors, and many open-ended materials that lend themselves to exploration and mastery (e.g., play dough, sand and water, building blocks). In addition, time, space, and materials that lend themselves to social play should always be available (including dolls, dress-up clothes, and blocks). However, organized games with rules, particularly competitive games, are beyond the ability of most preschoolers to understand and should not be part of the early childhood program.

Respecting Differences

Infants and young children have many characteristics in common and certainly share basic needs for affection, acceptance, consistency, respect, and appropriate challenges, yet there are many variations among children. The profiles of infants, toddlers, preschoolers, and primary-level children presented earlier reflect many

common characteristics of these ages, but they rarely describe any one child. While falling within the normal range of development, each child possesses a unique blend of attributes that makes him or her one of a kind. A Closer Look examines the concept of **inclusion** in the classroom. Inclusion is a concept that promotes the recognition of and respect for similarities and differences, or **diversity**, among children. Diversity includes factors such as the physical, intellectual, social, emotional, linguistic, creative, cultural, and financial. The concept of inclusion upholds all children's fundamental rights to access services and to grow and learn to their maximum potential.

THE CONCEPT OF INCLUSION—CHILDREN WITH DIVERSE NEEDS

Some children are born with or acquire conditions that place them outside the typical range of development for their age. They might have a **developmental delay**, meaning that they accomplish tasks in one or more developmental areas at a considerably later age than their peers. Some children are considered at risk for delay, with a significant probability that problems will occur because of adverse environmental factors such as poverty or low birth weight. With appropriate help, children who have developmental delays may well catch up to age norms. Other children may have an impairment, indicating development that is in some way different (not just slower) from that of most children. Children with hearing, visual, intellectual, or motor disabilities are part of this category. Similarly, children have different learning styles, behaviour patterns, temperaments, emotional and social needs, stressors, experiences, and cultural, religious, and financial parameters that need to be addressed.

We'd like to propose that all children have special needs. These needs are diverse yet equally important. We recognize that they require different approaches. Accepting and welcoming diversity among children means we can accept and welcome it into our schools and classrooms. Understanding diversity means reducing misconceptions and fears we might have about it. This is the first step toward an inclusive classroom—one that embraces all children and provides for their unique needs.

Children's differences reflect both inborn and external factors that have moulded who they are. Some children are born with an easy-going temperament; for instance, they have a moderate activity level, a predictable schedule of sleeping and eating, and a positive attitude toward, and curiosity about, new experiences. Other children have more difficult temperaments and are, for example, more irritable, unpredictable, and difficult to calm down (Thomas, Chess, & Birch, 1968; Chess & Thomas, 1987). Although children are born with such temperamental characteristics, these gradually tend to affect the adults around them so that parents and teachers may begin to think of children as difficult or easy, thereby expecting and reinforcing these behavioural traits. In turn, then, adults' perceptions of children contribute to children's self-perceptions.

A child's individuality is also shaped by the family. In most cases, the family is the most potent force in the young child's life. Consequently, it is important that early childhood educators endeavour to learn as much as possible about the families of young children. We must consider how to develop programs that respect and value the differences in the cultural, ethnic, religious, linguistic, and economic backgrounds of children's families. Early childhood teachers need to be sensitive to family diversity and genuinely value different cultures and backgrounds. Children mirror their primary environment—their home and family—as, of course, they should. If teachers, either consciously or unconsciously, put down, ignore, or negate what children experience and learn at home, they will convey that the family, including the child, is in some way inferior and undesirable. What a detrimental impact this would have on children's self-concepts!

Inclusion

One of the provisions often made is that children with disabilities be placed in the "least restricted" environment. First, this description itself implies restriction. A description with a more positive connotation such as "most enriching" would be more suitable (Spodek & Saracho, 1994). Second, we need to remember that children should be afforded the most enriching environment. A classroom, school, community, and government that support the diversity of children—whether developmental, cultural, racial, or financial—support the concept that all children belong to, and benefit from, being together.

Initially inclusion, formerly called integration or mainstreaming, meant that children that had been kept at home or institutionalized could be physically integrated (i.e., attend a segregated classroom within a school for typical children). This model is still prevalent today even though the champions of inclusion are clear: inclusion means inclusion in every respect. In this sense, inclusion is looked at as a human rights issue, not an education issue, in that it specifies children's rights to be included and to have access to the same learning opportunities and experiences as their peers, with their peers, in their own neighbourhood. It also affords parents the right to choose. Some parents still choose segregated programs feeling these best meet the needs of their children, but the point is they were provided with options. In the past, segregation was the only option available.

Helping parents make informed choices, providing a range of options that includes inclusion, and providing the necessary supports to implement the chosen option are critical to the success and acceptance of an inclusionary model. This concept has led to the expansion of inclusion—the integration of children with special needs into regular programs. Inclusion is certainly not new, having informally been part of many early childhood programs throughout this century.

An inclusive program is founded on the premise that young children, whether disabled or not, are much more similar than different (Wilderstrom, 1986). Children with special needs can benefit from a good inclusionary program by experiencing success in a variety of developmentally appropriate activities, through contact with age-mates who can be both models and friends, and by exposure to the many opportunities for informal incidental learning that take place in all early childhood programs (Deiner, 1993). At the same time, children with no disabilities benefit from inclusion by learning that children who are in some way different from them nonetheless have far more commonalities than differences (Karnes & Lee, 1979). An increasing number of young children with disabilities are enrolled in early childhood programs (Wolery et al., 1993).

Although inclusion has many potential benefits, the benefits do not happen automatically. In other words, inclusion does not simply mean enrolling children with special needs in an early childhood program. Careful planning, preparation, modification, evaluation, and support are necessary for successful inclusion.

Early childhood educators, because they know a great deal about children and how best to work with them, have many skills needed for working with children with disabilities. However, placement of children with special needs in early childhood classes also requires teachers to learn some additional skills. It often means having to acquire and use new teaching strategies, new terminology, and different evaluation tools. It also involves working with a wider range of professionals (e.g., speech and physical therapists or psychologists) and more focused involvement with parents. In addition, early childhood educators may find themselves with unexpectedly strong emotional reactions such as pity for the child, anger that the child has to suffer, fear of the disability, or self-doubt in their own abilities, which they must face and resolve as fear and ignorance prove to be the major blockers to inclusion.

One of the keys to successful inclusion is to view each child, whether disabled or not, as an individual with unique characteristics, strengths, and needs. This involves an attitude that sees *a child,* not a child with Down syndrome or a child who is blind or a child who stutters. For example, Ted may have Down syndrome, but he loves to paint, enjoys listening to stories at group time, and gives terrific hugs. Similarly, Noni's visual impairment does not diminish her enjoyment of the sand table, her budding friendship with Connie, or her ability to make others laugh through her language play. And Manuel, while often tripping over his words, can throw and catch a ball accurately. Many times he is the one who notices a colourful butterfly passing or the first buds of spring, and he has a totally winning smile. Working with a group of children means recognizing, encouraging, and building on each child's strengths. In this way, children's self-concept and self-assurance are boosted so they can meet the challenges posed by their disabilities.

Early childhood education principles are based on knowledge of child development, learning, and developmentally appropriate practices using a team approach. This makes early childhood education somewhat intrinsically inclusive in that it recognizes and addresses the developmental range of children and the need for programs to accommodate this.

It is beyond the scope of this text to discuss in depth such topics as characteristics of children with special needs, appropriate teaching methods, testing and assessment tools, interdisciplinary team models, legislation, and the unique needs of children at risk, or the parents of children with disabilities. This field combines the traditional skills of teachers of young children with those of special educators, therapists, and medical personnel.

Most early childhood educators, however, will inevitably find themselves in the following situations:

- One or more children with special needs will be included in their class.
- They will have concerns about a child who seems to experience consistent difficulties in one or more areas of development.
- They will be members of a team that supports and represents the child and family through their decision-making processes.

Communication within the team makes all team members informed, responsible, and accountable to the concept and process of inclusion.

It is important that teachers work with parents and specialists to make the inclusion experience successful. Likewise, teachers concerned about a child's functioning need to document their concerns and discuss them with the parents, as well as offer some concrete suggestions, for instance, about how to begin the referral process so the child is seen by an appropriate specialist. For these reasons, it is important that teachers of young children seek basic information about the characteristics of children with special needs, their families, and the importance of providing an inclusive environment for all children.

Now let us look more closely at these families to which children belong as we move to Chapter 3.

Key Terms

absorbent mind
accommodation
adaptation
assimilation
atelier
atelierista
behaviourism
behaviour modification
behavioural theory
casa dei bambini (children's house)
child-centred approach
child study movement
cognitive developmental theory
collaboration
concrete operations period
conservation
constructivist
constructivist theory
developmental delay
developmental domain

discrimination
disequilibrium
diversity
early childhood
emergent curriculum
equilibrium
formal operations period
Froebel gifts
garden of children
guided assistance
human development theory
image of the child
inclusion
infant school
interactionist
kindergartens
logico-mathematical knowledge
maturation
maturational theory
nature versus nurture

negative reinforcement
norms
object permanence
organization
perceived competence
personal control
physical knowledge
positive reinforcement
preoperational period
prepared environment
progressive education
projects
psychoanalytic theory
psychosocial theory
punishment
reinforcement

scaffolding
schemata
school readiness
self-concept
self-correcting materials
self-esteem
sensitive periods
sensorimotor period
social knowledge
social mediation
social reinforcers
sociohistoric theory
stage theorist
tangible reinforcers
zone of proximal development (ZPD)

Key Points

- Current practices are based on a blend of ideas and traditions evolved over centuries. Therefore, when questioned about your practices, you can refer to the appropriate theories.

- Early childhood in this text refers to children from birth to 8 years.

- Nineteenth-century changes in attitude regarding children are reflected when the first North American kindergarten was founded in 1873 in Toronto by Dr. J.L. Hughes.

- Other important changes include Head Start in the 1960s to rescue children of poverty through compensatory education programs and an increase in the need for improved child care due to recent changes in the economy, family life, and the workforce.

- The theories of influential people in the history of childhood are examples of how early childhood education has developed over the years.

- Parental involvement at all levels is essential.

- The need for a healthy self-concept (brought about by successful experiences and a sense of personal control) is vital to all areas of a child's development.

- Children's need for play provides a way to assimilate and integrate life experiences but must be geared to their age and particular personality.

- Inclusive programs are beneficial to all children as they lead to many incidental learning opportunities in the formative years.

Chapter 3

Families

While children are central in early childhood education, their families are equally important. Children are integral members of their family systems, and, conversely, family values and culture are an inseparable part of children.

Families are also at the core of early childhood education because the early childhood staff shares with families the responsibility for socializing young

children. It is important to provide for children a sense of continuity between home and school experiences, which can best be assured through a carefully fostered partnership between the family and the staff (Powell, 1989). This relationship implies mutual respect and equal power regarding ownership of rights, roles, and responsibilities of everyone involved.

Families—A Theoretical Perspective

Just as it is imperative you are familiar with developmental stages of early childhood educators and of children, it is equally important to understand family func-

tioning from a theoretical and developmental perspective. The **family systems theory** provides a useful approach to understanding the family as an ever-developing and changing social unit in which members constantly have to accommodate and adapt to one another's demands as well as to demands from outside the family. This theory provides a dynamic rather than static view of how families function.

From the perspective of the family systems theory, the influence that family members have on one another is not one-way but rather interactive and reciprocal. This interaction causes changes in the individual, between individuals within the family, and between the family and others. It is impossible to understand the family by gaining an understanding of just its individual members because the family is more than the sum of its parts. It is necessary to view its

interaction patterns and the unspoken rules that govern the members' behaviours. As in any healthy relationship, healthy families work well together, communicate often, are able to make effective decisions, and can handle change. In addition, understanding the family means looking at its functioning within the larger context, for instance, the extended family, the community, and the neighbourhood. The early childhood centre becomes part of that larger context in which families function (Bronfenbrenner, 1986; Walker & Crocker, 1988).

Each individual's development occurs in a broader ecological context, within different but

overlapping systems. This is called the **ecological model** since it looks at the ecosystems or habitats that the individual grows in, affects, and is affected by. The **microsystem** is the most immediate system that affects the individual; it could be the family, classroom, or workplace. These components of the microsystem are linked together in the **mesosystem** through such relationships as parent–teacher interaction or employment practices that affect the family (e.g., employer-supported child care or maternity-leave benefits that make up any difference between the employee's regular salary and unemployment insurance benefits).

The **exosystem** includes broader components of the neighbourhood and community that affect the functioning of the family, for example, government agencies or mass media. Finally, the broadest system to affect families is the **macrosystem,** which includes cultural, political, and economic forces (Bronfenbrenner & Crouter, 1983). From such an ecological perspective, the child and family are seen more clearly as part of and affected by many other systems, each of which influences their development and functioning.

Perceiving children and families as parts of various systems helps us to avoid seeking simple explanations and to acknowledge the complex interactions that often underlie children's and parents' behaviours. We must take time to look at the many factors affecting behaviour before jumping to conclusions. It is also important to recognize that families and schools interact to affect children's development in myriad possible directions (Goelman, 1988). This perspective makes good communication between home and school an imperative, not a choice. Finally, a systems approach helps us see the interrelatedness of all aspects of children's lives. We simply cannot assume that the child's home exists in one isolated compartment, while the school is in another. In the same way, we cannot presume that families' lives can be segmented into isolated facets.

The Changing Canadian Family

The family is and always has been the most important element in most children's lives. The family is where children experience the emotional and physical care and sustenance vital to their well-being. But the family has no simple definition or boundaries. Several decades ago, most Canadian children might have been part of a traditional family—working father, housewife mother, and two or three children. However, that image of the traditional family is the exception rather than the rule in Canada in the 1990s. Douglas Powell (1989) summarized this change well in a recent monograph on families and early childhood programs:

> Early childhood educators increasingly serve families characterized by single-parent households, cultural diversity and ethnic minority status, dual-worker or dual-career lifestyles, reconstituted ("blended") family arrangements, struggles with real or perceived economic pressures, and geographic mobility that decreases access to support traditionally available from extended family members (p. 15).

Family Forms

Just a short while ago, the **nuclear family**—a **married** couple with children—was virtually the only family form one might encounter growing up or teaching. Today parents may live **common law,** a family may be made up of one parent and one child, or a family may be part of an **extended family** of grandparents, uncles, aunts, cousins, and many other relatives who are in frequent, close contact. Families may have one, two, or more parents: these may be the **biological parents, step-parents, adoptive parents, legal guardians,** or **foster parents. Single parents** may never have been married or may be divorced, separated, or widowed; as part of this group, an increasing number of young children live with single fathers (Briggs & Walters, 1985).

If the family has undergone a divorce, children may live with the same single or remarried parent all of the time, may alternate between two parents who have joint custody, or may see the non-custodial parent for brief times during weekends or holidays. For some children, grandparents or other relatives take on some of the functions of parents, especially when **teenage parents** are involved. Some divorced parents find alternate living arrangements, perhaps moving back in with their own parents, sharing housing with another adult or single parent, or joining a group housing arrangement. This is known as the **blended family.** Because of divorce and remarriage, today's children may also acquire various natural and adoptive brothers and sisters, as well as half-siblings, step-siblings, or unrelated "siblings" in less formal family arrangements. In larger urban communities, in particular, it is also becoming more common to find children living with a **gay or lesbian parent,** the parent's mate, and often the children of that mate. While most individuals would not have been open about such a relationship two decades ago, they are becoming a more visible segment of society. Similarly, there may be a **single-wage earner, dual-wage earners, or no-wage earner** creating new family forms and varieties of care arrangements unfamiliar in past generations.

Whatever the family form, a wide range of people can make up a child's network of significant family members, as defined by emotional as well as legal ties. It is necessary, as a teacher of young children, that you also consider and acknowledge the unrelated but significant people as part of a child's family. Anyone who is important in the child's mind should be considered as important by you as well.

It is also vital that you are aware of legal restrictions that might affect children's relationships with adults in their lives. You should ensure that such information is accurately and promptly recorded in your files. During some divorce proceedings, for example, one parent may file a **restraining order** against the other, legally limiting or forbidding contact with the child. Although such situations are usually upsetting for everyone involved, it is necessary to be aware of and make appropriate provisions for complying with any legal action. As a professional, you are bound by the restraining order, even if you are not in agreement with it. Other legal terms such as "joint custody," "access," "supervised visits," and "joint guardianship" need to be understood by staff, and the entire centre needs to take ownership of the knowledge and the well-being of the child. A child care centre is busy and chaotic, often making use of supply staff, parents, and guests. Having a release form on file at the school is one important way of ensuring that only authorized persons pick up the child. After all, the majority of child kidnappings are committed by a divorced parent who does not have custody of the child (Sheldon, 1983). Barbara Young, a Vancouver-based lawyer, in describing the experiences she has had with "abductions" of children from an early childhood program by the non-custodial parent, outlines some cautionary measures. These include erring on the side of caution since "no responsible parent will begrudge your taking a little extra time to ensure that his or her child is safe and is leaving with a person of authority" (Essa & Young, 1994, p. 134).

In this chapter we have a Special Feature that addresses the very real issue of adoption and the responsibilities of the child care system.

SPECIAL FEATURE
Adoption Is Underrated in Our Child Care System

By now most of us have gotten the message: the child-protection system botches the job. It needs major-league repairs in every department, from philosophy to design and delivery. (We hear governments will study what's wrong. Please, someone tell me this is wrong. Both the problems and fixes have been documented to death.)

But there's one message that we almost never get. Adoption is part of the solution.

Either adoption doesn't figure into the discussion at all, or if it does, we're told no one short of Mother Teresa welcomes troubled, older kids. Adoption gets blacklisted for various reasons, often traceable to this belief: it is just paper, not binding like birth. Think of all the infertile couples who go to the ends of reproductive engineering. Men and women put themselves through hell to conceive, but few succeed. Yet, only a fraction go on to adopt. Though everyone has their own reasons for forgoing a family, for many, it's a cultural reflex: an adoptive family is fake.

The deep vein of suspicion that adoptive families aren't the real thing runs through the child-protection world as well. There, reuniting biological families is the gospel. Don't get me wrong. It's a worthy catechism provided the system helps the worst parents reclaim their demoralized lives and keeps their children safe—which it rarely does. However, it does repeatedly give them back their kids, who often suffer again. Yet somehow, a childhood lost in the foster care/home care drift suits child-welfare authorities better than the alternative. Better than wrapping an abused child in a loving, permanent home with "strangers."

Some of these strangers, not incidentally, gladly help their adoptee maintain links with his or her dysfunctional birth family. Some fost-adopters (foster first, adopt later), for example, have a working relationship with birth kin. In the United States more than here, other non-traditional adopters, such as single women, embrace system kids with whatever baggage they bring, from relatives to developmental delays.

Indeed, there's a family out there, albeit a newfangled version, for every child. Yet, all we ever hear: families can't be found. The truth is: the system has a pathetic record at reaching out. In a good year, it places under ten percent of adoptable Canadian youngsters, which means, excluding Quebec, homes for approximately 1,250 to 18,000 waiting kids. This tally excludes thousands more stuck in legal limbo.

All the stalled kids could join a permanent family through adoption or through a variation on adoption, such as guardianship. But families for keeps can't be found if the system continues its infatuation with the mom-and-pop icon of the '50s; if the system gets the jitters when would-be adopters are 40-something or childless or common-law couples or disabled or low-income or, heaven forbid, some combo of these; if the system's still nervous about straight single women, let alone lesbians; if the system goes into high alert when gay men try to adopt.

Families can't be found if the system keeps waiting kids a secret, if it offers paltry training, puny subsidies, inadequate support services and hardly any respite for adoptive parents of special-needs children. They can't be found in face of the myth that racial minority families don't adopt.

Families can't be found if red tape and bad laws block potential takers. In Ontario, for instance, crown wards with "access orders" can't be adopted. What does that mean? Although parents have lost custody, the court grants them supervised visits. (This isn't to argue against continuing contact. Remember, kids love even abusive parents.) Access orders cover about 80 percent of foster kids. Except—and here's the rub—almost none get regular visits from their parents.

Families can't be found if comers, most after years of battling infertility, have to wait two more years to be matched with an adoptee. It's not an accident that Canadians tuck more foreign than homegrown children into their families. Who can blame them? It's faster and easier to adopt abroad. Ironically, globetrotters now tend to bring home not babies but orphanage survivors with mind-boggling challenges, the same youngsters needing families here.

Hard as it is to pry children from Big Brother's clutches, many parent wannabes try. What happens? Some get lucky. They hit the rare office or renegade worker who rolls out the red carpet, even if applicants fit some hackneyed formula for family. They might even luck into a child-placer who manages to buck the system, to fast-track the screening and matching process, and actually deliver a child quickly.

What usually happens? Exactly what greeted me earlier this decade—systematic discouragement. The intake worker couldn't get me off the phone fast enough. There are no babies here, lady, and even if there were, they wouldn't go to you (I was past 40, then cohabitating). She didn't even mention waiting kids, let alone nudge me to consider one. Try the private system, she advised. Bye-bye.

We went the user-pay route—not for the average earner—ultimately adopting in the States. By the time we got our son, we'd conferred with about a dozen licensed adoption practitioners. Not one tried to educate us about kids marooned in foster care, to gentle us away from the nursery toward a preschooler. Our contacts were in the consumer-service and new baby business. Finding homes for system kids wasn't their role. Nor is it, seemingly, the public system's responsibility, since it neither publicizes the plight of family-less kids in a big way nor beats the bushes for prospective placements. Worse, it doesn't always welcome candidates with open arms when they walk in the door on their own steam.

Here's the good news: glossing the adoptive family image and finding nurturing homes for children are doable. We have to start by bringing together everyone outside and inside the system who are fed up with the status quo. Plus we have to pump up the volume and the pressure to get adoption, and the children, into the limelight.

Family Variations

Not only is there great variation in family form and composition, but other characteristics differentiate families as well. Some of these include economic, racial, cultural, ethnic, religious, linguistic, and geographic factors. The many ways in which families vary can affect not only family customs and traditions but also more fundamental issues, such as defining values and relationships (Jenkins,

1987). In some cases, a family's uniqueness includes a mixture of cultures, religions, races, and generations. The teacher can learn about characteristics of various cultural, racial, or religious groups by reading, but it is very important to avoid making large-scale generalizations about a family based on group traits. Families are complex, and only through genuine interest can a teacher get to know them well. Effective and frequent communication helps the teacher become aware of family attributes that can affect the child and family as participants in the early childhood program.

Increasing numbers of families of varied cultural, ethnic, and religious backgrounds are finding the need or making the choice to enroll their children in early childhood programs. It is of utmost importance that teachers are sensitive to differences in values, cultural expectations, and child-rearing practices. Effective communication is the key to promoting and achieving mutual understanding between families and centres which, in turn, help provide a consistent, positive experience for the children.

Families in Poverty

Poverty, as one factor in the lives of many families, bears closer scrutiny. Canada's Aboriginals stand out as being among the poorest people in the country. Poverty is also far more frequent in single-parent families (Pence, 1992).

A number of Canadian early childhood education programs have been aimed at helping economically disadvantaged families. Children who live in poverty often, but not always, have greater needs than children from more advantaged homes, as do their parents. Poverty does not pose a problem for children who have competent, stable parents who meet their needs. However, a variety of problems, including psychological instability, marital breakdowns, violence, and alcoholism, for example, are more common in poverty-stricken homes. Children from troubled disadvantaged homes are likely to exhibit delays in their cognitive and language skills, in their socio-emotional functioning, and in their physical development. They present a special challenge to early childhood educators. Nevertheless, teachers in high-quality early childhood programs can have a significant and lasting impact on the lives of disadvantaged children and their families. Rigorous research has shown that these high-quality early childhood programs, particularly those in which family support has been included, have a dramatic effect not only in terms of children's later school achievement but also on their families (Chafel, 1990; Seitz, Rosenbaum & Apfel, 1985; Zigler & Freedman, 1987; Doherty-Derkowski, 1995).

Teachers in quality settings also have an impact on the lives of families that are more fortunate. Many affluent families have a variety of concerns and difficulties such as illness, marital discord, substance abuse, and work-related problems. Other families are faced with fewer difficulties, but still welcome and profit from a supportive relationship with their children's teachers.

The Needs of Families

The fact that a child is enrolled in an early childhood program indicates that the family has a need that the program is able to meet. The most common and certainly the most obvious family need is provision of child care while the parents are at work. The growth of child care centres and family child care homes over the past three decades has been in response to the dramatic increase in the number of working single-parent and dual-income families.

But beyond the overall need for responsible and knowledgeable adults to provide care for children while their parents work, families have other needs that the early childhood centre can help meet. Some of these needs concern helping the parents, as individuals, meet the demands of their multiple roles. Others revolve around coordination of home and school routines and practices. One note to keep in mind: although it would be ideal if early childhood educators could meet everyone's needs—children's, parents', co-workers'—sometimes this is just not possible. Setting realistic goals within the particular early childhood education work setting can help establish priorities.

Parenthood

We typically view parenthood from the perspective of children's development and how parents facilitate, support, and promote it. Rarely is parenthood seen from the viewpoint of parents and their needs. Erik Erikson (1963), whose theory of human development was one of the first to span adulthood as well as childhood, believed that the most important need of the mature adult in the stage of **generativity** is to care for and nurture others. The tasks of this stage are often carried out in parenthood, through which the adult is concerned with meeting the needs of the next generation. Implied in this process is growth of the adult as an individual, which is separate from the nurturance extended to children. This acknowledgment of adulthood as a period of continued development has been advanced in recent years by other writers (i.e., Gould, 1978; Levinson, 1978; Sheehy, 1976).

Parenthood as a distinct process has also been examined in greater depth. Ellen Galinsky (1981), after extensive research and interviews with scores of individuals, suggested that parents change and develop in their roles, just as children do, by moving through six stages of parenthood. Each stage involves issues to be faced and a crisis that the parent has to resolve successfully. The parents of an infant are in the **nurturing stage,** forming a strong attachment and integrating this new member into the family unit. The parents of a young preschooler are enmeshed in the **authority stage,** defining rules and their own roles. Toward the end of the preschool years, parents enter the **interpretive stage** in which they are confronted with the task of explaining and clarifying the world to their children.

Galinsky was particularly concerned with the "images" that parents create, images of what they expect the child to be like before it is born, images of how they and their children will act and interact, or images of the loving relationship they expect. These images, especially what they wish to re-create or what they would like to change, emerge from parents' past experiences. Often, however, images and reality are different. Growth occurs when parents modify images so they become more consistent with reality or adjust their behaviour to come closer to the image.

Galinsky emphasized that parents frequently feel their responses and emotions are unique, and are unaware that other parents also experience them. Yet, as she pointed out, during each of the stages of parenthood, parents face predictable issues and strong emotions. It helps parents to discuss and recognize their shared experiences as well as to have opportunities to observe the behaviour of others' children. It is also helpful when professionals explain common reactions and feelings, for instance, to a child's first day at school. In working with children, then, it is very important to acknowledge that parents undergo personal development that parallels their children's growth but has separate issues and conflicts that need to be resolved.

Empowerment, Partnerships, and Advocacy

When parents feel confident and competent in their abilities as mothers and fathers and members of the larger community, their children benefit. Unfortunately, some parents feel that they are powerless in controlling what happens to them and to their children. Early childhood programs can fill a crucial need for families by promoting **empowerment,** a sense of control or power over events in one's life. This

is particularly important as families deal with a variety of agencies and professionals, for instance, school, welfare, and political systems.

Parental empowerment has been a direct aim or an unexpected outcome in some programs designed for low-income families (Cochran, 1988; Ramey, Dorvall, & Baker-Ward, 1983; Seitz et al., 1985). As cited in one report of such a program, "Intangible but crucial shifts in attitude took place in parents who were often severely demoralized at the start" (Nauta & Hewett, 1988, p. 401). Parents began to see that they could have an impact. Professionals can use a wide variety of techniques to help parents attain this sense of control, including approaches described in a number of excellent publications, for instance, Alice Honig's *Parent Involvement in Early Childhood Education* (1990).

One of the forces behind the concept of parental empowerment has been the move toward viewing parents and teachers as equals. This relationship, with mutual respect and an equal balance of power regarding decision making, can be called a **partnership.** Not too many years ago, the pervasive attitude was that professionals were experts whereas parents were the passive recipients of their expertise (Powell, 1989). Such a view does not provide parents with the security that they know their child best and that they should be full participants in any decisions that affect the child. As equal partners, both parents and teachers need to be treated with respect, their opinions should be asked for and taken seriously, and both partners must be involved in decisions about the child. Often parents need to be encouraged to advocate for their children and need to feel they have an ally, not an adversary, in the school. Part of the school's role is to educate the parents on and appreciate the parents' role in the advocacy process. Understanding the concepts of communication and relationships helps raise parents' awareness about their rights and responsibilities in their role as empowered equals. In addition, when early childhood professionals and parents share child development information, both have tools with which to make informed decisions about the children's needs. Thus, involving, consulting and collaborating with, and providing relevant education for parents and teachers can have a far-reaching impact by helping both recognize their own importance, competence, and integral and mutual role in the child's quality care (Swick, 1994).

In A Canadian Professional Speaks Out, Kathy and Ken Byrka, parents from Manitoba, and Janet and Gregg Hayes, from Ontario, offer two different perspectives on parenting and child care.

Coordinating Needs and Programs

Helping parents reach their potential as effective adults may be a goal in some programs that work extensively with families, particularly those from impoverished backgrounds. In all early childhood programs, there are additional points of contact between parents and teachers, at times revolving around seemingly mundane matters but nonetheless important. A flexible, good-humoured attitude can help establish and maintain positive home–school relationships.

Parents' busy lives or unforeseen events are sometimes at odds with the schedule and routine of the early childhood centre. For instance, one mother expressed concern that the centre's afternoon snack, provided at 3:30, was served too late and that the child was not interested in dinner at 5:30. Another parent preferred that her child not take a nap at school because when he slept during the day, he was just not ready to sleep at home until quite late in the evening. Other

A CANADIAN PROFESSIONAL SPEAKS OUT
Parents on Caring for Children

With the arrival of our first child, Rachel, over two years ago, my husband and I were overwhelmed with excitement. Contrary to what people were telling us about how our life would change, we really didn't find this to be the case. We still carried on our day to day lives in much the same way, taking Rachel with us wherever we went whether it be hiking, biking, canoeing, or in the car. Yes, the chances of sleeping in had slowly dimished, but this was a small price to pay for the enjoyment of our little bundle. By the time Mallory, our second child, was born only 18 months later, we were again overjoyed and began feeling a little busier, a little more tied down, and definitely more exhausted. With two kids, everything people were telling us about how our lives would never be the same definitely became a reality. However, we've accepted this and I have made a commitment to be at home and take part in the raising of our kids. My husband has also decreased his workload to be at home more with the kids until they are in school. These are the critical years we don't want to miss. The bottom line is that there are more sleepless nights, less time to do our own things, but it's worth it and we wouldn't change anything. In fact, we're even thinking of a third addition!

Kathy and Ken Byrka, Winnipeg

Despite all our homework, the first day we left our child in someone else's care was heart-wrenching. Far more tears were shed by us than by our child. But telling us or our child that it will be okay does not make it okay. We have to learn this. We know we have provided a strong, secure base for our child and that they will learn to trust and love you, as we will. But this takes time and patience on all our parts.

We choose to work because we love our jobs and we feel it makes us better people. As happy people, we feel we make happy parents with so much to teach and share with our children.

Child care to us is not academics. To us it means our child is recognized as an individual and is respected as such. Our child is sincerely cared about. He is safe, yet he is allowed to explore. He is hugged and comforted and encouraged. He is listened to. He has role models that understand his strengths and needs and who are genuinely interested in what he has to say. He is protected from harm—physically, mentally, and emotionally—and he is nurtured in his overall development.

As a caregiver, you are now part of our family with rights, roles, and responsibilities. We welcome you into it with all its ups and downs and with all its love!

Janet and Gregg Hayes, Rockwood, Ontario

problems (e.g., car trouble, a traffic snarl, or unexpected overtime at work) may keep a parent from arriving until after the centre has closed.

All of these situations can cause conflict but also provide an opportunity to evaluate what is best for the child, the parents, the other children, and the teachers. Sometimes such predicaments can be resolved fairly easily, but there are times when the needs of the child, the parent, and the school directly conflict. For instance, there is no simple solution as to whether a child should take a nap, particularly when he appears to need it, or not take a nap because a delayed evening bedtime keeps his mother from getting the sleep she needs. Teachers must carefully weigh their own professional judgment of what is best for the child, taking into account the child's need for sleep, the potential effect of being sleepy and cranky on the ability to function well at school, and the fact that the child would be treated differently from the other children by not napping (Ethics Commission, 1987). One way of resolving such conflicts—whether they involve naps, snacks, or pick-up time—is communication, our next topic.

Communicating with Families

Effective, positive communication is the key to any successful relationship, especially with families, and is vital to providing a consistent and congruent experience for young children. There is no simple formula for ensuring that such contact does, indeed, take place. But ensuring that it does take place is a right, role, and responsibility of both family and teachers. Families are an excellent resource and advocate not only for their children but also for child care in general. As partners, we rely on and trust each other to take ownership of children's overall positive growth and development and to effectively communicate in order to achieve this. Each family is unique and brings to the early childhood program distinctive strengths and needs. Just as the teacher deals with each child as a unique individual by employing a variety of teaching and guidance methods, so must a flexible approach be maintained in communicating with families to meet their individual requirements.

Communication with families should be viewed as a way to foster between the teachers and the family a bond that enhances the child's experiences in both school and home settings, and not simply as an opportunity to report inappropriate behaviour. Even if inappropriate behaviour is among the topics discussed, meetings and case conferences about individual children should be supportive and affirm the child's and family's strengths. Parents should leave such meetings feeling they have learned something, have contributed as an equal partner in the relationship, and would like to return.

Of course, formal meetings and conferences are not the only way to communicate. There are many bits of information that need to be shared by teachers and the family. For instance, both sides will benefit from discussing the child. In addition, there is often more general information about various aspects of the program that must be shared with families. The type of information to be conveyed often determines the communication method used. Communication, as we will discuss, can be carried out using both individual and group methods. Most early childhood centres utilize a combination of these approaches. However, parents and teachers should feel equally comfortable in initiating and requesting communication, be it a formal meeting or an informal chat.

Individual Communication Methods

The best way to get to know each family is through interaction and contact with individuals. Informally, such contact can take place daily, for instance, when children are dropped off and picked up from school. More formally, scheduled conferences between teacher and parents or other family members provide an avenue for exchange of information.

Informal Contact with Families

Daily Exchanges At the beginning and end of each day, at least one teacher should be available to exchange a few words with family members who drop off or pick up their children. Such informal interactions can make teachers more sensitive to the needs of children and families, can establish mutual trust, can convey a feeling of caring and interest to parents, and can heighten parents' involvement

in the program. "By being open, receptive, and chatty, teachers encourage parent interest and commitment" (Reiber & Embry, 1983, p. 162).

Notes and Phone Calls Because frequent school–family contacts are important, it makes sense to structure the schedule so that staff are free to participate in such exchanges (Tizard, Mortimer, & Burchell, 1981). The informal dialogues at the start and end of the day tend to be the most pervasive form of family involvement in early childhood programs (Gestwicki, 1987), especially those primarily involving working parents. In programs where children arrive by bus or come in car pools, the teacher needs to make an extra effort to maintain contact with parents, for instance, through notes or telephone calls (Gestwicki, 1987).

Some schools send home "happy notes"—brief, personalized notes that share with the parents something positive that happened during the day (Bundy, 1991). Telephone calls provide a comfortable way of talking to parents, particularly if the calls are made often enough and not only when they signal a problem.

Open-Door Policy Parents should always be welcome at the school. They have entrusted the care of their child to you. Working parents need a link to the children and need to spend whatever time they can with their children. In addition, the more time you spend together, the more you begin to understand and appreciate each other's needs. Parents are an excellent source of information, comfort, and strength. As partners, you share the responsibilities of caring.

Formal Contact with Families

Informal daily contacts between teachers and family members can create a mutually respectful and non-intimidating atmosphere. When teachers and parents feel comfortable with each other, communication will more likely be honest. In addition to such day-to-day encounters, more formal opportunities should be structured, when a sizable block of uninterrupted time is set aside for in-depth discussion. Such formal contacts can take the form of a parent–teacher conference or a home visit.

Parent–Teacher Conferences This is a regularly scheduled meeting that can satisfy different objectives. It can focus on getting acquainted; sharing information about the child and presenting a progress report; or, at the initiation of either teacher or parents, solving problems or discussing specific issues (Bullock, 1986; Reiber & Embry, 1983). Conferences often have negative connotations for the participants, who may view them as a time to share complaints and problems, perhaps even as a last resort when all else fails. But routinely scheduled conferences should be positive, affirming, and supportive.

A conference should never be an impromptu event. Both the teacher and the parents need to be well prepared ahead of time, reviewing relevant information and thinking about how best to present it. In fact, preparing for conferences should be an ongoing process, beginning when the child first enters the program (Bjorklund & Burger, 1987). Being ready with some anecdotes to support what you tell the parents helps convey to them that you know their child well. It is also important to think through what questions you might want to ask of the parents to help you to better understand and work with their child.

Equally important, you should facilitate a relaxed and easy forum for conversation. Sometimes sharing something with the parents, for instance, a picture painted by the child or a favourite recipe for play dough, contributes toward creating a positive atmosphere. The Partnerships box presents some helpful strategies, suggested by Carol Gestwicki in her book *Home, School, and Community Relations: A Guide to Working with Parents* (1987), to use when conducting a parent–teacher conference.

PARTNERSHIPS
Helpful Strategies for Parent–Teacher Conferences

1. Use common, not technical, terms. Avoid jargon that is not readily understood by someone unfamiliar with child development terminology. Don't tell the parents, "Halie functions one standard deviation below her age norm in fine motor development," when you could convey the message by saying, "Halie is still learning to cut with scissors and string small beads; we've been working on such tasks."

2. Use an egalitarian, not an authoritarian, approach. Parents can easily be put off when confronted with a teacher who is the expert and knows it all, telling them what they "should," "have to," or "must not" do. An authoritarian approach conveys that only the teacher is right and, by implication, the parents are wrong. Nothing prevents give-and-take discussion more quickly!

3. Provide an objective evaluation of the child. Teachers have to be sensitive to how closely parents' self-esteem is tied to their children. When a teacher seems critical of the child, the parents may quickly feel hurt and defensive. This does not mean that you should avoid sharing your concerns about the child. This can be better accomplished, however, by providing the parents with objective descriptions of the child's behaviour rather than by using labels and negative words. Examples of words to avoid include "problem," "immature," "hyperactive," and "slow."

4. Provide privacy and maintain a professional tone in conversations. It is important to ensure confidentiality in all information about children and families. A parent–teacher conference should never include discussions about other children and parents. Such talk can only make the parents wonder what the teacher might say about them.

5. Provide alternatives rather than answers. Problem situations, shared by parents, are seldom simple and easily solved because the teacher cannot know all the complexities. Furthermore, there are usually many possible ways of dealing with problems. It is important to ask the parents what they have tried and what has worked for them. In addition, it is helpful to provide alternatives for parents. You might provide several suggestions that have "worked for other parents" or that "we've tried in the classroom" as ideas for the parent to consider. When parents come to their own conclusions and chart a course of action, these suggestions are much more likely to be effective.

6. Take your time in approaching solutions. It is not realistic to expect that complex problems can be solved during a parent–teacher conference (Gestwicki, 1987). The teacher may suggest that both she (or he) and the parents take time to observe before jumping to premature conclusions.

7. Be sure to check back with the family to see if the suggestions are working. If they are not effective, meet again and formulate new strategies. If they are working, continue to provide support and feedback.

Home Visits   Home visits share some of the same objectives and procedures as parent–teacher conferences, but they contribute some added benefits as well. A teacher who visits a family at home conveys a sense of caring and interest in the child's world beyond the classroom. Children are usually delighted to introduce their room, toys, pets, and siblings to the teacher and feel very special that the teacher is visiting them at home. Parents can observe firsthand the interaction between the child and the teacher, and may become more relaxed with the teacher who has shown this special interest. In addition, teachers can observe firsthand the family's home environment and parent–child interactions in order to understand better the child's behaviour. In some instances, especially once a sense of trust has been established, home visits can become an extremely important source of support (e.g., for teenage parents).

Although there are very important benefits in conducting home visits, they are also quite time-consuming and may (though certainly not inevitably) intimidate the parents. On the other hand, a teacher from a suburban home may be intimidated by visiting an inner-city home. A teacher's commitment to learning as much as possible about the children in the class and their families must be weighed against other factors, including perceived risks to the teacher, comfort level of the parents and teacher, and time. There are instances when meeting at the centre or school, for example, is preferable or when it is necessary for a colleague to accompany you to the child's home for support and an additional source of information.

Brag Book   Some programs send a brag book back and forth with the child daily between home and school. Teachers can write about the child's day while parents can write about exciting news, sleep patterns, anecdotes, or influential events that might lend insight into the child's behaviour for that day. It is important to remember that it is not mandatory for parents to write in the book daily but that it is there as a tool if they need to use it.

Solving Problems between Parents and Teachers

Regardless of the type of contact initiated, it is critical that teachers and parents ensure they follow through on recommendations made. Holding a meeting to determine solutions is simply a step in the process. Through proactive means such as listening, asking, encouraging, and validating, we diminish barriers to communication (e.g., feelings of fear, anger, anxiety, resentment, or intimidation) and keep the lines of communication open. Monitoring progress, doing what you said you would do, reporting back, and being supportive and open-minded with a framework of positive expectations serves only to strengthen the mutual respect established between parents and teachers.

Ideally, parents and teachers cooperate fully to provide positive experiences for children at home and at school. Unfortunately, there are times when this ideal is not always realized. In fact, parent–teacher disharmony is quite common (Galinsky, 1990). Parents and teachers may disagree, particularly when they feel rushed and tired or when they are preoccupied with other aspects of their lives. In addition, both may harbour some unacknowledged negative feelings, for instance, disapproval of working mothers, jealousy or competition for the child's affection, or criticism of the other's child guidance approach (Galinsky, 1988, 1990). Although the child provices a common bond between parents and teachers, there are many other factors that affect their moods and impinge on their interactions. The job stress experienced by parents as well as by teachers can certainly spill over into the brief contact between them as children are dropped off or picked up at school during what Ellen Galinsky called the "arsenic hour" (1988). In addition, teachers sometimes resent certain parents. For example, there may be parents who convey the impression that they do not value the teacher and his or her work. In other cases, the teacher may feel that she or he is the only person who is an advocate for the child. There also is the case of the parent who is always late picking up the child from the centre.

Galinsky (1988) offered some concrete suggestions for working more effectively with parents. She suggested that when teachers become upset with parents, it is often because teachers' underlying expectations are somehow not realized; teachers need to examine whether their expectations are realistic. Similarly, teachers should scrutinize their attitudes toward the parents, looking for hidden resentments or prejudices. Teachers also need to make an effort to see the situation from the parents' point of view, asking themselves how they might feel if they were in the parents' shoes.

It can be very helpful for teachers to develop a support system, whether within their own program or even outside of it, which allows them to express and explore their feelings in an accepting and safe atmosphere. Teachers must also recognize and convey to parents the limits of their role. This includes being familiar with community resources to which parents can be referred when a problem is beyond the scope of the teacher's role and expertise.

Parents also need support, and establishing a school parent support group may give them the necessary outlet they need to calm fears and ease pressures.

There is no simple formula for effective parent–teacher communication. The parent–teacher relationship is founded on trust and respect, which grow out of many small but significant daily contacts. Greeting parents by name, writing personalized notes, making phone calls to parents whom the teacher does not see often, being sensitive to parents' needs, and sharing brief, positive anecdotes about their children all contribute to a good relationship (Morgan, 1989).

Group Communication Methods

In addition to personalized, individual contact between parents and teachers, early childhood programs generally also utilize other communication methods for getting information to the parents as a group. These methods can serve a functional purpose, for instance, to let parents know that the school will be closed Monday when Canada Day falls on a Saturday. They may also take on an educational role, for example, to give parents insight into an aspect of child development. We will review four such methods: physical environment, written communiqués, bulletin boards, and meetings.

Physical Environment

Setting the stage for communication is the first step. If parents feel comfortable in the school, they will be more likely to voice concerns, make suggestions, participate, or praise. An inviting atmosphere and welcoming tone is so important. Are there people smiling and greeting parents? Is there a parent information board at the front door? A family achievement wall of fame? A creed posted that boasts about the importance of family and team? A calendar of social events? A multitude of pictures of these events? A parent lounge? Is time always made available in the schedule to meet with parents? Are parents always invited to events and meetings? Is there a parent–teacher association set up? Is there evidence of mutual respect, admiration, and camaraderie? Is there an open-door policy? Is a mentor system in place? Do parents and teachers seem well informed and eager to participate. Is there a system in place to evaluate this to ensure it occurs and is successful? Parents are an integral, vital, and key component to the program, and their comfort and acceptance are pivotal if communication and, therefore, success are to occur.

Written Communiqués

Newsletters, memos, or other written material can be an effective way of getting information to all families. In addition, they provide parents with an overview of current happenings in the program and thus facilitate parent–child discussions about the program. It is, of course, important to match written information to the reading abilities of the parents. If many or all of the families in the program are non-English-speaking, for instance, communiqués should be written in the parents' primary language. In larger communities with a high percentage of immigrants, translation services, if not available through a parent, are often available through an ethnic group's cultural association. Community social workers and psychologists also have access to a list of translators. It is also important that all such materials be neat, attractive, and accurately written. A sloppy, misspelled, and ungrammatical letter conveys that the teacher does not care enough about the families to produce a thoughtful document. Today many schools have access to a computer, which makes it simpler than ever to compose attractively arranged letters or newsletters, check the grammar and spelling, and incorporate graphics. Other factors to consider are the type and size of print, amount of print, visual effects, type of paper (is it recycled, supporting the school's stated environmental policy), use of colour, and so on. These factors signify time, effort, care, and professionalism.

Many programs produce a regular newsletter that may contain announcements, news of what the teachers have planned for the upcoming time period, new policies, relevant community information, child development research summaries, columns by local experts, and other information of interest to families. A newsletter is only effective if it is read. Thus, its length, the information included, and the writing style need to be carefully considered.

Another form of written communication that can convey a great deal of information to parents is a school handbook, which parents are given when they enrol their children in the early childhood program. Such a handbook should contain relevant information about school policies and procedures, fees, hours of operation, holidays, sick child care, birthday routines, and other important matters. In addition, it should include a clear statement of the school's philosophy (Bundy, 1991).

Bulletin Boards

Bulletin boards can either be a useful means of conveying information or a cluttered mass of overlaid memos that no one bothers to look at. To be effective, a bulletin board should be attractively laid out, feature contents that are current, and have items that do not compete with one another for attention. Further, if family members know that only current and important items will be posted on a specific bulletin board, they are more likely to pay attention to it.

Bulletin boards can be used for a variety of purposes. They can be informative, for instance, letting parents know that the children will be taking a field trip the following week or that a child in the group is home with the chicken pox. Many centres include a notice of the day's activities on a bulletin board, which lets parents know the highlights of their child's day.

Bulletin boards can also be educational, conveying relevant information in a way that appeals to those who look at it. At one centre, for instance, the teachers wanted to follow up on comments from several parents that their children were just scribbling rather than drawing something recognizable. The teachers wanted to help parents understand that children's art follows a developmental pattern. They matted selections of the children's pictures, arranged them attractively on bulletin boards organized by the children's ages, and interspersed the pictures with quotes from experts on children's art. The pictures supported the quotations, thus conveying the messages that children gradually move toward representational art and that there are common steps children go through in their development of art. Many parents commented on how helpful they found this bulletin board information. It proved to be a most effective teaching tool.

In another centre, a Canadian cooperative nursery school, the teacher became concerned when she noticed that some parents were not using seat belts for their children when on a trip to the sugar bush, even though they are mandatory. An inviting bulletin board display on the merits of seat belts was her diplomatic approach to this concern.

Meetings and Other Group Functions

Group gatherings can provide another effective way of reaching family members. Such functions can take the form of meetings, the traditional forum for formal

parent education, or they can be social. In addition, parent discussion groups may be part of the early childhood program. When planning any kind of group function, however, keep in mind that family members are busy people who will weigh the benefits of attending a school program against other demands on their time. In fact, for some parents the pressure of one more thing to do might be so stressful that it would outweigh the advantages of the program. Because each family's needs are different, the early childhood program must facilitate communication with parents in many different ways and be prepared to individualize ways of meeting these needs.

If the supervisor and teachers feel that parent meetings can serve a positive function in meeting the needs of some of the families, they must ensure that what they plan will interest potential participants. One way to assess what might be relevant to parents is to conduct an interest survey. A brief form can solicit preferences about topic choices, time and day, and type of meeting. If the teachers or the supervisor plan parent functions without input from the parents, these functions may well fail to match the interest of the parents and result in very low attendance (Gestwicki, 1987). Also, parents are often more likely to come to a meeting if a meal or snack is included and if child care is provided. On the other hand, keep in mind that if children have already spent 9 or 10 hours at the centre, adding 2 evening hours may be more than is reasonable.

Parent get-togethers may feature a speaker with expertise on a topic of common interest, or they may revolve around discussion led by a facilitator. It is important to remember that parents' shared experiences are a valuable source of information and support (Kelly, 1981). Thus, if the main part of the program includes a speaker, time should also be allocated for discussion.

One particularly enjoyable way of presenting some topics is to illustrate them with slides or videotapes taken of the children at the school. Such subjects as children's play, social development, or developmentally appropriate toys can be enhanced with such visuals. In addition to gaining insight into an aspect of their children's development, parents will feel great pride in seeing their youngsters depicted on the screen.

Small groups are generally more effective than large groups in encouraging participation (Gestwicki, 1987). A common interest can also create a more intimate atmosphere for a meeting, for instance, involving parents whose children will enter kindergarten the following year or just the parents of children in one class rather than those from the entire early childhood centre.

Some centres generate considerable enthusiasm for social events during which parents and teachers have the opportunity to exchange information in a relaxed atmosphere. These can include holiday parties, meals, or an open house, and they can involve all family members. One university program sponsored a potluck dinner for families, staff, and student-teachers each semester. Prearranged seating assured that student-teachers sat with the families of children they were observing. This event attracted almost all of the families and proved to be enjoyable as well as valuable for all involved.

Family Involvement

We have been discussing various ways in which communication between teachers and families can be maintained. However this communication takes place, it implies involvement on the part of the family. Let's look at family involvement in more detail. Later, A Closer Look examines the parents' role in the early childhood environment.

Family involvement in the early childhood program is a multifaceted concept, embracing a wide range of options and levels. It can mean that parents and other family members are passive recipients of information; parents may be more intensely engaged by serving as volunteers in the program; or, at an even more complex level of involvement, they can be participants in the decision-making process of the program (Honig, 1979). Whatever the level, however, ample research has shown that such involvement has positive benefits for children as well as for families (Becher, 1986; Powell, 1989).

The **family-centred model** encompasses all aspects of involvement and acknowledges the family as the focal point of care. Remembering that the family is a system, the advocates of this model focus on empowering and strengthening the family as a whole. Early childhood educators using this model go beyond just linking or directing families to employment agencies, social service agencies, or support groups. They help provide and coordinate services and become members of the family's interdisciplinary team.

There is a reciprocal relationship between the family and the early childhood program, each providing support and help to the other as they are able. Family involvement will vary according to each family's ability to contribute and to its needs. Some families invest a great deal of their time and energy in the program, whereas others need all their resources to cope with the stresses they face. Some families support the program by participating in and contributing time to various school activities; others seek support from the program in facing their personal strains. As a teacher in an early childhood program, you will need to be flexible to be able to recognize each family's capabilities and needs and to set expectations or provide support accordingly. While this may seem like a formidable task early on in your studies, the qualities that drew you to the early childhood profession, coupled with the knowledge and experience you acquire during your studies, will help you to be sensitive to each family's needs.

You will also find that you can involve families in your program in a variety of ways. For example, you might involve family members as resources, as volunteers in the classroom, and/or as decision-makers. Regardless of the extent or type of involvement, an involved parent is a far greater asset to the program than an uninvolved one since planning, implementing, and evaluating becomes a team effort. A comprehensive family-centred model utilizes all these approaches, making the family the focus, rather than the program.

Families as Resources

Family members have many talents and abilities to contribute to the program. Many early childhood programs invite parents or relatives to participate on occasions when their job skills, hobbies, or other special expertise can augment and enrich the curriculum. For instance, a teacher may invite Ronnie's mother, who is a dentist, to help the children understand the importance of good dental hygiene and care; the teacher may take the children to visit the bakery owned by Annie's uncle, because the class is discussing foods; she can ask Carmelo's father to show the children how he makes pottery; or she may invite Ivan's mother and new baby brother when the class talks about babies and growing up. All family members— parents, siblings, grandparents, other relatives, and even pets—can be considered part of the program, extending its resource base.

Family members can also help out with maintenance and construction tasks that are part of the program. In some early childhood programs, especially parent cooperatives, parents routinely take home the dress-up clothes and other classroom items to wash or clean. In others, regularly scheduled clean-up days bring teachers and family members to the centre on specified weekends to deep clean the facility, materials, and equipment. Family members with carpentry skills may construct or repair equipment. Others may develop learning materials and games at home that will expand the activity options available to the children.

There are other ways in which family members can serve as program resources. For instance, they can help orient new families to the early childhood program, serve as role models, and provide support to other families. Their suggestions and ideas can enrich the program. Family members can also be extremely effective in providing local and provincial support for legislation that affects children and families, and can help provide program visibility in the community if the school is seeking outside funding. Family support can be a potent force in maintaining a high-quality early childhood program.

Family Members in the Classroom

Family members may also volunteer as teacher aides. Programs such as parent-cooperative preschools require parent involvement on a regular basis. Some programs modelled after Project Head Start also require that parents spend time in the classroom, although forced participation can be counterproductive (Honig, 1979; 1990). In most programs, particularly in child care centres, parents participate occasionally or not at all because parents are usually working while their children are at school. Some teachers relish such involvement; others feel skeptical and reluctant, fearing a clash with the parents' child-rearing practices, feeling stress about being under constant observation, or worrying that the children will get overexcited (Gestwicki, 1987).

Having parents in the classroom can have many benefits for children, parents, and teachers. Children can benefit from having their parents participate in the classroom, feeling pride and a sense of security "as they see parents and teachers working together cooperatively, each respecting the other's contribution" (Gestwicki, 1987, p. 205). For parents, such firsthand experience can provide insight into how their children spend their time at school, a basis for observing their own children in relation to age-mates, and a chance to note guidance techniques used by teachers. Teachers can benefit from the support parents offer, the added pair of hands that can expand activity possibilities, and the opportunity to gain insight into parent–child interactions (Gestwicki, 1987). There are, however, some consequences of having parents in the class that teachers and parents should expect.

The full-time teachers in parent cooperatives perhaps have the most experience with parents in the classroom as the staffing schedule includes a rotating staff of parents. Teachers in cooperatives find that most children behave differently when their own parents are there as helpers, although this change is most pronounced on the first few occasions when a parent is present. It is important to let parents know that children's behaviour tends to be different when a parent is present, since parents often become concerned about their children's behaviour in the program. For example, some children become aggressive and loud with a parent present, while others, who are independent most days, might become clingy and whiny.

Family Members as Decision Makers

Some programs ask parents to serve on an advisory or a policy board. Some university-based programs, for instance, invite parents to participate in parent advisory councils. Many not-for-profit child care or preschool centres also require a governing board of which parents are members. Effective decision-making boards can promote a true partnership between families and the school program (Dunst & Trivette, 1988), providing support for the school, empowerment of parents, and increased mutual understanding.

Adult Education and Lifelong Learning

All forms of family involvement potentially serve an educational function, since parents have the chance to gain insights into their children's development and the

---

A Closer Look

PARENTS' ROLE IN THE EARLY CHILDHOOD ENVIRONMENT

Parents can be active participants in matters related to the early childhood environment. To begin with, the parents' choice of a preschool or child care centre can be viewed as part of an environmental decision. Early childhood facilities, as part of a larger environment, contribute to and reflect the total character of their community. Often children's programs mirror the community's purpose and ethnic or cultural characteristics. For instance, there are distinct differences in an inner-city centre, an employer-supported program located on the premises of a factory, a suburban child care facility for dual-income parents, or a bilingual preschool in a predominantly immigrant community. By enrolling their children in their community's early childhood facilities, parents lend support to the wider community (Berns, 1989).

In addition, parents can contribute in a variety of ways to selecting, modifying, or maintaining various aspects of the environment. Some programs have advisory or policymaking parent councils that may be involved in decisions about major purchases or construction. Parents also often have a strong commitment to their children's program and are willing to spend a few weekend hours helping to paint, clean, varnish, or construct. Many parents contribute to their child's centre by making learning materials or contributing throwaways that children can use for creative activities. As in all areas of the early childhood centre's functioning, parents can be a tremendous resource in matters related to the environment.

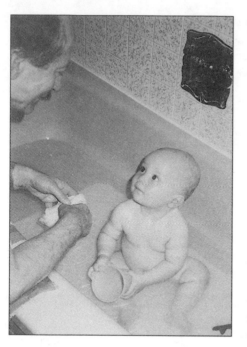

school's program. Often, however, early childhood programs provide specific **parent education** aimed at enhancing parent–child relations and improving parenting competence. Given the numbers of children who grow up in abusive homes and in poverty, some professionals even consider that high-quality parent education programs should be mandatory to prevent needless impairment of children through abuse, neglect, and deprivation (Anastasiow, 1988). Evaluation of many parent education programs aimed at economically disadvantaged families has indicated that such programs can be very effective, although much still remains to be learned through systematic research (Clarke-Stewart, 1983; Powell, 1986). In addition, there is limited evidence that parent education enhances the parenting skills of middle-class families as well (Harris & Larsen, 1989).

The scope of parent education programs is not easy to capture in a single definition because there is great diversity in the field. Douglas Powell (1986) spelled out some of the contrasts in parent education:

> Some programs focus on family–community relations while others teach parents how to stimulate a child's cognitive development. Some programs prescribe specific skills and styles in relating to young children.... Some programs are highly structured while others let parents select activities they wish to pursue. In some programs the staff serve as child development experts while other programs adhere to a self-help model with staff in non-directive facilitator roles. There are important differences in the use of professionals, assistants, or volunteers, program length (weeks versus years), and program setting (group- versus home-based). (p. 47)

Parent education can take many forms. Often informal, one-to-one interactions at pick-up and drop-off times are valuable, especially because they are tailored to the individual. Parent get-togethers or meetings are another frequently used forum. The content of such programs can vary widely, depending on parents' interests and needs. Christine Cataldo, in her book *Parent Education for Early Childhood* (1987), suggests a wide variety of subjects. Popular topics often revolve around children's development, including characteristics and common problems of various ages. Other topics can focus on various aspects of caring for children, for instance, nutrition, health and fitness, self-care and protection, and selecting child care services. Family composition, challenges, and crises offer many program possibilities as well. Children's play and appropriate toys provide other topic choices of interest to parents. In addition, most parents are concerned with issues related to children's behaviours, discipline, guidance, fears, sexual development and interest, personality development, and self-esteem. Finally, the family's involvement in and promotion of children's education include many areas of interest to parents.

Programs can be presented by the early childhood staff, based on their own expertise, or by local resource persons. It is important that presenters be well informed on the topic chosen and that they provide accurate information. In addition, a variety of packaged parent education materials are also available. Such packages may include extensive manuals and provide the facilitator with all the necessary resources to conduct the program. Two popular examples of such parent education programs that focus on development of child guidance skills are Parent Effectiveness Training (P.E.T.) (Gordon, 1976) and Systematic Training for Effective Parenting (STEP) (Dinkmeyer & McKay, 1976). A final note is that there is a wide range of education levels among parents at centres. As well, many parents are also students. These diverse and rich facets of parents' lives should be recognized, respected, and supported.

Key Terms

adoptive parents
authority stage
biological parents
blended family
brag book
common law
ecological model
empowerment
exosystem
extended family
family-centred model
family involvement
family sytems theory
foster parents
gay or lesbian parent
generativity

interpretive stage
legal guardians
macrosystem
married
mesosystem
microsystem
nuclear family
nurturing stage
parent education
partnership
restraining order
single parents
single wage earner, dual wage earners or no
    wage earner
step-parents
teenage parents

Key Points

- The Canadian family is changing very rapidly, and this presents additional responsibilities to the teacher (e.g., poverty and legal problems of the parents).

- It is important to acknowledge that parents undergo personal development which parallels their children's growth but that they have separate conflicts and issues which need to be resolved.

- Teachers and parents need to work closely to determine what is best for the child and the family. This is accomplished by effective, positive communication.

- When problems arise, teachers need to develop a support system that allows them to express and explore their feelings in a safe and accepting atmosphere.
- There are many ways to avoid communication problems (e.g., parental bulletin boards, parent lounge, PTA, newsletters, handbooks).
- Extended families (including pets) can have positive benefits for the children as well as the family.
- Parental education is important at the centre and can include not only children's development but also nutrition, self-care, fitness, and selection of childcare services.

Part 3

The Profession

Now that you are comfortable with your role, and the characteristics of children and families you will work with, you will want to familiarize yourself with the terminology of the field of early childhood education. Knowing terminology will make it easier to determine factors affecting quality in programs and to evaluate several program models that are featured. In Part 3, we investigate both terminology and the components of quality child care.

- Chapter 4, "The Field of Early Childhood Education," pulls together all the terms surrounding children, programs, funding, and human resources which you will undoubtedly encounter. This knowledge will facilitate the study of upcoming chapters in greater detail as you encounter quality in child care, curriculum, the specifics of provincial regulations, and the history and future of early childhood education in Canada.

- Chapter 5, "Quality in Early Childhood Programs," encompasses all the variables that must be addressed for child care to be considered of high quality. Included in these are teacher–child ratio, group size, centre size, and teacher training. We look at how Canada measures up to legislation governing these variables, and we examine some research findings. We provide an overview of various program models to "centre" you regarding the wide range of child care options available. We conclude with a look at the effects that low- and high- quality programs have on children.

Chapter 4

The Field of Early Childhood Education

Early childhood education—this is the field, the system, you are exploring through this text and the course in which you are enrolled. What is included in early childhood education? What is the terminology of the field? What influences act upon it? Who works in early childhood education? Who governs early childhood education?

As you begin learning about this field of study, the answers to some of these questions will gain greater significance and become more focused. This chapter presents an overview of the growth of a need for the field of early childhood edu-

cation and the systems that belong to it. We define children, staff, and programs. We look at child care not just in terms of full-day child care, but also in terms of a variety of programs that offer a combination of care, education, part-time relief for parents, and/or opportunities for parents and for children to play and socialize even if full-time care is not required. Hence, child care encompasses day care, after-school programs, nursery school, and drop-in centres, together with many other programs that we will discuss. Quality care and parental choice—parents' right to work, right to access quality care, and right to a diversity of programs— are essential. Quality care is defined and discussed in Chapter 5 following your orientation to the field in this chapter. As you read, remember that systems are influenced by the interactions within and between them. You are a system yet belong also to the system of staff, the system of family, and the system of community—the system of early childhood education. You are affected by and affect each of the systems with every interaction. We begin by defining "a system."

The System of Early Childhood Education

A system is an **organizational structure,** such as a family, a particular program setting, a corporation, or a profession. The structure is defined by individuals, or the **human resources,** who are in some way connected with it and who have a stake or interest in the system. Of course, individuals belong to many systems. A

systems approach is a particular way of looking at this structure. The approach relies on the principles of **wholistic thinking.** That is, it gathers and considers as much information (i.e., ideas, opinions, facts) from as many sources and perspectives as possible and attempts to integrate this information into an effective decision that mutually benefits all of its members. The components of the system are considered in relation to one another—their interactions and the results of these interactions.

Communication and relationships are the tools used to establish an open system that invites interaction between and within systems. This promotes shared decision making and, therefore, shared responsibilities and shared benefits, hence the terms "team" or "partnerships." This is a system that is dynamic. Since it is ever-changing, accommodating, adapting, and evolving, it has a history. A system has a goal, or mission statement, much as you have a philosophy, as we discussed in Chapter 1. It is based on what it has learned through history, research, evidence, and experience and what it hopes to accomplish by stating identified need. The system also needs resources to help it achieve this goal. This chapter examines the system of early childhood education—the growth and need for early childhood education, the purpose of programs, types of programs, information regarding individuals, such as children and families, and resources, such as human and financial.

The Growth of and Need for Early Childhood Education

As in any system, there are factors that influence its operation, identity, acceptance, and function. Four factors—historical events, changes in family life, evidence of the benefits of early childhood education, and advocating on behalf of

children—have led to the growth and need for early childhood education. Although the importance and value of education in the early years of life have been acknowledged for more than 2000 years (Carter, 1987), these relatively recent factors have brought early childhood education to the forefront of public awareness.

Historical events have served as a catalyst in establishing the need for and growth of child care in this century. Fundamental changes in the economy, family life, public awareness, and public support have had a profound effect on early childhood education. You have undoubtedly seen recent newspaper headlines and national magazine covers that have directed a spotlight on child care. Much of their focus has been on changes in family life that have brought about the need for child care outside the home. These changes result from an interplay of many complex factors including the rising cost of living, a growing number of dual-income families, an increase in single-parent families, an increased number of teenage parents, greater family mobility, and a decrease in the impact of the extended family.

But the needs of working families are not the only reason that early childhood education has been in the public eye. Over the past quarter-century, the success of some publicly funded early childhood programs in Canada and the United States has shown us that high-quality early educational intervention can combat poverty and dysfunction. There has also been increased attention on the needs of special populations of young children and how to bring them into the mainstream of society; for instance, children who are developmentally challenged, abused, or culturally different have benefited from such programs.

Finally, many professionals are outspoken and eloquent advocates for the rights of children. They continue to lobby for governmental changes that will improve the lives of young children. Below we discuss the four key factors mentioned above in defining the growth of early childhood education.

Historical Events in Early Childhood Education

With the exception of the flurry of activity during World War II, there was little change in early childhood education from the 1920s until the 1960s. Dewey and Hall's emphasis on child-centred programs became popular, and criticisms of the teacher-centred approach of Froebel led to the demise of his model in North America. Similarly, Montessori programs, which were popular in the United States between 1910 and 1918, were attacked by William Heard Kilpatrick in his 1914 work, *The Montessori System Examined*. Kilpatrick was a lecturer at Teachers' College in New York, where he was known as "the million-dollar professor" (Hunt, 1968, p. 108). Kilpatrick was an ardent follower of Dewey and was "compelled to say that in the content of her [Montessori's] doctrine, she belongs to the mid-nineteenth century, some fifty years behind the present development of educational theory" (Kilpatrick, 1914, pp. 62–63). Kilpatrick's work was circulated widely to both students and educators, and led to the demise of Montessori programs until the 1960s.

Gesell's emphasis on maturation seemed to govern thinking about education in the early years until the 1960s: there was little to do with young children other than wait for them to unfold, except in the area of social development. Thus, most early childhood programs, which were patronized by middle-class families, emphasized social growth and avoided interfering with cognitive development. Allowing the child to flourish in a supportive environment was sufficient. While day care centres were available, they had a welfare orientation (except during the war) and were a service to those families who needed daytime care for their children (Young, 1981).

During the late 1940s and throughout the 1950s, there was strong pressure on families to have the mother stay at home with children, at least until they were 3 years of age. Studies of infants and young children who were reared in orphanages where there was little human contact and virtually no stimulation had repeatedly found significant delays in the development of these unfortunate youngsters (Skeels, 1966; Spitz, 1945). Moreover, these problems persisted through adolescence when personality problems also were apparent (Goldfarb, 1943). These studies culminated in John Bowlby's now classic 1951 monograph, *Maternal Care and Mental Health*. Bowlby, after reviewing the orphanage studies, concluded that the best environment for a child, at least until age 3, was at home with his or her mother or permanent mother substitute. While this guiding principle was accepted in the 1950s, partly because it was consistent with the social and political climate of the times, it was quickly debunked in the 1960s (Caldwell, 1968, 1971, 1973a, 1973b). At that time, many researchers (Casler, 1961; Yarrow, 1961) realized that the sensory deprivation experienced by institutionalized infants and children bore no resemblance to short-term intermittent separations from a mother.

Sputnik and Educational Upheaval

In 1957, the Russians launched the first space satellite, *Sputnik*. The success of the Soviet space program and, conversely, the failure of the Americans to be the first in space also led to an attack on the school system in the United States that soon filtered up to Canada. Outmoded teaching techniques, dull curriculums, and too little emphasis on the sciences were seen as part of the reason the Americans lagged behind the Russians. The U.S. civil rights movement in the 1950s and 1960s spawned further examinations of the school system. The schools were seen to be failing the middle classes and not producing the desired rocket scientists, poor children did worse in school than their middle-class counterparts, and Black children in the U.S. south were the poorest in terms of their educational accomplishments (see Coleman, 1966; Riessman, 1962). While the school system could be held accountable for the performance of children of poor families, marked differences between poor children and their more advantaged peers were found at the time of school entry. These latter differences pointed to the importance of experience in the preschool years.

Changes in Family Life

Typical family life has changed considerably since the end of World War II. Demographic information began indicating that increasing numbers of women were entering the workforce (e.g., Statistics Canada, 1985; Women's Bureau, 1990). No longer do most mothers stay at home to rear their young children. In some families, both parents work because of the desire for personal and professional development rather than for economic reasons. In other cases, economic need forces families to rely on two salaries because one simply does not provide for all of their financial needs. And in some families, both parents work for both personal and economic reasons.

Whereas in 1951, only 11 percent of Canadian married women worked, that figure had risen to 44 percent in 1975, 56 percent in 1987, 60 percent in 1989, and almost 70 percent in 1993 (Doxey, 1990; Women's Bureau, 1970a, 1970b, 1990; Statistics Canada, 1993). Unfortunately, government studies of women in the workforce in the 1950s and 1960s had an unusual definition of working mothers: in addition to having children under 14, they had to have been married at some time (e.g., Women's Bureau, 1970a). Of course, that definition of a working mother eliminates single parents, thus making comparisons with more recent studies of working mothers, which include all mothers regardless of marital status, somewhat difficult. Nevertheless, it is clear that there has been a steady increase in the number of married and unmarried women in the workplace since 1975.

There is some regional variation in these figures that is related, at least in part, to employment opportunities. Nevertheless, women in all areas of the country are far less likely to be home rearing their children in the 1990s than they were in the 1950s. Both parents in two-parent families with children 5 years and younger work in about 50 percent of the cases. They are even more likely to work if their children are 6 years or older. The pattern is similar for single parents. About 40 percent of single parents with children aged 5 and under work, as do over 60 percent of those with school-aged children.

Recent projections (e.g., Jones, Marsden, & Tepperman, 1990) suggest that the number of women in the workforce will continue to increase and that by the year 2000, their rate of participation in the workforce will approach that of men. In 1989, 77 percent of Canadian men were in the workforce (Women's Bureau, 1990). In fact, in the 1990s, Canada Employment and Immigration Centre publications across the country (see Employment and Immigration Canada, 1992) project that child care will be one of the top 10 high-demand occupations throughout the decade. Even in economically depressed regions (e.g., the Niagara region in Ontario), they predict that the number of child care workers in the workforce will increase by 23 percent between 1992 and 1999.

Another family change that has increased the demand for child care is the rise in the number of single parents. Prior to changes in Canada's divorce laws in 1968, divorces were rare—only 1.6 married women per 1000 divorced in 1961 (Ram, 1990). That figure jumped to 6.1 in 1971, 11.3 in 1981, and 12.4 in 1986 (Ram, 1990). While the divorce rate has been levelling off after the flurry of activity that followed the 1968 Divorce Act, the marriage rate also has steadily declined. In 1961, 93.1 per 1000 single women over 15 married in Canada (Ram, 1990). By 1986, that figure had dropped to 71.9 per 1000. While the majority of single-parent families are created through divorce, there also is a growing number of never-married parents, some still finishing their high-school education and some older who choose to remain single. The percentage of single-parent families varies somewhat by province and territory, from a low of 11 percent in Saskatchewan, Ontario, and Newfoundland to a high of 30 percent of the parents of preschoolers in the Yukon.

The divorced single parent with custody of the children, most frequently the mother, typically experiences a significant decrease in income and standard of living. In addition, the single parent usually has to work (or work longer hours) to support the family. Of course, to work outside the home, the single, divorced parent, male or female, needs to find appropriate child care. Single parents who have never married face similar challenges when it comes to child care. A number of them—teenage mothers, for example—generally do not yet have the skills required to enter the workforce. As indicated in the National Council of Welfare's 1990 report, *Women and Poverty Revisited*, many of these mothers have not completed even grade 11. If they are to find alternatives to relying on social assistance for their livelihood, they must return to school. For this reason, child care facilities attached to secondary schools are becoming more common.

A third change in family life is the increasing mobility of many of today's families. Work demands cause some families to move away from relatives who might otherwise provide support. Family mobility, involving only the small nuclear family, has contributed to the declining influence of the extended family, that network of relatives such as grandparents, uncles, aunts, and adult brothers and sisters beyond the immediate family.

Traditionally, the most prevalent form of child care was having a relative look after the children. Many parents seem more comfortable leaving a young child with a relative than with a stranger, and relatives may charge little or no money, making this a financially attractive alternative. While relatives are still a frequently used source of care, the **Canadian National Child Care Study (CNCCS)** (Pence, Read, Lero, Goelman, & Brockman, 1992) found that non-relatives are now more likely to care for Canadian children than relatives. Quite often female relatives, who traditionally would have been home, are working (Wash & Brand, 1990).

Changes such as increasing numbers of dual-income families and single-parent families, and a decline in the impact of the extended family, have dramatically raised the demand for child care and brought early childhood education to the forefront of public attention. "Child care is now as essential to family life as the automobile or the refrigerator" (Scarr, Phillips, & McCartney, 1990, p. 26).

Exhibit 4.1 examines the scope of and need for child care arrangements in Canada. Although we define licensed, centre-based care and home- or family-

EXHIBIT 4.1 SCOPE OF CHILD CARE AND NEEDS OF PARENTS IN CANADA

Province or Territory	Canadian Children 0–9 Years of Age	Number of Children 0–9 Years in Some Form of Care	Number of Licensed Centre-Based Spaces	Number of Licensed Family Child Care Spaces
B.C.	404 300	283 300	41 331	7 155
Alta.	389 900	272 300	50 120	6 962
Sask.	157 900	112 600	3 795	1 980
Man.	144 900	103 000	16 939	2 623
Ont.	1 288 200	909 400	102 762	11 762
Yukon	NA	NA	564	84
Que.	881 900	569 400	77 801	7 273
N.B.	96 300	59 300	5 568	96
P.E.I.	191 500	12 300	1 913	35
N.S.	119 500	79 600	5 977	123
Nfld.	83 300	44 900	3 264	0
N.W.T.	NA	NA	694	66

NA = Not available

Sources: Pence et al. (1992); National Child Care Information Centre (1991); Young (1993b).

based care shortly, it is worthwhile noting at this point the sheer numbers of children in care versus the availability of licensed spaces. In Nova Scotia, for example, of 119 500 children, 79 600 require care, yet there are only a little over 6000 licensed spaces, leaving over 70 000 children in unlicensed care. This pattern is strikingly similar across the country.

Evidence of the Benefits of Early Childhood Education

The need of working parents for child care makes early childhood education a topic of national prominence, but this is not the only reason for its increasing importance. A great deal of research, which we will discuss in Chapter 5, has shown that high-quality child care programs have positive effects on the development of young children. On a parallel though separate track, much discussion and research have centred on the benefits of early education for special populations of children and families. Thus, children from poverty backgrounds, children with disabilities, and children at risk for other reasons have been enrolled in publicly funded programs. Since the mid-1960s, financial support has increased as a result of mounting evidence that high-quality early childhood programs can and do make a long-term difference that carries into adulthood. Researchers have concluded that good early childhood programs not only improve the lives of the children and families involved but also result in substantial economic benefits for society. Although early intervention programs are expensive, their cost is more than recovered in subsequent years through greater schooling success, decreased need for special education, lowered delinquency and arrest rates, and decreased welfare dependence (Berrueta-Clement, Schweinhart, Barnett, Epstein, & Weikart, 1984; Wright, 1983).

Need for Child Advocacy

A fourth factor that has brought early childhood education into the public consciousness is the urgency with which many professionals view the plight of increasing numbers of children and families. Of particular concern are the many families that face extreme poverty, lacking the most basic necessities.

In Canada, one in five children, on average, lives in circumstances that fall below the poverty line; in some regions of the country (e.g., the Atlantic region), that figure is higher while it is lower in other areas. Yet the social problems reach beyond the needs of the poor, to working parents with moderate incomes who are beset by the scarcity of affordable, high-quality care. A report from the **National Day Care Study (NDCS),** *Status of Day Care in Canada 1990* (National Child Care Information Centre, 1991), suggested that available licensed child care settings may serve less than 8 percent of Canadian children under 3 years who need child care and only 27 percent of children between 3 and 5 years who need child care.

Organizations such as the Childcare Advocacy Association of Canada and the Canadian Child Care Federation, as well as many provincial organizations, actively campaign for high-quality early childhood programs.

The needs of children and families have become political concerns. They have come to the attention of both political leaders and the public at large through the astute efforts of children's rights advocates, including early childhood professionals. But there is a continuing need to promote a common concern for the welfare of all children.

What Is Included in Early Childhood Education Programs?

We have looked at some of the historical roots of early childhood education and reasons for the rapid growth of the field. But early childhood education is a broad term and includes a variety of approaches and programs. Nursery schools, child care centres (formerly referred to as day care centres), parent cooperative preschools, infant stimulation programs, junior kindergartens, and kindergartens are but a few of the early childhood programs that exist in Canada. Toy-lending libraries, home-based child care, and employer-sponsored child care centres also fall within the definition of early childhood education programs. Winnipeg's Assiniboia Downs Race Track Child Care Centre as well as the Edmonton Hospital Workers' Day Care are early childhood programs that are offered by the workplace. Other programs include the Pairiviq Child Care Centre, an Inuit child care centre in Iqaluit, Northwest Territories, and *Gizhaadaawgamik,* a day care centre for Indian children in Toronto, which derives its name from the Ojibwa word that means a place to care for children. Some early childhood programs, such as drop-in centres, do not have explicit educational goals while other programs, such as babysitting cooperatives and drop-off child centres, do not have formal programs. All of these programs, however, aim to provide experiences for young children in addition to those they receive from their parents at home.

Clearly, the term "early childhood education" refers to a wide variety of programs with various purposes. As well, it includes children of various ages and enlists staff in many roles. Early childhood education encompasses a number of dimensions, and just some of them are shown in Exhibit 4.2 and explained in detail in the remainder of this chapter.

Children and Programming

Without children, of course, there would be no early childhood education. Recognizing that there even was such a thing as childhood, we learned in Chapter

2, is a recent phenomenon. The classification of early childhood spans the period from birth to age 8. This includes what we have come to call infants, toddlers, and children of kindergarten, primary, and preschool age. Needless to say, working parents need quality and a variety of child care for children of varying ages and at varying stages of their development. The field defines these terms for purposes of such issues as program design and legislation.

Infants and Toddlers

One of the most dramatic increases in recent years has been in infant and toddler programs. But what is an infant and what is a toddler? The answer is not as clear as it might seem. In 7 of the 12 provinces and territories, **infants** are defined as being between 0 and 18 months of age, so we will use the majority's definition. Canadians seem to have more difficulty with the term "toddler," so we will use the most common definition: **toddlers** range from 19 to 35 months of age.

Not all infant/toddler programs fall under the heading of child care, however. A number of compensatory programs, such as **infant stimulation programs** for infants at risk for developmental delays, enrol children from infancy. Programs for infants and toddlers with special needs, such as a visual or hearing impairment, also start early parent–child education programs as soon as possible. Other programs with a compensatory focus involve infants and toddlers and their families in programs as a way of intervening in the poverty cycle.

Preschoolers

The largest segment of children in licensed Canadian early childhood programs is between 3 and 5 years of age (Pence et al., 1992). Though typically we think of **preschoolers** as 2.5 to 5 years of age, about 22.5 percent of the parents in the CNCCS indicated they used nursery schools, child care centres, and kindergartens for their 3- to 5-year-old children. Another 20.3 percent of children in this age group were in family child care homes while 15.5 percent were cared for in their own homes by a relative or non-relative. The 1991 NDCS suggested that the available licensed child care spaces would serve only 27.7 percent of Canadian working women, and about 24 percent of the CNCCS sample reported using these facilities. Again these numbers suggest that there are simply not enough licensed spaces to meet parental needs.

There are many different types of preschool programs, some more developmentally appropriate than others. A number of different models will be discussed later.

Kindergarten and Primary Children

Most definitions of early childhood include children up to age 8. Children typically start junior kindergarten the year they turn 4 and kindergarten in the year they turn 5. **Primary children** are those in grades 1 to 3. Thus, directions for curriculum, teaching strategies, and the environment in kindergartens and primary classrooms derive (or should) from what is known about the development and mode of learning of young school-aged children.

Developmentally appropriate practice for this age group, just as for earlier ages, involves an integrated approach. An **integrated curriculum** acknowledges the importance of all aspects of human development—social, emotional, physical, cognitive, language, and creative—rather than focusing primarily on the cognitive. It also involves learning experiences that promote all aspects of development and does not segment the day into separate times, such as for math, reading, physical education, or social studies. Through the use of learning centres, themes, and the concept of emergent curriculum, such subjects are fully integrated and considered an inseparable part of one another (Bredekamp, 1987).

School-Aged Children

Elementary school-aged children, typically up to age 12, whose parents work full time also require care when they are not in school. This is often provided through before- and after-school programs and full-day holiday and summer care. Such programs generally focus on recreation and care rather than education, and particularly on self-directed and self-initiated activities, since the children spend the bulk of their day in school (Alexander, 1986). The 1991 NDCS indicated that **school-aged child** care is growing faster than any other kind of program in Canada. However, the NDCS also indicated that there were only spaces for 5.56 percent of the children of all Canadian working women. In fact, the CNCCS (see Exhibit 4.3) found just under 5 percent of school-aged children in these programs.

The parents of 15.6 percent (134 900) of Canadian 6 to 9-year-olds in the CNCCS had made no child care arrangements (Pence et al., 1992). In another 5.3 percent or 45 800 cases, the parents said the children looked after themselves.

Children without formal before- and after-school programs are often labelled **latch-key** or **self-care children**. They arrive at school with the latch-key around their necks and return to an empty home after school. Concerns about the safety, vulnerability, and lack of judgment of young school-aged children have prompted an increase in before- and after-school programs. Most Canadian early childhood education programs now include courses on the school-aged child. Since early childhood education professionals run many of theses before- and after-school programs, legislation governing child care has begun to include children to age 12. Relatively little research, however, has been carried out to measure the long-term effects of various arrangements for the school-aged children of working parents (Powell, 1987a). There are different purposes for such care and reasons why children require it. Thus, different care settings and program types are available.

Programs vary for different ages. As well, there are many people involved in the care of these children. Next we will look at the purpose of programs, types of programs, and the people who work in these programs.

Purpose of Programs

Care

We have already touched on some basic differences in programs that stem from their underlying thrust. The major purpose of many programs is to care for chil-

dren while their parents work. The rapid rise in recent years in the numbers of children in full day care, either in child care centres or in family child care homes, has paralleled the increasing prevalence of working mothers. The primary goal of child care programs is to provide safe and nurturing care in a developmentally appropriate setting for children.

Enrichment

Enrichment, a second aim, is particularly prevalent in part-time preschools. Such programs usually include specific activities to enhance socialization, cognitive skills, or overall development of young children. The underlying notion is that children will benefit from experiences that they might not otherwise receive (e.g., participating in group activities, playing with a group of age-mates, learning specific concepts from specially trained teachers). One phenomenon that has been growing recently is that of the **hurried child** or **hothousing,** apt terms that have become popular. Hothousing is aimed at accelerating some aspect of young children's development and is of considerable concern to many early childhood professionals (e.g., Elkind, 1981, 1987b; Gallagher & Coche, 1987; Hills, 1987; Sigel, 1987). It differs from enrichment by the nature of its activities (often drill-type exercises) and by its lack of developmental appropriateness.

Compensation

A third major purpose, found particularly in publicly funded programs, is compensation. Compensatory programs aim to make up for some lack in children's backgrounds. The basic philosophy of compensatory programs, such as Mary Wright's University of Western Ontario Preschool, is to provide experiences that will help children enter the mainstream of society more successfully (Wright, 1983). Such experiences sometimes include a range of services, encompassing early childhood education, nutrition, and parent education.

Preservation

An additional purpose of programs like *Gizhaadaawgamik* mentioned previously is the preservation and transmission of cultural traditions and languages. Similarly, some but by no means all church-based schools aim to provide educational programs in a religious context.

These categories, although descriptive of some underlying differences among programs, are not mutually exclusive. Few child care centres are concerned with only the physical well-being and care of children. Most also provide enriching experiences that further children's development. At the same time, preschool programs have to be concerned with the nurture and safety of children in their care. Similarly, compensatory programs are concerned with enriching experiences and caring for children, while child care or preschool programs may serve to compensate for something lacking in the backgrounds of some of the children.

Program Terminology

The child care profession in Canada is complicated to understand since it is multilayered and multifaceted. Unlike the United States with its federal (national)

system of education and child care, we have a provincial system. There is no federal program or guidelines. The provinces administer funds and set legislation and regulations. What you need to grasp is the idea that child care can occur in different settings in a centre-based or home-based care. These can be licensed or unlicensed by government. They can also be partially funded (cost-sharing by municipality, province, or federal government) or privately funded, and they can be for-profit or not-for-profit programs. The programs can be run by corporations, schools, governments, individuals, boards of directors, or agencies. These dimensions of early childhood education are highlighted in Exhibit 4.2. Exhibit 4.3 presents percentages of children in each type of care setting as outlined below. We will now take a close look at some of these dimensions.

EXHIBIT 4.2 PROGRAM TERMINOLOGY IN CANADIAN EARLY CHILDHOOD EDUCATION

Definition of Children	Purpose of Programs	Types of Settings	Sources of Support
Neonates (newborn) Infants (0–18 mo.) Toddlers (18–35 mo.) Preschoolers (3–5 yrs.) Junior Kindergarten (4 yrs.) Kindergarten (5 yrs.) Primary (6–8 yrs.)[2] School age (9–12 yrs.)[2]	Care Enrichment Compensation Preservation	May be licensed or unlicensed *Home-Based* Informal care (unlicensed) – Child's own home – Parents – Nannies (some regulations apply) – Relatives – Babysitters Formal care – Family child care homes (licensed) – Regulations and funding by municipalities and provinces – Caregiver cares for children in own home but is licensed, paid, and visited by family child care worker from an agency or the municipality, town, or city. *ECE Home Visitors* – Infant stimulation workers – Resource teachers – Therapy assistants – Special needs at-home workers – Child care workers – Early intervention specialists – Respite care *Centre-Based* – Full-day child care centres (licensed) – Nursery schools – Private preschools, junior kindergartens, kindergartens – Private school (e.g., Montessori) – Parent cooperatives – Before- and after-school child care programs	*For-Profit* – Called private, commercial, or proprietary care *Non-Profit: Publicly Funded* – Until 1996, Canada cost-shared with provinces 50% through CAP[1] to families who qualified for subsidized child care (parents pay none or some of cost). – Provinces decide who is eligible and administer the funds. – Some municipalities share funding. – Funding and regulations regarding children fall under the ministry or department that governs social services in the province (Minister of Health may be involved with children with special needs). – Ministries or departments of education govern curriculum for children of legal school age (usually 6 yrs.) and provide funding to public schools. *Non-Profit: Privately Funded* – Corporations – Employers – Agencies (e.g., YMCA, United Way), organizations (e.g., churches), school settings (e.g., colleges or universities), parents, individual (e.g., owner) *Scenarios* A. A child may attend a private, licensed, for-profit child care centre but be eligible for public funds (subsidy) and parents pay no or some fee. B. A child may be in a non-profit, licensed municipality-run child care centre and be ineligible for public funds. The parents must pay the full fee. However, this fee is still not representative of the true cost of child care since the centre on the whole is publicly funded. C. A child attends a Montessori or private junior kindergarten. Parents pay full fees for these programs. Programs run by private operators (individual or group) who get money from parents, sponsors, investments, or any private person, group, agency, or corporation who wishes to sponsor and invest in it.

Definition of Children	Purpose of Programs	Types of Settings	Sources of Support
		– Drop-in centres, play groups (may or may not have a fee, usually not licensed) – Toy-lending libraries – Treatment centres – Hospital playrooms – Recreational programs (e.g., kindergym)	who wishes to sponsor and invest in it. If a child needs care before or after the program, he/she goes to a child care setting (may or may not be located in the same building).

1. CAP stands for Canadian Assistance Plan.
2. Primary and school age together termed "elementary age."

Program Settings

Programs for young children can be divided into home-based and centre-based settings. The Canadian National Child Care Study (CNCCS) (Pence et al., 1992) examined the types of caregiving arrangements Canadian parents reported using for children between birth and 9 years of age.

The results, shown in Exhibit 4.3, clearly show that home-based care is more frequent than centre-based care even though Exhibit 4.1 shows that there are significantly fewer licensed home or family care spaces. However, parents favour different types of care for children of different ages, with centre-based care being most frequent for preschoolers.

Centre-Based Programs

Centre-based programs include child care centres, nursery schools, and preschools and are typically located in either a separate building of their own or any variety of buildings that have extra space available, a need for child care or child-related programs, and the desire to offer them. Schools, churches, colleges and universities, hospitals, YWCA and YMCA buildings, and office towers are among the many locations with child-centred programs.

EXHIBIT 4.3: CANADIAN CHILD CARE ARRANGEMENTS: PERCENTAGE OF TOTAL NUMBER OF CHILDREN IN EACH CAREGIVING SETTING BY AGE

Type of Care	0–17 Months	18–35 Months	3–5 Years	6–9 Years
parents—at work	10.0	11.2	10.7	9.3
parents—at home	20.0	15.6	17.5	24.6
sibling(s)	[1]	[1]	[1]	6.9
self	[2]	[2]	[1]	5.3
relatives in child's home	10.4	7.5	7.5	5.9
relatives not in child's home	14.3	11.8	8.3	6.5
non-relative in child's home	9.3	10.5	8.0	6.0
non-relative not in child's home—licensed	[1]	2.7[3]	1.7[3]	0.83
non-relative not in child's home—unlicensed	26.3	25.1	18.7	12.7
preschool	[2]	[2]	2.8	[1]
kindergarten	[2]	[2]	6.0	[1]
child care centre	5.4	12.5	13.9	1.6
before/after-school program	[2]	[2]	1.13	4.7
no arrangement	[1]	[1]	2.4	15.6
Total	223 300	269 600	570 200	862 600

1. Too small a sample
2. Nil
3. Estimate

Source: A. Pence et al. (1992), "An overview of NCCS data for British Columbia," in A. Pence (ed.), *Canadian child care in context: Perspectives from the provinces and territories* (p. 83) (Ottawa: Statistics Canada and Health and Welfare Canada).

Nursery Schools, Private Preschools, and Kindergarten Programs

Nursery schools, preschools, and private kindergartens (run by a person or organization outside of the public school board) are usually part-day programs with primarily an educational orientation, that serve children from 2 to 5 years of age. Colleges and universities often have schools attached to them which are used as demonstration centres for teacher education courses and as laboratories for research on child development and education.

Parent-cooperative nursery schools, which emerged in Toronto in the 1930s, and in Victoria, Saskatoon, Montreal, and Vancouver in the 1940s (Stevenson, 1990), are another type of setting created and managed by parents. The parents employ the teachers and historically have assisted in the program.

Child Care Centres

Child care centres, in contrast with nursery schools, offer full-day programs for infants and children of working parents, so the custodial aspect of child care must be included as *one* of their purposes. However, child care centres and nursery schools are by no means mutually exclusive. The better nursery schools emphasize education and care, as do the better child care centres. Moreover, child care centres often have half-day options or operate as before- and after-school programs, and nursery schools sometimes have before- and after-school options. Nevertheless, the child care centre typically is open for a minimum of 10 hours a day. Consequently, child care programs must provide meals and opportunities for naps or quiet times, and must deal with the realities of diaper changes, toilet training, and toothbrushes and combs. Historically, many child care centres provided only custodial care, but there has been a gradual shift in focus and it probably would be difficult to find a Canadian child care centre in the 1990s that did not at least express an interest in the education of the children. Frequently, the interest is not just expressed but clearly exemplified in child care centres that offer a comprehensive program which encourages development in all areas.

Treatment/Hospital Centres

Children in short- or long-term care for medical reasons often also need a high-quality early childhood education program during the day to assist in their overall development and to provide an excellent forum for play and socialization. Thus, many hospital and treatment centres provide such programs on location.

Recreational Programs

Early childhood educators have run excellent programs for children through municipal, private, and public agencies such as the YMCA, the municipality, the local school board, and social services. These programs include day camp, kindergym, music, art camp, and so on.

Toy-Lending Libraries/Resource Centres

These may be situated in a permanent location or may be mobile and travel from location to location. They are stocked with toys, books, and resources that can be utilized by early childhood education programs and families who are lacking equipment and materials that would improve the quality of their child care.

Drop-in Centres/Play Groups

Drop-in centres or play groups often do not fall under licensing regulations. Sometimes they require parents to remain with the child, or they may provide short-term care, such as in a shopping mall drop-in centre where parents need care while shopping or in a fitness facility where parents need care while they work out. Though many of these are run by well-regulated agencies like the YMCA and follow strict guidelines, it is important to help parents understand aspects of quality care as outlined later in this chapter.

In Canada, centre-based programs have increased more than any other type of child care. While in 1971 only 17 000 Canadian children were cared for in centre-based settings, close to 300 000 Canadian children were in licensed child care settings in 1990 (National Child Care Information Centre, 1991).

Home-Based Programs

In Canada, like the United States (Hofferth & Phillips, 1987), when all ages of children are considered, the largest number is cared for in homes. Some children are cared for in their own homes, some in others' homes. As you will see below,

these homes may or may not be licensed, and the quality of care ranges from excellent to atrocious. Canadian infants and toddlers, in particular, are cared for more in home settings (Pence et al., 1992). In some cases, this is because parents of very young children prefer a more intimate, homelike setting. Parents with several children often prefer this setting since it means that they do not have to drop off three children, for example, at three different locations on their way to work. Still other parents choose this arrangement for very young children because they do not want them exposed to the many illnesses often prevalent in a large centre. But for many parents, the main reason they choose family child care is that it is readily available and often considerably cheaper than centre-based care. In Saskatchewan and Newfoundland, centre-based care for infants is still not permitted, so home care may be the only alternative in those areas.

Family Child Care Homes

A caregiver may be licensed by the government to care for children in her or his home. Most provinces require licensing or registration of family child care homes that receive government funding, but the vast majority of homes are unlicensed (Halpern, 1987; Pence, 1992). Unlicensed care is sometimes called informal care. Certainly the vast majority of Canadian children in family child care are in unlicensed facilities (see Exhibit 4.3). This type of informal care generally means the parents bring the child to a neighbour's, friend's, babysitter's, or relative's home.

While licensing does not ensure quality, it does provide some safeguards. For example, the home must be safe and conform to fire regulations, and there are limits on the number and ages of children who can be in the home at any given time. Moreover, licensed homes are inspected on a regular basis. Usually an early childhood education worker visits and helps the caregiver learn about developmentally appropriate practices such as snacks and songs. Training is often provided, and some provinces have associations for licenced family child care homes. In each province, the number of licensed spaces—particularly for infants and toddlers—is low in both family- and centre-based child care programs. It is possible that parents would choose licensed centre-based care for the very young more frequently if more spaces were available. From 1971 to 1991, the number of children cared for in licensed family child care homes increased from 600 to 38 000 (National Child Care Information Centre, 1991).

Unlicensed In-Home Care

Exhibit 4.3 also shows that many Canadian children under 5 years are cared for in their own homes, by a relative or non-relative, but this arrangement is less frequent for school-aged children.

Nannies

Frequently parents arrange to have a **nanny** come into the home on a daily basis or a live-in basis. Nannies have become an attractive child care option for families where both parents work and/or have schedules that do not conform to centre-based programs. Some nannies have training in child care, and they may attend to other household tasks like cooking and light cleaning. In 1993, Canada's immigration policies required that nannies from abroad have grade 12 education and six months of on-the-job-training to enter the country.

Home Visitors

Home visitors can also be part of a home-based program since they visit homes to assist and support families with program and care needs or with special needs children, or to assist licensed caregivers who provide care in their own homes.

Sources of Support for Programs

One way of grouping early childhood programs is by the base of their support, especially financial. Many early childhood programs are privately owned, for-profit businesses, whereas others are not-for-profit enterprises operated through public funds or sponsored by an agency or church. A growing number of early childhood programs are also supported by employers.

For-Profit Programs

In for-profit early childhood programs, the monies left over after expenses are paid are profit, and they go back to the owners or stockholders. Generally, all

monies taken in are from parents or private investors. In Canada, only 35 percent of all licensed child care centres are operated for profit (National Child Care Information Centre, 1991). For-profit centres are sometimes called private proprietary or commercial business. The number of Canadian profit-making centres has dropped sharply since 1968, when 75 percent of all the licensed Canadian child care spaces were in for-profit centres. However, there is considerable regional disparity in these figures. Presumably, government incentives for non-profit centres have played a significant role in this decline. In Saskatchewan, for example, only non-profit centres were eligible for government funds until 1990, and there were no profit-making centres in the province then. However, one might expect to see a change in the distribution of centres there now that funding is available. Other provinces, such as Manitoba and Ontario, have at times given non-profit centres subsidies that allow them to increase teacher salaries.

The Canadian figures stand in sharp contrast to those for the United States, where about 60 percent of all child care programs are operated for profit, either as single, independently owned businesses or as part of regional or national chains (Wash & Brand, 1990). This percentage is rapidly rising in the United States, and it is expected to continue to increase. For many years, the majority of child care in most American communities was provided by local owners who operated one or two centres. In the 1970s and 1980s, child care chains that experienced tremendous growth—as much as a thousandfold—moved into virtually every metropolitan area (Neugebauer, 1988). There is some concern that they may want to move into the Canadian market in the future. Child care chains are big business. Some sell stock that is traded on the New York Stock Exchange, deal in mergers and takeovers, and utilize sophisticated marketing strategies.

In both Canada and the United States, a series of concerns about the quality of for-profit child care have emerged (e.g., Baynham, Russell, & Ross, 1988; Kagan & Newton, 1989; McIntosh & Rauhala, 1989; Meisels & Sternberg, 1989; National Child Care Staffing Study, 1989; Neugebauer, 1991; West, 1988). Political parties, such as the one currently in power in Ontario, that slash thousands of subsidized spaces and promote informal non-licensed care perpetuate privatization. Privatization without government funding results in centres charging enormous fees to parents in order to fund the quality programs and to make a profit. Most families in need cannot afford such fees. To keep care expenses and fees low, centres' practices border on the unsafe as they stretch every dollar to meet even minimum standards. A poorer quality of care, lower salaries and poorer benefits, less educated teaching staff, and more frequent licensing violations in for-profit centres have been documented in both Canada and the United States.

Without question, some of these difficulties stem from these centres' need to make a profit and keep fees low. In Canada, the National Council of Welfare (1988) has clearly outlined the source of the difficulties: "Profits are made by keeping costs down—paying low salaries to caregivers, raising child–staff ratios or compromising health, safety, or nutritional standards—all of which hurt children" (p. 27).

This is not to say that every for-profit centre does this and that every non-profit centre does not. In the United States, Neugebauer (1991) found that there was a wide range of quality in for-profit centres as in other types of centres. Kagan and Newton (1989) reported similar findings about overall quality but noted that non-profit centres had more favourable teacher–child ratios, more services, better management, and more child-centred environments. The controversy continues, and, more and more in Canada, there is a tendency for provincial and territorial governments to provide subsidies only to non-profit centres. But as these subsidies are cut and spaces dwindle, families are forced to seek private, informal, or unlicensed care where quality can be in jeopardy.

Non-Profit Programs

In non-profit programs, profits generally are poured back into the program or are returned to the sponsoring agency. You may wonder about the difference between returning the money to the non-profit sponsoring agent versus the owner of a profit-making centre; undoubtedly, in some cases, there is no major difference. However, if the profits are returned to the program, this is likely to have a positive effect on all aspects of the program.

Non-profit centres gain their status through incorporation or sponsorship from an entity that is, itself, not operated for profit. Groups such as the United Way, parent-run organizations, social service agencies, churches, YMCAs/YWCAs, municipalities, hospitals, colleges, and universities are the most common sponsors of non-profit early childhood programs. However, you probably can find non-profit programs where the operators are paid very large salaries and little profit returns to the program.

Nonetheless, non-profit child care centres in Canada generally have been founded by groups sincerely interested in providing affordable, high-quality child care. In the 1970s and 1980s, when the need for child care for working parents became a more pressing social concern, many groups like churches and the YMCA/YWCA responded to that need by opening their facilities during the week or offering them to non-profit groups. Often YMCA, YWCA, and church buildings included nursery, preschool, or recreational rooms that were used primarily on weekends. Some church programs are affiliated with and incorporate the religion of their churches, but many are secular. Not all church-based programs are non-profit, however. Sometimes an enterprising member of a congregation arranges to rent the facilities to a for-profit centre.

A unique form of non-profit early childhood program is the parent cooperative. Parent cooperatives, usually part-day preschool programs, are based on a staffing structure that includes a paid professional head teacher and a rotating staff of parents. As part of enrolling their children in the program, parents are required to assist a specified number of days in the classroom. This arrangement serves both a staffing and a parent education function. With increasing numbers of parents entering the workforce full time, however, fewer parents have the time to participate in cooperative programs. Nonetheless, they continue to be popular with families with a stay-at-home parent, and with those who work part time. Cooperative groups are also finding ways of offering full-day child care programs by having working parents involved in fundraising and maintenance activities.

Publicly Supported Programs

Another significant supporter of early childhood programs is the public sector, whether it be the federal, provincial, or territorial governments or the municipalities. Although there was some activity in the field of early childhood education during the war years, the **Canada Assistance Plan (CAP),** enacted in 1966, was the first piece of federal legislation that had a significant impact on child care arrangements in the provinces and territories (Clifford, 1992; Townson, 1985). The long-term aim of the CAP was to alleviate the effects of poverty, and it included provisions regarding social assistance or welfare as well as child care services, rehabilitation and homemaker services, and counselling for those who qualified for social assistance. The CAP permitted the federal government to share 50 percent of the costs of child care with the provinces and territories, but *only for those persons in need.* There was considerable variation, however, between the provincial and territorial definitions of "in need." The CAP ceased to exist in 1996 and is slated to be replaced with a comparable program. The absence of these funds in the meantime may have a severe impact on programs.

The federal government also provides some support for child care on Indian reserve lands through Indian and Northern Affairs Canada (Child Care, 1990). Some provinces and territories (e.g., Ontario, the Yukon) also fund Indian and Inuit programs, while others do not (e.g., Manitoba, Newfoundland). A very recent move by the federal government is to fund reserve and non-reserve day cares for Aboriginal children.

Similarly, it is worth noting that the provinces and territories, as well as many municipalities in Canada, make significant financial contributions to early childhood programs. In fact, some provinces provide more support for early childhood programs than the CAP requires, and many municipalities provide early childhood programs for their residents. Some ministries of education also are involved in providing child care to school-aged children when they are not in school.

Privately Supported Programs

Privately supported programs may or may not be funded in part by the public sector or government and may or may not be for profit. But the program is run by a member of the private sector—a business or an individual.

Agencies

As mentioned throughout, many agencies (e.g., YMCA, United Way, Children and Family Services) provide child care services, directly or indirectly, by providing funds to those who run the programs and, hence, serve as a sponsor rather than as a direct owner-operator.

Employer- or Corporate-Supported Programs

One of the fastest-growing groups with a stake in early childhood programs is employers. Many companies maintain that their interest in the needs and concerns of parent-employees has resulted in a more productive and stable workforce. For the working parents of young children, work and family are not separable and, in fact, often overlap. Child care, in particular, is not just a family issue but also a concern to employers. Employees with young children, as compared with other workers, more often are late for work, leave work early, miss work altogether, and deal with personal issues while at work. When employers support child care in some way, they often report that the result is lower absenteeism, greater stability and loyalty, better morale, decreased stress, and less distraction among their employees (Fernandez, 1986; Mayfield, 1990; Milkovich & Gomez, 1976; Rothman Beach Associates, 1985). However, research has not yet fully documented these claims.

There are many ways in which employers can support their workers' child care needs. Some large companies have created child care centres in or near the place of work. For example, Statistics Canada in Ottawa, the National Film Board in St. Laurent, and Nanisivik Mines in the Northwest Territories have established workplace child care centres. In some instances, employers make arrangements with community child care centres and may offer vouchers or direct subsidies. Such an arrangement can ensure that employees are given priority when child care openings are available. Another way in which employers help their workers is by banding together with several other employers to support a child care centre that meets the joint needs of their employees. The Edmonton Hospital Workers Day Care, for example, is run by a consortium of employers. As part of a strike settlement, several Edmonton hospitals banded together to form a non-profit child care facility that includes family-based child care for the young children of shift workers as well as a child care centre for the older children of day workers. Larger corporations also are expressing a greater interest in employee child care and in elder care. In July 1992, 12 large North American companies, including giant corporations such as IBM, AT&T, Xerox, and Kodak, announced they were committing millions of dollars to build and expand facilities for the care of their employees' children and elderly relatives (U.S. Firms, 1992).

Not all employers, however, operate on such a large scale. Some provide referral services to help match employees' needs with available resources in the community. Other companies have helped develop and train a community network of family child care homes to meet their workers' needs. A growing trend among employers is to provide more responsive scheduling options, for instance, job sharing or flextime. Child care is increasingly becoming a benefits option as companies, rather than provide a common benefits package for all, allow their employees to select from a menu. Some companies, recognizing the significant problem posed by children who are ill, have begun to explore sick-child care options (Friedman, 1989; NAEYC Information Service, 1990).

University- and College-Affiliated Programs

A sizable number of early childhood programs are linked to higher education. The institution in which you are enrolled may, in fact, have such a program. Some are specifically laboratory or training programs that support student practice-teaching experiences and provide subjects for research; others serve primarily as campus child care centres for the young children of students, staff, and faculty. Many combine these two functions, offering child care to the campus community while utilizing the children and families for practicum and research purposes.

Some programs are operated as a joint campus venture, others are affiliated with a specific department or unit, and still others are independent and only rent space from the university or college. Campus programs that are laboratory schools are generally high quality, incorporating what has been learned about young children and early childhood programs from research, theory, and professional practice. However, not all campus programs are high quality. In some cases, universities and colleges simply rent space to child care programs so that there will be some child care on campus.

Public-School Involvement

A relatively recent development in early childhood program sponsorship is the involvement of public schools. A few provinces have provided services to young children below kindergarten age for a number of years, and more public schools are considering extending their programs to preschoolers. Some provinces have appropriated monies for prekindergarten programs, and others have placed early childhood programs high on their agendas.

In addition, public schools have provided early childhood centres for many years as part of high-school or vocational training programs. Recent additions of secondary-school courses on the family are accelerating this trend.

Although many early childhood educators feel that public-school involvement is a natural and inevitable step, some persistent issues surround this move. One of the most serious concerns is that prekindergarten programs in public schools will focus on school readiness rather than on developmental appropriateness, simply offering a downward extension of the kindergarten and first-grade curriculum and methods (Elkind, 1988; Morado, 1986).

A recent U.S. study of public-school prekindergartens provides support that such fears may, in many instances, be legitimate. "We saw some wonderful programs, full of child-centred and interesting activities. Others were rigid and boring. Still others sounded good on paper, but observations revealed that classroom practice in no way resembled written philosophy" (Mitchell & Modigliani, 1989, p. 57). The authors of this report go on to say, however, that their finding of a mix of good and inappropriate practices in public-school programs was not so different from what they saw in community-based early childhood programs.

Public-school sponsorship of early childhood programs is, of course, subject to the same limited supply of money that constrains other publicly supported programs. Typically, therefore, existing programs serve a limited group of children, and they are most likely to be available in large urban centres. Review Exhibit 4.2 for an overview of what we have discussed in this chapter in terms of children, purpose, setting, and program terminology.

Of course, it is often overwhelming for parents to sort through and choose care for their children. In A Closer Look, we describe two very different schools. Then, in Partnerships, we discuss how to help when parents ask for advice about choosing a school.

Certainly it is the people who work in these settings that make the most difference in families' lives. We turn our attention now to the human resources factor in early childhood education.

Human Resources in Early Childhood Programs— Relationships and Team Building

The people, or human resources, who make up the early childhood program are a system in their own right. This system, of course, affects the systems it interfaces with—the children, the families, the community, the field. The early childhood educator works within this system along with others who share the tasks of the program. Staff members, from the supervisor or director to the custodian, contribute toward making the program successful, the lives of children important, and the profession of early childhood education respectable. There can be a variety of staffing patterns depending on the type, size, and philosophy of the program as well as on its funding source.

The distribution and allocation of responsibility also varies in different programs. Some have a hierarchical structure, fashioned as a pyramid, where power trickles down from the top and each level in the structure reports to that above. Thus, in some classrooms that follow this model, one teacher is designated as the

ST. PETER'S AND JACK SPRAT—
A CONTRAST IN PROGRAMS

A look at two early childhood centres in one community illustrates the two extremes of child care facilities that exist in North America: in one there is great teacher satisfaction and stability, while in the other there is a high rate of teacher burnout, which results in frequent staff turnover.

St. Peter's Child Care Centre is a church-sponsored facility begun by a group of interested parents in the 1970s. It has an active and supportive board made up of church, parent, and community professional representatives. Most of the staff have worked at St. Peter's for 10 years or more, and the rare job openings tend to attract many applicants. Salaries are a little above the average for the community but not as high as at some other centres.

The staff report high job satisfaction: they enjoy their work with the children, appreciate their colleagues, and value having input into the decision-making process. The director meets weekly with the staff, discussing concerns and promoting group problem-solving strategies. She spends a good part of each day in the classrooms, with the staff and children. A child–adult ratio of 7 to 1, team teaching, flexible scheduling to accommodate the staff's personal needs, and response to staff requests for material and equipment also contribute to the staff's level of satisfaction. One staff member summed up the feelings of her colleagues by saying, "I love this job and wouldn't trade it for the world. I work with a very special group of people whom I highly respect as well as really like. It's a pleasure to come to work. Each day is a challenge, and it's exhilarating. I suppose I could make more money at another job, but where else could I find this special combination of great people, little and big, and the chance to grow and develop personally as I have done in the 12 years I have been here?"

Jack Sprat, a privately owned child care program in the same community, suffers from constant staff turnover. Seven months is the longest any staff member has been at Jack Sprat. Most of the children have had as many teachers as the number of months they have been in the program. A director spends part of her time at this facility and part of her time at another one which belongs to the same owner. Each teacher has charge of a group of 13 to 17 children in isolated rooms, and there is little interaction between staff. The owner subscribes to a monthly curriculum service and teachers are expected to follow this program, which involves letter and number recognition activities, worksheets, and group discussions that focus on specific letters, numbers, names of the months, animals, and occupations. Each child is expected to complete a specific number of worksheets each day. Teachers complain about feeling isolated, having no say over what they do with the children, being forced to carry out activities neither they nor the children enjoy, a lack of resources, an inability to request additional supplies, and a lack of support in dealing with the children.

The contrast between St. Peter's and Jack Sprat is underlined by the frequent teacher turnover in the latter and the almost total absence of staff changes in the former. St. Peter's places a priority on meeting the needs of children and staff, allows staff to participate in decision making, promotes communication and camaraderie among staff, and provides an atmosphere of mutual respect among teachers, administration, and children.

senior teacher or teacher supervisor, and other teachers work under her or him, following the senior teacher's direction and guidance.

Yet, in the early childhood field, there is often an alternative to this pyramidal structure because of the strong interdependence and interconnectedness between teachers, who frequently make decisions by consensus. This can be depicted as a web, which allows for more flexible and dynamic relationships than the hierarchical model, in which the power structure tends to be static and individuals' responsibilities depend on their position in the structure (Dresden & Myers, 1989).

In other programs, classes are co-taught by team teachers who share responsibilities. Team teaching is based on a relationship of trust and communication among the teachers, something that takes time to build. A good team finds many bonuses in this relationship such as added flexibility, creativity, problem-solving capabilities, and focus on what each member of the team enjoys most or does best. In addition, the collaboration between teachers provides the children with a model for cooperative behaviour (Thornton, 1990).

The concept of **organizational development** is prevalent in business and has begun to transcend the boundaries of education. **Change agents** or **management consultants** help leaders and organizations restructure to develop relationships that maximize both the humanistic and business practices of the workplace. The goal is to achieve maximum efficiency through relationships, communication, empowerment, ownership, and collaboration. These practices reflect the attitudes of an **entrepreneur.** This paradigm shift, or change in the way things are done, in which staff train and consult with others in a team approach, is seen as the trend in the child care field. This trend includes family involvement, collaboration with other community professionals, the move to professionalism, the evolution of the emergent (rather than imposed) curriculum, and the ecological concept that people and systems are inter- and intradependent. This merging of systems involves the **transdisciplinary team** whose members communicate and interact both within the field (e.g., teacher to teacher), outside the field (e.g., doctor to parent), and between fields (e.g., doctor and parent to teacher) to coordinate efforts.

Whatever the structure, it makes sense to determine at the outset the lines of responsibility in terms of providing direction, feedback, evaluation, and resources. By learning the lines of authority and communication, teachers in a program will know whom to seek out for instructions and information, with whom to discuss

problems, and where ultimate responsibility for various decisions lies. Smooth functioning depends on a clear understanding of these responsibilities, the lines of communication, and cooperation among the staff. We will now briefly examine some of the positions and their responsibilities held by staff members in early childhood programs (Click & Click, 1990; Sciarra & Dorsey, 1990; Seaver & Cartwright, 1986).

Director and/or Supervisor

Directors and/or **supervisors** perform a variety of tasks, depending on the size and scope of the program. Very large centres may have both an administrative director and teacher supervisor. While the director would play an administrative role, the supervisor would have more direct involvement with the children as well as some supervisory responsibilities. In smaller programs, the director may double as a teacher and supervisor for part of the day. Traditionally, the director is responsible for financial, personnel, policy, and facility decisions; provides community linkages; handles licensing and regulation; and is the ultimate decision-maker in the chain of responsibility in all matters that pertain to the program. In addition, the job description often involves staff selection, training, monitoring, and evaluation. In programs that depend on grants and other outside sources of funding, the director may spend much time writing proposals and meeting with influential decision-makers.

A teacher supervisor, working under a director, usually works with the children, has some administrative duties, and does some staff supervision. Larger programs even have assistant supervisors, whereas smaller programs seldom need one. However, in a team-teaching-centred approach, everyone has input into decisions and delegation of roles and responsibilities. This creates a sense of group ownership for all of the aspects of the program. It is an "ours" rather than a "hers" or "mine" or "theirs" atmosphere.

Administrators, as well as having their ECE diploma, need additional training. Courses at colleges and universities across Canada offer additional qualifications in business administration, human resources, development, accounting and computer applications, Internet training, and management and leadership skill development.

Resource Teacher

Many communities and, in fact, many centres have a **resource teacher** on staff to assist in the inclusion of children with special needs into programs. This position requires additional qualifications too—often a one-year certificate or diploma following the two-year Early Childhood Education diploma. The resource teacher's role is exactly what it seems—a resource. It is not his or her job to take over the programming or the disciplining for the children with special needs. It is, instead, to help train all staff in understanding and therefore accepting the principles of inclusion. By educating and training each and every person involved—the teachers, the parents, the cook, the custodian, the other children, and the volunteers—everyone has ownership of the success of inclusion. By increasing the knowledge and confidence of the team, fear and ignorance—two of the biggest barriers in working effectively with children with special needs—are reduced. Everyone becomes a competent and proficient team member and advocate, thereby creating a positive, supportive environment which fosters the overall development and endless potential of each and every individual within it.

Some provinces have associations of resource teachers. In Ontario, the association is called Early Childhood Resource Teacher Network of Ontario.

Home Visitors

Infant stimulation (or education) workers are often people with their Early Childhood Education certification. They belong to a team, which includes speech, physical, and occupational therapists, that helps develop a program for the child with special needs once he/she arrives home from the hospital. The infant stimulation worker visits the home on a regular basis, helping the parents work with their child from newborn to 2 years. Special needs children may also attend a centre-based program part time. Due to the high medical needs of these children, these programs are often funded by ministries of Health, or jointly by Health, Social Services, and Education ministries.

Home visits are often part of the centre or program mandates for itinerant resource teachers (those who travel from centre to centre from a base centre or agency). This helps bridge programming from home to school or home to community and provides families with additional support systems.

Early childhood educators have also held positions as child care workers for children's aid societies. They have also acted as therapy assistants carrying out the therapy programs developed for children with special needs by speech, physical, occupational, or psychosocial therapists.

Early childhood educators have also been trained as early intervention specialists, assessing children's developmental progress throughout their specialized programs, or as special needs workers at homes through such agencies as Community Living. Communication of all team members, together with families, is essential to the family's overall well-being and the child's growth and development.

Teaching Staff

Those who work directly with children may hold a variety of titles, and these titles vary from one Canadian jurisdiction to another. Staff composition varies greatly with the actual physical layout of a program and group size. Group-size regulations vary greatly across the country, and they affect the staffing structure. In locations that have strict group-size regulations, you would usually find two teachers per room. In another setting, however, you may find a large open room with four or five teachers present, while only one teacher may be in yet another setting. Nevertheless, there are certain roles that are relatively common across the country. We will look at two common teaching positions in more depth—the senior teacher and the assistant teacher. We will also examine a team teaching approach to the role of the teacher.

The Senior Teacher

In many jurisdictions that require teacher training, the teacher with more education and experience acts as the **senior teacher** when there are two or more teachers in a room. However, the titles used vary greatly not only from province to province but also even within cities. Typically, the more senior teacher, **lead teacher, team leader, coach,** or **mentor** is responsible for coordinating the planning and implementing of the daily program. This involves knowing each child and family well and individualizing the program to meet each one's specific needs; responsibility for the physical environment of the classroom, setting up equipment, rotating materials, and ensuring a good match between what is available and the children's skill levels; maintaining records for the children in the class; initiating and maintaining family interactions, both informally at the start and end of each day and formally through conferences or meetings; and facilitating an atmosphere of communication and support with other staff members who work in the class by providing direction, guidance, and feedback.

The Assistant Teacher

In many settings, one or more teachers function in an **assistant teacher** role. Assistants have a variety of titles within a municipality, and the range of titles is greater when you cross provincial and territorial boundaries. Some terms that are used include "auxiliary teacher," "associate teacher," "small-group leader," "aide," and "helper." In the assistant role, the teacher works with the senior teacher to provide a high-quality program for the children in the class and their families. Frequently the assistant has less education and experience than the senior teacher, but this is not always the case. Depending on the assistant's skill level and experience, this teacher may share many of the senior teacher's responsibilities, for instance, participating in curriculum planning, leading large- and small-group activities, being involved in parent interactions, and arranging the environment. Because of the assistant teacher's close working relationship with the senior teacher, open and honest communication and mutual respect are vital between the two. In some schools, an assistant teacher may serve as a floater, moving among classrooms to help with special activities or during specific times of the day.

Some colleges, as we saw in our list of Canadian programs in Chapter 1 (Exhibit 1.2), such as Sheridan College in Ontario, offer an early childhood assistant (ECA) certificate program that runs as a one-year rather than the typical two-year early childhood education program.

Team Teaching

In many settings, the senior teacher position does not exist; teachers work as a team, under the direction of the program supervisor and/or director. Mary Wright's (1983) University of Western Ontario program, for example, had a program director (Wright), who also had teaching responsibilities at the university level, and four highly qualified teachers. One of the teachers was the supervisor of the school, while a second one was the assistant supervisor. The four teachers rotated through four different teaching timetables, one per week, which Wright describes in great detail in her very readable text (Wright, 1983).

The team teaching approach allows each teacher to interact with all the children and to work in all areas of the program. It also maximizes the children's flexibility since each area is supervised by a teacher, allowing the children to move freely from one activity to another. Finally, the teachers experience more variety in their work with this approach, and no one individual is always stuck with the less appealing duties (e.g., paint cleanup and washroom duty).

Volunteers

Some centres use volunteers to help with various aspects of the early childhood program. Volunteers can include parents, student-teachers or interns, members of volunteer organizations, foster grandparents, and other interested community members. To use volunteers most effectively, however, there has to be a well-planned orientation, training, and monitoring component that helps the volunteer understand the program, its philosophy, and its operation. Volunteers, as much as any other component of your program, are a reflection of your program and are advocates for it in the community. They must be as well-versed and as much an integral and equal team member as any paid personnel. Although volunteers can provide a wonderful additional resource to a program, the reality is that volunteers are not as plentiful as the potential need for them.

Support Staff

Depending on the size and scope of the centre, some people usually serve in a support capacity. These might include (although they certainly are not limited to) people involved in food preparation, maintenance, and office management. They, too, are essential and equal team members who must clearly understand the centre's mission statement, program goals, policies and procedures, the principles of inclusion, developmentally appropriate practices, and the key concepts of early childhood education. Support staff are in contact with children and families each day and must reflect and advocate the standards the profession demands. This reflects the true impact of the need for and role of effective communication, team problem-solving skills, solid organizational restructuring, training, evaluation, and accountability. Large programs often have a cook who is in charge of meal preparation, shopping, and sanitation and maintenance of the kitchen. The cook may also plan meals, if that person has an appropriate background in nutrition, or may participate in classroom cooking projects. A dietitian may serve as a consultant to the program to ensure that children's nutritional needs are appropriately met through the program's meals. In smaller programs, particularly those not serving lunch or dinner, the teaching staff or director may take responsibility for snack planning and preparation.

One of the most important yet difficult tasks of any centre serving busy and active young children is maintenance. Daily cleaning, sweeping, vacuuming, sanitizing, and garbage disposal are vital, though usually unpopular, functions. Large programs may have a custodian as part of the staff, whereas others hold contracts with a janitorial service. Often the expense of a maintenance crew or custodian has to be weighed against other important needs, and the teaching staff may find that its responsibilities include many maintenance chores. Most centres compromise by having the staff maintain cleanliness and order, while a cleaning service is responsible for intermittent deep cleaning of the facility.

Other support staff take care of office needs. Large programs often have a secretary who maintains records, answers phone calls, manages typing needs, and may handle some accounting tasks. In smaller programs, such tasks may fall to the director. Some programs may employ a part-time accountant or have a receptionist in addition to the secretary. Programs that are part of or housed with other agencies may share custodial and secretarial staff.

Board of Directors

Particularly in non-profit centres, some type of policymaking governing board holds the ultimate responsibility for the program. This board of trustees or **board of directors** may be a very powerful force, making all pertinent decisions that the director then carries out, or it may be only a nominal group that gives the director responsibility to make these decisions. Ideally, a board of directors' role falls somewhere between these extremes (Sciarra & Dorsey, 1990).

Boards of directors are usually made up of program parents and community members who come from a variety of spheres of expertise and influence, most of which are not likely to be related to early childhood education. It is wise, however, to include one child development expert on the board. The director serves as a liaison, helping the board understand the rationale for decisions made based on child development knowledge, while utilizing the expertise of board members in areas in which the director is not as well versed. Boards can be very effective, for instance, in fiscal management, fundraising, construction and expansion projects, or lobbying for children's rights.

Community Professionals

The resources of a centre can be expanded through other professionals in the larger community, for instance, health and mental health professionals, social

workers, speech pathologists, occupational therapists, and physiotherapists. In some programs, especially those involving subsidized children, families may be referred to the early childhood program by a community agency. In these cases, the program and referring agency frequently work together to maximize the help provided to the child and family. In other cases, the early childhood program may help connect families with community agencies and professionals to provide needed services. It is important for teachers to recognize the "boundaries of their own professional expertise" and know when other professionals need to be consulted (Sciarra & Dorsey, 1990, p. 369).

Coordinating and supporting staff to create an atmosphere of caring is difficult yet rewarding. Effective communication through team problem solving, solid organizational structure, training, and evaluation creates a sense of unity and trust that translates into accountability. Everyone shares in the responsible, professional, and successful operation of the program. In A Canadian Professional Speaks Out, team building and collaboration are expanded upon.

The factors we have discussed—ages of children, purposes of programs, types of programs, and human resources in programs—meld together to form a sound structure within which the daily program can run. But what makes a program a quality program? Before looking in depth at the heart of our day—play, guidance,

A CANADIAN PROFESSIONAL SPEAKS OUT
Team Building and Collaboration

Working directly with preschool and primary children has, without a doubt, been the most deeply satisfying work that I have done in my career as an early childhood educator. This work with children has also involved collaborating with parents and other professionals—to ensure the greatest possible continuity of education and care for the children I served. Though I understood this collaboration to be an essential aspect of my job, I often felt a bit insecure about the role I ought to be playing with parents and other professionals—speech therapists, public health nurses, doctors, and social workers—all of whom invariably spoke with great clarity and authority. They sounded so much more sure of themselves than I ever felt. Often I left interdisciplinary meetings where provisions for an individual child were being discussed feeling, somehow, that I had adequately represented neither the child's needs nor my professional capacity to meet those needs.

It was not until I participated in the New Brunswick Maternal Literacies project that I discovered working with parents and other professionals to be a pleasure comparable to that of working directly with the children. The New Brunswick Maternal Literacies project, a collaborative action research project funded by the Social Sciences and Humanities Research Council under the category of Women and Work, involved primary teachers, mothers, graduate students, and university professors working together over a two-year period to promote positive literacy interchanges between home and school. We wanted in particular to document and honour the literacies that rural mothers teach to their children and to find workable ways to integrate these maternal literacies into schooled literacies.

Our collaborative research involved regular meetings between parents and professionals—just the sort of meetings I had come to dread earlier in my career! But Lissa Paul, my colleague at the University of New Brunswick and a co-investigator in this project, was unconcerned. A feminist scholar of children's literature, she knew how to make room for everyone's voice. We adopted a rotating chair for our meetings; everyone had the opportunity to preside once or twice. We took turns at setting an agenda. We sat in a circle so no one would be "head" of the table. We chose a lounge to meet in rather than a more formal meeting room and determinedly replaced "discussion" with "conversation," respecting no one as the "expert" but honouring the expertise and experience of everyone. We dispensed with formal titles, which might imply a hierarchy. We preserving everyone's dignity, and made sure that no one's viewpoint was privileged, was paramount. Collectively we saw to that. We chatted, gossiped, and laughed our way through our monthly day-long meetings, and at the end of each, without having made a single formal resolution, we always came up with wonderful plans for the coming month. When we parted we felt good about the contributions we had made. And perhaps more importantly, we parted as friends.

When it came to publishing our research, it was Lissa who suggested that teachers, mothers, graduate students, and professors all write from their own perspective, in their own voice. Instead of writing about mothers and teachers, as academics typically do, Lissa and I wrote *with* them (Blake, Christine, Fulton, Gorham, Graham, Kershaw, Leavitt, Nason, and Paul, 1995; Gorham and Nason, 1997). And when we presented papers at academic conferences—the Learneds in Montreal and the Atlantic Educators conference in St. John's—everyone spoke their own part.

These practices enabled me to find my voice, and I now take immense pleasure in collaborating with other adults for the betterment of young children.

Pamela Nuttall Nason, Professor in Early Childhood Education, University of New Brunswick

Sources: Frankie Blake, Maria Christine, Winnifred Fulton, Peter Gorham, Marilyn Graham, Janet Kershaw, Midge Leavitt, Pam Nason, and Lissa Paul (1995), *The Pig's Tale: Exploring Maternal Literacies,* Primary Teaching Studies, University of North London Press, Vol. 9, No. 2; Peter Gorham and Pam Nason (1997), Why Make Teachers' Work More Visible to Parents? *Young Children*, Vol. 52, No. 5.

appropriate practices, and curriculum—as we do in chapters 6 through 9, we must first establish and recognize what factors contribute to the quality of care and, therefore, the well-being of the children we serve. We consider these factors in Chapter 5.

Key Terms

assistant teacher
board of directors
Canada Assistance Plan (CAP)
Canadian National Child Care
    Study (CNCCS)
centre-based programs
change agents
coach
community professionals
directors
entrepreneur
home-based programs
hothousing
human resources
hurried child
infants
infant stimulation programs
integrated curriculum
latch-key
lead teacher
management consultants

mentor
nanny
National Day Care Study (NDCS)
organizational development
organizational structure
parent cooperative
parent-cooperative nursery schools
preschooler
primary children
resource teacher
school age children
self-care children
senior teacher
supervisors
support staff
team teacher
team teaching
toddlers
transdisciplinary team
volunteers
wholistic thinking

Key Points

- The system of early childhood education is a wholistic organizational structure defined by individuals who are connected to it.
- This dynamic system uses communication and relationships to promote the team or partnership and its philosophy.
- The system is affected by historical events, changes in family life, evidence of the benefits of early childhood education, and need for child advocacy.
- The purposes of the programs are to provide safe and nurturing care, enrichment, compensation, parental education, and preservation of cultural traditions and languages.
- Child care in Canada is run by the provinces which administer funds and set legislation and regulations.
- Early childhood education programs include home-based operations, home visitors, and centre-based operations for infants through school age and receive various forms of funding.
- There can be a variety of staffing patterns depending on the type, size, and philosophy of the program as well as its funding source.

Chapter 5

Quality in Early Childhood Programs

Now that we have looked at some program terminology, we will explore the factors that affect the quality of a program and the effects of program quality on the well-being of children. In this chapter, we explore factors of quality care, examine research that supports quality care, and look at how Canada measures up in terms of quality care. We finish by looking at some program models and evidence supporting various types of childhood programs.

Program quality—the impact a program has on children and families—should be examined in terms of how it meets the needs and considers the well-being of children and their families.

Current research is focusing on identifying factors that create good early childhood programming for young children. The old question "Is child care necessary?" is now obsolete. Close to 2.5 million Canadian children are in some form of care (see Exhibit 4.1). Knowing this fact, and knowing too that critical development occurs in the early years, today's researchers try to find out how to make child care better for young children (Phillips, 1987). The emerging picture

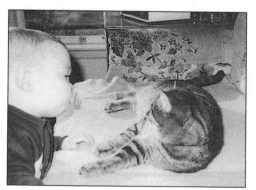

tells us that quality in child care is not dependent on single, separable factors but is a result of the presence and interaction among a variety of complex elements (Clarke-Stewart, 1987a). A landmark publication by Canadian educator Gillian Doherty-Derkowski, entitled *Quality Matters* (1995), outlines and emphasizes many critical factors and research studies related to quality in child care. Her emphasis focuses on the quality of the interactions and the interrelationships among factors. In the areas of language, play, social skills, behaviour, and academics, not only do quality programs have positive effects

on children, but also poor or low-quality programs have severe and often irreversible effects that cannot be compensated for by the home or school (Doherty-Derkowski, 1995). Doherty-Derkowski points out that

> until recently, recommended practice for early childhood programs was based on theory and the informed opinion of practitioners with years of experience. Reviews of research have concluded there is now sufficient consistency in the findings to reliably identify the components of early childhood programs that are associated with child well-being and development. As a result, we can confidently say we *know* what is required, not merely that we *think* that such and such is necessary for quality in early childhood programs. (Doherty-Kerkowski, 1995, p. 151)

Of course, as a student with interest in the field, you will be pleased to know that teacher training, including the knowledge you acquire in your courses, has been identified as one of the factors that lead to better teaching, as you will see below.

Factors Affecting Quality

Developmental Appropriateness of the Program

Child development theory and research have given us a good understanding of what young children are like and under what conditions they thrive and learn best. From such information, we are able to plan environments, develop activities, provide materials, and set expectations that match children's needs and characteristics (Bredekamp, 1987). This concept was formally articulated in the National Association for the Education of Young Children's publication *Developmentally Appropriate Practice in Early Childhood Programs Serving Children from Birth through Age 8* (Bredekamp, 1987; 1997). We will continue to focus on developmentally appropriate practice in upcoming chapters.

In recent years, there has been increasing concern that public education is not adequately preparing children for the challenges of the future. This concern, expressed by those in the **back-to-basics movement**, has led to a push to return to "the basics" in education. Some have interpreted this to include young children, with the idea that an earlier introduction to academics will result

in better-prepared and better-educated children. Early childhood professionals and researchers have expressed grave apprehensions about this trend, aptly termed "hothousing," which pushes preschoolers into inappropriate tasks for which they are not developmentally ready (Gallagher & Coche, 1987). Young children can learn a lot of material in a mechanistic, rote manner, but if these experiences are meaningless, such information has little relevance (Sigel, 1987). Thus, for an early childhood program to meet quality criteria, it must respect the emerging abilities of young children without imposing inappropriate expectations.

Teacher Qualifications

Research has given us some indication about the type of teachers who are most likely to provide a high-quality early childhood program. The National Day Care Study (Ruopp, Travers, Glantz, & Coelen, 1979) found a significant variable to be staff with *specific training in early childhood education and development*. Such teachers engaged in more interactions with the children, and the children showed greater social and cognitive abilities compared with those whose teachers lacked such training. These findings, particularly in relation to children's more advanced cognitive and language ability, have been supported in other research (Clarke-Stewart, 1987a; Clarke-Stewart & Gruber, 1984; Howes, 1983). In addition, teachers with early childhood training were rated as more positive and less punitive, employing a less authoritarian style of interaction with the children (Arnett, 1987). Furthermore, teachers who understand child development are more readily able to plan an environment that promotes and guides children's development in a play-based curriculum.

Given our understanding of relationships and systems theory, *all* persons who are concerned with the care of the children, and who interact regularly with them, need to be fully trained and versed in the policies and procedures of the centre as well as be made to feel integral and valued members of the team. It makes no sense to educate only the teachers since teachers do not work in isolation and since everyone concerned is working toward the same goal—quality care for the child.

Adult–Child Interaction

Although many factors contribute to the quality of an early childhood program, perhaps the most important factor is the interaction between the adults and the children. In a good program, all adults, regardless of their role at the centre, are involved with children. They are nurturing and responsive, there is ample verbal exchange, and interactions aim to teach, not just to control (Clarke-Stewart, 1987a). A wonderful physical facility, an exemplary teacher–child ratio, and a favourable group size would all be negated by uncaring and unresponsive adult–child interaction. It is, after all, the teachers and other adults who determine the tone and the character, in effect, the quality, of a program.

Teacher Consistency

A serious concern among professionals and parents alike is the high rate of staff turnover in early childhood programs. The low wages of professionals in the field, documented by a current Canadian study, *Caring for a Living* (Canadian Child Day Care Federation [CCDCF], 1992), have been identified as a significant factor in this turnover. Nevertheless, many young children spend the bulk of their waking hours in child care, with adults other than their parents, and consistency in caregivers is important. One important task of the early years is forming a secure attachment relationship to adults. Although primary attachment is with parents, research has shown that young children certainly do become attached to their teachers and the other adults in their lives. When children lose a teacher or adult with whom they have formed such an attachment, the loss can be profound (Phillips & Howes, 1987).

One study found that there is less teacher–child interaction in centres with a high teacher-turnover rate (Phillips, Scarr, & McCartney 1987). This is not surprising when interaction is dependent in part on establishing a relationship, something that takes time to develop. In general, research supports the finding that children seem to be better adjusted, less dependent, less anxious, and more sociable in programs with a low staff-turnover rate (Clarke-Stewart, 1987a).

Adult–Child Ratio

It has generally been assumed that when caregivers are responsible for large numbers of children, the quality of care is affected adversely. A number of studies have addressed this assumption and found that the ratio significantly affects children's behaviour and teacher–child interactions (Phillips & Howes, 1987).

Ratio is a concept that many people have difficulty understanding. A *high* **adult–child ratio** means there are fewer children per adult, while a *low* adult–child ratio means there are more children per adult.

Researchers have found that when there is a low ratio (larger numbers of children per adult), there is less verbal interaction among adults and children than when the adult–child ratio is higher. Conversations are brief and routine and contain more prohibitions (Smith & Connolly, 1981). A significant factor in providing quality care has to do with giving children individualized attention and confirming their unique identity and worth as individuals. When an adult is responsible for a large number of children, that adult is less able to provide such attention and more concerned instead with controlling and managing the group.

What is an appropriate teacher–child ratio? There is no definitive answer although there are some suggested guidelines. The recent *National Statement on Quality Child Care* (Canadian Child Day Care Federation, 1991), developed by experts from across the country, has suggested guidelines for teacher–child ratios and **group size** for centre-based programs. Keep in mind, however, that teacher–child ratio is one variable that interacts with other factors, such as group size and teacher qualifications. "We should avoid blanket statements about high teacher–child ratios being good and low ratios being bad until we check out the *limits* beyond which a low ratio is bad and the *outcome* for which a high ratio is good" (Clarke-Stewart, 1987a, p. 114).

Group Size

In the late 1970s, the large-scale U.S. National Day Care Study (Ruopp et al., 1979) published its findings, and Canadians have found the report quite relevant to our early childhood programs. The study showed that group size was one of two consistently important variables that define quality of care for young children. In smaller groups, children were more cooperative, innovative, and verbal; they showed less hostility and conflict than children in larger groups; and they made greater gains over time on cognitive and language tests. The correlation between test gains and group size was particularly marked in centres serving low-income children. Children in smaller groups were also less likely to be uninvolved in activities and to be observed wandering aimlessly. Furthermore, teachers in smaller groups spent more time interacting with children and less time in detached observation. Another study found more elaborate play, including more pretend play, among children in smaller rather than larger groups (Bruner, 1980). One recent study summarized that with a moderate number of children in a group, children seem to demonstrate greater social competence (Clarke-Stewart, 1987b). When teachers are in charge of large groups of children, on the other hand, they tend to be less responsive to the children, and they provide less social stimulation (Howes, 1983). As group size increases beyond 18 children, teachers spend more time in management activities and show a marked increase in the time they spend passively observing activities and interactions (Ruopp et al., 1979).

Ideal group size cannot really be defined because other variables, including the parameters of the physical environment, need to be considered. The recommended group size varies across Canada with the age of the children.

Mixed-Age Grouping

Only in relatively recent times has our society stratified children into narrow groups defined by age, particularly in the educational context. "Although humans are not usually born in litters, we seem to insist that they be educated in them" (Katz, Evangelou, & Hartman, 1990, p. viii). Many theorists and researchers have expressed concern about the increasing separation of people into age-segregated groups in education, housing, recreation, work, and other aspects of life (Bronfenbrenner, 1971). It is more natural, they say, that people of all ages interact and share various aspects of their lives. Throughout history, socialization was facilitated because people of all ages learned from and helped one another.

Early childhood education programs are also often segregated into narrow, homogeneous age groups, with the 3-year-olds in one class, 4-year-olds across the hall in another, and the mature 5-year-olds in their own environment. But many educators suggest that heterogeneous or **mixed-age grouping** will benefit both younger and older children. Positive social behaviours such as sharing, turn-taking, and helpfulness are encouraged in mixed-age groups. Similarly, older children have more opportunities to practise leadership skills, and young children become involved in more complex forms of pretend play. Children also appear to reap cognitive benefits from mixed-age grouping (Katz, Evangelou, & Hartman, 1990). In addition, children in some mixed-age settings stay with the same teacher for several years, and this stability can be reassuring. Recently, a few public schools have been organizing mixed-age classes at the primary level, and teachers in those classes talk enthusiastically about the experience. However, other teachers, accustomed to single-age classes, pale at the suggestion that mixed-age classes may become more common.

As we have already mentioned, quality in early childhood programs depends on many factors. There are certainly many outstanding, high-quality programs in which children are grouped by narrow age criteria; other equally good programs utilize a mixed-age model. Nonetheless, research suggests that children receive some unique benefits from being placed in groups that contain a wider age range of children. For this reason, mixed-age grouping is included as a criterion of quality.

Physical Environment

The physical facility is another important factor that contributes to program quality. According to research, children demonstrate higher cognitive skill levels and greater social competence in schools that are safe and orderly, contain a wide variety of stimulating equipment and materials, and are organized into learning centres on the basis of similar materials and activities when compared with children in schools that lack these features (Clarke-Stewart, 1987b).

A child-oriented environment conveys to children that this place is meant for them. There are interesting and worthwhile things to do in a child-oriented environment because it was designed with the characteristics, ages, and abilities of the children in mind. A child-centred environment also requires fewer restrictions and prohibitions because it was fashioned specifically for children. This helps to create a positive and pleasant atmosphere. In short, a good environment conveys to children that this is a good place to be, that people here care about them, that they are able to satisfy their innate curiosity and desire to learn, and that it is safe to engage in activities without fear of failure.

Family Involvement

With increasing numbers of children spending many hours per day in child care, parents and teachers, more than ever before, are partners in many aspects of child rearing and socialization. Studies have shown that the children benefit when parents and the early childhood staff share a common commitment to acting in the best interests of the children, communicate openly, and have mutual respect. On the other hand, if there is a lack of communication so that parents do not know what happened at school and teachers are not informed of significant events in the child's home life, there is lack of continuity for the child. This home–school link is explored throughout this text.

Respect and Concern for Teachers

As we have discussed, a nurturing, well-trained, and consistent staff is important to a quality program, but a concern for the well-being of the teaching staff is also needed. Working with young children is a demanding, challenging job. Thus, it is in the best interests of the children, the families, and the employer if staff members receive appropriate pay and benefits and work in a satisfying environment. In such a setting, the needs of the staff are seriously considered, an atmosphere of camaraderie is fostered, autonomy is encouraged in planning an appropriate program for the children, and the physical environment includes space for adults (Jorde-Bloom, 1988).

Quality as a Combination of Factors

For the purposes of discussion, we have isolated a number of components that contribute to quality early childhood programming, including teacher–child ratio, group size, teacher qualifications, mixed-age grouping, developmental appropriateness of the program, teacher–child interaction, staff consistency, concern for staff, the physical environment, and family involvement. It is important to keep in mind, however, that quality can best be understood and studied as a combination of components (Phillips, 1987). As you further your understanding and knowledge of the field of early childhood education, remember that quality is not defined by a single factor, but rather depends on the complex interaction of a variety of elements in which you, as an early childhood professional, play a key role.

How Does Canada Measure Up Regarding Quality?

In April 1996, the Liberal government ended the Canada Assistance Plan established in 1966 to subsidize child care for children of low-income families. The Liberals campaigned in 1993 for a national child care program that would create 150 000 new child care spaces. To date, the program does not exist. In 1988, the Conservative Party had promised 200 000 new spaces and a Canadian Federal Child Care Act. These policies were never enacted.

The provinces have fared little better. In 1996, Ontario's Conservatives cut subsidized child care spaces by 2800, stating that parents needed to rely on informal care methods from relatives, neighbours, friends, or strangers. Given what we have learned about the changing family form, needs of parents for child care, and the changing economy, it is unrealistic to expect parents to find anyone to stay home to care for their children or to afford the true fee of an unsubsidized quality program. This government also proposed changes to the Day Nursery Act that would lower teacher training qualifications and increase the number of children per teacher. We know that this would have serious ramifications on quality care. As Varga (1997) states:

> In a private system, parents as individuals would be wholly responsible for determining the quality of child care purchased including having to know about standards of care, safety issues, caregiver qualifications and the child care curriculum. This is an unreasonable expectation. In the history of private sector nursery care, improved quality and increased quantity have only occurred when, through the public sector, there have been financial supports for such initiatives. (p. 139)

Varga warns about the return to philanthropy that we discussed in Chapter 1. Providing child care for good will and low pay results in children and caregivers becoming exploited and devalued under legislation that reduces standards of care (Varga, 1997). Looking at our current situation, ratios and group-size legislation in most provinces fall within the ranges research suggests. However, without funding it is difficult to uphold the legislation in some areas. Again, the issues of low wages, teacher training, consistency, and ratios emerge, strongly reinforcing the urgency for professional status and recognition of early childhood education as a vital field.

Here we examine those quality factors that are regulated by province—adult–child ratios, group size, teacher qualifications, and the physical environment (e.g., centre size, space recommendations). The other issues of quality that are not legislated, such as teacher pay, teacher consistency, and teacher turnover, are often direct results of poor legislation in the other areas.

Current Practices and Future Directions

There are many differences in the history of early childhood education across Canada. (See Progression, the final chapter of this text, which looks at the history of each province in depth.) Some of these variations in early childhood programs reflect the sociogeographical and political differences that mark the country. For example, the have-not provinces generally have been slower to fund programs. However, that is not always the case. Alberta, for example, despite its wealth, was most reluctant to acknowledge early childhood education as a provincial respon-

sibility. If it were not for the persistent demands of professionals, parents, and other advocates for regulations and training, that province would likely still be without legislation.

In some jurisdictions, early childhood programs have been available for over a century, while they are quite recent developments in others. The provinces with more progressive legislation (e.g., Manitoba) generally have had early childhood programs in place for a long time. This lengthy history generally leads to higher standards for teacher education. In addition, the regulations for early childhood programs differ greatly between jurisdictions, and sometimes even within them. Nevertheless, at least every province and territory now has some form of regulation. However, professionals in the field will have to continue to advocate uniform national standards for early childhood programs.

Teacher–Child Ratios, Group Size, and Centre Size

The research on quality in early childhood programs points to teacher–child ratios and group size as important variables in defining high-quality programs. The specific group and centre sizes and the teacher–child ratios for each Canadian jurisdiction are discussed below. Legislative definitions of terms like "infant," "toddler," and "preschooler" vary across the country, but some generalizations are possible. Exhibit 5.1 summarizes the name of the legal documents that legislate these variables in each province. The legislation does not ensure the best ratios and the most favourable group sizes throughout the country. Exhibit 5.2 tells us that group size is still not regulated in Nova Scotia, Newfoundland, and Yukon. The required teacher–child ratios in some locations are also quite low. The regulations on teacher–child ratios, group size, and centre size are anything but consistent across the country. Exhibit 5.3 outlines the teacher–child ratios recommended in the *National Statement on Quality Child Care* (Canadian Child Day Care Federation, 1991). If you look at Exhibit 5.4, you will see that only 5 of 12 jurisdictions conform to the recommendations for infants.

The situation is not much better for Canadian toddlers. As Exhibit 5.5 shows, in some locations the regulated group size is two to three times greater than the recommended size. Similarly, the teacher–child ratios are twice as high as those suggested in the *National Statement on Quality Child Care*. The teacher–child ratios specified in the regulations for 3- to 5-year-olds (see Exhibit 5.6) are closer to those being advocated in most areas, but the regulated group sizes are considerably higher in a number of provinces. Moreover, group size, which has such a pronounced impact on the quality of care, is still not regulated at all in Nova Scotia and the Yukon.

When you study Exhibit 5.7, you will have comparable concerns about the ratios and group sizes for children who are 5 years and older.

Inspection procedures and the regulations related to the physical facility are highly variable across the country. For example, there is a wide range of requirements regarding the actual amount of space each child needs. You may wonder why 2.75 m^2 is adequate indoor space in some provinces (see Exhibit 5.8), while other provinces require 5 m^2 per child. The situation is comparable for outdoor space.

While we have made great strides in improving the quality of licensed early childhood programs in the country, especially with the advent of CAP in 1966 and the wider availability of licensed child care that accompanied CAP funding, our regulations still have a distance to go. This is especially true now with the cessation of CAP funding and the current economical and political stresses placed on the Canadian family, leading to a greater need for quality child care. Advocates for young children across the country continue to express their concern about this failure to provide the optimum environment for young children.

Teacher Training

The research we discussed found that teacher training and knowledge of child development were excellent predictors of high-quality care. However, the Canadian legislation governing child care does not consistently reflect this research finding, you'll recall. Exhibit 1.2 in Chapter 1 summarized the regulation of teacher qualifications and the availability of training programs in the country.

In A Canadian Professional Speaks Out you will learn about the current regulations on teacher education in Newfoundland. Of course, the regulation of teacher qualifications and the availability of programs are closely related. In some locations (e.g., British Columbia, Manitoba, and Prince Edward Island), changes in legislation seem to have stimulated the provision of ECE training programs on a broader basis. In other locations (e g , Alberta and Quebec), teacher training programs have pre-dated legislation by a number of years. In these latter cases, a lengthy history of governmental reluctance, if not outright opposition, to be involved in child care seems to have been a factor in the long wait for legislation. In yet other locations like Newfoundland, the Yukon, and the Northwest Territories, however, programs did not become "readily available" until the late 1980s—and "readily available" programs in these locations may still be thousands of kilometres away. These jurisdictions have been reluctant to implement training requirements when local programs have just recently become available. Presumably, initiatives like those seen in Manitoba, coupled with a gradual phasing in of teacher training requirements, would encourage the maximum number of individuals to enrol in the courses.

EXHIBIT 5.1: LEGISLATIVE DOCUMENTS OUTLINING PROVINCIAL AND TERRITORIAL CHILD CARE REGULATIONS

Province/ Territory	Acts and Regulations
Yukon	**Child Care Act** (Statutes of the Yukon). 1990. **Child Care Centre Program Regulations,** Order-in-Council, 1990/115 (pursuant to section 40 of the Child Care Act). **Child Care Subsidy Regulations,** Order-in-Council, 1990/116 (pursuant to section 40 of the Child Care Act). **Family Day Home Program Regulations,** Order-in-Council, 1990/117 (pursuant to section 40 of the Child Care Act). **Child Care Act: School-Age Program Regulations,** May 18, 1995.
Northwest Territories	**Child Day Care Act**, 1987 (1), C.13 (as amended by S1-101-87 (1), C.13). **Child Day Care Standards Regulations**, 1987 (pursuant to subsection 39(1) of the Child Day Care Act).
British Columbia	**Community Care Facility Act,** Chapter 57, 1979. **Community Care Facility Act: Child Care Regulation,** Reg. 319/89, O.C.1476/89. **Guaranteed Available Income for Need Act,** R.S. Chapter 158, 1979. **Guaranteed Available Income for Need Act Regulations,** 1989.
Alberta	**Social Care Facilities Licensing Act, 1980**. **Day Care Regulation. Alberta Regulation 333/90.** This regulation refers only to the care of children under 7 years of age.
Saskatchewan	**The Child Care Act,** Chapter C-73 1989, (An Act to Promote the Growth and Development of Children and to Support the Provision of Child Care Services to Saskatchewan Families). **The Child Care Regulations 948/90,** Chapter C-73 Reg. 1 Section 27.
Manitoba	**The Community Child Day Care Standards Act,** Chapter C158 of L.R.M., 1987. **Manitoba Regulation 62/86.**
Ontario	**Day Nurseries Act, Regulation 262,** general (R.R.O. 1990, Reg. 262), March 1993. This legislation and regulation refers only to the care of children under 10 years of age, except for children with special needs who are covered from 2 years of age up to 18 years of age. **Ministry of Community and Social Services Act,** 1980. **Child and Family Services Act,** 1984. **Health Promotion and Protection Act,** 1989.
Quebec	**Act Respecting Child Day Care,** R.S.Q., Chapter 5-4.1 as amended October 1992. **Regulation Respecting Child Day Care Centres,** S-4.1, R.2 amended October 1991.
New Brunswick	**Family Services Act,** Chapter C-2.1, Part II Community Placement Resources, 1983.

Province/ Territory	Acts and Regulations
	Family Services Act Regulation 83–85, under Family Services Act O.C. 83–457 (consolidated to June 30, 1985). **Day Care Facilities Standards.** Department of Health and Community Services, June 1, 1985.
Nova Scotia	**Day Care Act and Regulations,** (Chapter 120 of the revised statutes, 1989), 1990. This legislation and regulations have been consolidated and revised from the Day Care Services Act and the Day Nurseries Act. The short title of this act is **Day Care Act,** 1978, c.6, s.1.
Prince Edward Island	**Child Care Facilities Act**, R.S.P.E.I., 1988, Cap. C-5. **Child Care Facilities Act: Regulations,** R.S.P.E.I., 1988, Cap. C-5 (incl. any amendments to December 31, 1990).
Newfoundland and Labrador	**The Day Care and Homemaker Services Act,** R.S.N., 1990. **The Day Care and Homemaker Services Regulations,** Newfoundland Regulations 219/82, 1982 (under The Day Care and Homemakers Services Act, 1975).

Source: Canadian Child Care Federation, 306–120 Holland, Ottawa, ON K1Y 0X6. Reprinted with permission.

EXHIBIT 5.2: LEGISLATION OF CHILD CARE, AND COVERAGE OF RATIOS AND GROUP SIZE IN THE CURRENT REGULATIONS

Province or Territory	Date of First Legislation	Are Ratios Regulated?	Is Group Size Regulated?
B.C.	1937	Yes	Yes
Alta.	1978	Yes	Yes
Sask.	1969	Yes	Yes
Man.	1982	Yes	Yes
Ont.	1946	Yes	Yes
Que.	1979	Yes	Yes
N.B.	1974	Yes	Yes
P.E.I.	1973	Yes	Yes
N.S.	1967	Yes	—
Nfld.	1975	Yes	—
Yukon	1975	Yes	—
N.W.T.	1988	Yes	Yes

— No regulations in place in 1996

Sources: Cairns et al. (1992b); Child Care (1990, 1993); Desjardins (1992); Friesen et al. (1992b); Gamble (1992a); Glassman (1992a); Irwin & Canning (1992b); Kyle (1992b); McDonell (1992); Nykyforuk (1992a); Read et al. (1992); Stapleford (1976); Young (1981, 1993b).

EXHIBIT 5.3: RECOMMENDATIONS FOR TEACHER–CHILD RATIOS WITHIN DIFFERENT GROUP SIZES

Group Size	Age						
	0–12 Months	12–24 Months	2 Years	3 Years	4–5 Years	5–6 Years	6–9 Years
6	1:3	1:3					
8		1:4	1:4				
10			1:5	1:5			
12				1:6			
14				1:7			
16					1:8	1:8	
18					1:9	1:9	
20							1:10
22							1:11
24							1:12

1. In mixed-age groupings, the teacher–child ratio and group size should be based on the age of the majority of children in the group. However, if there are infants, ratios and group sizes for infants should be maintained at all times.
2. The ratios assume that the teachers are full time in the program. If they have other duties such as administration or parent interviewing, an additional teacher should be present to maintain the ratios.

Source: Canadian Child Day Care Federation (1991), *National Statement on Quality Child Care* (p. 9) (Ottawa: Canadian Child Day Care Federation).

Exhibit 5.9 shows the types of available training programs and the legislative requirements for knowledge of child development and experience. By 1989, teacher education programs were in place in all of Canada, but some jurisdictions still do not require teachers to be trained. Furthermore, many do not require knowledge of child development.

You probably are surprised, especially as a student in the field, to see in Exhibit 5.9 that 5 of 12 Canadian jurisdictions do not require teachers to be knowledgeable about child development, despite the available research. Moreover, the failure of many legislators to recognize the value of experience is a concern. In three

EXHIBIT 5.4: TEACHER–CHILD RATIOS AND GROUP SIZE FOR CENTRE-BASED CARE, BREAKDOWN BY PROVINCE FOR INFANTS

Province or Territory	Ratios for Infants	Group Size	Centre Size
B.C.	1:4	12	36
Alta.	2:6[1]–2:8	6[1]–8	80
Sask.	1:3	6	90
Man.	1:3[1]–1:4	6[1]–8	70
Ont.	3:10	10	NA
Que.	1:5	15	60
N.B.	1:3	9	60
P.E.I.	1:3	6	50
N.S.	1:4[2]	25	50
Nfld.	NA	NA	50
Yukon	1:4	NA	NA
N.W.T.	1:3[1]–1:4	6[1]–8	30

In 7 of the 12 provinces and territories, infants are defined as being between 0 and 18 months of age.

1. Infants under 12 months
2. Recommended, not yet legislated
NA = Not applicable

Sources: Cairns et al. (1992b); Child Care (1990, 1993); Desjardins (1992); Friesen et al. (1992b); Gamble (1992a); Glassman (1992a); Irwin & Canning (1992b); Kyle (1992b); McDonell (1992); Nykyforuk (1992a); Read et al. (1992); Stapleford (1976); Young (1981, 1993b).

jurisdictions, no one in an early childhood education program has to be experienced in the field. In another three provinces, only the supervisor has to have experience in the field. While the supervisor is important in a program, quite frequently she or he spends a large proportion of time doing administrative tasks and relatively little time in direct contact with the children. Clearly, we still have to make a number of changes in our legislation if we want high-quality programs to be the norm in this country.

Scope of Licensed Child Care and Parental Needs

Another challenge emerged when we looked in Chapter 4 at the number of licensed child care spaces in Canada versus the need parents had for care (National Child Care, 1991; Pence et al., 1992). The number of spaces available is small compared with the number of newborns to 9-year-olds requiring some form of

EXHIBIT 5.5: TEACHER–CHILD RATIOS AND GROUP SIZE FOR CENTRE-BASED CARE, BREAKDOWN BY PROVINCE FOR TODDLERS

Province or Territory	Ratios for Toddlers	Group Size	Centre Size
B.C.	1:4	12	36
Alta.	1:4–1:6	8–12	80
Sask.	1:5–1:10	10–20	90
Man.	1:4–1:6	8–12	70
Ont.	1:5–1:8	15–16	NA
P.Q.	1:8	30	60
N.B.	1:3–1:5	30	60
P.E.I.	1:3–1:5	9–10	50
N.S.	1:7	NA	60
Nfld.	1:6	NA	50
Yukon	1:6	NA	NA
N.W.T.	1:4–1:6	8–12	30

Canadians seem to have difficulty with the term "toddler." There are three definitions across nine jurisdictions, and another four jurisdictions avoid the term. We will use the most common definition: toddlers range from 19 to 35 months of age. When there are several entries in a column, it is because that jurisdiction has cutoffs that do not conform to the definitions.

NA = Not applicable

Sources: Cairns et al. (1992b); Child Care (1990, 1993); Desjardins (1992); Friesen et al. (1992b); Gamble (1992a); Glassman (1992a); Irwin & Canning (1992b); Kyle (1992b); McDonell (1992); Nykyforuk (1992a); Read et al. (1992); Stapleford (1976); Young (1981, 1993b).

care, as the CNCCS demonstrated. Nonetheless, even more Canadian children are expected to need care in the future. As we approach the year 2000, with more women entering the workforce, whether by choice or necessity, fewer children will be cared for at home. A corresponding increase in the availability of licensed programs would be welcome, but a national child care policy may be required before we see more readily available licensed early childhood education programs and fewer latch-key children in this country. While licensed care is expensive, many parents want the assurances that licensing

EXHIBIT 5.6: TEACHER–CHILD RATIOS AND GROUP SIZE FOR CENTRE-BASED CARE, BREAKDOWN BY PROVINCE FOR CHILDREN 3 TO 5 YEARS

Province or Territory	Ratios for 3- to 5-Year-Olds	Group Size	Centre Size
B.C.	1:8–1:10	20–25	60–75
Alta.	1:8–1:10	60–20	80
Sask.	1:10	20	90
Man.	1:8–1:10	16–20	70
Ont.	1:8	16	NA
Que.	1:15	30	60
N.B.	1:7–1:12	20–24	60
P.E.I.	1:10	30	50
N.S.	1:7	NA	60
Nfld.	1:8	NA	50
Yukon	1:8	NA	NA
N.W.T.	1:8–1:9	16–18	30

Some jurisdictions have different requirements for children of the same age, depending on the type of facility they attend.

NA = Not applicable

Sources: Cairns et al. (1992b); Child Care (1990, 1993); Desjardins (1992); Friesen et al. (1992b); Gamble (1992a); Glassman (1992a); Irwin & Canning (1992b); Kyle (1992b); McDonell (1992); Nykyforuk (1992a); Read et al. (1992); Stapleford (1976); Young (1981, 1993b).

brings with it. They know that a licensed program in a centre or home is inspected and must conform to a set of regulations. They want some guarantee that their children are receiving high-quality care and education while they work. And they do not want to spend their time at work worrying about the well-being of their children.

The *National Statement on Quality Child Care* (Canadian Child Day Care Federation, 1991) sees child care as a partnership among parents, professionals (and their associations), training institutions, and all levels of government. That statement provides an outline of the role government should play in child care in this country. Government:

- encourages a variety of flexible delivery models to meet the diverse needs of families;
- recognizes current research and social policy issues as the foundation on which licensing standards are built;

EXHIBIT 5.7: TEACHER–CHILD RATIOS AND GROUP SIZE FOR CENTRE-BASED CARE, BREAKDOWN BY PROVINCE FOR CHILDREN 5 YEARS AND OLDER

Province or Territory	Ratios for over 5-Year-Olds	Group Size	Centre Size
B.C.	1:10–1:15	20–25	60–75
Alta.	NA	NA	80
Sask.	1:10–1:15	20–30	90
Man.	1:10–1:15	20–30	70
Ont.	1:12–1:15	24–30	NA
Que.	1:15–1:20	NA	60
N.B.	1:12–1:15	24–30	60
P.E.I.	1:12–1:15	36 & NA	50
N.S.	1:15	NA	60
Nfld.	1:15	25	50
Yukon	1:8 & NA	NA	NA
N.W.T.	1:10	20	30

Some jurisdictions have different requirements for children of the same age, depending on the type of facility they attend.

NA = Not applicable

Sources: Cairns et al. (1992b); Child Care (1990, 1993); Desjardins (1992); Friesen et al. (1992b); Gamble (1992a); Glassman (1992a); Irwin & Canning (1992b); Kyle (1992b); McDonell (1992); Nykyforuk (1992a); Read et al. (1992); Stapleford (1976); Young (1981, 1993b).

- employs individuals within the licensing body who have completed recognized advanced professional training and experience related specifically to the field;
- provides information to enable parents to make meaningful choices regarding quality care;
- ensures that quality care is accessible and affordable; and
- coordinates various departments and levels at the municipal, regional, provincial/territorial, and national levels to ensure quality child care (p. 15).

In light of the current state of affairs in Canada, which you have considered in this chapter, it would be difficult not to conclude that governments at all levels have a major challenge ahead if they hope to meet these objectives. As professionals entering the field, you will have to keep legislators reminded of and concerned about these objectives. In Partnerships, we examine the question What do we know about quality care?

EXHIBIT 5.8: SUMMARY OF SPACE REQUIREMENTS FOR CHILD CARE SETTINGS IN CANADA

Province or Territory	Indoor Space	Outdoor Space
B.C.	3.7 m²	7 m²
Ont.	5 m²	5.6 m² & fence
Alta.	3 m²	fence & 2 m² <19 months, 4.5 m² >19 months
Man.	3.3 m²	7 m² & fence
Sask.	3.7 m²—infants 3.25 m²	7 m²
Que.	2.75 m²	4 m² & fence
N.B.	3.25 m²	fenced & drained
N.S.	2.75 m²	5.46 m² & fence
P.E.I.	3.5 m²	7 m² or park near
Nfld.	3.3 m²	drained & safe
Yukon	4 m²	5 m², fenced & drained
N.W.T.	2.75 m²	5 m²

Source: Young (1993b).

Program Models

Quality is not defined by a specific program model, but models give us a base from which to identify and measure various aspects of quality. We also need to discuss quality in relation to the range of program models available to parents. In subsequent chapters we will look more closely at the core components that guide programming. How we approach the education and care of young children depends, to a great extent, on our beliefs about children. Programs for preschoolers are often structured around some underlying assumptions about the nature of children. For instance, a belief that children learn actively by exploring their environment would result in a different type of early education program than one based on the idea that children learn passively by being taught specific information and skills. Similarly, a belief that children are basically unruly and need strict control would result in a different approach than the notion that children generally strive toward social acceptance.

A number of **early childhood education program models** founded on particular theoretical perspectives have emerged over the years. These program

EXHIBIT 5.9: SUMMARY OF TEACHER EDUCATION PROGRAMS IN CANADA

Province or Territory	One-Year and/or Two-year Certificate Available	Degrees Available	Knowledge of Child Development Required	Experience Required
B.C.	both	yes	1 teacher per group & supervisor	supervisor & 1 teacher per group
Alta.	both	yes	supervisor & 1 of 6 teachers	supervisor & 1 of 4 teachers by 1993
Sask.	both	yes	supervisor	supervisor only
Man.	both	yes	supervisor and 1/2–2/3 of the staff	supervisor
Ont.	two-year only	yes	1 teacher per group & supervisor	supervisor & 1 teacher per group
Que.	both	yes	1/3 of the staff	1/3 of the staff
N.B.	both	yes	none required	none required
P.E.I.	two-year only	no	supervisor & 1 teacher	supervisor
N.S.	both	yes	supervisor & 2/3 of the staff	supervisor & 2/3 of the staff
Nfld.	both	yes	supervisor	supervisor & 1 teacher per 25 children
Yukon	two-year with distance education	no	none required	none required
N.W.T.	both	no	none required	none required

Source: Young (1993b).

models describe typical goals, materials, roles, and schedules, and they often specify a particular theoretical stance (e.g., behaviourist, maturationist). Some models are quite specific about the role of teachers, children, and parents in the program, while others are less rigid.

There was a great proliferation of early childhood models in the 1960s and 1970s when educators and researchers were encouraged (and funded) to develop alternative approaches for **Head Start** programs. Most of these models were designed to examine different ways of

A CANADIAN PROFESSIONAL SPEAKS OUT
Current Regulations on Teacher Education in Newfoundland

An exciting new initiative in the province of Newfoundland and Labrador is the development of a certification process for all staff of licensed centres, accompanied by an individualized program of study toward the diploma in early childhood education. This is a joint venture of the Department of Social Services as the licensing body, the Department of Education, which approves curriculum, and the College of the North Atlantic (formerly Cabot College of Applied Arts, Technology and Continuing Education) as the lead institute that is developing the provincially approved curriculum into distance education, including summer institutes. Primary funding for this initiative has been provided by the Child Care Initiatives fund, Health and Welfare Canada.

It was recognized several years ago that there were approximately 450 to 500 practising early childhood educators, of whom only a small percentage had formal training. The diploma program is offered on-site in two locations within the province for full-time studies. Evening courses had been tried unsuccessfully due to the cost-recoverable nature of these offerings. Limited access to training led to this program design in order to address the vast geographic distances that exist between communities. Training through distance education methodologies makes it accessible, and quality is built in through qualified advisers/tutors, regular performance evaluation, and summer institutes for practical and group work. Participants are able to continue their employment and upgrade at their own pace toward certification levels that recognize various levels of academic education.

A challenging component of this program is to evaluate each participant's experiential learning in order to award advanced standing in their studies. Participants develop a comprehensive portfolio through a credit course, documenting their learning, which is further verified by identified individuals and through a performance evaluation. This enables participants to begin their studies in areas they need to work on and to avoid repeating learning in areas in which they can already demonstrate competence.

Until now the legislation governing certification has not been enforceable due to the absence of accessible training. This initiative is viewed as having widespread significance in upgrading the quality of existing service delivery. Supervisors and lead staff of centres will be prioritized as having to meet certification standards. Provincial orientation courses will become available for those not wanting to pursue lead positions within a centre and will satisfy entry level certification. As the pool of qualified individuals grows throughout various regions within the province, others in training will gain the benefits of qualified advisers and field supervisors in their communities. It is also anticipated that education and certification will lead to a greater sense of professionalism within the field and greater public awareness of the importance of quality child care.

Joanne Morris, College of the North Atlantic, St. John's

PARTNERSHIPS
What Do We Know about the Quality of Child Care?

Parallelling Canada's release of *Quality Matters* (Doherty-Derkowski, 1995), as discussed throughout this chapter, a recent report entitled *Cost, Quality, and Child Outcomes in Child Care Centres* (Helburn et al., 1995) paints a poor picture of child care in the United States. The results of this large-scale study made national news in January 1995. Headlines reflected the major finding that the quality of most centres is poor to mediocre and quality is even lower in infant/toddler centres. Very few centres were considered to be excellent, with 14 percent of preschool and 8 percent of infant/toddler programs receiving such a rating. At the other end of the scale, however, 12 percent of preschool and 40 percent of infant/toddler programs were considered to have less than minimal quality.

The authors of the study found these results disturbing enough to conclude that quality in most American child care centres is sufficiently poor to affect young children's emotional and cognitive development. Regardless of their family backgrounds, children in lower-quality child care were found to be less competent in social ability, language, and other developmentally related skills than those in higher-quality programs. The difference was even more marked for at-risk children.

This study confirmed many previous studies' findings about the variables that contribute to quality in child care. The most significant factor was higher adult–child ratios. Also important was the staff's educational level, especially specialized training. In addition, the prior experience of the administrator and teachers' wages were correlated with quality.

One of the most provocative findings of this research is that while such a high percentage of programs was rated by professionals as being mediocre or poor, 90 percent of parents considered their children's centres to be very good. This is clearly an overestimation of quality on the part of the parents. What might be the reason for this discrepancy? The researchers speculate that one reason is the difficulty of monitoring a child care program since parents have relatively little opportunity to observe in the facility. Another reason may be that some parents have never seen high-quality child care and thus have no basis for comparison. Parents may also feel they have no choice; therefore, it is easier for them to consider that their children are cared for appropriately. Since this study found little difference in the cost between high- and low-quality child care, the researchers conclude that parents simply are not demanding quality, although they state that quality in their children's care is important to them.

The study underscores a number of important issues. Good child care is not readily available to most families, thus a majority of children are getting less than adequate care. Adverse outcomes are associated with this poor quality care, which puts the future of our children, indeed the future of countries in general, in jeopardy. Governments must make a strong commitment so that all children and their families have access to quality child care. This commitment involves educating parents to help them both understand and demand appropriate quality for their children. Your role, as an early childhood educator, is important in this endeavour because you can be a force in ensuring that the children you work with experience a quality program and you can help to educate parents about what quality means.

helping children who were at risk for later academic failure to improve school performance. But the research on these models has implications for all children (Evans, 1982).

Roopnarine and Johnson (1993) have described 14 early childhood education models, including home-based and centre-based ones. The centre-based models could be placed in one of three categories: (1) Montessori models, (2) behaviourist models, and (3) interactionist models. We should not, however, assume that all early childhood programs conform to one of these carefully prescribed views. Quite frequently, programs are very eclectic in their approach, combining quality components from each model.

It is beneficial to examine how some specific models have taken the views of a particular theorist (or theorists) and transformed these into program application. Exhibit 5.10 briefly examines only four models, although many alternative approaches exist. These four were selected to illustrate how particular views of child development can be implemented in practice. Included are a brief overview of Montessori programs as they exist today; the Bank Street or open education approach, which is in part based on the psychosocial view of Erikson; the High Scope/Cognitively Oriented Curriculum, based on Piaget's principles; and the Reggio Emilia approach, grounded in part on the theories of Piaget, Vygotsky, and Dewey. Note that the Reggio Emilia principles and curriculum are outlined in Part 1. Also note that A Closer Look examines yet another model, the Waldorf education model, pioneered by Rudolf Steiner.

Research Support for Early Childhood Education

Much of the research about the effectiveness of early childhood education has come from the evaluation of programs designed for high-risk children and

EXHIBIT 5.10: EARLY CHILDHOOD EDUCATION PROGRAM MODELS

The Program	Roots	Environment	Materials	Schedules	Curriculum	Teachers	Parents	Research
Montessori	Dr. Maria Montessori, 1870–1952, Italy Children have absorbent minds in the early years and sensitive periods during which they are most ready to learn.	▪ Sense of order ▪ Low noise level ▪ Child-sized furniture ▪ Attractive ▪ Specific areas for tasks ▪ Match between materials and what a child is ready to learn ▪ Set-up for independent work *Strong sense g respect for children*	Montessori materials are designed and manufactured specifically for Montessori programs. ▪ Didactic— ▪ have a specific purpose ▪ Self-correcting ▪ Simple to complex ▪ Isolate a single quality (e.g., size, shape, colour) ▪ Manipulative for hands-on learning	▪ Focus on individual time ▪ Occasional group times ▪ Scheduled snack ▪ Little outdoor time ▪ Half and full day available at preschool level	*Practical* ▪ Emphasizes daily living skills (e.g., self-help and environmental care) *Sensorial* ▪ Is oriented to senses ▪ Uses discrimination tasks to develop perceptual and cognitive areas *Conceptual/Academic* ▪ Is multisensory and manipulative to build on specific skills (e.g., math) ▪ Has no dramatic, creative, or outdoor (playground) play in very traditional Montessori program ▪ Emphasizes self-directed, hands-on learning	▪ Director guides rather than controls or teaches. ▪ Teaching is low key since materials are designed to be self-correcting.	Parents are not directly involved and must remain unobtrusive observers.	▪ IQs rose in first year of program, including verbal IQ. ▪ Gains persist through grades 6–10. ▪ No strong consistent differences between children of Montessori and traditional programs but gains made by Montessori children do persist. Banta, 1969; Chattin-McNichols, 1992; Gettman, 1987; Lazar & Darlington, 1992; Lillard, 1973; Lindauer, 1993; Miezitis, 1972; Miller & Bizzell, 1983; Simons & Simons, 1986. Read *The Absorbent Mind* by Maria Montessori. (1967)

The Program	Roots	Environment	Materials	Schedules	Curriculum	Teachers	Parents	Research
COC— Cognitively Oriented Curriculum (High Scope)	David Weikart, High Scope Foundation, Ypsilanti, Michigan, 1960s to present Piagetian: Children are active learners who construct their own knowledge.	▪ Abundant stimulation but also orderliness ▪ Lots of choice ▪ Clearly defined work areas with specific materials ▪ Learning centres such as house, block, art	▪ Materials are gathered as deemed appropriate. ▪ Materials are "real" (e.g., hammer).	▪ Plan, Do, Review Cycle (planning time, work time, recall and review or evaluate time) ▪ Schedule quite set to enforce consistency	Set of eight key concepts based on pre-operational child: 1. active learning 2. language 3. representing experience 4. classification 5. seriation 6. number concepts 7. spatial relations 8. time Freedom allowed within prepared environment. Average ratio of 1:8.	▪ Team approach is used. ▪ Teachers plan small and large group activities but also allow free play time.	Meetings are scheduled meetings with parents to discuss child's progress. Original COC included parents directly in program planning and implementation.	Long-term studies show that students are more likely to graduate from high school than control groups, attend post secondary education, and be employed. Students: ▪ have few special education placements ▪ have high literacy levels compared to controls ▪ achieve higher standard of living than controls Berrueta-Clement et al., 1984; Weikart & Schweinhart, 1985, 1993. More research is cited in next section. David Weikart continues to speak and publish research on the High Scope project. Read *Petit Piaget* by C.M. Charles (1974).

The Program	Roots	Environment	Materials	Schedules	Curriculum	Teachers	Parents	Research
Reggio Emilia	Loris Malaguzzi, Italy, town of Reggio Emilia, 1940s to present Dewey, Piagetian, Vygotskyian: Learning occurs through relationships and interactions. Learning is continuous and emergent.	▪ Design that encourages communication: inviting, personal, aesthetic ▪ Design that promotes emergence of ideas: projects and efforts of team everywhere	▪ No set materials—gathered as projects are determined and started. ▪ Art is a key vehicle to learning.	▪ Freedom within structure ▪ No set schedule ▪ Children help set timelines for projects to increase sense of ownership and independence ▪ Continuity and consistency help shape projects	Conversation, collaboration, and documentation ▪ Projects are the central concept ▪ Idea of emergent curriculum ▪ No pre-planned curriculum, rather based on the interests of the children and the team ▪ Immersion in the topic from conception to fruition via examination of current and prior knowledge ▪ Questioning, probing, researching, problem solving, and representing (e.g., through construction or artwork)	▪ Team teaching is used. ▪ Some teachers remain with children for three years. ▪ Focus is on dynamics among teachers, families, and children. ▪ Teacher's key role is as resource to child as a "learning partner" ▪ Teacher is supported by program coordinators and visual arts teachers. ▪ Communication, coordination, collaboration, and training are essential elements.	Parents are integral members of the learning team.	Program is so new that few studies are available yet, but as this most recent trend in ECE explodes, watch for an increased number of publications focusing on it. Joanne Hendricks edited an excellent book entitled *First Steps Toward Teaching the Reggio Way* (1997). (See Partnerships in Orientation chapter.) Read John Dewey's *Democracy and Education* (1916) and Vygotsky's *Mind in Society* (1978b) for roots of invitational education. (See A Closer Look in Chapter 1.)

The Program	Roots	Environment	Materials	Schedules	Curriculum	Teachers	Parents	Research
Open (Bank Street Model)	Lucy Sprague Mitchell and Barbara Biber, Bank Street Model since 1930s Susan and Nathan Isaacs, British Infant Schools since 1930s Margaret and Rachel McMillan, Open-Air Nursery Schools since 1911 Developmentalists—Piaget, Erikson, and Vygotsky. Social-emotional development is crucial to learning. Learn by doing and interacting.	• Open concept —no designated times or lessons • Activity and interest centres—free flow from room to room • Homemade equipment	• Abundant • Homemade by teachers, parents, and children • Sensory, discovery-oriented	• No set schedule • No set lessons • Lunch and physical activity integral components • Teachers work with small groups	• Integrated curriculum • Wholistic learning • Theming • Bridging learning to broader areas of community • Focus on autonomy, trust, competence, ownership, and relationships	• Keep careful records via observation and anecdotes • Support children's interests • Follow children's lead • Help children make choices • Help empower children • Guide children through their play • Try to match teaching and learning styles	• Parents are welcomed as visitors and volunteers. • Parents have a close relationship with staff and are part of team.	Observational rather than empirical methods support the development of teaching, reading, writing, and math. Biber, 1984; Evans, 1975; Shapiro & Biber, 1972; Silberman, 1990; Zimiles, 1993. Read L. E. Weber (1971) or Susan & Nathan Isaacs (1933) on beginnings of open education. The Bank Street Model has been written on extensively.

WALDORF EDUCATION

Waldorf schools are part of a movement of over 600 schools worldwide. Each school, although operated autonomously, shares in a common philosophy. At present there are 15 schools in Canada, with a number of new initiatives and kindergartens starting each year.

Waldorf schools began in Europe in 1919 and are based on the philosophy of Rudolf Steiner called "anthroposophy". Anthroposophy embraces a spiritual view of the human being and the cosmos, leading to an education that addresses the whole child. Waldorf education places as much emphasis on creativity and moral judgment as it does on intellectual growth.

According to Steiner, understanding the true nature and the developmental stages of the human being is central to the education of the child. Certain predictable intellectual, psychological, and spiritual changes occur as the child is physically maturing, which the curriculum must appropriately address.

For example, physical and growth forces predominate in the child up to the age of 6. The young child absorbs the world primarily through the senses and takes it in most actively through imitation. The Waldorf Nursery and Kindergarten program offers plenty of opportunity for meaningful imitative learning and play, which is the young child's knowledge.

Waldorf teachers of young children provide them with examples that are worthy of imitation in a setting that is full of beauty. Classrooms are awash with warm colours on the walls and naturally dyed cloths. Play things are from nature, such as stones, shells, bark, and pieces of wood. These simple objects give the children an opportunity for creative play, through which their power of imagination is strengthened. The teachers strive to do daily work worthy of imitation, such as cooking, sewing, gardening, and housekeeping, while the children either play or join the teachers.

The life of the Parent and Tot program, Nursery, or Kindergarten is based on daily, weekly, and seasonal rhythms. Seasonally there are little plays, crafts, marionette shows, and festival celebrations. The daily rhythm consists of play, stories, circle time, singing, a daily snack, and activities such as sewing, knitting, painting, and woodworking. These daily activities, based on a strong daily rhythm, prepare and strengthen the children for their school years and their adult life.

When the children begin the first grade, they enter into a different and distinct stage. The teacher's task is to transform knowledge into the language of feelings and imagination. It is a language that is as accurate and as responsible to reality as intellectual analysis is to the adult. Folktales, legends, and mythologies speak truth in parables and pictures. Later, historical accuracy replaces myths as knowledge becomes associated with relevant daily experiences. Science begins with nature stories and evolves into the various branches of scientific knowledge. The use of music, movement, drawing, and drama in each main lesson engages the children in their studies and brings knowledge into wholeness. Handwork and woodwork balance intellectual work.

After puberty, imaginative learning undergoes a metamorphosis to emerge as the rational, abstract power of the intellect, and the child is challenged to develop creative, critical thought. Through the glorious turbulence of adolescence, young people are seeking to understand the world in a new way. The curriculum matches their changing needs as their individualities emerge and strengthens their sense of self. It challenges them with subjects such as atomic theory, the periodic table, coastal navigation, Native studies, and a broad program including math and science each year of high school.

Proponents of the Waldorf method view the rapid spread of Waldorf education in this century as a testament to the power of a visionary curriculum and the striving of teachers working for the development of each human being, the transformation of society, and the renewal of the earth.

Enquiries about Waldorf teacher education may be directed to the Rudolf Steiner Centre in Toronto at 905-764-7570. Enquiries about Waldorf education in Canada may be directed to the Waldorf School Association at 905-889-2066.

Submitted by Arlene Thorn

children from impoverished backgrounds. The result of such research is important in gauging the value of compensatory education, but it also provides us with more general information about early childhood education. In addition, it is important to understand the effect of early childhood education on all youngsters, particularly with the large number of young children enrolled in child care programs. We will look at these two topics separately.

The Effects of Early Intervention on At-Risk Children

Head Start

The 1960s can be portrayed as a period of great optimism on the part of the educators and psychologists who had a hand in the development of Head Start in the United States. The movement aimed at providing children and families of poverty with enriched opportunities. Edward Zigler, one of the leaders in the Head Start movement, expressed this aim:

> Intervention was supposed to impact immediate benefits so that class differences would be eliminated by the time of school entry. Furthermore, many expected that the brief preschool experience would be so potent a counteraction to the deficits in poor children's lives that it could prevent further attenuation in age-appropriate performance and a recurrence of the gap between social classes in later grades. (Zigler & Berman, 1973, pp. 895–896)

Head Start, backed by years of research, did not live up to that idealistic expectation. Many of the early intervention programs showed some short-term results in improved IQs and achievement scores for the first few years of elementary school (Lee, Brooks-Gunn, Schnur, & Liaw, 1990; Royce, Darlington, & Murray, 1983; Schweinhart & Weikart, 1985). Given the relatively brief time that children spend in Head Start, it alone cannot make up for the wide variety of social ills that beset the children of poverty. Broader assessments of compensatory programs, however, have demonstrated that early intervention can have important and lasting effects.

Head Start began an expansion program in 1993 and had a 1996 budget in excess of $3 billion. However, it estimates it serves only 40 percent of children eligible for the program. Head Start, in its evolution, has since spawned other pro-

grams—Ever Start to counteract illiteracy, Home-Based Head Start, and Transition Head Start to ensure follow through of programming in the elementary years. Head Start is a federally funded giant in the United States. Canada has no federal (national) child care system.

Head Start is relevant to Canadians in the field of early childhood education for several reasons. First, the scope of the project and the emphasis it places on the importance of the early years had an impact that was felt far beyond the U.S. boundaries. Second, much of the significant research on the effectiveness of early childhood programs has been completed because Head Start emphasizes an evaluation component, and researchers acknowledge the importance of this activity. Finally, many Canadians have generic Head Start programs in their own communities, including at least one in Nova Scotia that predated the U.S. project.

Canadians heard legislators talk about making funds available for Head Start projects in the 1960s (a time when funds were available). For example, in 1965, inspired by Head Start, Ontario's minister of education, William G. Davis, spoke in the legislature of his concerns about early childhood education.

Not surprisingly, generic Head Start programs soon became available in larger urban centres in Ontario. Some were junior kindergartens, funded by school boards and the province (e.g., Toronto and Hamilton). Canadian university students, administrators, and alumni also founded a number of programs in the 1960s, the decade of social concern. The University of Western Ontario's

Community Action Project, for instance, was initiated by students who received funding from the university, various levels of government, and donations from corporations. The Varsity Downtown Education Project (VDEP) in Toronto was somewhat larger in scope and included two different centres. VDEP was funded for several years by contributions from a charitable foundation (Atkinson Foundation) and the University of Toronto's Students' Administrative Council, Board of Governors, and alumni. VDEP then turned into a full-time alternative school, primarily for "graduates" of the summer program, that relied on self-raised funds at first, and later on funds from the Toronto Board of Education.

The East Coast also saw a flurry of activity, as did the far North. Nova Scotia perhaps saw the greatest increase in Canadian Head Start projects in the 1960s, as the provincial government made funds available for disadvantaged communities (Irwin & Canning, 1992b). Some programs received both federal and provincial funding, while others searched for local funds. A number of the programs were interracial and aimed to improve relations between whites, Blacks, and Natives in communities like Halifax, Truro, and Hants County. In fact, one program, the Brunswick-Cornwallis Preschool Program, predated Project Head Start by two years. Alexa McDonough, in Nova Scotia, supervised 9 such programs with a staff of 30. In Newfoundland, the St. John's Club of the Canadian Federation of University Women initiated an 11-week pilot program that drew on the university and community volunteers for staff and evaluations (Glassman, 1992a). The program was extended and eventually received federal funding as a demonstration project. It continues today as a parent cooperative.

The Skookum Jim Society in Whitehorse, Yukon, also started a generic Head Start program in 1968 with funding from the Department of Indian Affairs and a lot of volunteer efforts (Johnson & Joe, 1992).

When the federal government made Local Initiatives Program and Opportunities for Youth funding available in the early 1970s, the number of generic Head Start programs in certain areas of the country multiplied rapidly. Many of those programs continue to serve young children in the 1990s.

Mary Wright's University of Western Ontario preschool was based on preserving "the best in the traditional Ontario preschool program, which had been developed in the 1940s at the University of Toronto's Institute for Child Study" (Wright, 1983, p. 333), and combining it with aspects of more recent Piagetian programs, like the Cognitively Oriented Curriculum. Wright's program included both high- and low-income children, but financial constraints resulted in the presence of only the low-income children in the school follow-up study. All children made gains in ability, achievement, and social skill measures when they were in the program, and the gains were greater if they were enrolled for two years. In grade school, the low-income preschool graduates were less likely to fail and less likely to be placed in special education classes relative to matched controls. Moreover, they were viewed by their teachers as better adjusted than matched controls. Finally, there was a tendency for those low-income graduates who had spent two years in the program to do better than those who had only one year in a high-quality program.

DISTAR

Not included in Exhibit 5.10 are models based on behaviourist theory. One such model known as DISTAR was originally designed by Carl Bereiter and Siegfried Engelmann in the 1960s for children at risk in order to accelerate their learning. Unlike the other models presented, this model utilized direct instruction in reading and math through "skill and drill" teacher-directed lessons. Play, active learning, and creativity were not part of the program. Results of this program in terms of developmental appropriateness, quality, and research evidence are given here in order to address the recent pitch for "back to basics" by some parents and governments.

Initial evaluation of this program showed that children had significantly improved IQs and achievement test scores, more so than the other groups studied; however, those gains declined quickly over the next few years.

The levels of curiosity and inventiveness of the children in the DISTAR model seemed lower than those of youngsters who participated in other types of compensatory programs (Miller & Dyer, 1975; Miller & Bizzell, 1983). This may be in part due to the high level of external reinforcement, which, according to research, tends to decrease the intrinsic interest children may have in learning (Lepper, Greene, & Nisbett, 1973).

More recent evaluation of adolescents who had participated in the DISTAR program as preschoolers showed some unexpected outcomes. The youths who had been in a DISTAR program, utilizing direct instruction, appeared to have higher rates of juvenile delinquency than youths involved in programs where the major teaching method involved self-selection (Schweinhart, Weikart, & Larner, 1986a). The authors of this study speculated in a subsequent publication that when we enable young children to have control over the activities they participate in, they may well develop a greater sense of responsibility and initiative (Schweinhart, Weikart, & Larner, 1986b). They pointed out that development of such traits is crucial in early childhood, as described by such theorists as Erik Erikson. Proponents of the direct instructional approach, however, have questioned these conclusions and expressed concern over the research procedures used in these studies (Bereiter, 1986; Gersten, 1986)

Cognitively Oriented Curriculum / High Scope

A most interesting set of results comes from the Cognitively Oriented Curriculum, which has been one of the most thoroughly researched early childhood programs for children from low-income families. The most notable of these are the Perry Preschool Project and the High Scope Curriculum of Ypsilanti, Michigan. It is there that David Weikhart has conducted his longitudinal studies. Follow-up data was collected through adolescence on youngsters who had been enrolled in the program, giving information on their subsequent experiences and functioning within the larger society. When contrasted with a comparable group that had not attended preschool, the cognitively oriented graduates were significantly more likely to have completed high school, experienced job success and satisfaction, and been self-supporting rather than dependent on welfare. They were also less likely to have required special education services, experienced a teen pregnancy, or been arrested.

Further follow-up at age 27 of those who had participated in the program as preschoolers showed continued positive results (Schweinhart, Barnes, & Weikart, 1993). Results indicated that, compared to the control group, these adults had higher earnings, were more likely to own a home, demonstrated a greater commitment to marriage, were less dependent on social services, and had considerably fewer arrests.

Such long-range results indicate that high-quality early childhood programs can and do make a difference, not just to the individual children involved but to society at large. These researchers have estimated that early childhood intervention is a good tax investment that can save up to seven times the amount spent during the early years by offsetting later welfare, special education, and crime costs (Schweinhart et al., 1993).

Similar, positive long-term results were also found for adolescents who had participated in Syracuse University's Family Development Research Program (FDRP) during their infant and preschool years. Most impressive was the highly significant difference in involvement in the juvenile justice system between these teenagers and a comparable (control) group that had not participated in an early intervention program. Not only had far fewer of the FDRP youngsters been involved in juvenile delinquency, but the severity of the offences, the number of incidents, and the cost of processing were far lower.

Another finding from this study showed that, particularly for girls, early intervention resulted in better school performance and lower absenteeism during adolescence than was found for the control group. The teachers also rated the FDRP girls, compared to the control-group girls, as higher in self-esteem and self-control (Lally, Mangione, & Honig, 1988). Follow-up studies such as these provide evidence that high-quality early childhood intervention programs can and do make a difference.

The Effects of Early Intervention on Minimal Risk Children

Although a considerable amount of research has examined the effects of an early childhood program on children who are at risk for later school failure, these typically being children of poverty, relatively little research has given us comparable information on middle-income children. Some studies have found that children in high-quality early childhood programs exhibit greater cognitive, language, and social competence than children without such experience (Clarke-Stewart, 1984; Howes & Olenick, 1986); others, however, have found greater levels of aggressiveness among children with child care experience (Haskins, 1985).

A recent study (Larsen & Robinson, 1989) followed children from advantaged families, those who had attended a high-quality preschool program, into third grade and compared them to children who had not had a similar early childhood experience. Results showed that, particularly for males, the early childhood program experience seems to be related to higher school achievement scores. Another study (Tietze, 1987), using a sampling of the general elementary school population of one state in Germany, found that children who had attended an early childhood program experienced greater school success than children who had not been in a preschool program (measured by retention and special-education placement information).

One interesting variation of such investigations evaluated a sample of middle-class 8-year-olds in a state with minimal child care standards. The researchers

(Vandell & Corasaniti, 1990) found that children who had been in full-time child care since infancy were rated lower on a variety of measures by both teachers and parents than children who had experienced part-time or no child care. The youngsters with full-time child care histories were considered to have poorer peer relations, work habits, emotional health, and academic performance and to be more difficult to discipline. The authors contrasted these findings with the positive results found in Sweden for children who had extensive child care histories. Sweden, as they pointed out, has high child care standards.

Goelman and Pence (1990) have conducted a series of studies in British Columbia. They examined centre-based and family child care, the quality of the child's care at home and in the child care setting, and language development as a function of these variables. In Goelman and Pence's Victoria study, parents developed higher levels of friendship with family-based caregivers, but they had fewer negative concerns about centre-based care. This is consistent with the higher turnover rates that were found in family-based care. The providers of family child care generally had lower educational levels than centre-based teachers, but they were more flexible about caregiving arrangements. Nevertheless, most of the home-based providers would have preferred to be employed in a different capacity.

The unlicensed family homes were more likely to be of low quality than the licensed homes and centres in Victoria. In the low-quality homes, children watched more television than in the higher-quality settings, and their language development lagged behind that of children in licensed homes. However, caregiver training and the mother's educational level also were positively related to the language development scores. Moreover, those families with limited resources (e.g., single-parent families and ones with low income, little education, and lower-paying jobs) were more likely to have their children in low-quality, unlicensed settings.

The Vancouver study followed the Victoria one and concentrated on family-based care. Both the child's home and the care home were rated for quality, as were the parents and providers. The children's language was studied in both settings. The analyses confirmed the trends in Victoria. As you might predict, the quality of language and cognitive stimulation in both the child's own home and the care home was related to the child's own language development. The social-emotional climate of the child's own family was also directly related to cognitive stimulation in the child's home and the care home, and to language development.

A study of infant day care, conducted in Toronto by William Fowler (1971, 1972, 1973, 1974, 1978; Fowler & Khan, 1974), found that infants and toddlers from middle-income families made very significant gains on ability measures. In fact, their gains were even greater than those of the lower-income children.

These findings were supported by the recent Cost, Quality, and Child Outcomes in Child Care Centres study (Helburn et al., 1995), which reinforces that child care quality is generally lower in areas with low licensing standards. As reported by Doherty-Derkowski (1995), child care in and of itself has no effects, whereas high-quality care has substantial positive effects and low quality care has substantial negative effects.

A recent study (Hestenes, Kontos, & Bryan, 1993) lends support and provides some explanation for such findings. Preschoolers' emotional expressions were found to be much more positive (more smiling and laughing) in centres in which caregivers were more engaged and supportive in their interactions with children than in centers in which teachers ignored or minimally interacted with the youngsters. As you will recall from earlier discussions, the calibre of child–adult interactions is an important indicator of quality in early childhood programs. Quality care comes with both high teacher–child ratios and good teacher qualifications. Two of perhaps the most important aspects of care—the quality of the child–parent attachment and the effects of working parents—have shown both

EXHIBIT 5.11: THE IMPACT OF QUALITY CARE ON CHILDREN

	High-Quality Care (Whether Home- or Centre-Based)	Low-Quality Care (Whether Home- or Centre-Based)
	▪ has two-way interactions ▪ is nurturing ▪ is encouraging ▪ is empowering	▪ has one-way interaction ▪ may be abusive ▪ shows neglect/ deprivation ▪ has extreme demands on learning
At-Risk Child	positive impact on child	negative impact on child
Minimal-Risk Child	positive impact on child	negative impact on child
	results in confidence— a firm trust, a feeling of certainty, self-reliance (*Oxford Dictionary*)	results in stress—a force acting on something, pressing, pulling, twisting, to distort it (*Oxford Dictionary*)

positive and negative results. In families where moms work, dads often acquire more household and child care duties. A diverse range of role models, a balance of shared family responsibilities, and a parent's job satisfaction coupled with the right and option to choose work and child care help make happier and thus more effective parents (Hoffman, 1989).

Typically children at risk have been studied primarily from a low-income perspective since poverty creates enormous stress on families. Keep in mind that children face risks through other factors such as cultural, medical, regional, social, or religious barriers that may affect the availability and quality of their care.

Clearly more research can help us better assess the impact of early childhood education on all children. Many factors, including home experience and environment, quality of the program and teachers, and program philosophy, need to be taken into account. All such information will help us to better understand how we contribute to the lives of young children and to maximize their chance of success in the future. This information can help us assist parents seeking advice on selecting a child care program and aid them in making an informed and wise decision. Exhibit 5.11 emphasizes the effects of quality care on children.

Key Terms

adult–child ratio	Head Start
back-to-basics movement	mixed-age grouping
COC/High Scope Model	Montessori
early childhood education program models	Open Model
	program quality
group size	Reggio Emilia

Key Points

- For an early childhood education program to meet the criteria for high quality, it must respect the emerging abilities of young children without imposing inappropriate expectations and be staffed by specifically trained individuals.

- Low teacher turnover and positive child interaction are essential.

- Studies show that smaller groups receive more stimulation than large ones, however, the parameters of the physical environment also need to be considered.

- Mixed-age groups benefit both younger and older children.

- A child-oriented environment, open communication, and family involvement benefit the child.

- Staff must be respected, receive appropriate benefits, and work in a satisfying environment. Qualified staff is an important factor in any quality program.

- Quality is not defined by a single factor but rather depends on the complex interaction of a variety of elements in which the professional plays a key role.

- There is no federal legislation for child ratios and group size or centre size. Each province regulates this separately.

Part 4

The Pedagogy

Here we explore the basic hows of early childhood education. In Part 4, we will examine the following fundamental intricacies of what you now know to be quality programs.

- Chapter 6, "Play and Guidance: A Framework for Emotional Development," draws your attention to the inseparable relationship that play, guidance, and emotional development share as the basis for all quality programs and for all interactions with children. Each component is explored in depth.

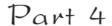

- Chapter 7, "Appropriate Practices in Early Childhood Education," examines some of the basic constructs in early childhood education programs including:

  1. the definition of developmentally appropriate practices, and environment, and
  2. the importance of a curriculum that promotes inclusion.

  Some basic components of that environment and curriculum, such as materials, and planning and implementation guidelines, are then addressed.

- Chapter 8, "Curriculum," introduces elements and contents of the curriculum. It then addresses the issue of accountability, examining observation, assessment, standards, learning outcomes, and evaluation.

- Chapter 9, "Development through the Curriculum," focuses on the developmental domains—creative, physical, cognitive, language, and social—in terms of the curriculum's role in fostering them.

- Chapter 10, "Helping Children Cope with Stress," highlights the very serious nature of stressors in children's lives. It provides excellent strategies for helping children and families cope with stress.

Chapter 6

Play and Guidance: A Framework for Emotional Development

As you know from Chapter 5, high-quality programs that combine the best of several different approaches have been successful, and you will want to select different components from different models when you design a program. In keeping with this eclectic approach, this text presents and combines many perspectives. However, it is the basic premise of all quality pro-

grams to support a play-based curriculum where children are guided in such a way as to nurture their emotional development.

In this chapter, we will examine play—the child's way of actively learning about and making sense of the world—and guidance—our way of helping children make decisions and choices that foster this learning. We view this interaction as one that nurtures and frames emotional development and well-being.

The Relationship between Play, Guidance, and Emotional Development

Play is the cornerstone of quality early childhood education programs because play behaviour occurs naturally in children and provides the foundation of devel-

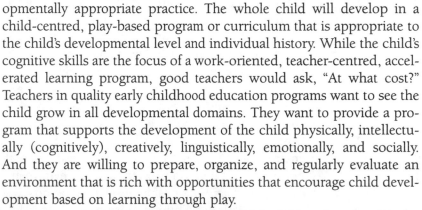

opmentally appropriate practice. The whole child will develop in a child-centred, play-based program or curriculum that is appropriate to the child's developmental level and individual history. While the child's cognitive skills are the focus of a work-oriented, teacher-centred, accelerated learning program, good teachers would ask, "At what cost?" Teachers in quality early childhood education programs want to see the child grow in all developmental domains. They want to provide a program that supports the development of the child physically, intellectually (cognitively), creatively, linguistically, emotionally, and socially. And they are willing to prepare, organize, and regularly evaluate an environment that is rich with opportunities that encourage child development based on learning through play.

Because play is the vehicle through which children learn, and is the focal point for children's interactions, a play-based curriculum is also one in which much guidance occurs. We do not teach play but help children to find ways to solve problems that they encounter in play and to access means for elaborating upon and extending the discoveries they make.

It may sound like a cliché, but today's children are tomorrow's adults, people we expect to be self-motivated, self-disciplined, and self-sufficient and to get along with others in a fair and just way. In that context, guiding the behaviour of young children takes on an important and delicate meaning. Every time you respond to an infant's cries, to a toddler's request for help, and to two toddlers' struggle over a toy, the children are learning about human responses. Every time you help a child to look at his or her behaviour and to evaluate its appropriateness, you are empowering the child, helping the child along the road to self-discipline and positive self-concept. Every time you give older children direction, ask for their help, help them prevent or solve a disagreement, or convey your expectations of them, you are affecting not just their immediate behaviour. You are shaping their future behaviour. You are, in essence, contributing another grain to the growing hill that is becoming the child's character. Play requires guidance and guidance requires interacting with children. Interacting with children is the most potent thing you do in contributing to their emotional development. The relationships between play, guidance, and emotional development are inseparable. In this chapter, then, we will view your guidance of children's behaviour in a play-based quality program as a framework for their healthy emotional development.

Your Role as Nurturer

Two components are integral to all adult-child interactions: play and guidance. Whether the adults are early childhood educators or not, these two elements encompass all relationships with children. Even knowing nothing about child development, early childhood education, or theories, we all know that children play. We know they depend on us for guidance as they interact with us, with other children and adults, and with their environment. Play is what children do. Guidance is what we do. How we do it is everything to children. It sets the tone of the relationship—either strengthens or weakens it, establishes trust or mistrust, encourages or hinders independence, and fosters or crushes self-esteem, all of which are components of emotional development.

Above being a teacher or a caregiver or a specialist, you are a nurturer, someone whom children depend on for their well-being in each of the developmental domains—physical, intellectual, social, emotional, language, creative, behavioural, and spiritual. You can be a nurturer in any type of program in any environment. Children play anywhere and where they play, they generally require non-intrusive, empowering strategies to help them to discover, gather, and utilize information and to problem solve in a positive, productive, and supportive

manner. Children rely on our dependability. They trust we will be there, that we will not harm them, that we will encourage and reassure them, that we trust them and realize their potential contribution, and that we will help them gain their confidence to discover, explore, and make sense of everything a safe world has to offer.

Emotional Development

A.F. Lieberman, in *The Emotional Life of the Toddler* (1994), emphasizes that the nurturing role of the early childhood educator is the most important. This is based on the belief that healthy emotional development is the foundation upon which all other development depends.

Healthy emotional development encompasses six milestones, according to Greenspan & Greenspan (1986). A child's inborn temperament coupled with the quality of the interactions children experience at each stage support children in their attainment of these milestones. Quality is meant to encompass adults who respond in fair, positive, sensitive, respectful, and appropriate ways.

1. *Self Regulation and Interest in the World—"Developing a Sense of Security"*—Children can organize and cope with all the new stimuli and sensations the world has to offer.

2. *Falling in Love—"Developing a Sense of Attachment"*—Children demonstrate an interest in the human world and take great pleasure in personal interactions. They enjoy the world—smiling, cooing, watching, kicking, reaching, and listening.

3. *Development of Intentional Communication—"Developing a Sense of Trust"*—Children gain an awareness that they can express needs in many ways through actions and sounds, and that they can expect these needs to be met by caring adults.

4. *Emergence of an Organized Sense of Self—"Developing a Sense of Independence"*—Children understand that they can have an effect on the world. They take initiative, explore, express themselves, assert needs, and gain a sense of autonomy, empowerment, pride, and confidence as they develop a positive self-concept and high self-esteem.

5. *Developing Emotional Ideas—"Developing a Sense of Empathy"*—Children explore and practise, through pretend play, ways to identify, label, manage, and use the many new emotions and ideas about emotions they observe and experience.

6. *Emotional Thinking: The Bases for Fantasy, Reality, and Self-Esteem—"Developing a Sense of Self-Control"*—Children develop interpersonal (between people) and intrapersonal (within self) skills to identify, express, and manage emotions. They understand the relationship between feelings, behaviour, and consequences and interact in socially appropriate ways.

As we read in Chapter 2, Erik Erikson's theory of child development was also seated in emotional growth. Children need to develop a sense of trust and security by having their needs met consistently, predictably, and positively. They need to develop a sense of autonomy through encouragement and opportunities for exploration. Children also need to develop a sense of initiative whereby they feel safe in expressing their ideas, taking risks, and making mistakes.

Abraham Maslow felt that the overall goal of development was to achieve **self-actualization,** which simply means realizing one's potential. Five basic needs must first be met. Maslow called this a **"hierarchy of needs"** because one level of needs had to be satisfied before moving to the next level. First, essential physical needs such as food and sleep must be satisfied. Maslow felt that fulfillment of emotional needs such as a sense of safety, security, belonging, and affection comes next. Only when these emotional needs are realized and met can children develop high self-esteem—a sense of personal worth and value and a positive self-concept.

Children's self-actualization—applying their knowledge and abilities confidently and appropriately—is only possible once their basic physical needs are met, they feel safe, secure, and loved, and they view themselves as worthy, competent, and responsible.

As an early childhood educator, you recognize that your role includes fostering healthy emotional development in children. See Exhibit 6.1, which is followed by examples of ways to foster this development.

EXHIBIT 6.1: POSITIVE EMOTIONAL DEVELOPMENT

Indicators of Positive Emotional Development in Children

- express self through play
- express their creativity
- exert independence
- problem solve
- investigate
- experiment
- make decisions
- take risks and accept mistakes
- make good judgments
- question
- help others
- respect others
- feel safe in asking adults for help, clarification, and guidance
- display competence
- take responsibility
- show initiative

Fostering Emotional Development

- model calmness in our approach—show self-control
- be reasonable
- provide a safe and secure environment that provides challenges and successes
- show that we trust and can be trusted
- model fairness in our methods
- help in solving problems and clarifying issues
- display accuracy in determining intent of children's behaviour
- model a respectful attitude of children as people
- foster and protect children's self-esteem
- be a positive role model for communication, interpersonal skills, and problem solving
- genuinely enjoy the children
- show understanding and tolerance of children's mistakes
- be flexible
- include children in the decision-making process
- believe children to be capable
- afford children the same rights and opportunities as any person

- provide a range of appropriate choices
- show unconditional acceptance (no bribes, bargains, or ifs)
- provide time and be flexible with our limits and routines to accommodate for individual differences and interests
- show that we will help solve problems in a fair and mutually beneficial way
- demonstrate that we are credible—we know about children and we know what we are doing
- be dependable and reliable
- be comforting
- show admiration, affection, approval, acceptance, and pride
- be encouraging
- listen
- create a beautiful environment with the children

This chapter defines guidance and presents guidelines that are meant not only to assist you in fostering play and guiding behaviour but also to ensure the healthy emotional development of children.

Play

One commonality of children throughout the world is their need to play, which we discussed briefly in Chapter 2. Through play, children come to know and understand their world. Most would agree that play is a source of joy, learning, and absorption, and no one need force children to do it. So why do you need to be concerned about play? Play is forever under attack in North America. David Elkind (1990), an eminent early childhood educator, who has raised so many concerns about the hurried child, hothousing, and people's belief that earlier is always better, comments:

The major victim of the earlier is better ideology has been the play of infants and young children…. Play is a bad word. Given children's sponge-like abilities to learn, the purported rapidity of brain growth, and the time-limited nature of this window of opportunity, play is extremely wasteful of time that might be put to more important and more long-lived activities…. Childhood is a period for work, not for play. (pp. 4–5)

Early lessons in almost everything become more and more prevalent, and the value of play is being questioned by more and more parents and members of the public. This places additional demands on teachers in early childhood education programs. They not only have to decide what to include in their programs, but also they have to be able to give cogent reasons for their practices to others. Far too frequently, teachers have adopted play-based program models without knowing why the approach was valid, and then they have been unable to articulate the reasons why they have play as a central feature in the curriculum (Monighan-Nourot, 1990). Teachers in play-based programs need to be familiar with the research on play and its effectiveness.

Theories of Play

Theories of play have proliferated over several centuries (Berlyne, 1969; Bruner, Jolly, & Sylva, 1976; Gilmore, 1971; Rubin, 1982; Rubin, Fein, & Vandenberg, 1983), and Canadians have been among the leaders in play research for a number of decades. In fact, three of the researchers in the foregoing list of references, Berlyne, Gilmore, and Rubin, have been based at Canadian universities. (The first two worked with Piaget in Geneva and at the University of Toronto, and Rubin worked at the University of Waterloo.) Most researchers (e.g., Rubin et al., 1983) agree that early play theories fall into four categories:

1. *The Surplus Energy Theory:* Play is a mechanism for burning off excess energy.
2. *The Relaxation and Recreation Theories of Play:* Play meets an adult's need for relaxation after a hard day's work.
3. *The Practice Theory of Play:* Play allows children to practise adult activities.
4. *The Recapitulation Theory of Play:* Children are the link in the evolutionary chain between animals and adults. In play, children go through or recapitulate all the steps humans passed before reaching their current evolutionary stage.

Roots of these theories can be found in 20th-century play theories, but all the early theories have been the subject of serious criticism and found lacking in a number of ways (Rubin et al., 1983). More recent theories of play have placed less emphasis on why people play and more on the actual *process* of play.

A comprehensive review of recent theories of play is beyond the scope of an introductory text. However, the views of Freud, Piaget, and Vygotsky on play merit consideration, especially because they have had considerable influence on early childhood education.

Freud's Theory of Play (Emotional)

According to Freud, play has anxiety-release and wish-fulfillment functions. Play allows the child a release from the real world and the opportunity to express impulses and wishes that are not acceptable in the real world. In that sense, play is healing as it permits children to relieve frustration and express their emotions.

Play therapy (see Anne Jernberg, Theraplay) evolved from the Freudian view of play, and it remains a common and powerful tool in therapeutic and hospital settings.

Piaget's Theory of Play (Cognitive)

One of Piaget's (1951) earlier works, *Play, Dreams, and Imitation in Childhood,* concentrated on play, including that of his own children. Piaget saw play as pure assimilation (see Chapter 2 on Piaget to refresh your memory about the terms he used). In play, the child assimilates a person, an event, or an object into current schemes or ways of thinking. Piaget also noted that play changes with age.

- *Practice Play*—In the sensorimotor stage of development (birth to 2 years), play is physical, not symbolic. **Practice play** is the term Piaget used to describe the repeated actions of the infant. Whether sucking, banging, or dropping an object, the infant repeats the behaviour that once was difficult and takes pleasure in mastering the skill. As motor development, such as the ability to grasp, bring hands to mouth, and reach, become refined, babies use practice, trial and error, and experimentation to gain control over the environment.

- *Symbolic Play*—As children enter the preoperational stage (2 to 7 years), **symbolic play** becomes possible as the child can mentally represent objects, events, and people. For instance, a block becomes an iron, a bowl becomes a hat, or a tube becomes a microphone. This is why simple materials with their limitless possibilities are far more appropriate than absolute toys with a single purpose. **Pretend play** is common during this period, and it becomes more social in nature, progressing from solitary to group pretend play.

- *Games with Rules*—**Games with rules** become possible once concrete operations (7 to 11 years) are achieved and children initiate an interest in organized games with simple rules. The rules become more complex as the child's cognitive capacities become more advanced.

Vygotsky's Theory of Play (Social)

Vygotsky (1976) was a Soviet psychologist who died before he completed work on his theory of mental development. However, his work on play in preschoolers has had a significant impact on research involving pretend play (Rubin et al., 1983). In keeping with Vygotsky's theory, play is a social interaction that builds knowledge. Other theories of play see children practising what they already know. Vygotsky saw children's interactions as a way to gain knowledge. Play is, in fact, the key to development. Play creates, facilitates, and imitates social interaction. Knowledge builds upon knowledge through social interactions and language (scaffolding is discussed in Chapter 2). Like other aspects of mental development, play initially demands action, but later it becomes imagination. The old adage that child's play is imagination in action can be reversed. We can say that imagination in adolescents and school children is play without action (Vygotsky, 1976, p. 539).

What Is Play?

No doubt you have heard that old, familiar saying that play is children's work. Though children would certainly not consider it work, they do realize it takes considerable energy, effort, and thought, and they do expect us to recognize and respect these efforts. This adult frame of reference does help us see children as

engaged in meaningful activity. The image of the little scientist helps some adults understand what it is children actually do as they play. Children, like all people, have many natural roles as they play—teacher, mentor, leader, manager, friend, confidant, learner. These actual roles are combined with the pretend roles children try on to gain insight and gather knowledge. As you will see, our primary role in play and guidance is to help children recognize and gain these insights to expand their knowledge base, not by telling or by continually questioning or by forever pointing out the obvious, but by careful observation, documentation, evaluation, and, most of all, timing. The

methods we use—labelling, elaborating, demonstrating, and challenging, the reasons we use them—to encourage, prompt, support, empower, and nurture, and how we use them—with a calm voice, at the child's level, respectfully, sincerely, confidently, and warmly—are equally important in facilitating and guiding play in order to foster healthy, emotional development.

Charlesworth (1987) described play as a sequence of four activities young children engage in when they encounter new objects and situations. These include:

- exploration—investigating the situation;
- manipulation—familiarizing self with its features;
- practice—experimenting; and
- repetition—mastering skills relative to the object/situation.

Children do this wherever they are, without fancy toys. They create their own learning environment. It is not the environment we see that is so important but the environment we don't see. Our role is to create, through our actions and words, an atmosphere of warmth and security where a child feels perfectly at ease doing what she or he does best—play.

Definitions of Play

Definitions of play have abounded over the years, with the most satisfactory ones focusing on play as an attitude. Children and adults enter into play with an attitude or *psychological disposition* or *set,* as the psychologists call it, that is different from their attitude when they work or study. That attitude distinguishes play from other forms of activity. A child who is playing has different intentions than one who is not. Rubin and his colleagues (1983) have outlined characteristics of play which theorists from different perspectives agree upon:

1. Play is *intrinsically motivated*: it comes from within the child and is not induced by needs for food or company, social demands, or promises of rewards.

2. In play, children focus on means, not ends. In play, the end-product is not important. Pleasure comes through the process of playing.

3. Play is more than exploration: play occurs with familiar objects, while exploration occurs with unfamiliar ones. In exploration, a child says, "What can this object do?" but in play, the question becomes, "What can I do with this object?"

4. Play is an "as if" activity: it involves pretending and has non-literal qualities.

5. Play has *no externally imposed rules*, whereas games do.

6. Play requires *active involvement*, whereas daydreaming does not.

7. Play is emergent and novel, not predetermined or scripted.

Play as Creativity

Given these characteristics, play can also be viewed as synonymous with creativity (discussed more in Chapter 9). Children approach their environment in a unique and novel way under their own initiative. They invent, discover, form hypotheses—in essence, they utilize scientific methodology. In so doing, they gather and construct knowledge. Children need an environment that does not restrict their creative nature. A restrictive, authoritarian environment can be frustrating and stressful to children as it inhibits and confines their natural drive and instinct to explore. Torrance (1963) argued that children's diminishing outward show of creativity and increasing conformity was a people-made rather than developmental phenomenon. Our progressively structured system of school environments gradually extinguish, or at least divert inwards, children's natural tendency to be creative thinkers It appears that children give in to the pressures of conformity. (We might wonder whether our attempts to socialize might better be replaced with attempts not to socialize.) You will see that guidance plays a pivotal role in facilitating and supporting children's drive to discover.

Overview of Play: Infants through School Age

Play in Infancy

Teachers working in settings that include infants and older preschoolers will tell you that their role in play differs substantially with the age of the child. In a preschool setting, for example, extended periods of time are allotted for self-directed play, whereas infants play for much shorter periods of time. Younger

infants also spend much of their day involved in caregiving routines, like feeding and changing. Play with infants often evolves during these caregiving sequences. The infant in the sensorimotor period of development also needs abundant opportunities to actively explore the environment—looking, smelling, tasting, banging, moving, listening, and shaking. Of course, arranging the environment so that sensorimotor play will occur is the responsibility of the caregiver. Teachers also are important facilitators of infant play, and they will be more likely to initiate play sequences with the very young than they would be with preschoolers.

To date, most studies of infant play have been descriptive in nature (Rubin et al., 1983). Most play during the first year is with single objects; the infant applies a sensorimotor action to the object. This type of play diminishes rapidly between 7 and 18 months, dropping from 90 percent of all play sequences to 20 percent. Symbolic play with objects (e.g., drinking from an empty cup) shows a marked increase between 11 and 18 months in a wide variety of settings and cultures.

The games parents play with infants also have been the subject of a number of investigations (Rubin et al., 1983). Parents initiate a number of play sequences (e.g., peek-a-boo, tickling, hiding), and infants coo, smile, and laugh in return. In the first few months of life, play is more likely to involve tactile, visual, auditory, and motor stimulation as opposed to toys. However, infants as young as 2 months respond to a responsive toy and try to maintain the stimulation. There is some suggestion that the language used in parent–infant game sequences introduces turn-taking conversational rules and social interaction.

The quality of play changes rapidly in the second year, and sensorimotor schemes are used less frequently. Pretend play with objects like toy cups, spoons, and pillows becomes more frequent. These sequences also come to involve others rather quickly; rather than self-feeding, the toddler will feed a doll, a parent, or a caregiver. Initially, this form of play involves an isolated event, but complex sequences soon emerge. These sequences are related to familiar activities like cooking, feeding, phoning, and changing. Substitute objects, rather than realistic objects, usually enter into play around 18 or 19 months, but the substitute needs to have some similarity to the real object for some months to come. Around 2 years, the toddler uses substitute objects more freely, and they contribute to an increase in the diversity of pretend-play sequences. Pretend play becomes more social in the third year as the following section indicates.

Play in the Preschool and Early School Years

Mildred Parten (1932) provided one of the landmark studies on play. Her work, still considered valid today (Sponseller, 1982), categorized young children's social

EXHIBIT 6.2A: PARTEN'S CATEGORIES OF SOCIAL PLAY

Types of Play	Definition	Example
Unoccupied behaviour	The child moves about the classroom going from one area to another, observing but not getting involved.	Sebastian wanders to the blocks and watches several children work together on a structure. After a few seconds he looks around, then walks over to the art table, where he looks at the finger-painting materials briefly but does not indicate a desire to paint. He continues to wander, going from area to area, watching but not participating.
Solitary play	The child plays alone, uninvolved with other children nearby. Children at all ages engage in this type of play, although older children's solitary play is more complex (Almy et al., 1984; Rubin, 1977).	Soon Yi works diligently at building a sand mountain, not looking at or speaking with the other children who are involved in other activities around her.
Onlooker play	Quite common among 2-year-olds, this type of play involves watching others nearby at play, without joining in.	Rajeef stands just outside the dramatic-play area and watches a group of children participate in doctor play using various medical props.
Parallel play	Children use similar materials or toys in similar ways but do not interact with one another.	Kalie alternates red and blue Lego blocks on a form board while Terrance, sitting next to her, uses Lego blocks to build a tall structure. They seem influenced by each other's activity but neither talk to each other nor suggest joining materials.
Cooperative play	Typical of older preschoolers, this is the most social form of play and involves children playing together in a shared activity.	On arriving at school one day, the children find an empty appliance box in their classroom. At first they climb in and out of the box, but then a few of them start talking about what it might be used for. Jointly they decide to make it into a house, and their discussion turns to how this could be accomplished. While continuing to discuss the project, they also begin the task of transforming the box, cutting, painting, and decorating to reach their common goal. It takes several days, but the children together create a house.

EXHIBIT 6.2B: SMILANSKY'S CATEGORIES OF COGNITIVE PLAY

Types of Play	Definition	Example
Functional play	Characteristic of infants and toddlers, this repetitive, motor play is used to explore what objects are like and what can be done with them.	Clark picks up a block, turns it, and looks at it from all sides. He bangs it on the floor, then picks up another block with his left hand and bangs the two blocks together. He alternates striking the blocks against each other and on the floor.
Constructive play	This involves creating something with the play objects.	Clark uses blocks to construct a tower. His activity now has a purpose.
Dramatic play	The child uses a play object to substitute for something imaginary.	Clark takes four blocks, puts one on each of four plates placed around the table, and says, "Here is your toast for breakfast."
Games with rules	These involve accepted, prearranged rules in play. This stage is more typical of older children.	In kindergarten, Clark and a group of peers play the game "Blockhead," agreeing on the game's rules.

play. She found that between 2 and 5 years children move from being asocial in their play to being associative. Although children at later ages engage in earlier forms of play, particularly solitary play (Hartup, 1983a), their play is typically more complex than it was when they were younger. Parten's six categories of social play are outlined in Exhibit 6.2.

Other researchers have viewed play from a different perspective. For instance, Sara Smilansky (1968) proposed play categories based on children's increasing cognitive abilities and measured by how children use play materials. This view is complementary to Parten's classifications because it focuses on a different aspect of play. Smilansky's categories are also highlighted in Exhibit 6.2

Pretend Play

The development of positive social traits is fostered in a variety of preschool activities and learning centres, but it is perhaps most naturally facilitated in pretend play. In pretend play, children use symbols such as words, actions, or other objects to represent the real world; in pretend play, they expand this symbolic play to include other children (Fein, 1979; Smilansky, 1968).

Theorists and researchers have postulated a relationship between pretend play and the development of social competencies. For instance, through such play, children have many opportunities to learn about social rules by taking on someone else's identity and enacting common situations, as well as by negotiating with peers when conflicts arise (Doyle & Connolly, 1989). Although research has found that not all children engage in pretend play (Christie, 1982; Smilansky, 1968, 1990), a number of programs have been successful in teaching young children how to do so.

The first of the series of pretend-play training studies was carried out in Israel by Sarah Smilansky (1968). She helped children from deprived backgrounds learn skills required in role taking, use of symbols, social and verbal interaction, and persistence. The level of teacher intervention depended on the skills and needs of the children. If children had very limited skills, the teacher facilitated pretend play by participating in the children's play directly. As children became more adept, the teacher became less obtrusive, taking on the role of an outside observer who made suggestions to enhance play rather than being a participant.

In many cases, children assist peers who are not as skilled in entering pretend play. For instance, 4-year-old Felix most often engaged in onlooker behaviour during child-selected activity times, usually standing on the outskirts of social groups. One day in November, Yasmine, age 5, deftly included Felix, who stood at the edge of the housekeeping corner observing a family group prepare dinner. The participants had assumed all the obvious roles, including that of family dog. The mother, Yasmine, took Felix by the hand, led him to the play oven, and declared, "You can be the turkey." She helped Felix fit himself into the oven and closed its door. A few seconds later, she opened the door, checked Felix's doneness by squeezing his thigh, and declared, "Turkey's done!" Everyone gathered around as the turkey was helped out of the oven. Felix's big grin testified to his delight at being assigned such an important role! Discussions ensued about children never getting into a real stove, fridge, and so on, for which the teacher checked, by listening, observing, and probing for prior, current, and new knowledge on the subject. In this way, the teacher identified those concepts that needed further guidance and discussion.

Most young children engage in dramatic pretend play naturally; however, such play should also be purposefully encouraged and enhanced in all early childhood settings. Every early childhood classroom should have an area set aside and equipped for dramatic play. Most commonly, dramatic-play props and children's engagement in dramatic play will centre on housekeeping because home-related roles and activities are most familiar to young children. Children re-create and enact what happens at home: meal preparation and consumption, bedtime routines, visitors, child rearing, even arguments. Home-related kitchen, living room, and bedroom items, as well as a selection of dolls, dress-up clothes, and mirrors, stimulate children's creative and social engagement in housekeeping play. Materials for younger preschoolers should be realistic, whereas they should be more abstract for older preschoolers, to encourage pretending (Fein, 1982). Children can be further encouraged to broaden their concepts and dramatic play through displays and pictures of people of all ages and different ethnic groups engaged in common household activities.

Dramatic play can also revolve around any other theme familiar to the children. Health care, shopping, and recreation are usually particularly relevant to young children because they invariably have visited the doctor, grocery store, or park. Children will also enact favourite book, television, or movie roles and stories. Ensuring children are familiar with a topic through concrete, firsthand experience before they engage in dramatic play also helps enhance their experiences. Ideally a program should have both a home centre and a dramatic play centre. If this is not possible, placing appropriate props for use in the dramatic play area following a field trip, for instance, can help children assimilate and integrate information from the trip.

You should make dramatic play kits available for children to integrate into the home centre rather than imposing a theme on the centre. Themes sometimes serve to restrict or impose play on children (e.g., children feel they must play "grocery store" because that is what is available). Without the choice between a home centre and a dramatic play centre, themes may actually rob the children of the value of the home centre where they often need to re-create circumstances to work them out. Kits, on the other hand, can be taken off the shelf as needed by the children. As well, number limits in the centre are usually not necessary. A more appropriate limit states that if everyone is cooperating, everything is fine!

Research and Value of Play

Research on pretend play has consistently found that this type of play increases with age in middle-class children from intact families, and it becomes more interactive with age. However, solitary pretend play decreases between 3 and 5 years and then increases again around age 6 (Rubin et al., 1983). Parallel pretend play remains frequent throughout the preschool years. A number of studies (Rubin et al., 1983; Shefatya, 1990) have suggested that pretend play is delayed and/or less mature in children from lower-income backgrounds. Some of these studies have not been well-controlled, and the differences may not be as great as was once suspected. Nevertheless, across several cultures, children who have parents with less formal education engage in less pretend play than children who have parents with more formal education. Children who watch a great deal of television also are less likely to engage in pretend play, and there is some suggestion that divorce reduces the occurrence of pretend play, especially in boys. Large toys that accommodate pretend play themes (e.g., a horse, a car) seem to produce more pretend play, as do more creative playgrounds.

Rubin and his colleagues (1983) and Smilansky (1990) also have reviewed the extensive literature on the effects of play on development, but the literature is clouded with methodological difficulties. The evidence suggests that problem solving, story making, classification skills, and scores on intelligence tasks are positively correlated with pretend play. Tutoring in pretend play also has been investigated (Rubin et al., 1983; Smilansky 1990) and found to lead to both an increase in pretend play in the class, improvement in related cognitive skills, and an increase in social participation. As peer interactions are significant influences on cognitive development, the increase in social participation may have far-reaching effects.

Smilansky (1990) noted that 12 independent studies, conducted over a 16-year period, have shown positive benefits from adult intervention in pretend play. The interventions were meant to improve and extend the play, not to make it adult-dominated. Subsequently, she conducted a survey of 120 preschool and kindergarten teachers in the United States and Israel to see if these results affected educational practices. While 100 percent of the teachers had a playhouse corner in their programs, 90 percent of the teachers did not expect all children to play there during the week, and none of the teachers assessed the children's play in that area. In fact, none of the teachers remembered any course that covered pretend play, and 90 percent of them did not think pretend play helped prepare children for school. Moreover, 50 percent of the teachers never intervened in pretend play, and another 30 percent only encouraged and facilitated pretend play. This gap between research and practice concerned Smilansky, who maintained that the cognitive learning potential of pretend play is being overlooked in many classrooms. Other teachers believe that provision of a proper setting and environment plus encouragement is sufficient for the child to grow. They look on intervention in socio-dramatic play activity with suspicion (Smilansky, 1990, p. 40).

Smilansky recommended a fundamental change in attitudes and pointed to teacher education as the force that can lead to such a change. With knowledge about the importance of pretend play, and appropriate assessment and intervention techniques, teachers are likely to make much greater use of this untapped resource. Wright (1983), for example, demonstrated that changes in the theme of the dramatic play centre (e.g., a store, hospital, hairdresser and barbershop) led to increased use of the centre, especially by older children. A study by Marcotte and Young (1992) in Hamilton, Ontario, also found that a switch in the dramatic play centre's theme was associated with a substantial increase in language use in the centre.

Smilansky (1990) and Rubin et al. (1983) have documented many studies that have demonstrated the value of play in the life of the young child. Teachers who are aware of this literature are able to defend play-based, developmentally appropriate programs and resist the push for academics.

A Note on Superheroes

Though superhero play has been criticized, proponents of this type of play emphasize the fact that children emulate the noble qualities in superheroes and strive toward these values and images. Kostelnik, Whiren, and Stein (1986) pointed out that children benefit from these play experiences in many ways:

- Children are empowered
- Children experience positive emotions (e.g., courage, strength, pride, glory, and wisdom in doing something good).
- Children gain confidence in themselves and adults.

- Children experience and imitate clear models of good behaviour and strive toward these roles.
- Children practise problem solving, decision making, conversational skills, and cooperation.
- Children can role play in a safe environment.

Saltz, Dixon and Johnson (1977) introduced thematic fantasy play to help children act out fantasy characters. Saltz and Saltz (1986) found that this play activity improved children's performance across social, emotional, and cognitive domains. As early childhood educators, we need to remember that children can learn good things through imitation and observation. Children usually want to play the good guys. They can choose what aspects they will learn. Conversely, they ignore aspects that are above their thinking, experience, or interest level. We provide dramatic play as an outlet for children to solve problems they have seen, heard, or experienced, yet we often preclude them from exploring selected aspects of these problems through play by assuming we know what the problems are.

How will we learn what hidden experiences or fears the children have if we impose biases on what they are able to express through play? Where, then, is the safe outlet for experience of fears, anxieties, and confusion? How can we guide what we cannot observe? We need to be aware that implementing blanket policies (e.g., no play involving pretend use of guns) may prevent children from showing us what we need to know since we cannot possibly know ahead of time what children need to express to us. Carlsson-Paige and Levin (1992) wrote an excellent guideline entitled "Who's Calling the Shots?" that deals practically with both sides of the debate concerning children's fascination with war play and war toys.

To guide, among other things, means to help children understand, to pose questions, to clarify and confirm, to help them research and investigate, and to provide information to help identify and work through problems and fears. Our curriculum should enable children to show what they know. Only then can we adequately and effectively guide them.

Cooperative Games

One prosocial goal that early childhood educators cite for young children is cooperation, the force that unites people into working together toward a common objective. Games can be easily adapted to keep the element of fun while minimizing competition. For instance, the game of musical chairs can be changed so that all the children share the decreasing number of chairs, until everyone is piled on (and around) the last chair.

Terry Orlick (1978a, 1978b, 1982) first turned our attention to the destructive outcome of some competitive games and proposed cooperative games as an alternative. The rationale for cooperative games is not just the avoidance of situations in which most of the participants lose but is much broader, extending to a general concern for the quality of life, emphasis on peace and harmony, and decrease in societal aggression.

Activities involving two or more players can be considered cooperative if one or more of the following is involved: shared goals, joint decision making, shared ideas and materials, negotiation and bargaining, coordination of efforts to meet goals, and evaluation of progress toward goals (Goffin, 1987). Although Orlick recommended organized group games as a vehicle for promoting cooperation, this trait can be encouraged in more indirect and less structured ways as well.

Classroom space can be organized to encourage interactions, and ample time blocks can be allocated for child-selected play. Cooperative endeavours may well require more space and more time than activities in which children act alone. In addition, materials should be selected for their cooperative properties. Open-ended materials such as dramatic-play props, blocks, water, sand, and puppets particularly promote cooperation.

Guidance

Certainly, understanding that children need to play, and knowing what play is, are major steps toward providing a quality program. Your role in guiding children's play is inextricably linked to your role in guiding children. The principles that govern our interactions with children apply throughout the day. In fact, the principles of guidance are, in many ways, the early childhood education program. If

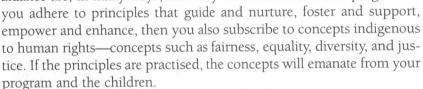

you adhere to principles that guide and nurture, foster and support, empower and enhance, then you also subscribe to concepts indigenous to human rights—concepts such as fairness, equality, diversity, and justice. If the principles are practised, the concepts will emanate from your program and the children.

As you are well aware, you could not go through a day of play-centred learning without a few occasions where misunderstandings and conflicts arise as children play to assert themselves, to figure things out, to gain a sense of achievement. Your role of guiding children in their development in a manner that keeps their self-esteem intact yet enriches the learning experience is a delicate yet fundamental one. As soon as you interact with children, you have an impact on them. There are two possible outcomes. This impact can be negative and debilitating or positive and nurturing. The goal of guidance is to nurture children's emotional development while helping them grow and learn as they play and interact with others.

What Guidance Is

In this chapter, when we use the term "discipline," we imply positive discipline or guidance. *Webster's Dictionary* defines **guidance** as "the act of directing ... to a particular end." This implies, as we discussed earlier, that guidance is an ongoing process and that techniques must be appropriate for the kind of people you want children to grow up to be. Guidance is also related to discipline, which, for too many adults, connotes a reaction to a misbehaviour by the child who did not follow the rules—rules that might have been inappropriate in the first place (Morrison, 1988). The word "discipline," however, comes from the Latin word meaning learning or teaching, and, in early childhood education, we need to focus on this positive aspect of discipline. **Positive discipline,** or guidance, helps children achieve self-discipline (Gordon & Browne, 1993); it is an empowering force, not a negative one. In essence, we are coaching children as they play to discover positive alternatives to inappropriate behaviours.

What Guidance Is Not

Undoubtedly, you will meet people who equate **punishment** with discipline. But punishment has a whole series of difficulties associated with it. For example, punishment emphasizes what the child should not do (e.g., "Don't hit!"), whereas discipline indicates what the desired behaviour is (e.g., "You need to use your words"). Punishment is a one-time rather than an ongoing occurrence; it focuses on obedience rather than on development of self-control; it undermines self-esteem by criticizing children, centring them out, or embarrassing them, thus creating a loss of enjoyment and negative feelings toward themselves and others (Bredekamp, 1987); and it makes decisions for the children rather than allowing the children to think through solutions (Gordon & Browne, 1993). In addition, physical punishment may, in fact, increase undesirable behaviours such as aggression (Maccoby & Martin, 1983; Patterson, 1982) because it models the very behaviour it is intended to discourage. Early childhood experts discourage punishment because of its *long-term ineffectiveness* in changing behaviour. Children will learn to dislike and avoid those who punish them, creating a paradox of conflicting emotions including guilt, anger, confusion, and remorse (Sheppard, 1973). Guidance or positive discipline has none of these difficulties, and it preserves the child's self-esteem.

An Atmosphere of Trust

To relax and learn effectively and to become confident individuals, children must trust their environment and the people in it. In Chapter 2, we discussed children's need for play and need for self-esteem and have elaborated on play and emotional development yet further in this chapter. These needs can only be met in an environment where the children trust us. Trust occurs when we are consistent, pre-

dictable, and fair in our interactions with children. The environment must be warm, safe, and nurturing. Children also learn to trust as they observe the behaviours we expect of them as reflected in the positive role models we present to them. Children expect us to be rational and logical and are taken aback when we are not. Their sense of trust and faith in their own judgment of perception is shaken when we do not behave predictably and sensibly.

Children respond to our voice tone perhaps even more than to our words since tone conveys our true intentions and feelings. Children need to trust that our voice tone and words match and that our intentions are sincere and honourable.

Children also learn to trust, and therefore grow and develop as confident and competent persons, when the limits we set are fair, logical, and consistent. Fairness implies a sensitivity toward individual needs, without bias, through a gentle and caring manner. Children put great trust in us that we know what is good for them and that we know what we are doing. This trust that we are capable and mature individuals frees them up to play without insecurity, stress, or worry. Understanding children comes from self-awareness and being able to put yourself in children's shoes. By understanding children, we can create an atmosphere of trust in which they can play and develop to their maximum potential. Below we elaborate on those factors that help create this all important atmosphere of trust.

A Warm, Nurturing, Safe Environment

One thing we expect of children is that they will play. Through their play, they construct knowledge about their world and they develop skills and traits that help them interact within that world. Knowing that children will and must play implies many things. It means we expect them to be noisy and busy and forgetful and assertive. Children expect that this is acceptable to us and when it is not, that we will address them calmly, justly, logically, and democratically. In doing so, we create an atmosphere where children feel secure, cared for, and cared about.

Positive Role Models

Parents and early childhood educators, in general, hope to help children develop so that they are friendly, sociable, responsible, helpful, collaborative, and considerate, and who acquire a conscience (Moore, 1982). This is because we also value adults (i.e., colleagues, parents, friends) who exhibit such qualities. Hence, if we expect these behaviours in children and admire them in adults, it follows that children expect to see these behaviours in the adults in their lives. Such a range of behaviours, however, does not emerge without thoughtful and consistent guidance from parents and teachers.

Logical Reasoning and Positive Interactions

Among the qualities of children that parents and teachers often value are the abilities to care about others, to share willingly, to be altruistic, to be empathetic, and to be understanding of the needs of others. Such prosocial behaviours are most likely to appear in children and grownups who come from a nurturing environment, where understanding and caring are modelled, where responsibility is expected, and where **inductive reasoning** is used (Mussen & Eisenberg-Berg, 1977). Inductive reasoning involves an approach in which adults help children see, through logic and reasoning (questioning to confirm or clarify, exploring, elaborating, demonstrating, and calming), the consequences of their behaviour.

One aspect of prosocial qualities in children appears to be the development of self-control. This, in turn, leads to self-regulation, in which the child's judgment about the situation dictates the response (Kopp, 1982). Internal rather than external control is critical, for it means that the child does what is right, not because she or he might be rewarded (or punished), but because she or he knows this action is the morally responsible thing to do. Development of inner control is fostered by giving the child many opportunities to make decisions and to experience the **logical and natural consequences** of those decisions which teach but do not harm (Kamii, 1984). It is during even the earliest years that the foundations for self-regulation are being constructed.

In an article entitled "Obedience Is Not Enough," Constance Kamii (1984) differentiates between **morality of autonomy,** based on an inner sense of integrity, and **morality of obedience,** based on doing what one is told to do. To achieve morality of autonomy, children need many opportunities, beginning at an early age, to develop a sense of personal values. The development of values comes from the opportunities to exchange viewpoints with others and to make decisions.

A climate in which such opportunities are offered is *child-centred and nurturing, respectful of the child's growing autonomy.* Adults in the child's world are careful to use inductive reasoning, focusing on explanations that provide rationale and stress the rights and feelings of others rather than on punitive insults or restrictions (Honig, 1985b; Maccoby & Martin, 1983). Thus, the child is told, "It really makes Ingrid feel unhappy and hurt when you tell her nobody likes her," rather than "Don't you say that, you selfish brat!"

An interactional style between adult and child, in which *the child is given a reason for what the adult expects,* has been shown to produce children who are socially competent; have positive interactions with peers; and are self-controlled, assertive, self-reliant, generally happy, and explorative (Baumrind, 1967). The adult engages in verbal give-and-take with the child, provides opportunities for decision making, and is consistent in setting and enforcing rules and expectations (Baumrind & Black, 1967).

Respectful Tone

Children expect and respond to a voice that is calm but firm, a gentle, confident voice that the child can trust and respect, not fear, a voice that reassures we love you and we are helping you. How we say things to children is as important as what we say. Often words are lost when tone is harsh, scary, and cutting. The voice is an exceptional guidance and teaching tool. It can be calming, affirming, soothing, and strengthening. As adults, it is our role to model the same respectful behaviour that we expect.

Gentle Actions

Children expect our actions to be comforting and supportive. If our actions are not congruent with our words, children are caught off balance. This creates insecurity and a sense of mistrust and trepidation or uneasiness. Children must believe and trust what we say, and our actions must confirm, not negate, the positive atmosphere we are attempting to create. Negative actions can erase all the good we have instilled. Our actions must also show we respect and value the dignity, differences, and worth of each child.

Fair and Sensitive Guidelines

Often we unintentionally give children messages in ways that say, "We trust you but we don't." The intent of setting guidelines—or limits—is to help children retain freedom of choice through decision making and problem solving within a safe environment. Guidelines are meant to prevent, not escalate, situations. We encourage children to develop independence and creativity, but when they exercise these traits at times that are inconvenient to us, we often reprimand them for it. When there is no apparent logical reason for our limits save that it is convenient, we might call these "limits of convenience." These limits of convenience do not make much sense to children, and they do not seem fair. Thus, they often create further problems that did not originally exist as child and adult engage in a power struggle to get what each wants. In this situation, there is always a loser—someone who leaves the situation feeling hurt, frustrated, or angry. If we are feeling exasperated in a situation, we need to remember that children are probably feeling the same way.

Examples of limits of convenience are "Blocks stay in the block centre" or "Only two allowed in the house centre." These limits are external controls that do not convey to children that they are responsible and capable. If a block is needed as an iron in the house centre and we have taught children that creativity, tidying up, and borrowing and returning things are admired qualities, we need to trust that (1) we have done a good job in teaching this to the children, and (2) the children will respect the limits and return the block when they are done. Similarly, if five children are getting along fabulously in the house centre, have we not met our goals of guidance—children who collaborate, cooperate, solve problems, respect others, and manage their own behaviour? If Sarah wishes to stay in role as a princess for snack, is it really a situation that warrants intervention? It is, only if you have set up a limit of convenience (e.g., "Clothes stay in the house centre"), which you are then forced to follow through on. Hence, you must deal with two discipline situations: (1) enforcing the limit and (2) dealing with the behaviour that results from enforcing the limit. You also end up disciplining children for the very behaviours that you have encouraged and that come naturally to them. When you say, "Clothes stay in the house centre" or "Blocks stay in the block centre," you are saying, "Your creativity is not valued here," "You've done something wrong," "Your initiative is not respected," "Your judgment is poor." This instils in children feelings of guilt, shame, doubt, and lack of confidence in their own self-assertion. They will be less likely to take initiative and express their creativity and autonomy next time. Are we accomplishing what we set out to do—or the opposite?

Simply requesting information to confirm a child's intent would prevent many problems. "John, I see you needed an iron for all that laundry. Tell me what you will do with the iron when it is time to tidy up." No doubt the child will exclaim (probably with surprise that you should even ask!), "Put it back in the block centre!" Here the child has verbalized exactly what is expected. You have now confirmed that he knows the limit, which is an appropriate (not a convenient) one. He, not you, is now responsible for his own behaviour. He now owns the decision. If he forgets, you can guide him back to his decision—a decision that is meaningful to him because he owns it. Having children help you set limits and discussing logical outcomes with them also assists in self-regulation of behaviour. Keeping limits few and simple works best.

Good Judgment

Children need to feel that we know and understand them and, therefore, have good judgment about them. One of the most common mistakes adults make is taking children's behaviour personally. In most cases, a child's actual intent is far different than the intent the adult perceives. For instance, when John removed the block from the block centre, we might assume his intent was to break the limit, so we would discipline him. If his intent was to be creative, then disciplining him will be inappropriate for his intent. At the least, John would be surprised at our actions and remorseful for his own. Children become confused when they are disciplined when they thought they were doing something good and right. At the very least, we need to ask or remind children to clarify their intent before stepping in to guide their behaviour (or not have unnecessary rules in the first place).

Dan Gartrell (1995) wrote an excellent article, "Misbehaviour or Mistaken Behaviour," in which he traced our traditional discipline techniques back to our historical values of children. In Chapter 2, we discussed that in the past children were seen as evil and naughty, so corporal punishment, forced obedience, and harsh discipline ensued to make the children into "good people." Though most of us believe children to be inherently good, we still fall victim to disciplining a child as a "good girl" or "bad boy." In this case, we are not separating the child from the behaviour.

Greenberg (1988) reminds us that as good early childhood educators, we should consider all children potentially good people with a great deal of motivation to please, be approved of, be loved, be cared for, and do the right thing (pp. 24–25). With this in mind, Gartwell (1985) said that we can view most behaviour as a mistake. If we see a child's behaviour as a mistake, we are less likely to view the child as bad or to take his or her behaviour personally. We are more likely to want to guide that child through the mistake—through the learning and developing process—just as we would guide a child who falls when learning to walk or who makes mistakes when learning to talk. Here Gartwell recommends we use the term "mistaken behaviour" rather than misbehaviour. Behaviour is also a developmental domain, one that must develop as the child grows and changes. And as much time as it took to develop, it takes as much time to redevelop.

Our view of children's behaviour also helps us deal with our perceptions. Children who are labelled "behaviour problems" often stand little chance of ever again being seen as behaving appropriately, of being a child worthy of acceptance, respect, and guidance. Every single behaviour that the child initiates is interpreted as a problem, so every behaviour is dealt with as if it were a problem, even if the behaviour is typical of any other child of the same age.

As early childhood educators, we must know what is typical behaviour for children at particular ages. This coupled with knowledge of child development will help us guide children fairly and justly so that each party retains dignity, trust, respect, and positive feelings.

Empathy—Putting Yourself in Children's Shoes

Children need empathy. Put yourself in their shoes. What were they trying to do? What method will work best without jeopardizing emotions? If you think you would feel hurt or scared by what you were about to do, stop and choose a different response. Children live moment to moment, so every moment is significant and powerful. Though you might forget the incident in a second, the child might never forget.

Can you remember an incident when the teacher disciplined you? You can possibly see clearly how he or she misperceived your intent, interpreting it as a bad or purposeful behaviour. The teacher's reaction to your innocent and unknowing ways surprised you at the time since you had no such intentions of "being bad," and you were confused and hurt by her or his reactions—and you still remember what that feels like. The teacher also did not have bad intentions; her or his discipline was momentary and casual with little insight into its impact. The teacher's mandate was to stick to the schedule, maintain order, and finish the lesson—a much different agenda than yours. The sooner we, as teachers, understand intent and realize the impact of our actions, the sooner we will reach our goals of guidance.

Self-Awareness

Where will you begin? What approach or approaches to guidance should you use? Some guidelines may help you select an approach to working with young children. First, try to think through your own values and expectations as they relate to the care of infants and young children. Do this in the context in which you were reared because your own background will affect your views. If you were raised in a family that used firmness and fairness, you will most likely bring your own experiences to the task of guiding young children. If your family was authoritarian, and you were expected to follow rules because someone bigger than you said these were the rules, then you will need to examine whether you will carry this attitude into your work.

Self-understanding is very important in working with young children. If you acknowledge your strengths and identify areas you might want to change, you will

emerge with a more solid foundation. As you examine your own values, keep in mind your aim in working with the children whose parents have entrusted them into your care. As was stated at the beginning of this chapter, guidance is a long-term process, contributing to the evolution of children into adults. If the aim is to develop caring, competent, self-directed adults, this process begins early in life. What matters is that the guidance principles applied are in line with the desired outcome.

Good early childhood educators generally follow an **eclectic approach** to guidance and, in so doing, hope to empower children with self-discipline and problem-solving skills. Developing a personal style of guidance takes time, and it may well change over the years of your professional involvement and development. What is important is that you are comfortable with the guidance approach you use because it is effective and supports children's development in a positive, nurturing manner.

Summary

Research supports the fact that the process of child rearing and child caregiving is tied to the characteristics that the child displays. A consistent, loving, firm, reasonable, inductive environment helps children become morally responsible, considerate of others, independent, and assertive. These findings give direction to early childhood educators, who are partners with parents in the process of nurturing children.

Some Guidance Techniques

Keep in mind that your attitude toward your job and children, your knowledge, your skill as a teacher, your ability to be consistent as well as flexible, and a good sense of humour all contribute to setting the tone for the classroom. A respect for all children and a willingness to get to know each child as an individual are basic ingredients in positive guidance. A sense of partnership with the children rather than a me-against-them attitude is also essential. There is no doubt that you, the teacher, are central to establishing a productive, lively, happy environment for all the children. Being firm while fair is a difficult concept for some, but it is a trademark of a good early childhood education teacher.

Prevention

It is much easier on you, as the teacher, as well as on the children if problems are prevented before they occur. As you will see, prevention and preparation are the mainstays of guidance when coupled with a calm, caring, fair, logical, consistent, empowering, and sincere approach.

Be Thorough and Creative in Your Planning

When children are afforded opportunities to become engrossed in meaningful activities which they find rewarding and interesting, they are much less likely to need guidance. Good curriculum is integrally tied to your guidance approach (Good Discipline, 1987) and will, in itself, provide a key preventive technique.

Be Consistent, Fair, and Logical

Children generally abide by guidelines that are logical, fair, consistent, simple, and few in number. There is no need to overwhelm children with too many rules. A simple, all-encompassing guideline is that children or adults cannot hurt themselves, others, or things.

As we discussed, usually children's behaviour is a function of not knowing, remembering, or understanding what is expected. When children engage in behaviours that you see as a problem, do not jump to the conclusion that they are misbehaving deliberately. They may simply be acting out of ignorance, may not understand your expectations, or may not have been given any expectations.

Involving children in establishing a few classroom guidelines helps children understand the rationale behind them. In determining the consequences as a group, the entire class understands the guidelines and takes responsibility for upholding them. The guidelines are not the teacher's alone. Thus, simple reminders are all that are required.

Inconsistencies confuse children. Setting limits that still allow for choice, problem solving, individual differences, and creativity are both appropriate and expected. Children expect us to be consistent with our discipline and they generally know the limits, but they feel safe and secure in the knowledge that you are there to monitor limits that protect them.

Observe

One way to use preventive guidance is to keep an eye on as much of the group as possible. Both inside and on the playground, position yourself with your back to a wall or fence where you can watch the majority of the children, even though generally you are with an individual child or a small group. Teachers often feel guilty observing. They equate being busy with teaching. But being busy means you may miss things. Observation allows you to get to know the children to learn what they like, what skills they possess, and what they need. Watching children play is perhaps the most enlightening of all experiences. Enjoy it. Also watch the children watching. Teachers tend to redirect them if they are just standing there watching, but children are rarely doing nothing. As they watch, they are processing, deciding, learning, and thinking.

Know the Children

Know what triggers certain children's behaviours. If Solomon tends to hit others when he gets frustrated, be available when you see him trying a difficult puzzle. If Rana cries when she does not get to be Mommy at the home centre, be available to guide the children's role selection if needed. If Jarrod hits children when the room is crowded, ensure that he has more space. If Shaheen has a difficult time sharing, watch the block centre when Andy approaches it. You are not stepping in to solve the children's problems but to be available to guide them if needed in learning problem-solving skills.

Stay Calm and Gentle

Remaining calm and not allowing anger to interfere with your own judgment or behaviour is critical to keeping others calm. Looking at the whole situation will give you the whole picture. Children are not intentionally doing something to you, as we discussed; they are making mistakes and they need help, time, and encouragement while they learn.

Listen

A few minutes at the beginning of the day spent encouraging children to discuss anything they wish undoubtedly reduces problems during the day since it allows children to unload and get ready to face their day with a renewed outlook. During the day, we must sincerely listen when children approach us to talk. Our tendency is to speak for them or hurry them along when what we really need to do is provide the time for children to express themselves.

Communicate

Communication means a message that is being given or received. This can occur through words and actions. Our goal is to ensure these messages are positive:

- Provide children with information—rationale, feelings, and descriptions of behaviour, and include them in your thinking and consequences.
- State directions and expectations positively. Speak to children as capable people—at their eye level, without baby talk, in a normal tone of voice.
- Encourage children to engage in conversation. This fosters turn taking, problem solving, and self expression.
- Include children in planning.
- Ask children for their input and respect their opinions.
- Your body language should be positive and inviting.
- Stay close to the children who need reassurance.
- Hug those who need it.
- Hold hands on walks.
- Sit between children who could present a potential problem at circle time.
- Lean forward, put your hand out, or signal a reminder to children that you are aware of the whole class.

Stone (1993) emphasizes that how we say things is certainly as important as what we say. Do we sound sincere? Are the words nice but the tone angry? Are your teeth clenched? Is your pitch elevated? Or are you genuinely calm, matter-of-fact, and sincerely interested? Stone terms the language we use with children as responsive because it conveys a positive tone of regard, respect, and acceptance of children's ideas and feelings. It is guiding and leading, helping the child toward more independent choices and alternatives. It empowers the child in the decision-making process.

Stone uses four categories:

1. Use reason and logic.
2. Encourage independence and autonomy.
3. Use nurturing control or commands: "You need to …"
4. Use elaboration to expand on ideas.

What we say and how we say it makes all the difference in the world as to whether a child goes on his or her way feeling empowered or deflated. As staff, monitor one another. Practise and uphold that school policy that embraces children's self-esteem, independence, and curious nature.

Provide Choice

The key here is providing choices that are all acceptable. In so doing, you maintain some structure and control, and the children are empowered by the ability to choose their own snack, activity, book, puzzle, or play centre. Be sure you ask questions that highlight the choices rather than questions that require a yes or no answer. Narrowing choices down, outlining them, and even having children decide on possible choices and the rationale behind them gives children parameters within which to work.

Use Redirection and Distraction

Another way to prevent potential problems is by **redirection.** For instance, distract Sylvia if she is about to kick over the block tower by steering her to the water table, or provide Yusuf with an alternative toy to replace the one he is about to snatch from Richie. Redirection works particularly well with very young preschoolers whose self-control is just emerging and who do not yet have the verbal and social skills required for sharing. Sensitive teachers can help 2-year-olds develop these skills and attributes over time through many positive interactions. However, redirection should not be used routinely with older preschoolers, who need practice in handling social situations effectively (Essa, 1990).

Distraction through humour is used very effectively by some teachers (Laughing, 1988). Many potential me-against-you situations, in which a heavy hand is needed, can be avoided by using a light touch—distraction from a problematic situation to something interesting and fun, directions in the form of a jingle or song, or a joke, *not* at the child's expense, of course (p. 41). Distraction works particularly well with younger children; most toddlers readily change focus when distracted.

Humour helps prevent power struggles because the teacher and children are joint participants in a fun-filled friendship. Telling a child, "Now … let … me … see … you … walk … slow … slow … like … a … turtle" will be more effective than saying, "How many times do I have to tell you not to run in the classroom?"

Use Positive Reinforcement

We briefly discussed the origins of the concept of positive reinforcement in Chapter 2 and its meaning and value at the beginning of this chapter. Positive reinforcement is perhaps the most widely used application of behaviour management, but it is one that teachers frequently forget to use in abundance. You use it every time you smile at the children who are playing cooperatively in the dramatic play centre, gently touch the head of the child who is engrossed in putting together a puzzle, or say thank you to the children for helping to clean up after snack. Such subtle social reinforcers come naturally to most teachers. In behaviour management, reinforcers are often used systematically to encourage specified behaviours. If Julio gets positive attention every time he hangs up his coat, he is more likely to repeat the behaviour. Eventually, Julio will provide his own inner reinforcement as he becomes independent, and the teacher can provide intermittent reinforcement to reassure Julio she still notices.

Positive reinforcement can be a powerful tool but ineffective praise, such as in general or gratuitous statements such as "Good job! "or "Good boy!" can actually be counterproductive (Hitz & Driscoll, 1988). Rather than foster positive self-concept and autonomy, ineffective praise can lower self-confidence and lead to dependency because the teacher has placed herself or himself in the position of telling children what is right or wrong (Kamii, 1984). Ineffective praise can also decrease motivation by making the reward, rather than the activity, the goal. When praising one child's appropriate behaviour is used to encourage the others to follow suit, children may react with anger and resentment because they feel manipulated.

Furthermore, insincere or indiscriminate praise reduces the children's respect and trust. Instead, it is recommended that you use **effective praise** or **encouragement,** which focuses on the activity and process, allows children to evaluate their own work, and discourages competition. Below are some examples of encouragement, as proposed by Hitz and Driscoll (1988, p. 12):

- Denise played with Jimmy at the sand table. They experimented with funnels for more than 20 minutes.

Encouraging statement: "You and Jimmy played together for a long time at the sand table."

- Sue seldom talks in the group, but today she told a short story about Hallowe'en.

Encouraging statement: "That was a very scary story you told. It gave me goosebumps."

- Daniel just finished a painting. He comes to you, the teacher, and says, "Look at my painting. Isn't it beautiful?"

Encouraging statement: You look happy about your painting. Look at all the colours you used!

Note that the statements are informational and descriptive yet are not value-aden or judgmental. They don't start with "I like the way you ..." We need to get in the habit of providing children with information about what they did coupled with *why* it made such a difference (the results of their choices). Rationale is an important tool for progress.

Provide Attention

Reinforcement is a form of attention, but attention is more than reinforcement. All human beings need acknowledgment of their existence, affirmation of their linkage to others, acceptance of their membership in the human race. Sometimes we communicate through nurturance, caring, gentleness, sensitivity, and tenderness; we do this not because we are reacting to a desired behaviour, as in reinforcement, but simply because we are responding to a human need.

Reinforcement is given conditional on the child responding in a specific way, but children also need **unconditional attention.** This type of attention given to them not because you want them to do something, because they did something, or only when they are good, but because they are inherently valued and worthy persons who deserve and need your attention. Such attention makes an enormous difference to a child. Unconditional acceptance and response begin in earliest infancy and lay the foundation for feelings of trust. As a result, many children receiving such attention in ample supply, at home and in infant and toddler care programs, have strong, trusting relationships in their lives. By 3 years, these children are full of independence and openness to new experiences. Other children whose foundation for trust is not as firmly established or has been shaken by a disruptive experience, such as divorce, may seem unduly demanding; they may constantly seek your attention, possibly through misbehaviour.

Unconditional attention tells children that you value *them,* as individuals in their own right, not because they behave as you want them to behave. You can give unconditional attention in a number of ways, such as greeting children at the beginning of the day with *genuine* statements, such as "Good morning, Jenny! I'm so glad to see you!" During the day, teachers also provide such attention when they smile at, glance at, hug, cuddle, or soothe a child or when they respond to the child who requests help or attention.

One mechanism for providing unconditional attention to a child who particularly seems to need extra attention is **special time** (Essa, 1990). The teacher sets aside just a few minutes a day, or even two or three times a week, just for the child. This one-on-one time is not conditional on the child behaving in a particular way (e.g., "If you …, then we will spend special time") but is unconditional, not at all tied to the child's behaviour. The teacher conveys the message, "I want to spend time with just you because you are you." The teacher can ask what the child would like to do for special time and then follow up on that suggestion, whether it is going for a short walk, reading a book, or playing a game; the specific activity is less important than the teacher's undivided attention during this time together.

Such a time investment can have great payoffs. Early childhood educators who have used special time with children who seem to be seeking extra attention have found that these children seem to feel better about themselves and greatly decrease their acting-out behaviour. Some schools also recommend this method to parents (Keele, 1966), with the result that children whose parents regularly spend a few minutes in one-on-one interaction seem much more self-assured and secure.

Provide Adequate Time and Space

Children need time to finish their projects, their snack, their conversations. Children need time to be alone—to think, to reflect, to daydream. What our child care centres lack most is a sense of privacy for children. Every move and all work is under the watchful eyes of the teacher. Playgrounds and playrooms need to be big enough for children to "escape" and yet, of course, still be safe. Children need time to whisper, conspire, giggle, fantasize, converse, and plan. So often a problem situation is created when teachers spring transition time on children. Children need warning so they can begin to plan and tidy up. We need flexibility in our schedules, especially if we want children growing up to control and plan their own time. This relates to setting guidelines and to communication. Everything can be discussed; everything can be solved.

Abandon Your Agenda

It is hard when you stayed up until 2:00 a.m. planning that wonderful lesson, but if it isn't working—and you've switched gears and been as creative and ingenious as you possibly could—live dangerously! Stop what you are doing, determine the group's needs, and move on with something that everyone will enjoy. If you are struggling in your delivery—you're frustrated, unhappy, tense—the children on the receiving end are too. Remember, they don't know you stayed up late, and they aren't doing this *to you*. They're children who are communicating to you that certain factors are affecting their behaviour, and they need your help in eliminating those. Being honest with children, discovering what is going on, and determining a solution are wonderful experiences. Children are sensitive, compassionate, empathetic, and oh so wise. As your partners, they will have no problem in telling you what they (or you) need (or what a good job you're doing).

Model

Modelling, advocated by social learning theorists, is effective because research has told us that children are likely to imitate those they admire and like. Observational learning occurs frequently in the classroom, and we use it when we model politeness, friendliness, or caring, although modelling is not a simple cause–effect phenomenon. Certain conditions, for instance, children seeing another child being reinforced (e.g., praised) will more likely result in imitation of the reinforced behaviour (Bandura, 1977).

Cue or Prompt Children

Cuing is a technique used to help children remember what is expected. Thus, teachers may use a specific cue such as a bell to tell children that it is time to come in from outside play or a specific song to signal a transition time. It may suffice for the teacher to catch a child's eye and give a nod of the head to remind the child of what is expected.

Discuss

Talking about a behaviour before and after its occurrence can be effective with some children, especially older preschoolers and school-aged children. Older children often respond well to such discussion, particularly if they have adequate verbal skills, the budding ability to look at themselves, and the motivation to change a behaviour that makes them unhappy. Infants and toddlers, in contrast, are quite unlikely to benefit from elaborate discussions but can be quite capable of short, specific interactions geared to their level. In essence, the teacher and child form a partnership: the child agrees to try to make some behavioural changes, while the teacher promises to support the child and be there to help or remind.

Problem Solve

Teachers can help children develop creative problem-solving skills and strategies. Our goal for children is that they will eventually learn constructive ways of preventing, dealing with, and resolving conflicts, whether among themselves or with adults. As children employ the problem-solving process, they circumvent conflicts and altercations as they discuss, plan, and decide. One of Gordon's (1974, 1976) strategies, in writing on parent and teacher effectiveness, involves a no-lose method of **conflict resolution** in which the outcome ensures that both the parties are winners and no one is the loser. This is congruent with his theory that guidance rests on mutual respect and acceptance.

The teacher's role in implementing this method begins with helping children identify and clarify the problem, done best through active listening by the teacher. Children are then enlisted in brainstorming some possible ways of dealing with the problem, evaluating these possibilities, selecting the one that best satisfies both parties, and finding ways of implementing and affirming the solution. The key to this approach is to avoid having one person, child or adult, impose his or her position on the other person. This method conveys a sense of mutual respect based on the equality of both parties rather than the power of one over the other.

Ignore

Just as giving positive reinforcement strengthens behaviours, withdrawing it, through **ignoring**, can weaken and eliminate behaviours. A cautioning note, though, is that ignoring can eliminate acceptable or unacceptable behaviour just as reinforcement can strengthen behaviour. The teacher must be able to ignore calmly and matter-of-factly, not in an agitated state. You have to determine whether what you perceive to be an annoying behaviour is annoying to everyone or only to you.

Some behaviours don't require any intervention. Sincerely look at whether the behaviour warrants acknowledgment. Personal temperaments, experience, and understanding typical behaviour and child development are important here. A grade 6 teacher supplying in an early childhood education class may (fruitlessly) be trying to keep the children from talking. Of course, this is impossible as well as inappropriate and creates many new problems that did not exist before she tried to intervene. Taking the time to step back or remove yourself from the situation to look at it as a whole will often provide you with the answers you need. Giving the situation ample time to resolve itself is also important.

A CANADIAN PROFESSIONAL SPEAKS OUT
Tailoring Curriculums to Ability and Interest

My desire for Canadian children enrolled in child care centres is that each child will receive quality, individualized care from educated, caring, and committed adults. Nice idea, you say, but hardly practical. I disagree. For many young children this idea is reality, and with some changes it can become a reality for all children. From my perspective, theme planning and "recipe card" manuals should be discarded. Play experiences for children should be planned using playroom staff's educational expertise and information gathered through frequent, firsthand observations of each child's needs, interests, and abilities.

Let's suppose from recent observations and conversations with children, parents, and other playroom staff that Timothy is interested in dinosaurs, Rachel in colours, and Kent in changes. Michael's mother had a new baby and he needs to learn how to understand and express his feelings, positive and negative, about his sibling. Attiya is thrilled about her newly acquired skill of printing the letters in her name. Heather and Pam are frustrated that their block structures continue to tumble. Just as you were leaving the centre yesterday, Sharon's mother called to say that their family dog had been killed by a car. This is the information that forms the backbone of your upcoming daily play programs. For each child you develop a variety of play experiences for active and quiet play throughout the planned environment.

Here are some possible play opportunities that meet the individual needs of the children and more than likely will appeal to several others:

- At the easel, primary colours of paint, large pieces of paper cut in circles, and one-inch, long-handled brushes (Rachel, Attiya, Michael, Kent).

- Beside the sandbox, a box of dinosaurs, a variety of twigs and branches gathered from yesterday's walk in the nearby park, and a container of water (Timothy, Kent).

- On the manipulative table, three different types of paper, preschool pencils, erasers, rulers, crayons, stencils, and scissors. At a nearby table, alphabet blocks with small people and animals (Attiya, Kent, Rachel, Michael, Sharon).

- At the science table, bean and onion seeds, soil, clear plastic cups for planting, watering can, and magnifying glasses with pictures of growing plants on the nearby bulletin board (Kent, Michael).

- In the dramatic play area, several stuffed [toy] baby zoo animals with appropriate foodstuffs, zookeeper shirts, hats, gloves, and cleaning supplies with a stack of hollow blocks that could be used to construct habitats (Michael, Sharon, Pam, Heather).

- Newborn babies [dolls], bottles, blankets, a carriage, and a cradle are available in the family area (Michael).
- The water table has clear water, and beside it are props for making bubbles (liquid soap, straws, tennis racquets, and plastic tubes with terry towel wrapped around one end) (Kent, Rachel, Michael).
- In the block area, several flat pieces of masonite are on the floor along with three large cardboard boxes (Heather, Pam, Kent).
- Added to the bookshelf are alphabet, dinosaur, plant, and animal books.
- For children who wish to join a group activity, there are scales for weighing and measuring people; conversations about growth of nails, hair, skin, and feet; and clothes of different sizes.
- When children arrive, Sharon's primary caregiver will be there to talk and support her in the playroom and is prepared to talk about her feelings about her dead pet at appropriate opportunities.
- Materials added to the outdoor playground will be sponges, chamois, cloths, brushes, buckets, and water for washing bikes, windows, and equipment, woodworking materials, and some musical instruments.
- Throughout the day adults will interact with children as they self-select play experiences.

Using all knowledge and information available, early childhood professionals must trust their own judgment on what is best for each child and provide daily, numerous, real, firsthand play experiences that allow children to self-select from a wide range of opportunities to foster their own growth and development with supportive guidance from competent, confident adults. Children will feel valued and respected; learning opportunities will be individually and developmentally appropriate; and individual and group needs will be met in a responsive environment that recognizes the uniqueness of each child in the playroom. The result will be quality care for each child.

Judy Wainwright
Mount Royal College
Calgary

Be a Team Player

Open and honest dialogue among children, parents, teachers, and community members creates a sense of ownership whereby all members feel responsible for the safety and well-being of one another. Each member brings to the table insights and experiences that are valuable in preventing, identifying, and solving conflicts. Team support means ideas are exchanged, encouragement is given, and resources are shared. Since a problem belongs to the team, the team works toward finding a solution that benefits and is agreed upon by all members. Everyone, then, takes part in its success.

A Note about Time-Out

Time out is an example of a very specific behaviour management technique that entered the mainstream of Canadian day care. Originally meant to be a short, cooling-down period, it has been abused in the field. It became a form of punishment and neglect as children were isolated for long periods of time without guidance, explanation, or understanding. Hence, the situation was not one of positive learning and growth but of negative and humiliating experiences.

A more empowering method is **self-selected time away** (Essa, 1990). This procedure gives children the responsibility of removing themselves from the class if they sense that they are about to lose control. This helps the children gauge their own inner emotions and choose an appropriate method to deal with them. They can also judge when they are ready to return. This sense of self goes a long way toward self-discipline. Exhibit 6.3 expands on self-selected time away.

EXHIBIT 6.3: SELF-SELECTED TIME AWAY

When $2\frac{1}{2}$-year-old J.D. started at the child care centre, he was almost immediately labelled as a "difficult child." Major tantrums, disruptive outbursts, and aggressive behaviour occurred on multiple occasions each day. The teachers tried talking to J.D., reinforcing appropriate behaviours, distracting him, ignoring the tantrums, putting him in time-out, holding and rocking him, and any other technique they could think of. But it was all to no avail. J.D. simply did not seem to respond. The staff was particularly perplexed because most of the time they had no idea what set off J.D.'s behaviour. A discussion with his parents indicated that they, too, had experienced difficulty; in fact, they felt overwhelmed and powerless in dealing with the unpredictable nature of J.D.'s behaviour.

When it became obvious that J.D. did not respond to conventional guidance techniques, the staff decided to approach the problem more systematically. One staff member was assigned to observe J.D. for several days and to pay particular attention to what triggered his outbursts. This teacher gradually became aware of a rather subtle change in J.D. just before he had a tantrum or hit out at another child. He seemed to visibly "wind up" before his outbursts, clenching his teeth and tightening the muscles of his whole body.

This observation was the turning point. The staff no longer considered this as a case of misbehaviour; rather, they thought they were dealing with a behaviour the child just could not control. They concluded that J.D. was unable to handle the level of stimulation of the class, and the way to deal with this was to provide J.D. with an opportunity to remove himself from the classroom. Because J.D.'s outbursts came on quickly with no observable warning, however, there seemed to be no way of preventing them. "Perhaps," suggested one staff member, "J.D. knows when he is losing control. Should we ask him?"

The next day one of the teachers asked J.D. whether he could "feel" when he started to get upset and mad. To her surprise, J.D. indicated that he could. "I tell you what, J.D.," she said. "Whenever you feel that you are getting really upset, you can leave the room." The staff had arranged for a supervised area to be available outside the classroom, equipped with a small table and some toys. This area was across the hall from J.D.'s classroom. J.D. was shown where he could go if he ever felt the need to leave the room. It was made very clear to him that this was not punishment but an aid to help him regain control. It was presented in an encouraging and positive way.

Having this option made all the difference for J.D. The frequency of his out-of-control behaviours dropped dramatically as J.D. removed himself from the classroom several times a day, usually returning after 5 or 10 minutes. He didn't seem to abuse the opportunity to leave the room and never went anywhere other than the identified area. Over the next three years, J.D. continued to remove himself from his classroom, although at a continually decreasing rate.

A persevering staff that genuinely wished to help J.D. turned a very frustrating situation for all (J.D. especially) into a warm, empowering scenario.

Understanding the Difference between Typical and Atypical Behaviour

If you view guidance as an ongoing process that contributes to the socialization of the child, it is easier to consider a solution to a problem behaviour as a change that has a far-reaching impact rather than as a stopgap measure to make your class run more smoothly. Although many children in their early years go through temporary periods that can be difficult for the adults around them, children pass through these without too many residual effects. The negative stage of many toddlers, for instance, often dissolves within a few months into a period of cooperation. But some behaviours persist and may become more problematic as children get older.

Atypical, persistent behaviours are one of the greatest challenges facing teachers of young children. Remember that it is normal for children to test the limits. Children can usually be rerouted by the adults around them. Some atypical behaviours are caused by medical conditions, and knowing the medical diagnoses gives you some direction for handling these behaviours. For instance, a child diagnosed with *hyperactivity,* known as **attention deficit-hyperactivity disorder (ADHD),** has particular needs which can be identified and met. Some children totally frustrate all their teachers' attempts to deal with them. Teachers can go through a series of up-and-down feelings about their own competence as they try to cope with such children in the classroom. Remember that the children must be frustrated too if they are impulsive and unable to conform to the classroom routines. If a child simply cannot sit, perhaps remaining mobile can become acceptable, provided that the basic rule of not hurting self, others, or things is still upheld.

Finally, what may be classified as problem behaviour to one teacher may not bother another. Unrealistic limits or expectations can cause, rather than prevent, behaviour problems. Analyze the environment and teaching techniques to ensure they are not part of the problem. So which behaviours are typical, and which should send up a red flag? The following guidelines can help you make that distinction:

• Know the developmental stages of the children in your class, particularly as they relate to social, emotional, and moral development. Many children of a given age go through a phase that will most likely pass. For instance, the tendency of 4-year-olds to blur the line between truth and fantasy does not predict a life of dishonesty and pathological lying.

• Realistic expectations for the age group, tempered with a recognition of individual variations among children, are important. However, if a child appears extremely immature in relation to her or his peers (e.g., a 4-year-old who acts more like a 2- to 3-year-old in social behaviour), the child may be developmentally delayed, particularly if other areas of development are also delayed.

• Look for signs of possible medical causes for problem behaviours. As we will discuss later in this chapter, a chronic infection, allergy, nutritional deficiency, or sensory deficit can profoundly affect behaviour. If, in addition to disruptive social behaviour, the child frequently rubs the eyes, winces when urinating, or appears unduly clumsy, consider a possible link between the social behaviour and an underlying health problem.

• When the behaviour of a child in your class is out of hand so frequently that you feel there are too many negative experiences between you and the child, *it is probably time to bring in assistance to help you deal with the situation.* Consulting an outside professional is particularly appropriate if other teachers, who are generally very effective in dealing with children, share your experience and feel as baffled and frustrated by this child as you do. Griffin (1982) suggested that if a child is frequently disruptive and not able to get along in the early childhood program without continuous help, that child needs professional, one-to-one help which cannot be given in a group school setting.

• As teachers, we generally notice acting-out children because they force our attention to their behaviour. But also be alert to the extremely withdrawn child who stays away from social interactions, is reluctant to participate in activities, avoids eye contact, and/or refuses to talk. Many children are shy, but extreme withdrawal might signal a deeper problem.

- A child whose behaviour changes suddenly and drastically may be signalling a problem requiring attention. You should feel concerned about the generally happy, outgoing child who suddenly becomes antisocial, or the active, assertive child who inexplicably becomes withdrawn and passive, particularly if the changed behaviour persists for more than a few days. Your first source of information, of course, is the child's parents. But if they, too, are baffled, a more thorough search for the cause of the change is in order.

- If you notice unexplainable bruises, abrasions, cuts, or burns on a child, consider the possibility of child abuse. Verbal and sexual abuse and/or neglect do not leave physical scars but are just as damaging as physical abuse. An abused child usually exhibits behavioural symptoms of the problem. If you have reason to suspect child abuse, speak to your supervisor or director so the concern can be followed up by notifying the appropriate authority. (We will discuss this issue further in Chapter 10.)

- One of the mistakes we often make is to look at a child as the cause of problems or as something that needs fixing. If the entire team is feeling overwhelmed or if discipline is a constant component of the day, it might be time to re-evaluate the program and guidance principles of the centre and staff.

- When you find that a particular child's behaviour is just beyond your capacity to cope, it is time to look beyond your own resources. Parents, of course, are your first resource. They, together with other team members can help brainstorm possible causes and solutions. Getting help is not a sign of weakness, but rather of your strength in being able to recognize the limits of your professional expertise. It is also your duty and responsibility. This may mean asking a colleague to relieve you for five minutes so that you can remove yourself from the situation in order to regroup or seeking a psychologist, psychiatrist, or other appropriate professional to help the team and child cope with a challenging behaviour. These community professionals also have a share of responsibility for the care and guidance of young children in your community.

A Closer Look provides insight into the plight of drug-exposed children and the challenge they present.

Other Factors That Affect Children's Behaviour

In dealing with children's behaviour, it is important to examine all potential factors that might be affecting that behaviour. All kinds of subtle influences undoubtedly

A Closer Look

THE PLIGHT OF DRUG-EXPOSED CHILDREN

Just a few years ago, the media began to reflect a concern about crack babies, children born of mothers who had taken crack cocaine during pregnancy. Now many of these babies are in their preschool and early elementary school years, and the focus of attention has turned to how these youngsters will function in the school environment. Some early childhood teachers have already experienced drug-exposed children who have been mainstreamed into their classrooms.

Over the years, many children exposed prenatally to drugs have been born. Stories of newborns suffering withdrawal symptoms are not new. Research has documented tremors, irritability, oversensitivity to stimuli, and other problems in infants whose mothers took a variety of illicit drugs. But one problem in studying this population of children is that it is difficult to tell what drugs or combination of drugs their mothers took, when during the pregnancy these children were exposed, how frequently they were exposed, and the quantity to which they were exposed. To complicate matters, many of the mothers had inadequate prenatal nutrition and no prenatal care.

Once they are born, drug-exposed babies are often taken away from addicted mothers and placed in foster care, subjecting already vulnerable children to a host of potential social risk factors. Thus, many unknown variables make it difficult to generalize about children who were exposed to drugs prenatally. There are no prototypes of drug-exposed children.

In recent years, several early childhood programs have been developed specifically to work with this group of children. Two such programs in California have concluded that the children do best in a high-quality early childhood environment.[1] The preschool program provides a secure base for children who are attached insecurely, according to one administrator. The focus of these programs is not on the children's history but on their current needs, which most often involve social-emotional and language problems.

Although there are no long-term studies to document the success of these children, staff members are very positive about the prognoses for those they have served. Several youngsters have moved into regular kindergarten classrooms, while others have required some limited special education services; none have required full special education placement. The staff feel that the children they have worked with would be served best in mainstreamed early childhood programs. Furthermore, they are very concerned that these youngsters not be stuck with a label that will follow them through their school years.

Other experts are not as optimistic, however. Many are particularly concerned about unexpected emotional swings that some drug-exposed children have demonstrated; such outbursts often result in unpredictable aggression. Although most children who react aggressively do so in response to some external provocation, the aggression of some drug-exposed children tends to come with no warning and often for no apparent reason. Some see this as a symptom of neurological damage. As with every issue, some feel that it is irresponsible to mainstream children who are so unpredictable. Unless a full-time aide is provided, the teacher should not be expected to add such a child to the class. Others feel it is irresponsible not to subscribe to the inclusive model.

The question of how to help children who were exposed to drugs before birth and often end up in unstable care once they are born is a difficult one to answer. As those who work with these youngsters in special programs indicate, the children can be helped, but the social service delivery system so often enmeshes them in a cumbersome and inconsistent bureaucracy. Some of the conflicting opinions and concerns about this group of children may be resolved as more research continues to follow their progress.

[1]From conversations in May 1991 with Mary Ann Nielsen, Assistant Superintendent, Diagnostic Center for Neurologically Handicapped Children, California State Department of Education, and Carol Cole, early childhood special education teacher with the Los Angeles Unified School District.

contribute to behaviour, for instance, the weather (Essa, Hilton, & Murray, 1990; Faust, Weidmann, & Wehner, 1974). But behaviours also have more identifiable causes, some external, others internal. When you are concerned about a particular behaviour, it is wise to give careful thought to what might be triggering it. We will now examine some of the factors that can affect children's behaviour.

Health-Related Problems

Children often react in unacceptable ways because their bodies are not functioning well or are sending messages of discomfort or pain. When children do not feel well, they cannot be expected to behave normally. Think about how most adults become very irritable when they are ill. Children are no different. In fact, children have fewer resources to control their behaviour when they don't feel well (Essa, 1990), which sometimes leads to the emergence of problem behaviours.

Some children are also affected by environmental or food **allergies,** which can change their behaviour in unpredictable ways.

Some children have an undetected **sensory deficit** which may be affecting their behaviour. Could the clumsy child who is unwilling to try anything new have

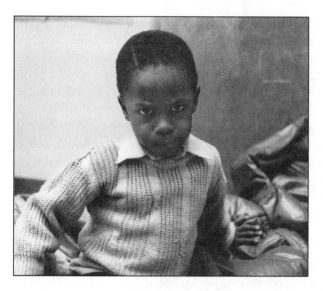

a vision deficit? Might the child who is often distracted and seems to ignore instructions have trouble hearing?

Nutrition, both the quality and the quantity of food, is another factor that can affect children's behaviour (Lozoff, 1989). A child who comes to school hungry or malnourished may be irritable or listless, may not work to potential, and/or may misbehave. Studies have linked nutrition to behaviour and learning (Barrett, 1986; Van Heerden, 1984). Canadian children from all social strata are at risk for malnutrition and undernutrition. Some do not get proper nutrients because of costs; others subsist on a diet high in sugar, fats, additives, and empty calories; and others become malnourished as well-intentioned parents provide low-fat yogourt and skim milk to infants requiring sustenance found in whole-milk products.

Individual Temperament

To a large degree, children's personalities are molded by their environment, but research has also shown that children are born with a certain **temperament** (Thomas & Chess, 1969). Thomas, Chess, and Birch (1968) found that the children they studied could be classified into three general categories: easy or flexible, slow to warm up or courteous, and intense. They concluded that the majority of children could be classified as flexible.

Easy children, from their earliest days, follow a regular cycle in sleeping, eating, and eliminating; are readily adaptable to change; have a reasonable attention span; display a moderate level of activity; are not overly sensitive to stimuli; and have a generally happy disposition. Intense children, on the other hand, show opposite traits such as irregularity, intensity in reactions, an inability to adapt, and a high activity level, and they are often out of sorts. Slow-to-warm-up children fall in between these two extremes.

A more important concept of Thomas, Chess, & Birch (1968; Chess & Thomas, 1987) is that of "goodness of fit." Inexperienced parents might interpret an infant's intense behaviour as purposeful—intentionally directed at the parents—and they begin to equate difficult behaviour with difficult or "bad" child. The parents' response to the behaviour would be an inappropriate method of discipline. Helping parents understand child development and behaviour also helps them change their discipline habits. A flexible child who grows up to be a parent is much better able to cope with a fussy new baby than an intense parent would. But what if an intense parent is paired with an intense baby? What if a parent who enjoys cuddling gets a child who does not like being touched? Since infants can't talk, they cannot tell us why they are irritable. An infant's distress at being touched might easily be translated by a new, inexperienced parent into "my baby doesn't like me." Helping parents understand that people have different temperaments helps them create a goodness of fit between themselves and their child. If parents match their approach to the child's temperament, interactions begin to become positive and rewarding, allowing parents to relax and enjoy their child.

Soderman (1985) advised teachers to deal with difficult children through respect, objectivity, environmental structure, effective limits, positive interaction, patience, and cooperation with colleagues and parents. She further warned against inappropriate reactions such as ignoring the difficult behaviours, coercing or bribing, compliance, shaming, labelling, or punishing.

As you pursue your early childhood teaching career, you will be entrusted with a variety of temperaments in children. Consistent, positive guidance skills and ingenuity can help you identify, adjust to, and accommodate this diversity. Rely on your teaching strengths, examine and acknowledge your own feelings, and then continue to view each child as a unique individual worthy of respect and support.

The Child's Family

A child's behaviour may be a reaction to stress or change at home. Statistics tell us that a large number of young children will experience their parents' divorce, enter a single-parent family where there will most likely be financial as well as emotional stresses, or experience reconstitution of a family as one of their parents remarries (Halpern, 1987). Such major changes, even when parents are very sensitive to and mindful of the needs and feelings of their youngsters, are invariably upsetting to children who cannot fully understand what is happening. Other changes, such as a new baby in the family, a visit from grandparents, a parent away on a business trip, the death of a family member or pet, or moving to a new house, can also trigger behavioural responses. (These topics are discussed further in Chapter 10, in which we will examine stress and young children.)

Patterson, DeBaryshe, and Ramsey (1989) proposed a developmental model of antisocial behaviour. Antisocial behaviour is more likely to develop in the children of families with a history of antisocial behaviour and stressors such as unemployment, marital conflict, and divorce. The authors, in summarizing the literature on intervention efforts, concluded that intervention at adolescence produced short-lived results. But intervention at earlier ages has proven to be more effective.

It is important to maintain frequent and open communication with parents to find out what is happening at home. If you know, for example, that Amy's parents are heading toward a divorce, you can better understand her sudden angry outbursts. You cannot put Amy's family back together, but you can convey to her that you understand her distress and are there for her. If Amy hits other children, you

PARTNERSHIPS
Supporting Parents in Positive Guidance Approaches

Parents and teachers often seek out each other's advice and support when they deal with their children's behaviours. It is important to keep in focus the concept of guidance as an ongoing, positive process. Your approach to guiding children is primarily concerned with helping them develop inner control and self-direction rather than merely dealing with problems. Many adults think of working with children in terms of discipline; however, you can help parents see guidance more broadly by viewing it in terms of laying a foundation for lifelong patterns of creative problem solving, positive interactions, and concern for the needs of others.

Being familiar with, discussing, and sharing resources (e.g., books, articles, videos, speakers) is one way to grow together as a positive guidance team. Ongoing communication is key to understanding, respecting, and trusting in each other's guidance approaches. Certainly children need to be understood in the context of school, family, and community, and this can only be achieved through dialogue and observation.

Although it is important to share your guidance philosophy with parents, also keep in mind that there are a wide variety of parenting approaches. Individual families have unique characteristics, including their way of guiding their children. As well, parents have a deep emotional investment in their children. Many factors, such as the way the parents themselves were raised, experiences, and culture, will have an impact.

One of the authors had an opportunity to observe this recently when she spent three weeks living within a different culture, observing adult–child interactions. At first she felt alarmed at the total lack of control she perceived adults exerting over young children. It seemed that children under 5 were allowed to do anything, including engage in behaviours that were dangerous (e.g., a 3-year-old took his grandfather's car keys and started the car). But as she observed further, it was clear that once children turned 6 or 11, they seemed to develop a responsibility and maturity beyond that of North American children of the same age. Somehow the freedom of early childhood also carried with it an unconditional trust that the children would make a successful transition from babyhood to adulthood. For the author, this experience reinforced the need to be aware of cultural differences, of not jumping to premature conclusions, and of valuing the great diversity in parenting approaches by giving parents the benefit of the doubt that they know their children well.

---

can let her know that you cannot condone her behaviour (most children know this and expect this from you) and will take measures to stop it, but that you do acknowledge her pain.

Key Terms

allergies
attention deficit-hyperactivity
  disorder (ADHD)
conflict resolution
cuing
distraction
eclectic approach
effective praise
encouragement
games with rules
guidance
hierarchy of needs
ignoring
inductive reasoning
logical and natural consequences
modelling

morality of autonomy
morality of obedience
nutrition
play
positive discipline
practice play
pretend play
punishment
redirection
self-actualization
self-selected time away
sensory deficit
special time
symbolic play
temperament
unconditional attention

Key Points

- A teacher is also a nurturer in each of the developmental domains—in any program, in any environment.

- Healthy emotional development encompasses developing a sense of security, attachment, trust, independence, empathy, and self-control (Greenspan & Greenspan, 1986).

- Children discover their world through play. Therefore, it is important to be familiar with research on play and its effectiveness (e.g., Freud—emotional, Piaget—cognitive, Vygotsky—social).

- Our progressively structured system of school environments may gradually extinguish, or at least divert inward, children's natural tendency to be creative thinkers.

- Pretend play, thematic fantasy play (superheroes), and cooperative games together act to produce a general concern for life, an emphasis on peace and harmony, and a decrease in social aggression by providing positive alternatives.

- Guidance helps children become morally responsible, considerate, independent, and assertive.

- An atmosphere of trust, necessary for learning, occurs when we are consistent, predictable, and fair in our interactions with children.

- Positive guidance consists of proper preparation and prevention of problems through consistency, flexibility, communication, positive reinforcement, and self-selected time away.

- Teacher observation helps to determine what methods are needed to help a child through disruptive behaviour patterns and, if necessary, what outside professional help should be called in.

- Health problems, individual temperament, and stress at home affect a child's behaviour.

Chapter 7

Appropriate Practices in Early Childhood Education

In previous chapters, we have examined factors that affect quality programs, factors such as teacher qualifications and group size. We have examined play and guidance as the cornerstones for positive learning. We have looked at our beliefs about children and the way they learn. We have discussed the interrelationships of teacher, child, and parent. We have explained

terminology and oriented you to this wonderful field. But in this chapter we examine the foundation upon which the child's daily life is built. The program model you choose, fancy toys, and a beautiful setting are all for naught if your stance—the way you interact with children—is inappropriate. Equally important is the interaction between child and program, for which you are the link.

The purpose of this chapter—and this text—is to convey the concept of appropriate practices in early childhood education rather than to prescribe a program outline with schedules, routines, and environments laid out like a recipe. We chose the chapter heading "Appropriate Practices" over "Developmentally Appropriate Practices" to broaden, rather than limit, the scope of this chapter. However, we do retain the term "developmentally" within the chapter since the term is used widely in the field itself. (In A Closer Look we feature developmentally appropriate programs in transition. See Page 303.) In your provincial legislation (see Chapter 5), standards can easily be looked up. This text is an introduction to early childhood education—a tour of the field—which your program elaborates on course by course. Appropriate practices, aside from being one of these courses, is portable from program to program. We would rather use this space to create a feel or sense of this ideal than to list schedules, furniture, space requirements, and so on.

Appropriate practices should include a commonsense approach to child care. Common sense dictates that you pay attention to the environment. Knowledge about child development, play, and learning help you determine what is appropriate for the environment. Is the room too hot or cold? Too light or dark? Too noisy or quiet? Is there time for privacy? For conversation? For outdoor play?

Think about your own situation. You come to a particular program setting—college or university. The setting is based on a particular model—adult learning. You choose a particular program—early childhood education. The teachers use their knowledge of adult learners when they engage in particular practices. These include setting up the physical environment, designing a schedule, and choosing activities (e.g., individual, small-group, large-group) and materials. Do you feel these practices were designed with your learning and developmental needs in mind?

In high-quality early childhood programs, *developmentally appropriate* means they meet the following criteria:

- The program is *age-appropriate* for the children it serves.
- The program is adapted to be *individually appropriate* for each child it serves. Every child in the program is different, and the program is responsive to developmental, temperamental, familial, cultural, and ethnic differences.
- The program promotes inclusion.

- The program provides adequate time for various pursuits. Children need time in a program—time to be alone, time to be with others, time to reflect, time to be noisy, time to be children. In planning a program, you will want to provide time for self-directed activity, indoor and outdoor play, group activities, meals and/or snacks, and napping in a full-day program. You will want to allow time to get outerwear on and off, but you do not want a child to be bored while waiting for others to get their outerwear on or off. A child's needs for time vary with the developmental level and history of the child.

- The program provides variety and choice.

- The program offers different experiences at varying levels of difficulty. Both self-selected and teacher-directed activities have value, but there must be a balance between them.

- The program provides flexibility and predictability. Striking a balance between versatility and stability is an ongoing challenge for teachers.

- The teachers, together with children and parents, plan the program, choose resources, and organize the environment so that play-based, child-centred learning will occur.

- The program should be evaluated on a daily basis. Evaluation is multidirectional and includes the children.

Developmentally Appropriate Programs

By the mid-1980s, the "earlier is better" ideology had led to the establishment of increasingly academic kindergarten programs in many parts of the United States. The National Association for the Education of Young Children (NAEYC) opposed this move to direct instruction and maintained that play-based programs, in which

children were active learners, were more developmentally appropriate. To support its position, it produced and subsequently expanded *Developmentally Appropriate Practice in Early Childhood Education Programs Serving Children from Birth through Age 8* (Bredekamp, 1987). This document generated considerable discussion. It also generated a number of changes to more **developmentally appropriate practices,** even at the elementary school level (e.g., Scales, Almy, Nicolopoulou, & Ervin-Tripp, 1992a; Smith, 1991). In 1997 NAEYC released the second edition of this document. The document is as relevant in Canada as it is in the United States. A full discussion of the policy is beyond the scope of this text, but it is likely to be covered in advanced courses on early childhood education. Nevertheless, the key points merit our attention.

Just what do these policy papers say? In 1987 the concept of developmental appropriateness had two components: *age appropriateness* and *individual appropriateness*. The concept of age appropriateness may already be somewhat familiar, especially if you have studied child development or developmental psychology. Bredekamp (1987) offers this definition of age appropriateness:

> Human development research indicates that there are universal, predictable sequences of growth and change that occur in children during the first nine years of life. These predictable changes occur in all domains of development—language, physical, emotional, social, and cognitive. Knowledge of typical development of children within the age span served by the program provides a framework from which teachers prepare the learning environment and plan appropriate experiences (pp. 3–4). [Language, creativity, and behaviour are also considered domains. Often they are lumped somewhere under the above headings.]

The concept of individual appropriateness is perhaps less familiar:

> Each child is a unique person with an individual pattern and timing of growth, as well as individual personality, learning style, and family background. Both the curriculum and adults' interactions with children should be responsive to individual differences. Learning in young children is the result of interaction between the child's thoughts and experiences with materials, ideas, and people. These experiences should match the child's developing abilities while also challenging the child's interest and understanding. (Bredekamp, 1987, pp. 3–4)

In the 1997 document, this concept of individual appropriateness was subdivided to elaborate on the importance of social and cultural contexts as well.

The policy continues with many examples of both appropriate and inappropriate practices for early childhood programs for newborn to 8-year-old children. The policy also comments on play: "Children's play is a primary vehicle for and indicator of their mental growth.... Therefore, child-initiated, child-directed, teacher-supported play is an essential component of developmentally appropriate practice" (Bredekamp, 1987, p. 4). (See also Bredekamp, 1997, p. 14.) NAEYC publications include *Developmentally Appropriate Practice in Early Childhood Programs Serving Infants* (1989a) and *Developmentally Appropriate Practice in Early Childhood Programs Serving Toddlers* (1989b). They deal with the special needs of the very young. Below we look a little more closely at age and individual appropriateness (which includes contextual—social, cultural, familial).

Age-Appropriate Programs

Developmentally appropriate programming supports children in their natural propensity for play rather than just teaches them directly. This is a delicate balance. Some studies show that simply leaving children to their own devices is detrimental to development. For instance, children in orphanages (Skeels, 1966) who experienced severe environmental deprivation acquired developmental delays. More recently, a similar situation was brought to our attention about Romanian orphans. Yet placing children in direct instruction programs that are beyond their developmental level in order to boost their IQ also creates stress and is detrimental to development, as pointed out by at least four well-known childhood experts of our time: Elkind (1986), Brazelton (1985), White (1984), and Greenberg (1988). Certainly the extremes of any practice are inappropriate. Similarly, taking sides or ignoring the virtues of opposing methodologies is equally worrisome. Simply teaching or simply playing is not enough. Developmentally appropriate practice "recognizes age-related human characteristics that permit general predictions within an age range about what activities, materials, interactions or experience will be safe, healthy, interesting, achievable and also challenging" (NAEYC, 1997, p. 9).

Perhaps one of the most important statements to come out of the NAEYC revision of 1997 is the recommendation, on page 23, to move from an either/or to a both/and way of thinking, as we did originally with the nature/nurture controversy. Hence, whole language *or* phonics becomes whole language *and* phonics. Many ideas can be compatible and effective in combination: play-based *and* direct instruction; routine *and* emergent curriculum; integrated theme *and* content area study; choice *and* limits—these are just a few examples. Balance is achievable and acceptable within the framework of "developmentally appropriate" and "high quality."

Individually Appropriate Inclusive Programs

A good early childhood program is intrinsically inclusive of all children because it accommodates a range of developmental, cultural, familial, social, financial, religious, and ethnic needs. Its freedom-within-structure environment is flexible enough to adapt to all children, and its staff is trained in child development, stages of play, and guidance so that they, too, can adjust their approaches for every child. The concepts of empowerment, respect, age and individual development, opportunity, and nurturing lend themselves to accepting children with a wide range of needs. As well, since we subscribe to the team and transdisciplinary approach, we know we have many resourceful partners to help us in embracing diversity.

Ignorance or indifference are certainly not the same as acceptance. Sensitivity to and awareness of individual differences are important. Fairness means you recognize these individual needs and address them. In order to provide an anti-biased, multicultural, inclusive program, teachers must be knowledgeable as to the implications of an activity to ensure that their program meets the needs of the children and families it serves and that it sets an example for the generations to come.

The concepts of *anti-bias, multicultural, inclusive education* (Derman-Sparks & Ramsey, 1993) will be apparent in every high-quality educational program. These programs actively confront—or proactively avoid—exclusion, prejudice, stereotypes, and the "isms" and phobias, including racism, sexism, and homophobia. The diversity of children and families in the program is respected and reflected throughout the program, the day-to-day environment, staffing, provision of opportunity, and all activities. Inclusion is a common thread, a philosophical base, that permeates every facet of the program. It is not represented by a special day, a unique toy, or a learning centre or a circle; it is a fundamental component of the program.

As this concept is so crucial to appropriate practice, both A Canadian Professional Speaks Out and Partnerships focus on it in more depth.

Developmentally Appropriate Expectations

An appropriate practice for encouraging responsible behaviour includes involving the children in identifying what is expected. As was mentioned in Chapter 6, you probably need only one rule: *you may not hurt yourself, others, or the things around you.* Children should know what the limits are and why they are set, and can often help with deciding on a few key rules. By discussing why a rule is necessary, children believe in and are more likely to honour and monitor it because they had a hand in making it.

Another important factor to consider in setting expectations for the group is the developmental level of the children. Carefully examine activities, the daily schedule, and materials to ensure they are appropriate to the strengths and needs

A CANADIAN PROFESSIONAL SPEAKS OUT
Anti-Bias Education: A Personal and Professional Challenge for Early Childhood Educators

For many early childhood educators in Canada today, anti-bias education is a new and challenging topic. For some educators, anti-bias, human rights, and social justice concepts and goals may seem far removed from the ECE environment. For others, working with young children is both a vocation and an avenue for political action, "for making a better world."

Whatever our current personal perspective, it is important to consider that what we choose *to do* or *not to do* has consequences for children in their immediate environment and in the long term. Do we intervene effectively when children or adults reveal bias or prejudice? Do we select materials for our program that portray and reflect human similarities and differences positively? Do we introduce developmentally appropriate experiences for exploring individual and group rights and responsibilities? When making choices that relate to anti-bias ECE practice, we are challenged to examine our actions, and to clarify how these actions reflect our values and support our goals.

As we review our own practice, we are engaging in some of the processes that are, ultimately, at the heart of anti-bias education: namely, reflection, action, and evaluation. In turn, we can also encourage children to explore anti-bias issues by considering such questions as, "What do we think is important about sharing and getting along with everyone?" (reflection), "What can each of us do to take care of ourselves and treat each other fairly?" (action), and "What areas of our own behaviour do we want to improve?" (evaluation). Questions like these promote children's connection with issues such as respect, fairness, and inclusion through action-oriented self-awareness, personal responsibility, and problem solving.

As we encourage these understandings and abilities in young children, we provide the foundation for their later consideration of broader social issues such as, "How do people share wealth and privilege, and get along without resorting to violence and war?", "What can individuals, organizations, and governments do to share more fairly and resolve differences more effectively?", and last, "How well are we, as a human family, dealing positively and creatively with our similarities and differences?" In considering these questions, we can see the links between the social challenges for children in the preschool environment and the challenges faced by society as a whole.

For early childhood educators, then, we return to consideration of how much or how little of an anti-bias approach we choose to implement within our programs. Some of us may feel that our knowledge is inadequate or that we lack the skills for addressing issues such as stereotyping or discrimination.

We may also have ambivalent feelings about exploring some areas or aspects of anti-bias with young children—perhaps we are comfortable talking about special needs, but feel less so about sexual orientation or poverty or religion. Such hesitations or concerns are valid and may be addressed through professional development and peer support. Yet when deliberating on the need to change our attitudes, knowledge, and practice, we should always consider the consequences of what we do or not do with children. Is not self-awareness, personal responsibility, and problem solving in the social sphere as important, or more important, than anything else we teach children? If we do not model how to reflect, act, and evaluate in relation to anti-bias issues, how and when will children learn these skills?

As individuals within a diverse society, and as educators guiding young children, it is important that we consider carefully our values and goals, and how they relate to anti-bias education. Many resources and options are now available for instructing developmentally appropriate anti-bias concepts and content within ECE settings. For early childhood educators committed to human rights and social justice goals, implementation of anti-bias ECE is one way to act on these values, thereby helping young children "begin well in the beginning" to identify with and protect the rights of the whole of the human family.

Ruth Fahlman
West Coast Child Care Resource Centre
Vancouver

of the children without trying to mould the children to your plan. Frequently refer to NAEYC's *Developmentally Appropriate Practice in Early Childhood Programs Serving Children from Birth through Age 8* as a guide (Bredekamp, 1987; 1997). If your expectations are either too simple or too complex for the children's abilities, behavioural problems and frustrations are likely to ensue.

Keep in mind that, although developmental guidelines help you identify appropriate expectations for the age of the children, each child is an individual and will conform to some but not to other developmental milestones. Be sensitive to the unique needs, characteristics, and ideas of every child.

Conveying Expectations

Young children are exuberant and active, so you may find times when their voices get too loud.

PARTNERSHIPS
Reflection of Family Culture and Values

Communication with parents is particularly important in clarifying home and school values about socialization and about children's cultural and racial identities. Although the school is responsible for conveying to parents what values it tries to instil in the children through the curriculum and guidance techniques, the school also is responsible for obtaining similar information from parents about what they value for their children. Teachers need to be sensitive to the many variations among families of different cultures, and they must be particularly aware of their own attitudes and biases. It is easier to convey positive messages to a family with whose parenting style and values you are familiar with and agree with than it is to understand and accept an approach different from your own.

Another reason that good parent–teacher communication is vital is to avoid making assumptions about children's home life based on cultural generalizations. There are wide variations within cultural groups. In addition, individual families' adaptation to Canadian culture will also affect their lifestyles and customs. One child care centre director, for instance, hired one of the parents to help with meal preparation. When this mother, who had recently come from Colombia, asked the director to explain the "tacos" on the menu, the director was taken aback, assuming that anyone from Central or South America would know what they were. As she quickly learned, Central and South America represent many countries with diverse and individual foods and customs.

Teachers can gain much information from parents about cultural and ethnic backgrounds and values. For instance, it is important to have the child's full name, the name the family uses, and the correct pronunciation. In some cultures such as the Vietnamese, the correct order in giving a name is last name first, followed by first and middle names (Morrow, 1989). Also some Asian families give a child one name to be used in public and another to be used at home. It is important, therefore, to have accurate information about what name to use in speaking to the child.

Also gather information about the child's family, special friends, pets, or any other people or objects that are important. This will help facilitate discussions and provide ways of involving what is closest to the child. In addition, obtain information about holidays and other special cultural, religious, or family celebrations, including when they are observed, their purpose, and how the children are involved. This will help incorporate cultural activities that are meaningful (*Culture and Children,* 1985).

Some teachers may face an additional challenge if some of the families whose children are enrolled in the program speak a primary language other than English. In some communities with a large population from another culture, early childhood programs may have teachers who speak the language of this group and can either facilitate communication or provide a bilingual program. This is often not the case, however. It is important to help children, parents, and teachers communicate. One way is for teachers and even other children to learn some common words and phrases that can help the child begin to integrate into the class. While children may quickly learn enough English to function effectively at school, their parents generally will not acquire the new language as rapidly, and communication with the school could be a problem.

Because communication between home and school is so important, the school can do several things. Finding an interpreter who can facilitate occasional parent–teacher meetings can be helpful. If there are older siblings, they are natural interpreters who can be asked to assist. You might also offer to locate an ESL (English as a second language) program if the parents are interested in improving their acquisition of English. For everyday interaction, try to learn and use a few common words and phrases in the family's language: this can convey your desire and willingness to communicate. If nothing else, your quaint pronunciation attempts will bring a smile to the parent's face and create a sense of shared effort.

Finally, Derman-Sparks (1989), in *Anti-Bias Curriculum,* suggested that in addition to open communication in which values and ideas can be shared by parents and teachers, the school can provide accurate information to parents about the development of children's sexual, racial, and ethnic identities and attitudes. A series of parent group meetings can inform and invite discussion about such topics as gender identity and sexism, the creation of non-sexist environments, the development of racial identity and awareness, the creation of anti-racist environments, and evaluation of children's books for sexist and racial stereotypes. Such groups can help parents gain information about the school's philosophy, help teachers attain insight into parents' values and attitudes, and provide parents with strategies for anti-biased socialization of children.

Shouting instructions to "Quiet down!" or "Settle down!" will add to the confusion and hurt feelings, but whispering softly helps. Move from small group to small group and speak in a soft, slow voice. Children will quiet their pitch so they can hear you. You will find the noise level quickly reduced by your modelling.

Similarly, an elevated activity level, if it seems unproductive, also can be reduced by a quiet voice, dimmed lights, quietly waiting, or soft music that induces relaxation rather than agitation.

As individual children quiet or settle down, let them know with a smile or nod that you appreciate it. Teachers will frequently praise the behaviour of one compliant child publicly in the hopes that others will behave similarly because they also want to be acknowledged. Hitz and Driscoll (1988), however, report that praise given in this manner can lead to resentment and anger. "Teachers of preschool-age children ... may get away with blatant manipulation and fool themselves into thinking that it works. But eventually most children come to resent this type of control" (p. 10).

Group Guidance

The actual sequence and timing of activities, as well as their length, will also have a bearing on group guidance and behaviour. There must be a logical rhythm and flow to the sequence of daily activities that relates to the developmental level and interests of the children. If children are expected to sit quietly for several activities in a row, they will tend to find unacceptable ways to release some of the energy that is pent up during this overly long period. If too many boisterous activities are scheduled one after another, the children may tire or get too keyed up. Boredom sets in when activities last too long, and frustration is evident when activities are not long enough. If children have too little or too much teacher assistance, this can also be discouraging.

Developmentally Appropriate Environment

Take a moment to think about a place where you enjoy spending time. What are its appealing features? Is it relaxing and soothing, stimulating and exciting, thought-provoking and challenging, orderly and methodical, comfortable and homey, or colourful and bright? Now think about a place that you do not particularly like, and consider why it is unappealing to you. It may be that this place is boring, messy, stark, disorganized, dark, or uninviting. Think about spending all day in each of these places. What feelings and attitudes does each place evoke? How do you think you would act and react in each place? Can you draw some conclusions about how and why the environment affects you?

According to research, when children are in a particular **behaviour setting,** they behave in a manner appropriate to that locale, following what might be viewed as unspoken rules. Kounin and Sherman (1979) observed the following:

It is apparent that preschoolers behave "schoolish" when in a preschool. They are diligent creatures who spend 95 percent of their time actively occupied with the facilities provided and they deal with the facilities appropriately. They do all of these things in a sort of unwritten private contract between themselves and the setting they enter: teachers and peers infrequently exert any pressure to either enter or leave these settings. (p. 146)

Such research underscores the importance of providing an environment that supports development and learning. If children's engagement in activities is largely prompted by the environment, then it is incumbent upon teachers to provide the most appropriate setting possible.

The quality of the environment has an impact on the behaviour of children as well as adults who spend time in that space (Kritchevsky, Prescott, & Walling, 1977). "Arrangement, organization, size, density, noise level, even the color of the classroom directly and indirectly invite a range of behaviors from children and teachers" (Thomson & Ashton-Lilo, 1983, p. 94).

More than a room's fixed features (i.e., room size, room shape, acoustics, storage, shelving units), it is the movable elements that allow you to arrange a well-planned, developmentally appropriate environment for children. Placement and grouping of equipment and furnishings communicate many messages. They convey the purpose of spaces, set limits on behaviour, establish boundaries, invite possible combinations of play through juxtaposition of areas, and encourage quiet or active involvement. Research has provided some guidelines for maximizing the effective use of space.

Phyfe-Perkins (1980), in a review of studies that examined the effect of physical arrangements on children's behaviour, proposed some helpful principles:

- Children in full-day care need privacy; thus, places where children can be alone should be provided in the environment.

- Soft areas such as beanbag chairs, pillows, or rugs allow children to snuggle and find comfort if "adult laps are in short supply" (p. 103).

- Small, enclosed areas promote quiet activities as well as interaction among small groups of children.

- Physical boundaries around areas can reduce distraction, which, in turn, increases attention to activities.

- Large spaces allow for active, large-group activities that are more boisterous and noisy.

- Clearly organized play space and clear paths can result in fewer disruptions and more goal-directed behaviour.

Exhibit 7.1 elaborates on guidelines for organizing classroom space.

EXHIBIT 7.1: GUIDELINES FOR ORGANIZING CLASSROOM SPACE

1. The room arrangement should reflect the program's philosophy. If the program's aim is to foster independent decision making, self-help skills, positive self-concept, social interaction, and more child-initiated than teacher-initiated activities, this should be promoted through room arrangement.

2. Keep in mind the children's ages and developmental levels. As children get older, provide more choices, a more complex environment, and greater opportunity for social play. For young preschoolers, it is best to offer a simple, uncluttered, clearly defined classroom with space for large motor activity.

3. Any environment in which children as well as adults spend blocks of time should be attractive and aesthetically pleasing. Thought and care should be given to such factors as the arrangement of furnishings, use of colours and textures, and display of artwork. Plants and flowers added to the classroom can enhance its attractiveness.

4. If children are encouraged to make independent choices, then materials should be stored at a level where children can easily see, reach, and return them.

5. If children are to develop self-help skills, toileting facilities and cubbies for coats and boots should be accessible to them. Access to learning materials also contributes to development of self-help skills.

6. If the program supports a positive self-concept in children, then there should be individual places for children's belongings, for their projects or art to be saved, and for their work to be displayed.

7. If development of social skills and friendships is encouraged, then the environment should be set up to allow children to participate in activities with small groups of other children without undue interference or disruption.

8. If children are to have many opportunities to select and direct their own activities, then the environment should be set up to offer a variety of activity choices.

9. There should be places for children to be alone if they so wish. Quiet, private spaces can be planned as part of the environment (e.g., a corner with large pillows, a cozy spot in the library area, a designated rocking chair with cushions).

10. There should be soft places in the environment where children can snuggle and find comfort.

11. An environment set up into learning centres should have clearly marked boundaries that indicate the space designated for each given area. Storage shelves and other furnishings can be used to define the edges.

12. Paths to each area should be clear and unobstructed. Children are less likely to use areas that are hard to reach.

13. A pathway to one area should never go through another activity centre. This only interferes with ongoing play and can cause anger and frustration.

14. Doorways and other exits should be unobstructed.

15. Quiet activities should be grouped near one another, and noisy ones should be placed at some distance from these (e.g., the block centre should not be next to the book centre).

16. Group those activities that have common elements near one another to extend children's play possibilities. Blocks and dramatic play are often placed next to each other to encourage the exchange of props and ideas.

17. Provide areas for individual, small-group, and large-group activities by setting up different-sized centres.

18. Some areas require more space than others (e.g., block play is enhanced by ample room to build and expand block structures).

19. The sizes of various learning centres will, to some extent, convey how many children can play in each area and how active that play should be. Small, cozy areas set natural limits on the number of children and the activity level, whereas large areas send the opposite message.

20. Decrease noise level by using carpeting or area rugs in noisy centres (e.g., block centre).

21. Place messy activities near a water source.

22. Place activities that are enhanced by natural light near windows. Ensure that all areas are well lit, however.

23. Place tables and chairs in or near centres where tabletop activities are carried out (e.g., art and manipulative areas). Tables scattered throughout the room can take on an added use during snack time.

24. Consider multipurpose uses for space, especially where room size is restricted. When your room allows for a limited number of areas to be set at any one time, some of these might be used for more than one activity (e.g., the area designated for large-group activities might also be the block centre, music centre, or place set aside for large motor activity).

25. Some learning centres may not be part of the classroom on a daily basis. Such centres as woodworking, music, or cooking may be brought into the classroom on a less frequent schedule or may be rotated with other areas for specified periods of time.

26. Be flexible in the use of space and open to rearranging it. As children mature and their interests change, so should the centres. Also, if repeated problems arise, try solving these by rearranging the environment.

27. Safety should be an overriding, primary concern in setting up an environment for young children.

Effects of the Environment on Children

"Developmentally appropriate" does not mean sterile, clean, or filled with expensive toys. Earlier we said that an environment devoid of materials or people with which to interact can result in serious developmental delay. Conversely, a beautifully planned and decorated environment, though it presents more opportunities for exploration and is appealing to the senses, can become developmentally inappropriate when combined with poor guidance, strict schedules and routines, or direct instructions.

Each province has its own legislation regarding environment, though usually this only sets out minimum standards which can be improved upon. In addition, the Early Childhood Environment Rating Scale (Harms & Clifford, 1980) is one instrument that assists teachers in beginning to assess some aspects of the developmental appropriateness of their centre. However, this tool is based on normative practices (Varga, 1997) and thus is somewhat culturally value-laden. It does not have the scope or flexibility to cover all aspects of a good program. But it is widely used since it is one of the first and only good tools that begins to assess the environment.

The early childhood environment should support the development of children. It has a direct effect on how children behave toward one another. Positive peer interaction is promoted when children are not crowded, when an ample number and variety of items are available, and when socially oriented materials are provided. Classroom arrangement and careful selection of materials also foster cognitive development by providing opportunities for children to classify, find relationships, measure, compare, match, sort, and label (Weinstein, 1987). The environment also enhances both fine and gross motor development through a range of appropriately challenging equipment and materials.

Children's growing sense of independence is supported when they can confidently and competently use equipment and when space and materials are arranged so that they can see what is available and make autonomous choices. At the same time, children develop a sense of responsibility when the environment makes it clear how and where materials are to be returned when they finish using them. Children are more productively involved in activities when the purpose of classroom spaces is clearly defined and when materials are developmentally appropriate (Phyfe-Perkins, 1980; Thomson & Ashton-Lilo, 1983). Children are more likely to follow classroom rules when the environment reinforces these; for instance, if it is important for reasons of safety that children not run inside, classroom furnishings should be arranged in a way that makes walking, rather than running, natural.

The environment also enhances children's self-esteem when it is designed with their needs and development in mind, when it provides space for personal belongings, and when it promotes competence by allowing children to function independently yet safely (Weinstein, 1987). In addition, the environment should convey a sense of security and comfort through a friendly, warm, and inviting atmosphere and through soft elements such as beanbag chairs, carpeting, or sling swings (Jones & Prescott, 1978; Weinstein, 1987).

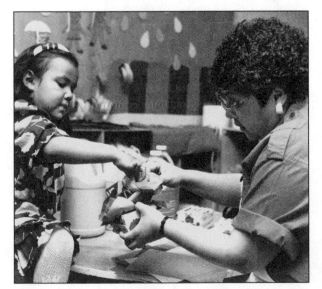

Effects of the Environment on Teachers

When the environment is set up to maximize children's development, prevent problem behaviours, and promote appropriate behaviours, teachers' well-being is indirectly supported. More directly, teachers' jobs are made more pleasant if they work in aesthetically pleasing surroundings, if they have a designated space where they can relax and plan, and if their needs are generally taken into consideration (Thomson

& Ashton-Lilo, 1983). Both personal comfort and professional needs should be supported (Harms & Clifford, 1980). Environmental factors such as temperature, light, colour, sound absorption, ventilation, and spatial arrangement can facilitate or hinder staff in carrying out their jobs (Jorde-Bloom, 1988). Thus, a carefully arranged environment can help prevent teacher burnout by supporting teachers' goals for the children and by making the work site a pleasant place to be.

Developmentally Appropriate Equipment

Early childhood **equipment** refers to furniture and other large items that represent the more expensive long-term investments in an early childhood facility. **Materials** refer to the smaller, often expendable items that are replaced and replenished more frequently. Because equipment can be expensive, its acquisition requires considerable thought. Exhibit 7.2 lists basic equipment and materials that should be included in a classroom for preschool-aged children.

Criteria for Selecting Equipment

We remind you that a list of commonsense questions is a far better guide than an actual list of specific equipment. Some important questions to ask when selecting equipment include the following:

- Does this piece of equipment support the program's philosophy?
- Is the equipment appropriately sized for the children?
- Is the equipment safe?
- Is the equipment durable?
- Is there room for this equipment?
- Can the equipment be constructed rather than purchased?
- Is the equipment aesthetically pleasing?
- Is the equipment easy to clean and maintain?
- Will it accommodate everyone?
- Is it compatible with the concept of diversity?

Computers

Over the past decade, early childhood programs have been investing in the purchase of computers and software for children's use. A growing number of people

EXHIBIT 7.2: BASIC EQUIPMENT AND MATERIALS FOR A PRESCHOOL CLASSROOM

A classroom for 16 to 20 young children should include, but not be restricted to, the following equipment and materials:

Equipment	Materials
Basic Furniture	
• 3–4 child-sized tables that each seat 6–8 (round, rectangular, or both) for meals and activities, as needed • 24–28 chairs • 1 child-sized rocking chair and 1 adult-sized rocking chair • 16–20 cubbies, one for each child, to store personal belongings at children's level	• bulletin boards (some at children's level)
Dramatic Play Centre	
• 1 small table • 2–4 chairs • 4 appliances • 1 large mirror • 1 ironing board • 4–6 dolls, different ethnic groups, both sexes • 1 doll bed or crib and stroller • appropriate storage shelves/bins	• dress-up clothes, both men's and women's, reflecting variety of cultures • empty food containers • set of dishes, pots/pans, utensils • telephones • doll clothes, blankets • dramatic play kits with props and writing utensils
Art Centre	
• 2 easels, two-sided • 1 storage shelf for materials	• variety of paper, paints, crayons, pencil crayons, scissors, glue, collage materials, and clay—self-serve • shelves for drying and storing
Block Centre	
• 1 set of unit blocks, 250–300 pieces, 12 shapes • 1 set of hollow blocks • 1 set of cardboard blocks • 3–6 large wooden vehicles	• various props, including animals, vehicles, people, and furniture
Manipulative Centre	
• 1 storage shelf with individual storage bins	• wide variety of puzzles, pegboards, construction toys, parquetry, beads, lotto, and other games

Equipment	Materials
Sensory Centre	
▪ 1 sand and water table ▪ 1 mixing station for experimenting ▪ plastic bins	▪ variety of props such as deep funnels, hoses, measuring cups, water wheels, scoops, containers, and shovels
Language Centre	
▪ 1 bookshelf ▪ 1 large flannel board ▪ 1 tape recorder, set of head-phones, and microphone ▪ 1 puppet theatre	▪ wide variety of books ▪ file of flannel-board stories ▪ writing materials ▪ variety of puppets ▪ magnetic letters ▪ dictionary
Music Centre	
▪ 1 CD player, tape recorder, set of headphones, and microphone ▪ 1 set of rhythm instruments ▪ 1 autoharp ▪ 3–4 tonal instruments such as xylophones or bells ▪ 1 storage unit for instruments	▪ variety of CDs/tapes ▪ props for movement activities, such as scarves or streamers ▪ writing utensils
Construction Centre	
▪ 1 woodworking bench with vise ▪ 1 set of tools ▪ 1 tool storage unit ▪ 1 pegboard with pegs and hooks ▪ bins and containers	▪ soft wood scraps ▪ thick Styrofoam sheets ▪ variety of nails and screws
Quiet Centre	
▪ beanbag chairs, couch ▪ 1 lamp	▪ magazines, books, pictures ▪ music
Outdoor Equipment	
▪ gross motor equipment that allows children to slide, climb swing, hang, balance, and crawl ▪ 8–10 wheeled vehicles: tricycles, wagons, scooters ▪ 1 play house or other space for quiet or dramatic play ▪ 1 shed for storage	▪ sensory materials such as fine-grained sand and access to water ▪ movable equipment such as crates, planks, cardboard boxes, and tires ▪ Balls, ropes, parachute

Equipment	Materials
World Centre	
▪ globe	▪ maps, books
Computer Centre	
▪ 1 computer and printer ▪ software—categorized ▪ simple posted directions	▪ computer paper
Science and Math Centre	
▪ animal homes, such as aquarium or cages	▪ animals and their care charts ▪ plants, garden supplies, and care charts ▪ wide variety of natural materials found in nearby environment ▪ variety of scientific instruments, such as microscopes, magnifiers, magnets, thermometers, and scales ▪ writing utensils ▪ relevant books ▪ variety of math materials, such as attribute blocks, Cuisinaire rods, items to sort, classify, or seriate, calendars, and timers ▪ variety of old mechanical objects to take apart, such as clocks, watches, cameras, or locks

Note: This suggested equipment and materials list is by no means exhaustive. Many other items could and should be added which suit the program, children, and staff.

have achieved **computer literacy**. In other words, they are knowledgeable about and capable of using a computer. It is often argued that young children are entering a world in which familiarity with computers will be a prerequisite for effective functioning. Therefore, exposure to computers and development of some basic computer skills should be part of early childhood programs.

NAEYC released its position statement "Technology and Young Children Ages Three through Eight" in 1996 in response to this trend.

Various concerns have been raised about the developmental appropriateness of using computers with young children (Barnes & Hill, 1983). However, research shows that young children are quite competent in using the symbols of computers appropriately (Clements, 1987). When computers first became widespread in early childhood education, an often-heard concern was that their use would be at the expense of peer interaction. This fear has been dispelled by a number of studies that document the positive effects of computers on socialization and cooperation (Essa, 1987; Swigger & Swigger, 1984; Ziajka, 1983). Another concern has been that the computer could decrease participation in other activities, but research has shown that it augments rather than replaces other centres (Essa, 1987).

The computer should be viewed as neither good nor bad but rather as a tool, similar to the many other educational resources used by children. It is the wisdom of the teachers, who structure the conditions and setting in which computers are used and who select the software, that makes such activities relevant and worthwhile (Clements, 1987; Haugland & Shade, 1990).

Acquiring a computer for children's use necessitates the purchase of **software,** the set of instructions that direct the computer to perform an activity (Davidson, 1989). Software, which is usually stored on a disk that is inserted into the computer, is available through a variety of commercial sources. More and more software packages for young children are being developed and put on the market, offering a confusing choice to a novice software buyer. Haugland and Shade (1990), in assessing more than one hundred software packages, suggested using the following criteria for judging developmental appropriateness:

1. *Age appropriateness*—The concepts taught and methods presented show realistic expectations of young children.

2. *Child control*—The children, as active participants, not the computer, decide the flow and direction of the activity.

3. *Clear instructions*—Verbal or graphic directions are simple and precise. Written instructions are not appropriate.

4. *Expanding complexity*—Software begins with a child's current skills then builds on these in a realistic learning sequence.

5. *Independence*—Children are able to use the computer and software with a minimum amount of adult supervision.

6. *Process orientation*—The intrinsic joys of exploring and discovering are what engage children on the computer. Completed work is not the primary objective and extrinsic rewards are unnecessary.

7. *Real-world models*—Objects used in software are reliable models of aspects of the world.

8. *Technical features*—Children's attention is better held by high-quality software, with colourful, uncluttered, animated, and realistic graphics, realistic sound effects, and minimal waiting times.

9. *Trial and error*—Children have unlimited opportunity for creative problem solving, exploring alternatives, and correcting their own errors.

10. *Transformations*—Children are able to change objects and situations and see the effects of their actions.

Developmentally Appropriate Materials

In addition to the more expensive equipment, an early childhood classroom requires a rich variety of play and learning materials. This includes commercially purchased items such as puzzles, crayons, or Lego blocks; teacher- or parent-made games and manipulatives; commercial or teacher-assembled kits that contain combinations of items for specific dramatic play themes or flannel-board stories; and donated scrap materials for art or construction activities. Review the recommended basics for an early childhood program listed in Exhibit 7.2.

Criteria for Selecting Materials

More than ever before, a great selection of early childhood materials is commercially available. Toy and variety stores, as well as catalogues, display variously priced toys and games that often promise to educate fully or entertain young children. In selecting learning and play materials, the following specific criteria must be met to ensure their suitability for young children:

- *Developmentally appropriate*—Materials should match the stage of development of the children. Infants need toys that are responsive to sensorimotor actions: mobiles to see and bright, durable books and pictures. Toddlers and very young preschoolers just mastering language and locomotion will benefit from play items that encourage vocabulary building, promote a sense of balance, exercise fingers, and feed their burgeoning sense of independence. Older preschoolers, on the other hand, need materials that utilize their more refined skills in all areas of development. All preschool materials, however, should actively involve children, be interesting, and be safe.

- *Active*—Young children need materials that promote interaction. They quickly get bored with items that require no action on their part. All early childhood materials should promote active involvement and exploration.

- *Open-ended*—Among the most popular and most frequently used materials are open-ended toys, ones that can be used flexibly and do not dictate how they are to be used. Not all materials in the early childhood program will be open-ended (e.g., puzzles have only one outcome), but the majority should be.

- *Feedback-oriented*—As children interact with materials, they should receive feedback on the success of their actions. A completed puzzle tells the child that the pieces have been fitted together correctly; when their bridge stays up, the children know that the blocks were stacked successfully; when there is a place setting for each of the four children at the table in the home centre, they know that they have matched children and dishes appropriately.
- *Multipurpose*—Materials or combinations of materials should suggest many possibilities for play. Children's problem-solving skills and imaginations will be enhanced by multipurpose materials. Children of different skill levels should be able to use materials successfully.
- *Safe and durable*—Items purchased for children's use should be sturdy and constructed from high-quality material. Preschoolers should not be given toys that require electricity. All materials should be checked regularly for loose parts, sharp edges, splinters, or chipping paint. All materials should be nontoxic and age approved.
- *Attractive and aesthetically pleasing*—Materials should be appealing and inviting. Colour, texture, and appearance should be considered when choosing materials in the same way you consider them when redecorating a kitchen.
- *Not stereotyped*—Materials should encourage a sense of equality and inclusion rather than reinforce sexist, racial, or cultural stereotypes.
- *Diverse*—A wide variety of materials that cater to different interests and that meet all developmental needs is necessary. There should be ample materials to develop fine and gross motor skills, to exercise cognitive processes, to promote language use, to encourage socialization, to provide outlets for emotional needs, and to invite creativity. Although variety gives children divergent ways through which they can develop skills, there should also be more than one of some items. This is particularly important with infants and toddlers. However, younger preschoolers, who have not yet mastered the art of sharing, especially need the assurance of multiples of some items.

Teacher-Made Materials and Resources

Some of the best early childhood materials are not purchased commercially but are ones that teachers, parents, and/or children construct as projects. Homemade toys often are tailored to fit the specific interests or needs of the children. Many resource books offer excellent suggestions and instructions for games and materials that enhance cognitive concepts, fine or gross motor skills, and language development (Baratta-Lorton, 1979; Debelack, Herr, & Jacobson, 1981; Linderman, 1979).

Projects evolve daily and require planning and collecting information through collaboration of teachers and children. Teachers and children also can develop and organize classroom resource materials to facilitate planning and programming. One helpful resource is the dramatic play kit, which contains a collection of props for common dramatic play themes. Contained in individually labelled boxes, dramatic play kits can include some of the following themes and items:

- *Health theme*—bandages, empty syringes, hospital gowns, stethoscope, bandages, empty medicine vials, and similar items donated by local doctors, hospitals, and other health-care providers.
- *Bakery theme*—rolling pins, cookie cutters, baking pans, muffin liners, and aprons.
- *Self-care theme*—small mirrors, combs, toothbrushes, hair rollers, empty shampoo bottles, and other cosmetic containers.
- *Grocery store theme*—empty food containers, cash register, cash register tapes, bags, and play money.
- *Plumbing theme*—taps, connectors, lengths of ABS piping, plugs, wrenches, and a hard-hat.

It is worthwhile to note that many typical early childhood education programs set up the dramatic play centre in a theme often arbitrarily chosen by the teacher (e.g., the grocery store). Current practice is moving toward involving the children in deciding on a relevant theme, by recognizing key experiences arising daily or by keeping dramatic play kits available for children to take off the shelf and use at any time. Numerous community resources can be tapped for useful materials. It is a good idea to canvas your community for possible resources to complement whatever marvellous ideas you and the children decide to pursue.

A Note about Learning Centres

Traditionally, indoor space is often organized into **learning centres** (also called interest or activity areas), which combine materials and equipment around common activities. Learning centres can include art, manipulatives, dramatic play, sensory experiences, blocks, music, science, math, computers, books, language arts, woodworking, cooking, and a variety of other areas that fit the unique interests, developmental needs, and characteristics of a group of children and teachers (Essa & Rogers, 1992).

Learning centres allow children to make choices from a range of available, developmentally appropriate activities. In the field of early childhood education, there have recently been modifications to this concept. We now include children in the design of these centres by inviting them to choose materials that would make the centres more enjoyable. Historically, each centre has been independent of the others. For example, we would say, "Go to the math centre to do math." This felt off-kilter to us as teachers because we knew that every other centre (e.g., blocks, language, construction) also supported math concepts. As early childhood educators, we supported the concept of an integrated curriculum, yet our centres existed separate from one another rather than being interconnected. When children play at home, they rarely go to a block centre or a math centre or a language centre. Rather, they access materials from their environment then engage in their activity—cooking, building, drawing, recording, pretending—based on projects that have evolved from their play, ideas, and discussions. Children might decide, "Wow, let's make a bird house!" and then ask "What do we need?" and then begin to plan.

With these modifications, learning centres can be seen more as storage centres, areas that house particular materials that children can access—paper, pencils, dress-up clothes, masking tape, a tape recorder, and so on. Hence, children don't go to the art centre to use clay to make a dinosaur on a particular day because that is the teacher-designated art activity. Rather, clay is available as a tool or medium if the children need to design or make something to enhance their idea, play, or project. The computer is set up not just with a predetermined software program like "Sticky Bears" but is there as a resource if the children want to design a fort or write a song. Writing utensils are used in many areas of the program for recording, planning, and drawing. In this sense, the teacher uses principles to guide the children through the day as their ideas emerge rather than imposing her or his ideas on the children through preplanned themes. We will elaborate more on this idea at the end of this chapter and in chapters 8 and 9 when we discuss curriculum.

Developmentally Appropriate Schedules

Obviously the schedule in a program will vary with the children's ages, their developmental histories, and the length of the day. This, too, is legislated by province to ensure that adequate time is allotted for children to rest, eat, play, and toilet. Unfortunately, legislation, despite its good intent, sometimes negates the purpose of developmentally appropriate programming as it regulates choice, flexibility, and the concepts of child centredness and individual appropriateness right out the centre door. Teachers have to use caution. Schedules of convenience are as detrimental as limits of convenience (see Chapter 6). Children are learning to pay attention to their internal clocks, and their private voices and to make decisions and voice them. Very early on, children know when they have to go to the bathroom, are hungry, and are tired. Just like you, they need time—down time, social time, planning time, time to finish, time alone—and they need space. Imagine how frustrated we would make them if we spent every minute of the day telling

them when, where, and what to do and how to do it!

Of course, infants and toddlers have unique needs, as any parent or teacher who has been with them knows. It is somewhat more difficult to determine what they are communicating to us. Rarely do they have predictable schedules. While time must be allocated for feeding, changing, and sleeping, the very young will always be somewhat unpredictable in their needs. Familiar teachers need to respond to them in a consistent manner and realize that the child's schedule will change in short order.

Programs for older preschoolers and school-aged children are more likely to have a general schedule in mind. Obviously, the outline of the day for a 2- or 3-hour preschool program will differ from that of a 9- to 11-hour child care centre program. But it is not only the difference in the number of hours but also *the needs of the children* that distinguish schedules for these two types of programs.

In planning the course of a typical day in an early childhood program, teachers typically allot times for self-selection, group activities, routines, and transitions. Children and their parents are greeted when they arrive and bid farewell at the end of the day. Both the indoors and outdoors are used whenever possible, and there is a balance between quiet and active times, and between group and individual times. The teachers know their responsibilities and thus ensure that no area of the program is unsupervised. However, they should in no way be rigid about their schedule.

A flexible daily schedule does provide security because it gives the day a predictable order. Children need predictability, and they soon know the general outline of the day. Thus, a schedule can give form without dictating exactly what happens each minute.

A schedule is simply an outline of a typical day that can be changed when children's interests and needs point to a need for change. For example, if children want to watch a large cement truck that comes into view just as the group is about to go indoors, the teachers should extend the outdoor period. If new materials are attracting considerable attention, activity time is extended. If it has been raining relentlessly for two weeks and today is a beautiful, sunny day, plan to spend a large portion of the day outside so everyone can enjoy the nice weather. Similarly, if, despite your best efforts, the children are restless and uninterested in your group activity, shorten the time rather than allow a negative situation to develop. In other words, use cues from the children—and your judgment—to adapt the schedule if it will improve the flow of the day and better meet the needs of the children. You might also ask the children what changes in the schedule they would suggest. Their insights will surprise you! And if the chickens start to hatch when you are about to read a story, always forget the story!

You will make appropriate age adjustments in your typical day. For example, you will extend the number of choices available for older children, who also are able to make some transitions as a group. With school-aged children, you also will have more teacher-initiated activities and they will usually last for a longer period of time. The materials you select will be developmentally appropriate as well. You may read a short story to an infant but read the same story and sing a song with several toddlers. Preschoolers who have some experience in the program may want to sing several songs after a more complex story, but on some days they will not. Kindergarten and primary-level children may spend even longer times with the group.

Some large early childhood centres present special challenges because they have multiple classes that share some common facilities. This can place some constraints on your flexibility but still allows for some latitude, especially when the team plans together rather than for individual classes. The self-contained parts of the program, such as activity or group time, can and should still be adapted freely.

As teachers, you will review the day's events and make adjustments on a regular basis. You will realize that schedules have to be tailor-made by teachers who know the needs of the children in their care. While the main scheduling consideration for child care centres is the needs of the children, the schedule must also take your needs into account. Early childhood teachers spend long and difficult hours working with their young charges, a job that can be both tiring and energizing, frustrating and rewarding. As a complement to the schedule you develop for the children, you need a schedule that provides rest, rejuvenation, and planning time for the adults. When the needs of the adults are considered, the children's needs will be better met, and teacher burnout is less likely to occur.

Components of the Developmentally Appropriate Program

Most early childhood programs contain some fairly standard elements. How these components are arranged and how much time is allocated to them reflect the ages and individual histories of the children, and the teachers' philosophy and goals. It would be absurd for an infant program to allocate large blocks of time for self-initiated play, but this would be a standard feature in developmentally appropriate preschool and primary programs.

The philosophy and goals of the program should reflect a respect for the child's growing independence, increasing decision-making skills, and ability to draw what is valuable from the day's experiences. The teacher facilitates play, structures the environment, and supports children's choices. The teacher offers group activities for older children, recognizes that some children are not yet ready for them, and supports projects that emerge from children's creative thinking. The teacher also keeps groups small and has faith in children's ability to learn and flourish in a well-planned program. Planning does not mean deciding on all the activities to offer the children but on preparing to support and follow through on things that arise during the day.

Let us now examine standard components of the early childhood programs for preschool and school-aged children. (If you intend to specialize in infant care, consult additional resources.)

Arrival and Departure

The first event of the day—the transition from home to school—must be considered carefully because leaving their parents can be very difficult for children. One factor affecting the ease of arrival at preschool or child care is children's general enjoyment of school. Feelings of separation anxiety are not uncommon in preschoolers, although they are more prevalent in younger children (Hinde, 1983). Other factors, particularly what happened at home the night before or as the child was getting ready that morning, also have an impact.

It is worth thinking through the arrival procedure and individual children's reactions and needs. Children arrive at different times of the morning and need time to adjust. They need an individual hello and welcome. They need time to talk before starting their day, just as you needed before starting yours. And they often have made plans in their minds of what they'd like to do that day. Respect this and ask about their plans. Parents need reassurance and a greeting too. Arrival is not a good time to bring up concerns with parents.

Children also need time to prepare to go home—to say goodbyes and finish projects. Set a time to share information casually, calmly, and confidentially with parents after school, and not in front of the child if that would be inappropriate. These are the keys: children and parents need to feel good as they arrive and leave, as you do. Find a way to make this so—smiles, welcomes, reassurances, redirection, a hug, a plan, sharing stories, or making an appointment when you and a parent can talk later.

When children cry, time, comfort, and proximity to a caring adult help them calm down. Distraction and redirection work sometimes, but every child is different. Children cannot stop crying because you say so, and you must be very careful not to trivialize a child's tears. Be patient and continue to monitor and acknowledge the child's mood and behaviour. Give the child space to regain composure, time to talk, and reassurance through words or actions when he or she is ready.

Activity Time

In many programs, **activity time** is also called self-selected learning activities, free play, play time, learning centre time, or other similar names suggestive of the fact that children make choices about the activities in which they engage (Hohmann, Banet & Weikart, 1979). A wide variety of well-planned activities or opportunities from which children can design projects should reinforce and support the objectives of the curriculum. Each day should also provide multiple opportunities for development of fine and gross motor, cognitive, creative, social, and language skills.

Early studies confirmed the importance of an adequately long time block for self-selected play. Christie, Johnsen, and Peckover (1988) compared 4- and 5-year-olds' social and cognitive levels of involvement in play during 15- and 30-minute free-play periods. They found that when the play period was longer, children engaged in more mature play. More specifically, in the longer play period, children engaged in considerably more group play than parallel or solitary play; in the shorter period, there was more onlooker and unoccupied behaviour. During the longer play period, there was significantly more constructive play, in which objects were used to make something.

Beginning teachers often are concerned that they are not active enough during activity time or free play, but being a careful listener and observer is not being idle. Try to think of this time as an opportunity to respond to child-initiated learning opportunities. When you are simply looking and listening, you are learning more about the developmental status of the children you observe. Your demeanour says that you are always approachable and that you are ready to guide children into productive activities and help them resolve disagreements. At other times, you engage in quiet, informal conversations with children, but you do not distract busy players. Your relationships with the children are strengthened, and their self-esteem is enhanced because you let them discover solutions to their problems, rather than provide them.

When planning the activity time block, you should consider safety and adequate supervision. Some activities require close attention by an adult, while others can be carried out relatively independently by the children. Such activities as cooking and woodworking require constant teacher attention. Water and sand play, other sensory activities, messy media, and blocks also need to be monitored on an ongoing basis.

Children can be involved in planning their time. This can include timelines, materials, evaluation methods, accessing resources, and procedures that might require the teacher's guidance. New teachers tend to want to limit the number of children in centres, but in our discussion both in this chapter on learning centres and in Chapter 6 on limits of convenience, we stated that this was not necessary since it often caused more problems than it intended to avoid. Children cooperate and solve problems quite readily when the environment enables them to do so.

For each activity time block, it is important to consider the balance between activities that should be closely supervised and those that are more self-directed, particularly in relation to the number of adults available in the class. It can be easy to lose sight of safety needs in an effort to provide a wide variety of interesting and stimulating activities.

Large-Group Activities

Most programs include one or more times when all of the children and teachers gather together. **Large-group times** such as *circle time,* which originated with Froebel, can be used for many purposes. Some teachers tend to use it in the same way day after day, and others use such times to meet various objectives. Some programs have several group times, each serving a different purpose. Examples include times for stories, music, and movement; sharing time, when children bring something special from home or present projects, ideas, or feelings; and times to share news with their peers.

Group times help the teacher meet a wide variety of objectives. For instance, they provide an excellent opportunity to introduce new topics and explore new materials, or to probe the children's comprehension of concepts and information (Essa & Rogers, 1992). They can also be used for discussions, stories and books, songs, finger plays, movement, socialization, poetry, games, dramatizations, sharing, relaxation exercises, planning and review, calendar or weather activities, and a host of other activities often carried out with the whole group (McAfee, 1985).

From interviews with and observations of early childhood teachers, McAfee (1985) found that the most popular and frequently observed circle activity was reading of books or stories, then music. As well, sharing time or "Show and Tell" was observed quite regularly, whereas other types of activities were seen relatively infrequently or not at all.

Group times are usually teacher-initiated and -led, although teachers always seek children's input. However, older preschoolers enjoy and are very competent in leading group activities, for instance, "reading" a familiar book, leading songs, and moving the group into transitions. Such opportunities to take over group leadership should, of course, never be imposed and should be conducted as the child chooses.

When guiding large-group (as well as small-group) activities, it is important to remember how children learn and what constitutes developmentally appropriate group activities. Children, as active learners, will gain more from activities that allow for their input, include active involvement, and encourage flexible problem solving. Asking children to answer questions for which there is a right or wrong response does not support their developmental needs and their growing self-esteem.

Teachers often get hung up on logistical details such as requiring all children to come to circle simply because it is circle time or insisting everyone sit on their bottoms. The guidelines, instead, should say: We trust you will get comfortable, respect your neighbour, and respect whoever is talking. So as long as children are following the "no hurt" rule, lying down should not be prohibited. The objective is for them to enjoy circle time without bothering anyone else. Our messages should give children the benefit of the doubt and convey trust.

Small-Group Activities

With infants and toddlers, the group size must be very small for most activities. For preschoolers and school-aged children, who usually are in larger groups, programs need to include a **small-group activity time** during which five or six children work with one teacher. This can be handled by staggering small groups throughout the program day or by having each teacher take a small group during a designated small-group time block. Usually such times focus on specific concepts and materials and are geared to the abilities and interests of the children in the group (Hohmann et al., 1979; Wright, 1983). Children should not be grouped by developmental level for activities. Hohmann and colleagues recommend that small groups represent a cross-section of the classroom population to promote cross-learning. In a small-group setting, the teacher has an opportunity to pay close attention to each individual child. As you might expect, careful planning is crucial for successful small-group activity times. In addition, children should be able to choose not to attend small-group activities.

Outdoor Activities

Outdoor play should be a large part of the daily schedule. Some adults think of outdoor play merely as a time for children to expend excess energy and for teachers to take a rest. But outdoor time contains far too many valuable opportunities for learning and development to be dismissed in this way, as the open-model schools have so aptly demonstrated. When you think of outdoor play as an integral part of the early childhood experience, it becomes natural to allocate a large period of time for it. Outdoor time still requires planning in the same way that indoor activity does, and it involves the same kinds of teacher–child interactions.

Just as during activity times, the teacher's role when outside includes setting up a stimulating and safe environment, providing for each child's individual needs, guiding children's behaviour, providing a variety of experiences, taking opportunities to teach concepts, and encouraging exploration and problem solving. An important skill that you, as the teacher, should develop is the ability to scan, to keep an eye on the entire outdoor play area. It is particularly important to pay attention to the fronts and backs of swings, slides, climbing equipment, tricycles and other wheeled toys, and the area in and around the sandbox.

Time for outdoor play may be affected by the weather, although the weather should never be used as an excuse for not going outside. Children do not catch cold from playing outside in the winter, and rain can be glorious. Children thoroughly enjoy the snow or rain, and proper dress is all that is required. Nevertheless, there are times in most areas of Canada when frostbite or heat stroke will be a concern. Outdoor time can work well as a free flow system if teachers, rather than groups, are assigned to the playground.

If inclement weather does prevent the children from enjoying outside time, gym time and games should be available so children can expend energy.

Many schools have a selection of large-motor equipment, such as tumbling mats or indoor climbing apparatus, to use on rainy days, but these should be available every day since physical activity is central to overall health and development.

Finally, teachers often consider the school playground as the limit of outdoor experience, but walks, parks, nature trails, farms, hikes, swims, and beaches are all valuable outdoor experiences. Common safety sense should prevail including permissions, emergency information, enough adults including parents, a first-aid kit, an attendance list, an emergency plan, assigned tasks and children, proper equipment, drinks, spare clothes, and a discussion with the children about safety and expectations in your usual calm, empowering way.

The Benefits of Outdoor Play

The outdoor area and the time children spend outdoors should be integral parts of the early childhood program because of their many inherent values. Lovell and Harms (1985) summarized some of the educational and developmental objectives that well-planned outdoor activities in a well-designed, safe playground can meet:

- Age-appropriate equipment should facilitate a wide range of **gross motor activities** at different levels of challenge, including balancing, throwing, lifting, climbing, pushing, pulling, crawling, skipping, swinging, and riding.
- **Social skills** such as sharing, cooperating, and planning together can be encouraged by such equipment as tire swings, on which several children can swing together, wide slides, or movable equipment with which children can build new structures.
- Activities and equipment should also enhance **development of concepts,** for instance, understanding spatial relations (e.g., up and down, in and out, under and over, low and high) and temporal relationships (e.g., fast and slow; first, second, and next).
- **Problem solving** that involves both physical and social skills should be encouraged as children figure out how to move a heavy object or how to share a popular item.
- Children can learn about their natural world by **observing,** helping to care for plants and animals, noting seasonal and weather changes, and learning about environmental concerns.
- A variety of activities carried out outdoors, such as art, woodworking, or music, can enhance **creative development.**
- Children can try out and **experience** various adult roles through dramatic play, for instance, re-creating the fire station, gas station, or airport.
- In addition to stationary equipment, movable components such as planks, climbing boxes, and ladders allow children to create new and different

possibilities to enhance their motor, social, language, cognitive, and creative development.

- **Exploration** and **increasing competence** help children develop positive self-image and independence.

Routines

Routines are regular, predictable behaviours that are repeated every day—or almost every day—in early childhood programs. They include arriving and departing, cleaning up the playroom and the playground, transitions, and personal care routines. How you approach personal care will vary greatly with the children's ages but will include eating, resting, washing, and toileting. Routines can provide valuable learning experiences, and they are also important for children's well-being. While routines are regular behaviours, it is important to remember that their timing should never be carved in stone.

Cleanup

With infants and toddlers, there is a constant balancing act in how much tidy-up is required to ensure safety, and encourage independence yet maintain a relaxed, low-key setting. With age, children are more likely to put toys away after they are finished with them. Gentle reminders about your class discussions on why cleanup is necessary are usually enough. Older children also are quite willing to assist in tidying up large toys like blocks. Children also enjoy helping to put outdoor toys in the storage shed. Since children need warning, cleanup should not be sprung on them.

Meals and Snacks

Sharing food provides a unique opportunity for socialization, learning, and fun. Thus, almost every program includes at least one snack, if not several meals. Children can assist in every aspect—meal planning, shopping, preparation, delivery, setup, serving, and cleanup. Discussions of fitness, nutrition and "Canada's Food Guide to Healthy Eating" (Health Canada), gardens, and anatomy can surround this activity. Children's involvement piques their interest, generates questions and ideas, and identifies interests, experiences, and prior knowledge while developing skills in all areas. The timing of meals, however, should be dictated by the children's needs, not by a rigid schedule. If it appears that some children get to school having had breakfast several hours before or not having eaten breakfast at all, then an early morning meal should be available. Snacks should be available for a period of time and children be allowed to eat as they feel the need to refuel. Having snack at a set time is unnatural and does not allow for individual differences or choices. Snacks should, of course, be self-serve and nutritious and offer variety.

Timing of lunch will depend on the ages of the children, the length of time they are at the centre, and when morning snack was served. Younger preschoolers may need lunch at 11:30 a.m. and be ready for a nap by noon. How much time is allocated for eating will depend on the children in the group and the type of meal. Generally, however, 15 to 20 minutes for snacks and 20 to 30 minutes for lunch is adequate. Most children can comfortably finish a meal in this period of time.

In any given class, you will find children who are vigorous eaters, enjoying whatever is served, and others who are picky and selective. Even individual children will vary considerably in appetite from day to day or meal to meal, just as you do (Alford & Bogle, 1982). Let's look at some suggestions for encouraging good eating habits and for dealing with some eating problems.

- A relaxed, comfortable atmosphere is vital to good eating. Eating is a time for sharing and talking.
- Teachers should sit and eat with the children during all meals.
- Children should never be forced to eat a food against their will, but they should be encouraged to try all menu items since food preferences and aversions are formed at an early age.
- Involve children in the mealtime.
- Children should be allowed to be as independent as possible at mealtimes.
- Teachers should not serve the meal. "Family style" means children must use their language (e.g., "Please pass the potatoes") and make decisions about what and how much to eat. Drinks should accompany meals; everyone needs to wash down the occasional mouthful.
- It is important to be aware of foods that put young children, especially those under the age of 3, at risk of choking and food allergies.
- Always have the children wash their hands before eating.
- Be sensitive and accommodating to cultural and religious food variations.

Sleep and Rest

Infants and young toddlers spend a considerable period of time napping. But older children need rest too. When children spend all day at a child care centre, a rest or nap time should be an important part of the day. Not all children need a nap, especially as they get older, but for children who are on the go all day, a time to slow down is important. According to Dr. Richard Ferber (1985), director of the

Center for Pediatric Sleep Disorders in Boston, most but not all children sleep 11 to 12 hours at night by age 2, with a 1- to 2-hour nap after lunch. Most children continue to take naps until at least age 3, though some children still nap until they are 5 while others stop at age 2.

A regular nap time is scheduled to help children have some sense of their day. Many children look forward to this quiet time. A variety of arrangements can be made for those children who do not take a nap in the middle of the day. In some programs, children may lie on a cot to relax. When they lie down in a relaxed atmosphere, some children will eventually fall asleep. Those who don't move into an activity apart from the sleepers, for instance, book browsing, playing quietly with manipulatives, or working on their projects.

Sleep, which is a natural part of the body's daily rhythm, requires that the body and mind be relaxed and at ease. If children are anxious or wound up, they will have a difficult time falling asleep. Children should not be expected to move directly from a high-energy activity, such as outdoor play, into napping; rather, a transition is needed to let children slow down gradually. A predictable pre-nap routine that is followed every day is as important as the nap itself (Ferber, 1985). A leisurely 10-minute period can be set aside for children to go to the bathroom, get a drink of water, take off shoes and tight clothing, get a favourite stuffed animal and blanket, engage in last minute chats, and settle down on cots. The lights may be dimmed and drapes or shades drawn. Once all the children are settled down, a teacher may read a story or play a story cassette, sing softly, or lead the children in relaxation exercises. Bob Munsch, the renowned and much-loved Canadian children's author, got his start telling stories to the children in the sleep room at the University of Guelph's child care centre.

After these preliminaries, the teachers can move from child to child, gently rubbing backs, whispering a soothing word, or stroking children's hair. Children who need a nap will fall asleep in a conducive atmosphere where lighting is dim, the temperature is comfortable, the room is relatively quiet, and the teachers convey a gentle, soft mood. Some children need time to wake up gradually, so an unstructured transition in which children can join the class at their own pace is helpful. The setting out of an afternoon snack, to which children can move when ready, often helps provide that transition.

Washroom

Toiletting is important because it helps children become more independent and establishes habits of good hygiene. Toiletting takes on particular significance in groups of toddlers and young preschoolers, who are in the process or mastering or have recently mastered bowel and bladder control. Even with older preschoolers, it is good to remind ourselves that these children were still in diapers just a couple of years ago.

Before toiletting becomes a matter-of-fact routine of life, young children may go through a period when they are especially interested in the acts of urinating and defecating, as well as everything that surrounds them. This is no wonder since adults have spent the first two years of their life praising them for it.

Though we might schedule washroom time, this should never imply that it is the only time that children can go. With young preschoolers who are just mastering bladder control, periodically ask them if they need to go to the bathroom. Be particularly aware of signs such as wiggling or holding, which indicate a need to urinate. Reassure children who fear losing an activity if they go the washroom that their places at the table will be there when they return and that their project will be safe.

It is imperative that teachers handle toilet accidents gently and sensitively. Children will react differently to toilet accidents. For some, an accident will be embarrassing and upsetting, whereas for others it will be, at most, a minor irritant. *In neither instance should a child ever be lectured, shamed, or chastised for a mishap.* Accidents should be handled in a matter-of-fact manner that does not call attention to the child and conveys acceptance of the accident as "no big deal."

Every school should have a supply of extra underwear, pants, and socks available in case of accidents. For a group of younger children, parents might be asked to bring several changes of clothing for possible mishaps. (Remember to ask parents to label them.)

It is beneficial to children if toilets and sinks are child-sized or easy to reach. Children should also be able to reach toilet paper, soap, and towels with ease. Having to overreach can cause accidents.

Washrooms adjacent to the classroom are easiest to supervise, and children are less likely to have accidents when they can go on their own as needed. Children should not be taken to the washroom in large groups; such a procedure only promotes pushing, shoving, frustration, and even toilet accidents.

Teeth Brushing

Especially in child care centres, teeth-brushing supplies are often located in the washroom. Wet toothbrushes should not be stored in a closed cabinet, but in an out-of-the-way place where they can air out after each use. Each child should have an individual, clearly marked brush; disposable paper cups can be used for rinsing. Once they are around age 2, the children can dispense the toothpaste, preferably from a pump, with supervision. In order to establish good hygiene habits, children should be allowed to brush their teeth after meals. Since teeth brushing often occurs after toileting, children should be supervised to ensure they wash their hands before brushing their teeth.

Developmentally Appropriate Guidelines for Program Planning

The components of the early childhood day—activity time, large-group activities, small-group activities, outdoor activity, cleanup, meals, nap or rest, and transitions—can be combined in your program in a wide variety of ways. Let's examine some guidelines that will help in planning an effective program.

Alternating Active and Quiet Times

Children need time both to expend energy and to rest. A useful rule in planning is to look at the total time in terms of cycles of activity and rest, boisterousness and quiet, or energy and relaxation. Categorize the descriptions of time blocks listed in your daily schedule in terms of active times (e.g., activity time, outdoor play, large-group activities that involve movement) and less active times (e.g., story, small-group activities, nap, snack).

In applying this guideline, think about providing the opportunity to be physically active after quiet times and to slow down after active involvement. Also consider the total consecutive time that children are expected to sit quietly. If you planned to have children sit at a large-group activity from 10:00 to 10:20, then move into a small-group activity from 10:20 to 10:35, and then have snack until 11:00, you would be courting chaos, if not disaster. Young children need periods of activity, and this plan has children shifting from one relatively inactive period to another for a full hour. Similarly, when children have been engaged in active exploration, a quieter time should follow. However, do not expect children to move immediately from very active involvement, such as outdoor play, to being very quiet, such as nap time. Plan a more gentle transition that helps children settle down gradually.

Ideally children understand the parameters, limits, and basic rules and can be responsible for choosing to move from place to place as their interest changes or as they've finished what they were doing.

Balancing Child-Initiated and Teacher-Initiated Activities

In quality early childhood programs, most of the day consists of large time blocks in which children can make decisions about the activities in which they will participate and how they will carry them out. Most programs also include times when teacher-directed group activities are available. Most of the day's activities should, however, be child-selected and allow children to move from activity to activity at their own pace (Miller, 1984). Typically, activity time and outdoor time accommodate child initiation, whereas small- and large-group times involve teacher initiation. Some functional activities, such as meals and nap, require some teacher direction, but these times also include opportunities for children to make choices.

Developmentally appropriate programs emphasize child-initiated, child-selected, and teacher-supported activities. When young children are allowed to decide how they will spend their time, they develop qualities such as autonomy, judgment, independent decision making, cooperation, initiative, adventurousness, and creativity. In addition, children develop a reasonable amount of compliance, they understand the rules of group behaviour, and they accept the authority and wisdom of their teachers in safety-related issues. Generally, if teachers convey respect for and trust in the ability of children to make appropriate decisions, children will reciprocate with enthusiastic participation in teacher-initiated, developmentally appropriate activities that engage their interest. Teachers who trust the children's abilities also allow children to leave group activities that do not interest them.

Activity Level of Children

By nature, young children are active and must have many opportunities for expending energy. Some children, however, are more active than others. Occasionally you will have a group in which a large proportion of the children are particularly active. If this occurs, a schedule that has worked for you in the past may not serve as well because the needs of the children are different. In such a case, adjusting the schedule as well as the classroom arrangement and the types of activities planned will help the class run more smoothly. Certainly children should not have to adjust to some predetermined schedules, but rather the schedule should adjust to them. Schedules can create more problems than they solve. However, if you are relaxed and flexible—and pay attention to the children, you will be able to judge their needs.

Developmental Level of Children

As children get older, their attention span noticeably increases; thus, your daily schedule should reflect the group's ages and developmental levels (Miller, 1984). For older preschoolers, plan longer time blocks for small-group and large-group activity times. On the other hand, younger preschoolers require added time for meals and nap. With even younger children, most teachers schedule regular times for toileting. It would be easier and more natural to get to know the children and offer/ask periodically about their need to go to the bathroom, for instance, before going outdoors and before nap. And with infants, you would want to check diapers and have bottles available before going outdoors.

The length of time you devote to large-group activities can be problematic. The time allocated to such activities will depend on the ages and attention spans of the children, but it will also depend on the length of time they have been in the program and on their activity level. At the start of the year, 5 minutes may be long enough for young preschoolers, but they may want to participate in a large-group activity for 15 minutes later on. Children entering kindergarten, with previous experience in an early childhood program, may be interested in spending 20 minutes in a group, whereas children new to a group experience may lose interest after 5 minutes. Children of all ages can, of course, sit for a longer period of time if the activity captivates their interest, but generally a well-paced, shorter group time is more rewarding for all. As the program year progresses, reassess the length of group time and adjust it according to the children's interest.

No matter how long or short the attention spans are in your group, it is important to remember that young children need to be *actively involved in problem solving*. A group time that just entailed listening to the teacher would not be a source of learning for young children.

Group Size

Group size may also influence your planning. A general rule is to keep groups as small as you can. If you happen to be in a province or territory that does not have group-size regulations—or has less than ideal ones—try to arrange the program so that the children are in smaller groups as much as possible. For example, while one group is outdoors, another group is indoors. While some children are involved in self-selected activities, offer a music activity or read a story for those who are interested. A free flow philosophy tends to keep group sizes manageable naturally.

Family Groupings

If you are in a program that has family groupings, the mix of ages will influence the length of your group activities and your program planning. You will also need to provide either a wider range of activities or variants of the same activity so that there is a selection of developmentally appropriate materials.

Wasted Time

Keep in mind that children spend most of their waking hours in the early childhood program. It is, therefore, particularly important to ensure that their daily experiences are meaningful. Davidson (1982) observed time use in child care centres and found that, when considered cumulatively, a considerable amount of time each day—often well over an hour—was wasted. She found wasted time particularly during routine activities such as lunch, nap, transitions, and special or

A Closer Look

DEVELOPMENTALLY APPROPRIATE PROGRAMS IN TRANSITION

Although developmentally appropriate programming has been the accepted practice, Varga (1997) pointed out some consequences if we keep our view too narrow. She warned that we do not want to become so absorbed in the notion of childhood that we forget children have characteristics of people as well. Children disagree; they have opinions; they need space. So often we create conflicts and power struggles with children by imposing on them time limits and transitions that make no sense save because the schedule says this is what we do now. Developmentally appropriate programming strives to respect the nature of the child through a child-centred curriculum. However, programs border on overdirection and disempowerment by imposing schedules and routines on children's personal time—when they eat, sleep, and toilet.

Spatial arrangements are made by the caregivers, themes are imposed, materials are determined off limits on certain days; a limited range of developmentally appropriate materials—often unrelated to the real world—are offered or allowed, and there is confined space without freedom of movement within and between indoors and out. Child-centred play and decisions can be made only within the confines of a self-contained learning centre and a set time with no room for suggestions or projects to emerge—and all this under the constant vigilance of the teacher.

Remember what play was really like? Parents ensured a safe environment; and there were all kinds of stuff to explore, play with, and discover in the house, the basement, your room, and your backyard. You could come and go within those boundaries: read in you room, build a fort, play school, dance to music, or plant a garden. It felt like all the space belonged to you, and you felt free and safe to travel within it. You would dream up little projects every day, and parents were there to help you find where to look and to ask the right questions. They didn't interfere in your play or private time but worked for hours on projects you created together. You knew there were limits and consistency and a proper place for things, that you had to ask about certain things, and that there were problems to solve. You helped choose your own markers, had your own art kit, and decided when you were sleepy and hungry.

The programs of the new millennium will strike a balance between old concepts and the new. We are beginning to recognize the need to value children as competent individuals without pushing them too early to learn academically or leaving them completely abandoned. Recognizing learning as a relationship that develops from interactions will no doubt help.

unexpected occasions. Berk (1976) found that children spent from 20 to 35 percent of their time in transition—waiting their turn or waiting for others. This is not fair and creates many frustrations for children and teachers. Wasted time, Davidson suggested, can lower self-esteem, encourage children to behave inappropriately, and make it more difficult for them to learn to value and use time wisely. Davidson found that the causes for ill-used time included poor organization, inadequate equipment or space, not enough teachers for the number of children, lack of respect for the children, and inappropriate activities.

One clarification should be made. The wasted time described by Davidson revolves around times that force inactivity on children. Children, however, may *choose* times when they refrain from activity, stand at the periphery to observe, or seem to be daydreaming. Such times represent a self-selected rest from activity rather than imposed inactivity.

Some realities of early childhood programs (e.g., a less than ideal number of teachers, too large a group size, and/or inadequate space) are beyond the teacher's control. Nevertheless, teachers who are caring and concerned about the needs of the children and plan an age-appropriate program are on the right track. Additional attention and sensitivity to times in the schedule during which waiting and inactivity could occur will help improve the program. Moreover, how you handle these times can make a major difference. For example, snowsuit time can be a time for conversation, singing, and developing self-help skills. Children who wake up early from a nap could look at a book with an adult or by themselves if they are old enough. Meal time is often rich with opportunities for socialization and conversation, as well as for learning about foods and enjoying them.

Key Terms

activity time	increasing competence
behaviour setting	large-group times
computer literacy	learning centres
creative development	materials
developmentally appropriate practices	observing
development of concepts	problem solving
equipment	routines
experience	small-group activity time
exploration	social skills
gross motor activities	software

Key Points

- Developmentally appropriate programming suggests supporting children in their natural propensity for play and not just teaching them directly. This is a delicate balance.
- The diversity of children in the program and their families is respected and reflected throughout the program, the day-to-day environment, the staffing, and all activities.

- To encourage responsible behaviour from the group, help the children to make some of the rules, thereby creating ownership of their world.
- A pleasant, safe, well-planned environment for both children and teachers will produce long-term positive effects on how children and teachers interact with one another.
- Equipment selections should support the program's philosophy, be appropriately sized, safe, and easy to maintain, and respect the concept of diversity.
- By including the children in the design and theme of learning centres, you enable children to make choices from a range of developmentally appropriate activities and materials.
- A flexible daily schedule provides security and predictability but also allows for the unexpected.
- The developmentally appropriate program includes diverse elements (i.e., indoor and outdoor time, small-group and large-group activities, routines which provide valuable learning experiences).
- Program planning reflects the needs of all the children and includes different levels of activity that teach the children problem-solving techniques.
- Routine activities create time for conversations, singing, and developing self-help skills when used creatively.

Chapter 8

Curriculum

Aprogram is the structure within which certain things occur. Program components, as we just discussed in Chapter 7, include such things as schedules, the environment, times for certain types of activities, and personal care, which are devised based on knowledge of child development and imply certain guidelines for incorporating these into the day. Curriculum, essentially, is what happens during these times.

Remember our scenario at the beginning of Chapter 7 when we asked you to think about your own situation at school. Your program, and even each particular class, may involve individual and group times, a variety of materials, and a balanced time frame, which are appropriate practices for adult learning. But it is the curriculum that you are learning during these times.

Curriculum can also be thought of as what happens during the course of the day for children. The term **lesson plan** almost always creeps into discussions concerning school-aged children. Notwithstanding the variations in terminology, quality early childhood education settings have developmentally and individually appropriate curriculums that have been carefully planned and regularly evaluated by their teachers and team.

In the following sections, we will consider some of the elements of the early childhood curriculum. Our goal is not to provide actual step-by-step lesson plans but to introduce you to a framework for planning. Content and applications are far more vital than format. Is your rationale sound? Is the content appropriate? Do you plan effectively? Do you know how to observe and document children as they engage in the activities? Can you assess and evaluate their development? We will then look in Chapter 9 at five developmental domains—creative, physical, cognitive, language, and social—and will provide guidelines for supporting them through the curriculum.

Of course, some ingredients will be found in all programs, regardless of the children's ages. Caring, warm adults who welcome parent involvement in a developmentally appropriate program are taken as givens. Choice, variety, and challenge in an anti-bias program are also basics. But young children also need the sense of security that a predictable, yet fully flexible, program can offer. Finally, young children—especially children in full-day programs—also need time, time to do what comes naturally, time to pause and reflect, time to be alone, and time to be with others. If the program has all of these ingredients, the environment will also have children and adults who are enjoying each day. You will hear sounds of delight, joy, pleasure, and humour from both children and teachers who approach each day with enthusiasm.

Elements of the Curriculum

The early childhood curriculum is the result of both long-range and short-term planning, and the children's developmental levels. Long-term planning is perhaps

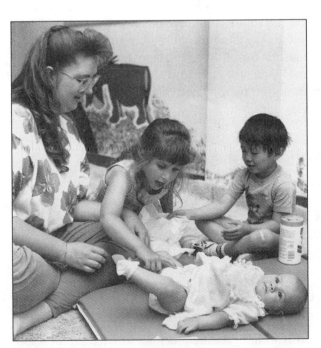

inappropriate for infants and toddlers because they change so quickly—almost daily. In contrast, in late August, a kindergarten teacher might outline what she or he would like to accomplish over the year, and then revise and refine the outline upon meeting the children in the program in September.

Curriculum has to be integrally related to several important factors—program philosophy, learning outcomes, observation, and evaluation—as we will discuss (Langenbach & Neskora, 1977). These factors form a cyclical pattern: program philosophy guides goals and objectives, which are part of learning outcomes or expectations; these, coupled with observation, lead to development of content and activities; content and activities are evaluated on an ongoing basis; and, learning outcomes are reassessed and adjusted as needed, starting the cycle anew (Lawton, 1988).

Program Philosophy and Curriculum

Curriculum takes its direction from the overall philosophy of your program. For instance, underlying beliefs and values about how children learn will have an impact. Another factor shaping the curriculum will be reliance on a particular theorist's works. For instance, programs derived from the theory of Jean Piaget will focus on developmentally appropriate cognitive tasks, whereas programs based on behaviourist theory may rely more on a direct instructional approach. Montessori programs will have equipment and activities, some of which you are unlikely to find in a Piagetian or behavioural program. Likewise, Reggio Emilia takes its approach from Piaget, Vygotsky, and Dewey's perspectives.

Finally, the children in your program and your assumptions about how best to meet their specific requirements will also affect the curriculum. For instance, you might increase the language component of your program if you have children from low-income families. You would also adjust your program if you think that some children in your program have special needs, including a need for positive socialization experiences, an improved self-concept, or cognitive stimulation.

Standards, Learning Outcomes, and Curriculum

From the program's philosophy comes a set of standards (sometimes called goals), which are then translated into learning outcomes (sometimes called expectations or objectives). Both standards and learning outcomes are expectations of what we want a person (i.e., student or staff member) to know or be able to do—a set of knowledge and skills over a range of topics and developmental domains. These provide the basis for the curriculum, elevating activities above a utilitarian rationale, such as "We have to keep the kids busy!" Standards are designed both to promote and facilitate growth in developmental areas and to convey specific content related to the curriculum. Outcomes, in turn, give direction to the activities that are planned and the learning to be done.

Observation and Curriculum

It would be impossible to determine if your outcomes were appropriate or had been achieved without observation. Outcomes must be describable and measurable. We have to see and recognize progress, and we need to be able to make changes where necessary. Observation is one of the most critical tools for curriculum planning and will be looked at more closely later in this chapter.

Assessment, Evaluation, and Curriculum

A curriculum has to be closely matched to the needs of the children in the program. For this reason, evaluation is an important element in curriculum development. It is essential to evaluate, on an ongoing basis, whether the topics and activities of the curriculum are appropriate and meaningful for the children. This can be done by observing and documenting the children's engagement in activities and by reviewing not only their comprehension of concepts you deem important but the emergence of concepts you were not planning or looking for. If your assessment leads you to question aspects of the program, then modify or change the objectives and the curriculum as needed.

Children's Development and Curriculum

You know from our earlier discussion in Chapter 7 of developmentally appropriate practices and individually appropriate, anti-bias, multicultural, inclusive programs that what you include in the curriculum must be directly related to the children in your program. A curriculum that does not accommodate and adjust for the comprehension levels, abilities, needs, and interests of the children is meaningless. To plan an appropriate program requires knowledge about the age group of your class, family characteristics and backgrounds, and individual variations among the children in the class.

A valuable guide in developing curriculum is the NAEYC's brochure, discussed earlier—*Developmentally Appropriate Practice in Early Childhood Programs Serving Children from Birth through Age 8* (Bredekamp, 1987; 1997). This resource provides a philosophical rationale as well as specific and pragmatic information on appropriate and inappropriate practices when working with young children. Exhibit 8.1 outlines "A Systems Approach to Planning" that includes these elements and acts as an integration of information contained in the text to this point.

Curriculum Content

What, then, is appropriate in an early childhood curriculum? What interests the children in your program? What is relevant to them? What is developmentally relevant (Hohmann et al., 1979)?

Perhaps the best way to define what is appropriate in a curriculum is to say that it should be derived from the children's life experiences, based on what is concrete, and tied to their emerging skills. Consider that young children have been part of their physical and social world for only a very short time. They have so much to learn about the people, places, objects, and experiences in their environment. When you give careful consideration to making the elements of the environment meaningful and understandable to children, you need not seek esoteric and unusual topics. Children's lives offer a wide variety of topics on which to build a curriculum, including learning about themselves, their families, and the larger community in which they live (Essa & Rogers, 1992).

EXHIBIT 8.1: A SYSTEMS APPROACH TO PLANNING

Program Includes:

Philosophy

based on historical, theoretical, and empirical evidence

Developmental Framework

domains of creative, emotional, social, language, cognitive, and physical

Ongoing

- assessment
- observation
- documentation
- evaluation
- modification

through

- interaction
- communication

with

team using positive guidance principles that reflect appropriate practices and uphold quality to nurture relationships which create an atmosphere of respect and trust so that learning will occur

Standards (Long-Term Goals)

based on philosophical and developmental framework

- reflect rationale
- identify strength and needs

Learning Outcomes (Objectives)

1. developmental objectives—information on domains
2. content objectives—information on subject/topic
3. behaviour objectives—information on observable and measurable actions and skills
4. personal objectives—information on individual or group progress and satisfaction

Action

- plan, develop, implement time frames (schedules), routines, activities, projects, opportunities, experiences, resources (i.e., materials, equipment, people, environment)
- learning related back to guide development

Children as the Focus of the Curriculum

The most crucial attributes with which young children can be armed to face the future are feelings of self-worth and competence. Children are well equipped for success if they are secure about their identities, feel good about themselves, and meet day-to-day tasks and challenges with a conviction that they can tackle almost anything. The curriculum can foster such attributes by contributing to children's self-understanding and providing repeated reinforcement and affirmation of their capabilities, individual uniqueness, and importance.

Self-understanding comes from learning more about oneself—one's identity, uniqueness, body, feelings, physical and emotional needs, likes and dislikes, skills and abilities, and self-care. Children enjoy learning about themselves, so a focus on children as part of the curriculum can and should take up a significant portion of time. It is important, however, to ensure that planned activities are age-appropriate so they contribute to both self-understanding and positive self-esteem. Infants will enjoy playing patty-cake, for example. Two-year-olds are still absorbed in learning to label body parts; thus, activities that contribute to sharpening this language skill are appropriate. Older preschoolers, on the other hand, are more interested in finer details. For example, they enjoy examining hair follicles under a microscope or observing how the joints of a skeleton move in comparison with their own bodies. Still older children are interested in processes like digestion and respiration, when presented in a concrete way. But all children are interested in exploring through doing and creating, so this should become the cornerstone of practice.

The Family as the Focus of the Curriculum

The family is vitally relevant to children and provides another rich basis for curriculum topics. We can help children build an understanding and appreciation of the roles of the family, similarities among families, the uniqueness of each family, different family forms, the tasks of families, and relationships between family members. An examination of the children's family homes, means of transportation, food preferences, celebrations, parental occupations, and patterns of communication also provide appropriate curriculum topics. You might invite family members to come into the classroom and share special knowledge and talents. Alternatively, children as well as teachers might bring photographs of their families to share.

A curriculum focus on the family contributes to children's feelings of self-esteem and pride. They can share information about something central to their lives while, at the same time, expanding their understanding of the family life of the other children. While such learning strengthens children's emerging socialization, it also contributes to cognitive development. Teachers help children make comparisons, note similarities and differences, organize information, and classify various aspects of family structure.

The Community as the Focus of the Curriculum

The open schools have aptly demonstrated that children's awareness of their world can particularly be expanded through the community. Older toddlers and preschoolers have had experience with numerous aspects of their community, especially shopping, medical, and recreational elements. School-aged children know even more about it. The community and those who live and work in it can certainly extend the walls of your program and offer a wealth of learning opportunities and curriculum material.

From the community and the people who work in it, children can learn, through projects and investigations, about local forms of transportation; food growing, processing, and distribution; health services, including the role of doctors, nurses, dentists, dental hygienists, health clinics, and hospitals; safety provisions such as fire and police departments; communications facilities, including radio and television stations, newspapers, telephone services, and libraries; and local recreational facilities, such as parks and museums. Children can visit an endless variety of appropriate places through field trips. In addition, community professionals can be invited to visit your class and share information and tools of their professions with the children.

You can help children begin to build an understanding of the community as a social system by focusing on the interrelatedness of the people who live and work in your area. For instance, people are both providers and consumers of goods and services; the dentist buys bread that the baker produces, and the baker visits the dentist.

In addition, the larger physical environment of the area in which you live provides a setting worth exploring with the children in your class. Your approach will differ depending on whether your community is nestled in the mountains, by the ocean, or in the midst of rolling prairies. Most young children living in Saskatchewan, for instance, will not have experienced the ocean. It is difficult to convey what the ocean is like to someone who has never seen it, and this is particularly true for children who rely on concrete, firsthand experience. Therefore, it makes little sense to plan a unit on the ocean when it is more than a thousand miles away. Instead, focus on what is nearby and real in the environment, on what children are familiar with and can actually experience. You may choose a unit on farming if it is harvest time in Saskatchewan, whereas you may choose shellfish as a topic in Nova Scotia during lobster season. If you are visiting a barn with horses and pigs, you will not select tender fruit farming as a topic.

In Exhibit 8.2 we provide an example of a curriculum that begins with the child and builds outward. In the past, the arrows often moved inwards, imposing the outside world onto the child. In this sense, developmental objectives for what the child should know dictated learning. In this model, the arrows move outward. The curriculum evolves as the child learns. In this sense, learning is leading development. This model is child-centred, open-ended, divergent, and flexible.

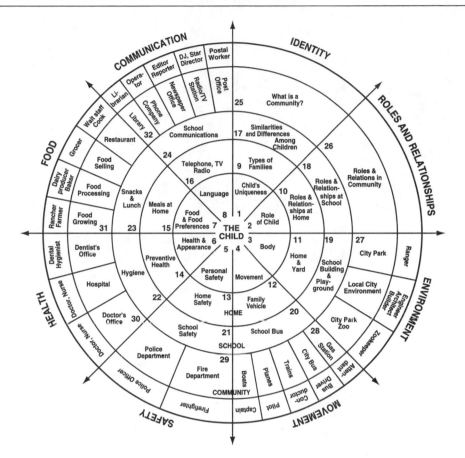

Adapted from Essa, E.L., & Rogers, P.R. (1992), *An Early Childhood Curriculum: From Developmental Model to Application* (Albany, NY: Delmar Publishers, Inc.).

Planning the Curriculum

In some programs, especially those with infants and toddlers, long-term plans and objectives are inappropriate. Short-term objectives, however, are reasonable. With older preschoolers and school-aged children, your plans and objectives may cover a longer time span. Flexible long-term objectives also are appropriate at the primary-school level. Teachers try to plan their programs so that the whole child is challenged every day. Quite frequently, the only effective way of making sure you do this is to develop global plans for each week and more specific ones for each

day. This means planning not what is done and said each minute since we wish to be flexible enough to accommodate the unexpected, but rather your approach to the day, some of the things you and the children would like to accomplish, and what you need to accomplish them.

Planning precedes and goes far beyond the actual implementation. Planning means coming up with ideas. Think about the difference between the following two scenarios and how it relates to teaching and learning. An architect shows up and says, "Here is the blueprint I designed. This is the building we will build." In contrast, there is the architectural team who collaborate. The team members, including the client, know they want to build a building, but they first discuss the type of building; investigate possible sites; research; design; and determine needed materials and equipment, staff requirements, length of project, and ways to measure its progress and evaluate their work. Changes are welcome along the way as new information arises and problems are solved. Which scenario would engage you and teach you more?

Daily plans describe each activity planned for that day, objectives for the activities, and the time frame within which they are carried out. In addition, a daily plan can indicate which teacher will be in charge of an activity, in what part of the classroom each activity is to be carried out, and what materials are needed. Plans can take many forms, but they should be complete enough so that any teacher can pick them up and know for any given day what activities are planned and why they are planned.

Each plan may be part of a project or theme and, as such, related to broader goals and objectives. But each plan should also be complete in itself by providing a balanced day for the children. Within each plan, there should be provision for activities that meet needs in all developmental domains. There should be activities that promote creative expression. Communication should be woven throughout activities, so children exercise receptive and expressive language, as well as a variety of non-verbal means of communication. And there should be opportunity for exploring new topics in a variety of ways through multiple activities in a leisurely, unrushed manner.

While beginning teachers find planning time-consuming, they also find that written plans are useful as they help to organize thinking about objectives, materials, and evaluation. Written plans are also helpful when teachers work in teams and when unexpected illness necessitates a supply teacher. Plans for older children who are working on themes keep parents informed about what their child has been experiencing, discussing, and investigating. But for plans, as for schedules, flexibility is critical. You may need to abandon your plan completely, or you may need to revise it as you go along. With older preschoolers and school-aged children, you probably will also want to consider using projects and themes in your program.

Themes and Projects

Themes and projects, which can be traced back to the Open Education model and to Dewey in North America, provide a unifying element around which activities are planned (Katz & Chard, 1993). While **theme** and **project** are often used to mean the same thing, themes are generally less specific than projects. You might have a theme titled "Spring," but that does not provide much information on what you will do. A related project would be more specific, for example, "What happens in the garden—or fields or the ranch or fisheries—during spring?" (The term **unit** is often used to mean theme. However, a unit also is used to describe a series of teacher-initiated, prearranged lessons on specific topics. As such, a unit would be more appropriate at the upper limits of the early childhood years, especially if provincial or territorial directives require teachers to cover certain topics.)

A project or theme can last any length of time, from a day or two to a month or more. The interest-value and relevance of the topic to the children should dictate how much time is spent on a theme. Furthermore, the length of a project or theme should be flexible enough so you can spend more time if the topic intrigues the children or cut it shorter if the children seem ready to move on.

Planning a project or theme should begin with a careful consideration of your objectives and the children's interests. What is it that you and the children want to learn about the topic? What concepts, skills, and information can this project convey? Most important, are these relevant, age-appropriate, and of interest to the children, and will the children enjoy them? Children have to be the starting point for planning, and they can be involved in the planning. Consult them when you are planning to find out what their ideas are, and incorporate these ideas into your plan. Prior knowledge is critical. Teachers so often create elaborate lessons and teach this new knowledge without first exploring what the children already know. Don't you find it tedious to be taught something you already know? If the group is planning a project on "How to Make Bread," you might hope to cover the following concepts:

- Bread is baked at the bakery.
- The baker is the person who bakes bread.
- Many loaves of bread are baked at the bakery (mass production).
- Bread is made up of many ingredients.
- Bread is taken by trucks to grocery stores, where it is sold to people such as those in the children's families.
- Different bakeries make different types of bread (e.g., Rajeev's baker makes chapatis and puris, Rana's baker makes pita bread, Maria's baker makes tortillas, Albino's baker makes crusty cornbread).

A project usually begins with an introduction in which the theme is initially presented or arises out of the children's interests, and often this introduction is a field trip or investigation of prior knowledge and experiences. Early on in a project, you will want to focus on the children's familiarity with the subject or closely related areas, and adjust your plans to fit with their existing knowledge. Thus, if you plan a theme on the topic "bread," you can discuss types of bread with which the children are familiar, the food group to which bread belongs (if you have already spent time discussing nutrition and the four basic food groups), the process of baking (for those children who have helped their parents make bread), and the different ways in which bread is used in meals.

New ideas and activities can be introduced logically and sequentially. New material should always be presented first in a concrete manner. While field trips are frequent starting points, concrete experiences also can be brought into the classroom through objects or guests. In the case of the bread unit, you may want to plan a field trip to the local bakery at the beginning of the unit so the children can see how bread is made. On the other hand, some in-class experiences with bread baking can be a wonderful preparation for a trip to the bakery. Alternatively, Rajeev's and/or Maria's mother and father may agree to help the children make chapatis and tortillas. In either case, *it cannot be emphasized enough that any new concept should begin with the concrete, with firsthand experience.*

Once children have had a chance to observe and learn through firsthand experience, they can begin to assimilate this information through subsequent activities. After the field trip, children should have opportunities to represent factually what they observed by talking about and dictating accounts of the visit to the bakery, drawing pictures of what they saw on the field trip, and otherwise recalling and replicating their visit. This factual recounting allows children to fix the experience in their minds.

Children can begin to use new information in creative ways once it has been integrated into their existing memory and experiential store. They can play with the information through such activities as art, dramatic play, puppets, or blocks. This element of the project offers a wide variety of possibilities that children can approach in their unique ways.

Finally, a project is ended through a summarizing component. Younger children may enact baking in the bakery they have made in the home or dramatic play centre. Older children may have individual and group projects they would like to share with others. Visitors also may be invited to see the children's creations—and to taste them. Usually, the teacher also evaluates the children's responses to the project and makes notes about changes for future years.

Activities

The play in which children are involved is as important as any planning for from this emerges new ideas, new insights, and new questions upon which more planning can be based. Children at play are constructing new knowledge, for which we could not possibly plan, as they bring their unique experiences and dispositions to the situation.

It is important to be aware of the objectives of a given activity as well as to think through how the activity will be carried out so that the children will gain the intended knowledge and skills. However, there is a danger in creating lesson plans that focus on very specific skills: you tend to watch only for those skills to determine whether they were achieved. With this narrow focus, it is easy to overlook other important learning that is occurring.

Environment

An environment that is designed to promote play and learning opportunities facilitates children's propensity to explore and investigate. This, in turn, piques their curiosity and desire to find out more, which generates questions. It is from these queries that teachers and children discover interests and generate ideas for projects. In A Closer Look, we examine two environments. We enter a playground that, through design, provides opportunities for play, creativity, spontaneity, planned events, and ongoing projects, and acts as a springboard for endless new activities. Some of these activities are child-initiated, some teacher-initiated, but all activities are agreeable to both children and staff based on common interests and mutual respect. Next we observe a classroom based on a curriculum that supports emergent literacy. The environment provides materials that immerse the child in literacy, and the teacher has a set of general goals and objectives for the children. However, rather than present structured lessons, the teacher is guided by principles that she can apply in either an emergent or a planned way.

Team Planning

Planning for an individual child or class without regard for the system to which they belong is fruitless. The school as a whole must buy into the philosophy, goals, and curriculum. Teachers must work as an interconnected, interrelated system so that continuity is evident through the program. The entire program must reflect the attitude of respect toward all persons and uphold the value and worth of children, families, and teachers.

Working as a group ensures that all members are familiar with, accountable to, and responsible for objectives and activities because they took part in their development. It can also lead to greater commitment to the program because everyone's ideas were incorporated. Personal investment in the curriculum can contribute to the overall cohesiveness of the program. In A Canadian Professional Speaks Out, Carolyn Simpson relates how team planning, program planning, program philosophy, children's development, and accountability (our next topic) merge to create a high-quality inclusive program.

ENVIRONMENTS THAT SUPPORT CURRICULUM:
1. A PLAYGROUND FOR LEARNING

St. Elizabeth's Child Care Center, in a metropolitan community in northern California, serves a large population of children from low-income families. Several years ago, one of the staff members was particularly interested in transforming the original blacktop playground—with its traditional swings, slides, and jungle gyms—into a more exciting and flexible outdoor area that would enhance and extend learning. She devised a plan that, through extensive fundraising and the cooperative efforts of staff, parents, and the community, eventually became a reality.

This new outdoor area now includes multiple, well-defined learning centres. Included in this carefully and aesthetically landscaped space are an amphitheatre for storytelling and dramatic play; a fenced animal care area for rabbits; a covered art area; a "freeway" network of paths for riding toys; an extensive sand area; a woodworking centre; a "meditation garden" or quiet area surrounding a shady willow tree; a boat-shaped centre with props and equipment for housekeeping dramatic play as well as a car engine with which children can tinker; a five-opening drainage pipe tunnel; and many places that can be used to climb, swing, and build. Storage spaces are provided wherever materials and props are needed.

Building materials throughout the area were selected and arranged to provide various textures, multiple sizes, and aesthetic appeal. Equipment was selected to encourage children to observe and classify, make comparisons, and note similarities and differences. Movable equipment, such as planks and tires, was added to promote problem-solving skills. In addition, this outdoor play area is a delight to the senses, with its dwarf-tree fruit orchard, vegetable garden, strawberry patch, raised herb garden for easy sniffing, and flower beds, all of which children and teachers help tend. This playground has a wide range of activities to engage children, activities that promote all areas of development. Through the imaginative planning of one teacher and the efforts of the many people who helped make it a reality, this playground has enriched the play of many young children (Essa, 1981).

Not all early childhood programs have the luxury of such an exciting playground because each school is unique in its approach as well as limited by space, weather, funding, and other resources. All playgrounds have the potential to be improved, however, through added movable props, the enhancement of natural features, and the careful arrangement of learning centres.

2. A CLASSROOM FOR EMERGENT LITERACY

Mary was hired to teach a class of fifteen 5-year-olds at a school in which most of the children came from low-income families. Her first task was to get rid of the desks, both the small ones and the one intended for the teacher, and to set up a developmentally appropriate environment with learning centres. She particularly focused on providing a whole-language environment. She carefully selected materials and arranged the room to reinforce language in as many ways as possible, also using day-to-day spontaneous conversations and planned activities.

As she found on the first day, many of the children came to school having had few or no experiences with art materials. From that very first day, she encouraged each child to draw many pictures on any topic. "I remember one little boy who drew a line and said, 'It's a dog,'" Mary recalled. She wrote the word "dog" next to his line and encouraged him to make other pictures. "His picture was typical of this group's artwork in September," she said. In addition to the daily art, Mary posted labels around the room, talked about the labels, sounded them out, read many stories, had the children discuss and act out the stories, talked and encouraged the children to talk all the time, included letters and letter lotto games to allow the children to manipulate them, and generally enriched their environment with lots of written and oral language.

Mary also enlisted the help and support of the parents, who became very interested in what their children's teacher was doing. She talked with parents every day, showed them what the children were doing, and explained the importance of the children's work. She sent notes home and made phone calls to those parents she did not see. In addition, she put together a "writing suitcase," an old briefcase with a variety of writing and reading materials that the children took turns taking home.

By January, some of the children were drawing very detailed pictures and taking an interest in the letters of their names. One day, Lishana, after spending considerable time working on a complex picture that featured a lot of red, suddenly jumped up screaming, "I did it! I did it!" Mary went to Lishana to see what the excitement was about. She found, to her delight, the phrase "i lik red" written at the top of the picture. "Obviously she had been thinking about what letters mean, and from that time on, she put letters into words. It clicked for her," explained Mary.

By the end of the school year, all 15 children were writing often long and complex stories on their own. They continued to use invented spelling, to read many of the words in their environment and in books, and to use a lot of verbal language. According to Mary, "Given the right environment, these children could do a lot. They just blossomed!"

Accountability

As with anything we do, we need to provide a sound rationale for why we do things, a plan for getting them done, and evidence that we did them. We must also have some way of measuring our success and our satisfaction. In essence, we must be held accountable for our actions. Accountability means setting goals based on observation and information, documenting progress and evidence, and evaluating the results so that improvements and achievements can be addressed.

Working with young children and planning a program for them requires a sense of direction and purpose. In order to plan, we need to assess situations. Assessment involves such components as observation, documentation, and collaboration. These can be expressed as a set of standards and learning outcomes that include broad goals and more specific objectives. Goals and objectives provide the road map for the early childhood program journey. But not just any map will provide the specific information needed for your specific program. Goals and objectives should reflect the individual character and uniqueness of your class, school, and program. One way of identifying that individuality is through systematic evaluation.

In order to determine if you accomplished what you set out to do, to learn what new knowledge and skills emerged or how existing knowledge and skills were applied, you must evaluate the process and the outcomes. Evaluation holds you accountable to your plan and actions and helps you to make adjustments. It also helps gather the evidence and support you need to keep your program credible. This process occurs at all levels of the system. We assess and evaluate individual children, our curriculum, our program, our environment, the model of service delivery, and our practices. Staff is evaluated on an ongoing basis as well, and this includes reciprocal and self-evaluation. The information we glean from this process assists us in making decisions, recommendations, and modifications with regard to the children, family programs, the team, and ourselves. In this section, we look at accountability and its constituents, including standards and learning outcomes, observation and documentation, and assessment and the process of evaluation.

Standards and Learning Outcomes

Standards

Standards provide a general overview of what you and the team expect the children, yourself, the family, the team, and the centre to gain from the program. They

A CANADIAN PROFESSIONAL SPEAKS OUT
Inclusion in Early Childhood Education

Making the decision to utilize an early childhood program is often difficult for parents, and especially so for parents with children who have special needs. Matching the service to family needs can prove especially challenging. These parents must also match the quality and philosophy of services with other resources that may be required to meet their children's needs.

In Prince Edward Island, once the parent and ECE supervisor agree that his service will best meet the needs of the family, the supervisor can apply for funding under the Ministry of Health and Community Services (formerly the Department of Health and Social Services) for a Special Needs Grant. Prior to 1988, funding for specialized programming was available to families through either the Child Care Subsidy Program or Family Support Program; eligibility was determined by an income test. With the implementation of the Special Needs Grant in 1988, funding is now granted to licensed centres directly. The grant allows for a higher child–staff ratio and for the purchase of additional resources (i.e., materials, equipment, or environmental modifications) as required, thus enabling the centre to be in a better position to deliver a high-quality inclusive program.

The grant is individualized, and approval is based on an assessment of the child's needs, the appropriateness of proposed program activities and curriculum, the availability of funds, and the agreement of the centre to administer any funds according to the policies of the Special Needs Grant.

Another strength of the program is its accountability. Centres are required to submit quarterly progress reports and salary reports, and to hold annual case conferences, the first being six months into the program, with the transdisciplinary team. As well, should this team decide that a child of school age would benefit from one year longer in the ECE environment, the Department of Education and Health and Social Services [now the Ministry of Health and Community Services] have worked together to provide services for this child.

As a result of the Special Needs Grant, Island children and their families are receiving early education and intervention that may not otherwise have been possible.

Carolyn Simpson, Holland College, Prince Edward Island

are long-term (i.e., for the year) and are commonly referred to as "aims" or **goals**. Goals should be based on a sound understanding of process and needs, reflecting appropriate expectations and practices. Goals are often based on facilitating and encouraging healthy development in the social, emotional, cognitive, creative, language, behavioural, and physical domains; the acquisition of skills; and the construction of new knowledge in and about these domains. Hence, as a teacher and, therefore, an employee, you would require a written plan about your career goals. The program must have goals which are conveyed to parents. The families clearly have goals they expect of the centre. Of course, the teachers, centre, and families have goals for the children. The children, too, have goals. The common thread that ties these goals together is communication and collaboration. Goals reflect the theoretical rationale on which the program is based.

Another way of identifying goals, related to a developmental approach, focuses on important processes that we all begin to acquire in the early years. Frazier (1980) suggested that these might include:

- *communicating*—expressing, taking in, responding
- *relating* to others
- *finding out*—inquiring, investigating
- *discovering*
- *making*—constructing, creating, inventing
- *choosing*—seeking, preferring, holding on to
- *controlling*—directing, leading, managing
- *persisting*—staying with, enduring

Keep in mind that there is no one way of wording goals and objectives.

Learning Outcomes

A **learning outcome** is a more specific interpretation of a general goal, and it provides a more practical and direct tool for planning. Goals can be identified at the beginning of the program year to provide direction; learning outcomes are useful for short-term planning (i.e., lesson and daily planning) and should be an integral part of it. Learning outcomes have often been referred to as **objectives**. However, recent thinking has differentiated objectives and outcomes; objectives tend to refer to what the child should do, whereas outcomes reflect what the child should learn. We will use the terms interchangeably while the field sorts out the transition. Objectives will differ depending on whether they are developed for a group as a whole or for an individual. The inherent danger with objectives is that they can be limiting. They are often very teacher-determined and can limit the teacher to observing only that which she or he has deemed important. This is one reason why team input is so vital.

Objectives must include not only what you want to teach the children or what you want to learn about them but the conviction that you want to learn about them. They help you evaluate what you do with the children, what the children know and have learned, and how they approached learning. This evaluation helps you to determine the children's learning styles and problem-solving skills over and above the actual facts they have accumulated. Often what you intend children to get out of a lesson and what they actually get out of it are quite different. You must be able to tie together what you planned, what you did, and what you saw.

Objectives encompass several areas to help you plan for, observe, assess, and evaluate an activity, a skill, knowledge, or performance.

Developmental Objectives   These help you focus on the developmental domains by directing your attention to development and the wholeness of your activity. Is it open-ended enough to enlist all the domains in its implementation?

Content Objectives   Objectives are also identified for the content or subject matter of the curriculum (Essa & Rogers, 1992; Lawton, 1988; Peters, Neisworth, & Yawkey, 1985). A **content objective** relates to the information that an individual activity conveys. Appropriate topics can be drawn from meaningful aspects of the children's environment to expand their understanding of the world. They also help you focus on the wholeness of your activities.

A content objective also gives direction to the teacher carrying out an activity (Essa & Rogers, 1992). Assume the lesson plan indicates that you will help the children make fruit salad. What direction does this activity description give you? What will you discuss with the children? Where is your focus? Do you talk about the colour of the fruit, its texture, and its sweetness? Do you help children label the individual fruits? Do you relate the fruit salad to what might be served in a restaurant? What about at home? Do you discuss the fact that chefs, or mothers and fathers, make fruit salad? Do you focus on safety and health? Or should you incorporate measurement and math concepts? The objectives will determine the focus and purpose of the activity and will help guide your teaching style and handling of the activity.

Behavioural Objectives   Although developmental and content objectives usually apply to planning for the total group, a **behavioural objective** is generally used in planning for an individual. Behavioural objectives are very specific and are based on observable and measurable actions or skills. Behavioural objectives can help you to document program and teacher effectiveness as well as individual progress. Words such as "label," "name," "identify," "match," "sort," "classify," or "order from largest to smallest" relate to a child's actions which you can observe. On the other hand, words such as "think," "enjoy," "consider," "appreciate," or "be aware of" describe an internalized process. If, for instance, an objective stated that Simon would *understand* the colour red, you would have no way to measure this because you cannot see Simon understanding the concept of redness (Deiner, 1983).

Behavioural objectives can be useful, particularly in planning for an individual child in an area needing attention. Such objectives have also been criticized, however. Because they specify how a child will behave, they eliminate spontaneity, creativity, and playfulness; by spelling out and directing the content of activities, they ignore a child's internal motivation to master a topic or skill; they demand a great deal of work from the teacher because each identified behaviour will require developing a list of objectives; they also encourage teachers to "teach the objective" rather than to observe for it in context; and, because they are broken into such small components, it is sometimes difficult to keep in touch with the larger goals for the child (Lawton, 1988). However, it is possible to write objectives that are open-ended yet measurable.

Personal Objectives   These include the individual in determining what she or he views as necessary knowledge and skills for personal growth, progress, success, and satisfaction.

Observation and Documentation

It would be impossible to set standards and learning outcomes without observation and documentation to provide evidence and rationale for your plans. One of the most effective informal methods of assessment, program planning, and evalu-

ation is focused observation. Early childhood teachers use observation as a primary method of gaining insight into the various facets of children's development at different times and in different contexts (Wortham, 1990). As well, observation is integral to making program and curriculum changes. Environment and approach have strong impacts on behaviour. As we stressed in Chapter 6, watching children's play is very rewarding. Often, however, we tend to look for something specific. If we get in the habit of watching with an open mind, we will learn a great deal about the children and gain many insights. As well, we remind you to watch children watching and you'll note they are continually processing, deciding, analyzing, and absorbing. Their facial expressions, body language, language, and actions reveal much about their overall development.

Observation is valuable as a team tool in improving team function and sharing teaching strategies. Observation can provide us with detailed information about behaviour, help us understand it, and provide the basis for predicting behaviour (Richarz, 1980). One of the most appealing features of observation is that it is unobtrusive and natural. It does not interfere with the child's ongoing activity and behaviour, in contrast with more formal tests that require the child to perform specified tasks in an isolated setting.

Confidentiality and Objectivity

Observation, assessment, and evaluation are meant to be a positive, supportive tool to improve the lives of those it measures. Information is shared verbally or written, only with permission of all parties and only as a tool that will positively enhance the lives of the participants. Being objective supports fairness and confidentiality protects the rights and privacy and therefore the integrity and dignity of all.

Documentation

Obviously observation and assessment imply documentation since you must record what you see and hear. Writing is the most common method of recording. However, videotapes, audiotapes, photographs, interviews, and children's work all lend insight to observations. Formal and informal assessment methods provide concrete information primarily about children's overall development.

Parental Involvement

Parental consent is mandatory as is their input. Their input must be actively sought and supported from the very beginning. Parents should not be simply the recipients of information after the process is concluded. Their observations, interpretations, experience, and recommendations are integral to the true picture of the child or situation.

Types of Observations

Anecdotal Record   Observation can take a variety of forms. One of the most often used is the **anecdotal record,** a brief description or "word picture" of an event or behaviour (Cartwright & Cartwright, 1974). A collection of well-written and accurate anecdotes can provide a very descriptive characterization of a child. Anecdotal records come only from direct observation, are written down promptly and accurately, describe the context of the behaviour, are factual rather than interpretive, and can focus either on a typical or unusual aspect of the child's behaviour (Wortham, 1990).

Running Record   A **running record** is a more detailed account of a child's behaviour over a period of time (Wortham, 1990). Whereas the anecdote focuses on a single event, the running record keeps track of everything that happens in a specified time period, whether it is a half-hour or several months. Such a record can be very useful when you are trying to pinpoint the source of a problem. It was most helpful in getting a handle on the disruptions in one class, where 3-year-old Erin seemed to be always at the centre of aggressive outbursts. A careful running record, kept over a period of three days, helped the teachers see that Erin was responding to rather subtle taunts from two other children.

ABC Analysis   One helpful device in keeping a running record is the **ABC analysis,** in which three columns identify the antecedent (what occurred just prior to the episode), the behaviour, and the consequence of incidents (Bijou, Peterson, & Ault, 1968). This helps you focus not only on the child's behaviour but also on what precipitates and what follows it.

Time Sampling   Time sampling provides a way of measuring the frequency of a behaviour over a period of time (Wortham, 1990). Time sampling is a quantitative method of observation in that you count how often a behaviour occurs at uniform time intervals (Genishi, 1982). You may, for instance, want to know just how often the adults in the classroom attend to Yanik because you suspect he is often overlooked and neglected. Since you don't have time to observe Yanik all day long, you might determine that every half-hour you will spend five minutes watching Yanik, noting every time a teacher attends to or interacts with him. Over a period of a week, you should have a representative sampling of the attention Yanik receives from adults. You might also decide, for purposes of comparison, to observe Brittany at the same time because Brittany appears to get frequent adult attention.

Event Sampling   When you want to observe a less frequent behaviour, **event sampling** can be used (Genishi, 1982; Wortham, 1990). In this case, you wait until a given behaviour occurs and then write a descriptive record of the event. Event sampling can be useful if you have noted that Kareem has periodic crying spells, and you have trouble pinpointing the cause. Thus, each time Kareem engages in this behaviour, one of the teachers stands back and records carefully what is happening. The ABC analysis can be very useful in recording such an event because you are trying to get a sense of its causes and consequences (Wortham, 1990).

Characteristics of Good Observations

One of the requirements of good observation is that it be *objective*. Your role as observer is to be as impartial as possible, to stand back and record what you see rather than what you think the child is feeling or experiencing. Compare the two records in Exhibit 8.3. What distinguishes the two? The first observation tells you how the observer is interpreting the incident; the second describes what is happening. Can the first observer really know that Letitia does not like Erica? Can she

---

EXHIBIT 8.3: OBSERVATIONS

Observation 1

Letitia comes into the classroom and immediately decides to pick on Erica, whom she doesn't like. She approaches Erica and, in her usual, aggressive way, grabs the doll with which Erica is playing. Letitia doesn't really want the doll; she just wants what Erica has. When the teacher sees what has happened, she gets upset with Letitia and makes her give the doll back to Erica. Because of this, Letitia gets really angry and has one of her nasty tantrums, which upsets everyone in the class.

Observation 2

Letitia marches into the classroom. She looks around for a few seconds then ambles to the dramatic play area, where Erica is putting a doll into the cradle. Letitia stops two feet in front of the cradle, standing with her legs apart and hands on hips. She watches Erica put a blanket on the doll then steps right up to it, grabs the doll by an arm, and pulls it roughly out of the cradle. She runs with the doll into the block area and turns around to look back at Erica. As Letitia is running off, Erica yells, "No! I was playing with the doll." Erica looks at Mrs. Wendell, whose eyes move toward the dramatic play area. Erica's shoulders drop and she says in a softer whimper, "Letitia took the doll I was playing with," then starts to cry. As Mrs. Wendell walks toward Letitia, Letitia drops the doll and darts to the art area. Mrs. Wendell catches up with Letitia, and urges her back to the block area by pointing and stating matter-of-factly, "Go back to the block centre." She picks up the doll. "Letitia, we need to give this doll back to Erica. She was playing with it." Letitia, her lips pressed together over clenched jaws, pulls away from Mrs. Wendell and throws herself on the floor, kicking her feet and screaming.

---

be certain that the teacher is angry and that Letitia made a conscious decision to pick on Erica?

Another characteristic of good observation is that it is *adequately descriptive*. Cohen and Stern (1978) provide some helpful suggestions to beginning observers in the use of descriptive vocabulary. The verb "run," for instance, has many synonyms that can evoke a clearer image of what is being described. Examples include "stampede," "whirl," "dart," "gallop," "speed," "shoot across," "bolt," "fly," "hippety-hop," or "dash." Adding descriptive adverbs, adjectives, and phrases will also enliven an anecdote. Although synonyms can add authenticity and life to your observational anecdote, be sure to use the dictionary to ensure that the word means what you intend. What descriptive words in the second example of Exhibit 8.3 make the incident come alive?

Good observations also describe **non-verbal cues,** some of the nuances of body language as well as voice inflection which can give deeper meaning to an anecdote. Children, like adults, share subtle movements of face and body and shadings of voice that describe common feelings and reactions. Izard (1982), for instance, used common facial nuances in infants and children to measure emotion. Body language is not easy to read, requiring experience and practice to interpret accurately. In Exhibit 8.3 do you see some descriptions of such non-verbal signs?

Interpreting Observations

As we have indicated, observational information must be gathered objectively, without inserting personal bias. But there comes a point, once you have gathered a collection of anecdotes, when you can look for patterns (Cohen & Stern, 1978). Interpretations, however, should always be kept clearly separate from observations (Cartwright & Cartwright, 1974). In reviewing observations that span a period of time, you should be able to find clues to children's unique ways of behaving and responding. When a set of observations shows repeatedly that a child reacts aggressively to conflict or becomes pleasurably involved in messy media or talks to adults far more than to other children, you can see a characteristic pattern for that child.

Interpretation should be undertaken cautiously and consensus reached through team effort. Human behaviour is complex, not easily pigeon-holed, and there is the danger of overzealous interpretation when a pattern is more in the mind of the observer than representative of the child.

Some Observational Techniques

Finding time to observe can be challenging for the busy teacher. Cartwright and Cartwright (1974) recommended developing a pattern and time frame for carrying out observations. Hymes (1981) further suggested setting a goal, a fixed number of anecdotes to record each day. It is helpful to carry a pencil and pad in your pocket while working with children so you can jot down some quick notes, and to set aside a few minutes at the end of the day to write up the records. Keeping such records can also pinpoint children who are being overlooked when, over a period of time, you find very few or no records on some youngsters (Hymes, 1981). Beaty (1990) offered a comprehensive approach in her text *Observing the Development of the Young Child.*

Early childhood student-teachers and, in some programs, teachers, may be asked specifically to record observations for a period of time. If you are assigned a role as an outside observer rather than as a teacher, try to be as unobtrusive as possible so that children's behaviour is minimally affected by your presence. If children come to you to ask what you are doing, as invariably they will, give a simple answer that does not invite further conversation (e.g., "I am writing").

Assessment

Instruments

Checklists for Children

A checklist itemizes behaviours, skills, concepts, or attributes and contains a space for noting their presence or absence at a point in time or over a period of time.

Rating Scales for Children

Rating scales provide more qualitative information than checklists because they indicate to what extent the child engages in or has mastered a behaviour. For example, as a student, you are judged on a rating scale that usually takes the form of letter grades ranging from A (excellent) to F (unsatisfactory).

The dimensions of ratings applied to children will depend on what you want to measure. You may, for instance, want to determine the frequency of each child's participation in various types of activities. In that case, you might graph the children on a continuum that goes from "daily" to "never" (Cartwright & Cartwright, 1974; Wortham, 1990). Rating scales can also be used to show where a child is in the process of mastering certain tasks by using such words as "emerging," "developing," and "developed."

Standardized Tests

Whereas observations and teacher-devised instruments are informal methods of gathering information about children, standardized tests are considered formal assessments. Such instruments are developed by professionals and are distributed commercially. Standardized tests are developed, tested, and refined so that they have **validity** and **reliability.** "Validity" means that tests measure what they purport to measure. "Reliability" means that tests are stable and consistent; you know that when a child's score changes, it is because the child has changed, not the test (NAEYC, 1988). When standardized tests are administered, specific standards for testing conditions are required to ensure uniformity. Over the past few years, the use of standardized tests to evaluate caregiving environments and young children's development has increased. While a comprehensive overview of standardized tests may be offered in advanced courses you will take, we will just briefly examine some general test categories and consider several sample instruments.

Environmental Checklists and Rating Scales Several standardized rating scales and checklists have been developed and published that help in the evaluation of early childhood programs. The **Early Childhood Environment**

Rating Scale, developed by Harms and Clifford in 1980, is perhaps the best known. The Family Day Care Home Rating Scale (Harms, Clifford, & Padan-Belkin, 1983) and the Infant/Toddler Environment Rating Scale (Harms, Cryer, & Clifford, 1990) are useful for evaluating family child care and infant programs respectively.

These rating scales are helpful both when you are evaluating a program and when you are comparing several programs. The results can help you pinpoint areas of the program that need improvement. The results also are useful if you are doing research related to early childhood education. Goelman and Pence (1990), for example, used the Early Childhood Environment

Rating Scale and the Family Day Care Home Rating Scale in the Victoria and Vancouver studies.

Goelman and Pence also used Caldwell and Bradley's (1979) **Home Observation for Measurement of the Environment (HOME)** in the Vancouver study. HOME is used to assess the quality of stimulation in the home environment, and this makes it useful for home-based child care. A number of studies (e.g., Bradley & Caldwell, 1984; Gottfried, 1984) have demonstrated that HOME scores are highly correlated with child development. A parent or caregiver who scores highly on HOME:

1. is verbally and emotionally responsive;
2. does not restrict the child's activity and does not punish the child;
3. provides age-appropriate play materials;
4. arranges the environment so it is safe and organized;

5. is involved with the child and usually is within sight; and

6. provides variety in the available stimulation. In addition to reading to the child several times a week, the parent or caregiver takes the child on outings and arranges for the child to eat meals with the family at least once a day.

Of course, these behaviours also can be found in good teachers in centre-based programs.

Screening Tests   **Screening tests** provide a quick method of identifying children who may be at risk for a specified condition, for instance, developmental delay. Screening is not an end in itself but *is meant to be followed by more thorough diagnostic testing* if screening shows a possible problem. Because most screening tests are quick and easy to administer, they can be used by a wide variety of people who may have no specialized training.

A wide variety of tests are available. One widely used test is the **Denver Developmental Screening Test (DDST)** (Frankenburg, Dodds, Fandal, Kajuk, & Cohr, 1975), which is used with infants and children up to age 6. This test, often used by medical as well as early childhood professionals, examines the child's functioning in self-help, social, language, fine motor, and gross motor areas. The child's test scores are compared with **norm-referenced** scores. By testing a large number of children at each age, the test developers were able to determine what the average child of each age could do—or what the norm was for each age. For each item on the test, you can determine if the child is functioning around the norm or average level, or above or below average. If a child appears to be well below or above average, then more testing might be recommended.

Developmental Tests   Frequently a screening test will indicate the necessity for more complete assessment and is then followed by a more thorough and time-intensive **developmental test.** Such tests usually measure the child's functioning in most or all areas of development. Developmental assessments are usually **criterion-referenced** rather than norm-referenced. Thus, children are measured against the test developer's educated understanding of what children, at various ages, can be expected to achieve.

One widely used developmental test is the **Brigance Diagnostic Inventory of Early Development** (Brigance, 1978). With some training, early childhood teachers can use this test. It contains subtests for fine motor, gross motor, language, cognitive, and self-help areas for children from birth to age 7.

Intelligence or IQ Tests   One of the oldest types of standardized assessments is the **intelligence test.** Such tests have stirred considerable controversy, much of it loaded with emotion, because they raise the question of whether intelligence is a fixed biological trait or whether it is malleable and can be raised through an enriched environment (Jensen, 1985a; Woodrich, 1984). Another volatile controversy about such tests has been the concern over culture bias (Goodwin

& Goodwin, 1982), that is, tests are slanted to white, middle-class norms and experiences.

The **Wechsler Preschool and Primary Scale of Intelligence—Revised (WPPSI—R)** (1989) is another commonly used test for 3- to 7-year-old children. The **Wechsler Intelligence Scale for Children—III (WISC—III)** (1991) is also available for use with children from 6 to 16 years of age. Both Wechsler tests have been revised recently, and the norms are current.

Readiness Tests The specific purpose of **readiness tests**—to determine whether a child is prepared to enter a program such as kindergarten or first grade—differentiates them from other types of assessments. Such tests should not be used to predict school success because they merely measure a child's level of achievement of specified academic tasks at the time of testing (Meisels, 1986). A recent study, in fact, found that the **predictive validity** of one widely used readiness test, when compared with first-grade teacher judgment and report cards, was very modest, raising questions about the usefulness of the test and about the potential harm to the many children misidentified as not ready for school (Graue & Shepard, 1989). Increasingly, early childhood educators have questioned why school is not ready for children!

Success on readiness tests, as you might suspect, depends on the child's having been exposed to the concepts, not on innate ability. Unfortunately, readiness tests do not distinguish between the child who has had limited exposure to the concepts and the child who has actual learning difficulties. The use of these tests has driven many prekindergarten programs to incorporate activities designed to prepare children for readiness testing, often at the expense of other appropriate activities, particularly exploratory, hands-on experiences (Schickedanz, Hansen, & Forsyth, 1990). Moreover, virtually all of the available readiness tests have technical problems in the areas of reliability and predictive validity (Salvia & Ysseldyke, 1991). Unless the appropriate research is conducted to determine the ability of these tests to predict school achievement, they should not be used to make major educational decisions.

Learning-Style Inventories These are designed to assess how a person best learns and, therefore, how she or he approaches tasks, problems and people. Employers use these to plan teams and match employees to positions that best suit them.

Aptitude Tests Employers and academic institutions often use these to assess your potential for a particular position or program.

Concerns about Using Assessment Instruments

All of these informal and formal evaluation instruments can give us useful insights into the environments we provide and the children in our care. Although using a variety of methods to better understand children has always been an important part of early childhood education, there is a growing concern about potential misuses, particularly of standardized evaluations.

The 1980s brought an increased emphasis on testing, particularly as a way of proving that educational goals are being met (Wortham, 1990). The back-to-basics movement has become a powerful lobby group, and it is asking for more frequent standardized testing, especially for school-aged children. In the 1990s, the provincial and territorial ministers of education have been meeting on a regular basis to develop a national testing program. Pilot testing of selected grades across the country began in the 1993–94 school year.

One major concern involves the misuse of readiness tests. With increasing frequency, such tests are being used to decide children's placement. For instance, a test is used to decide which children will be allowed to move on to first grade, which ones will be placed in a transitional class, and which ones will be retained in kindergarten (Wortham, 1990). Thus, children are often labelled as failures when, in fact, they are expected to conform to inappropriate expectations (NAEYC, 1988). How devastating such practices are on children's self-concepts! Read the eloquent discussion of these concerns in NAEYC's "Position Statement on Standardized Testing of Young Children 3 through 8 Years of Age," which was published in *Young Children* in 1988.

Tests are being used by prestigious (and expensive) private schools, not just in large cities like New York but also in smaller cities in Canada, to determine which children will be admitted. A corollary to this testing trend is that many early childhood programs have adopted curriculums whose main aim is to prepare children for readiness tests (Bredekamp & Shepard, 1989). Thus, preschool and kindergarten programs promote developmentally inappropriate methods to meet such goals, intensifying the problem of "failures" and children who are "unready" (NAEYC, 1988). In fact, the NAEYC became so concerned about this that it had Constance Kamii, an eminent early childhood educator, edit a book on the topic. *Achievement Testing in the Early Grades: The Games Grown-ups Play* (Kamii, 1990) is a book you will want to consult if testing becomes a problem in your community.

It has long been acknowledged that standardized tests have a variety of limitations. For instance, a test cannot ask every possible question to evaluate what a child knows on a topic. Another criticism of standardized tests is that they are culture-biased. However, test designers have found it impossible to devise tests that are completely culture-free (Wortham, 1990). In addition, it is very difficult to establish reliable and valid instruments for young children, given the rapid changes that occur in development as well as the normal individual variations among children (NAEYC, 1988). This also calls into question the use of norm groups against which individuals are rated.

In addition to the potential problems with tests, there are difficulties in evaluating young children that can affect the accuracy of test results. These might include the child's attention and interest, the familiarity (or unfamiliarity) with the surroundings, the trust the child has in the adult tester (or whether the child has even seen this person before), the time of day, the fact that the child slept poorly the night before, or the fact that the mother forgot to kiss the child goodbye. In too many instances, tests are given to young children in large groups, a practice that further decreases reliability (NAEYC, 1988).

In a number of Canadian settings, there also is concern that tests are *not* always administered and interpreted by individuals with the qualifications to do so. Even some major school boards (but by no means all) in some Canadian jurisdictions rely upon unqualified individuals to complete the testing process, much to the chagrin of Canadian psychologists. An unqualified tester is likely to obtain misleading, unreliable results which might still be used in educational decisions regarding a young child. Parents are frequently upset if testing is recommended and tend to be overwhelmed by the testing process. They often do not know—or feel they know—what cautions and questions are appropriate and are reluctant to seek a second opinion, which can be invaluable.

If so many problems are inherent in standardized tests, what is the answer to the dilemma of their increasing use with young children? NAEYC (1988) recommends that the relevance of tests be carefully evaluated by administrators: Will results from the test contribute to improving the program for the children? Will the children benefit from the test? If the benefits are meager in relation to the cost (expense and time), perhaps the test should not be used. Furthermore, it is recommended that:

- tests be carefully reviewed for reliability and validity;
- tests match the program's philosophy and goals;
- only knowledgeable and qualified persons administer and interpret results;
- testers be sensitive to individual and cultural diversity;
- tests be used only for the purpose for which they were intended; and
- no major decision related to enrollment, retention, or placement in a remedial program be made based on only one test, but that multiple sources of information be used for this purpose.

It is important to keep in mind that any information gathered about children and their families—whether from test results, observations, or something a parent shared—needs to be treated with complete **confidentiality** and respect.

Evaluation

Evaluation is closely tied to goals, objectives, observation, and assessment as a beginning, an ending, and an ongoing process. To set appropriate goals and objectives, we need to know something about the group. **Preassessment** can help us

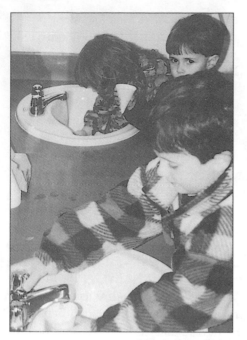

learn about the children in the group. Later, to find out whether the children (or group) have met our goals and objectives, we can conduct a **summative evaluation** at the ends of units, for example. In addition, ongoing **formative evaluation** is characteristic in good early childhood programs as it allows us to determine if our planned activities, methods, and topics are accomplishing what we want them to. Evaluation can be carried out in many ways, by different disciplines of qualified persons, depending on whether they are informal or formal types of assessment.

Evaluation is a two-directional interaction. However, you will find that it is often only used one way. For instance, in your course, your instructor will hand you a course evaluation so you can comment on the strengths and needs of the course's goals and objectives, course content, and teaching methods, as well as how you, as a student, contributed to the class's success. But not very often does the instructor get to evaluate the class. This would allow for a comparison between what both parties felt, observed, and experienced and therefore would be more accurate in identifying the needs that changed and why. Together the two-way evaluation gives a more wholistic view by combining and comparing vantage points. Similarly, when you are evaluated on your job, you

should complete an evaluation on yourself which can be compared to the one that peers, administrators, and parents complete on the work enviroment. Once the evaluations are compared, they should be discussed with you, and changes, comments, goals, recommendations, timelines, and responsibilities should be agreed upon, recorded, and signed. This process is repeated for each team member. Families are part of this process since their input on teacher, school, and program is an essential team component.

Selecting and Using Assessment and Evaluation Methods

We have looked at formal and informal methods of gathering information. Selecting an appropriate method will depend on how the results are to be used. The key is to use a combination of methods that involve the entire team in the process from beginning to end. But how will we use this information? Once information is gathered, we must make sense of it and then apply it. We gain knowledge that we must share (1) about children, (2) for program planning purposes, and (3) for parent feedback. In Partnerships we discuss sharing evaluations with parents.

Information about Children

Effective teaching depends on knowing as much as possible about the children in the class. A variety of data-gathering methods can be used as follows:

- Ongoing observation and documentation, including a portfolio of their work, can provide valuable insight into all children, their functioning as part of the class, and their growth in all developmental areas.

- A screening test coupled with parent interviews might help with those children who, on the basis of your observations, seem to have problems.

- A developmental assessment can be given to children whose performance on the screening test indicated a need for further evaluation. Periodic reassessment may be appropriate.

- You may decide that a referral to an outside professional (e.g., psychologist, speech pathologist, doctor) is needed.

- Feedback from each team member can be solicited.

Utilizing a combination of evaluation and assessment methods is the most comprehensive approach to planning.

Information for Program Planning

One of the main purposes of assessment is to help direct program development. Once you have an idea of strengths and areas that need attention, both for individual children and for the group as a whole, you can plan a prescriptive curriculum (Hendrick, 1986; Wright, 1983). Some useful data-gathering methods include the following:

- Information from observations and documentation can provide excellent programming direction.

- Checklists and rating scales allow you to evaluate the functioning of the group of children on a variety of factors that the team identified as being important.

Evaluation as a team—of the team itself, the children, the team members, and the program provides a forum for improvement.

Information for Parent Feedback

All forms of evaluation provide information to share with parents from the beginning to the end of the process. It is important to examine the child's strengths, and it is vital that all information be as accurate, realistic, and unbiased as possible. Data that is carefully collected over a period of time and thoughtfully evaluated provides the basis for good parent-feedback conferences. As well, parents shed tremendous light on their children's behaviour.

PARTNERSHIPS
Sharing Evaluations with Parents

The results of tests, observations, and other measures provide valuable information that can be shared with parents. As you read this information, you might also briefly review the discussion of parent conferences in Chapter 3 for the methods described are important to sharing evaluation results. We expect that any evaluation that teachers administer to a child is used because the teachers expect it to offer relevant insights. Thus, if this information is important to teachers, it will also be important to parents, who certainly have a right to know how their child is performing (Wortham, 1990).

There are a number of points to keep in mind when sharing evaluation results with parents. In all instances, tests or other evaluation information should never be given in isolation, out of the context of the child's overall nature. As we will continue to stress throughout this book, children cannot be divided into separate developmental compartments. Thus, to tell parents that their 4-year-old daughter is performing below (or, for that matter, above) the norm in fine motor skills is only part of the picture. It is equally important to tell them that their child has excellent social skills, that she shows leadership qualities, that she has a delightful sense of humour, that she particularly seems to enjoy sensory activities, and so forth. Such information does not rely just on the results of a developmental assessment, which yielded the fine motor score, but is reinforced by observations, anecdotes, and the teacher's reflections about this child.

Another point to remember when sharing evaluation results with parents is that you should be able to explain the measures that were applied. Some standardized tests are rather complicated to use, score, and interpret. Be sure that you understand what the test results mean and that you can explain them. It does not help a parent who asks, "What do you mean she scored below the norm?" to be told, "Well, I'm not exactly sure what 'norm' means." If your school uses any kind of standardized test, read its manual carefully, understand how the test was constructed, know how results should be interpreted and used, and be familiar with the terminology.

At the same time, it is also important to keep in mind and convey to parents that tests have their limitations. Consider the preceding discussion about the shortcomings of and concerns about tests, and let parents know that the test results represent only part of the input used in evaluation. Also remind parents, as well as yourself, that young children are amazingly flexible and often will experience a quick change or growth spurt in their development that could suddenly modify the test findings. Do not present any evaluation results as the definitive answer about the child's abilities and functioning.

A similar point is that each child is individual and unique, and test results will show a wide variety of profiles that fall within a normal range. It is reassuring to parents to be reminded that many factors affect a child's performance, particularly when parents compare the child with siblings or other children (Wortham, 1990). Keep in mind, however, that when you share test scores or other evaluation results, you should present only the child's scores, not the child's score in relation to other children's.

Finally, when sharing evaluation results with parents, be prepared to defend the measures you used. A parent may well ask you, "Why did you give this test to my child?" Be able to answer such a question because it is certainly logical and valid. You need to feel that the test provides valuable information, and you should be able to specify how such information will be used. For instance, such measures should help plan relevant and appropriate learning experiences for the child (Wortham, 1990).

Key Terms

ABC analysis
anecdotal record
behavioural objective
Brigance Diagnostic Inventory of
    Early Development
confidentiality
content objective
criterion-referenced
Denver Developmental Screening
    Test (DDST)
developmental objective
developmental test
Early Childhood Environment
    Rating Scale
environmental checklists
event sampling
formative evaluation
goals
Home Observation for Measurement
    of the Environment (HOME)
intelligence tests
learning outcome

lesson plan
non-verbal cues
norm-referenced
objectives
personal objective
preassessment
predictive validity
project
readiness tests
reliability
running record
screening tests
standards
summative evaluation
theme
time sampling
unit
validity
Wechsler Intelligence Scale for
    Children—III (WISC—III)
Wechsler Preschool and Primary Scale of
    Intelligence—Revised (WPPSI—R)

Key Points

• Elements of the curriculum include both long- and short-term planning based on ongoing philosophy, knowledge of development, observation, assessment, and evaluation.

- Curriculum has three focal points—the children themselves, their families, and their community, and it evolves continuously from here.

- To ensure continuity, the school and team as a whole must buy into the philosophy, goals, and curriculum and agree to be accountable and make necessary adjustments.

- A project begins with an introduction that arises from the children's interests and experiences, and then new ideas are presented sequentially and completed with a summarizing component.

- A learning outcome (objective) is a more specific interpretation of a standard general goal, and it provides a practical and direct tool for planning.

- Although developmental and content objectives usually apply to planning for the total group, behavioural and personal objectives are generally used in planning for an individual.

- Observation must be unobtrusive and as natural as possible, objective, descriptive, and carefully interpreted.

- Formal and informal assessment and evaluation instruments give us useful insight into the environments we provide and the children in our care but are subject to misinterpretation and potential misuse.

- A combination of assessment and evaluation methods provides a more comprehensive portrait of the child (family, program, etc.).

Chapter 9

Development through the Curriculum

art 1 of this text provided a narrative of a day in a quality child care program. Part 2 introduced you to the partners you would encounter—teachers, children, and parents. Part 3 oriented you to the intricacies of the terms you would hear and the components of quality care you should watch for. Part 4 examines curriculum from the general to the specific. In Chapter 6, we looked at play and guidance because they occur wherever there are children. Teachers gently and positively guide as children play. When you enter a child care program, the very first thing you will likely see is children playing. Eventually you will observe the teacher guiding and the result of this interaction. Each interaction impacts upon the child's emotional development and well-being.

Accepting this, we looked a little more closely in Chapter 7 at the structure of play, including small- and large-group times, routines, equipment and materials, schedules, the physical environment, and appropriate practices for guiding and planning for children. Chapter 8 expanded on how to plan effectively, focusing on curriculum. We examined elements of the curriculum and curriculum content, and looked at accountability for our planning, which encompassed standards and learning outcomes, observation, assessment, and evaluation. We used the analogy of your attending school to clarify appropriate practices and curriculum. There is a general schedule, appropriate content is determined, and different types of activities are planned (i.e., individual or group), all in the context of experience- (play-) based learning with a teacher who uses positive guidance techniques. How does the teacher support your construction of new knowledge?

This chapter looks at supporting the development of five domains—creative, physical, cognitive, language, and social—in relationship to the curriculum. It is not focused on activities (e.g., art activities), developmental milestones (e.g., children walk at 12 months), or on theories (e.g., Piaget's theory of cognitive development). This chapter focuses on defining each domain (i.e., by asking, for example, What is creativity?), looking at environments and attitudes that foster this development, and providing guidelines for supporting its development across the curriculum. A good teacher—one armed with knowledge on child development, excellent guidance techniques, and strategies—will have little difficulty in supporting, creating, locating, assessing, planning, implementing, and evaluating activities that are appropriate, enriching, and rewarding for children.

Having read Judy Wainwright's article in Chapter 6's A Canadian Professional Speaks Out and about Reggio Emilia in the Orientation to this text and in Chapter 5, you will have gained some insight into the principles of the emergent curriculum. In it, the traditional word-for-word themed curriculum, planned in advance, is abandoned. Instead, a broad set of goals and guiding principles, based on knowledge of development, is coupled with observation and dialogue to help teachers and children plan and create projects that are meaningful. The image of the child as a competent partner suggests a relationship fostered through dynamic and ongoing communication. Hence, there is not necessarily a standard art centre or home centre or science centre. Projects, by their very nature, and teachers, through their interaction, foster all the domains. As you read, think about how the children's emerging interest in, say, birds could evolve into projects—not preplanned by you but planned in relation to what has happened, is happening, and could happen.

In this sense, curriculum does not guide development. Rather, development guides curriculum. Instead of children adjusting to a preplanned curriculum, the curriculum is adjusted to adapt to the changing interests, strengths, and needs of the children. Planning is definitely required, but rather than a preplanned lesson based on an arbitrary theme, it would entail a well-planned project based on real interests.

Creative Development

The preschool years have been described as a "golden age of creativity, a time when every child sparkles with artistry" (Gardner, 1982, p. 86). One of the most rewarding joys of working with young children is watching them approach experiences with that spark of freshness and exuberance that opens the door to cre-

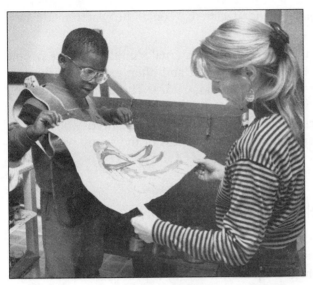

ativity. Each of us possesses some measure of creativity—some more, some less. This is especially true of young children. Unfortunately, there is the danger of their creativity being stifled through increasing pressure to conform to adult expectations (Mayesky, 1990).

What Is Creativity?

Creativity has been defined in a number of ways. Most definitions include such concepts as originality, imagination, divergent thinking (seeing things from different viewpoints), and the ability to create something new or to combine things in novel but meaningful ways. Creativity is more likely to occur when the person possesses traits such as curiosity, flexibility, and interest in investigation and exploration (traits manifested by most children).

J.P. Guilford (1962), dissatisfied with the limited definition of intelligence imposed by tests that measure it by a series of single, "correct" answers, developed a new way of looking at intelligence that includes some of these traits. In Guilford's structure of the intellect, divergent thinking is differentiated from convergent thinking, both of which are involved in the creative process.

- **Divergent thinking**, by one definition, is "the making in the mind of many from one," for instance, by elaborating on a topic as in brainstorming (Hampden-Turner, 1981, p. 104).

- **Convergent thinking** is defined as "the making of one from many" through narrowing down many ideas to a single, focused point (Hampden-Turner, 1981, p. 104).

- **Fluency** is the ability to generate many relevant ideas on a given topic in a limited time. Five-year-old Michelle wonderfully displayed fluency when she was confronted with a sheet of paper containing 20 circles. She drew as many different items from these circles as she could—face, balloon, ball, sun, orange, and flower. She then created an ashtray, glass, light bulb, and pencil eraser as they would be seen from the top. She had used all but one row of the circles when the teacher reminded her that she needed to finish up. Michelle, after a moment's thought, drew two parallel lines under the remaining row of circles, connected them with crosshatches, then put boxes on top of the circles, creating a quick but recognizable train.

- **Flexibility** is the ability to adapt readily to change in a positive, productive manner. Three-year-old Ramon showed flexibility when another child accidentally knocked water on the lines that he had carefully painted in different hues of water colours. After a fleeting look of dismay crossed his face,

Ramon surveyed his picture and declared, "Look, the water made new colours!"

- **Sensitivity** is a receptivity to external and internal stimuli. Creative people have a heightened awareness of their world and often experience through their senses what others miss (Lowenfeld, 1962). The creative child will more likely be the one who points out that a cloud looks like a speeding motorboat, appreciatively sniffs the aroma of freshly sawed wood at the woodworking activity, or delights in the softness of the soapy water when blowing bubbles.

Aesthetic Appreciation

Aesthetics, an enjoyment and appreciation of beauty, is related to art in all its forms. Evans (1984) considers the inclusion of aesthetics in education as contributing to a "quality of life that is uniquely human" by exposing children to "sublime experiences" (p. 74), that sense of wonder and enjoyment when we are touched by beauty. Aesthetics includes sensitivity and appreciation for both natural beauty and synthetic creations (Feeney & Moravcik, 1987). A teacher who is sensitive to beauty can help children find it in their surroundings.

The early childhood setting should provide an environment in which these traits are encouraged and valued. Such an environment, however, goes far beyond providing materials for artistic and other expression. The creative environment is made up not just of the physical arrangement, but is permeated by an attitude of openness, acceptance, and encouragement. We will examine both of these aspects—the physical parameters of such an environment and the attitudes that promote creativity.

Environments That Encourage Creativity

The physical setting can support creativity through provision of and access to a wide range of **open-ended materials,** that is, materials that lend themselves to various uses. Children have to make choices about how to use open-ended materials and employ their imagination in doing so because these materials do not dictate a single outcome. Furthermore, each time they use the materials, they can do so in a unique way. They love to practise familiar songs over and over, to read and act out favourite stories, to participate in both open-ended and themed dramatic play centre, and to create endlessly with art materials. In art, for example, *children do not need a different art activity each day*. When a different set of limited materials is provided every day, children never get the chance to explore in depth or experiment with common, basic materials (Clemens, 1991).The easel should be out every single day, and the creative shelf should be stocked with ample materials from which the children can create limitless things.

A well-stocked early childhood program will be full of open-ended materials. Examples include a wide variety of art materials, manipulatives, blocks, sensory materials, puppets, dramatic play props, musical instruments, and versatile outdoor equipment. (This is not to say that single-purpose materials (e.g., puzzles) are unimportant, but they meet different developmental needs and are not particularly suited to creative development.) One study demonstrated that children who were offered a large selection of art materials from which to choose, rather than provided with materials limited to a single project, produced significantly more creative artwork, as judged by a panel of artists (Amabile & Gitomer, 1984).

The physical arrangement of the room can also facilitate creativity. Clearly organized classroom areas let children know where they can engage in various creative activities, for instance, where they can build or where they might experiment with messy media. Classroom areas should be set up so that traffic flow does not interfere or disrupt ongoing activity.

At the same time, children should be able to move freely from one activity to another. When materials are organized and visible on accessible shelves, the children know what is available for their independent use. These materials should be attractively displayed and uncluttered so that children can see possible new combinations they might try. You may also want to label the materials available. Such orderly display also conveys a respect for the materials. Similarly, a display area for children's work tells the children that their creative endeavours are valued and respected. Even though many children will not be interested in the finished product, it is also important to have an area where you can store the children's work.

Creativity can and should occur in every aspect of the early childhood program. Although art and music foster creativity, they also promote cognition, socialization, language, emotional release, sensory stimulation, and muscle development. Similarly, language, outdoor motor, and manipulative activities can be very creative. As you read on, keep in mind that good early childhood activities serve many purposes, meet many needs, and, above all, contribute to the development of the whole child. Creativity is not limited to art, music, or drama but is the essence of process in everything the child (and teacher) does. "Creativity in Art: An Expression of the Inner Self" is explained in A Canadian Professional Speaks Out.

A CANADIAN PROFESSIONAL SPEAKS OUT
Guidelines for Supporting Creative Development

Creativity in Art: An Expression of the Inner Self

Young children come to our day care centres as avid participants in the discovery of their world. They are curious, excited, and creative when they arrive at our door. It is our responsibility and challenge, as child care professionals, to ensure they maintain these positive qualities.

Our child care facilities should provide programs that meet the social, physical, emotional, and intellectual needs of the young child. Such a program enables each child to develop to his or her fullest potential, feeling confident and willing to take risks. Having opportunities to participate in creative art activities enhances all areas of development in a relaxed, positive atmosphere. Through creative activities, children grow socially as they share materials and ideas. Fine and gross motor skills are developed as they manipulate a variety of art media. Intellectually, children learn about spatial awareness, colours, textures, and problem solving. The children learn to express their emotions in a positive manner and gain confidence in their capabilities.

As adults we must learn to appreciate the uniqueness of each child's artistic presentations. We should share in their joy as they utilize paints, crayons, clay, and other art media to produce original works of art. Frequently, as adults, we are tempted to try to channel the child's art by providing predesigned crafts or gifts, colouring sheets, glue and paste activities, or stencils for them to complete. These types of activities stifle imaginative thought and rob the children of the freedom to express their own ideas. According to Piaget's stages of intellectual development, children do not perceive the world as adults do. Neither are they developmentally capable of representing their world in an artistic form determined by adult standards. Robert Schirrmacher believes that as the creative process blossoms within each child, "the emphasis is on the making and doing rather than on the finished product." The making and doing of creative activities comes naturally from within the child, and adults do not need to impose their ideas on them.

The child care professional plays an important role in the development of the children's creativity. One of our greatest creative resources is the environment. By providing daily access to an art centre with a variety of art media, children are given the freedom to explore the materials and create as they desire to do so. The materials in the art centre should be changed frequently to maintain interest and stimulate creative thought.

In addition to the art centre, the adult needs to plan a variety of sensory experiences for the children. As they participate in the experiences, they will acquire information that will then be expressed through their artistic representations. An effective creative art program encourages children to portray their perceptions of the world in a variety of ways. Only through an open-ended approach will we create an atmosphere where children will become creative, confident people who are willing to risk sharing their ideas and feelings.

Elizabeth Wood, Early Childhood Studies
Nova Scotia Community College, Cumberland Campus

Attitudes That Encourage Creativity

Creativity, as you have seen, is related to flexibility, divergent thinking, and openness to new ideas. Young children's minds strive to make sense of their world by organizing information and input. Once they become familiar with and master new concepts, they are free to use these in various ways. If we use what we learn in only one way, we are limited and rigid in our approach. Flexible or creative thinking is a mindset that can be encouraged in an open classroom atmosphere. A creative environment promotes new perceptions of and responses to the world.

Creativity has to be nurtured; it does not develop on its own. The teacher plays an important role in fostering creativity by providing a variety of materials and encouraging imaginative use of them. When children are allowed creative expression, each child will produce a different outcome. The teacher's acceptance of each child's work and unique responses gives children the opportunity to learn that people feel and think differently, and to value this difference.

Creativity does not always result in a product, although we traditionally tend to think of the song, the picture, the story, or the dance as the creative product. It is the *process,* not the product, that is important for young children—and the younger they are, the more this applies. All too frequently, you see adults imposing their desire for a finished product on young children. Infants and toddlers are not inclined to take paintings home. And preschoolers may have painted a beautiful picture in red, yellow, and blue that they then cover with black paint. By the time they are school-aged, however, many children will want a completed product to take home. But this product should still be a result of the child's chosen process as opposed to a teacher-imposed craft.

If you watch young children involved in creative activities, you will better understand why the process is so valuable. In the process, the child can:

- experiment ("What will happen if I put this block across the top of these two?");
- enjoy the sensory experience ("Squishing the play dough between my fingers feels nice!");
- communicate ("I'm a bird!");
- relive experiences ("I'll tell the 'baby' she has to go to bed because that's what big people always tell me."); and
- work out fears ("I'll be the doctor, and my dolly will be the baby who gets the shot!").

As children mature, as their motor and perceptual skills improve, and as they plan ahead more, their creative efforts may well result in purposeful products. But young preschoolers are much more involved in the process of creative experiences. For children up to 4 years, any end product is usually secondary to the enjoyment of doing the activity.

By encouraging children to solve problems, the teacher also fosters creativity. By helping children think through different alternatives and find various solutions, the teacher expands their creative capacity. The teacher, however, is a facilitator rather than the one who comes up with answers or solutions. Divergent thinking involves the opportunity to go off in different directions and to explore various strategies. The teacher's acceptance of children's suggestions and willingness to try these tells them that they are capable of worthwhile ideas.

Another way of accepting and encouraging children's creative work is through uncritical acknowledgment. Well-intentioned praise ("I like your picture") can stifle creativity because it imposes a value judgment, or becomes meaningless when it is repeated to every child. Rather than evaluate, compare, or try to read meaning into non-representational art, a teacher can remark on the process ("You glued the squares on first, then you glued circles over them"), recognize the work that has gone into the picture ("You've worked 20 minutes on this sculpture!"); or comment on its design qualities ("You're using lots of big circles!") (Schirrmacher, 1986).

In setting up an appropriate climate for creativity, it is important to provide enough time for children to get involved in and complete their projects. When the time set aside for child-selected activity is short, children tend not to get very involved (Christie, Johnsen, & Peckover, 1988), thus missing opportunities to engage in creative activity. Children may continue to pursue a creative project over a period of time.

Factors That Decrease Creativity

A discussion about creative development should include a few words about the all-too-present factors in our society that often blunt children's creative impulses. As we have discussed, creativity depends on flexible, open, divergent thinking, which is encouraged in children through a flexible and open environment.

Conversely, creativity can be diminished by socializing factors that narrow, stereotype, or limit ideas. An atmosphere that promotes racial, cultural, or sex stereotypes, for instance, imposes a narrow view of people that restricts potential. An environment in which the adult is always right and children are expected to do what they are told without asking questions is not conducive to creativity. When children are always shown how to do tasks, they will not have the opportunity to engage in problem solving and creative thinking. When adults laugh at, rather than appreciate, a child's unique or unusual response, that child is discouraged from expressing other creative ideas.

Television and Creativity

One pervasive factor in children's lives that can affect creativity is television and, increasingly, videotapes. On average, children spend more time watching television than they do engaging in any other activity except sleep (Huston, Watkins, & Kunkel, 1989). What children see—program content—as well as how much time they spend in front of the TV set can decrease creative thinking.

Programs on this medium tend to convey a very stereotyped view of people, one in which recognition and respect are accorded primarily to those who are white, male, young, and beautiful (Liebert & Sprafkin, 1988). Television also generally promotes the view that an effective way of solving problems is through violence, another narrow attitude that often does not model a variety of constructive problem-solving strategies.

Even more disturbing are the results from a number of studies showing that frequent and consistent viewing of violent television programming is strongly related to aggressive behaviour (e.g., Huesmann, Lagerspetz, & Eron, 1984; Joy, Kimball, & Zabrack, 1986; Singer, Singer, & Rapaczynski, 1984).

The amount of viewing time can also affect creativity. Creative learning is an active process, dependent on ample time spent exploring, investigating, manipulating, and reflecting. Television viewing is basically a passive occupation; thus, the more a child sits in front of the TV, the less time there is for active, self-directed play. On the other hand, some researchers feel that television is active in that children process what they see in relation to their own background and experience (Anderson & Lorch, 1983).

Dr. MacBeth Williams and her colleagues at the University of British Columbia confirmed findings of increased aggression, decreased creativity, interference of reading skills, and negative reinforcement of stereotypes. Certainly watching television, in and of itself, does not cause these problems. If children can learn negative stereotypes, they can also emulate positive role models.

There are worthwhile children's programs on television that model and teach children positive, **prosocial behaviours** and promote appreciation of nature, aesthetics, and culture. Four rules can help ensure that young children benefit from the positive values of television:

1. Parents at home and teachers at school must carefully monitor the content so children watch only age-appropriate programs.

2. Television viewing should be allowed only in small doses.

3. Adults should watch television with children so discussion can take place.

4. Videos may be a better choice if you cannot be with the children throughout the program. You can choose an age-appropriate, commercial-free video with which you are familiar.

Physical Development

One of the major aspects of the early years is physical growth and development. At no other time in life is there such a rapid rate of change in size, weight, and body proportion, as well as in increased control and refinement in the use of body parts (Allen & Marotz, 1989). Physical changes, which are readily observable,

profoundly affect and are affected by all areas of development.

What Is Physical Development?

As children start the preschool years, they have rudimentary movement ability and control, but by the time they enter middle childhood, their movements have become much more refined and competent, allowing for a wider repertoire of activities and choices. This is due to an integration of three components

- **Gross motor development** is involved in control of the large muscles of the legs, arms, back, and shoulders needed for movements such as running, jumping, and climbing. The preschool development of six important elements of body control—walking, running, jumping, hopping, throwing, and balancing—have been described by Keogh and Sugden (1985). Walking is the basic means of locomotion or self-movement from place to place; running, jumping, hopping, and throwing are fundamental play skills; and balancing provides one way of assessing postural control. All of these important skills become more accurate, controlled, and efficient as children develop coordination during the preschool years.

- **Fine motor development** is involved in use of the small muscles of the fingers and hands necessary for such tasks as writing, drawing, and buttoning. During the infant and toddler years, children develop basic grasping and manipulation skills, which are refined during the preschool years. The preschooler becomes quite adept in self-help (i.e., feeding, dressing, toileting), construction (i.e., building and manipulating materials), **holding grips** (i.e., for writing, grasping, and drawing) (Keogh & Sugden, 1985), and **bimanual control** tasks requiring use of both hands.

Toys, which require some kind of manipulation with fingers and hands, can be categorized as **manipulatives.** Manipulative materials enhance fine motor development because they require controlled use of hand and finger muscles. But they contribute much more. Manipulatives are sensory materials, involving visual and tactile discrimination and **eye–hand coordination**; they require skill in coordinating the eyes with what the hands do. Manipulatives can reinforce a variety of concepts such as colour, shape, number, and size, as well as encourage one-to-one correspondence, matching, patterning, sequencing, and grouping.

Some manipulative toys, such as puzzles, are **self-correcting**, fitting together in only one specific way. Such toys allow children to work independently and know when they have achieved success. These toys contribute to children's growing attention span and the satisfaction of staying at a task until it is completed (*Table Toys*, 1979).

- **Sensory-perceptual development** involves conveying information that comes through the senses and the meaning that it is given. Closely intertwined with motor development are sensory and perceptual functioning. Sensory input involves the collection of information through the senses of sight, hearing, taste, smell, and touch. The **kinesthetic sense** provides people with a sense of awareness, a feel, for their body in space so that they can make judgments about movement. Perceptual input involves attention to, recognition of, and interpretation of that information to give it personal meaning. Thus, perception is a cognitive process as it integrates sensory and kinesthetic information into knowledge and behaviour.

  Any activity involves a sensory component because we use sight, hearing, or touch almost all of the time. But some activities are specifically geared to enhance sensory awareness. Most young children seem to enjoy and become thoroughly immersed in activities such as sand and water play. These are completely open-ended, tactile, and soothing.

Environments That Encourage Physical Development

In addition to internal influences, external factors also influence physical development (Keogh and Sugden, 1985). Early childhood educators should arrange the environment to facilitate children's exploration, creativity, and discovery. Through movement, in interacting with the environment, children engage in problem solving (Curtis, 1987). In other words, the environment provides materials, equipment, and activities that motivate, challenge, and stimulate the child. The child exercises his or her muscles while engaging in thinking, socialization, language, and creative development at the same time.

In a quality setting, teachers ensure that infants and toddlers are given a responsive environment to explore, one that enhances their existing schemes of the world. Teachers who have physically challenged children in their class can ensure that these children also have a responsive environment.

Attitudes That Encourage Physical Fitness, Health, and Well Being

Physical Fitness

Physical fitness is concerned with overall health—nutrition, alertness and energy level, and integration of the range of skills covered by gross motor, fine motor, and

sensory-perceptual skills such as eye–hand coordination, dexterity, heightened senses, quickness, precision, and accuracy. Physical fitness is important to every aspect of daily living and stress reduction. Specifically, it contributes to the development and maintenance of an "adequate level of cardiovascular endurance, muscular strength, muscular endurance, flexibility, and body leanness" (Poest, Williams, Witt, & Atwood, 1990, p. 5), also imperative to health and daily functioning. The sizable and growing number of overweight North American preschool-aged children further attests to a need for physical fitness.

Exercise occurs in many early childhood activities. Vigorous, active play is important not only to muscle development but also to the establishment of lifelong health habits (Seefeldt, 1984). Yet a recent large-scale survey found that preschool children are not engaging in enough physical activity (Poest, Williams, Witt, & Atwood, 1989, 1990). Children whose parents engage in exercise are more likely to do so as well.

Javernick (1988) feels that teachers of young children often neglect gross motor development, paying it only lip service, and instead emphasize fine motor, cognitive, and social areas in the curriculum. A number of physical education proponents express the concern that free play alone does not adequately meet the motor development needs of young children (Seefeldt, 1984; Skinner, 1979). They advocate that regular physical fitness activities (not organized sports) be part of the early childhood curriculum. It is important to note, however, that no norms exist for what physical fitness in preschoolers should involve (Poest et al., 1990).

The term "physical fitness" often conjures up our own childhood experiences involving games and sports. Play, games, and sports have characteristics that are tied to developmental readiness and appropriateness (Coleman & Skeen, 1985). Play is free from time, space, and rule constraints, and reward is inherent in the play rather than dependent on winning. Play involves such activities as creeping, running, crawling, climbing, and throwing. Games are more structured than play. Although time limitations and rules can be altered to meet the needs of the players involved, games with more than a few simple rules are beyond the ability of most preschoolers. However, non-rule-based jumping and running games can be played. Children are famous for making up games, which encourages creativity and cognitive, language, and social development. Teacher-imposed competition can have detrimental effects on children, and teachers' interference in children's devised games, which sometimes involve competition, places value judgments on them and minimizes group skills. If the group is cooperating and the basic rule of no hurting is being respected, then the teacher must respect the group's decision to follow through with its devised game.

Young children need to develop physical capabilities through many play experiences in which they can explore their world (Coleman & Skeen, 1985). The challenge to early childhood educators is not just to develop appropriate gross motor and physical fitness activities but to allow time to play, to be active, to observe people in action, to discuss the value of activity, health, and fitness, and to plan as a group for it. Early childhood educators must model fitness and health practices as part of everyday living. Javernick (1988) suggested some guidelines for teachers of young children as shown in Exhibit 9.1.

The research implies that early childhood teachers need to be more concerned with providing physical fitness as part of the daily program. Vigorous daily activities that are fun and enjoyable contribute to establishing a foundation for lifelong health habits and attitudes.

Caring for the Body

The early childhood program should help lay the foundation for good health habits. In addition to establishing routines and activities that emphasize the importance of physical exercise, the preschool or child care centre also can help children of all ages learn about appropriate nutrition, health, and safety concepts.

EXHIBIT 9.1: GUIDELINES FOR SUPPORTING PHYSICAL DEVELOPMENT

- Activities should be presented in ways that will interest and intrigue children.
- Physical activities such as calisthenics, "adventurecises," walks, hikes, bike rides, swimming, or obstacle courses should be planned for each day.
- Music and movement activities should also be part of every day. Many excellent children's tapes and CDs are available to enhance exercise and movement activities.
- Children should be provided with opportunities to make choices from a diverse range of materials and should have input into suggesting activities, events, equipment, and projects.
- The teacher must be an active participant in physical activity. Children are much more attracted to activities in which a teacher is enthusiastically involved.
- Outside and inside activities must provide and encourage a mix of game time, active and passive time, individual and group time, teacher- and child-initiated activities, materials that promote doing, and play time within and away from the playground and the classroom.
- Materials need to be open-ended with varying attributes of size, shape, colour, and texture to encourage a variety of physical and creative uses.
- Many open-ended sensory activities like sand and water provide excellent forums for physical, social, language, and creative skills. These activities are very soothing and relaxing.

Nutrition   Because food is a basic human need and so often provides great pleasure, nutrition education experiences should be an integral part of the curriculum. Nutrition concepts can be explored with the children in an understandable, interesting manner, and they can be reinforced by such things as hands-on cooking activities. Nutrition and cooking, while promoting understanding of a basic physical need, equally involve cognitive, language, creative, and social areas of development.

Nutrition education, attitudes toward food, and food behaviours are all of interest to children. The following list of nutrition-related concepts may help in planning activities (Herr & Morse, 1982, p. 154).

1. There is a wide variety of food.

2. Plants and animals are sources of food.

3. Foods vary in colour, flavour, texture, smell, size, shape, and sound.

4. A food may be prepared and eaten in many different ways—raw, cooked, dried, frozen, or canned—and with utensils or hands.

5. Good foods are important to health, growth, and energy.

6. Nutrition is how our bodies use the foods we eat for health, growth, and energy.

7. Foods may be classified according to the following categories:

   • milk and dairy products

   • meat and fish

   • dried peas, beans

   • breads and cereals

   • fruits

   • vegetables

8. A good diet includes a wide variety of foods from each of the food categories.

9. Many factors influence eating, such as:

   • attractiveness of food

   • method of preparation

   • cleanliness, manners

10. We choose the foods we eat for many reasons, such as:

   • availability and cost

   • family and individual habits

   • taste

11. Food is available from many locations.

If you are in a full-day setting, where meals are a standard feature, you will probably discuss many of these topics informally while eating. Exploring children's prior knowledge, interests, and questions will provide an excellent starting point for determining what the group can investigate in more depth. Limitless options for projects will unfold from the children's growing of their own food, planning a banquet, or studying anatomy. Herr and Morse (1982) recommended that nutrition be an integral part of the early childhood program, covered on an ongoing basis. Local and provincial marketing boards (e.g., egg, beef, and milk producers' boards) often have excellent photographs, activities, or speakers available free of charge for teachers. Local markets, restaurants, agricultural associations, public health departments, and provincial bodies are also excellent resources.

Cooking Experiences

Among the most enjoyable activities for young children are those that involve food preparation. Such activities are multisensory; involve children in a process they have observed but in which they may not have participated; teach and reinforce a variety of concepts related to nutrition, mathematics, science, and language; and are very satisfying because they result in a tangible (and delicious) end product (Cosgrove, 1991).

Some cooking activities are more appropriate than others and should be carefully selected to meet specific criteria and objectives. The following are guidelines to keep in mind when planning food activities:

- The activity should be matched to the children. Older infants might help poke some bread dough, for example, but they would not be able to knead it, whereas older children could. Heat, sharp utensils, and a need for precise fine motor control place age constraints on activities, so for younger children think of activities that do not require them. Examples include tearing lettuce for a salad, plucking grapes from the stem for fruit salad, mixing yogurt and fruit in individual cups, or spreading tuna salad on crackers with a spoon. Older preschoolers and school-aged children have more refined muscle control and can follow more complex instructions. More involved recipes that might require use of knives, electrical appliances, and multiple ingredients can be planned.

- Safety is of utmost importance. Many cooking tools are potentially dangerous, and careful adult supervision is required. Some steps in cooking require that only one child at a time be involved with a teacher (e.g., flipping pancakes in an electric skillet or griddle). Other cooking activities may well require that the number of children be limited, for instance, to five or six at a time, so that the adult can supervise and observe all of the children adequately. The process can then be repeated with additional groups of children so that everyone who is interested has the opportunity to participate. However, limitations on the number of children who can be involved at one time have to be thought out before the activity is presented to the children.

- The recipe should involve enough steps so that all of the children in the group make a significant contribution. Some recipes can be prepared individually by each child in single-serving sizes. Other recipes will require group cooperation. Such an appealing activity as cooking should have enough ingredients and steps (i.e., five or six) so that each child in the group is an active participant. If children are making muffins, for instance, one child can break and stir the eggs while others add and stir in the butter, flour, milk, honey, nuts, raisins, flavourings, and leavening; then they can take turns stirring the dough.

- Children can be helped to understand the entire process. It is helpful to prepare a pictorial recipe chart (or use one that is commercially made) that shows ingredients and amounts, allowing children to experience measuring as well as mixing. Point out the changes in ingredients as they are mixed with others (e.g., the flour loses its dry "powderiness" as it joins the liquids). Discuss and point out the effect of heat, which changes the semi-liquid dough into firm muffins, for instance.

- The activity should focus on wholesome, nutritious foods. It is important to set a good example in the planned cooking activities to reinforce nutritional concepts. A wide selection of available cookbooks focus on healthy recipes for preschoolers.

- The importance of hygiene and cleanliness must be stressed. Require that children as well as adults wash their hands before participating in cooking experiences. Make sure that cooking surfaces and tools are clean. Multisensory learning is enhanced if you allow children to taste at various points during the cooking process; however, instead of letting children use their fingers for tasting, provide individual spoons or popsicle sticks.

Health and Hygiene   Young children get many messages about health needs and practices from what is expected of them, what they are told, and what adults model. School routines (discussed in Chapter 7) set many expectations and structure the schedule to encourage and facilitate increasing self-care in toileting, cleanliness, and eating. But health information should also be conveyed as part of the curriculum. Discussions and activities can heighten children's awareness of such topics as the relationship between health and growth, the body's need for both activity and rest, temperature regulation through appropriate clothing, hygiene practices as part of disease prevention, the importance of medical and dental care, and health professionals and facilities that care for children in the community. In addition, if a child in the class has a specific allergy or a chronic illness, you can help all of the children to understand this condition better by sensitively including the topic in the curriculum.

It was helpful in one preschool program, for instance, when the teacher discussed why Dorothea could not eat certain foods. The children became more sensitive to Dorothea's allergies and the restrictions it caused, and they saw that her special snacks were not a privilege but a necessity.

Safety   Young children begin to acquire safety information and precautions, although it is important to remember that adults must be responsible for ensuring children's safety by providing a safe environment and preventing accidents. Because toddlers and very young preschoolers may not process safety information accurately, it should be conveyed with a great deal of caution. Some 2-year-olds, or young 3-year-olds, may fail to understand the negative message in "Don't do …" or may get ideas from well-intentioned cautions (Essa & Rogers, 1992). Through curriculum topics, older preschoolers can gradually acquire information and learn some preventive precautions related to fire, electricity, tools, traffic, potential poisons, and strangers, as well as learn about community safety personnel and resources, and what to do in case of an accident.

Cognitive Development

Young children's thinking ability is quite amazing. Within just a few years of their birth, preschoolers have acquired an immense repertoire of information and cognitive skills. A child, who two or three or four years before was a helpless baby responding to the environment mainly through reflexes, is now a competent, thinking, communicating, reasoning, problem-solving, exploring person. In studying children's cognition, you should be concerned more with the *process* of knowing than with *what* children know. In particular, we are interested in how children acquire, organize, and apply knowledge (Copple, DeLisi, & Sigel, 1982).

What Is Cognition?

Most people think of **cognition** only as knowledge, and many think of knowledge simply as facts. Cognition goes far beyond this. It involves:

- **modes** (i.e., some people learn best by seeing, others by touch, others by hearing, and most of us in combinations)
- **strategies** (i.e., some people write things down, others repeat them over and over)

- **skills** (e.g., reading, writing)
- **acquisition** (i.e., resourcefulness)
- **processing** (which involves memory and the storing and retrieving of information)
- **comprehension** (i.e., some people know a lot of facts but do not know what they mean; comprehension is understanding meaning)
- **application** (i.e., some people have the knowledge, for example, that smoking is dangerous, but they do not use it; application is using the knowledge)

Virtually every activity involves cognition. Children actively learn, use problem-solving strategies, construct new knowledge, and use new knowledge in all activities, be they science and math or art, music, movement, manipulatives, storytelling, or dramatic play. Some specific cognitive skills include:

- **classification**—the ability to sort and group objects, ideas, and information into categories
- **seriation**—the ability to understand and relate to the order of things, ideas, and events
- **number concepts**—the understanding of quantity
- **temporal concepts**—the understanding and awareness of the principles of time
- **spatial concepts**—the understanding and awareness of the principles of space

These skills are not strictly mathematical concepts but ones that transcend all facets of daily interactions and decisions from passing in traffic to meal planning to deciding what to wear to planning your day. As these skills develop in children, their knowledge and ideas about the world, people, and things grow and develop.

Children develop their own **theories of mind.** These are theories about thinking and how the mind works. Children have theories on just about everything though. This is what Piaget found so fascinating about interviewing children—their answers to questions such as, Why is the sky blue? Children of different ages would, of course, give very different answers, but most children answer confidently and without hesitation, secure in the conviction that the answer is obvious and therefore correct. Intelligence is generally related to facts and how many of these one knows. As we saw in Chapter 2, however, Piaget and Gardner felt there were several types of knowledge.

People gather knowledge, approach a task, use knowledge, and remember and understand things differently. We sometimes call this a person's "learning style." There are learning style inventories on the market which are interesting to do with a team since they build understanding of one another's style and approach to problem solving. Early childhood philosophy caters well to a classroom of diverse learning styles since it is open-ended and therefore accommodating and flexible.

Many elementary, secondary, and postsecondary programs, as well as corporations, have recognized this open-ended, accommodating style as an excellent approach to teaching and learning and have begun to adapt it to their environments.

A Closer Look depicts an environment that recognizes, supports, and extends children's learning

Environments and Attitudes That Encourage Cognitive Development

While young children learn about the properties of objects, compare objects to discover what makes them similar and different, begin to understand quantity and number concepts, and start to develop a sense of time and space, they also learn

a wide variety of facts and information. Some of this information emerges from repeated daily experiences; other items seem to pique children's interest and stick in their memories.

Young children generally do not discriminate or differentiate between facts, but collect and store much information. The early childhood curriculum helps support children as they learn to sort and classify. Attitudes that provide for and encourage opportunities to explore, question, practise, and discuss enable children to construct new knowledge.

As we discussed in Chapter 8, appropriate topics for curriculum development can revolve around children, families, and the community. These familiar subjects, which offer innumerable learning possibilities, hook into a child's prior or current knowledge about a topic and can then be expanded and built on to help children gain additional information that has relevance in the context of their lives and experiences. Teachers must realize that each child brings unique experiences and interests to school.

Acquisition of information, as well as of the concepts related to classification, seriation, numbers, time, and space, occurs in many ways in the early childhood program. Just about any activity in which young children engage involves one or several of these concepts. Although the acquisition of information and concepts is often associated with specific curriculum areas, especially math and science, it is not that easy to place them in discrete categories. *Children's thinking is ongoing and involves a constant taking in, sifting, connecting, and storing of experiences, concepts, and information.* Teachers are constantly listening, observing, questioning, and adjusting to these processes as the children engage in learning.

A Closer Look

MAP MAKING

Through many experiences and discussions, the children expressed detailed interest in maps and wanted to make one of their neighbourhood. It was decided the first thing they needed to do was to take a walk to take a closer look at their surroundings.

The children were taking a walk around the block. Teachers Ardith and Jason encouraged them to pay close attention to everything they saw on the way, including buildings, trees, stop signs, the parking lot next to the dentist's office, and other features. "Remember, when we get back, we're going to make a map of our block. So we have to pay really close attention to everything we see," Jason cued them.

The children discussed and described all sorts of features that, on previous walks, had gone unnoticed. Lynette, for instance, found a doghouse in the yard behind the brown house. Chad noticed a bed of tulips and daffodils along the side of the blue house.

When the children got back to their classroom, Ardith put out a large sheet of butcher paper as a starting point for the map. The children decided to start their map at the school. "Our school is on the corner, so we should put it right here," said James, pointing to the lower left-hand corner of the paper.

"Let's build the school," suggested Miriam and got some blocks from the block area. She and James built the school with several unit blocks and enclosed it with a fence of connected longer blocks.

"I want to put in the doghouse," said Lynette.

"Where is the brown house?" asked Ardith.

"Let's put it here," said Lynette, pointing next to the school.

"Is the brown house next to our school?" asked Ardith.

"No, it's on this side of the block," said Pradeep, pointing along the other side of the map.

Because the brown house was not on the map yet, Lynette decided to draw a picture of the doghouse. She got a piece of paper and crayons from the art shelf.

"Maybe we should think about what we saw in the order that we saw it on our walk," suggested Ardith. "What was the first thing we saw when we got past the playground fence?" The children discussed the various buildings and houses, and soon they began putting up more block structures as they recalled the spatial relationships of the various features.

Lynette finished her drawing of the doghouse and cut it out with the scissors. It was placed behind the brown house when that was put on the map. Chad wanted to paint the blocks for the blue house so they would be the right colour.

"I don't think we ought to paint our blocks, Chad. What else could you use to make the blue house?" Ardith asked.

After a moment's thought, Chad said he would find the materials for the house in the woodworking area. He found a piece of scrap lumber that was just the right size and painted it blue. Later, Chad and Melissa drew flowers on the butcher paper along the house's side. Stop signs, trees, cars, the snail that the children had seen along the side of the road, and the sign outside the dentist's office were all added to the map.

The teachers left the map out for several days. Children continued to add items to it, particularly things they noticed on following days on their way to and from school. Teachers took pictures of the progress, noted the major developments along the way, and kept detailed anecdotal records on the children. Some children made sketches of the map, others made models, and still others extended their interests to the globes and maps in the class and library. This culmination of prior, emerging, and new knowledge, skills, and interests was a fascinating process for both teachers and children as they observed, documented, discussed, and presented. This example demonstrates the balance between emergent curriculum and daily planning that accommodates the project to ensure it can be realized.

A Word about Math and Science

Remember that math and science are as much a part of other activities (e.g., blocks, cooking, woodworking, manipulatives, dramatic play, art) as they are separate activities. It is easy to see that the acquisition of number concepts is central to math. But math is not central to the acquisition of number concepts. Classification, seriation, and temporal and spatial concepts are equally integral to both math and science. Yet, these concepts supply some of the tools required to carry out many other endeavours, for instance, measuring, grouping, and comparing which are crucial for managing in all aspects of one's day.

Having children take part in artificial activities to learn math, asking them endless "test" questions (e.g., What is 2 + 2? How many fingers?) or cornering them to make every instance a teachable moment is unrealistic and inappropriate. So much of what children know is demonstrated as they play, and we need to watch for this. Though we must always help children find ways to explain and explore phenomena and answer their queries, math, as with anything, is best learned in the context of experience and guided learning. Math can be identified, pointed out, explored, and enhanced in many indirect, as well as direct, ways throughout the curriculum, both by children and teachers, as interests and circumstances warrant. Remember that the goal of teaching is not to show how much you know but to learn about what the children know. The math centre should not contain math worksheets but the tools of math that can be utilized over the entire curriculum throughout the day. Measuring tapes, rulers, scales, counters, calculators, pencils and paper, and software are only a few examples. If children wish to make comparisons, predictions, or plans on the playground, in the block centre, in the art centre, or in home centre or kitchen, they can!

Science, as well, needs to be woven throughout the curriculum. A science centre, consisting of a pine cone and magnifying glass is insufficient. Caring for plants and animals, using binoculars, keeping records, using observations, and making predictions help children not only acquire the facts but also acquire the tools for getting the facts. Children's scientific needs can be identified, supported, and enhanced through both the context of the day and their interests and experiences. Exhibit 9.2 outlines guidelines for supporting children in their growth.

EXHIBIT 9.2: GUIDELINES FOR SUPPORTING COGNITIVE DEVELOPMENT

Recognize interests, respect ideas, and support efforts.

Encourage children to use the same strategies you use to create an atmosphere of exploration, discovery, excitement, warmth, teamwork, respect, and positive relationships:

▪ observe	▪ evaluate
▪ predict	▪ plan
▪ record	▪ listen
▪ hypothesize	▪ present
▪ discuss	▪ elaborate
▪ experiment	▪ expand
▪ question	▪ explain
▪ research	▪ attend to
▪ brainstorm ideas	▪ compare
▪ problem solve	▪ support
▪ implement	▪ encourage
▪ assess	

This list is by no means complete. How we implement these guidelines is demonstrated through positive words and actions and voice tone, as well as all the other guidance techniques we discussed in Chapter 6 for building learning, self-esteem, and prosocial behaviours. These strategies, or ways of doing things to acquire and use information, can be applied in any situation with any project, short- or long-term, in any area of the curriculum throughout the day. Help children to understand these words and to use them. As children learn about learning, they gain lifelong strategies for learning and interacting in a positive and productive way.

Language Development

Children's early development is particularly astounding when we consider the acquisition of language. Infants arrive in the world with no language, but within a 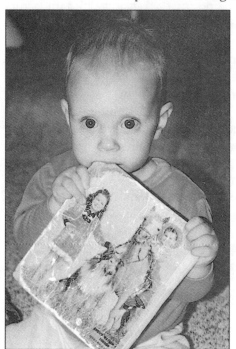 year they are starting to converse. And they have done this without any direct instruction in one of the most complex cognitive tasks, one that is unique to humans. The toddler makes rapid gains in language and by the preschool years has acquired an enormous vocabulary, a fundamental grasp of the rules of grammar, and an understanding of the subtleties of the social aspects of communication. In addition, young children begin to develop the skills needed for the complex process of reading and writing, which they begin to tackle soon after they enter school.

These are truly amazing accomplishments. We know much about this language acquisition process, although language researchers certainly are far from understanding completely how children learn to communicate with such speed and accuracy (Gineshi, 1987).

What Is Language?

Language is a complex system involving a variety of components. Included are:

- **vocabulary**—learning words
- **semantics**—understanding word meaning
- **morphology**—knowing the rules for creating and using words accurately
- **grammar and syntax**—learning the rules for putting words together meaningfully
- **pragmatics**—obtaining a growing grasp of the appropriateness of what is being communicated

Any theory of language development indicates that children's early years are particularly crucial in the evolution of language skills.

What Is Communication?

Language is only part of the communication process. Children can communicate well even when they are unable to talk. Gestures; body language; eye contact; use of picture symbols; assistive devices that replace or augment talking such as picture boards, voice synthesizers, or sign language; facial expressions; sounds; written symbols; and creative media such as art, dance, music, audio and visual effects, pictures, and drama all communicate ideas and messages.

Language is simply one tool of many that we use to interact with others to share and exchange information and ideas. A conversation is a good example of a communicative interaction. But a dance between two people, exchanging letters, or a chat room on the Internet are also examples, each of which have their own unique characteristics. The interaction can be positive or negative. Certain factors can extend the communication, that is, keep it going. Other factors can stop or prevent the communication.

To keep the communication going , especially in a conversation, we generally do things such as nod, ask questions for clarification or more information, confirm what we heard, pay attention, give eye contact, listen, give positive reinforcement, use body language that says we are interested (e.g., leaning forward), and use an expressive tone and face. Things that typically end communication quickly are a lack of acknowledgment, interruptions, negative comments, inattentiveness, misunderstandings, and a lack of response.

In early childhood education, our aim is to keep the communication and the interactions going, whether they are verbal, written, or expressed through actions or activity. We strive to communicate many positive messages to parents, children, and others through what we do and say and how we present the environment. Messages such as "Welcome," "It is safe here," "I will help you," "You can trust me," "I respect you," and "You can do it" are all evident in the many ways in which we present information and interact.

What Is Multilingualism?

Canadian early childhood educators in some areas of the country have been familiar with the issue of **bilingualism** for a long time. However, with our changing immigration patterns, **multilingualism** in the program is now an issue, especially in some of our larger urban centres. Early childhood programs increasingly include children from varied linguistic and cultural backgrounds, children who may speak only a language other than English, children who are in the process of acquiring English as a second language, and children who have grown up acquiring more than one language simultaneously.

In some programs, English-speaking children are also exposed to a second language, particularly if that language and culture are important parts of the community. Bilingualism and multilingualism, although often considered a matter of language learning, are intricately tied to cultural and social dimensions (Hakuta & Garcia, 1989). Awareness of and sensitivity to family values is particularly important in working with children learning English as a second language (Sholtys, 1989). In general, young children have little difficulty acquiring more than one language and eventually speaking each language with no interference from the other (Obler, 1985).

Second-Language Teaching Strategies

Although there are no definitive guidelines for helping children learn a second language, the following strategies, which are important for all young children, can also be helpful to those learning a new language (Saville-Troike, 1982; Sholtys, 1989).

- A new experience such as preschool can be bewildering to any young child, particularly if the child cannot understand the language. A friendly, consistent, supportive atmosphere can help make the child feel welcome and comfortable, which, in turn, will facilitate learning English.

- If someone who speaks the child's first language is available, enlist that person to help the child learn the routines and expectations, as well as the new language. If another child in the class speaks the language, interaction between the two should be encouraged, although certainly not forced.

- Encourage all of the children to talk to and include the child in activities.

- Use the child's name frequently, being sure to pronounce it properly when talking to the child.

- A non-English-speaking child should not be forced to speak because the natural process of learning a second language usually entails a time of silent assimilation.

- Involve the child in the classroom through non-language activities (e.g., helping to set the table for snack) to help the child become part of the group.

- Language should be presented in a natural, meaningful way in the context of the child's experiences and interests.

- Concrete objects or demonstration of actions should be paired with new words. For example, say the word "milk" when helping the child pour it at snack.

- Repetition of new language learning is important, provided it is done naturally. Meaningless drill does not help. Consistently using the same wording each day, for instance, to signal classroom transitions, will help the child connect words and meaning more easily.

- When a child shares feelings or an idea verbally, such communication should be encouraged through uncritical acceptance. Correcting grammar or pronunciation tends to inhibit rather than foster language.

Environments and Attitudes That Encourage Language Development

The following sections will examine several important aspects of language. First, we will discuss the spontaneous, informal, ongoing use of language that should be a natural accompaniment to whatever children are doing. We next look at the story as a means to enhance language development. Finally, we will examine children's emerging literacy, their awareness that language extends to reading and writing, and how this is supported through integrated language experiences.

Spontaneous Language

Because language is used in almost everything children do, it must be central to the early childhood program. Children are constantly involved in communication—in listening, hearing, talking, interpreting, representing, writing, and reading. All forms of language surround them as they interact with one another, with adults, with media, with activities, and with varied materials. Language activities do not need to be structured to teach language because preschool-aged children have already acquired an elaborate and complex language system. Rather, early childhood language experiences should emerge from natural and meaningful conversations, interactions, and experiences between adults and children and among children. Such talk is used to inform, tell stories, pretend, plan, argue, discuss, express humour, and so on (Gineshi, 1987). Classrooms for young children, therefore, are not quiet. They are abuzz with language almost all of the time.

Almost every aspect of the early childhood environment and program facilitates language. For instance, the knowledgeable teacher, who values what children have to say and listens to them carefully, promotes language development. Similarly, a daily program that provides large blocks of time in which children can become immersed in activities and interactions fosters language usage. In addition, language growth is encouraged by a curriculum that introduces interesting and stimulating objects, experiences, and concepts, just as a classroom environment that is set up to invite small groups of children to work together promotes language.

Conversations   A natural way of using language is through conversation. In good early childhood programs, there is an almost constant, ongoing buzz of conversations between children and teachers and among children. For children, conversation is an art that takes time to develop since it involves learning a number of elements, such as how to initiate and end conversations, maintain coherent dialogue, take turns, and "repair" a conversation that breaks down (McTear, 1985). It is important, therefore, that there be many opportunities for children to practise their emerging conversational skills.

Teachers' ability to engage in effective conversations with children is also an art. Dialogue between adults and small groups or individual children is essential in teaching preschoolers (Lay-Dopyera & Dopyera, 1987a). Unfortunately, research has found that there is generally little extended conversation between teachers and young children.

An in-depth study of one skilled teacher's conversational strategies revealed some significant findings (Rogers, Perrin, & Waller, 1987). "Cathy" (the teacher) maintained an equal relationship in her conversation; the number of words and length of sentences were relatively equal to those used by the child. Particularly important was Cathy's genuine interest in what the child was telling her. Cathy's interactions were based on the child's actions and interests and, more often than not, were in response to the child's initiation.

The most significant observation of this study was Cathy's avoidance of "know-answer questions," questions to which the teacher already knows the answer (e.g., "What colour did you paint the sky?" or "How many cookies are on your plate?"). Such questions are answered by a simple response from the child and may be evaluated by the teacher. Children may fear giving a wrong answer and therefore avoid conversation with the teacher. Thus, teacher–child conversations should arise from natural situations and be based on genuine interest in what the child is doing.

Playing with Language Another facet of language that teachers can use to enrich its use in the early childhood setting is children's language play. Once children have a good grasp of the principles of language and the correctness of a concept, they delight in confirming this by expressing the opposite, usually accompanied by much laughter and giggling (Geller, 1985). Expressions of humour through silliness, nonsense words, or rhymes particularly enthrall preschoolers. Children enjoy humour, and teachers can use it to capture and maintain children's attention, both in the stories they read or tell and in their conversations with children.

Stories

In a language-rich early childhood program, you will find that language permeates every activity. You will hear it in the washroom, at the meal table, in the block centre, and on the playground. You will hear children talking to themselves, with their teachers, and with their peers. A quiet program is cause for concern. In addition to the ongoing use of language in the early childhood program, specific activities based on language use and elaboration are also incorporated. Such activities are often presented at large- or small-group times, enhancing not just language but listening skills, group social skills, creative thinking, concept formation, and other areas of development. The story is at the core of many of those experiences.

Stories, in their various forms, are the most popular vehicle for language activities. Stories can be told or read by teachers, children, or both together; they can be enacted by children or with flannel-board pieces, puppets, or play dough; or they can come from the rich store of children's literature or from the children's own experiences. Stories can exist in a variety of forms such as poems, rhymes, songs, actions, pictures, videos, dramas, writing, or drawing. In this section, we discuss the significance for development of preschool experiences with stories.

The Story Schema   As adults, you know that most simple stories have a regular, predictable structure—a beginning, a middle, and an end. Preschoolers, in communicating, tell us their stories constantly in relaying events about their day, families, projects, experiences, play, ideas, and other matters. Everything in life has this basic structure of a beginning, a middle, and an end. In essence, you have a story. The beginning of the "story," or "*once upon a time*" section, introduces the setting, the time, and the characters. In the middle, there is a complication—something unusual or unexpected happens. Then, in the end, or the "*lived happily ever after*" section, the complication is resolved or settled and the characters reach a more stable state. This simple structure is known as the **story schema.** Children need to gain a sense of this sequence in order to communicate effectively and to understand the world around them. It has been the subject of fairly extensive research since the 1980s.

Both children and adults use the story schema to help them understand, remember, and retell stories. As long as stories follow that structure or schema, they are easy to understand and to remember. Experience with stories in the preschool years is critical for the development of the story schema (Young, 1987, 1993a).

By reading lots of stories in your program, you are helping children to learn about the story schema and to develop cognitive skills they will need throughout their lives. And you are contributing to significant cognitive growth through a developmentally appropriate activity.

Emergent Literacy

As we have seen, children learn to understand and express language in a natural way through a process that begins very early in life. They also learn about the story schema without direct instruction. Similarly, preschool children begin to form an understanding of reading and writing, something that has only come to interest researchers and educators relatively recently. The term "emergent literacy" acknowledges that learning to read and write (in other words, to become literate) is a dynamic, ongoing, emerging process. In fact, all aspects of language—listening, speaking, writing, and reading—are intertwined and develop concurrently, not sequentially (Teale & Sulzby, 1986).

Children develop an understanding of reading and writing through a supportive, literate environment, starting at home and continuing in the early childhood program. And this is done without formal instruction. If a young child is in a story- and print-rich environment, the child will develop the foundations of literacy that are required for reading and writing.

Catherine Snow concluded that when parents read to and with their young children, the children's language is more complex than it is during other times of play. Furthermore, in the process of early reading, teachers and parents help their children acquire some of the basic rules of literacy—learning that books are for reading rather than manipulating or that books represent a separate, fictional world (Snow & Ninio, 1986). Both home and school experiences with books provide children with further insights, for example, that print should make sense, that print and speech are related, that book language is different from speech, and that books are enjoyable (Schickedanz, 1986). Out of many experiences with the printed form of the language come the foundations for writing and reading.

Learning to Write   The beginnings of writing emerge early in life through a number of steps. Vygotsky (1978a) traced the roots of writing to earliest infant gestures, described as "writing in the air." In late infancy, infants will try to copy a parent's list writing, and a toddler engages in more complex writing behaviours. During the preschool years, children become aware of the differences between drawing and writing, a distinction that is evident in their own efforts. By age 3, many children begin to use **mock writing**, a series of wavy, circular, or vertical lines that deliberately imitate adult writing and are distinctly different from drawing. Within the next couple of years, mock writing increasingly becomes a mixture of real letters and innovative symbols.

By late kindergarten or grade 1, most children who have grown up in a pleasurable, literate environment and who recognize most or all of the letters of the alphabet begin to use **invented spelling** by finding the speech sound that most closely fits what they want to write (Atkins, 1984). Five-year-old Abby wrote, "I M GNG TO DRV MI KAR AT HOM" (I am going to drive my car at home) in one of her stories, which was accompanied by a picture of Abby atop a blue vehicle. Analysis of the errors seen in invented spelling indicates that children are trying to work out a system of rules, just as they did as toddlers when they were acquiring oral language. Because reading and writing are intertwined processes, such early attempts at spelling are soon replaced with more conventional forms as children repeatedly come across the same words in their reading (Atkins, 1984).

Learning to Read   When children read and write, they are "making sense out of or through print," although this sense does not require an understanding of a conventional alphabetic code (Goodman, 1986, p. 5). Eventually, children do acquire this understanding as they learn the consistent relationship between the letters of the alphabet and their use in the written form. Early literacy, however, is based on the growing awareness that print means something, for instance, that a stop sign indicates that a driver should step on the brake.

Some 2-year-olds already display such awareness, for example, pointing to a word in a book and saying, "That's my name" (Walton, 1989). By age 3, children clearly have substantial understanding of why and how print is used. Many 4-year-olds have developed the ability to recognize a variety of words when these are presented in their appropriate context, for instance, common labels and signs.

Experiences in recognizing words in their environmental context help children learn about the process of reading and lead to eventual recognition of these words out of their context (Kontos, 1986).

Children actively seek to make sense of print in their environment by using a variety of strategies that they themselves invent (Willert & Kamii, 1985). Younger preschoolers' strategies focus on such clues as the first letter of a word ("That's my name," says Paul, "because it's got a 'P'"); looking at the shape of the word, such as its length or spacing if there is more than one word in a configuration; and using pictures as clues to help decipher accompanying words. As children get older and more experienced in acquiring reading skills, they use some additional strategies. Included are looking for familiar letters or combinations of letters in words; spontaneously and repeatedly practising the spelling and copying of words; and inventing a phonological system, similar to that used in invented spelling, to sound out words.

Implications   As the preceding discussions suggest, young children have a natural interest in the print environment around them, an interest most of them express through their own inventive attempts at writing and reading. This developmentally appropriate view of how children learn to read and write is far removed from some of the stereotyped notions of reading and writing as formal subjects best begun in first grade. Thinking of literacy merely as recognizing words or the sounds of letters "is as dangerous as it is erroneous" (Gibson, 1989, p. 30).

Yet, all too often, young children are placed into high-powered, rigid, formalized programs that focus on isolated skills involved in the reading process rather than on the integration of all aspects of language. In fact, a statement expressing concern over this developmentally inappropriate practice was jointly prepared by a group of relevant organizations (International Reading Association, 1986).

Reading and writing emerge from many successful and enjoyable experiences with language, both oral and written. According to research, literacy best develops through meaningful context in an informal, supportive environment (Kontos, 1986). As Judith Schickedanz (1982), one of the leading authorities in children's emergent literacy, wrote:

> We need to abandon ideas and practices that assume early literacy development to be simply a matter of teaching children a few basic skills such as alphabet recognition or letter–sound associations. Much more is involved. Limiting children's reading experiences to contacts with bits and pieces of print isolated from meaningful contexts may actually prevent them from developing broader and more complex insights that are key to understanding what written language is all about. (p. 259)

Promoting Literacy Development   Literacy, like oral language, emerges in a natural way that does not require formal teaching to prompt interest. What it does need is a language-rich environment to encourage its development. Literacy is best promoted in the context of a **whole language approach,** one in which high-quality oral and print language surrounds children, children can observe others using literacy skills, and children are encouraged to experiment with all forms of language. Such an approach integrates all forms of communication, including speaking, listening, writing, reading, art, music, and math (International Reading Association, 1986). Exhibit 9.3 provides excellent ideas for promoting literacy and language development.

EXHIBIT 9.3: Guidelines for Supporting Language and Literacy Development

---

The following suggestions for supporting literacy development come from a variety of sources. The term "story" can be interchanged with "project" or another medium where appropriate.

- The aim of supporting literacy development in young children should be to enhance their desire to read and write by building on their intrinsic motivation to learn these skills (Willert & Kamii, 1985).

- A language-rich environment must contain many materials, opportunities, and experiences for planned and spontaneous interaction with language, both oral and written. This means providing appropriate materials and scheduled time blocks for children to pursue language activities (Machado, 1985; Teale & Martinez, 1988).

- A carefully selected library of high-quality children's books must be available for children to browse through or to ask a teacher to read.

- Stories should not just be read but also discussed when the children want to do so. Children understand stories better when they have opportunities to ask and answer questions about the plot and characters of a story and to relate the story to their own lives (Teale & Martinez, 1988; Walton, 1989). But stories need not be stopped and interrupted with a barrage of questions. A few key questions can be used to assess prior knowledge and experience, to check for key concepts, and to check for understanding occasionally to ensure the children are following the story line.

- Children need many story-reading experiences to acquire the story schema. Knowing, for instance, how a story begins and ends and the story's sequence of events is important to literacy development (Jensen, 1985b; Young, 1987, 1993a).

- Books should be read more than once. Children are more likely to re-enact a book on their own if they have heard it at least three times (Teale & Martinez, 1988).

- Children should be encouraged to "read" to one another, whether or not they actually know how to read. Such activities promote emergent literacy (Teale & Martinez, 1988).

- If some children in the class seem to have had few one-on-one reading experiences at home, time should be set aside when a teacher can spend time reading to just one or two children (Jensen, 1985b).

- Print awareness can be supported through books as well as through other forms of print in the school environment. Charts, lists, labels, and bulletin boards that surround children in the environment contribute to print awareness, as does a teacher who interprets, calls attention to, and gets the children's input when creating print (Goodman, Smith, Meredith, & Goodman, 1987; Schickedanz, 1986).

- Children gradually learn that there is a relationship between written and spoken words. When children read certain books frequently, they often become so familiar with the stories that they know which words correspond with which pages. Such experiences contribute to making the connection between speech and print (Schickedanz, 1986).

- Children should be provided with a variety of reading and writing materials to incorporate into their play. For example, paper, pencils, markers, and other implements in the art, language arts, dramatic play, science, and math centres should be included to suggest a link between the activities that go on in those areas and reading/writing.

- Given a supportive atmosphere, older children will engage in storywriting. Although children may not be using conventional letters and words, their stories as well as the writing process are still full of meaning. The sensitive teacher must carefully attend to what children are conveying to understand that meaning (Harste, Short, & Burke, 1988).

- One way of promoting storytelling and writing is to include a "publishers workshop" as an ongoing activity centre in the classroom (Bakst & Essa, 1990). The teacher writes down children's dictated stories but also encourages the children to write their stories. Books are designed, made, and presented and stories are displayed and recorded.

- Stories should be shared, something that can be done informally as other children come to the publishing area or more formally during a large-group activity. When their stories are shared, children develop **audience awareness,** an appreciation that their stories are a form of communication that should make sense to others (Bakst & Essa, 1990).

- Some children show little interest in reading and writing, perhaps because they have had little access to materials that promote these activities. One successful strategy to stimulate this interest is to provide a "writing suitcase" that the children can take home overnight or over a weekend. This suitcase can include such materials as various sizes and shapes of paper and notebooks; chalk and chalkboard, pencils, crayons, and markers; magnet, cardboard, or plastic letters and stencils; favourite picture books; scissors; and tape, glue, stapler, hole punch, and ruler (Rich, 1985).

- Stories can be input on the computer.

- Stories can be represented through creative media

- Post children's work everywhere.

- Share books and stories between home and school.

- Make comparisons between salient features of books, such as authors' backgrounds, illustrators' methods, themes, size, shape, colour, and texture of the book.
- Stories should be read often for the sheer pleasure they give with no strings attached!

Social Development

One major function of the early childhood program is to support the process of **socialization**, the means through which children become a functioning part of society and learn society's rules and values. Although socialization is a lifelong

process, it is particularly crucial early in life, when the foundation for later attitudes, values, and behaviours is laid. Unquestionably, socialization begins with the parent–child and caretaker–infant relationships in infancy, where patterns of response, need fulfillment, and give-and-take have their roots. Children who do not come to an early childhood program until they are older already have had numerous socializing experiences. They may have learned to trust or be wary of others, to meet new experiences enthusiastically or with caution, to care about others' feelings because their needs have always been considered, or to think of others as competitors for affection or resources. The term "curriculum" includes all the elements in the environment that lead to conversations and activities that promote socialization.

What Is Social Development?

As increasing numbers of infants, toddlers, and preschoolers enter group care, these children experience increasingly intimate peer contact (Howes, 1987). By age 3 or 4, most children are part of a social world that is truly egalitarian, a world of peers who are equals (Moore, 1982). In this world, as young children go through this process of becoming socialized to the peer society, they are expected to:

- share and cooperate;
- learn the rules and expectations;
- gain skill and competence in peer interaction;

- enter into friendships;
- develop gender identity;
- adopt racial and cultural attitudes;
- form a sense of morals and values; and
- acquire a host of prosocial behaviours.

The opportunity to develop multicultural, multiracial, and multieconomic acceptance will, to a large extent, depend on the integrative nature of the early childhood program. Environment, attitude, and actions combine to guide social development.

Environments and Attitudes That Encourage Social Development

Peer Interaction

Peer interaction is an essential ingredient in the process of childhood socialization, in fact, in the total development of the child (Hartup, 1983a). As with any skill, it is through practice in real situations that children develop competence in peer interaction. The many naturally occurring opportunities of day-to-day life allow children to be sympathetic and helpful to peers (Honig, 1982). These social skills include the many strategies children learn to help them initiate and continue social interactions, negotiate, and settle conflicts (Smith, 1982).

For young children who are just entering peer relationships, adult guidance—not interference—is important; as children get older and less egocentric, the presence of an adult becomes less necessary (Howes, 1987; Oden, 1982). The teacher, in facilitating social development, must first of all provide children with ample time and space, and appropriate materials, to facilitate social interaction. A child who has difficulty engaging in social play can be helped through sensitive teacher guidance, for instance, directing that child to a group with similar play interests or pairing the child with a more socially competent peer (Rogers & Ross, 1986).

Older children also provide excellent models for younger ones. In one study, the pretend play of 2-year-olds was characterized as much more cooperative and complex when they were paired with 5-year-olds than with fellow toddlers (Howes & Farver, 1987). This research supports the idea of providing children in early childhood programs with some opportunities for mixed-age interaction.

Friendship

One special type of peer relationship is friendship, that close link between people typified by mutual concern, sharing, and companionship. Recent research points to the importance of early friendship to later emotional well-being (Flaste, 1991). Young children's concept of friendship primarily revolves around the immediate situation. As children grow older, their friendships typically become more stable (Damon, 1983).

Preschoolers view friends in terms of their accessibility, physical attributes, and actions (Rubin, 1980). In other words, a friend is "someone you play with a lot," "someone who wears a Batman T-shirt," "someone who invites you to her birthday party," or "someone who isn't mean." Another insight into early friendship can be found in the often-heard question, "Are you my friend?" which can be translated to mean, "Will you play with me?" (Edwards, 1986).

Preschoolers expect friendships to maximize enjoyment, entertainment, and satisfaction in play (Parker & Gottman, 1989). Typically young children are focused on themselves—their own feelings and needs (Rubin, 1980). Yet, as many observers have noted, young children are surprisingly capable of caring about and giving emotional support to one another (Levinger & Levinger, 1986); for instance, observe the concern of onlookers when a child cries because he or she is hurt or distressed.

Trust is the basic foundation on which friendship is built. Children who are trustworthy, who share and cooperate, are more likely to be considered as friends by their peers. Trust in the peer relationship, however, does not simply emerge but is built on the sense of trust that children established early in life (as described by Erikson), when nurturing adults met their needs consistently. Teachers can help children develop a sense of trust, which can enhance friendships, through their support and guidance. More specifically, they can help children recognize their own needs and goals and those of others, develop more effective social skills, recognize how their behaviour affects others, and become aware of their own social successes so they can be repeated (Buzzelli & File, 1989).

It is wise to remember that friendships cannot be imposed or forced. To tell children, "We are all friends at school" or "Go find another friend to play with" sends a mixed message about the meaning of friendship. Young children will develop friendships based on trust and criteria meaningful to them. Teachers should respect their right to choose friends.

Inclusion and Diversity

The theme of inclusion and diversity—respecting, valuing, and including all people by affording them the same access to rights, choices, and opportunities and acknowledging their commonalities while respecting their individuality and unique strengths and needs—is a thread we have attempted to weave throughout this text. Here we look at three areas, gender, race and culture, and special needs, in order to provide helpful strategies that incorporate awareness, advocacy, sensitivity, and empathy in the curriculum so that inclusion becomes a way of life for the children as they grow.

Gender Role Development

Research has shown that one of the most powerful determinants of peer interaction and friendship is the children's sex. If you work with young children, you will have observed that the majority of their playmate choices are of the same sex. This holds true in all cultural settings, not just in North America (Maccoby, 1990). Cross-sex friends are not uncommon; however, as they get older, girls increasingly choose to play with other girls, and boys seek out other boys as play partners.

Children choose same-sex friends spontaneously, and attempts to change or influence their choices to encourage more cross-sex interaction have generally not been very successful (Howes, 1988; Katz, 1986; Maccoby, 1990).

Children value the concrete symbols of their gender that confirm their maleness or femaleness, and they construct and adopt a rigid set of rules and stereotypes about what is gender-appropriate. This rigidity is consistent with a similar approach to other cognitive concepts. In acquiring same-sex values, children also form an identity with same-sex people.

This rigidity, children's gravitation toward same-sex peers, and their engagement in gender-stereotyped activities are often troublesome to adults who want children to be broad-minded and tolerant of others. Despite many parents' and teachers' efforts to present non-sexist models to the children in their lives, these same children will often display highly sex-stereotyped behaviours and attitudes. Some guidelines can help the early childhood teacher lay the foundation for non-biased attitudes toward the sexes based on respect for each person as an individual, which includes their unique gender. These are found in Exhibit 9.4.

Racial and Cultural Awareness and Attitudes

Similar to their early recognition of gender differences, children also develop an awareness of racial variations at an early age. Preschoolers use the most readily visible physical differences as cues; skin colour in particular, as well as hair and eye colour, provide a basis for comparison and classification.

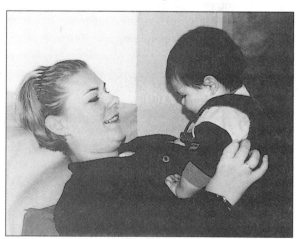

A rather subtle variation in learning about different people arises when children begin to discover cultural differences. Family, neighbourhood, school, church, books, and mass media can introduce children to the fact that people meet their daily needs in different ways. All people need to communicate, but they may do so in different languages; all people need to eat, but they don't all eat the same types of foods; all people require clothing, shelter, and transportation, but they meet these needs in different ways.

Although children's cognitive development steers them toward noting differences and classifying accordingly, society applies the comparative values that lead to stereotypes and prejudice. Children are bombarded with subtle and not-so-subtle messages about the worth of people. Parents, as the primary socializers of their children, seem the obvious transmitters of racial and cultural attitudes; yet, research has shown little relationship between children and their

Non-Sexist Teaching

- *Value each child as an individual.* Focus on the strengths and abilities of each child as a person, and help children recognize and value these characteristics.

- *Help children learn that gender identity is biologically determined.* Before they develop gender constancy, children may feel that it is their preference for boy or girl activities that makes them boys or girls. Reassure them that their bodies, not their activities, determine their sex (Derman-Sparks, 1989).

- *Be aware of possible gender biases in your own behaviour.* Studies have shown, for instance, that adults tend to protect girls more, react to boys' misbehaviours more, encourage independence more in boys, and expect girls to be more fearful (Honig, 1983).

- *Listen carefully to all children.* Adults tend to interrupt or speak simultaneously more with girls than with boys, suggesting that what girls have to say is less important (Honig, 1983).

- *Help children find the words to get their nurturance needs met.* Little boys are not as likely to ask for a hug or a lap to sit on as girls. Teachers can help all children find the right words to communicate their needs for affection (Honig, 1983).

- *Use language carefully, avoiding bias toward male identity.* The English language tends to assume male identity when sex is not clear. We generally say "he" when we don't know whether an animal, person, or storybook character is male or female, and this tricks children into thinking that "he's" are more important than "she's" (Sheldon, 1990).

- *Provide materials that show males and females in a variety of roles.* Puzzles, lotto games, posters, and photographs can portray males and females in non-traditional roles. Dramatic play props can draw children into a variety of roles sometimes stereotyped as male or female.

- *Select children's books that portray non-sexist models.* Children's literature includes a range of characters from the very sex-stereotyped to the very non-sexist. A study of widely read children's books, including award-winning ones, showed that male and female roles are often distorted and stereotyped. Males appear far more often; females, when they are portrayed, tend to be shown as passive and dependent (Flerx, Fidler, & Rogers, 1976).

- *Plan a wide range of activities, and encourage all children to participate.* Children will participate in and enjoy a variety of activities—cooking, woodworking, blocks, housekeeping, book browsing, sewing, sand and water, art—if they are well planned and the teacher's words or attitudes do not promote sex stereotyping.

- *Discuss obvious sex stereotyping with children.* Older preschoolers and school-aged children, especially if they have been around adults who are sensitive to using non-biased concepts and vocabulary, can engage in discussions about sex stereotypes in books, favourite television programs, or movies.

parents in this respect (Katz, 1982). A more plausible source of racial and cultural information may be television, movies, and books that, by their portrayals or omissions, imply superiority of some and inferiority of other groups.

In forming their own attitudes, young children continually strive to fit together the multiple and often contradictory sources of information about other people. The early childhood program is an ideal place to help children learn about themselves and others, learn to value and have pride in themselves, and learn to respect others. This involves conveying accurate knowledge about and pride in children's own racial and cultural groups, accurate knowledge about and appreciation of other racial and cultural groups, and an understanding of racism and how to counter it (Derman-Sparks, Higa, & Sparks, 1980). One excellent resource for helping teachers of young children in this task is Louise Derman-Sparks's *Anti-Bias Curriculum: Tools for Empowering Young Children* (1989). This book sensitively and succinctly discusses and suggests strategies for helping children learn about and respect racial, gender, cultural, and physical differences and promotes anti-discrimination and activism. Derman-Sparks and Ramsey's 1993 article, *Early Childhood Multicultural, Anti-Bias Education in the 1990s: Toward the 21st Century,* would also be a useful resource. Exhibit 9.5 outlines guidelines, gleaned from various sources, that can help you provide children with a developmentally appropriate understanding of other races and cultures.

Sensitivity toward People with Diverse Abilities

Children learn attitudes of understanding, acceptance, and sensitivity toward those who have special needs. More and more children with disabilities are included in early childhood programs. In Prince Edward Island, for example, direct funding to licensed centres for children with disabilities has been available since 1988. Consequently, the number of children with disabilities included in the province's child care centres has risen quickly. The following factors are important considerations in helping children develop sensitivity.

Spending Time Together   Children with special needs can benefit from a quality inclusive program by experiencing success in a variety of developmentally appropriate activities through relationships with age-mates, where both assume roles of model and friend, and through exposure to the many opportunities for informal, incidental learning that take place in all early childhood programs (Deiner, 1983; Spodek, Saracho, & Lee, 1984). At the same time, all children benefit by learning that children who are in some way different from them have, nonetheless, far more commonalities than differences (Karnes & Lee, 1979). Inclusion provides children with the opportunity for positive experiences that build a good foundation for lifelong learning about and from others. Its intent is to decrease isolation from others and increase knowledge about others. This, in turn, decreases prejudice toward and stereotypes of those initially perceived as different (Deiner, 1983, p. 14).

Racial and Cultural Awareness and Attitudes

- *When children bring up racial/cultural differences, discuss them honestly.* Help children recognize that there are differences among people but that these differences do not make them superior or inferior to others.

- *Help children develop pride through positive racial/cultural identity.* Children's self-concepts are tied to feeling good about all aspects of their beings. Acknowledgment and positive comments about the beauty of different skin, hair, and eye colours is important to developing feelings about self-worth.

- *Help children develop positive attitudes about other races.* Children need accurate information about other races. Modelling acceptance and appreciation of all races is an important factor.

- *Help children see skin colour variations as a continuum rather than as extremes.* Colour charts to which children can match their own skin colour can help them recognize that everyone is a shade of brown.

- *Help children learn that darker colours are not dirty.* A common misconception among children is that a child of a darker colour is dirty or unwashed. Be careful in your choice of words (e.g., do not say, "Wash that black dirt off your hands"). Doll-washing activities, for instance, bathing an obviously dirty white doll and a clean black doll, can help begin to dispel this notion.

- *Post photographs of children and their families.* This can help children begin to acquire the concept of racial constancy as teachers point out similarities (as well as differences) among family members. Help dispel misconceptions about racial constancy as these come up spontaneously. Be prepared for questions if a child in your class was adopted by parents of a different race.

- *Ensure that the environment contains materials representing many races and cultures.* Books, dolls, pictures, posters, dramatic play props, manipulatives, puzzles, and other materials should portray people of all colours and cultures in very positive ways. This is particularly important if your class is racially/culturally mixed. It is also important, however, to expose children in homogeneous classes to different racial and cultural groups through the environment.

- *Discuss incidents of racism and racial stereotypes with the children.* Model anti-racist behaviours by challenging incidents of racism or racial stereotyping. Help children find alternative words if they use racial slurs in arguments with one another.

- *Focus curriculum material about cultures on similarities among people rather than on differences.* Children can identify with shared experiences engaged in by people of other cultures. All people eat, wear clothes, need shelter, share special occasions, and value family activities. Focusing on "exotic" aspects of a culture only points out how different these are and robs them of the shared human factor.

- *Avoid a "tourist" approach to teaching about cultures.* Do not teach children about other cultures out of context. For instance, avoid using only the holidays celebrated by other cultures or a one-shot "cultures week" to focus on this topic (e.g., Monday—Mexico, Tuesday—Japan, Wednesday—Africa, Thursday—

Germany, and Friday—France). Also avoid using an ethnic cooking activity and a display of ceremonial clothing as the main components of these occasions. Such an approach is disconnected from everyday life, trivializes cultural diversity, and merely represents multiculturalism as a token gesture rather than as a genuine reflection of life around the world.

- *Make cultural diversity part of daily classroom activity.* Integrate aspects of the children's cultures into the everyday life of your class. Consider that the typical housekeeping centre in many early childhood classrooms conveys a single culture: a white, middle-class model. Many ways of life should be reflected throughout the classroom. For instance, you can include dolls of different races, post pictures showing different ethnic groups, introduce in the housekeeping cupboard food packages that reflect cultural preferences, or include home or cooking implements used by families of children from different cultures.

- *Convey the diversity of cultures through their common themes.* Read about different cultures to find out how various cultural groups meet their physical needs, engage in celebrations, and adapt to their environment. For instance, although Canadians and Americans carve pumpkins into jack-o'-lanterns at Halloween, other cultures also commonly carve fruits and vegetables on certain occasions.

- *Consider the complexity involved in celebrating holidays when their observance might be counter, even offensive, to some families' beliefs or cultures.* The celebration of Christmas could offend the non-Christian families with children in your program. Thanksgiving as a holiday might be an occasion of loss rather than celebration for Canadian Aboriginal families. The celebration of holidays should not be avoided but should be considered carefully, taking into account the attitudes, needs, and feelings of the children, families, and staff. Holiday celebrations should focus on respect and understanding of cultural observances.

- *Do not single out a child in a way that would make that child feel different.* Learning about a child's culture should be done in the context of learning about all of the children's cultures. Help such a child and the others in the class recognize that a particular culture is shared by many other people in the world.

- *Involve children's families.* Families are a prime source of information about cultural diversity. Invite parents to participate in the class and share ideas about how all of the children can learn more about their unique backgrounds. Particularly in child care centres, parents may not have the time to join the class, but they should always feel welcome.

Sources: Derman-Sparks (1989); Derman-Sparks & Ramsey (1993); Dimidjian (1989); Edwards (1986); Phenice & Hildebrand (1988); Ramsey (1982, 1987); "Suggestions for Developing Positive Racial Attitudes" (1980).

Planning   As we discussed in Chapter 2, simply including children with and without disabilities does not ensure interaction and acceptance. The benefits do not happen automatically. Inclusion does not mean simply enrolling children with special needs in a preschool or child care program. Current information and ongoing planning, preparation, modification, evaluation, and support inclusive of the team are necessary for success. Early childhood educators, because they know a great deal about children and how best to work with them, have many skills needed for working with all children, including those with special needs.

Team Effort   Teachers need to recognize their skills and the influence they have. Just as we attempt to empower children by involving them in the decision-making process and creating ownership—a vested personal interest—so the entire school needs to be involved in the process of inclusion. Making decisions together holds each team member responsible and accountable for the success of the process.

In working with children and their families, you will find that the greatest emotion is the fear of the unknown. Parents of typical children will worry about the effect inclusion will have on their child. Parents of the child with special needs will worry about their child being able to manage. Children will have questions. The new child will have all the anxieties of any new child plus the additional fears of being taken care of adequately. Teachers will worry whether they are prepared to handle the situation.

To reduce these fears, schools often arrange for the child to spend some time in the program before they are to start. The teacher can spend time in the child's current program as well. Each gets an opportunity to know and understand the other. Then a planning session with all parties helps address needs, answer questions, and delegate responsibilities and develops a network of support for parents. Following this, parents and teachers often state that their fears were unfounded or addressed and that they felt confident, prepared, and excited about having the child in the class.

Continuity and Communication   Continuity between teachers and programs can be a serious barrier to inclusion. Teams need to include the transitional partner from the very beginning in a gradual process of transfer in which trust, goals, needs, and information are clearly defined and considered in the context of the family. Ongoing communication and interaction is essential before, during, and after the process has been initiated. This is done with the family as the central focus. No decisions or discussions should occur without the parents present and actively involved.

As well, too much or too little information can be damaging by creating either unnecessary bias or work. Parental consent, presence, and review of information to be exchanged is critical before exchanging information.

Honesty   Children need accurate information, presented in a sensitive manner, about why a peer (or a teacher) looks, moves, sounds, or behaves differently from themselves. Children need the chance to express fears or misgivings and to ask questions. It is not unusual for children to be apprehensive about things that are unfamiliar and different or to worry that the disability could happen to them as well. Children's questions are honest and without value judgments. Offering a simple, honest explanation will answer the child's concern and respect the person's disability (Derman-Sparks, 1989).

When a child with cerebral palsy was enrolled at one school, one student called her a "baby." Initially, the teacher thought of an explanation: "Roberta cannot walk because there is something wrong with the muscles in her legs. She can get around on this scooter board by using her arm muscles. Would you like to ask Roberta if you can try her scooter board so you can see what it feels like?" However, the teacher concluded there were three difficulties with this answer:

1. The teacher felt she needed to explore with the child why she thought Roberta was a baby. Sometimes children's questions have nothing to do with the disability, yet we assume they do. Perhaps Roberta *was* acting like a baby as many children do when they play. Or perhaps it was because Roberta was so small. Asking for reasons for, and clarification of, a child's comments or queries helps us provide the child with the appropriate response. This is a springboard for discussion to clarify the child's misconceptions or fears.

2. The teacher realized she needed to word statements objectively and without value. "Something wrong" would devalue Roberta as a person. Children can identify and accept matter-of-fact statements, so "Roberta was born with cerebral palsy" would prove a better choice. It is simply a statement and does not imply good or bad or right or wrong.

3. The teacher realized Roberta's scooter board was very personal, and she did not want to put Roberta in the awkward position of choosing between a yes and no answer. She decided to provide some additional scooter boards in the class so that children could use them as they wished. This would create natural instances for discussion as the children compared their self-directed activities and experiences.

Sincerity, Credibility, and Trust   Think how often we say we are going to "help" children accept and include peers with disabilities. Relationships are two-way and both parties must do the accepting. People can't accept others simply because they are told to or because they live next door. Acceptance is based on credibility and trust, so children need opportunities to establish this. Having a disability is not a basis for friendship or permission to behave in a hurtful way. Children need the skills to go beyond the disability to determine the personality of the person who has it and pursue genuine friendships.

Moral Development

One primary aim of socialization is for children to learn and internalize standards of what is right and wrong, in other words, to develop a conscience. **Moral development** is a long-term process to which many factors contribute. Children are surrounded by a social climate in which the actions of others convey degrees of fairness, consistency, respect, and concern for others. Children's observations of how others behave, how they are treated, and their own cognitive maturation contribute to their emerging sense of morality.

Children adopt a more mature set of standards if they are raised in an atmosphere of clearly set and enforced standards, support and nurturance, open communication in which their viewpoint is valued, and other-oriented reasons for expected behaviour (Maccoby & Martin, 1983). There is also evidence that the onset of the distinction between right and wrong may be an inborn trait, emerging by children's second birthday (Kagan, 1987).

Another factor with which children have to contend, especially in a diverse society such as ours, is that moral standards vary in different cultures. Some universal **interpersonal moral rules**—ones prohibiting harm to others, murder, incest, and theft—are found across cultures. Other **conventional moral rules** are arrived at by general consensus and are more culture-specific, such as wearing clothes in public or chewing with your mouth closed. In addition, each society specifies some regulations that ensure orderly and safe functioning, for instance, stopping at red traffic lights. Implied in this differentiation is that some rules are more important than others. This is usually reflected in the classroom, where some transgressions, for instance, harm to others, are considered more serious than others (Edwards, 1986).

Much of today's theoretical writing about moral development derived from Piaget's work on children's developing understanding of rules (1932). From his observations of children at play, Piaget formulated a stage theory of moral development that moves from an early childhood view, in which rules are unchangeable and derived from a higher authority (e.g., God or parents), to the more mature perspective that rules are made by and can be changed through mutual consent of the players.

Lawrence Kohlberg (1969) took Piaget's stage theory and developed a more elaborate framework for considering moral development based on why people make certain choices rather than on what those choices are (Edwards, 1986).William Damon (1977, 1983) further delineated children's thought processes as they move from the very concrete to the wider range of self in relation to others. It is important for caregivers to help children attend to inner cues to label and interpret emotions as they begin to make decisions based as much on their "rightness" and internal reward as for their external rewards. Exhibit 9.6 outlines some helpful strategies for promoting moral development.

Development of Prosocial Behaviours

Peer interactions, friendship, gender role acquisition, racial and cultural awareness, and moral development are all part of an intertwined process that involves the emergence of a number of other related traits. Researchers have looked at how such social characteristics as nurturance, empathy, altruism, generosity, sharing, and tolerance evolve in young children. Children's social cognition will affect how

Exhibit 9.6: GUIDELINES FOR SUPPORTING SOCIAL DEVELOPMENT III

Promoting Moral Development

It is important to recognize children's abilities and limits in terms of moral reasoning and to guide them on the road to moral understanding. The following guidelines will help in this task.

- *Use other-oriented reasoning with children.* For example, rather than state, "Our rule is that we don't run inside," say, "We don't run inside because we could hurt other children by bumping into them."

- *Use stories to promote thinking and discussion about moral issues.* Favourite children's stories often pose interesting moral dilemmas that, with teacher guidance, encourage discussion. Krogh and Lamme (1985) recommended such books as *The Little Red Hen* by Paul Galdone (1973), *Angus and the Cat* by Marjorie Flack (1931), and *Peter's Chair* by Ezra Jack Keats (1967) for this purpose.

- *Provide ample time for child-selected play and materials that promote cooperation.* Dramatic play, for example, allows children to take the viewpoints of others; equipment that requires more than one child to operate it encourages cooperation.

- *Provide activities that help children become more aware of how the face conveys emotions.* Collages, masks, photos, acting out feelings, and "emotion puzzles" can strengthen this awareness.

- *Initiate thinking games that encourage children to seek multiple alternatives for social problems.* Puppets can enact a common social dilemma, for instance, one dealing with a refusal to share, and children can generate alternative solutions to the situation.

- *Plan thinking games that deal with moral intentionality.* Children over the age of 4 can begin to differentiate between intended naughtiness and an accident that happened while a child was trying to help. Discuss the context of consequences in each instance.

- *Use any teachable moments that arise to encourage moral development.* For example, if you accidentally spill a large jug of juice, discuss the concept of intent regarding accidentally or purposely spilling a small glass of juice.

- *Realize that not all cultures share the same values.* Communication with parents can help teachers find which values are important to families and reinforce these as appropriate with the children (Edwards, 1986; Krogh & Lamme, 1985).

---

they respond to others. With age comes greater comprehension, although a higher level of understanding will not ensure that children's responses will necessarily be appropriate. Other factors contributing to the emergence of prosocial behaviours include the modelling by the significant people in children's lives as well as the kinds of other-oriented values that have been stressed (Schickedanz, Hansen, & Forsyth, 1990).

PARTNERSHIPS
Parental Involvement in the Curriculum

As we've indicated many times, the curriculum should reflect the backgrounds, needs, and interests of the children and their families. One excellent resource, as you plan the curriculum for your group of children, is their parents. Frequent parent–teacher communication and an open-door policy that conveys the school's emphasis on the importance of the family can encourage parents to be part of the early childhood program. As parents investigate your school in order to decide whether to enrol their child, your open-door policy regarding family should be explained and discussed. As the central focus toward ensuring quality, parent involvement in the curriculum can take many forms. Helping parents feel welcome and genuinely soliciting their ongoing input benefits both parties. Each feels reciprocally valued and respected as an integral component in the overall well-being of the child.

Most parents are interested in what their children do each day. The overall curriculum, the units, and the daily lesson plans should be available for the parents' review and input. A Parents' Night should be planned early in the year to discuss plans and responsibilities. A school newsletter might be the place to share information about the overall curriculum and philosophy throughout the year. Lesson and unit plans, as well as progress reports of ongoing projects, can be posted in a prominent place, for instance, just outside the classroom door or on a parent bulletin board, where parents can look at the activities, objectives, and outcomes. The children can be videotaped and the video presented on a Parents' Night, or photos of the children in action can be sent home. Parents appreciate knowing what activities their children engaged in during their day at school, something that is often a topic of conversation between parent and child on the way home from school. Anything that highlights their child and the positive experiences of his or her day helps parents to relax and share in the successes of the program and child.

Parents can also be called on to participate in the curriculum. There are many areas in which their expertise and input can greatly enhance the program. Parents can provide information about special family, cultural, religious, or ethnic customs, celebrations, foods, or dress. They can visit the classroom to share occupational information or special skills. A parent who makes pottery, weaves baskets, plays an instrument, or knows origami will contribute a fascinating element to the classroom. Knowing parents' interests is as important as knowing their children's. Whether parents prefer to work behind the scenes or in the class, asking for, supporting, and honouring parents' suggestions and encouraging their participation will prove a strengthening factor in the overall integrity of the curriculum.

An early childhood program in which adults model, emphasize, and value prosocial behaviours will facilitate development of such traits in children. Alice Honig (1988a), who considers a prosocial curriculum based on caring and kindness as a crucial goal of early childhood programs, has highlighted the importance of such behaviours. Previous sections of this chapter presented activities and strategies that can encourage developmentally appropriate and positive social attitudes and behaviours. In the context of a supportive atmosphere, understanding of child development, concern for children's needs, respect for their opinions, encouragement of their autonomy, support for their individuality, and provision of a stimulating program and environment, such activities will help promote positive socialization.

Parents and teachers must, of course, work together toward creating such an atmosphere and must communicate regularly to build a bridge between home and school. When children see parents working together in a positive, prosocial manner, they trust that their own strengths and needs will be cared for. Partnerships suggests ways parents can foster development by being involved in the curriculum.

Key Terms

acquisition	interpersonal moral rules
aesthetics	invented spelling
application	kinesthetic sense
audience awareness	manipulatives
bilingualism	mock writing
bimanual control	modes
classification	moral development
cognition	morphology
comprehension	multilingualism
conventional moral rules	number concepts
convergent thinking	open-ended materials
divergent thinking	pragmatics
eye–hand coordination	processing
fine motor development	prosocial behaviours
flexibility	self-correcting
fluency	semantics
grammar and syntax	sensitivity
gross motor development	sensory-perceptual development
holding grips	seriation

skills
socialization
spatial concepts
story schema
strategies

temporal concepts
theories of mind
vocabulary
whole language approach

Key Points

- Creativity includes originality, imagination, divergent thinking, and the ability to create something novel in meaningful ways when combined with flexibility, investigation, and exploration.

- Creativity can be diminished by socializing factors and thoughtless actions by adults.

- Television and prerecorded videotapes can enhance creativity when used properly.

- Vigourous daily activities that are fun and enjoyable help establish a foundation for life-long health habits and attitudes.

- Children's thinking is ongoing and involves a constant taking in, sifting, connecting, and storing of experiences, concepts, and information.

- Language involves vocabulary, semantics, morphology, grammar and syntax, and pragmatics, whereas communication involves body language, sounds, and creative media such as art and dance.

- Conversation with and reading to children aid them in acquiring the basic rules of literacy in the context of the whole language approach.

- Socialization is a crucial process early in life, created by peer interaction, friendships, and racial and cultural attitudes, for developing the beginnings of a conscience in children.

- Due to the recent inclusion in early childhood programs of children with special needs, it is essential to help children develop sensitivity to and acceptance of others unlike themselves.

Chapter 10

Helping Children
Cope with Stress

Stress is inevitably a part of life. Hans Selye (1980), the father of stress research, considered stress to be any demand on our ability to adapt. Stress causes disequilibrium to which we have to make some kind of adjustment (Doyle, Gold, & Moskowitz, 1984). Sometimes stress leads to positive changes, but too much stress can have a negative impact on a person's well-being. Undoubtedly, you have experienced some stress in your life and can think of positive and negative effects of stress on your physical and/or mental health.

A variety of internal and external causes of stress are an inevitable part of life for young children as well. As early childhood educators, we are reminded all too often of the devastating effects of stress on ourselves through burnout syndrome. However, we often don't think of children as having any stress in their lives. This is because we tend to define stress as it relates to our adult lives—finances, jobs,

family matters. But children have their own sources of stress, which can affect them greatly. Today's demands place greater responsibility and expectations on children. Knowing this, we must identify causes of stress, symptoms of stress, and methods for relieving and coping with stress as it relates to children. In this chapter, we will examine stress in young children and our role in its identification and alleviation.

Defining Stress and Coping

Stress has proved a difficult term to define, surrounded by "conceptual cloudiness" (Garmezy, 1984, p. 44), because researchers who study stress use the word in different ways. A broad definition, however, would include an environmental change that triggers the stress and some kind of resulting emotional tension in the individual that interferes with normal functioning (Garmezy, 1984). Yet stress is not in itself a negative force and, in fact, often provides the challenge and motivation to improve, grow, and mature. In her excellent two-part research review of stress and coping in children, Alice Honig (1986a, 1986b) pointed out that:

> Stress continues to mark the achievement of developmental milestones. How often an infant, on the verge of toddling, stumbles, lurches, falls, crashes, and recommences bravely. Not all stresses are harmful. The struggle to learn to walk is a good example of how some stresses can be perceived as challenges that impel a child to strive toward more mature forms of behaviour. (1986a, p. 51)

Other stressful experiences can be more negative, however, requiring the child to deal with an emotional or physical situation that is unsettling, frustrating, painful, or harmful. More often than not, the child is helpless and unable to cope with this kind of stress (Arent, 1984). It appears to many professionals that the number and severity of childhood stresses have greatly increased over the past two decades. To add to this concern about increased stresses, "people who work with children report an uneasy sense that youngsters today have fewer sources of adult support, affirmation, and love than in the recent past" (Brenner, 1984, p. 1).

From our own experience, we are aware that stress causes emotional reactions, such as anxiety, fear, guilt, anger, and frustration in some cases or joy, euphoria, and happiness in other instances. Behind these emotional responses are physiological,

neurochemical reactions involving many bodily changes, such as in hormones, heart rate, blood flow, skin, and muscles (Ciaranello, 1983). It is important to recognize that stress is as much a physical as an emotional phenomenon because children often respond to stress in physical ways. The complexity of responses to stress has made its study a challenge to researchers and those who work with young children.

In response to stress, we use different **coping strategies** to ease the tension. Coping always involves mental and/or physical action and can take such forms as denial, regression, withdrawal, impulsive acting out, or suppression, as well as humour (Brenner, 1984) and creative problem solving. Coping reactions vary according to the stressful situation, and they depend on such inborn factors as temperament, the age and cognitive functioning of the child, and a variety of learned responses and social factors (Allen, 1988; Brenner, 1984). Children also begin to develop certain patterns of coping with specific stressors through **habituation** (i.e., becoming accustomed to them) and adaptation (Brenner, 1984). Some coping strategies are more effective and more socially acceptable than others. When a child uses aggression as a coping reaction to rejection by peers, we view such behaviour as less acceptable than if the child uses a problem-solving approach. Later in this chapter, we will discuss in more detail how to help children cope with stress.

Stages of Stress

Alice Honig (1986a) has identified four stages of response to stress:

1. The *stage of alarm* involves involuntary physical changes. For example, adrenaline may be released into the bloodstream or acid may be produced by the stomach. If stress persists, such responses can result in psychosomatic illness (not an imaginary illness but a case of the mind and body working together to produce a physical problem).

2. The *stage of appraisal* is concerned with the cognitive process of evaluating and giving personal meaning to the stressful situation. The child's age and psychological makeup will affect this process.

3. The *stage of searching for a coping strategy* can include both adaptive and maladaptive responses. A child may, for instance, cry, throw a tantrum, ignore the situation, find a compromise, or find a substitute.

4. In the *stage of implementing coping responses,* children will react in different ways depending on their personal experiences and resources. A child responding defensively may distort, deny, or respond with rigid and compulsive behaviours. Responding through **externalization** means tending to blame others rather than looking at using one's own resources in coping. On the other hand, a child who uses **internalization** is more likely to

accept responsibility for dealing with the stressor. With either internalization or externalization, it is not blame for the cause of the stress but the responsibility for dealing with it that is at issue.

Sources of Stress in Children's Lives

Today's children grow up in a complex world that contains a host of potential and actual stressors. A helpful framework for viewing sources of tension for children is the ecological model discussed in Chapter 3 developed by such researchers as

Urie Bronfenbrenner (1979). Stress sources, as well as potential moderating influences within the social system, can come from any of the interacting and overlapping systems (Doyle, Gold, & Moskowitz, 1984). These systems can include the family (the microsystem); its interactions (the mesosystem); the family's social network, friends, school, and extended family (the exosystem); and the larger society, with its values and beliefs (the macrosystem).

Because stress is an individual's unique reaction to a specific event or circumstance, there is an infinite variety of possible stressors. Young children's stressors most often have their roots in the microsystem, the mesosystem, and, to some extent, the exosystem; however, the larger macrosystem also affects young children since social forces and policies have an impact on their families. For purposes of discussion, we will focus on some common contemporary sources of stress, many of which have received the attention of researchers and theorists.

Family Stressors

Children's security is anchored in their families. Ideally, this security is created by a caring family that provides a protected, predictable, consistent environment in which challenges and new experiences occur as the child is able to handle them successfully. But families do not have such control over the environment and increasingly are caught up as victims of forces that produce enormous stress. Today's families face innumerable struggles—family violence, hostile divorces, custody battles, poverty, homelessness, unemployment, hunger, slum environments, neighbourhood gang wars, AIDS, and drug and alcohol abuse—that can shatter their control and sense of security.

Divorce

One of the most common stressors that today's children face is divorce. It is estimated that 40 to 50 percent of the children growing up in this decade will

experience their parents' divorce, live in a single-parent family for a period of time, and probably experience their parents' remarriage (Hetherington, Stanley-Hagan, & Anderson, 1989). Although divorce is stressful for everyone involved, it is probably most difficult for children, particularly young ones (Medeiros, Porter, & Welch, 1983).

Preschoolers in the midst of a divorce see what is happening from an egocentric viewpoint. They tend to attribute the departure of one parent to their own "bad" behaviour, in essence a punishment for something they did wrong (Brenner, 1984). Accompanying this anxiety is the worry that the other parent may also abandon them (Wallerstein, Corbin, & Lewis, 1988), a situation stirringly depicted in the 1979 film *Kramer vs. Kramer*. Wallerstein (1983) found that after a divorce, preschoolers are likely to experience behavioural difficulties, such as sleep disturbances, irritability, increased sensitivity, and heightened aggression.

Divorce is usually accompanied by a range of other occurrences that can have a profound effect on young children. Before the divorce, there is often parental anger, discord, and open fighting, which can be very frightening to children. After the divorce, about 90 percent of children end up living with the custodial mother (Hetherington, Stanley-Hagan, & Anderson, 1989). Not only do the children experience a shift from a two-parent to a single-parent arrangement, but often they also shift to a lower income bracket, have fewer resources, live in less expensive housing or with a transitional family (e.g., grandparents or mother's new friend), live with a parent who is stressed in new ways, and perhaps enter or spend more hours in child care (Hilton, Essa, & Murray, 1991). All these changes, on top of what amounts to the loss of one parent, can be very traumatic.

Poverty, Homelessness, and Depression

Another area of stress, on which increasing attention has been focused recently, is the plight of children whose families lack adequate resources to meet basic needs. In Canada, one of five children live in poverty. Chronic poverty can interfere intrusively with effective parenting and may lead to insecure mother–child attachment (Honig, 1986a).

The number of homeless families with children in Canada is increasing, as is the use of food banks. Such children tend to suffer health and emotional problems, developmental delays, nutritional deficits, and irregular school attendance. The capacity for effective parent–child bonding is affected by the lack of privacy experienced by homeless families. Homeless children "are robbed of the most basic and essential element of childhood—reliable, predictable, safe routines" (Boxhill, 1989, p. 1). A small but growing number of public and non-profit organizations are starting to provide services, including child care, to homeless families and children.

In 1993, a series of teenage suicides, coupled with rampant substance abuse, in relocated Inuit communities like Davis Inlet, received a great deal of media attention—but perhaps not enough professional and government attention. Many of the adolescents in these communities are depressed and have a sense of hopelessness since their future is not promising. Undoubtedly, the younger children in these communities are affected by the marked stress that their elders are experiencing with these events.

Fast-Paced Family Life

Some children, who at first glance might appear to be privileged, actually experience a great deal of stress. Many dual-income professional families, in which both parents work 60 or more hours a week to keep up with their careers, produce a different kind of stress for themselves and their children. Parents are frequently rushed and beset by the constant need to make quick and important decisions. Children are so "scheduled" that there is little down time for spontaneity, creativity, play, or reflection.

When looking at the child from a high-powered family, surrounded by abundant material possessions, keep in mind that this child might be involved in a fast-paced and stressful lifestyle, which can take its toll.

Additional Stressors

We can easily recognize that experiences such as divorce, poverty, homelessness, and hopelessness can be grave sources of stress for young children. Children may also experience stress from family occurrences that to adults may not appear on the surface to be as stressful. For some children, for instance, the birth of a new sibling triggers regression to earlier behaviours, increased crying, and sleep problems (Honig, 1986a). Other stressors can include any event that causes a change, such as the death of a pet, relatives who are visiting, or a parent's prolonged business trip. Partnerships discusses helping families cope with stress.

Abuse, Neglect, and Violence in Children's Lives

Stress is certainly an issue for children who are victims of abuse or neglect, although the more pervasive danger is that serious harm can befall them. Because

PARTNERSHIPS
Helping Families Cope with Stress

A stressed child usually comes from a stressed family. Although all families experience stress, the circumstances and their available resources for coping with stress will differ. Early childhood programs can function as important family support systems for parents of young children, although traditionally they have focused more on the child than on the family system (Powell, 1987b). Certainly from an ecological perspective, the child cannot be separated from the family (Weiss, 1987); thus, a good early childhood program includes a family support component.

As an early childhood educator, you can help families cope with life stressors, whether through your support, modelling, education, or referrals. Gestwicki, in her book *Home, School, and Community Relations* (1987), provides some helpful guidelines for teachers interacting and working with stressed parents:

- *Reassure parents.* Through empathy and caring, teachers can encourage parents and reassure them about such things as the amount of time needed to readjust after a divorce or the grief process. Suggesting books for both children and adults can also provide reassurance.

- *Know about available community resources.* Teachers' expertise is in working with children rather than in professional counselling. Thus, their role with highly stressed parents is to provide emotional support, information, and a listening ear. Beyond that, they should refer parents to appropriate community agencies. It is important that early childhood teachers be aware of services available in their own areas. Different communities have different services, for instance, family and children's services or United Way agencies. There are also support groups such as Parents without Partners, organizations for parents who have abused their children, and associations for parents of children with disabilities. The yellow pages of the telephone directory often have appropriate listings under the heading "Social Services."

- *Be aware of legal agreements.* It is important to know both legal and informal agreements between parents, particularly when custody battles are involved. A written statement from every family listing authorized persons who can pick up the child should be on file.

- *Keep requests light.* It is important to be sensitive to the stress level of parents and not to ask an overwhelmed, single parent to bake two-dozen cookies for tomorrow's snack.

- *Be aware of your own attitudes and feelings.* It is sometimes easy to lay blame, be judgmental, or get angry at parents, especially when you perceive them as inadequate. Teachers should examine their own attitudes and work especially hard to get to know the parents and their special circumstances so that true empathy can develop.

In addition, teachers can assist parents by modelling positive guidance techniques, respect for children's ideas, and enforcement of reasonable limits. For some parents, it may be necessary to accompany modelling with verbal explanations and a discussion of alternatives (*Day Care, Families, and Stress,* 1985).

It is important to differentiate between a family that is coping adequately and continuing to carry out its family functions in the face of stress and a family that is in trouble and may require intervention. Some signs of a parent who may be at the breaking point include the following:

- *Disorganized behaviour*—Parents frequently forget vital things, for instance, the child's jacket on subzero days or the child's lunch.

- *Frustration*—Parents have perpetually worried expressions, are unduly impatient with a slow child, threaten punishment, express lack of confidence in their parenting ability, or appear confused about how to handle the child.

- *Inability to accept help*—Parents get defensive and become verbally aggressive or walk away from a teacher who tries to discuss the child, perhaps in response to their own sense of guilt, failure, or inadequacy.

- *More concern for themselves than for their child*—Parents seem more focused on their own problems and bring them up any time the teacher tries to talk about the child. (*Day Care, Families, and Stress,* 1985)

If you suspect that a parent is under so much stress that she or he is temporarily unable to cope, discuss your concerns with other teachers who interact with the parent, as well as with the director. A poorly functioning parent puts the child at risk. Your school's decision may be to contact a social service agency, which, in turn, may recommend that the child be temporarily removed from the home, that parental counselling be required, or that some other form of support be provided for the parent.

---

young children are inexperienced and because they depend on adults to meet their needs, they are particularly vulnerable to abuse.

Most often, though certainly not always, **child abuse and neglect** occur within the family. Garbarino (1990) identified three basic causes of child abuse:

1. Our culture supports domestic violence by permitting a range of behaviours perpetrated by adults against children.
2. We have strong ideas about family privacy which reduce community responsibility for children, so that problems are viewed as someone else's rather than everyone's.
3. Family stresses stemming from social and economic factors often lead to parental feelings of inadequacy and frustration, which can explode into abuse against children.

Ray Helfer, one of the world's leading authorities on the subject, views child abuse and neglect as disrupters in the normal developmental process of children, with long-term repercussions. During childhood, youngsters begin to formulate and practise many skills that are precursors to important adult skills; opportunities for such practice occur naturally, as part of normal development. Parents and other adults who interact with the child have a great impact on this process. When the normal course of development is disrupted through what Helfer terms "the world of abnormal rearing" (W.A.R.), serious developmental deficiencies occur. "Adults who are victims of the W.A.R. truly have 'missed out on childhood,' that is, missed learning many of those basic skills necessary to interact with others" (Helfer, 1987, p. 68).

Meddin and Rosen (1986) defined child abuse and/or neglect as "any action or inaction that results in the harm or potential risk of harm to a child" (p. 26), including the following:

- *Physical abuse* is manifest in such signs as cuts, welts, bruises, and burns.
- *Sexual abuse* includes molestation, exploitation, and intercourse.
- *Physical neglect* involves such signs as medical or educational neglect and inadequate food, clothing, shelter, or supervision.
- *Emotional abuse* occurs through any action that may significantly harm the child's intellectual, emotional, or social functioning or development.
- *Emotional neglect* is considered inaction by the adult to meet the child's needs for nurture and support.

We typically think of abuse, neglect, and violence as being inflicted directly on the child. However, we must remember that children's witnessing of abusive and violent acts on other family members can be just as stressful and debilitating. Physical marks or unusual behaviour may tell you that a child has been or is at risk of being abused or neglected, although it is not always easy to read such signs. For instance, cigarette burns on a child's body are more recognizable as abuse than a child's inability to sit for any length of time because of sexual molestation (Meddin & Rosen, 1986). Emotional abuse and neglect are particularly difficult to read because the behavioural symptoms could be the result of any number of causes. Exhibit 10.1 lists some physical signs of child abuse, while Exhibit 10.2 outlines some behavioural indicators of physical and emotional abuse that can help identify children who are being victimized. It is your skill as a careful observer, combined with your knowledge of child development, that can best provide clues about abnormal or unusual evidence indicating possible abuse or neglect (Meddin & Rosen, 1986).

Another source of information about whether a child has been or is at risk of being abused or neglected is the cues you might pick up from the child's parents. As you interact with parents informally, you might note whether parents convey unrealistic expectations for the child, seem to rely on the child to meet their own social or emotional needs, lack basic knowledge and skills related to child rearing, or show signs of substance abuse (Meddin & Rosen, 1986). Chronic family problems and frustrations stemming from unemployment, illness, and poverty often also result in child abuse and neglect. The majority of parents who abuse or neglect their children can be helped through intervention (Kempe & Kempe, 1978).

It is important to stress that it is your ethical as well as legal responsibility as a professional to report suspected child abuse or neglect to an appropriate children's aid society or agency. Every province and territory has regulations about professionals reporting suspected cases, and specific laws protect them from any liability for that report. A number of professional associations in different parts of the country also have guidelines for teachers to follow (e.g., provincial associations in British Columbia, Alberta, and Ontario have guidelines) that you may wish to consult.

It is not easy to make the decision to report a family for suspected child abuse or neglect. You may be aware of stress afflicting the family and be reluctant to add

Exhibit 10.1: Physical Signs of Child Abuse and Neglect

- The child has bruises or wounds in various stages of healing, indicating repeated injuries.
- Multiple injuries are evident on two or more planes of the body, for instance, a head injury and bruises on the ribs, which are not likely to have happened in a single fall.
- Injuries are reported to be caused by falling but do not include the hands, knees, or forehead, the areas most likely to be hurt when a child attempts to break a fall.
- The child has oval burns left by a cigarette, shows doughnut-shaped or stocking-mark signs of being immersed in a hot substance, or has identifiable burn imprints of such items as an electric stove burner.
- A child shows discomfort when sitting, which could be caused by sexual abuse.
- A child has sexual knowledge too sophisticated for the child's age, evident in conversations or through inappropriate play, which may indicate a victim of sexual abuse.
- A child is dressed inappropriately for the weather, for instance, wears sandals or no coat on a snowy day, which could be reason to suspect neglect.
- A child steals food because he or she does not get enough to eat at home, which may be another sign of neglect.

Source: Adapted from N.J. Meddin and A.L. Rosen (1986), Child abuse and neglect: Prevention and reporting, in *Young Children, 41*(4), 28.

EXHIBIT 10.2: BEHAVIOUR PATTERNS OF ABUSED CHILDREN YOUNGER THAN AGE 5

Physically Abused Children

Expressiveness and apparent sense of self

- displays bland affect, no tears, no laughter
- shows no curiosity/exploration
- is unable to play; has no sense of joy
- shows no affect when attacking another child
- is afraid of dark, being hurt, being alone
- is reluctant to try messy activities
- is aggressive, hyperactive, or withdrawn

Response to frustration or adversity

- withdraws or has tantrums

Language and learning

- displays lack of speech or delayed language development
- has delayed motor development
- has short attention span

Relationships with peers

- grabs objects from others without trying to retain them
- displays inept social skills
- avoids or is aggressive toward peers
- can't wait or take turns

Relationships with parents

- shows no expectation of being comforted; shows no distress at separation
- is alert to danger
- is solicitous of parents' needs
- is constantly aware of parents' reactions
- may defy parents' commands
- is difficult to toilet train

Relationships with other adults

- relates indiscriminately to adults in charming and agreeable ways; seeks affection from any adult
- avoids being touched
- responds negatively to praise
- always seems to want/need more objects, attention, and so forth

Emotionally Abused Children

Expressiveness and apparent sense of self

- comforts self through rocking and sucking

- does not play
- has difficulty sleeping
- is passive and compliant or aggressive and defiant
- rarely smiles

Language and learning

- has speech disorders or delayed language development

Relationships with peers

- has inept social skills

Relationships with parents

- is affectless: is detached from parents or solicitous of them
- is fussy, unresponsive, irritable
- is watchful yet avoids eye contact

Relationships with other adults

- relates indiscriminately to adults in agreeable ways
- seeks attention and always seems to want/need more

Source: Adapted from A. Brenner (1984), *Helping children cope with stress* (Lexington, MA: Lexington Books, pp. 98–99, 101).

to it through your report. The evidence of abuse may not be clear-cut, or the child may tell you that he or she fell rather than that he or she was hit. But it is your responsibility as an early childhood educator and caregiver to act on your concern and speak for and protect young children.

Self-Protection Program

With increased social awareness and concern about child sexual abuse has come a host of programs aimed at teaching children self-protection techniques. Specially designed programs are usually presented to preschool groups by volunteer, law enforcement, or social agencies. They address such topics as the difference between "good" and "bad" touching and the child's right to say no, and they present some specific protective techniques, including running away from a potential assailant and rudimentary karate moves.

Although such programs are well intentioned, their effectiveness has been questioned. In fact, a critical review of research evaluating child sexual-abuse prevention programs found little evidence that such programs for preschoolers actually meet their goals (Reppucci & Haugaard, 1989). These authors raised serious questions about the developmental readiness of young children for meaningful understanding of the concepts these programs teach. It is a fundamentally important point that adults, not children, are responsible for providing protection against abuse (Furman, 1987; Jordan, 1993). Young children are too inexperienced to be given such a serious responsibility. We need to protect them through our consistent and constant supervision, modelling of appropriate interaction with strangers, and teaching respect and ownership of the body through nurturing care.

Community Violence

Increasingly, focus has been placed on children who grow up in violence-riddled inner cities, which have been likened to "war zones" (Garbarino, Dubrow,

Kostelny, & Pardo, 1992). Every day young children witness or fall victim to violent acts, assaults, and death in their communities. Often an early childhood program is the only safe haven in young children's lives; thus, early childhood educators have taken the plight of children from violent neighbourhoods seriously.

In 1993, NAEYC, concerned about the escalation of community violence to which increasing numbers of young children are subjected, adopted a Position Statement on Violence in the Lives of Children (1993). This statement articulated two goals. The first goal is to decrease violence to children's lives through advocacy; the second is to enhance educators' ability to help children and families cope with violence through improved professional practice in early childhood programs.

Health Stressors

Another source of childhood stress derives from health-related problems. Children suffering from chronic asthma, facing a tonsillectomy, undergoing chemotherapy for cancer, or enduring the aftermath of a serious automobile accident experience stress. This stress is a combination of factors surrounding the physical problem— pain and discomfort—as well as related elements such as fear of the unknown, limited understanding of what is happening, a strange environment populated by strangers, terrifying medical terms, and, perhaps most frightening, fear of being abandoned by the parents (Medeiros, Porter, & Welch, 1983). This last factor causes particular distress for young preschoolers facing hospitalization because attachment and separation are important issues at this age. In addition, children who are seriously ill or face surgery are aware of their parents' anxiety, and this adds further to their own stress (Rutter, 1983).

A parent's serious health problem, whether physical or mental, is also a source of stress for children. If a parent is hospitalized, the child's familiar routine is disrupted and the remaining parent or another adult fulfils some of the absent parent's functions. These changes produce stress, particularly if a new caretaker is involved. During the parent's convalescence, the child may also have to adapt to changes in the ill parent's personality, energy level, and preoccupation with health.

Death

Inevitably, as a teacher of young children, you will find a need to discuss and explain death, perhaps because the classroom parakeet was lying stiffly on the floor of the birdcage when the children arrived in the morning or because one of the children's relatives has died. Most young children encounter death, whether it is the death of a grandparent, friend, sibling, parent, family or classroom pet, or dead worm found in the backyard.

Preschoolers' Understanding of Death

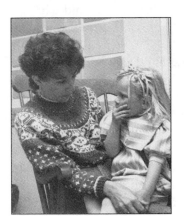

Young children's understanding of death is a function of their cognitive development. Their "conceptualization of death … is marked by a general immaturity, though death is by no means foreign to children of this age" (Smilansky, 1987, p. 43). Children in the preoperational stage of cognitive development do not yet have the mental ability to grasp fully the concepts involved in understanding death. This can lead to misconceptions based on the child's "magical or other pre-logical explanation" (Wass, 1984, p. 12) when they come face to face with death. Some preschoolers' reactions cited by Wass (1984) include:

- "My grandfather died by eating too much dinner."
- "If people don't go for a walk, they die."
- "Boys don't die unless they get run over. If they go to a hospital, I think they come out living" (from Schilder & Wechsler, 1934, and Anthony, 1972).

Smilansky (1987) described five concepts involved in preschoolers' misunderstanding or partial understanding of death:

1. *Irreversibility,* an understanding that the dead cannot return to life, whether they have been buried or not, is not yet understood by many young children.

2. *Finality,* the fact that life processes end with death, is easier for young children to grasp in terms of tangible processes such as sight or hearing ("When you're dead, you can't hear any more") but less easy to grasp in terms of more complex processes such as sensation, thought, and consciousness.

3. *Causality of death,* such as illness or accident, is only partially understood by preschoolers, who may also think that people can die from a headache or sadness.

4. *Old age,* the fact that all people grow old, and the connection of aging to death, is difficult for young children to grasp because of their egocentric focus.

5. *Inevitability of death* is another difficult concept because young children perceive that if death results from an illness or accident, all they have to do is avoid accidents and take care of themselves not to die.

Bereavement

Young children's limited understanding of death does not mean that they do not experience genuine grief at the loss of someone who was important in their lives. **Bereavement** is a natural process, an essential reaction to loss, which needs to be worked out and supported (Ketchel, 1986). Children's reactions to death vary. Although some children show no overt signs of mourning or may even seem indifferent to the death, others may react with anger, tantrums, and destructive rages. Children, like adults, pass through stages of mourning that include denial, anger, bargaining, depression, and, finally, acceptance (Kubler-Ross, 1969).

It is important that the adults in children's lives provide strong support and help in the mourning process. The early childhood teacher can offer such support by being willing to discuss the death, recognize and accept the child's feelings, and answer questions (Furman, 1982). This is particularly crucial for a child who has lost a parent, "the worst bereavement," because no other loss or separation is like it (Furman, 1982, p. 239).

A special example of death occurs when a young child in your class battles cancer unsuccessfully or is killed in an accident. Almost a year after the death of 5-year-old Robbie, one of the children in the University of Oklahoma centre, there was still considerable discussion and expressions of grief by peers in his class. During his 10 months of illness, chemotherapy, and hospitalizations, Robbie continued to see his friends and visited his class a few times. When Robbie died, the grief process involved the children, their parents, and the centre staff. Frequent discussions, prompted by questions or angry outbursts, continued. Some of the older children expressed anger that they had lost a good friend whom they would never see again, while the younger children sought frequent affirmation of the finality of Robbie's death (e.g., "Robbie won't be back because he is dead, right?"). Underlying many of the children's comments was a sense of their own vulnerability, the fear that they, too, might die. The staff and some of the parents also engaged in discussions, both to deal with their own fears and grief and to consider how best to help the children. Robbie's death was a painful experience but also one that brought growth and understanding for everyone involved.

Children's Fears

Lisl's mother had gone to the apartment next door when the thunderstorm broke. Lisl was 5 years old, and the remembered boom of that thunderclap, while she was all alone, continued to frighten her for many years. Even long after Lisl learned about the physical workings of storms, thunder had the power to cause stress, accelerate her heartbeat, and make her mouth feel dry.

This early experience is not uncommon, and you can undoubtedly recall some generalized feeling of unease or a precise incident that caused a specific fear for you. Everyone experiences fear at some time because "fear is a normal emotional response to a perceived threat that may be real or imagined" (Sarafino,

1986, p. 15). Fear is an important self-protective response because it alerts us to danger. Children facing an unknown situation for the first time, for example, a visit to the dentist, will experience natural apprehension. In other instances, a fear can turn into a **phobia**, which is intense and irrational and stems directly from a specific event such as the thunderstorm just mentioned. A more generalized, vague feeling of uneasiness that cannot be traced to any specific source is labelled **anxiety**, and it is the most difficult form of fear to deal with (Sarafino, 1986). Overcoming phobias and anxieties often requires professional help, although teachers can support children as they struggle to understand the source of the fears and their feelings.

Preschool-aged children's cognitive characteristics influence the types of fears they experience. For example:

- Young children often confuse reality, dreams, and fantasy.
- Preschoolers often attribute human or lifelike qualities to inanimate objects.
- Concepts of size and relationship are just developing during the preschool years.
- The relationship between cause and effect is not yet well understood at this age.
- Young children are often helpless and not in control of what is happening around them.

These characteristics, reflecting incomplete or inaccurate understanding, combine to contribute to children's fears (Myers-Walls & Fry-Miller, 1984).

It is not always easy to recognize fearfulness in young children. Hyson (1986) gave three examples of children who are afraid of dogs: one child runs away from an approaching dog, another stands frozen in panic, a third constantly asks questions about and looks for dogs. The source of these three children's fear is the same, but their different reactions do not make it equally easy to recognize their fear. The third child's response, for instance, might be mistaken for interest or fascination rather than fear.

Although all people develop fears based on their unique experiences, some common fears of preschoolers can be identified. Pervasive fears for young children include abandonment and the unknown, apprehensions that commonly emerge when children deal with divorce, hospitalization, and death. Other frequent sources of fears are animals, the dark, doctors, heights, school, monsters,

YOUNG CHILDREN AND WAR

Canada's involvement in peacekeeping initiatives in war-torn countries like Bosnia and Somalia are very visible to children. In early 1991, when the United States engaged in war against Iraq, there was unprecedented media coverage of every aspect of this event. Adults in countries around the world were kept abreast of the latest developments almost as soon as they happened. Children also were exposed to this news. Much of the news conveyed anxiety, uncertainty, and unpredictability. Even very young children, not surprisingly, were affected by these feelings.

The United States' media decided to respond to children's fears about war, and Canadian children benefited from this media coverage just as they had been alarmed by the other aspects of the media stories. Major television networks broadcast prime-time programs aimed at providing understandable, factual answers to children's questions and apprehensions. Articles and features appeared in a variety of national and local newspapers, magazines, and journals. The magazine *Young Children* provided an article, co-authored by Fred Rogers (from *Mister Rogers' Neighborhood*), on helping adults deal with children's concerns about war. While this wide-scale media focus on children and war was taking place, early childhood teachers dealt with issues of war and peace in their classrooms. We will consider one teacher's experiences with children's reactions.

During a group discussion soon after the war began, one child mentioned that she was afraid of the dark. The mention of a specific fear opened the door to further discussion. Mike said, "I'm afraid of bombs. What if one falls on my house?" Others also chimed in. They expressed various concerns on the same theme: What if a bomb hurts me? My family? My dog? The teacher allowed the children to share their fears, accepting their emotions as valid and genuine. They talked about the limited range that missiles could fly.

Discussion on the war continued in this class during the entire time of extensive media coverage. The children were particularly interested in labelling a "good team" and a "bad team." Words such as kill and hate, rarely heard in this class before, crept into the vocabulary. Music activities in which the children made up new verses to familiar songs began to take on a violent, war-related tone. School-aged children's artwork became very focused on war themes. Flags, missiles, bombs, and guns became prominent features. At the writing table, children wrote stories and made posters about the war. While the children's fears continued to surface in group discussions, a less self-focused concern also began to emerge. Many of the children expressed their wish that no one would be hurt.

Once the war ended and the television coverage stopped, the children's interest quickly disappeared. In retrospect, several important guidelines helped many parents and teachers help their young children cope with the war. These included the following practical suggestions made by Rogers and Sharapan (1991) in the previously cited article in *Young Children*.

- Children need reassurance that adults will take care of them and ensure their safety. Such a message can be conveyed through verbal assurances as well as in non-verbal ways.

- An open environment allows children to share their concerns and anxieties without fear of being ridiculed or ignored.

- Adults who listen with empathy and understanding make it safe for children to discuss their feelings.

- An understanding of children's egocentric thinking helps adults accept children's fears. It is developmentally consistent that preschoolers will worry about a bomb hurting them or their families, even though the war is many thousands of miles away.

- Children's war play, like all play, may be one way that children can work through their concerns. However, the teacher, will want to ensure, through judicious supervision, that such play does not become overly scary.

Additional resources on this topic include *Who's Calling the Shots? How to Respond Effectively to Children's Fascination with War Play and War Toys* (1990) and *Helping Young Children Understand Peace, War, and the Nuclear Threat* (1985), both by N. Carlsson-Paige and D.E. Levin.

nightmares, storms, and water (Sarafino, 1986). Children have experienced such fears throughout time. In addition, modern society has created the sources of some unique fears for children. Today's children worry not just about the dark or the "boogie man"; they also are victims of feelings of powerlessness and helplessness in an age of nuclear war, meltdown, and sophisticated missiles (Allen & Pettit, 1987). Canadian children have had parents involved in the Bosnia-Herzogovina war in 1992 and 1993, for example. Canadian children in many locations, thanks to the pervasiveness of the media, also reacted with stress to the 1991 Desert Storm operation in Iraq, which television covered so graphically. A Closer Look discusses war as one fear children encounter. Fears are powerful stressors for young children.

Children's Reactions to Stress

Stress can result in a wide variety of reactions. The reaction will depend on the child as well as on the nature of the stressful event. Behavioural reactions have been classified into four categories (Blom, Cheney, & Snoddy, 1986) as follows:

1. *Feeling*—This category includes such reactions as crying, temper tantrums, shyness, fearfulness, loneliness, low self-confidence, sadness, anger, and depression.
2. *Thinking*—Such reactions may involve short attention span, distractibility, and confusion.
3. *Action*—Active reactions could include fighting, stealing, teasing, withdrawal, overdependency, impulsiveness, hiding, and running away.

4. *Body response*—Physical manifestations of stress might entail tics, hyperactivity, headaches, stuttering, loss of bladder or bowel control, clumsiness, nail biting, stomach complaints, and thumb sucking.

As we discussed in Chapter 6, on guiding children's behaviours, it is important to consider what triggers a problem. The previous categorization indicates that children may respond to stressful events in a variety of negative ways. But behind the overt behaviour is often a stressor that precipitates the behaviour. Getting to the root of problem behaviours requires a thoughtful, observant teacher who gathers pertinent information and considers many factors when dealing with a child.

Resilient Children

It is important to be aware of what factors cause stress and that stress can result in a variety of undesirable or harmful behaviours. Yet, such a focus on the negative effects of stress should be balanced by considering that not all children respond adversely to stress. Some researchers have focused their attention on children who appear to be stable, healthy, outgoing, and optimistic in spite of incredibly stressful lives. They have been called **resilient children**—resistant, vulnerable but invincible—and "superkids" (Werner, 1984). Honig (1986b), however, cautions that although some children are incredibly resilient, "there are no super children who are impervious to all stresses in life" (p. 51).

Researchers have found some shared characteristics among resilient children. They tend to have an inborn temperamental character that elicits positive responses from adults, being cuddly, affectionate, good-natured, and easy to deal with as infants. They have established a close bond with at least one caregiver, enabling them to establish a basic sense of trust. As preschoolers, they have been shown to have a marked independence, playing vigorously, seeking out novel experiences, showing fearlessness, and being self-reliant. They are highly sociable and often develop a close bond with a favourite teacher. In fact, they have been described as being adept at actively recruiting surrogate parents. In spite of poverty, abuse, a broken home life, and other chronic distress, resilient children grow up to feel in control of their destinies, loving, and compassionate (Werner, 1984).

An awareness of the "self-righting tendencies" of children under stress can help early childhood teachers focus on development of traits that contribute to such resilience. Werner (1984) suggested that to "tilt the balance from vulnerability to resiliency" (p. 71), teachers need to be accepting of children's individuality and allow them to be challenged but not overwhelmed, convey a sense of responsibility and caring and reward cooperation and helpfulness, encourage special interests as a source of gratification, model a positive outlook despite adversities, and encourage children to reach out to adults outside their family for support.

Techniques to Help Children Cope with Stress

As an early childhood educator, you have the power to help children cope with some of the stresses in their lives, although you do not have the ability to change the source of most of their stressors. You cannot reconcile divorcing parents, make the new baby sister go away, change the rushed pace of hectic lives, or disperse the monsters in the closet. But you can help children develop some of the skills that will enable them to handle stress more effectively. As we will discuss, the kind of atmosphere you establish and your skills as a good communicator are part of a stress-reducing approach. We will also examine bibliotherapy, relaxation techniques, and play as they contribute to stress reduction in young children. In addition, you may want to consult Alice Honig's (1986b) invaluable list of suggested strategies for teachers to help children cope with stress.

A Consistent, Supportive Environment

A good early childhood program—one that is child-oriented, supports children's development, is consistent and predictable, provides experiences that are neither boring nor overly demanding, affords appropriately paced challenges, and is staffed by knowledgeable and nurturing teachers—is one important element in reducing children's stress. Establishing such a program allows you to provide direct help to stressed children. One underlying component of stress is that it results from something unknown and potentially scary over which the child has little control. Thus, a safe and predictable school environment, in which children can experience success and their actions are valued, will contribute to reduced stress.

The NAEYC publication *Reducing Stress in Young Children's Lives* (J.B. McCracken, 1986) contains a collection of articles drawn from the journal *Young Children*. Many of the papers deal with helping children cope with stressful events in their lives and with ways of strengthening families. In addition, about half of the articles, under the heading "Making Sure We Don't Contribute to Children's Stress," focus on ensuring that the early childhood setting is developmentally appropriate. Similarly, a child care provider's guide entitled *Day Care, Families, and Stress* (1985) focuses much of its discussion on providing a well-thought-out program for young children.

These publications underscore the importance of the early childhood program's role in providing some elements of stability and security for young children under stress. The tentative results of a recent study support the basic premises of these publications. The researchers compared a developmentally appropriate and a developmentally inappropriate classroom and found significantly higher rates of stress in the children involved in the latter (Burts, Hart, Charlesworth, & Kirk, 1990).

Communication

One of the most important ways that you, as a teacher of young children, can help eliminate stress is by how and what you communicate. Both the process (how you communicate) and content (what you say) of communication are important. Thus, it is important that someone share the child's concern, acknowledge how the child feels, and provide reassurance by hugging, holding, or rocking. Allen (1988) suggested that such responses are particularly important for very young children and for older children who are extremely distressed. Listening carefully to what children say and encouraging them to ask questions, express feelings, and discuss their perceptions are important in helping children deal with stress in their lives.

In addition to such responses, it is also important to give accurate and developmentally appropriate explanations and information to preschoolers old enough to understand. Vague reassurances such as "Don't worry about the doctor" do not help the child develop control and alternative coping skills. On the other hand, information about what the doctor will do and what instruments will be used will help reduce the child's sense of helplessness (Hyson, 1986, p. 5).

Four-year-old Percy, whose parents were in the process of getting a divorce, spent most of his time at the child care centre involved in activities and play. But when he was confronted with minor frustrations, he would fly into angry outbursts, engaging in abusive language and unmanageable behaviour. Such conduct was quite different from Percy's former competent approach to life. His teacher, Ann, had been in close contact with Percy's mother and recognized his behaviour as resulting from stress. Ann did several things for Percy. She spent extra time with him, encouraging him to talk about his father, his fears, and his anxieties. She also tried to give Percy accurate information about the divorce, based on what she had learned from his mother. When Percy flew into one of his rages, Ann would immediately pick him up, take him away from centres of activity in the class, hold him in her lap, and rock him. This calmed him, and within 5 or 10 minutes he was generally ready to return to an activity or sit quietly looking at a book.

Bibliotherapy

The term "bibliotherapy" refers to the use of books that deal with emotionally sensitive topics in a developmentally appropriate way, and that help children gain accurate information and learn coping strategies. Jalongo (1986) defined bibliotherapy as "using literature for the purpose of promoting mental health or the use of books in a therapeutic sense" (p. 42). Bibliotherapy provides a relatively comfortable form of dealing with difficult topics because book reading is a familiar activity for both teachers and children (Blom, Cheney, & Snoddy, 1986). Jalongo (1986) identified three potential advantages of such books:

1. *Information*—They stimulate the adult–child exchange of ideas on significant topics.
2. *Relevance*—They encourage the child to make meaningful connections between school experiences and daily life.
3. *Acceptance*—They legitimize the child's emotional responses to crisis situations (pp. 42–43).

Today many books are available that deal with such issues as death, divorce, new siblings, separation, sexuality, handicapping conditions, hospitalization, and fears (*Day Care, Families, and Stress,* 1985; Jalongo, 1986). Books can help children replace a frightening mental image with a more realistic one by presenting accurate facts about a topic, for instance, helping children relieve the anxiety of facing the first day of school (Kleckner & Engel, 1988).

But, as Jalongo (1986) cautioned, just because a book deals with a sensitive topic does not necessarily make it a good book for young children. General guidelines for evaluating children's literature are presented in Appendix I. In particular, crisis-oriented children's books must have settings and characters with which children can identify, and must accurately depict and explain the crisis situation, examine the origins of emotional reactions, consider individual differences, model good coping strategies, and display optimism (Jalongo, 1986). Exhibit 10.3 lists selected books for bibliotherapeutic use with young children.

EXHIBIT 10.3: SUGGESTED BIBLIOTHERAPEUTIC BOOKS

Loss, Death, and Dying

Burningham, J. (1984). *Granpa.* New York: Crown. Ages 3–8.

Buscaglia, L. (1982). *The fall of Freddie the Leaf: A story of life for all ages.* Thorofare, NJ: Charles B. Slack. Ages 4 and up.

Clifton, L. (1983). *Everett Anderson's goodbye.* New York: Holt, Rinehart & Winston. Ages 3–8.

DePaola, T. (1981). *Now one foot, now the other.* New York: Putnam. Ages 4–8.

Hickman, M.W. (1984). *Last week my brother Anthony died.* Nashville, TN: Abingdon. Ages 3–8.

Sharmat, M.W. (1977). *I don't care.* New York: Macmillan. Ages 3–5.

Wilhelm, H. (1985). *I'll always love you.* New York: Crown. Ages 3–8.

Family-Related Matters

Alexander, M. (1979). *When the new baby comes, I'm moving out.* New York: Dial Press Books. Ages 3–7.

Baum, L. (1986). *One more time.* New York: Morrow. Ages 4–8.

Cain, B.S., & E.P. Benedek (1976). *What would you do? A child's book about divorce.* New York: Saturday Evening Post. Ages 4–7.

Caines, J. (1977). *Daddy.* New York: Harper & Row. Ages 4–8.

Drescher, J. (1986). *My mother is getting married.* New York: Dial Press Books. Ages 4–8.

Galloway, P. (1985). *Jennifer has two daddies.* Toronto: Women's Educational Press. Ages 3–8.

Girard, L.W. (1987). *At daddy's on Saturday.* Niles, IL: Albert Whitman. Ages 3–8.

Lapsley, S. (1975). *I am adopted.* New York: Bradburg. Ages $2\frac{1}{2}$–6.

Lasky, J., & M.B. Knight (1984). *A baby for Max.* New York: Scribner. Ages 4–7.

Perry, P., & M. Lynch (1978). *Mommy and Daddy are divorced.* New York: Dial Press Books. Ages 4–8.

Smith, P. (1981). *Jenny's baby brother.* New York: Viking Press. Ages $3\frac{1}{2}$–7.

Stinson, K., & N.L. Reynolds (1985). *Mom and Dad don't live together anymore.* Toronto: Annick Press. Ages 3–5.

Vigna, J. (1982). *Daddy's new baby.* Niles, IL: Albert Whitman. Ages 4–7.

———. (1988). *I wish daddy didn't drink so much.* Niles, IL: Albert Whitman. Ages 3–7.

Fears

Aylesworth, J. (1985). *The bad dream.* New York: Albert Whitman. Ages 4–8.

Bunting, E. (1987). *Ghost's hour, spook's hour.* New York: Clarion. Ages 3–7.

Dragonwagon, C. (1977). *Will it be OK?* New York: Harper & Row. Ages 4–8.

Howe, J. (1986). *There's a monster under my bed.* New York: Atheneum Press. Ages 4–7.

Jonas, A. (1984). *Holes and peeks.* New York: Greenwillow. Ages 2–5.

Jones, R. (1982). *The biggest, meanest, ugliest dog in the whole wide world.* New York: Macmillan. Ages 3–7.

Mayer, M. (1969). *There's a nightmare in my closet.* New York: Dial Press Books. Ages 4–7.

Robinson, D. (1981). *No elephants allowed.* New York: Houghton Mifflin. Ages 4–7.

Szilagyi, M. (1985). *Thunderstorm.* New York: Bradbury Press. Ages 3–6.

Viorst, J. (1972). *Alexander and the terrible, horrible, no good, very bad day.* New York: Atheneum Press. Ages 3–6.

———. (1988). *The good-bye book.* New York: Atheneum Press. Ages 3–7.

Illness and Hospitalization

Brandenberg, F. (1978). *I wish I was sick, too!* New York: Puffin. Ages 3–8.

Hautzig, D. (1985). *A visit to the Sesame Street hospital.* New York: Random/ Children's Television Workshop. Ages 2–7.

Krementz, J. (1986). *Taryn goes to the dentist.* New York: Crown. Ages 3–4.

Rockwell, A., & H. Rockwell (1982). *Sick in bed.* New York: Macmillan. Ages 3–6.

———. (1985). *The emergency room.* New York: Macmillan. Ages 2–5.

Rockwell, H. (1973). *My doctor.* New York: Macmillan. Ages 2–6.

Rogers, F. (1986). *Going to the doctor.* New York: Putnam. Ages 3–6.

Wolde, G. (1976). *Betsy and the chicken pox.* New York: Random House. Ages 3–6.

First Day at School

Bram, E. (1977). *I don't want to go to school.* New York: Greenwillow. Ages 3–6.

Frandsen, K. (1984). *I started school today.* Chicago: Children's Press. Ages 4–7.

Gross, A. (1982). *The I don't want to go to school book.* Chicago: Children's Press. Ages 5–8.

Hamilton-Merritt, J. (1982). *My first days of school.* New York: Simon & Shuster. Ages 4–6.

Howe, J. (1986). *When you go to kindergarten.* New York: Alfred A. Knopf. Ages 5–6.

Oxenbury, H. (1983). *First day of school.* New York: Dial Press Books. Ages $2\frac{1}{2}$–4.

Roger, F. (1985). *Going to day care.* New York: Putnam. Ages 3–6.

Wolde, G. (1976). *Betsy's first day at nursery school.* New York: Random House. Ages 3–6.

Sources: M. Cuddigan, & M.B. Hanson (1988), *Growing pains: Helping children deal with everyday problems through reading* (Chicago: American Library Association); *Day care, families, and stress* (1985) (Austin, TX: Child Development Program Division, Texas Department of Human Resources); M.R. Jalongo (1986), "Using crisis-oriented books with young children," in J.B. McCracken (ed.), *Reducing stress in young children's lives* (Washington, DC: National Association for the Education of Young Children), p. 46; *The bookfinder: A guide to children's literature about the needs and problems of youth aged 2–15,* vol. 1 (1977) (Circle Pines, MN: American Guidance Service).

Relaxation Techniques

Older children, ones who are able to understand language fairly well, can be helped to reduce some of the physical tension associated with stress through guided relaxation exercises. Relaxation routines can easily be incorporated into the early childhood program, for instance, as part of movement activities or during rest or pre-nap time. Some programs schedule a regular relaxation period for specific exercises.

One approach to relaxation is to experience muscle tension followed by muscle relaxation (Humphrey & Humphrey, 1985). For instance, children can be instructed to make themselves stiff as a board then to become as floppy as a Raggedy Ann or Andy doll. A more systematic approach, called **progressive relaxation**, asks children to tense and then relax various specified muscle groups. For instance, the children could be instructed, "Squeeze your eyes shut tightly, then relax; make fists with both hands, then relax; push your knees together hard, then relax" (Humphrey & Humphrey, 1985). A game such as Simon Says can be used to promote relaxation activities.

Imagery, a mental image that helps in the process of relaxation, can also be used effectively with young children. After children are lying in a comfortable position, they can be asked to float like a feather or melt like ice. A poem or story read very slowly and softly can help children visualize an image in their own way.

Play and Coping with Stress

Play provides a natural outlet for children to cope with and work out stressors in their lives. Play furnishes a safe setting in which children can confront fears and anxieties, express anger, and find solutions to problems. Role playing or pretend play, in particular, allows children to re-enact frightening experiences, feel what it is like to take on the perspective or role of others, and make reality more acceptable (Allen, 1988). Taking on the role of the doctor by using a stethoscope or giving a doll an injection with an empty syringe can help dispel some of the fears associated with an upcoming visit to the doctor's office.

Another effective approach to decreasing fear is to increase understanding about something unknown. For instance, one study reported that children who used the game "Hospital Windows," a medically oriented lotto game that helps children gain accurate information, increased their knowledge of healthcare concepts significantly, while decreasing their fear of medical equipment and procedures (Henkens-Matzke & Abbott, 1990).

Gunsberg (1989) noted that abused and neglected children often exhibit primitive and disorganized play behaviour, are disruptive, and are hostile toward, or

avoid, adults. Gunsberg cited the case of a 4-year-old abused child whom the teacher engaged in a repeated, simple play episode. By structuring play that responded repeatedly and predictably to the actions of the child—that was contingent on the child's behaviour—the teacher helped her form a perception of a nurturing and attentive adult. Repeated, positive play experience was used not only to help the child develop more mature and effective play patterns but also to promote trust, a sense of control and power, and enjoyment.

Outdoor play, is an excellent outlet for children's stress and a medium for encouraging fitness and a healthy, balanced lifestyle. Yet, as you will see in A Canadian Professional Speaks Out, adequate space, time or importance are not placed on the value of outdoor play. Releasing energy, exploring, and appreciating nature, as well as having one's own time and space, are critical factors in preventing and alleviating stress in all people. Exhibit 10.4 outlines many additional ways teachers can help children cope with stress.

A CANADIAN PROFESSIONAL SPEAKS OUT
Playing Outdoors: Time, Space, and a Positive Attitude

In the mid-1990s close to 200 000 young children between 6 months and 5 years of age will attend an early childhood program in Canada. Some of these children will spend up to 12 000 hours of the first 5 years of their lives in the care of early childhood educators or other private care providers. This is more than the collective time that they will spend in school for the next 12 years. Increasingly, young children spend their early years in day care centres, family day care homes, or alternative care arrangements. Some travel great distances to the child care centres, others remain close to home in the residential community. What they have in common, however, is that the physical space in which they live has largely been built based on standards established in the 1960s that may not respond to the needs of the 21st century.

Standards for outdoor play areas in North America range between 20 and 25 m^2 per child in licensed day care centres. These requirements have remained unchanged and relatively unchallenged since the early 1960s. In 1984, the Child Welfare League of America (CWLA) recommended that 60m^2 of space per child be available for outdoor play. Unfortunately, the minimal outdoor space required by licensing standards is often waived and many centres do not have space readily accessible for children to play outdoors. Experience and research have shown that the CWLA recommendation is legitimate; unfortunately, in most cases, land is no longer available and children and early childhood educators are forced to spend the majority of their time indoors. In 1991, the Canadian Institute of Child Health undertook a National Survey of Day Care Centres to assess the types of physical activity programs available. Almost 50 percent of respondents reported that they had no outdoor gross motor play activity area. A significant number (60 percent) reported that children spend less than 10 percent of time in structured outdoor gross motor play. Finally, 36 percent of respondents reported that children spend less than 10 percent of time in free outdoor gross motor play.

Playing outdoors in all seasons has to become an integral part of the daily lives of young children. Research evidence confirms that regular physical activity started early in childhood is essential to building healthy and vigorous adults and to reducing stress.

Playing outdoors requires a positive attitude toward the importance of play, and early childhood educators have a critical role to play in changing attitudes and professional practice, which has more often than not neglected the outdoor play experience. In addition to attitude, time and space are essential ingredients to making outdoor play experiences possible for the children of the next century. Hopefully it will not be too late to secure some high-quality outdoor play experiences for young children growing up in day care centres.

Steen B. Esbensen, Université du Québec à Hull, Hull, Québec

EXHIBIT 10.4: HOW TEACHERS HELP CHILDREN COPE WITH STRESS

Considering the large number and variety of stressors affecting children's lives, and the fragility of coping skills and the scarcity of buffering supports in some children's lives, what can parents and teachers do to help children cope with stress? Most of the suggestions given here focus on preschoolers and school-aged children rather than infants. Some will be useful for caregivers of children of all ages. Adults who care for children in stressful life situations need to have a *wide* variety of techniques and ideas to help young children adjust better in classrooms, at home, and in stressful situations such as temporary foster care or hospitalization.

1. To be able to help children cope with stress, adults must *develop noticing skills.* Recognize when a child is stressed. Be alert to changes in behaviour

(e.g., more quarrels with playmates, bedwetting, poor concentration) that signal stress. Parents and teachers who are sensitive to telltale signs of stress can tune in more effectively. Learn the signs of stress.

2. *Demonstrate self-control and coping skills yourself.* Be fair and sensitive to differences and problems. Demonstrate brave behaviours: keep calm even when classroom problems arise and stresses (e.g., crying, diarrhea, acting out) seem to be especially prevalent or aggravating on a particular day. If a teacher's voice is exasperated, whiny, disappointed, aggrieved, or angry fairly often, then young children learn that these are acceptable models of coping with stress.

    As a parent or teacher, *find social supports in your own life* so that you are energized for adaptive coping with problems that arise with young children. Your "feeling of confidence or faith that things will work out as well as can be reasonably expected and that the odds can be surmounted" contributes to children's effective coping (Werner, 1986, p. 192).

3. *Enhance children's self-esteem* wherever and whenever possible through encouragement, caring, focused attention, and warm personal regard. You are the mirror that reflects the personal worth of each child (Briggs, 1975).

4. *Encourage each child to develop a special interest or skill* that can serve as an inner source of pride and self esteem (Werner, 1986).

5. *Use proactive intervention to avoid unnecessary stress.* Give children plenty of time before a transition. For example, use verbal, musical, or light-dimming signals so children can gradually put away toys and get ready for lunch. Anticipate stressful occasions.

    Preventive actions lessen the possibility and impact of stressful events. Frequent fire drills make children less terrified of loud alarms or sudden commotions. Children who have experienced drills and other such procedures become used to their occurrence and the rules to be followed so that a fire drill does not become an occasion for panic.

6. *Help children understand the consequences and implications of negative, acting-out behaviours* on others and on themselves. Shure and Spivack (1978) provide daily activities to help young children improve skills in *consequential thinking.*

7. *Acknowledge children's feelings and encourage verbal mediation.* Help children learn that they are not alone in having uncomfortable feelings. Give them permission to feel scared, lonely, or angry (e.g., when a peer squashes their sandpie). Help them *decenter*—become able to see how others also feel upset if their play or rights are interfered with. Give children *words* to express their negative feelings so that they will not have to be aggressive or disorganized when stressed. "I" statements help a child communicate personal upset and strong wills rather than accusing, hurting, or threatening others (Gordon, 1970).

    Impulsive behaviour often causes peer troubles. Help children think about the situation and their impatient feelings so they can avoid a fuss with friends. Use Gordon's (1970) active listening: "You wish you could have the new trike all morning, but other children want to ride too, so we need to take turns." "You are trying so hard to sit still until the crackers are passed to you. You are wiggling and *waiting.* Good for you."

    The "Think Aloud" lessons (Camp & Bash, 1981) teach children to deal with cognitive and interpersonal problems through verbal mediation. Children learn to talk to themselves in effective and skillful ways to identify their problem, to make plans for coping, and to weigh the merits of different solutions.

8. *Help children distinguish reality from fantasy.* Explain to them, for example, that having strong, angry wishes about a brother did not cause that brother to become ill or that Papa did not leave home because you were a sloppy eater or were mad at him for not buying you two ice cream cones.

9. *Use gentle humour when possible to help children reframe their negative thoughts and feelings.* Then they can perceive mild stressors as possible opportunities or challenges. For example, if Jonathan accidentally knocked down his own block tower, you could comment matter-of-factly with a smile, "Jonathan, your elbow sure was a giant tower-smasher. Now you have a chance to design on even fancier and taller tower."

10. *Focus directly on the stressor if it is peer aggression.* If a class bully gets others to tease or jeer at a child, *you must stop the bullying.* Talk to the children in your class about attitudes and values that permit bullying or threatening. Speak with the children and their parents separately. Aggression that is not addressed does not go away (Caldwell, 1977). Teachers need to be brave and direct in handling hurting. Children cannot be allowed to hurt others. A child who scapegoats needs to have other ways to feel good about herself or himself.

11. *Help children view their situation more positively.* Some stressors make a child feel ashamed as well as hurt. *Shame eats at a child's self-esteem.* Having a single parent can be such a stressor. As Blom, Cheney, and Snoddy (1986) have noted in their excellent resource for teachers: "A child can be helped to view the single-parenthood status of his mother as acceptable, not uncommon, and preferable to having both parents together and quarreling. [The child's] perception can be altered and the impact of the stress thereby reduced" (p. 82).

12. *Structure classroom activities to enhance cooperation* rather than competition. A cooperative climate in the classroom can help reduce stress. Children will flourish where they can grow and achieve at comfortable a pace. Required helpfulness has been found to increase children's sense of effectiveness and coping. Devise cooperative games to play (Honig, 1985a; Honig 1985b; Honig, Wittmer, & Gibralter, in press; Sobel, 1983).

    If a child in unpopular with peers, arrange for *cooperative activities* that require children to work together. When you provide friendly younger children as companions in mixed-age classes, unpopular children increase their social skills (Roopnarine & Honig, 1985).

13. *Modify classroom situations and rules.* Make choices and expectations easier to understand and to meet. *Rearrange environments to decrease stress.* Quiet reading corners should not be set up adjacent to tricycle riding or block building areas. Define activity areas with clear rules so that fewer tensions will arise in play.

14. *Find individual talk time* with troubled children. Find out how children perceive threats or stresses. A child may feel picked on or that nobody likes her or him. Help the child think of a variety of possible solutions for his or her problems. *Generating alternatives* will increase a child's coping resources.

15. *Mobilize other children to help.* For example, if a disabled child is entering a preschool class, talk with the children about strengths and troubles that every child, and particularly the disabled child, might have in making friends, using materials, and negotiating spaces. Honig and McCarron (1986) have shown that normal preschool children in a mainstreamed classroom can be very helpful, empathic, and prosocial toward disabled peers. If a child

has a seriously ill sibling, enlist classmates of the well child to provide peer support and attention.

16. *Use bibliotherapy.* Adults can find many materials to read aloud with children to help them identify with stressed characters and earn how they cope. Some representative titles from the Human Sciences Press are *My Grandpa Died Today, The Secret Worry, Two Homes to Live In: A Child's Eye View of Divorce,* and *Dusty Was My Friend.* Walker Publishers have books such as *That New Baby* and *About Handicaps.* Sunal and Hatcher (1985), Jalongo (1986), and Fassler (1978) provided guides to the use of such books when children are having troubles in their lives.

17. *Have regular classroom talks, in a safe calm atmosphere, about different stressors.* Ask children who are comfortable about their experiences to share what it was like to go to the hospital for surgery, to move to a new house or school, when a new baby was born in the family, when a parent had to go away for a long while, when there was a violent storm, when a fierce-looking dog barked at them, or when a child thought he or she was lost while shopping with a parent.

    Arent (1984) has written a guide to symptoms, situations, and strategies for dealing with child stress, which can stimulate your ideas for talks. Such talks give courage to a child who may be hiding secret sorrows, thinking she or he is all alone with these troubles or the only one scared by them.

    In Bessell and Palomares' "Magic Circle" program (1973), children sit in circles and share pleasant and unpleasant feelings, secure that they will not be judged.

    Provide verbal stems for children who may find it difficult to talk in circle time: "One time when I really felt scared, I ..."; "My friend made me feel really good when ..."; "One time I was very worried when ..." Such openers help a teacher evaluate the appraisal reactions of young children to stressors and to learn the range and efficacy of coping strategies that children have used.

18. *Use art.* Many young children cannot verbally express fears and anger about the painful stressors in their lives. Paint, clay, and other art media allow a child to express upsets and act out private feelings. A big, brown, smeary painting can be the way a child feels about the ambulance that came to take Papa away when he suddenly became ill.

19. *Encourage children to act out coping skills with dolls and in other dramatic play.* For example, if a particular child is stressed because of a recent or future move, "doll houses, housekeeping equipment and boxes are good for helping a child act out a moving experience. Toy telephones allow imaginary communication with friends in other places and friends that the child would like to know better" (Long, 1985, p. 8). Early in the school year, doll play can help children deal with separation from home.

    Use puppets to act out positive problem-solving responses to ordinary daily stressors that a child might encounter. Some sample topics might be forgetting to bring a lunch or lunch money to school; wanting a turn on the slide and finding a lot of children ahead of you; wanting a teacher to read to you right away when she or he is busy helping another child; and feeling another child unfairly got a bigger portion than you.

20. *Involve parents.* Recommend good books about recognizing and managing child stress (Arent, 1984; Brenner, 1984; Kersey, 1985; Wolff, 1969). Remind parents how important rest and good nutrition are for coping with stressful situations (see Honig and Oski, 1984, for a discussion of iron deficiency symptoms of irritability and solemnity in infants and young children).

Listen empathetically if parents are able to share some of their life's stressors. Together, you and the child's family can be a mutually supportive human system that reduces stress effects and enhances the security of a child who is troubled.

Key Terms

anxiety	imagery
bereavement	internalization
child abuse and neglect	phobia
coping strategies	progressive relaxation
externalization	resilient children
habituation	stress

Key Points

- Since today's demands place greater responsibility and expectations on children, teachers must identify the causes of stress, symptoms of stress, and methods for relieving and coping with stress.

- Family stressors include divorce, poverty, homelessness, depression, fast-paced family life, and any event that causes a change.

- In the case of child abuse or neglect, it is the teacher's skill as a careful observer combined with knowledge of child development that can best provide clues to the stress caused by inappropriate actions toward (or in the presence of) the child.

- It is a teacher's ethical and legal responsibility as a professional to report suspected child abuse or neglect to the appropriate authorities.

- Health problems, death of a loved one, and unexplained fears all create stress in children, and getting to the root of the problem behaviours requires a thoughtful, observant teacher.

- By developing positive techniques such as bibliotherapy, communication, relaxation, and play therapy, teachers can help children cope with their stress.

Part 5

The Promise

We began this text with an orientation to a child care centre. Now that you are thoroughly familiar with the field of early childhood education, you will embark on your field placements and career choices better prepared and equipped with the history, theory, research, knowledge, skills, ideas, and ambition to have an impact on, and be inspired by, the lives of those you will meet.

- Progression: "Early Childhood Education in Canada" considers in depth the history and regulations of each province in Canada and ends with future directives for our field—a field to which we welcome you to as a pioneer in the care of our nation's children.

Progression

Early Childhood Education in Canada

We have attempted to weave Canadian information throughout this text using examples, statistics, and research whenever and wherever possible. For instance, the name of your provincial legal document (legislation) that governs ratios, group size, and qualifications is found in Chapter 5 (Exhibit 5.1) because such documents affect quality care. For instance, the legislation relating to the Yukon is called Child Care Act Bill 77. We elaborate somewhat on these documents in this chapter. Provincial and federal early childhood education associations are found in Chapter 1, as are early childhood education

college and university training programs, since these directly relate to you, the early childhood educator.

In this chapter, we list the provincial administering bodies that oversee child care services. We impart a truly Canadian note by highlighting the history of early childhood education in each province and summarizing the regulations that govern child care across the country. We convey some general current issues and advances in early childhood education and in Canadian research and projects. We also introduce you to some of the excellent members of our Canadian early childhood education field. We left this historical tour to the end because by now you will have a clear grasp of the field in general and a broader perspective from which to view past events and future trends.

As a student in an introductory course, you will probably be most interested in the section on your own province or territory. However, you may want to see how the services, legislation, and/or teacher education programs in your area compare with others. Perhaps you plan to enter the profession or have young children requiring care or are thinking about relocating after you graduate. If that is the case, you may be interested in learning about practices and alternatives in other parts of the country.

Assembling the information for this chapter was less challenging than seemed likely at first due to the publication of *Canadian Child Care in Context: Perspectives from the Provinces and Territories* (Pence, 1992), a two-volume work of almost one thousand pages. As part of the government-funded Canadian National Child Care Study (CNCCS), teams of authors from each province, the Yukon, and the Northwest Territories were asked to compile articles on their province or territory, the history of early childhood education there, and current ECE regulations and practices. In addition, information on the scope of licensed child care and parents' child care needs and use was compiled for each province and territory. Those documents are a valuable resource but could not be fully covered in most ECE courses. Hence, they will be summarized below.

In addition to Pence's invaluable volumes, most institutions in the country that offer ECE courses responded willingly to the original and subsequent requests for information about their programs. In addition to their published data (Child Care, 1990), the Child Care Resource and Research Unit at the University of Toronto also shared unpublished data on child care in Canada that was presented at the third National Child Care Conference in May 1993 (Child Care, 1993). Governments from across the country also responded to the authors' requests for information about their legislation for ECE programs. National organizations such as the Canadian Child Care Federation and the National Day Care Information Centre, provincial associations of early childhood education, and, of course, the

Internet were also valuable resources. Our local Early Childhood Community Resource Development Centre was also helpful. Thus, it was only through the collaborative efforts of ECE professionals and government officials across the country that this chapter, based on Young (1993b), could be assembled. As students in ECE courses, you will gain a stronger sense of the field in this country than virtually all of your predecessors. This perspective may subsequently influence your decision about where to pursue your career either as an ECE professional and/or as a parent of children requiring a high-quality program.

The Roots of Early Childhood Education in Canada and Regulation in the Field

British Columbia

Ritch and Griffin (1992) provided an overview of British Columbia, the third most populous province in Canada, for the CNCCS. Over half of British Columbia's three million people live in urban centres, and 50 percent of the people are concentrated in the Greater Vancouver area. The province has been ethnically diverse since the Canadian Pacific Railway was built in the 1880s. Even in the early 1900s, Vancouver had the largest Chinese community in Canada. In recent years, British Columbia has seen a large influx of immigrants from the Pacific Rim as well as from the rest of Canada. Over 50 percent of the children in Vancouver come from homes where English is not the first language.

Traditionally, British Columbia had a resource-based economy with forestry, fishing, mining, and agriculture being its mainstays. However, the service-based industries now employ 70 percent of the workforce. Average incomes are high in British Columbia, and it continues to be one of the more affluent provinces.

Historical Overview

Linda McDonell's 1992 article, "An Historical Overview of Child Care in British Columbia," provides an excellent summary of developments in early childhood in British Columbia from 1910 to the present. In 1910, the only early childhood facility was the City Crèche, located in a hospital in downtown Vancouver. The crèche was a facility where working mothers could leave their children for the day when they found work as domestics. The crèche closed at the onset of the Depression, and nursery schools and private kindergartens did not appear until the 1940s. There were some family day care homes available to working mothers in the interim, mainly in Vancouver, where there was some concern about having high-quality substitute care. World War II led to an increase in day care facilities, but British Columbia did not have enough women working in war-related industries to qualify for federal funds.

British Columbia led the country when it initiated the licensing of child care facilities in 1937. By 1939, the province had 20 licensed programs. The nursery school movement became visible in the 1940s, as did cooperative preschools which steadily multiplied. Some private kindergartens also were established. There were 170 licensed programs in British Columbia by 1945, and concern was expressed about the need to establish standards for these facilities. In 1955, the province, responding to mounting pressure, added training requirements to the legislation, and the Faculty of Education at the University of British Columbia (UBC) began to offer these courses. Trained early childhood educators became the norm in urban areas. However, despite considerable effort to offer courses in rural areas, few teachers in the remote areas of British Columbia were qualified, even in 1975. Training programs became more widely available during the 1970s and the early 1980s, and courses in infant and toddler care also were established.

In 1989, the regulations were revised so that centres could have programs for infants under 18 months of age (Griffin, 1992). Training requirements were also clarified. In addition, the maximum number of hours a child could spend in a centre per day was increased from 10 to 13. A review of the regulations was initiated in 1993, and changes were finalized in 1994 (Child Care, 1993).

Regulation

Early childhood programs in British Columbia are regulated by several different bodies (Child Care, 1990, 1993; Griffin, 1992; McDonell & Griffin, 1992). School-based programs, including kindergartens (now known as Primary I classes), fall under the Ministry of Education. Non-school-based early childhood programs are governed by three ministries (Child Care, 1990; McDonell & Griffin, 1992). The Ministry of Advanced Education, Training, and Technology is responsible for teacher training. Funding of those eligible for assistance under the Canada Assistance Plan came from the Ministry of Social Services and Housing. The licensing of programs, inspections, certification of teachers, and approval of early childhood training programs all fall in the hands of the Ministry of Health. One does not have to have had many dealings with governments to suspect that this tri-ministerial involvement brings additional challenges to the field of early childhood education.

The 1979 Community Care Facility Act and the British Columbia Child Care Regulations, as amended in 1990, specify requirements for early childhood programs in the province (Child Care, 1990, 1993; Griffin, 1992; McDonell &

Griffin, 1992) and regulate teacher–child ratios, group size, facility size, and teacher qualifications. The revised regulations also contain an extensive account of appropriate programming for the young child's physical, intellectual, language, social, and emotional development.

Alberta

The population of Alberta has almost quadrupled from 1921 to the time of the 1986 census, and that growth seems to have occurred primarily in the urban areas (Greenwood-Church & Crozier-Smith, 1992). While over two-thirds of the province's population were in rural settings in the 1930s, 80 percent lived in urban settings in the 1980s (Greenwood-Church & Crozier-Smith, 1992). A large number of European immigrants moved to Alberta prior to World War I, giving the province a long tradition of ethnic diversity. While Alberta's fluctuating oil market has led to waves of immigration and emigration, the province has not experienced the significant increases in foreign immigrants witnessed by British Columbia and Ontario.

Historical Overview

"An Historical Overview of Child Care in Alberta" (Read, Greenwood-Church, Hautman, Roche, & Bagley, 1992) traces the development of early childhood education in Alberta until 1988, while Read (1992) discusses developments from

1988 until 1990. Child care has a comparatively brief history in Alberta where it was not generally available until the late 1960s. Until that time, the few child care centres that existed were privately owned and received little attention from the government beyond routine fire and health inspections. With the advent of the CAP in 1966 and Alberta's Preventive Social Service Act in the same year, the onus was on the province to provide preventive, rather than custodial, services including child care. The province provided 80 percent of the funding to any municipality that opened a non-profit child care centre, and the cities of Edmonton and Calgary quickly took advantage of the new funding agreement. Similar growth occurred in smaller urban centres, but the two major cities provided a model for high-quality programs. However, the municipal centres were primarily for children from low-income and single-parent families. As a consequence, profit-making child care continued to predominate in Alberta, and child care chains and franchises found the province a receptive home.

The first training programs for ECE teachers within the province were not instituted until 1970 when several two-year diploma courses and some extension courses were established. The demand for graduates of these programs increased after 1973 when the province finally agreed to provide funding for kindergarten programs offered by either the school boards or private non-profit organizations.

Legislation governing child care licensing was not introduced until 1978 after the Alberta Association for Young Children (AAYC) had applied consistent pressure on the government to adopt and enforce standards. Interestingly, the standards were lower than those that Edmonton and Calgary had adopted from the Child Welfare League of America in the 1960s and actually led to a decline in ECE standards, if not quality, in these two cities. Nonetheless, requirements for physical facilities and teacher–child ratios were stated in the Social Care Facilities Licensing Act. Training requirements were not included, however, much to the dismay of the AAYC. Group-size requirements were added to the legislation in 1980, and teacher–child ratios were improved.

Inspections of child care facilities in Alberta after the 1978 Licensing Act seemed to be inconsistent and often cursory. Concerns about the inspection procedures and the continued lack of training requirements were expressed by a number of groups and resulted in a commission of inquiry into child welfare during the 1980s. Moreover, the failure of the government to tie financial subsidies for child care centres to the quality of care in those centres was subject to criticism. Making subsidies contingent on strict conformity to the regulations is usually an effective method of ensuring compliance with the legislation.

The ongoing barrage of criticism of the government's policies (and lack of policies), led by groups like the AAYC, finally led to the 1990 publication of *Alberta Day Care Reforms*. In that document, the province outlined training requirements that were to be fully implemented by 1995 (Read, 1992). By September 1995, all supervisors of child care facilities had to have completed a two-year diploma in ECE or have equivalent education and experience. By September 1992, one in six teachers in an ECE centre had to have completed a one-year ECE certificate program. In 1994, the ratio changed to one in five, and in 1995, one in six. Teachers without those certificates had to complete an orientation course. Centres that provide care for school-aged children have to be licensed. However, they still do not have to conform to the teacher–child ratios set down in the regulations.

Regulation

Because of early childhood education's recent history in the province, many of the current regulations in Alberta have been discussed above. In 1990, new regulations regarding teacher–child ratios, group size, and teacher qualifications were added to the Social Care Facilities Act (Read, 1992). Teacher–child ratios and group size are not regulated for school-aged children. According to the new regulations, the program must meet the children's physical, social, intellectual, creative, and emotional needs. The new requirements for teachers have been discussed above, and, especially in view of the research on quality of care and teacher education, these regulations are welcome.

Saskatchewan

Jean Nykyforuk (1992b) provided an excellent overview of this province in a 1992 article, "A Socio-Geographic Overview of Saskatchewan." The province is vast, but its population is just over one million. While it is seen as a primarily rural province, over 60 percent of the population lived in urban centres at the time of the 1986 census. Like Alberta, Saskatchewan had a large wave of immigrants in the first few decades of the 20th century, and it again experienced growth after World War II. However, since 1987, with the slump in its economy, Saskatchewan has experienced a net loss in population. The province continues to be ethnically diverse and includes a large Aboriginal population. The province's economy is still tied to agriculture and mineral production, and manufacturing is secondary. Weather also remains a critical factor for Saskatchewan's well-being. The drought in the late 1980s had a marked effect on the province's economy.

Historical Overview

Nykyforuk (1992a) detailed the history of child care for the National Child Care Study in her article "An Historical Overview of Child Care in Saskatchewan." World War II did not have an impact on child care in Saskatchewan as there were too few war-related industries for the province to qualify for the federal government's funding. It was not until the 1960s that a substantial number of women entered the workforce and began to need child care facilities. This growing need for child care, coupled with the financial assistance offered under CAP in 1966, led to a steady increase in the number of unregulated centres. Most were privately owned and operated as business ventures.

In 1969, the province enacted child care legislation, passing the Child Welfare Act. All advertised centres were to be inspected by a social worker who had the authority to close a centre; apparently this provision was not very effective. Several advocacy groups, including the Saskatchewan Day Care Development Committee, the Saskatoon Steering Committee, and the People for Child Care Action, were relentless in pressuring the government for improved legislation, more accessible child care, and larger government grants. In 1974, the government announced its intention to implement a new program and to increase funding. In 1975, new day care regulations were passed.

Significantly, the regulations required that all licensed facilities (except those already in existence in 1975) be non-profit organizations run by a board that included more than 50 percent of parent users of the centres. The regulations also included procedures and standards for licensing, requirements for centre size, and details of financing. Training requirements, however, were minimal, consisting of a 42-hour in-service program for centre-based teachers and nothing for family child care providers. Interestingly, nursery schools were exempt from the act and are not regulated by the province. Nykyforuk reported that 97 percent of all facilities were non-profit by 1987.

A number of difficulties with the parent-board model have occurred, perhaps mainly because the boards did not have business training. In fact, the preschool-cooperative movement has found it necessary to develop training programs, which they offer each year for incoming board members.

The 1980 provincial review of child care services reported a number of difficulties, including the lack of any in-province training programs other than the 42-hour government course. Both one- and two-year programs in early childhood development (initially, they were called the Child Care Worker Program) were established in 1981 at the Kelsey Institute in Saskatoon, which followed an outreach system to make programs available across the province through the community colleges.

Advocacy groups were active in Saskatchewan in the 1980s, seeking both expanded services and increased funding for child care. They also successfully

lobbied against the Grant Devine government's 1984 intent to allow profit-making child care. A provincial organization, the Saskatchewan Child Care Association (SCCA), was formed in 1988 to express concerns about the profession as well as advocacy issues. Nykyforuk (1992a) suggested that the advocacy groups were needed as the government had not been increasing the number of licensed spaces, even though demand was increasing. Due to increased demand, a number of unlicensed, unregulated facilities sprang up, and the 1975 legislation did not limit the number of children who could be cared for in an unlicensed facility. While the unlicensed centres received no government funding, they also were not subject to the regulations.

In 1989, the Child Care Act was passed, replacing the 1975 regulations (Dill, 1992). Under the new act, profit-making centres could be established, but they had to have parents on their boards. The legislation also insisted that all centres be licensed, and it restricted the number of children who could be cared for in family child care homes whether or not they were licensed (Dill, 1992). In addition, the act permitted centre-based care for infants. The regulations that accompany the act now require supervisors of child care centres to have completed a one-year certificate program.

Regulation

The 1990 regulations noted above introduced new requirements for centre size and group size as well as for the care of infants under 18 months (Child Care, 1993; Dill, 1992; Truemner, 1992). Nursery schools, however, are still not regulated. The new act requires programs to provide a developmentally appropriate environment. As noted above, supervisors now have to have a certificate or its equivalent, but teachers only have to be over 16 and to take an orientation course within six months of being hired.

SPECIAL FEATURE
Rural Child Care: A Saskatchewan Perspective

What is it like to live on a farm and experience a lack of child care services? Nettie Wiebe from Laura, Saskatchewan, is the Women's President of the National Farmers' Union. She knows all too well what lack of child care services is like. She and fellow farm women have experienced many stressful situations in regard to child care arrangements. Nettie, who has four young children, has had to take the children along with her on the grain truck out to the field. Other farm mothers have had to leave their children alone napping in the farm house while they are in the field summer fallowing. Regular trips have to be made back and forth to the house to check on the children. This makes for very anxious times for parent and children.

Another farm mom went through *six* different child care arrangements in a short period of time. Flexible child care could not be found.

Farm children are exposed to many dangerous situations. Heavy equipment is a part of farm life, as are various kinds of chemicals. Many parents have no option but to leave children by themselves. In 1991–92, 41 Saskatchewan children under the age of 15 were hospitalized due to farm accidents.

Other problems that hinder rural families are distance and relative cost. Families must travel long distances for child care services. In the 1989–91 Federated Women's Survey, which questioned 1740 rural families across Canada with at least one child, more than 50 percent of the respondents had to travel 15 km or more to the child care centre. In Saskatchewan, some parents have to travel more than 100 km to a centre. The population density is often too small to support the urban type of child care program; therefore, smaller, more flexible programs are needed.

Farm families have seasonal fluctuations in their income. Paying for child care services requires a regular monthly income. Therefore, farm families cannot obtain child care services at certain times because of irregular income. With low grain prices, many families cannot afford child care at any time of the year.

Rural parents may often need child care on a seasonal basis. Activities such as calving, planting, cultivating, haying, and harvesting occur at different times of the year. At these times flexible child care is needed. For example, full day care is needed in April, May, June, August, and September.

In November 1992 the National Conference on Farm Women Employment was held in Quebec. The following is a summary of their proposal for rural child care:

Needs and Services:

- Recognition and development of child care services at the farm residence as well as local, community-based, diversified child care services.

- Assurance of children's safety through the recognized training of child care workers.

- Recognition of the farm as the place of residence and work.

Financial Support:

- Recognition by Revenue Canada that child care expenses are farm business expenses.

- Subsidized child care reciprocally based on the net income of farm families.

- Subsidies for sparsely populated regions.

- Recognition of subsidization for in-home as well as financial support for local community-based child care centres.

Decision-makers must now recognize the needs of rural child care. They have the reports and recommendations. Now they must implement them so that families like Nettie Wiebe's will have quality child care.

Karen Troughton, Instructor, Early Childhood Development Program, Kelsey Institute
Saskatchewan Institute of Applied Science and Technology, Saskatoon

---

Manitoba

Manitoba's population of 1 063 015 people in the 1986 census, 75 percent of whom live in urban settings, makes it the fifth most populous province (Stevens, 1992). Stevens provided an overview of the province for the CNCCS that helped to place child care in Manitoba in context. Manitoba's economy has shifted from its total reliance on native resources in the 19th century to an economy dependent on the service industries (Stevens, 1992). Manitobans have a history of ethnic diversity, but they have not experienced significant immigration waves in recent years.

Historical Overview

Friesen, Humphrey, and Brockman (1992b) prepared an article, "An Historical Overview of Child Care in Manitoba," for the CNCCS that provided much of the following information on the development of the child care profession, facilities, and policies in Manitoba. Child care has a lengthier history in Manitoba than it does in the other Prairie provinces, and can be traced back to the turn of the century when the Mothers' Association started advocating on behalf of the children of immigrants in Winnipeg. Several day care centres were established prior to World War I, and crèches sprang up over the years in communities where mothers worked for long shifts and volunteers identified a need for care. Churches were also involved in founding day nurseries when they perceived a need.

After World War II, child care services continued to evolve, and Friesen et al. (1992b) identified three periods of development that will be outlined below: (1) 1945–1974, (2) 1974–1981, and (3) 1982–present. Between 1945 and 1974, there was a steady increase in the number of child care facilities, and their growth was more marked when federal funds became available under CAP in 1966. Part-day nursery schools that offered enrichment opportunities for more affluent children and compensatory programs for the less fortunate also grew in number beginning in the early 1940s. A laboratory nursery school was established at the University of Manitoba in 1943 during the period when the child study movement was flourishing. Licensing of centres was a municipal responsibility during this time, and the requirements focused on issues of health and safety rather than curriculum, teacher education, group size, and teacher–child ratios. A series of government studies and briefs submitted to the government pointed to problems with the lack of consistent licensing standards as well as the lack of training programs in the province. A pilot training program was established at Red River Community College in the late 1960s. Then, in 1970, the University of Manitoba began a four-year program in Family Studies, while the University of Winnipeg introduced a three-year degree program in Developmental Studies in 1971.

Friesen et al. (1992b) identified the years from 1974 to 1981 as the second period of development of child care services in the province. In 1974, the government began to fund its Child Day Care Program, and in the first year, about 1500 spaces were included in this non-profit program that was available to families eligible for subsidies. The new program apparently had more of a social-service orientation than the previous programs, which had a welfare bias. While private centres that had been in operation from 1974 to 1977 were permitted to take subsidized children, up to 50 percent of their capacity, as of 1977 non-profit centres and family child care were generally favoured by the government's funding policies.

Licensing and inspections did not become uniform in Manitoba until 1982 when the new government introduced the Community Child Day Care Standards Act and Regulations (Friesen et al., 1992b). The act also included standards for teacher training, teacher–child ratios, programming, equipment, health and safety, and behaviour management, as well as requirements for the physical facility and fire safety. Funding for non-profit organizations that had a parent-elected board was also outlined in the act, and capital grants were made available. Teacher training standards that had to be implemented in full by 1988 led to a rapid increase in the number of teachers who were knowledgeable in the area of child development. Between 1984 and 1988, the number of teachers who had completed a two-year diploma in ECE rose from 17 percent to 62 percent. The availability of funding for substitute teachers, who were employed while untrained teachers upgraded their training in intensive programs, presumably was a significant factor facilitating this rapid change. A competency-based assessment procedure also was introduced for people with experience in the field but no formal training. Salary enhancement grants (SEGs) for eligible non-profit centres were introduced in 1986, partly in recognition of the educational requirements teachers had to meet and partly in recognition of the negative effects of low salaries.

During the period 1982 to 1988, the integration of children with exceptionalities also expanded, and funds for the additional teachers required were made available. School-based child care also received capital allowances. In addition, the government demonstrated its interest in child care by working with the federal government to try to develop a comprehensive national system of child care.

The 1988 Manitoba Child Care Task Force demonstrated a continuing interest in the quality child care system which the NDP government had begun to implement, and a number of the Task Force's recommendations were adopted. Although SEGs had been increased, teachers staged a one-day walkout from their centres in October 1989 to protest the still inadequate salaries (Friesen et al., 1992a). The Manitoba Child Care Association, founded in 1974, accepted the government's plan to have a working group study the salary complaints, and in February 1990, the group's recommendations for short-term changes were adopted. SEGs were increased, as was funding. Non-profit workplace child care centres also became eligible for capital grants. A number of groups, including the Assiniboia Downs Race Track Child Care Centre, have taken advantage of the available funding.

Regulation

Non-school-based ECE programs fall under the Ministry of Family Services in Manitoba, and the Community Child Day Care Act and Regulations mentioned above are the relevant pieces of legislation (Child Care, 1990, 1993; Friesen, 1992; Friesen et al., 1992a). The legislation on group size and teacher–child ratios is extremely strict and perhaps the best in the country, at least for centre-based care. A play-based program is described in the legislation, and, as noted above, teachers must meet training requirements.

Ontario

Ontario, with close to 10 million people, is the most populous province in Canada. Over 80 percent of the population is urban, and 90 percent of the residents live in the small area of southern Ontario that makes up less than 10 percent of the province's land mass (Kyle, 1992d). Kyle (1992a) sketched an overview of social and demographic trends in Ontario that will help you place child care in its provincial context. Immigration to Ontario has been steady since World War II, and less than 50 percent of Ontario's population have British ancestors (Kyle, 1992d). In major urban centres like Toronto, as many as 40 percent of children in educational settings may not have English as a first language, and in some neighbourhoods, there may not be any children with English as their native tongue (Kyle, 1992d). The needs of immigrant families, coupled with a high percentage of two-working-parent families, has led to a proliferation of early childhood programs: often both parents in immigrant families must work, and the families frequently require language classes.

Ontario also has close to 100 000 Aboriginal people, more than any other province. However, Aboriginal people constitute only 10 percent of the province's population. Special early childhood programs have been developed to meet the needs of Aboriginal children living on reserves and in some urban centres.

Historical Overview

Young (1981) traced the development of early childhood education in Ontario to the 1980s, and Irene Kyle (1992b), in her article "An Historical Overview of Child Care in Ontario," discussed more recent developments. Early childhood education has had a long but fragmented history in Ontario. One of the first public kindergartens in North America, if not the first (Morrison, 1991), was established in 1871 in Ontario by Dr. J.L. Hughes (Stapleford, 1976). Dr. Hughes, who provided the impetus for the optional kindergartens, later became interested in child care as a consequence of discussions with Hester Howe, a public school principal (Stapleford, 1976). Howe had many pupils in her school who brought their preschool-aged siblings to school because their widowed or deserted mothers were working and unable to care for their children during the day. Hughes suggested the establishment of a crèche to care for these preschoolers, and thus, the crèche, which is now known as Victoria Day Care Services in Toronto, was opened in 1892. Unfortunately, the subsequent history of early childhood education programs in Ontario has not been marked by the coordinating force of people such as Dr. Hughes.

In 1885, Ontario again established itself as a pioneer in education when it passed legislation making kindergartens for 5-year-olds an integral part of the public school system (Fleming, 1971). However, it was not until after World War II that kindergartens were established in virtually in all Ontario schools.

Junior kindergartens are a more recent phenomenon in Ontario. In 1943, the first junior kindergarten for 3- to 4-year-old children was established by the Ottawa Public School Board (Young, 1981). Dr. McGregor Easson, the chief inspector of Ottawa public schools at the time, cited the positive effects that British and American nursery schools had on children's development as a rationale for these programs. Four years later, the Toronto Board of Education introduced a junior kindergarten program that was made available only to children from deprived environments (Young, 1981). Although the 1950 *Report of the Royal Commission on Education in Ontario* recommended that half-day, optional programs for 3- and 4-year-old children be established by the public school boards, the increase in the number of junior kindergarten programs throughout the 1950s was minimal (Young, 1981).

The establishment of early childhood education programs for children under 5 years of age, including nursery schools and child care centres, was much more sporadic and subject to the political and social pressures of the time than the establishment of kindergartens. Although the number of child care centres increased after the 1892 establishment of the crèche and peaked during World

War I, the 1920 Ontario Mother's Allowance Act, which provided unsupported mothers with sufficient funds to remain at home, resulted in a declining need for child care (Stapleford, 1976). In 1926, however, the St. George's School for Child Study, now the Institute for Child Study, was established under sponsorship of the Department of Psychology at the University of Toronto with funds from the Laura Spelman Rockefeller Foundation (Fleming, 1971; Northway, 1973; Stapleford, 1976). The introduction of the study of child development at the university seemed to prompt a recognition of the educational aspects of care for children under 5. A number of half-day nursery schools that catered to middle-class children were established in subsequent years, and child care centres began to offer both education and care.

World War II marked a period of significant and rapid change for child care in the province (Stapleford, 1976). Mothers were needed to staff the war-related industries, and thus the provision of extensive child care services became an urgent matter. A number of child care facilities were opened in response to this demand during the early war years (Stapleford, 1976). Early in 1942, a report by the Welfare Council of Toronto and District indicated that the available child care services were inadequate (Stapleford 1976). Consequently, the council pressured the provincial and federal governments to provide appropriate care for the children of employed mothers. By July 1942, the Dominion-Provincial Wartime Day Nursery Agreement, a cost-sharing arrangement, was negotiated, and Ontario established an advisory committee to direct efforts aimed at the rapid provision of day care. A wartime day nursery, which doubled as a demonstration and training centre for teachers, was in operation within two months (Stapleford, 1976). Parents paid fees covering approximately a third of the centre's costs, and the federal and provincial governments shared the remaining expense.

The province established a Day Nursery Branch in the Department of Public Welfare to promote and administer the establishment of additional "day nurseries," as they were called at the time. Dorothy Millichamp, the Assistant Director of the Institute for Child Study, was appointed to head the newly created Day Nursery Branch (Stapleford, 1976). By the end of the war, 20 day nurseries with 1200 children between the ages of 2 and 5 had been established throughout the province. Moreover, an additional 42 child care centres had been established in the public schools for 3000 children ranging from 6 to 14 years (Stapleford, 1976). These facilities for some 4200 children reflected an unusually strong commitment to the full development of each child, especially given the haste with which the centres were conceived and opened (Stapleford, 1976). In large part, the developmental nature of these centres is attributable to the influence that Millichamp and her colleagues at the institute had on ideas of appropriate day care. However, many of the unsupervised day nurseries that opened during the early war years, in response to the demand for child care facilities, did not have the same commitment to high-quality care (Stapleford, 1976).

The end of the war marked the end of federal government support for child care centres in the province. Contrary to popular expectation, the return of the veterans to the workforce did not mean that all the working mothers wanted to return to the home. Consequently, in 1946, the government passed the Day Nurseries Act and became one of the first jurisdictions in North America to have both licensing and inspection of child care centres and provincial and municipal sharing of the operating costs. By the end of 1947, there were 146 licensed centres in the province, including 25 full-day and 139 half-day programs. Growth was slow throughout the 1950s, which is not surprising in view of Bowlby's assertion (discussed in Chapter 4) that short-term separations from the mother were comparable to being placed in a sterile orphanage. Once Bowlby's work was reassessed, confidence in child care grew, and by 1960 there were approximately 360 licensed day nurseries in the province (Stapleford, 1976).

The growth of preschools and child care centres in Ontario during the 1960s and 1970s was particularly rapid. By September 1980, a total of 66 998 children were enrolled in 1400 centre-based facilities licensed under the Ontario Day Nurseries Act (Young, 1981). Most spaces were for children 3 years and older; only 910 infants under 18 months and 2474 toddlers, ranging from 18 to 30 months, were in such centres in 1980. Junior kindergartens also multiplied in the 1960s and 1970s, and kindergartens were available in all school boards by the 1970s.

Given the lengthy history of early childhood education in the province, it is perhaps surprising to find that teacher education continues to be fragmented. Fleming (1971, vol. 5, p.1), commented that Ontario has never been noted for the importance it has placed on the formal preparation of teachers. With the exception of the Institute for Child Study's graduate education and training program for nursery school and child care teachers, there were no facilities for the preparation of preschool teachers prior to the war. The provincially operated demonstration and training child care centre, established in 1942 to meet wartime needs, ceased operations shortly after the expiry of the War Measures Act.

In the years that followed the war, the primary impetus for the establishment of education and training programs for preschool teachers came from the Toronto Nursery Education Association (TNEA) (now the Association for Early Childhood Education, Toronto [AECET]) and subsequently the Nursery Education Association of Ontario (NEAO) (now the Association for Early Childhood Education, Ontario [AECEO]), which were founded in 1946 and 1950 respectively. The first success these associations had was in persuading the government and Ryerson Polytechnical Institute (now Ryerson Polytechnic University) to establish an ECE program. Shortly afterwards, the NEAO succeeded in convincing several universities to offer three-part extension courses for preschool teachers (Fleming 1971; Stapleford, 1976). Following successful completion of the first two sessions of these courses, students were given a letter of standing "recommending the holder as a student assistant" (Fleming, 1971, vol. 5, p. 17). Students who demonstrated their competence as teachers in a nursery school or child care setting for a period of a year, and who completed the third part of the course, were eligible to apply for NEAO certification. The NEAO, a voluntary professional organization, had instituted a voluntary system of certification to regulate the competence of the members of the profession. NEAO certification provided prospective employers with an effective means of identifying competent staff.

Since 1960, there have been a number of significant developments in terms of the availability of teacher education and training programs for early childhood educators in the province. In 1965, when the Ontario Colleges of Applied Arts and Technology were proposed, the NEAO saw them as educational institutions that could meet the growing demand for competent early childhood educators to staff the rapidly increasing number of child care centres and preschools in the province (Young, 1981). Early in 1966, NEAO representatives and Department of Education personnel began to prepare a series of guidelines for the development of ECE programs in the colleges. In September of the same year, the first program opened at Centennial College and attracted far more applicants than enrollment capacity would allow. In 1967, an additional eight colleges offering the ECE program were opened, and all had a capacity enrollment that year.

Despite the availability of trained teachers, the government continued to see child care as a welfare service, and professionals in the field grew more vocal (Kyle, 1992b). In the early 1980s, the Ontario Federation of Labour organized a child care conference, which led to the establishment of the Ontario coalition for Better Day Care (now Child Care). The coalition was very active in the 1980s, and eventually the Conservative government, in a pre-election package, announced a program that would increase funding and child care spaces. The defeat of that government in 1985 was followed by a Liberal–NDP coalition, then a Liberal majority in 1987, and subsequently an NDP government in 1990. These frequent changes in government have meant that some policies developed by one party were later questioned and their implementation delayed by another party. Nonetheless, there were some significant developments in this period.

The Liberal–NDP coalition developed a child care plan that became a reality in 1987 when the New Directions for Child Care policy was included in the new government's throne speech. This policy injected over $165 million into child care, which was clearly recognized as a public service rather than a welfare benefit. School-aged programs were made a priority, and capital funding for child care centres in all new schools became available. Direct operating grants (DOGs) were given to all non-profit centres in 1988 in an effort to improve teacher salaries; later, 50 percent of the DOGs were given to profit-making centres.

Concerns about the quality of care, especially in profit-making centres, emerged during this period. A series of articles in *The Globe and Mail* (McIntosh & Rauhala, 1989) and the provincial auditor's report in the same year pointed to inadequate enforcement of the regulations across the province. Subsequent government initiatives have tried to rectify this situation. A shortage of trained teachers, due primarily to the rapid turnover of underpaid teachers in the field, is a continuing concern.

In 1990, funding for full-day kindergartens became available, and school boards were given a 1994 deadline for implementing junior kindergarten programs. In 1992, the Peel Board of Education, having hastily established junior kindergartens in 1990, ended them when cuts in provincial funding were announced. Other school boards suggested they would follow Peel's example, and in the spring of 1993, the impoverished Ontario government revoked its deadline that would have made all school boards offer junior kindergarten programs by September 1994. However, reports of a leaked Cabinet document suggested that universally available school-based programs for all children between 3 and 5 years will become available, and they will conform to the Day Nurseries Act, not the Education Act (Critics Challenge, 1993).

Regulation

Kyle (1992c, 1992d) outlined the Ontario regulations for child care for the CNCCS. Two ministries are involved in early childhood education. School-based programs, including junior and senior kindergartens, are regulated by the Ministry of Education. However, child care centres housed in schools and all non-school-based child care settings, including nursery schools and parent–child resource centres, are regulated by the Ministry of Community and Social Services (MCSS). The Day Nurseries Act and Ontario Regulation 143/88, discussed above, specify requirements for centre-based and family child care in Ontario. The legislation outlines minimum requirements for the physical setting, teacher qualifications, teacher–child ratios, group size, nutrition, and safety in licensed facilities. The legislation also specifies that centres must provide appropriate programs that enhance motor skills, language, and cognitive and socio-emotional development.

The Education Act does not have comparable requirements regarding group size, teacher–child ratios, and indoor and outdoor space; teachers do not have to have a background in early childhood education. This leads to some serious discrepancies in the program requirements for 4- and 5-year-old children in the province. For example, a 4-year-old in a junior kindergarten may be in a class of 25 children with a teacher who has minimal experience with children of this age, while a 4-year-old in a child care centre would be in a class with 2 teachers, at least one of whom has studied young children in depth, and no more than 16 children.

Quebec

Carrière's (1992) article, "A Socio-Geographic Overview of Quebec," provides an overview of this distinct province in which more than 90 percent of its 6.5 million inhabitants are of French origin. While Quebec is the largest province physically, most of its population lives in the St. Lawrence Valley, and 80 percent were in urban centres during the 1986 census. While pulp and paper production, mining, and hydroelectric power generation remain factors in the economy, manufacturing and the service sector have become major forces in Quebec. The province continues to be a destination point for a number of immigrants, especially native French speakers. Of course, all immigrant children must enrol in francophone schools.

Historical Overview

Desjardins (1992) provide a detailed account of the lengthy history of child care in Quebec, which dates back to the first half of the 19th century. Families moving into the cities to find work in new industries led to the creation of facilities to care for their children. As factory work by children under 12 did not become illegal until 1885, parents could not rely on older siblings or neighbours for child care while they were working. Children's shelters, run by the Grey Nuns and Sisters of Providence, were established in Montreal and some smaller locations as early as 1858. Over 60 000 preschoolers attended these centres between 1858 and 1922, but did the centres in no way come close to meeting the need for child care in the province. Children under 2 years were not permitted to attend the shelters, and, typically, the eldest girl in a family left school at 10 or 11 to care for the younger children in her family. A labour journalist for *La Presse*, Jean-Baptiste Gagne Petit, campaigned against this practice and day care centres eventually received some provincial government funding in the 1890s. English-speaking mothers had even more difficulty finding care. Desjardins reported that the Montreal Day Nursery, founded in 1887 by wealthy volunteer women, was the only centre for English children in the 19th century.

Many of the shelters were closed early in the 20th century, while others became orphanages. Although several child care centres were established with the advent of World War I, orphanages became the more common form of care for single parents. Apparently, only a tenth of the children in orphanages in Quebec were real orphans. Despite recommendations by the Liberal government that child care facilities and junior kindergartens be funded during the Depression, the Duplessis government firmly opposed women who worked outside the home and refused to assist them. World War II forced the government to abandon, at least temporarily, its view of working women as immoral, and six centres were opened in Montreal with federal funding. The Catholic Church, a potent force in Quebec society, denounced the child care centres, and most francophone women who worked during the war relied on informal methods of care. Duplessis closed the centres as soon as the war ended despite considerable protest, and unregulated, unsubsidized child care was the norm in the province throughout the 1950s. The city of Montreal had 27 private centres at that time, and a number of them offered a five-day residential program for children with working parents, so they could return to their homes each weekend. The Montreal Day Nursery also continued its service, and several religious groups offered help to needy children.

Despite the advent of CAP in 1966, the Quebec government remained steadfast in its opposition to child care by anyone other than parents, and it was not until the 1970s that any significant changes occurred. Federal government funding came through the Local Initiatives Program (LIP), a federally funded job creation program that provided startup funds for many child care programs throughout the country. In addition, the Perspectives Jeunesse or Focus on Youth program, a federally funded job creation program targeted at youths, led to the creation of around 70 child care centres in Quebec, much to the dismay of the provincial government. When the funding stopped in 1973, occupations of government offices and street protests followed, pressuring Bourassa's Liberal government to develop a child care policy. The Bacon Plan, implemented in 1974, allowed needy children to be subsidized but favoured for-profit centres as non-profit centres no longer received any public funds. Desjardins noted that 54 of the 70 non-profit centres had to close for financial reasons several months after the Bacon Plan was implemented.

Pressure on the government to play a role in child care continued throughout the 1970s, and, finally, in 1978, the government issued a policy statement on child care. The policy favoured parental choice of services, joint parent–government funding of child care, and additional options such as family child care and school-aged care facilities. In 1979, the government passed the Child Care Services Act and created a new government office, the Office of Child Care Services (Office des services de garde à l'enfance [OSGE]), which now falls under the jurisdication of the Minister for Women's Issues (i.e., Ministre déléguée à la condition féminine), to deal with children's issues. The OSGE, among other responsibilities, was to ensure that quality child care was available, was to monitor centres, and was to improve teacher training.

The Act Respecting Day Care recognized five types of child care: the group child care centre (garderie), family child care homes (milieu familial), drop-off centres (halte garderie), school-aged child care (milieu scolaire), and nursery schools. The new legislation set standards for these facilities, which have undergone several revisions in recent years. Teacher training, teacher–child ratios, group sizes, and centre sizes were regulated, as were health and safety, equipment, and the physical setting.

Regulation

The OSGE, a unique institution in Canadian child care, is a semi-autonomous body that has the power to set standards and regulations for child care and to ensure that the legislation is followed (Child Care, 1990; Fullum, 1992a, 1992b). The Ministère de la main-d'oeuvre et de la sécurité du revenu (MMS) et l'information professionnel and the Ministère de l'éducation (ME) are also involved in child care (Fullum, 1992a, 1992b). The MMS administers the subsidy program for child care for the OSGE. The ME administers the startup and operating grants that are available to school boards that want to establish child care in their schools. The ME also is responsible for the university and college programs for teacher training. Teacher–child group size are regulated, as is centre size. Teacher qualifications are also specified in the legislation. While centres must outline their developmental objectives in order to receive a licence, the legislation does not contain information about a prescribed curriculum.

New Brunswick

New Brunswick's population of 709 445 in the 1986 census made it the third smallest province in the country (Gamble, 1992b). Joan Gamble (1992b), an ECE professor at the University of Moncton, prepared "A Socio-Geographic Overview of New Brunswick" for the Canadian National Child Care Study. In the article, she provides an outsider with a picture of the province's economy and people. Almost

two-thirds of New Brunswick's population are English-speaking, while a third of the population is French-speaking. The province also has close to 5000 Micmac and Maliseet Indians. The population is evenly split between urban and rural settings. While fishing, logging, trapping, and other resource-based occupations used to be the mainstay of the New Brunswick economy, industries such as tourism, education, information technology, and governments also are important employers. The province is one of the poorer ones, and many young people have moved away during periods when jobs were plentiful in places such as Alberta and Ontario. Women have moved into the workforce in increasing numbers, but the unemployment rate is chronically high.

Historical Overview

Gamble (1992a) also prepared "An Historical Overview of Child Care in New Brunswick" for the CNCCS. The history of child care in New Brunswick, as in many provinces, is brief. During the first half of the century, the extended family was responsible for child care in the province. If one could not call on that informal network, the only option was to turn to the child welfare services. Prior to the 1950s, that usually meant allowing one's children to be placed in an orphanage, and those institutions were underfunded and of very questionable quality. Many served both children and adults who needed care. Large institutions for children in New Brunswick remained in existence until the mid-1970s, even though the research showing their negative effects on development had been available since the 1940s.

A number of unregulated child care centres were established in the 1960s and early 1970s in New Brunswick, and professionals in the field were becoming concerned about the quality of care in these centres. The formation of the Garde de Jour NB Day Care Association in 1973 was significant, and the association helped to accelerate changes in child care policies. In September 1974, the government proclaimed the Day Care Act, and teacher–child ratios and health and safety requirements finally became a reality. However, as we have seen in so many other jurisdictions, enforcement of the act was sporadic as there was only one supervisor to inspect all centres in the province. More comprehensive regulations were included in the 1980 Child and Family Services and Family Relations Act. The new legislation also differed in tone: child care was seen as a child development service rather than as a welfare issue.

Since 1974, excellent degree programs in education with a specialization in ECE have been available at the University of New Brunswick and the Université de Moncton, and some of the key experts in the field were graduates of these programs. However, college programs were needed. The Garde de Jour NB Day Care Association and other interested groups persistently urged the government to establish teacher-training programs. Finally, several college-based training programs were established in the early 1980s. Subsequently, a competency-based program was developed for teachers with experience but no formal training so that they became eligible for an equivalency certificate. Then, in 1987, the Canada Employment Centre agreed to fund teachers in a part-time, formal training program, and many have taken advantage of this opportunity.

A number of significant developments in ECE occurred in the early 1990s. For example, kindergartens became part of the school system, and government-funded early intervention programs became available. *Excellence in Education,* a 1992 provincial government report, also recommended significant changes in teacher education. Although the province still does not have any training regulations, a review of the child care legislation was initiated in 1992 (Child Care, 1993). Subsequently, a working group was established by the government in 1993 (Child Care, 1993) to discuss teacher training, standardization of regulations, and wage enhancement grants.

Regulation

Lutes (1992) and Lutes and Gamble (1992) outlined New Brunswick's regulations for the CNCCS. School-based ECE programs fall under the Department of Education, while non-school-based programs are under the Department of Health and Community Services. The 1980 Family Services and Family Relations Act and the 1983 Regulations 83–85 for the act contain regulations for non-school-based ECE programs. The 1985 Day Care Facilities Standards also apply to these programs. Centre size, teacher–child ratios, and group sizes are regulated in centre- and family-based ECE programs. The legislation does require centres to provide stimulating, developmentally oriented programs, but there are still no requirements for teachers other than that they be 16 or older and willing to take training. Primary staff must be 19 as of 1993 and must supervise staff under that age (Child Care, 1993).

Prince Edward Island

Mullen (1992) provides an overview of Prince Edward Island, Canada's smallest but most densely populated province. The 1986 census found that close to 50 000 of the island's almost 130 000 people live in urban settings, while 70 000 live in rural, non-farm settings. The economy of Prince Edward Island has become far more service-based in the past 30 years, and service industries now employ two-thirds of the labour force.

Historical Overview

Flanagan-Rochon and Rice (1992) documented the history of child care in the province for the CNCCS. Orphanages and informal mechanisms of child care, often involving relatives, were the norm in Prince Edward Island until the late 1960s when unregulated kindergartens developed, especially in the urban areas. Social workers saw these programs as potentially beneficial for disadvantaged children and soon wanted full-day programs. Some federally funded, unregulated, unlicensed full-day programs were developed for children from impoverished families, and private operators opened centres in urban areas like Charlottetown.

Significant growth in centre-based child care in Prince Edward Island was not seen until the mid-1970s. Nevertheless, concern mounted about the crowding, inadequate ventilation and lighting, and poor programming that characterized the few available settings in Charlottetown. In 1971, the provincial Department of Social Services assumed responsibility for regulating and funding child care. The province continued to fund several of the Head Start–type programs that had been federally funded until 1971, as well as the University of Prince Edward Island and Charlottetown child care centres. Moreover, the province established a two-year ECE program at Holland College. Then, in 1973, the Child Care Facilities Act was enacted, but it addressed only basic concerns like health and safety. However, the government initiated discussions about additional regulations with child care centre operators, who, in turn, formed the Early Childhood Development Association (ECDA).

The ECDA gained prominence through a variety of public education programs and through ongoing submission to the government of proposals for better regulations and training requirements. The ECDA was instrumental in having the government undertake its 1983 *Study of Child Care Services in Prince Edward Island*, which led to the introduction of teacher-training requirements and other far-reaching revisions to the regulations for the act. The revised regulations were introduced in 1986, and the Child Care Facilities Act and the regulations were revised in 1987. The province, with the assistance of the federal government, funded a part-time program in early childhood education at Holland College for teachers seeking to upgrade their qualifications. The University of Prince Edward Island also introduced extension courses in early childhood education. As well, the government issued a long-range policy paper on child care and increased available funding. The Direct Funding Program, announced in 1987 and improved in 1990, not only allocates maintenance funds for centres but also provides operating grants with a portion designated for teachers' salaries (Flanagan-Rochon & Rice, 1992; Flanagan-Rochon, 1992a, 1992b). Consequently, salaries have increased substantially since 1987.

Regulation

The Ministry of Health and Social Services is responsible for non-school-based ECE programs, including kindergarten, in Prince Edward Island, while the Department of Education oversees school-based ECE programs (Flanagan-Rochon, 1992a, 1992b). The five-member, multidisciplinary Child Care Facilities Board, which, by law, includes two ECDA members, is responsible for licensing and enforcement of the Child Care Facilities Act. The Coordinator of Early Childhood Services, the Assistant Coordinator, and their administrative assistant are resources for the board, and they act as inspectors in the province. They ensure that the regulations related to group size, teacher–child ratios, centre size, and teacher training are followed. The curriculum must include group and individual activities, active and quiet play, and developmentally appropriate activities.

Nova Scotia

Canning and Irwin (1992) prepared "A Socio-Geographic Overview of Nova Scotia" for the CNCCS. In 1986, 46 percent of Nova Scotia's 880 000 people lived in rural settings, but a large proportion of them lived adjacent to urban areas where they worked. Forestry, construction, mining, and fishing remain important to Nova Scotia's economy, but the service sector provides two-thirds of the available jobs. Unemployment rates are typically higher in Nova Scotia than the national average, even if they are lower than in the rest of the Atlantic region. The lack of employment opportunities forces many people to move to central and western Canada during economically bleak times, and this accounts for the relatively slow population growth. While more ethnically diverse than the other Maritime provinces, almost 90 percent of Nova Scotians are of British or French origin.

Historical Overview

Irwin and Canning (1992b) documented the history of child care in Nova Scotia for the CNCCS. Child care was not regulated until 1967 when the Day Nurseries Act was proclaimed, and CAP funding did not become available until 1972. However, there were child care programs in the province before that time. Several centres were established in Halifax in 1910 for the children of working women, and orphanages became common institutions in the following decades. A centre for underprivileged children that charged 10 cents a day for milk and a snack was established by the Protestant Orphans' Home in Halifax in 1946, perhaps in an attempt to keep the children from becoming residents of their home. In addition to the child care centres opened by several orphanages, there were some generic Head Start programs, some parent-run programs, and a student-run child care centre that operated on a non-profit basis before licensing became a reality. In addition, some profit-making centres were founded, sometimes by mothers who could not find adequate child care for their own children. Part-day preschool programs with an educational, rather than custodial, orientation also were available for those who could afford them.

The 1967 Day Nurseries Act emphasized the importance of the physical environment for licensing but did not address teacher training or curriculum. However, a government committee looking at child care in the province just prior to the creation of the act suggested that training programs were needed. The committee also suggested that CAP assistance be available only if children were in non-profit centres, and that recommendation was adopted as policy. Part-time summer and evening ECE courses, organized by professionals in the field, were offered as early as 1968, and the program has continued since then, both with and without provincial funding. A Child Study option was established in Dalhousie University's Faculty of Education in 1970, and soon after, Mount St. Vincent University began a one-year ECE diploma program and then a four-year degree program. The Nova Scotia Teachers' College also offers a two-year diploma course in child development through its Froebel Institute.

A number of child care centres were established in the early 1970s with the federal funding that was available through the Local Initiatives Program (LIP). Citizens involved in these centres pressured the province to continue funding these centres when LIP ended, and eventually received limited assistance. While additional assistance was offered in 1974 by the newly elected Liberals, they soon put a freeze on subsidized places that remained in effect until 1989. Centres were permitted to extra-bill on several occasions between 1975 and 1979 to keep solvent, and this led to an outcry about the lack of support for child care in the province. After a task force was appointed in 1979 to look at financing, improved funding, including yearly increments to the available subsidies, became a reality. Subsequently, a 1983 task force made far-reaching recommendations about teacher training, funding, infant care, and ECE-trained government employees. The teacher-training recommendations, which required two-thirds of centre teachers to have ECE training by 1989, were accepted. Many of the other recommendations were accepted in principle, subject to the availability of federal approval of a cost-sharing plan. However, the federal approval did not materialize, and issues such as separate infant care standards and subsidies continue to be discussed. Nonetheless, the recommendations to government continued through the following years, but the advocacy groups extracted firm promises only from the losing parties in the 1988 election.

Rural areas remained underserviced, subsidized spaces remained frozen, teachers remained underpaid, and protest grew. Finally, in March 1990, 80 percent of the province's non-profit centres closed. Teachers filled the legislative gallery, and the media focused on parental and community support for teachers' demands for increased wages and better funding (Irwin & Canning, 1992a). Salary-enhancement grants were announced within days, and the government created a Round Table on Day Care which was to review salaries, legislation, training, certification, and involvement of the private sector in child care by 1991. The Round Table released its interim report in April 1991, and one hundred new subsidized spaces, fewer than were recommended, were created in 1992. The Round Table was still meeting regularly as of 1993, while the need for more quality child care continued.

Regulation

The Day Care Services Section of the Department of Community Services is responsible for child care in Nova Scotia. All facilities with four or more children are required to have licences. The 1978 Day Care Act and Regulations, amended in 1984 and 1987, outlines requirements for licensed, non-school-based centres. Centre size, teacher–child ratios, and group size are regulated for some ages, but not all. The act specifies that the program must be designed to stimulate all areas of development, and the 1990 *Guidelines for Operating a Day Care Facility for Children in Nova Scotia* notes that a variety of models, including Montessori, the Cognitively Oriented Curriculum, and thematic approaches are acceptable. Two-thirds of the teachers in a centre must have ECE training or, for those teachers who began work in centres prior to the change in the act, the equivalent combination of experience and courses.

Newfoundland

Marc Glassman (1992a, 1992b) provided an overview of Newfoundland's socio-geographic features for the CNCCS and traced the history of child care in that context. In the 1986 census, 60 percent of the province's 568 349 people were found to be in urban areas. Only 2 percent of Newfoundland's population have non-British, non-French origins. A small percentage of the population is Aboriginal. Fishing, mining, logging, and their related industries remain important in the province's economy, but the 1992 and 1993 moratorium on the fishery was devastating for the province. While the service sector accounts for a larger portion of the economy, this sector depends heavily on federal transfer payments and government employment. The Hibernia oil fields project and the Churchill Falls hydroelectric project were viewed as possible means of enriching the economy of one of the poorest provinces.

Like the other Atlantic provinces, Newfoundland had many people leave during the 1980s, the boom years in central and western Canada, as employment was difficult to find at home. Newfoundland has had the dubious distinction of leading the country in unemployment rates and poverty statistics since the 1970s.

Historical Overview

As noted above, Glassman (1992a) compiled a history of child care in Newfoundland. Several accounts suggest that a group of nuns operated a child care centre at the turn of the century in Renews, and unregulated kindergarten programs were available by at least the mid-1920s. Private preschool and kindergarten programs for fee-paying parents became more plentiful in St. John's between the 1940s and 1960s, and workplace child care grew in St. John's in the 1960s. Play groups and generic Head Start programs also multiplied in the capital city during the 1960s. In addition, several child care centres and preschools were established in Labrador. It is interesting that the government prohibited care for children under 2 years in any licensed facility as of 1968, even though they did nothing about licensing existing facilities until 1975. The Day Care and Homemaker Services Act was not passed until 1975 when licensing and regulations for child care were introduced. Moreover, kindergarten was not available across the province until the 1973–1974 school year.

After a review of 1971 census data pointed to the great shortage of child care in Newfoundland, the province launched a review committee in 1974. The committee's recommendations led to the enactment of the aforementioned child care act in 1975, as well as the Day Care and Homemaker Services Regulations in 1976. Although the act seemed to emphasize the custodial aspects of child care and ignore teacher education, it did bring standards and licensing into being ahead of more affluent provinces like Alberta. Until 1980, subsidies were available only if children were in non-profit child care, but they were then extended to include up to 50 percent of the spaces in any private child care centre in the province. Centres became more common in the St. John's area, but concerns still remain about the lack of facilities in the rural areas.

The Early Childhood Development Association (ECDA), founded in 1971, persisted in asking the government to implement regulations, teacher education programs, and funding policies that would enhance the quality of child care in the province. Many of their recommendations have been accepted, although the waiting period was often extended. As of 1989, supervisors of child care centres had to have a one-year ECE certificate and a year of experience, a two-year diploma, a degree in ECE, or a related degree (e.g., child development) and a year of experience. In addition, one teacher in programs with less than 25 children (two teachers if there are more than 25) had to have a year of supervised experience or training.

The ECDA convinced Memorial University to offer a nine-course certificate program in ECE in the early 1970s, and it was extended to include a Corner Brook location. In 1980, however, the university cancelled the program, assuming that what is now Cabot College and the Faculty of Education at Memorial Universtiy would soon be offering respectively two-year and four-year degree programs in ECE. Finally, in 1983, a year-long certificate program was established with Canada Employment and Immigration funding. The long-awaited two-year diploma program did not come into being until 1986. In 1988, both certificate and diploma programs were established in Corner Brook, some eight years after the university had cancelled the original program, fearing redundancy.

The issue of junior kindergarten was raised several times during the 1980s, both by teachers and government committees concerned about how unprepared many children are for kindergarten. The teachers were successful in reorganizing kindergarten programs to be more play-based and child-centred, but junior kindergartens are still not a reality in most school boards. Infant care, or the lack thereof, also remains a concern; the province still does not permit licensed care for children under 2 years. The Association of Early Childhood Educators of Newfoundland and Labrador, founded in 1989, seems to have replaced the ECDA, and, along with several child care advocacy groups, aims to ensure that affordable, high-quality child care is available in the province. In A Canadian Professional Speaks Out, in Chapter 5, Joanne Morris described some very significant developments in teacher education that were initiated in 1991.

Regulation

The Department of Social Services is responsible for ECE programs in the province, and a 10-member Provincial Licensing Board oversees licensing and subsidies (Randall, 1992a, 1992b). Nursery schools and preschools in private schools also fall under the Day Care and Homemaker Services Act, which means that ECE programs receive equal treatment which is lacking in some provinces, such as Ontario. The Department of Education oversees the curriculum in kindergartens and primary programs and is represented on the Licensing Board. A full-time ECE consultant with the Department of Social Services develops programming standards and may inspect centres to see if they comply with the standards, at the request of the Licensing Board. The Department of Health is represented on the Licensing Board and is responsible for building, fire, health, and electrical code inspections. Finally, the Department of Education, Postsecondary Studies, is responsible for postsecondary ECE programs. Teacher–child ratios, group size, and centre size are regulated. Minimal teacher qualification requirements are in place in a province that didn't see its first ECE graduates until 1988.

Yukon Territory

Mauch (1992c) described this territory in "A Socio-Geographic Overview of the Yukon." Almost 75 percent of the territory's 30 000 residents are likely to live in Whitehorse, Faro, Dawson City, or Watson Lake. There is a large Aboriginal population, of whom the Inuvialuit are the best known. Around 25 percent of the population are Native Canadians; in rural settings, they are usually the majority group. Mining and tourism are the major industries, and both are quite susceptible to fluctuations in the economy. Mining and tourism also attract a transient labour force that leaves the territory after earning high wages for a while. Single-parent families are especially common in the Yukon; 30 percent of all preschoolers, for example, live in single-parent families. The birthrate is high, exceeded in Canada only by that in the Northwest Territories. Moreover, over 70 percent of working-age females are employed. These characteristics of the Yukon's population have a number of implications for child care.

Historical Overview

Linda Johnson and Mary Jane Joe (1992) documented the history of child care in the Yukon and included a fascinating overview of Yukon life before the gold rush, which would be good supplementary reading material. Prior to the influx of people that came with the discovery of gold, most Native people led a traditional life, living in small bands and supporting themselves through hunting and fishing.

The extended family was a reality, there were few non-Native people, and major urban centres did not exist. The 1896 rush to the Klondike quickly ended the tranquillity. Schools were established in the Yukon with the arrival of non-Native parents, but Native children were excluded from these schools. In addition, Native people became foreigners in their own land, the wildlife and resources of which were being disrupted by the newcomers.

The rush came to a fairly abrupt halt in 1904, but the practices of the foreigners had become part of life for many in the Yukon. Native children were frequently sent to residential schools run by missionaries (some of which are currently under investigation because of accusations of abuse), and were thus uprooted from their families, language, and customs. In 1942, with the arrival of construction crews for the Alaska Highway, the population multiplied to almost six times its prewar size. Wildlife disruption, social disorder, and epidemics of non-Native diseases were pronounced. While growth slowed after the war, the population of 9000 was double what it had been in pre-highway years, and urban centres started to spring up along the highway, further disrupting traditional ways of life.

Federal funding for schools was provided on the condition that Native children be allowed to attend them, and these children were slowly integrated into public schools. Nonetheless, many schools were still residential because they were concentrated in larger towns and cities, and racism was a reality for most Native students (and adults) in these urban centres. Kindergartens were not available in the 1960s in the Yukon, but a generic Head Start kindergarten was opened in Whitehorse in 1968 with the aim of more gradually introducing Native children to English and school. The first child care centre opened the same year in Whitehorse. A subsequent boom that accompanied the opening of a zinc mine at Faro led to more demand for child care, and a number of child care centres and preschools opened in the early 1970s. However, there was no legislation, and any government funding for child care programs was on an ad hoc basis.

Finally, in 1974, the Yukon Child Care Association (YCCA) was formed, at the government's suggestion, and, in conjunction with the Department of Welfare, it began to draft legislation, arrange for inspections, draft funding policies, and lobby the politicians. While its proposals were ready by 1975, it took five years of persistent work before the government finally adopted the Day Care Act and

A CANADIAN PROFESSIONAL SPEAKS OUT
Child Care Issues for First Nations

The First Nations people make up one-fifth of the Yukon's population. There are four First Nations band-operated day care centres in the Yukon, as well as a First Nations family day home in an isolated northern community. Caregivers in the rural communities as well as the larger centres understand the need to include language, heritage, values, and learning styles of First Nations people in the day care programs.

At Yukon College, our mission statement mandates all programs to incorporate a native component as an integral part of courses, not just an add-on. The Council for Yukon Indians has developed a day care curriculum manual and curriculum resource guide entitled *Show Us the Way*, which is used in numerous day care centres and family day homes throughout the territory.

In a discussion of First Nations early childhood education, several points must be stressed:

1. A strong emphasis on verbal communication is vital; enriched programming is necessary to prepare First Nations children for our school system and increase success in postsecondary education.

2. There must be accessibility of child care training support for First Nations people wishing to enter the early childhood field. In the Yukon, this means offering courses in the rural communities to enable single parents and/or parents of young children to further their education without leaving their home or family. Yukon College has addressed this need, offering early childhood courses to various rural communities each term. Distance education will enable us to reach even more students.

3. Training for child care workers and administrators must recognize and provide programming for fetal alcohol syndrome and fetal alcohol effects. Agencies providing funding and/or support staff are overburdened, and rural day care centres cannot acquire or afford staff specifically trained in this area.

4. Strong, clear cultural role models are necessary. The caregiver is the most powerful part of the curriculum, providing consistent patterns that value First Nations history and traditions. This is evident in the remote family day home, where the operator provides opportunities for the children to observe meat drying, berry picking, smoking fish, and snaring rabbits.

5. Programming must include involvement from parents, elders, and the extended family. The First Nations day cares are extensions of the community. Children develop a positive sense of identity, which in

turn leads to increased self-esteem when they have clear cultural role models and learn how their heritage is related to the present.

6. Each band-operated day care, as well as the family day home, stresses the need to introduce the traditional language to the children. First Nations children in our child care centres need to be given the tools to adjust to non-native environments, yet should have ample opportunity to preserve and maintain their cultural traditions. The First Nations elders say the seed is the tree, the tree is the forest. Children are like the seeds of a tree. They contain not only the information of the one tree, but hold the potentiality of all the forests to come.

To the parent(s), elder(s), and caregiver(s), each child is important. Although all children share some common characteristics, they believe each is a special being. It is the responsibility of the extended family, which includes the day care, to help each child reach his or her full potential.

Sandra Beckman, Yukon College, Whitehorse

Regulations. The legislation required centres with more than seven children to be licensed, and it set out teacher–child ratios and maximum centre sizes. Funding for new centres was not provided and standards for teachers were not included, but some form of regulation was welcome.

In 1979, the Yukon attained a fully elected Cabinet and responsible government, and the politicians became more responsive to concerns. This change in governing procedures was associated with a number of improvements for child care in the Yukon, including a new subsidy program and a half-time staff position to help enforce legislation. The election of the NDP government in 1985 led to further changes. Standards were improved in revised legislation, a full-time coordinator for child care services was hired, and funding was increased. Startup grants and improvement funds also became available for group and family child care. Nevertheless, concerns remained. Most children in the Yukon were not in licensed child care, and there were only three trained teachers in the territory. Most centres were in Whitehorse, while 50 only licensed spaces were to be found in other communities in 1987. A series of discussion papers followed the flurry of legislation, and, in January 1989, the government released its policy paper, *Working Together: A Child Care Strategy for the Yukon*. Substantial funds were made available, subsidies were increased, training programs were established, and new legislation was promised. The new Child Care Act was passed in 1990.

Regulation

Mauch (1992a,1992b) outlined the relevant legislation for the CNCCS. All senior kindergartens fall under the Ministry of Education in the Yukon, as do primary programs. Other ECE programs are under the jurisdiction of the Ministry of Health and

Human Resources. The legislation covers teacher–child ratios but not group size. It also specifies that centres should provide experiences for children that will encourage development in all areas, but it does not yet regulate teacher qualifications.

Northwest Territories

Cairns, Moore, Redshaw, and Wilson have described the socio-geography of the Northwest Territories (1992d), documented the historical roots of child care there (1992b), and reviewed legislation and training programs for the CNCCS (1992a, 1992c). The territories are a vast expanse of land, covering four time zones, yet the total population was just over 53 000 in 1988. While 25 percent of the people live in Yellowknife and almost 50 percent in the small communities around Great Slave Lake close to Fort Smith, the rest of the population lives in very small communities and fluctuating locations. Native people, including the Inuit, the Dene, and the Métis, comprise 58 percent of the territories' population. Hunting, trapping, and fishing are important both as sources of food and cash for the Aboriginal people, but municipal, provincial, and federal government positions account for 80 percent of the 18 561 employed people. Mining and oil production also are significant forces in the economy. Though salaries may at first look appealing, the cost of living is high, especially in areas north of Yellowknife, where supplies must be brought by air once a year. See A Closer Look.

Historical Overview

The Dene and Inuit followed a traditional hunting and gathering way of life into

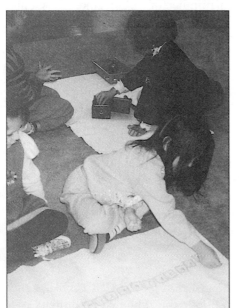

the 1950s and 1960s, and child care, as we know it, was not an issue. However, moving to communities where their children could attend school has meant an end to that way of life for most Native people. Residential schools, established at the turn of the century, also disrupted life since many children forgot their Native language and some of their traditions, never learned others, and were not exposed to familial and cultural practices.

The first child care centres were not established until the 1970s, and government regulation and funding were not firmly in place until 1987. Limited subsidies were available from 1971, but funding centres was not seen as a government concern. Short-term funds, including the federal LIP grants, were often used to set up centres, and parents and communities struggled to keep budgets low and the centres affordable. In one centre, "bare-bones" budgeting meant that teachers even brought bones from home to make soup each day! The Pairivik Centre in Iqaluit (then Frobisher Bay) was established in 1971 by Inuit women who were working and returning to school. The centre was bilingual, and children attended on a drop-in basis, which was consistent with community needs. Sometimes the children would attend for several months, then leave to visit relatives in another area, and then return for several months again. A similar facility opened in Baker Lake, but received less government funding. Organizations like the YWCA and companies such as the Nanisivik Mine opened centres to meet the needs of working parents. A number of centres also were established in the early 1970s with LIP funding in far-ranging locations, including Fort Simpson, Pangnirtung, Inuvik, and Coppermine.

In 1976, the government adopted a subsidy policy but avoided regulating and licensing policies. In 1980, the policy was changed so that funds were made available to eligible families, rather than centres with eligible children. This revision made child care services more readily available to families in small communities that did not have centres. While this did allow parents to find family child care homes and babysitters, it led to the closing of the Yellowknife YWCA centre, which had previously received deficit funding. A group of parents subsequently took over the centre, which continues to operate. Several private facilities were opened in the early 1980s, and a prekindergarten centre was opened in Fort Norman with funding from the National Native and Drug Abuse Program.

The second national child care conference, in Winnipeg in 1982, was a significant event for child care in the Northwest Territories. A number of delegates from there attended, and ultimately they formed the Northwest Territories Child Care Association (NWTCCA). The association was concerned about the lack of regulations but knew that strict rules would prevent centres from opening in many small communities. It developed voluntary standards for Yellowknife and shared them with small communities. Subsequently, a discussion paper stimulated the government to fund a family child care program in Yellowknife and eventually to review child care needs, as public demand for services was growing in small communities as well as in Yellowknife. Finally, in 1988, the Northwest Territories Child Day Care Act and the Child Day Care Standards Regulations became law (Cairns et al., 1992a, 1992c), and all of Canada had child care legislation. The act covered licensing, health and safety, teacher–child ratios, nutrition, and space. Teacher education was not covered since there were no available programs. However, significant progress has been made in this area since 1988.

Since the late 1980s, professionals in the Northwest Territories have been emphasizing the development of culturally appropriate child care practices and culturally appropriate teacher education practices for people in that vast expanse. The geography of the Northwest Territories poses special problems for inspection and monitoring, and for professional development, as many communities are accessible only by plane. In 1989, the government introduced startup, maintenance, and operating grants for non-profit centres and homes, and Cairns et al. (1992a) reported there were requests for funding for over four hundred new spaces.

ECE TEACHER SALARIES IN
THE NORTHWEST TERRITORIES

Many Canadians consider the north to be a romantic land of the midnight sun where fortunes are easily made. They anticipate working in the north for a few years, earning a large salary, and returning to the south with a substantial bank account. While it is true that incomes in the north are typically higher than those in the south, living and working in the isolation of northern Canada involves a variety of different factors that affect the cost of living. Any discussion of salary levels for people employed in the north must take into account these factors.

In 1991, the Canadian Child Care Federation and the Canadian Day Care Advocacy Association completed a joint project entitled "Caring for a Living." Their recently published report included salary averages of early childhood educators for four different position levels across the country based on studies from 1990–91. The Northwest Territories ranked first in average salaries for the positions of Assistant Teacher and Administrative Director and second only to Ontario for the positions of Teacher and Teacher Director. What this report fails to indicate are the differences in the cost of living across the country that make higher salaries necessary for residents of the north.

Ignorance of the conditions and difficulties faced by residents in Canada's north is widespread. Few people are aware that the Northwest Territories accounts for almost half of Canada's land mass and yet is inhabited by less than 60 000 people. Moreover, the majority of the inhabitants are located in small communities of less than 3000 people spread across four time zones. In fact, only 15 of approximately 66 communities have year-round access by road; although some communities can be reached by ice road in winter, most communities can only be accessed by plane. This means that all the supplies for these communities (food, building materials, clothes, toys, furniture) must be brought in by plane or via the once-a-year sea lift. Imagine putting together your grocery list and having to plan for an entire year. Imagine living in Iqaluit on Baffin Island and paying over $12 for four litres of milk. Even in Yellowknife, which is accessible by road virtually all year, people are expected to pay 66 cents for a litre of gas and $800 a month for a one-bedroom apartment. Secondary expenses add to the cost of living. To visit family or to go on vacation, residents of Yellowknife face airfares topping $1800 to Toronto. People living in the more remote communities face even higher travel costs.

In an effort to counterbalance these differences in costs, the Northwest Territories government has two minimum wages to accommodate the cost of living in a remote community without road access. Moreover, many salaries include housing allowances to help offset the high cost of housing in the Northwest Territories.

Statistics Canada considers the cost of living in the north to be roughly 25 to 30 percent higher than in southern Canada, the percentage increasing for more remote and isolated settlements. If one were to subtract 25 to 30 percent from the reported average wages for child care workers in the Northwest Territories, perhaps a more accurate comparison of wages with southern child care workers could be made.

So don't cast an envious eye on the salaries paid to the northern child care worker. While "income" is higher, "outgo" is also substantially higher. In the end, when compared with salaries paid in southern Canada, the real income earned by northern child care professionals may, in fact, be less.

Gillian Moir, Arctic College, Yellowknife

EXHIBIT P.1 GOVERNMENT DEPARTMENTS RESPONSIBLE FOR CHILD CARE

Provinces/Territories	Department
British Columbia	Ministry for Women's Equality
Alberta	Alberta Family and Social Services—Day Care Programmes
Saskatchewan	Dept. of Social Services—Child Care Branch
Manitoba	Dept. of Family Services, Child Care
Ontario	Ministry of Community & Social Services, Child Care Branch
Quebec	L'Office des services de garde à l'enfance
New Brunswick	Office for Childhood Services in Dept. of Health & Community Services
Nova Scotia	Daycare Services, Dept. of Community Services
Prince Edward Island	Early Childhood Services, Division of Special Services, Dept. of Health & Social Services
Newfoundland & Labrador	Day Care and Homemaker Services, Dept. of Social Services
Northwest Territories	Dept. of Social Services
Yukon	Child Services Unit, Dept. of Health & Human Resources

Source: Based on Child Care Resource and Research Unit. (1993). *Child Care in Canada: Provinces and Territories*. Toronto: CRRU, University of Toronto.

Regulation

The Department of Education, Culture, and Employment's Child Day Care Section administers the Northwest Territories Child Day Care Act, and two inspectors are responsible for all licensing, monitoring of group and centre sizes, and teacher–child ratios. Programs are to facilitate development and reflect the ethnic and cultural backgrounds of the children. Currently, teachers are only required to be 19 years of age, and they must supervise any support staff under 19. The children's cultural background also is to be reflected in staffing patterns.

Canadian Initiatives in Child Care

Child Care Visions

Child Care Visions (CCV) was created in 1995 as a National Child Care Research and Development program, administered by Human Resources Development Canada. Its mandate is to support the production of new knowledge on current and emerging child care issues, especially those most in need of investigation. Annual calls for proposals (*Child Care Visions Call for Proposals*, 1997) may address need areas such as on-reserve care, flexible-hours care, and quality issues; projects must address implications for service planning, delivery, and evaluation. Through these competitions the program hopes to produce results applicable to community, government, and funding bodies.

Canadian Child Care Federation

Project Highlights

The Canadian Child Care Federation is embarking upon several exciting and important studies for the child care field. All of these projects involve partnerships with other organizations that have a keen interest in improving the quality of child care for Canadian children and families. All of these projects include extensive consultation with the field.

Quality Assurance Project

Under the co-sponsorship of the CCCF and its 13 affiliate organizations, and with the leadership of principal researchers Gillian Doherty and Alan Pence, this project will develop a framework for quality assurance in Canada that includes processes, mechanisms, and tools for child care providers, parents, governments, training programs, and communities. The model for quality assurance will be based on community development principles and will be developed using an inclusive process of consultation with the community.

Partners In Practice: Successful Canadian Mentoring Programs Pilot Project

Human Resources Development Canada (HRDC), in partnership with the Early Childhood Community Development Centre (St. Catharines, Ontario), Niagara College (Welland, Ontario), College of the North Atlantic (St. John's, Newfoundland), Child Care Connections Nova Scotia, and the Certification Council of Early Childhood Educators of Nova Scotia will look at the development of reflective practice by early childhood practitioners. The project will pair mentors and protégés at different stages in their career development.

Education and training modules will be designed and delivered for both mentors and protégés. Data will be collected on mentoring strategies, the demonstration of reflective thinking, the effects that the pilots have on the equality of the programs provided to the children in the protégés' classrooms, and the job satisfaction of the participants.

The project outlines the following definitions and program objectives:

1. What is mentoring?

It is the pairing of an experienced practitioner who practises with excellence (MENTOR) with a less experienced practitioner (PROTÉGÉ) to help the latter become a more effective, reflective practitioner.

2. Who is an early childhood mentor?

She or he is an experienced early childhood practitioner who practises with excellence and is concerned not only with how children grow and learn but also in gaining skills to help other adults become more effective practitioners.

3. Who is an early childhood protégé?

She or he is an early childhood educator who works with a mentor for the purpose of furthering her or his career through reflecting upon personal practice with children and enhancing skills.

4. What is reflective practice?

Reflective practice is the process of questioning, analyzing, reconsidering, and evaluating practice which enables teachers and students to gain insight into their practices and explore new ways of doing things in the future.

5. What are the overall objectives of the Partners in Practice: Successful Canadian Mentoring Programs Pilot Project?

The objectives are:

- to compare mentoring tools and strategies and their effect on the development of reflective thinking in early childhood education students, trained novice child care teachers with less than two years of experience, and experienced child care teachers with more than two years of experience in the process of being certified;

- to develop a mentoring model that develops reflective practice in the child care practitioner and that can be implemented at various stages of his or her development as a child care practitioner. The model will be inclusive, portable, affordable, accessible, sustainable, and adaptable to various local/provincial/territorial and national contexts;

- to identify roles of each partner (postsecondary early childhood education programs, child care organizations, and child care practices) in developing reflective practice in child care practitioners;

- to contribute to the enhancement of quality child care at the individual, centre, and system (infrastructure) levels; and

- to identify gaps and recommend areas for further study relative to mentoring and reflective practice.

The final report is expected by the fall of 1998.

Source: *Niagara Early Childhood Mentoring Program Information Package* (1997), Early Childhood Community Development Centre, St. Catharines, Ontario. Reprinted with permission.

Family Child Care Training Project

The objectives of this project are to develop guidelines for family day care training that meet the needs of caregivers and of the children and their families; to identify best practices in family day care training; and to develop a framework for the delivery of family day care training that is flexible, innovative, and responsive to individual and community needs. Co-sponsors of this project are the Canadian Child Care Federation, Canadian Association of Family Resource Programs, Alberta Association of Family Day Home Agencies, Family Dare Care Association of Manitoba, Family Home Day Care Association of Newfoundland and Labrador, Home Child Care Association of Ontario, Ontario Network of Home Child Care Provider Groups, and Western Canada Family Child Care Association of BC. The principal researcher is June Pollard and the project manager is Lee Dunster.

Early Childhood Education Training Study

The Association of Canadian Community Colleges and the CCCF are sponsors of this important new project that will analyze the content, methodology of delivery, and evaluation mechanisms of the programs for the preparation of child care providers in Canada. The goal is to derive models of education and training.

The Future of Early Childhood Education in Canada

In Chapter 1, we examined issues that Canadian early childhood teachers face as a profession. As we approach the end of the 20th century, we can look back and examine some of the factors that have shaped the field as it exists today.

But what lies ahead? Are there more changes in store? Will unresolved social issues be addressed? Will early childhood education become an important force in considering these issues? Lacking the aid of a crystal ball, we might, nonetheless, try to predict what lies ahead by looking at current trends:

- From all economic and social indications, it is reasonable to expect that a high percentage of families will continue to have two parents in the workforce. Thus, while they are at work, dual-income families, along with working single parents, will continue to need care for their young children.

- The increase in the percentage of women in the childbearing years slows as we approach the end of the century. Nonetheless, the actual number of children potentially requiring child care will still be higher as we move beyond the year 2000 (Jones, Marsden, & Tepperman, 1990).

- Employment and Immigration Canada (1992) projected that child care would be one of the top ten high-demand occupations throughout the decade. Employment opportunities in early childhood education will continue to increase.

- The number of young children who live in poverty is also expected to increase (Halpern, 1987; Wash & Brand, 1990). However, recent economic and political realities in Canada have not made people optimistic about federal increases in funding for child care.

- Employer involvement in child care sponsorship has been one of the fastest-growing trends during the past decade. This interest is likely to increase as employers recognize the need to provide child care benefits for parent-employees to help maintain a productive workforce. A shift in type of program sponsorship, along with new job opportunities, is likely to accompany such a trend.

- All indications are that the number of positions for early childhood professionals will continue to rise because of the ongoing need of families for child care, projected expansion in publicly funded programs for children at risk, and increasing numbers of employer-sponsored programs. Yet, there are and will continue to be grave concerns about the stability of the early childhood workforce. In no other industry is there such a high turnover of employees as in child care. Unless wages become more attractive, this turnover is likely to continue.

- Professionals working with young children are realizing that teacher training programs for those specializing in early childhood education are fragmented in most Canadian jurisdictions. Programs for elementary school teachers often do not place a great enough emphasis on the early years, while programs for child care teachers do not place enough stress on school-related issues. Joint offerings and more formal liaison mechanisms between programs are likely to increase. An example of such a liaison is found in Ontario, where faculty from the early childhood education programs at Durham College (Oshawa) and Seneca College (Toronto) are involved in discussions with York University's education faculty about developing a degree program that emphasizes the early years and draws on the resources of all three institutions.

- As more children are in school-aged care, new issues emerge. The need for improved communication between child care facilities and elementary schools is becoming more urgent. Similarly, there will be a greater opportunity for teacher training programs to broaden their focus to include non-school-based care in the curriculum.

- As we have discussed, stability of staff is an important element in the quality of early childhood programs because children's trust and attachment to the adults in their lives depends on that stability. As a result, there has been increasing concern about the interplay among the needs of children for quality care, the needs of parents for affordable child care, and the needs of early childhood professionals for appropriate compensation and status (Willer, 1987). This concern, expressed both within and outside the early childhood profession, will continue to be articulated. We can expect greater focus on, and increasing public awareness of, this issue in the future.

- As issues related to early care and education continue to occupy public attention, it becomes more and more apparent that our country lacks a cohesive and consolidated social policy within which to consider child and family matters. For instance, a wide variety of agencies initiate, license, administer, and evaluate varying programs for children and families, often relying on different philosophies, approaches, and regulations. Even within provinces, there are different regulations governing variables like teacher–child ratios, depending on which ministry is involved. But, at the same time, because of increased public attention, there also seems to be greater willingness to address such issues with more depth, integration, and forethought. It can be expected, therefore, that efforts to coordinate early childhood policies and approaches will continue in the future, and perhaps a national policy will eventually be a reality. Many programs for young children, for example, compensatory education and kindergarten programs, often are operated only on a part-day basis. Such scheduling is problematic for working parents who need full-day care for their children. This conflict may prevent youngsters, who would potentially benefit, from participating in such programs (Washington & Oyemade, 1985). Because limited funding is the major stumbling block to extending these programs to meet working parents' needs, this issue will continue to be raised.

- Within the early childhood profession, there is a continued focus on the pluralistic nature of our society and the shrinking world in which children are growing up. Many early childhood programs can be expected to focus more than ever on an unbiased curriculum that includes children and families from all cultural, ethnic, linguistic, and economic backgrounds, as well as children with disabilities. Special programs that preserve the culture of Aboriginal groups also are likely to become more numerous. Sandra Beckman from Yukon College in Whitehorse outlined some child care issues for First Nations in A Canadian Professional Speaks Out, page 446.

- Because of legislation in some provinces, which ensures that young children with disabilities are included in early education, there will be continued efforts to ensure that this occurs. The parent groups representing children with disabilities are a powerful lobby, and they are likely to pressure provinces to enact legislation about integration.

Conclusion

As we leave you to study, we trust we have stirred your emotions, stimulated questions, and provided some answers. You belong to a field that is rapidly gaining momentum, professional status, and a cohesion that will empower its members immensely as we move into the new millennium. This is a field in its infancy, and you can have a profound impact on its development and direction, as you will on each and every child each and every day. Welcome to early childhood education!

Appendix 1

The books you select for children should meet the best standards, both for literary and artistic quality. Although more than 2000 children's books are published every year, the fact that a book is in print does not necessarily assure that it is good (Sword, 1987). There are some published guides to selecting high-quality children's books (for instance, the monthly *Bulletin of the Center for Children's Books*, the bimonthly *Horn Book Magazine*, or the American Library Association's *Notable Children's Books*), and resource persons such as children's librarians can prove extremely helpful. But it is also important to develop a sense of what constitutes a good book (Glazer, 1986). As you review books to read to children, apply the following guidelines (Glazer, 1986; Goodman et al. 1987; Machado, 1985; Sword, 1987).

Overall Impression

- The length of the book should be appropriate to the ages of the children. Although engrossing stories of increasing length should be presented as children get older, 5 to 10 minutes (not including discussion) is generally a good time limit for children over age 3.

- The amount of text per page should also be considered. Especially young preschoolers will find long text with few pictures difficult.

- The size of the book is important, particularly when you read to a group of children. Very small books should be kept for one-on-one reading sessions. Children do enjoy many of the new oversized books.

- The binding of a book is important if you are planning to buy it for the school library. Sturdy binding will ensure durability. Some schools prefer buying less expensive books such as paperbacks, which won't last long but the cost is only one third or one fourth that of the hardbound books.

Text Elements

- Read the book carefully and consider whether the plot or story line is coherent and interesting. The plot doesn't have to be complex, but it should be plausible and logical. The adventure of Max in Maurice Sendak's *Where the Wild Things Are* is a good example of a well-written plot that appeals to young children.

- The characters of the book should be distinctive and memorable, should not be stereotyped, and should provide children something with which they can identify. Children have no trouble remembering mischievous Curious George or spunky Madeline from their books.

- Many books revolve around a theme, for instance, friendship, emotional reactions, or exploration (Smith, 1989). If there is a theme, it should not sound like a sermon. A theme should also be relevant to young children's lives and worth sharing with them. Ann Scott's *On Mother's Lap* contains the common theme of jealousy over a new sibling, an experience to which many children can relate.

- As you review a book, pay close attention to the style of writing. Language should be simple but vivid and evoke appropriate mood and images. Because children delight in repetition and humour, look for some books that incorporate these elements. Children love to chime in the refrain of Wanda Gag's *Millions of Cats* as the old couple's acquisition of cats reaches the ludicrous stage with "hundreds of cats, thousands of cats, millions, and billions, and trillions of cats!"

Illustrations

- Above all, pictures should be aesthetically pleasing, complementing and enlivening the words of the story. Many skilled artists' talents enrich children's books. Illustrators use numerous, effective ways to convey the story in pictures. As you browse through some children's classics, compare the whimsical characters of Dr. Seuss, the humorous pen-and-ink drawings of Maurice Sendak, or the impressionistic watercolours of Brian Wildsmith.

- Pictures should be placed adjacent to the text so the story and illustrations work in harmony.

Appendix 2

1. "Sticky Popcorn"
   Children begin by jumping or hopping up as they "pop." Because the popcorn is sticky, whenever a piece of popcorn touches another they stick together. Once stuck, they continue to pop together until all the popcorn kernels make one big popcorn ball.

2. "Musical Hugs"
   With energetic music playing, children skip around the room. When the music first stops, children give a big hug to someone nearby. When the music starts again, pairs of huggers can skip together if they want. The next time the music stops at least three children hug together, and so on, until everyone is joined in one massive hug.

3. "Shoe Twister"
   The children each remove one shoe and place the shoes in a pile. While holding hands in a circle around the shoe pile, the children pick up someone else's shoe (the method for doing this is left up to the children's imagination). After locating the owners of the shoes, they exchange the footwear without breaking the circle.

4. "Big Turtle"
   Seven or eight children get on their hands and knees under a "turtle shell"—a tumbling mat, tarp, or blanket. Children have to work together to move without dropping the shell.

5. "Toesies"
   With bare feet, pairs of children lie stretched out on the floor, toes touching. They try to roll across the floor while maintaining their toe touch.

6. "Beach Ball Balance"
   Pairs of children try to hold a large ball between them without using their hands. They try to find as many different ways of doing this as possible (between their stomachs, knees, foreheads, hips, and so on). Next they try to walk without losing the ball.

7. "Lap Ball"
   The children sit close together in a circle and try to pass a large ball from lap to lap without using their hands. A less difficult version of "Lap Ball" and "Beach Ball Bounce" can be arranged by having four children each hold a corner of a towel and and keeping a ball bouncing on a towel through cooperative effort.

8. "Elbow-Nose Reverse"
   With the children in a circle, one child starts by pointing to her or his elbow and saying, "This is my nose." The second child passes this message to the next one, and so on. When this has gone around the circle, a new confusing message is sent.

Sources: Orlick, T. (1978), *The cooperative sports and games book* (New York: Pantheon Books); Sobel, J. (1983), *Everybody wins: Non-competitive games for young children* (New York: Walker & Co.).

Appendix 3A

The development of young children's art can be seen in these pictures. Typical of two-year-olds' art. Zena's and Ryan's work contain many of the basic scribbles, while Jessie's and Tommy's depictions contain combinations that suggest a face. Jessica's work shows the emergence of shapes and combines. As he was scribbling, three-year-old Bret saw a suggestion of Snoopy emerge; he added some details to enhance the image and named the picture "Snoopy," The older children's work is much more deliberate and recognizable, moving from the crude dinosaurs, sun, and flowers of the four- and five-year-olds to the greater sophistication and humor shown by the school-aged children.

Appendix 3B

Art Recipes

1. Noncooked Play Dough
Mix together:
   3 cups flour
   $1\frac{1}{2}$ cups salt
Stir in:
   1 cup water
   $\frac{1}{4}$ cup cooking oil
   food coloring or dry tempera paint
Knead ingredients together until well mixed. Add more water if too dry or more flour if too sticky. Store in an airtight container or plastic bag.

2. Cooked Play Dough
Mix together in an aluminum pot:
   2 cups flour
   1 cup salt
   2 cups water
   $\frac{1}{4}$ cup oil
   1 tablespoon cream of tartar
   food coloring
Cook these ingredients over medium heat, stirring constantly, until they thicken. Place on a plate to cool enough to handle comfortably. Knead, and then store mixture in an airtight container.

3. Cornstarch Dough
In a pot, bring to a boil:
   3 cups salt
   1 cup water
In a separate bowl, mix:
   $1\frac{1}{2}$ cups cornstarch
   1 cup water
Add the cornstarch mixture to the boiling saltwater mixture and cook over low heat for several more minutes, until thick. Place on a plate and let the dough cool enough to handle comfortably. Knead well, then store airtight in the refrigerator.

4. Peanut Butter Clay
Combine and knead:
$1\frac{1}{2}$ cups peanut butter
1 cup powdered milk

5. Soap Flake Finger Paints
2 cups soap *flakes* (not soap powder)
water
food coloring
In a bowl, gradually add water to soap flakes while beating with a rotary or electric mixer. The soap should be the consistency of beaten egg whites, holding soft peaks. Add food color to make desired shade.

6. Liquid Starch Finger Paints
Pour 1 tablespoon of starch on heavy paper; add liquid color.

A Guide to Daily Food Choices

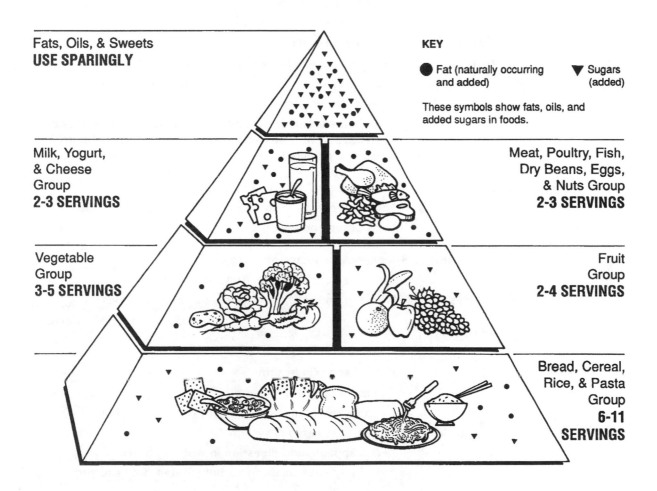

Fats, Oils, & Sweets
USE SPARINGLY

KEY

● Fat (naturally occurring and added)

▼ Sugars (added)

These symbols show fats, oils, and added sugars in foods.

Milk, Yogurt, & Cheese Group
2-3 SERVINGS

Meat, Poultry, Fish, Dry Beans, Eggs, & Nuts Group
2-3 SERVINGS

Vegetable Group
3-5 SERVINGS

Fruit Group
2-4 SERVINGS

Bread, Cereal, Rice, & Pasta Group
6-11 SERVINGS

Appendix 4B

Protein
- Essential for growth and lifelong body maintenance.
- Builds resistance to disease.

Sources: Animals foods and plant foods such as dry peas or beans.

Minerals

Calcium
- Forms healthy bones and teeth.
- Aids in normal blood clotting.
- Helps nerves and muscles react normally.

Sources: Milk and other dairy products.

Iron:
- Helps blood cells carry oxygen from the lungs to body cells.
- Protects against some forms of nutritional anemia.

Sources: Liver, meat, egg yolks, dry beans, dark greens.
- Other minerals are important too, such as **zinc, iodine, phosphorus,** and **magnesium.** Eating a wide variety of nutritious foods will provide them.

Fats
- Carry vitamins A, D, E, and K.
- Source of energy (calories); best used in limited amounts.

Sources: Meat group and milk group.

Carbohydrates
- Inexpensive source of energy.
- Best when consumed as fruit sugar or starch.

Sources: Whole-grain bread, cereal, rice, pasta, or potatoes.

Vitamins

A
- Protects eyes and night vision.
- Helps keep skin healthy.
- Builds resistance to disease.

Sources: Deep yellow/orange or very dark green vegetables.

B-complex
- Protects the nervous system.
- Keeps appetite and digestion in working order.
- Aids body cells in using carbohydrates, fat, and protein for energy.

(*The more important B-complex vitamins include **thiamin, riboflavin, folic acid, niacin, B_6, B_{12}.**)

Sources: Whole-grain products, enriched rice, wheat germ, beans, peas, nuts, peanut butter, fish, and leafy green vegetables.

C	▪ Keeps body cells and tissues strong and healthy.
	▪ Aids in healing wounds and broken bones.
Sources:	Citrus fruit, melon, strawberries, broccoli, tomatoes, raw cabbage.
D	▪ Aids in absorption and use of calcium and phosphorus by body cells.
	▪ Helps build strong bones and teeth.
Source:	Vitamin-D fortified milk.

Adapted from Rothlein, L. (1989), Nutrition tips revisited: On a daily basis, do we implement what we know? in *Young Children, 44*(6), 30–36.

Appendix 4C

SELECTED COOKBOOKS THAT FOCUS ON NUTRITIOUS RECIPES

Croft, K. B. (1971). *The good for me cookbook.* San Francisco, CA: R and E Research Associates.

Gooch, S. (1983). *If you love me don't feed me junk!* Reston, VA: Reston Publishing Co.

Goodwin, M. T., & Pollen, G. (1980). *Creative food experiences for young children.* Washington, DC: Center for Science in the Public Interest.

Haney-Clark, R., Essa, E., & Read, M. (1983). *SHINE!: School-home involvement in nutrition education.* Reno, NV: Child and Family Center, University of Nevada, Reno.

Harms, T., & Veitch, B. (1980). *Cook and learn.* Menlo Park, CA: Addison-Wesley.

Johnson, B., & Plemons, B. (1984). *Individual child portion cooking: Picture recipes.* Mount Rainier, MD: Gryphon House Press.

Katzen, M. (1977). *Moosewood cookbook.* Berkeley, CA: Ten Speed Press.

Wanamaker, N., Hearn, K., & Richarz, S. (1979). *More than graham crackers: Nutrition education and food preparation with young children.* Washington, DC: National Association for the Education of Young Children.

Appendix 5A

EXAMPLES OF COMMON UNIT BLOCKS

Square or Half Unit		Roof Boards	
Unit		Intersection	
Double Unit			
Quadruple Unit			
Ramp		Half Roman Arch and Small Buttress	
Large Triangle and Small Triangle		Large Buttress	
Pillar and Half Pillar		Ellipse, Curve and Quarter Circle	
Unit Arch and Half Circle			
Large Column or Cylinder and Small Column or Cylinder		Side Road	
Small Switch		Large Switch and Gothic Door	

Appendix 5B

BASIC WOODWORKING TOOLS FOR EARLY CHILDHOOD

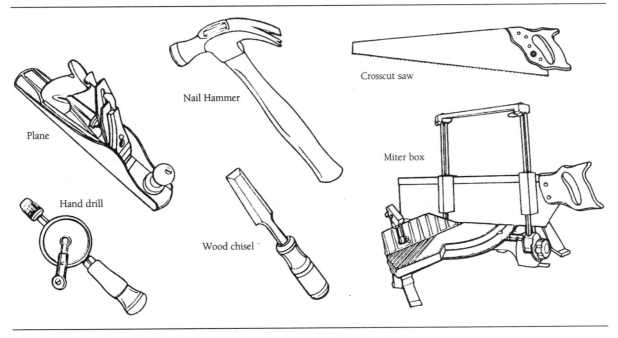

Plane

Nail Hammer

Crosscut saw

Hand drill

Wood chisel

Miter box

Glossary

ABC analysis   An observational technique in which the observer records observations in three columns, identifying antecedent, behaviour, and consequence.

Absorbent mind   Maria Montessori's term to describe the capacity of young children to learn a great deal during the early years.

Abstract thinking   According to Jean Piaget, the ability to solve a variety of problems abstractly, without a need to manipulate concrete objects.

Academic materials   *See* **Conceptual materials.**

Accommodation   According to Jean Piaget, one form of adaptation that takes place when an existing concept is modified or a new concept is formed to incorporate new information or a new experience.

Accountability   To be responsible for one's actions.

Acquisition   To gain or acquire (i.e., a skill or knowledge).

Active learning   A teaching style in which children are active seekers of knowledge, not passive recipients of it.

Active listening   Thomas Gordon's term for the technique of reflecting back to children what they have said as a way to help them find their own solutions to problems.

Activities   Well-planned, self-selected learning opportunities, usually placed in activity centres, for children in an active learning program.

Activity centre (also called learning or interest area)   An area in which materials and equipment are combined around common activities, such as art, science, or language arts.

Activity time   The largest block (or blocks) of time in the early childhood program day during which children can select from a variety of activities.

Adaptation   Jean Piaget's term for the process that occurs any time new information or a new experience occurs.

Adoptive parents   A person (or persons) who become parents through a legal process.

Adult–child ratio   *See* **Child–adult ratio.**

Advanced entry   *See* **Equivalency.**

Adventure playground   A European innovation, a type of outdoor play area in which children use a wide range of available "junk" materials to create their own environment.

Advocates   People speaking out on behalf of another.

Aesthetics   The enjoyment and appreciation of beauty, particularly the beauty in forms of art.

Aggregates   Rhoda Kellogg's term for the step in the development of art in which children combine three or more simple diagrams.

Aggression   Behaviour deliberately intended to hurt others.

Allergies   Physiological reactions to environmental or food substances that can affect or alter behaviour.

Anal stage   The second stage of development described by Sigmund Freud, occurring during the second two years of life, in which pleasure and conflict derive from bowel control and elimination.

Anecdotal record   A method of observation involving a written "word picture" of an event or behaviour.

Anxiety   A general sense of uneasiness that cannot be traced to a specific cause.

Application   The ability to implement one's knowledge and skills.

Appropriate practices   *See* **Developmentally appropriate practices.**

Assimilation   According to Jean Piaget, one form of adaptation that takes place when the person tries to make new information or a new experience fit into an existing concept.

Assistant teacher   A person who works under the guidance of the head teacher in providing a high-quality program for the children and families in the class. (Also called aide, helper, auxiliary teacher, associate teacher, or small-group leader.)

Associative play   A category of play in which children interact to some extent and may share materials but are not engaged in a common activity.

Atelier   A workshop that provides learning through visual arts and an aesthetically pleasing environment.

Atelierista   A teacher who provided the framework for learning through visual arts and an aesthetically pleasing environment.

Attachment   The child's bond with the mother, established during the first year of life.

Attention deficit-hyperactivity disorder (ADHD)   Disorder characterized by short attention span, restlessness, poor impulse control, tendency to be distracted, and inability to concentrate.

Audience awareness   Children's growing awareness that their stories are a form of communication and thus should make sense to others.

Authority stage   The stage of parenting defined by Ellen Galinsky typifying parents of young preschoolers who are defining rules as well as their own parenting role.

Auto-education   *See* **Self-education.**

Autonomy   The ability to care for oneself (to be independent).

Autonomy vs. shame and doubt   The second stage of development described by Erik Erikson, occurring during the second two years of life, in which toddlers assert their growing motor, language, and cognitive abilities by trying to become more independent.

Back-to-basics movement   A movement that advocates a return to teacher/subject-centred education that stresses the basic subject areas.

Bank Street Model   An early childhood education program model, developed at the Bank Street College of Education in New York, that draws on progressive education and the open education model seen in the British Infant Schools.

Basic scribbles   According to Rhoda Kellogg, the twenty fundamental markings found in all art.

Behaviour management   The behavioural approach to guidance, according to which the child's behaviour is under the control of the environment, which includes space, objects, and people.

Behaviour modification   The systematic application of principles of reinforcement to modify behaviour.

Behaviour setting   According to Kounin and Sherman, different environments elicit behaviours that are fitted to the setting; thus, children act "schoolish" at school.

Behavioural objective   An aim or goal, usually set for an individual child, that describes in specific and observable terms what the child is expected to master.

Behaviourism   The theoretical viewpoint, espoused by theorists such as B.F. Skinner, that behaviour is shaped by environmental forces, specifically in response to reward and punishment.

Behaviourist view of language development   *See* **Behaviourism.**

Bereavement   The grief over a loss such as the death of a loved one.

Bibliotherapy   The use of books that deal with emotionally sensitive topics in a developmentally appropriate way to help children gain accurate information and learn coping strategies.

Bilingualism   The ability to use two languages.

Bimanual control   The ability to use both hands in tasks for which each hand assumes a different function.

Biological parents   Natural mother and father of a child.

Black English   A term identifying the dialect that is spoken by some black children and that has a complex grammatical system of its own.

Blended family   The merging of two or more families.

Board of directors   Policy-making or governing board that holds ultimate responsibility, particularly for not-for-profit programs.

Brag book   A journal, sent back and forth daily with a child, containing events that pertain to the child's daily activities and behaviour.

Brigance Diagnostic Inventory of Early Development   A developmental assessment tool for children from birth to age 7.

British Infant School   Schools for 5- to 8-year-olds where the open model was developed.

Burn-out syndrome   A condition that is experienced by professionals as a result of undue job stress, and that is characterized by loss of energy, irritability, and a feeling of being exploited.

Canada Assistance Plan (CAP)   Canadian federal legislation that requires the federal government to share child care funding—only for those in need—with the provinces on a 50–50 basis.

Canadian Child Care Federation (CCCF)   National early childhood organization, founded by the federal government in 1987, that aims to improve the quality of child care in Canada by providing services to those in the field.

Canadian Childcare Advocacy Association (CCAA)   National early childhood organization, founded in 1983, that aims to make high-quality, affordable, nonprofit child care accessible to all Canadians who need it.

Canadian National Child Care Study (CNCCS)   A federally funded study of child care in Canada.

CAP   *See* **Canada Assistance Plan.**

Caregiver   A term traditionally used to describe a person who works in a child care setting.

Casa dei bambini (children's house)   Montessori's first school in Rome, founded in 1907.

Centre-based program   A school program for young children that usually includes larger groups of children than are found in home-based programs.

Change agents   These agents help leaders and organizations restructure to develop relationships that maximize both the humanistic and business practices.

Checklist   A method of evaluating children that consists of a list of behaviours, skills, concepts, or attributes that the observer uses by checking off an item as a child masters it.

Child abuse and neglect   Any action or inaction that harms or puts a child at risk.

Child–adult ratio   The number of children for whom an adult is responsible, calculated by dividing the total number of adults into the total number of children. A high ratio means there are fewer children per teacher; a low ratio means there are more children.

Child advocacy   Political and legislative activism by parents and professionals who urge consideration of social issues affecting children.

Child care centre   *See* **Centre-based program**.

Child care worker   *See* **Caregiver**.

Child-centred approach   An approach that allows children to select activities themselves.

Child Development Associate (CDA)   An early childhood teacher who has been assessed and found competent through the national CDA credentialling program.

Childhood   Pertaining to those who are under adult legal age.

Child study movement   A movement that occurred in the 20th century in the United States in which many university preschools were established to develop scientific methods for studying children.

Classical conditioning   A learning technique in which a stimulus that usually evokes a reflex is paired with one that does not usually evoke the reflex, until the latter eventually evokes the reflex by itself.

Classification   The ability to sort and group objects by some common attribute or property, such as colour or size.

Coach   *See* **Senior teacher**.

Code of ethics   Agreed-upon professional standards that guide behaviour and facilitate decision making in work situations.

Code switching   The ability to switch appropriately from one language system to another.

Cognition   The process of mental development that is concerned more with how children learn than with the content of what they know.

Cognitive developmental theory   The theory, formulated by Jean Piaget, that focuses on how children's intelligence and thinking abilities emerge through distinct stages.

Cognitive interactionist view of language development   The view that children's language is rooted in cognitive development, requiring, for instance, the ability to represent objects mentally.

Collaboration   Working together for the common good.

Collage   A type of art activity in which a creative combination of materials is assembled.

Colour tablets   In Montessori programs, two sets of wooden tablets of many colours that children match and sort by shades.

Combines   According to Rhoda Kellogg, a step in the development of art in which children combine two simple diagrams.

Common law   Legally binding partnership without the ceremony of marriage.

Communicative competence   A term that describes the ability to use language in socially appropriate ways.

Competency-based program   A program that gives paraprofessionals credit for the knowledge they acquire through experience, thereby facilitating in-service training of early childhood professionals.

Comprehension   One's understanding of information.

Computer literacy   Familiarity with and knowledge about computers.

Conceptual materials   A Montessori classroom area that focuses on academic materials related to math, reading, and writing.

Concrete operations period   According to Jean Piaget, the period of development spanning approximately ages 7 to 11, when children do not depend solely on visual cues but can apply logic to explain physical tasks or operations.

Confidentiality   A requirement that means that results of evaluations and assessments be shared only with the parents and appropriate school personnel.

Conservation   The ability to recognize that objects remain the same in amount despite perceptual changes, usually acquired during the period of concrete operations.

Constructive play   Category of play involving creating something with play objects.

Constructivist   A person who believes that children construct or build their own knowledge through meaningful experiences.

Constructivist theory   A theory, such as that of Jean Piaget, based on the belief that children construct knowledge for themselves rather than have it conveyed to them by some external source.

Content objective   The purpose or rationale for an activity that specifies that the activity is intended to promote specific subject matter.

Conventional level of moral development   According to Lawrence Kohlberg, the stage concerned with pleasing others and respect for authority.

Conventional moral rules   Standards, which are generally culture-specific, arrived at through general consensus.

Convergent thinking   The act of narrowing many ideas into a single, focused point.

Cooperative play   A category of play, typical of older preschoolers, in which children play together in a shared activity.

Coping strategies   Mental or physical reactions, which can be effective or ineffective, to help deal with stress.

Core knowledge base   The framework within which to work and improve.

Creative development   A variety of activities such as art, woodworking, or music.

Creative playground   Outdoor play area that uses innovative materials such as tires, telephone poles, nets, and cable spools.

Creativity   The ability to bring an idea into being.

Credibility   Making believable.

Criterion-referenced   A characteristic of tests in which children are measured against a predetermined level of mastery rather than against an average score of children of the same age.

Cross-modal intersensory activity   The use and integration of more than one sensory modality—for instance, matching an object that is perceived visually to an identical object that is selected through touch only.

Cuing   A technique used to help children remember what is expected by giving them a specific signal.

Curriculum   The master plan of the early childhood program that reflects its philosophy and into which specific activities are fit.

Daily living   Montessori classroom area that focuses on practical tasks involved in self-care and environment care.

Deep structure   According to Noam Chomsky, inborn understanding of underlying rules of grammar and meaning that are universal across all languages.

Denver Developmental Screening Test (DDST)   A quick test for possible developmental delays in children from infancy to age 6.

Developmental delay   Accomplishing tasks in one or more developmental domains at considerably later age than their peers.

Developmental domain   Consists of areas in which children learn, believe, and change in their physical development, cognitive or intellectual development, social development, emotional development, language development, and creative development.

Developmental Indicators for the Assessment of Learning—Revised (DIAL-R)   A developmental screening test, for children ages 2 to 6, that assesses motor, concept, and language development.

Developmental objective   Purpose or rationale for an activity that specifies that the activity is intended to promote an aspect of physical, social, emotional, or cognitive development.

Developmental test   A test that measures the child's functioning in most or all areas of development, though some such tests apply to only one or two areas.

Developmentally appropriate practice   A term coined by the NAEYC to describe programs that match children's developmental and personal histories.

Development of concepts   Actions that help children to understand and form a mental image or thought (idea) about something.

Diagnostic testing   Another term for screening, which might indicate that more thorough testing should be carried out.

Diagrams   According to Rhoda Kellogg, the stage in children's art when they begin to use the six recognizable shapes: rectangle, oval, triangle, X, cross, and deliberate odd shape.

Dialect   A regional variation of a language that differs in some features of vocabulary, grammar, and pronunciation.

Didactic   A term often applied to teaching materials, indicating a built-in intent to provide specific instruction.

Direction   Management/administration. Making choices for oneself.

Director   A label often used for the teacher in Montessori programs.

Discipline   Generally considered a response to children's misbehaviour.

Discovery learning   *See* **Active learning.**

Discrimination   The ability to distinguish among different features of objects.

Distraction   By using humour or diversion effectively with children the potential me-against-you situations (power struggle) can be avoided.

Disequilibrium   According to Jean Piaget, the lack of balance experienced when existing mental structures and new experience do not fit exactly.

Diversity   Variety.

Divergent thinking   The act of expanding or elaborating on an idea, such as in brain-storming.

Dramatic play   Type of play in which children use play objects as a substitute for something imaginary.

Early childhood   The period between birth and 8 years of age.

Early childhood education   A term encompassing developmentally appropriate programs that serve children from birth through age 8; a field of study that trains students to work effectively with young children.

Early childhood education program model   An approach to early childhood education, based on a specific theoretical foundation—for instance, the behavioural, Piagetian, or Montessori view.

Early childhood educator   *See* **Early childhood teacher.**

Early childhood teacher   A specifically trained professional who works with children from infancy to age 8.

Early Childhood Environment Rating Scale   A rating scale to help in the evaluation of early childhood programs.

Eclectic model   An approach in which various desirable features from different theories or methods are selected.

Ecological model   A framework for viewing development that takes into account the various interconnected contexts within which individuals exist—for instance, the family, the neighbourhood, the community.

Effective praise   A form of encouragement that focuses on children's activities rather than on teacher evaluation of their work; praise that is meaningful to children rather than general or gratuitous.

Ego   According to Sigmund Freud, the rational facet of personality that helps find appropriate ways of achieving the pleasure goals of the id and mediating between the id's demands and the superego's restrictions.

Egocentricity   A characteristic of young children in which they see things from their own subjective perspectives.

Elaboration   A memory strategy in which imaginary connections are made among items where no logical links among those items exist.

Emergent curriculum   Education through continuous dialogue and documentation.

Emergent literacy   The ongoing dynamic process of learning to read and write, which starts in the early years.

Empirical   The condition of an idea that has been researched and tested.

Employer-supported programs   Provision by businesses of child care programs or support for child care costs incurred by employees' children.

Empowering   Raising self-confidence and autonomy.

Empowerment   Helping parents gain a sense of control over events in their lives.

Encouragement   *See* **Effective praise.**

Entrepreneur   One who creates and implements new ideas.

Entrepreneurial spirit   The ability to create and implement new ideas.

Environmental awareness   An appreciation of the natural world.

Equilibrium   According to Jean Piaget, the state of balance each person seeks between existing mental structures and new experiences.

Equipment   The furniture and other large items that represent the more expensive long-term investments in an early childhood facility.

Equivalency   Granting of an early childhood diploma through alternate methods.

Event sampling   A method of observation in which the observer records a specific behaviour only when it occurs.

Experience   Guiding children through various adult roles through dramatic play.

Exploration   To search for knowledge through various activities.

Externalization   When dealing with stress, the child blames others rather than using his or her own resources to cope with the stress. *See* **Internalization.**

Exosystem   According to ecological theory, that part of the environment that includes the broader components of the community (e.g., government agencies or mass media) that affect the functioning of the family.

Extended family   Family members beyond the immediate nuclear family—for example, aunts and uncles, grandparents, and cousins.

Extinction   In behavioural theory, a method of eliminating a previously reinforced behaviour by taking away all reinforcement—by totally ignoring the behaviour, for instance.

Eye–hand coordination   Integrative ability to use the hands as guided by information from the eyes.

Family centered model   Encompasses all aspects of involvement and acknowledges the family as the focal point of care.

Family child care home   Care for a relatively small number of children in a family home that has been licensed or registered for that purpose.

Family involvement   The commitment of parents to the early childhood program through a wide variety of options.

Family systems theory   A view of the family as a developing and changing social unit in which members constantly accommodate and adapt to each other's demands as well as to outside demands.

Fast tracking   *See* **Equivalency.**

Feral children   Children who, lost or abandoned by their parents, were thought to have been reared by animals in the wild.

Fine motor development Development of skills, involving the small muscles of the fingers and hands, used in such tasks as writing, drawing, and buttoning.

Flexibility A measure of creativity involving the capability to adapt readily to change in a positive, productive manner.

Fluency A measure of creativity involving the ability to generate, in a limited time, many relevant ideas on a given topic.

Formal operations period According to Jean Piaget, the last period of development, spanning approximately ages 11 to 15 and characterized by sophisticated, abstract thinking and logical reasoning abilities.

Formative evaluation Ongoing assessment to ensure that planned activities and methods accomplish what the teacher intended.

For-profit program Privately owned early childhood program in which any money left over after expenses goes to the owner or shareholders.

Foster parents People assigned to the care of minors by a legal agency.

Froebel gifts Toys consisting of solid geometrical shapes, tablets, lines, and points, which allow the child to build her inner world objectively as well as to imitate the outer environment.

Functional play Category of play, characteristic of very young children, that is repetitive motor play used to explore what objects are like and what can be done with them.

Games with rules Type of play, usually engaged in by older children, subject to accepted, prearranged rules.

Garden of children The English translation of the German phrase "kindergarten," coined by Friedrich Froebel of Germany. The school setting in which children are likened to plants—tended and cultivated.

Gay Homosexual. A term applied to a person who desires members of the same sex.

Gender identity Identification with the same sex.

Gender stability The recognition by children aged 5 to 7 that gender is constant and cannot change.

Generativity According to Erik Erikson, the stage of human development in which the mature adult focuses on the care and nurture of the young.

Genital stage The last stage of development described by Sigmund Freud, beginning with the onset of puberty, during which adolescents become increasingly aware of sexuality.

Genre Category or type—in music, for example, classical, jazz, and country.

Goal A general overview of what children are expected to gain from a program.

Golden beads Montessori manipulative materials that represent the decimal system in a concrete way. A single bead is one unit, while rows of ten and cubes of 100 and 1000 beads represent larger units.

Grammar and syntax The rules for putting words together meaningfully.

Gross motor activities Activities or actions that provide different levels of physical challenge, including balancing, throwing, lifting, climbing, pushing, pulling, crawling, skipping, swinging, and riding.

Gross motor development Development of skills, involving the large muscles of the legs, arms, back, and shoulders, that are used in such activities as running, jumping, and climbing.

Group size The number of children together in a room in an early childhood setting. Distinct from *teacher–child ratio,* which see.

Guidance Ongoing process of directing children's behaviour based on the types of adults children are expected to become.

Guided assistance Helping a child as he needs it.

Habituation Becoming accustomed to an action or event.

Head Start Comprehensive, federally funded early childhood program in the United States, designed for children from poverty backgrounds.

Healthy development To grow in a meaningful manner.

Historical Series of events.

Holding grip Placement of the hands in using a tool for drawing or writing.

Holistic *See* **Wholistic.**

Home visit An interaction between the teacher and the parent(s) of the child that takes place in the child's home.

HOME observation An evaluation tool used to assess the quality of stimulation in the home environment. Useful for home-based child care.

Honesty Truthfulness, integrity.

Hothousing Term taken from horticulture in which plant growth is quickened by forced fertilization, heat, and light; refers to accelerated learning programs for young children.

Human development theory A theory that describes changes in individuals as they move from infancy through adulthood, identifying significant events experienced by all people and explaining why changes occur.

Human resources Any structure defined by individuals who are connected with it or have a stake or interest in the system.

Hurried child Term coined by David Elkind to describe children who are rushed into academics and lessons or hothoused in other ways.

Hyperactivity *See* **Attention deficit-hyperactivity disorder.**

Ignoring A principle of behaviour management in which all reinforcement for a given behaviour is removed in order to eliminate that behaviour.

Image of the child A view of the child and childhood that varies according to culture, history, and theory.

Imagery A relaxation technique in which a mental image such as "float like a feather" or "melt like ice" is invoked.

Immersion program A program that involves teaching a second language to children by surrounding or immersing them in that language.

Inclusion The integration of children with special needs into regular programs by recognizing their rights as children first and affording them the same choices and opportunities granted to any child.

Inclusive education *See* **Inclusion.**

Increasing competence   The process by which children gain skills.

Inductive reasoning   A guidance approach in which the adult helps the child see, through logic and reasoning, the consequences of a behaviour on other people.

Industry vs. inferiority   The fourth stage of development described by Erik Erikson, starting at the end of the preschool years and lasting until puberty, in which the child focuses on development of competence.

Infant   In seven of the twelve provinces and territories, infants are persons between the ages of 0 and 18 months.

Infant school   *See* **British Infant School.**

Infant stimulation program   A compensatory program for infants at risk for developmental delay.

Initiative vs. guilt   The third stage of development described by Erik Erikson, occurring during the preschool years, in which the child's curiosity and enthusiasm lead to a need to explore and learn about the world, and in which rules and expectations begin to take effect.

Integrated curriculum   A program that focuses on all aspects of children's development, not just cognitive development.

Interaction   Working together for the good of everyone.

Interactionists   Interactionists think that children's development is determined by an interaction between inborn and external factors.

Internalization   The process in which a child, when dealing with stress, accepts responsibility for dealing with the stressor. *See* **Externation.**

Interpersonal moral rules   Rules considered as universal, including prohibitions against harm (murder, incest, theft) to others.

Interpretive stage   Stage of parenting defined by Ellen Galinsky, typifying the parent of an older preschooler who faces the task of explaining and clarifying the world to the child.

Invented spelling   Used by young children in their early attempts to write by finding the letters that best fit the speech sound of the words they want to convey.

Key experiences   In the cognitively oriented curriculum, the eight cognitive concepts on which activities are built.

Kindergarten   A German word, literally meaning "garden for children," coined by Friedrich Froebel for his program for young children.

Kinesthetic sense   Information from the body's system that provides knowledge about the body, its parts, and its movement; involves the "feel" of movement without reference to visual or verbal cues.

Large-group time (also called circle, story, or group time)   Time block(s) during the day in which all children and teachers join in a common activity.

Latch-key or self-care children   School-aged children who, after school, return to an empty home because their parents are at work.

Latency stage   The fourth stage of development described by Sigmund Freud, occurring during middle childhood, during which sexuality is repressed until adolescence.

Lateralization   The division of the human brain, marked by a specialization in analytical and logical tasks in the left half and intuitive and creative functions in the right half.

Lead teacher   *See* **Senior teacher.**

Learning   Acquiring and applying knowledge.

Learning centre   *See* **Activity centre.**

Learning outcome   A specific interpretation of a general goal that provides a more practical and direct tool for planning and evaluation.

Learning style   The various methods in which a person gathers knowledge, approaches a task, and uses knowledge to remember and understand things.

Legal guardians   Persons with legal authority to care for and/or make decisions for a child.

Lesbian   *See* **Gay.**

Lesson plan   The working document from which the daily program is run, specifying directions for activities.

Lifelong learning   The process of continued education during one's life.

Locomotion   Self-movement from place to place, as in walking.

Logical and natural consequences   Positive guidance strategy that teaches children to understand the outcomes and effects of their actions so they can change their behaviour.

Logical thinking   According to Jean Piaget, the ability that begins to emerge around age 7 in which children use mental processes to solve problems rather than rely solely on perceived information.

Logico-mathematical knowledge   A type of knowledge described by Jean Piaget that involves learning about the relationships among objects as well as their relationships in time and space.

Long-term (or permanent) memory   In information-processing theory, the vast store of information and knowledge that is held for a long time.

Macrosystem   According to ecological theory, the broadest part of the environment, which includes the cultural, political, and economic forces that affect families.

Mainstreaming   The integration of children with and without disabilities in a school program.

Malting House School   The name of Susan Isaac's famous nursery school in Cambridge, England, where open education was refined and exemplified.

Management consultants   *See* **Change agents.**

Manipulatives   Toys and materials that require the use of the fingers and hands—for instance, puzzles, beads, and pegboards.

Mapping   A mapmaking activity involving spatial relations in which space is represented creatively through such media as marking pens or blocks.

Married   A legal ceremony uniting a man and a woman in matrimony.

Materials   The smaller, often expendable, items used in early childhood programs that are replaced and replenished frequently.

Maturation   The nature side of the nature–nurture controversy emphasizes maturation, which is the unfolding of inherited potential.

Maturational theory   Explanation of human development that depends on information about when children achieve specific skills.

McCarthy Scales of Children's Abilities   An intelligence test, used particularly with children who are mildly retarded or who have learning disabilities.

Mean length of utterance (MLU)   A measure that calculates the average length of a child's sentences.

Memory strategies   Various approaches used especially by older children and adults to help them remember information.

Mentor   *See* **Senior teacher.**

Mesosystem   According to ecological theory, the linkages between family and immediate neighbourhood and community.

Metamemory   The ability to think about one's own memory.

Microsystem   According to ecological theory, that part of the environment that most immediately affects a person, such as the family, school, or workplace.

Mission statement   A statement of what an organization believes and intends to accomplish.

Mixed-age grouping   Programs in which children of different ages—for instance, 3- to 6-year-olds—are together in one class.

Mock writing   Young child's imitation of writing through wavy, circular, or vertical lines; distinct from drawing or scribbling.

Model   In social learning theory, those whom children imitate, particularly because of some desirable feature or attribute.

Model of communication   A belief that the system of education is analogous to communication in that it is an interaction and a relationship that is nurtured through trust and respect.

Modelling   In social learning theory, the process of imitating a model.

Modes   The senses through which people learn, such as auditory (hearing), visual (seeing), kinesthetic (touching), olfactory (smelling), oral (tasting).

Montessori equipment   Early childhood learning materials derived from and part of the Montessori approach.

Moral development   The long-term process of learning and internalizing the rules and standards of right and wrong.

Morality of autonomy   A sense of morality based on self-integrity.

Morality of obedience   A sense of morality based on doing what one is told to do.

Morpheme   A meaningful part of a word.

Morphology   The study of word rules, for instance, tense, plurals, and possessives.

Movable alphabet   Montessori-designed individual wooden letters that can be combined to form words.

Multilingualism   Ability to use multiple (more than two) languages.

Multimodality   Referring to information that depends on input from several of the senses.

Nanny   A caregiver who comes to the child's home; the child's home is the primary residence of some nannies.

National Association for the Education of Young Children (NAEYC)   Largest American early childhood professional organization that examines issues associated with children from birth to age 8 and those who work with young children.

National Day Care Study (NDCS)   A study of child care availability in Canada summarized in the *Status of Day Care in Canada 1990* (National Child Care Information Centre, 1991).

Nature   Theorists in the nature camp believe that a child's development follows an inborn plan—that is, it is determined largely by heredity.

Nature versus nurture   Debate concerning the issue of whether learning and behaviour depends on, or is shaped by, natural inborn characteristics (heredity characteristics) and a biological time clock or outside environmental forces.

Negative punishment   The removal of a pleasant stimulus.

Negative reinforcement   The removal of an unpleasant stimulus.

Non-immersion program   An approach to teaching a new language that involves using both the primary and second languages, with a gradual shift from emphasis on the first to the second.

Nonverbal cues   Some of the subtle cues of body language or voice inflection that can give an observer deeper meaning in a record of behaviour.

Norm-referenced   A test in which scores are determined by using a large group of same-age children as the basis for comparison rather than by using a predetermined criterion or standard of performance.

Norms   A term used to describe what is usual, average, or customary in terms of development, behaviour, or expectations.

Not-for-profit program   Incorporated program or one sponsored by a public entity, such as a church or school, in which profits are put back into the program or returned to the sponsoring agency.

Nuclear family   The smallest family unit, consisting of a couple or one or two parents with children.

Number concepts   One of the cognitive concepts young children begin to acquire, involving an understanding of quantity.

Nursery school   A term used to describe a half-day program for preschoolers that has an educational emphasis.

Nurture   Theorists in the nurture camp contend that children's development is affected primarily by external, environmental factors, not heredity.

Nurturing stage   A period of development that parents of an infant are expected to experience.

Nutrition   Encompasses both the quality and quantity of food consumed for healthful living.

Object permanence   As part of Jean Piaget's theory, the recognition that objects exist even when out of view, a concept that children begin to develop toward the end of their first year of life.

Objective   An aim; a specific interpretation of general goals, providing a practical and directive tool for day-to-day program planning.

Observable behaviour   Actions that can be seen, as opposed to those that are inferred.

Observational learning   In social learning theory, the process of learning that comes from watching, noting the behaviour of, and imitating models.

One-to-one correspondence A way in which young preschoolers begin to acquire an understanding of number concepts by matching items to each other—for instance, one napkin beside each plate.

Onlooker play Category of play in which a child watches others at play nearby without joining in.

Open education A program that operates on the assumption that children, when provided with a well-conceived environment, are capable of selecting and learning from appropriate activities.

Open-ended materials Early childhood materials that are flexible rather than structured and can be used in a variety of ways rather than in only one manner.

Operant conditioning The principle of behavioural theory whereby a person attempts to increase or decrease behaviour by controlling consequences.

Oral stage The first stage of development described by Sigmund Freud, in which, during infancy, pleasure is derived from the mouth.

Organization According to Jean Piaget, the mental process by which a person organizes experiences and information in relation to each other.

Organizational development The process by which a system grows and changes.

Organizational structure A system such as a family, a program setting, a corporation, or a profession.

Overextension The application, especially by toddlers, of a word to a variety of related objects.

Overregularization A term that describes a child's overuse of grammatical rules. For example, the child who learns to add -s to form a plural will use words like *mouses, gooses,* and *sheeps* for a short time after learning the rule.

Ownership Belonging to an individual; therefore, the individual has rights to it.

Palmar grasp A way of holding tools in which the pencil or crayon lies across the palm of the hand with the fingers curled around it, and the arm rather than the wrist moves the tool.

Parallel play Category of play in which children use similar materials but do not interact with one another.

Parent-cooperative A program staffed by one professional teacher and a rotating staff of parents.

Parent education Programs aimed at enhancing parent–child relations and improving parenting competence.

Parent–teacher conference An interaction between the teacher and the child's parent(s).

Partners Those who work together effectively for a specific purpose.

Partnership A relationship with mutual respect and an equal balance of power regarding decision making.

Parquetry blocks Variously shaped flat blocks, including diamonds and parallelograms, that can be assembled into different patterns on a form board.

Pay equity Equal pay for equal work, regardless of gender.

Perceived competence Children's belief in their ability to succeed in a given task.

Perceptual motor model   A theoretical view of physical development that holds that motor behaviours are a prerequisite for, and lead to, cognitive abilities.

Personal control   The feeling that a person has the power to make things happen.

Phallic stage   The third stage of development described by Sigmund Freud, occurring during the preschool years, in which pleasure is derived from the genitals.

Philosophy   A statement of beliefs reflecting one's value system. It is often based on theory and guided by research.

Phobia   An intense, irrational fear.

Physical knowledge   A type of knowledge described by Jean Piaget that involves learning about objects in the environment and their properties, such as colour, size, weight, and shape.

Pictorialism   According to Rhoda Kellogg, the stage in the development of art in which children draw recognizable objects.

Pink tower   A set of ten pink wooden cubes, developed by Montessori, that vary from 1 cm^3 to 10 cm^3 and are used to build a tower.

Place identity   Considered part of self-identity because it relates to the environmental context in which a child's needs are met, competence is developed, and control over the physical world is gained.

Placement patterns   According to Rhoda Kellogg, a way of analyzing children's art by examining the seventeen ways in which the total picture or design is framed or placed on the paper.

Plan–do–review cycle   The heart of the cognitively oriented curriculum, in which children are encouraged to make deliberate, systematic choices with the help of teachers by planning each day's activities, carrying them out, then recalling them.

Planning time   In the cognitively oriented curriculum, the time set aside during which children decide what activities they would like to participate in during the ensuing work time.

Play based   Using play as the basis for learning.

Playscapes   Contemporary, often innovative, playground structures that combine a variety of materials.

Pleasure principle   According to Sigmund Freud, the principle of maximizing what is pleasant and avoiding anything unpleasant, which motivates all behaviour.

Positive discipline   Synonymous with guidance, an approach that allows the child to develop self-discipline gradually.

Positive guidance (teaching)   Encouraging and exploring alternatives in a manner that is meaningful, relevant, and respectful. *See also* **Guidance.**

Positive punishment   The addition of an unpleasant stimulus.

Positive reinforcement   The addition of a pleasant stimulus.

Postconventional level of moral development   According to Lawrence Kohlberg, the stage in which moral decisions are made in accordance with universal considerations of what is right.

Practice play   A term used by Piaget to describe repeated actions, such as banging or playing patty-cake, that infants make.

Pragmatics   Rules that govern language use in social contexts.

Preassessment   A form of evaluation given before teaching a specific concept or topic to assess how much children know about it; the information is used later in a comparison to determine how much the children learned.

Preconventional level of moral development   According to Lawrence Kohlberg, the stage during which moral decisions are made based on personal preference or avoidance of punishment.

Predictive validity   A term that means a test is a valid predictor of future events, such as school achievement.

Preoperational period   In Jean Piaget's theory, the second stage of cognitive development, spanning roughly the preschool years, in which children are able to use various forms of mental representation but do not yet think logically.

Prepared environment   Maria Montessori's term to describe the careful match between appropriate materials and what the child is most ready to learn at any given time.

Preschematic stage   The stage in the development of art in which children have a subject in mind when they begin a picture but in which the finished picture is a crude and inaccurate representation of that subject.

Preschool   The setting for children who are not yet of elementary school age.

Pretend play   Children's dramatic or symbolic play that involves more than one child in social interaction.

Prior knowledge   What one already knows.

Problem solving   Involves physical and social skills to encourage and guide children in creating and/or finding solutions.

Processing   A set of steps to achieve an end result.

Profession   Employment that requires specialized training.

Professional development   Growth in a manner congruent with a particular code of ethics.

Program   A schedule of events.

Progressive education   A term used to describe the type of education advocated by John Dewey, who maintained that teachers should use the child's interests and that education should emphasize active learning through real experiences.

Progressive relaxation   A technique in which various specified muscle groups are tensed and relaxed systematically.

Project   Similar to themes, because they provide a unifying element around which activities are planned, but projects are more specific. A theme might be titled "Spring," while a related project would be more specific—for example, "What happens at the fishery during spring?"

Prosocial behaviour   Positive, commonly valued social behaviour such as sharing, empathy, and understanding.

Psychoanalytic theory   The branch of psychology founded by Sigmund Freud that focuses on unconscious drives and the importance of the early years in later personality development.

Psychosocial theory   The branch of psychology founded by Erik Erikson, in which development is described in terms of eight stages that span childhood and adulthood, each stage offering opportunity for personality growth and development.

Punishment An aversive consequence that follows a behaviour for the purpose of decreasing or eliminating the behaviour; not recommended as an effective means of changing behaviour.

Quality program A system made up of components that are observable and measurable. A set of requirements deemed necessary by the profession to ensure the program meets its goals.

Rating scale An assessment of specific skills or concepts that are rated on some qualitative dimension of excellence or accomplishment.

Rational counting Accurately attaching a numeric name to a series of objects being counted.

Rationale Arriving at a conclusion by a process of reasoning.

Reality principle According to Sigmund Freud, the reality-based principle by which the ego functions to counter the pleasure-seeking goals of the id.

Recall time In the cognitively oriented curriculum, the time when children review their work-time activities.

Redirection A method of distracting young children to prevent potential problems while their self-control is just emerging.

Reflective abstraction According to Jean Piaget, the part of a child's self-directed activity that allows the child to think about and reflect on what he or she is doing; leads to the development of new mental abilities.

Reggio Emilia An approach to teaching and learning that originated in Italy under the supervision of Loris Malaguzzi (1920–1994); the approach believes in the Emergent Curriculum, projects, and collaboration. It has received worldwide attention and its popularity is growing in the 1990s.

Reflective practice The constant questioning, evaluation, and modification of one's beliefs, decisions, and actions as new knowledge and experience are gained. The purpose is to develop professionally.

Rehearsal The mental repetition of information over and over, as is commonly done with phone numbers.

Reinforcement In behavioural theory, any response following a behaviour that encourages repetition of that behaviour.

Relationship A connection for a common purpose.

Reliability A measure of a test indicating that the test is stable and consistent; ensures that changes in score are due to the child, not the test.

Representation According to Jean Piaget, the ability to depict an object, person, action, or experience mentally, even if it is not present in the immediate environment.

Resilient children Children who, despite their extremely stressful lives, appear to be stable, outgoing, and optimistic.

Respect Esteem. The value that one feels in oneself or in another.

Respect for children An unusual feature of Montessori's original program.

Responsibility Being accountable for one's actions.

Restraining order A court order that prevents someone from seeing someone else.

Role   A characteristic or expected social behaviour.

Rote counting   Reciting numbers from memory in the context of objects in a series, without attaching meaning to them.

Running record   A type of observation that provides an account of all the child's behaviour over a period of time.

Scaffolding   Assistance to the child, adjusted as he masters the task at hand.

Schemata (*schema* is the singular form)   According to Jean Piaget, cognitive structures into which cognitive concepts or mental representations are organized.

Schematic stage   Stage at which a child's representations become more realistic and accurate.

School readiness   A term used to describe the age and stage at which a child is prepared to enter school.

Screening test   A quick method of identifying children who might exhibit developmental delay; only an indicator, though—must be followed up with more thorough testing.

Scribbling stage   The stage in the development of art in which children experiment with marks on a page.

Self-care children   *See* **Latch-key children**.

Self-concept   Perceptions and feelings children have about themselves, gathered largely from how the important people in their world respond to them.

Self-correcting materials   Learning materials such as puzzles that give the child immediate feedback on success when the task is completed.

Self-education   A term used by Montessori to describe how a child educates herself or himself through activity in the prepared environment.

Self-esteem   Children's evaluation of their worth in positive or negative terms.

Self-help skills   Tasks involving caring for oneself, such as dressing, feeding, toileting, and grooming.

Self-selected natural activity   Those actions that child choose on their own accord.

Self-selected time away   A guidance technique to help children determine when they need to take a moment to calm down and think over a situation.

Semantic network   The interrelationship among words, particularly in regard to word meaning.

Semantics   Related to the understanding and study of word meaning.

Senior teacher   The person in charge of a class and ultimately responsible for all aspects of class functioning.

Sensitive periods   Maria Montessori's term to describe the times when children are most receptive to absorbing specific learning.

Sensitivity   A term related to creativity that refers to receptivity to external and internal stimuli.

Sensorial materials   Learning materials in Montessori classroom area that help children develop, organize, broaden, and refine sensory perceptions of sight, sound, touch, smell, and taste.

Sensorimotor period   In Jean Piaget's theory, the first stage of cognitive development, covering approximately the first two years of life, in which the child learns primarily through movement and the senses.

Sensory deficit   A problem, particularly of sight or hearing.

Sensory education   A term used to describe the emphasis Montessori placed on education through the senses.

Sensory integration   The ability to translate sensory information into intelligent behaviour.

Sensory-perceptual development   Giving meaning to information that comes through the senses.

Separation anxiety   Emotional difficulty experienced by some young children when leaving their mothers.

Seriation   A relationship among objects in which they are placed in a logical order, as from longest to shortest.

Sex cleavage   Distinct separation based on gender, evident in children at a very young age.

Shaping   In behavioural theory, a method used to teach a child a new behaviour by breaking it into small steps and systematically reinforcing the attainment of each step.

Short-term (or working) memory   Cognitive theory uses the term to describe the limited capacity memory used for temporarily remembering information such as a telephone number.

Show-and-Tell   A common group activity in which children share something special and personal with their classmates.

Single-, dual-, or no-wage earner   *See* **Wage earner.**

Single parent   A person who has the major responsibility for a child on a day-to-day basis.

Simultaneous language acquisition   A child learning two languages at the same time or before the age of 3.

Skill   Ease and ability with which one accomplishes a task.

Small-group activity time   Time set aside for children to work with a teacher in a smaller group than usual.

Social cognition   Organization of knowledge and information about people and relationships.

Social interactionist view of language development   Theoretical view that considers language as closely tied to and dependent on social processes.

Social knowledge   According to Piaget, a knowledge conveyed by people and defined by culture; it involves the many social rules, morals, and values children must learn in order to function in society.

Social learning theory   Derived from but going beyond behaviourism, this theoretical view holds that children learn not just from reinforcement but from observing and imitating others.

Social reinforcer   In behavioural theory, a reward that conveys approval through such responses as a smile, hug, or attention.

Social skills   Actions that encourage sharing, cooperating, and planning, in a context in which several children can interact.

Socialization   The process through which children become a functioning part of society and learn society's rules and values.

Sociohistoric theory   Believes social and historic forces shape intellectual ability.

Software   The program—containing a set of "instructions"—that an operator can use to direct a computer to perform certain functions; usually stored on a disk or directly in the computer. Many programs are available for young children.

Solitary play   Category of play in which a child plays alone, uninvolved with other children.

Sound boxes   Montessori equipment that includes two sets of cylinders, both of which are filled with various materials (e.g., rice, beans, or salt) and then matched by the sounds they make.

Spatial concepts   A cognitive ability to understand how objects and people occupy, move in, and use space.

Spatial relationship   The relative positions of objects and people in space.

Special time   A method for spending a few minutes a day with just one child as a way of providing unconditional attention.

Split brain   The term that describes the brain as having two distinct sides or hemispheres (left and right), each with different functions.

Stage theory   Any theory that delineates specific stages in which development is marked by qualitatively different characteristics and accomplishments; each stage builds on the previous one.

Stage theorist   One who agrees with Piaget's theory of qualitatively different characteristics and accomplishments in cognitive ability during four stages of development.

Stanford-Binet Intelligence Scale   A widely used test that yields an intelligence quotient (IQ).

Stepparent   The spouse of a child's biological parent.

Story schema   The regular, predictable structure of simple stories.

Story structure   The order in which events occur in a tale.

Strategy   The method that a person uses (or plans to use) to accomplish a task or approach a situation to make it meaningful.

Stress   Internal or external demand on a person's ability to adapt.

Successive approximations   Breaking a complex behaviour into smaller steps and reinforcing the child at each step as she or he comes closer to attaining the final behaviour.

Successive language acquisition   Learning a second language after the age of 3.

Summative evaluation   An assessment that follows a specific lesson or unit and determines whether the children have met the objectives.

Superego   According to Sigmund Freud, the facet of personality called the conscience, which is based on the moral norms of society as passed on by parents and other adults.

Surface structure   According to Noam Chomsky, specific aspects of language that vary from one language to another.

Symbolic play   A term used by Piaget to describe play by children who can mentally represent objects and therefore can pretend.

Symbolic representation   The ability acquired by young children to use mental images to stand for something else.

Syntax   The grammatical rules that govern the structure of sentences.

System   The merging of ideas, methods, and people to achieve a goal.

Systems approach   Has many parts that work both dependently and independently to keep the system working.

Tangible reinforcers   Concrete rewards such as stickers, candy, money.

Teacher   *See* **Early childhood educator.**

Teacher–child ratio   *See* **Child–adult ratio.**

Team   A group of people working together for a purpose.

Team approach   Working together in appropriate roles to achieve a goal.

Team teacher   *See* **Senior teacher.**

Team teaching   An approach to co-teaching in which status and responsibility are equal rather than structured in a pyramid of authority, with one person in charge and others subordinate.

Teenage parents   13–19-year-old person(s) who conceive a child.

Temperament   A child's inborn characteristics (e.g., regularity, adaptability, and disposition) that affect behaviour.

Temporal concept   Cognitive ability as it pertains to a child's growing awareness of time as a continuum.

Temporal sequencing   The ability to place a series of events in the order of their occurrence.

Theme   Themes—such as spring or community helpers, for example—provide a unifying element around which activities are planned. *See also* **Project.**

Theoretical   Pertaining to ideas that are of a speculative nature.

Theories of mind   Ideas about thinking and how the mind works.

Time-out   A technique in which the child is removed briefly from the reinforcement and stimulation of the classroom.

Time sampling   A quantitative measure or count of how often a specific behaviour occurs within a given amount of time.

Toddler   In the majority of Canadian jurisdictions, toddlers are defined as persons between the ages of 19 months and 35 months.

Tonal bells   Two sets of bells (one brown, one white) that children in Montessori programs match by the sound they make.

Transdisciplinary team   A group in which members communicate and interact within the profession, outside the profession, and between professions.

Tripod grasp   A way of holding tools in which the pencil or crayon is held by the fingers; the wrist, rather than the whole arm, moves the tool.

Trust   Having confidence in.

Trust vs. mistrust   The first stage of development described by Erik Erikson, occurring during infancy, in which the child's needs should be met consistently and predictably.

Unconditional attention   A way of conveying acceptance to children by letting them know they are valued and liked; attention that is not given in response to a specific behaviour.

Understanding   To make sense of.

Unit blocks   The most common type of blocks, precision-made of hard wood in standardized sizes and shapes.

Units   A segment of the curriculum, based on a unifying theme, around which activities are planned.

Unoccupied behaviour   Category of play in which a child moves about the classroom, observing but otherwise not involved.

Validity   A characteristic of a test that indicates the test actually measures what it purports to measure.

Vocabulary   A collection of words.

Wage earner   May be single-, dual-, or no-.

Wechsler Intelligence Scale for Children—III (WISC-III)   An intelligence test for 6- to 16-year-olds that gives a verbal IQ score, a performance IQ score, and an overall IQ score. A score of 100 is average for the WISC-III.

Wechsler Preschool and Primary Scale of Intelligence—Revised (WPPSI)   An intelligence test, like the WISC-III, but for 3- to 7-year-old children.

Whole language approach   Strategy for promoting literacy by surrounding children with high-quality oral and print language.

Wholistic   Encompassing every aspect of the idea, belief, approach. Information gathered from as many sources and perspectives as possible and integrated.

Work time   In the cognitively-oriented curriculum, the large block of time in which children engage in self-selected activities.

5 Ws, H questions   Who, What, Where, When, Why, and How.

Zone of Proximal Development   The area in which a child finds a task too difficult to complete alone but can with assistance.

References

Adler, S. (1993). Teacher education research as reflective practice. *Teacher and Education, 9*, 159–167.

Alexander, N.P. (1986). School-age child care: Concerns and challenges. *Young Children, 42*(1), 3–10.

Alford, B.B., & Bogle, M.L. (1982). *Nutrition during the life cycle.* Englewood Cliffs, NJ: Prentice-Hall.

Alger, H.A. (1984). Transitions: Alternatives to manipulative management techniques. *Young Children, 39*(6), 16–25.

Allen, J. (1988). Children's cognition of stressful events. *Day Care and Early Education, 16*(3), 21–25.

Allen, J., & Pettit, R.B. (1987). Mighty Mouse and MX missiles: Children in a violent society. *Day Care and Early Education, 15*(1), 6–9.

Allen, K.E., & Marotz, L. (1989). *Developmental profiles: Birth through eight.* Albany, NY: Delmar.

Allen, K.E., & Marotz, L. (1994). *Developmental profiles: Birth to six.* Albany, NY: Delmar.

Almy, M. (1975). *The early childhood educator at work.* New York: McGraw-Hill.

Almy, M., Monighan, P., Scales, B., & Van Hoorn, J. (1984). Recent research on play: The teacher's perspective. In L.G. Katz (Ed.), *Current topics in early childhood education* (Vol. 5, pp. 1–26). Norwood, NJ: Ablex Publishing.

Alper, C.D. (1987). Early childhood music education. In C. Seefeldt (Ed.), *The early childhood curriculum: A review of current research* (pp. 211–236). New York: Teachers College Press, Columbia University.

Amabile, T.M., & Gitomer, J. (1984). Children's artistic creativity: Effects of choice in task materials. *Personality and Social Psychology Bulletin, 10,* 209–215.

American Academy of Pediatrics. (1985). *Pediatric nutrition handbook* (2nd ed.). Elk Grove Village, IL: American Academy of Pediatrics.

Ames, L.B., Gillespie, C., Haines, J., & Ilg, F.L. (1980). *The child from one to six: Evaluating the behaviour of the preschool child.* London: Hamish Hamilton.

Anastasiow, N. (1988). Should parenting education be mandatory? *Topics in Early Childhood Special Education, 8*(1), 60–72.

Anderson, D.R., & Lorch, E.P. (1983). Looking at television: Action or reaction. In J. Bryant & D.R. Anderson (Eds.), *Understanding TV: Research in children's attention and comprehension* (pp. 1–33). New York: Academic Press.

Andrews, J.H. (1988). Poetry: Tool of the classroom magician. *Young Children, 43*(4), 17–25.

Anthony, S. (1972). *The discovery of death in childhood and after.* New York: Basic Books.

Arent, R.P. (1984). *Stress and your child: A parent's guide to symptoms, strategies and benefits.* Englewood Cliffs, NJ: Prentice-Hall.

Aries, P. (1962). *Centuries of childhood: A social history of family life* (R. Baldick, Trans.). New York: Alfred A. Knopf.

Arnett, J. (1987). *Caregivers in day care centers: Does training matter?* Paper presented at the biennial meeting of the Society for Research in Child Development, Baltimore, MD.

Atkins, C. (1984). Writing: Doing something constructive. *Young Children, 40*(1), 3–7.

Ayers, W. (1989). *The good preschool teacher: Six teachers reflect on their lives.* New York: Teachers College Press, Columbia University.

Baker, B.B. (1982). *The planning board: Ideas for construction and use with young children.* (ERIC Microfiche No. ED 233 801) APA, Appendix 3A, section 43, p. 208.

Bakst, K., & Essa, E.L. (1990). The writing table: Emergent writers and editors. *Childhood Education, 66,* 145–150.

Balaban, N. (1992). The role of child care professionals in caring for infants, toddlers and their families. *Young Children, 47*(5), 66–71.

Bandura, A. (1977). *Social learning theory.* Englewood Cliffs, NJ: Prentice-Hall.

Banta, T. (1969). Research on Montessori and the disadvantaged. In R. Orem (Ed.), *Montessori and the special child.* New York: Putnam.

Baratta-Lorton, M. (1979). *Workjobs: Activity-centred learning for early childhood education.* Menlo Park, CA: Addison-Wesley.

Barnes, B.J., & Hill, S. (1983). Should young children use micro-computers: LOGO before LEGO? *The Computing Teacher, 10*(9), 11–14.

Barrett, D.E. (1986). Behaviour as an outcome in nutrition research. *Nutrition Reviews, 44,* 224–236.

Baumrind, D. (1967). Child care practices anteceding three patterns of preschool behaviour. *Genetic Psychological Monographs, 75,* 43–88.

Baumrind, D., & Black, A.E. (1967). Socialization practices associated with dimensions of competence in preschool boys and girls. *Child Development, 38,* 291–327.

Bayless, K.M., & Ramsey, M.E. (1982). *Music: A way of life for the young child.* St. Louis, MO: C.V. Mosby.

Baynham, P., Russell, L., & Ross, L. (1988). Wages and work experience survey of child care staff in an Ontario community. *The Canadian Journal of Research in Early Childhood Education, 2*(2), 159–164.

Beaty, J. (1990) *Observing the development of the young child.* Columbus, OH: Merrill.

Becher, R.M. (1986). Parent involvement: A review of research and principles of successful practice. In L.G. Katz (Ed.), *Current topics in early childhood education* (Vol. 6, pp. 85–122). Norwood, NJ: Ablex Publishing.

Bereiter, C. (1967). *Acceleration of intellectual development in early childhood.* Washington, DC: Department of Health, Education & Welfare, U.S. Office of Education, Bureau of Research.

Bereiter, C. (1986). Does direct instruction cause delinquency? *Early Childhood Research Quarterly, 1,* 289–292.

Bereiter, C., & Engelmann, S. (1966). *Teaching disadvantaged children in the preschool.* Englewood Cliffs, NJ: Prentice-Hall.

Berk, L.E. (1976). How well do classroom practices reflect teacher goals? *Young Children, 32*(1), 64–81.

Berlyne, D. (1969). Laughter, humor, and play. In G. Lindzey & E. Aronson (Eds.), *The handbook of social psychology* (Vol. 3). Reading, MA: Addison-Wesley.

Berns, R.M. (1989). *Child, family, community: Socialization and support* (2nd ed.). New York: Holt, Rinehart & Winston.

Berrueta-Clement, J.R., Schweinhart, L.J., Barnett, W.S., Epstein, A.S., & Weikart, D.P. (1984). Changed lives: The effects of the Perry preschool program on youths through age 19. *Monographs of the High/Scope Educational Research Foundation, 8.* Ypsilanti, MI: High/Scope Press.

Biber, B. (1984). *Early education and psychological development.* New Haven, CT: Yale University Press.

Bijou, S.W., Peterson, R.F., & Ault, M.H. (1968). A method to integrate descriptive and experimental field studies at the level of data and empirical concepts. *Journal of Applied Behaviour Analysis, 1,* 175–191.

Birch, L.L. (1980a). Effects of peer models' food choices and eating behaviours on preschoolers' food preferences. *Child Development, 51,* 489–496.

Birch, L.L. (1980b). Experiential determinants of children's food preferences. In L.G. Katz (Ed.), *Current topics in early childhood education* (Vol. 3, pp. 29–46). Norwood, NJ: Ablex Publishing.

Birch, L.L., Marlin, D.W., & Rotter, J. (1984). Eating as the "means" activity in a contingency: Effects on young children's food preferences. *Child Development, 55,* 431–439.

Bjorklund, G., & Burger, C. (1987). Making conferences work for parents, teachers, and children. *Young Children, 42*(3), 26–31.

Blanco, R. (1982). *Prescriptions for children with learning and adjustment problems* (2nd ed.). Springfield, IL: Charles C. Thomas.

Blocks: A creative curriculum for early childhood. (1979). Washington, DC: Creative Associates.

Blom, G.E., Cheney, B.D., & Snoddy, J.E. (1986). *Stress in childhood: An intervention model for teachers and other professionals.* New York: Teachers College Press, Columbia University.

Bloom, B. (1964). *Stability and change in human characteristics.* New York: John Wiley.

Bohannon, J.N., & Warren-Leubecker, A. (1985). Theoretical approaches to language acquisition. In J.B. Gleason (Ed.), *The development of language* (pp. 173–226). Columbus, OH: Merrill.

The Bookfinder: A guide to children's literature about the needs and problems of youth aged 2–15 (Vol.1). (1977). Circle Pines, NM: American Guidance Service.

Borstelmann, L.J. (1983). Children before psychology: Ideas about children from antiquity to the late 1800s. In P.H. Mussen (Ed.), *Handbook of child psychology* (4th ed., *History, theory, and methods: Vol. 1.,* pp. 1–40). New York: John Wiley.

Bowlby, J. (1951). *Maternal care and mental health.* Geneva: World Health Organization.

Boxhill, N.A. (1989, December). Quoted in S. Landers, Homeless children lose childhood. *The APA Monitor,* pp. 1, 33.

Bradley, R., & Caldwell, B.M. (1984). The relation of infants' home environments to achievement test performance in first grade: A follow-up study. *Child Development, 55,* 803–809.

Braun, S.J., & Edwards, E.P. (1972). *History and theory of early childhood education.* Worthington, OH: Charles A. Jones.

Brazelton, T.B. (1992). *On becoming a family: The growth of attachment.* New York: Delacorte Press.

Bredekamp, S. (Ed.). (1987). *Developmentally appropriate practice in early childhood programs serving children from birth through age 8.* Washington, DC: National Association for the Education of Young Children.

Bredekamp, S. (Ed.). (1997). *Developmentally appropriate practice in early childhood programs serving children from birth through age 8* (2nd ed.). Washington, DC: National Association for the Education of Young Children.

Bredekamp, S. Quoted in E.R. Shell (1989, December). Now, which kind of preschool? *Psychology Today,* pp. 52–57.

Bredekamp, S., & Shepard, L. (1989). How best to protect children from inappropriate school expectations, practices, and policies. *Young Children, 44*(3), 14–24.

Brenner, A. (1984). *Helping children cope with stress.* Lexington, MA: Lexington Books.

Brigance, A.H. (1978). *Brigance Diagnostic Inventory of Early Development.* Woburn, MA: Curriculum Associates.

Briggs, B.A., & Walters, C.M. (1985). Single-father families. *Young Children, 40*(3), 23–27.

Briggs, D. (1975). *Your child's self-esteem.* New York: Doubleday.

Bronfenbrenner, U. (1971). Who cares for America's children? *Young Children, 26*(3), 157–163.

Bronfenbrenner, U. (1979). *The ecology of human development.* Cambridge, MA: Harvard University Press.

Bronfenbrenner, U. (1986). Ecology of the family as a context for human development: Research perspectives. *Developmental Psychology, 22,* 723–742.

Bronfenbrenner, U., & Crouter, A.C. (1983). Ecology of the family as a context for human development research perspectives. In P.H. Mussen (Ed.), *Handbook of child psychology: Vol. 1. History, theory and methods* (4th ed., pp. 357–414). New York: John Wiley.

Brooks, R.L., & Obrzut, J.E. (1981). Brain lateralization: Implications for infant stimulation and development. *Young Children, 36*(3), 9–16.

Brown, R. (1973). *A first language.* Cambridge, MA: Harvard University Press.

Bruner, J. (1980). *Under five in Britain.* Ypsilanti, MI: High/Scope Press.

Bruner, J., Jolly, A., & Sylva, K. (1976). *Play—Its role in development and evolution.* Markham, ON: Penguin.

Bullock, J. (1986). Teacher–parent conferences: Learning from each other. *Day Care and Early Education, 14*(2), 17–19.

Bundy, B.F. (1989). Effective record keeping. *Day Care and Early Education, 17*(1), 7–9.

Bundy, B.F. (1991). Fostering communication between parents and preschools. *Young Children, 46*(2), 12–17.

Burts, D.C., Hart, C.H., Charlesworth, R., & Kirk, L. (1990). A comparison of frequencies of stress behaviours observed in kindergarten children in classrooms with developmentally appropriate versus developmentally inappropriate instructional practices. *Early Childhood Research Quarterly, 5,* 407–423.

Bushell, D. (1982). The behavior analysis model for early education. In B. Spodek (Ed.), *Handbook of research in early childhood education* (pp. 156–184). New York: Free Press.

Buzzelli, C.A., & File, N. (1989). Building trust in friends. *Young Children, 44*(3), 70–75.

Cairns, R.B. (1983). The emergence of developmental psychology. In P.H. Mussen (Ed.), *Handbook of child psychology: Vol. 1. History, theory, and methods* (4th ed., pp. 41–102). New York: John Wiley.

Cairns, R., Moore, C., Redshaw, D., & Wilson, T. (1992a). Addendum: Child care in the Northwest Territories, 1988–1990. In A. Pence (Ed.). (1992). *Canadian child care in context: Perspectives from the provinces and territories.* Ottawa: Statistics Canada & Health and Welfare Canada.

Cairns, R., Moore, C., Redshaw, D., & Wilson, T. (1992b). An historical overview of child care in the Northwest Territories. In A. Pence (Ed.), *Canadian child care in context: Perspectives from the provinces and territories.* Ottawa: Statistics Canada & Health and Welfare Canada.

Cairns, R., Moore, C., Redshaw, D., & Wilson, T. (1992c). An overview of child care legislation in the Northwest Territories. In A. Pence (Ed.), *Canadian child care in context: Perspectives from the provinces and territories.* Ottawa: Statistics Canada & Health and Welfare Canada.

Cairns, R., Moore, C., Redshaw, D., & Wilson, T. (1992d). A socio-geographic overview of the Northwest Territories. In A. Pence (Ed.), *Canadian child care in context: Perspectives from the provinces and territories.* Ottawa: Statistics Canada & Health and Welfare Canada.

Caldwell, B.M. (1968). The fourth dimension in early childhood education. In R.D. Hess & R.M. Bear (Eds.) *Early education.* Chicago: Aldine-Atherton.

Caldwell, B.M. (1971). Impact of interest in early cognitive stimulation. In H. Rie (Ed.), *Perspectives in child psychopathology.* New York: Aldine-Atherton.

Caldwell, B.M. (1973a). What does research teach us about day care? *Young Children, 29,* 197–208.

Caldwell, B.M. (1973b). Infant day care—The outcast gains respectability. In P. Roby (Ed.), *Child care—Who cares?* New York: Basic Books.

Caldwell, B.M. (1977). Aggression and hostility in young children. *Young Children, 32*(2), 4–13.

Caldwell, B., & Bradley, R. (1979). *Home observation of the environment.* Little Rock: University of Arkansas Press.

Canadian Child Care Federation Proposal. (1996). In *Visions special research and development competition on child care,* pp. 6–7. Ottawa: Canadian Child Care Federation.

Canadian Child Day Care Federation. (1991). *National statement on quality child care.* Ottawa: CCDCF.

Canadian Child Care Federation. Inside the Federation: Partnerships and Projects. *Interaction* (Fall), 2. Ottawa: Canadian Child Care Federation.

Canadian Child Day Care Federation & Canadian Day Care Advocacy Association. (1992). *Caring for a living: Executive summary.* Ottawa: CCDCF.

Canning, P., & Irwin, S. (1992). A socio-geographic overview of Nova Scotia. In A. Pence (Ed.), *Canadian child care in context: Perspectives from the provinces and territories.* Ottawa: Statistics Canada & Health and Welfare Canada.

Canning, P., Irwin, S., & Lewis, L. (1992). An overview of child care legislation in Nova Scotia. In A. Pence (Ed.), *Canadian child care in context: Perspectives from the provinces and territories.* Ottawa: Statistics Canada & Health and Welfare Canada.

Caplan, F., & Caplan, T. (1974). *The power of play*. New York: Anchor Press.

Carlsson-Paige, N., & Levin, D.E. (1985). *Helping young children understand peace, war, and the nuclear threat*. Washington, DC: National Association for the Education of Young Children.

Carlsson-Paige, N., & Levin, D.E. (1990). *Who's calling the shots? How to respond effectively to children's fascination with war play and war toys*. Philadelphia, PA: New Society Publishers.

Carrière, Y. (1992). A socio-geographic overview of Quebec. In A. Pence (Ed.), *Canadian child care in context: Perspectives from the provinces and territories*. Ottawa: Statistics Canada & Health and Welfare Canada.

Carter, D.B. (1987). Early childhood education: A historical perspective. In J.L. Roopnarine & J.E. Johnson (Eds.), *Approaches to early childhood education* (pp. 1–14). Columbus, OH: Merrill.

Cartwright, C.A., & Cartwright, G.P. (1974). *Developing observation skills*. New York: McGraw-Hill.

Cartwright, S. (1990). Learning with large blocks. *Young Children, 45*(3), 38–41.

Casler, L. (1961). Maternal deprivation: A critical review of the literature. *Monographs of the Society for Research in Child Development, 26* (2, Serial No. 80).

Cass, J.E. (1973). *Helping children grow through play*. New York: Schocken Books.

Cataldo, C.Z. (1987). *Parent education for early childhood: Child-rearing concepts and program content for the student and practicing professional*. New York: Teachers College Press, Columbia University.

Chafel, J.A. (1990). Children in poverty: Policy perspectives on a national crisis. *Young Children, 45*(5), 31–37.

Charles, C.M. (1974). *Teachers*. Belmont, CA: Petit Piaget Pitman Learning.

Charlesworth, R. (1987). *Understanding child development*. Albany, NY: Delmar Publishers.

Charlesworth, R., & Lind, K.K. (1990). *Math and science for young children*. Albany, NY: Delmar.

Chattin-McNichols, J. (1992). *The Montessori controversy*. Albany, NY: Delmar.

Chattin-McNichols, J.P. (1981). The effects of Montessori school experience. *Young Children, 36*(5), 49–66.

Chess, S., & Thomas, A. (1987). *Know your child: An authoritarian guide for today's parents*. New York: Basic Books.

Child Care Resource and Research Unit. (1993). *Child care in Canada. Practices and territories*. Toronto: CRRU.

Child Care Resource Unit. (1990). *Child care information sheets*. Toronto: Centre for Urban and Community Studies, University of Toronto.

Child Care Resource Unit. (1993, May). *What's happening in child care policy: A cross Canada overview*. Paper presented at the Canadian Child Care Federation's third National Child Care Conference.

Child Care Visions Call for Proposals. (1997). Hull, PQ: Employability and Social Partnerships Division, Human Resources Development Canada.

Chomsky, N. (1972). *Language and mind*. New York: Harcourt Brace Jovanovich.

Christie, J.F. (1982). Sociodramatic play training. *Young Children, 37*(4), 25–32.

Christie, J.F., Johnsen, E.P., & Peckover, R.B. (1988). The effects of play period duration on children's play patterns. *Journal of Research in Early Childhood, 3*, 123–131.

Ciaranello, R.D. (1983). Neurochemical aspects of stress. In N. Garmezy & M. Rutter (Eds.), *Stress, coping and development in children* (pp. 85–105). New York: McGraw-Hill.

Cicirelli, V. (1969). *The impact of Head Start: An evaluation of the effects of Head Start on children's cognitive and affective development.* Athens, OH: Westinghouse Learning.

Clark, E.V. (1978a). Non-linguistic strategies and the acquisition of word meaning. In L. Bloom (Ed.), *Readings in language development* (pp. 433–451). New York: John Wiley.

Clark, E.V. (1978b). Strategies for communicating. *Child Development, 49*, 953–959.

Clarke-Stewart, A. (1988). The "effects" of infant day care reconsidered. *Early Childhood Research Quarterly, 3*, 293–318.

Clarke-Stewart, K.A. (1983). Exploring the assumptions of parent education. In R. Haskins & D. Adams (Eds.), *Parent education and public policy* (pp. 257–276). Norwood, NJ: Ablex Publishing.

Clarke-Stewart, K.A. (1984). Day care: A new context for research and development. In M. Perlmutter (Ed.), *Parent–child interaction and parent–child relations in child development: The Minnesota symposia on child psychology* (Vol. 17, pp. 61–100). Hillsdale, NJ: Lawrence Erlbaum.

Clarke-Stewart, K.A. (1987a). In search of consistencies in child care research. In D.A. Phillips (Ed.), *Quality in child care: What does research tell us?* (pp. 105–120). Washington, DC: National Association for the Education of Young Children.

Clarke-Stewart, K.A. (1987b). Predicting child development from child care forms and features: The Chicago Study. In D.A. Phillips (Ed.), *Quality in child care: What does research tell us?* (pp. 21–41). Washington, DC: National Association for the Education of Young Children.

Clarke-Stewart, K.A. (1988). Evolving issues in early childhood education: A personal perspective. *Early Childhood Research Quarterly, 3*, 13–19.

Clarke-Stewart, K.A. (1989). Infant day care: Maligned or malignant? *American Psychologist, 44*, 266–273.

Clarke-Stewart, K.A., & Fein, G. (1983). Early childhood programs. In P.H. Mussen (Ed.), *Handbook of child psychology: Vol. 2. Infancy and developmental psychobiology* (4th ed., pp. 917–1000). New York: John Wiley.

Clarke-Stewart, K.A., & Gruber, C. (1984). Daycare forms and features. In R.C. Ainslie (Ed.), *Quality variations in daycare* (pp. 35–62). New York: Praeger.

Clemens, S.G. (1991). Art in the classroom: Making every day special. *Young Children, 46*(2), 4–11.

Clements, D.H. (1987). Computers and young children: A review of research. *Young Children, 43*(1), 34–44.

Click, P.M., & Click, D.W. (1990). *Administration of schools for young children* (3rd ed.). Albany, NY: Delmar.

Clifford, H. (1992). Foreword. In A. Pence (Ed.), *Canadian child care in context: Perspectives from the provinces and territories* (pp. xiii–xvii). Ottawa: Statistics Canada & Health and Welfare Canada.

Cochran, M. (1988). Between cause and effect: The ecology of program impacts. In A.R. Pence (Ed.), *Ecological research with children and families: From concepts to methodology* (pp. 143–169). New York: Teachers College Press, Columbia University.

Cohen, D.H., & Stern, V. (1978). *Observing and recording the behavior of young children* (2nd ed.). New York: Teachers College Press, Columbia University.

Cole, E., & Schaefer, C. (1990). Can young children be art critics? *Young Children, 45*(2), 33–38.

Coleman, J.S., et al. (1966). *Equality of Educational Opportunity*. Washington, DC: United States Government Printing Office.

Coleman, M., & Skeen, P. (1985). Play, games, and sports: Their use and misuse. *Childhood Education, 61*, 192–198.

Comenius, J. (1967). *The great didactic* (M.W. Keating, Ed. & Trans.). New York: Russell & Russell. (Original work published 1896 & 1910)

Cook, R.E., Tessier, A., & Armbruster, V.B. (1987). *Adapting early childhood curricula for children with special needs*. Columbus, OH: Merrill.

Copple, C.E., DeLisi, R., & Sigel, E. (1982). Cognitive development. In B. Spodek (Ed.), *Handbook of research in early childhood education* (pp. 3–26). New York: Free Press.

Corbett, B. (1994). Froebel Education in Canada. In E. Essa & R. Young (Eds.), *Introduction to early childhood education* (p. 38). Toronto: Nelson Canada.

Cosgrove, M.S. (1991). Cooking in the classroom: The doorway to nutrition. *Young Children, 46*(3), 43–45.

Cox, M.V. (1986). *The child's point of view: The development of cognition and language*. New York: St. Martin's Press.

Cratty, B.J. (1982). Motor development in early childhood: Critical issues for researchers in the 1980s. In B. Spodek (Ed.), *Handbook of research in early childhood education* (pp. 27–46). New York: Free Press.

Critics Challenge. (1993, February 24). Critics challenge proposed program for preschoolers. *The St. Catharines Standard*, p. 8.

Cuddigan, M., & Hanson, M.B. (1988). *Growing pains: Helping children deal with everyday problems through reading*. Chicago: American Library Association.

Culture and children. (1985). Austin, TX: Texas Department of Human Resources.

Curtis, S.R. (1987). New views on movement development and the implications for curriculum in early childhood. In C. Seefeldt (Ed.), *The early childhood curriculum: A review of current research* (pp. 257–270). New York: Teachers College Press, Columbia University.

Daehler, M.W., & Bukatko, D. (1985). *Cognitive development*. New York: Alfred A. Knopf.

Dale, P. (1976). *Language development* (2nd ed.). New York: Holt, Rinehart & Winston.

Damon, W. (1977). *The social world of the child*. San Francisco: Jossey-Bass.

Damon, W. (1983). The nature of social-cognitive change in the developing child. In W.F. Overton (Ed.), *The relationship between social and cognitive development* (pp. 103–141). Hillsdale, NJ: Lawrence Erlbaum.

Davidson, J.I. (1982). Wasted time: The ignored dilemma. In J.F. Brown (Ed.), *Curriculum planning for young children* (pp. 196–204). Washington, DC: National Association for the Education of Young Children.

Davidson, J.I. (1989). *Children and computers together in the early childhood classroom.* Albany, NY: Delmar.

Day care, families, and stress: A day care provider's guide. (1985). Austin, TX: Child Development Program Division, Texas Department of Human Resources.

Debelack, M., Herr, J., & Jacobson, M. (1981). *Creating innovative classroom materials for teaching young children.* New York: Harcourt Brace Jovanovich.

Deiner, P.L. (1983). *Resources for teaching young children with special needs.* New York: Harcourt Brace Jovanovich.

Delacato, C.H. (1964). *The diagnosis and treatment of speech and reading problems.* Springfield, IL: Thomas Publishers.

Delacato, C.H. (1966). *Neurological organization and reading.* Springfield, IL: Thomas Publishers.

deMause, L. (Ed.). (1974). *The history of childhood.* New York: Harper & Row.

Derman-Sparks, L. (1989). *Anti-bias curriculum: Tools for empowering young children.* Washington, DC: National Association for the Education of Young Children.

Derman-Sparks, L., Higa, C.T., & Sparks, B. (1980). Children, race and racism: How race awareness develops. *Interracial Books for Children Bulletin, 11*(3–4), 3–9.

Derman-Sparks, L., & Ramsey, P. (1993). Early childhood multicultural, anti-bias education in the 1990s: Toward the 21st century. In J.L. Roopnarine & J.E. Johnson (Eds.), *Approaches to early childhood education* (2nd ed., pp. 47–70). New York: Merrill.

Desjardins, G. (1992). An historical overview of child care in Quebec. In A. Pence (Ed.), *Canadian child care in context: Perspectives from the provinces and territories.* Ottawa: Statistics Canada & Health and Welfare Canada.

deVilliers, J.G., & deVilliers, P.A. (1973). A cross-sectional study of the acquisition of grammatical morphemes in child speech. *Journal of Psycho-linguistic Research, 2,* 267–278.

deVilliers, P.A., & deVilliers, J.G. (1979). *Early language.* Cambridge, MA: Harvard University Press.

Dewey, J. (1897). *My pedagogic creed.* Washington, DC: The Progressive Education Association.

Dewey, J. (1900). *The school and society.* New York: McLure, Phillips & Company.

Dewey, J. (1902). *The child and the curriculum.* Chicago, IL: University of Chicago Press.

Dewey, J. (1916). *Democracy and education: An introduction to the philosophy of education.* New York: Macmillan.

Dill, N. (1992). Addendum: Child care in Saskatchewan, 1988–1990. In A. Pence (Ed.), *Canadian child care in context: Perspectives from the provinces and territories.* Ottawa: Statistics Canada & Health and Welfare Canada.

Dimidjian, V.J. (1989). Holidays, holy days, and wholly dazed: Approaches to special days. *Young Children, 44*(6), 70–74.

Dinkmeyer, D., & McKay, G.D. (1976). *Systematic training for effective parenting: Parent's handbook.* Circle Pines, MN: American Guidance Services.

Doherty-Derkowski, G. (1995). *Quality matters.* Don Mills, ON: Addison-Wesley.

Doman, R.J., Spitz, E.B., Zucman, E., & Delacato, C.H. (1960). Children with severe brain injuries: Neurological organization in terms of mobility. *Journal of the American Medical Association, 174,* 257–262.

Douvan, E. (1990). Psychoanalytic theory of human development. In R.M. Thomas (Ed.), *The encyclopedia of human development and education: Theory, research, and studies* (pp. 83–88). New York: Pergamon Press.

Doxey, I. (1990). The Canadian child. In I. Doxey (Ed.), *Child care and education: Canadian dimensions* (pp. 3–12). Toronto: Nelson Canada.

Doyle, A.B., & Connolly, J. (1989). Negotiation and enactment in social pretend play: Relations to social acceptance and social cognition. *Early Childhood Research Quarterly, 4,* 289–302.

Doyle, A.B., Gold, D., & Moskowitz, D.S. (Eds.). (1984). *Children and families under stress.* San Francisco: Jossey-Bass.

Drabman, R.S., Cordua, G.D., Hammer, D., Jarvie, G.J., & Horton, W. (1979). Developmental trends in eating rates of normal and overweight preschool children. *Child Development, 50,* 211–216.

Dresden, J., & Myers, B.K. (1989). Early childhood professionals: Toward self-definition. *Young Children, 44*(2), 62–66.

Dunst, C.J., & Trivette, C.M. (1988). Toward experimental evaluation of the family, infant, and preschool program. In H.B. Weiss & F.H. Jacobs (Eds.), *Evaluating family programs* (pp. 315–346). New York: Aldine de Gruyter.

Early Childhood Educators of British Columbia. (1997). *Code of ethics.* Vancouver: ECEBC.

Edwards, C.P. (1986). *Promoting social and moral development in young children.* New York: Teachers College Press, Columbia University.

Elkind, D. (1983). Montessori education: Abiding contributions and contemporary challenges. *Young Children, 38*(2), 3–10.

Elkind, D. (1986). Formal education and early childhood education: An essential difference. *Phi Delta Kappan, 67,* 631–636.

Elkind, D. (1987a). The child yesterday, today, and tomorrow. *Young Children, 42*(4), 6–11.

Elkind, D. (1987b). *Miseducation: Preschoolers at risk.* New York: Alfred A. Knopf.

Elkind, D. (1988). *The hurried child: Growing up too fast too soon.* Reading, MA: Addison-Wesley.

Elkind, D. (1988). The resistance to developmentally appropriate educational practice with young children: The real issue. In C. Warger (Ed.), *A resource guide to public school early childhood programs* (pp. 53–62). Alexandria, VA: Association for Supervision and Curriculum Development.

Elkind, D. (1990). Academic pressures—too much, too soon. The demise of play. In E. Klugman & S. Smilansky (Eds.), *Children's play and learning* (pp. 3–17). New York: Teachers College Press, Columbia University.

Employment and Immigration Canada. (1992). *Labour market information.* St. Catharines, ON: Author.

Eriksen, A. (1985). *Playground design: Outdoor environments for learning and development.* New York: Van Nostrand Reinhold.

Erikson, E.H. (1963). *Childhood and society* (2nd ed.). New York: Norton.

Esbensen, S. (1990). Designing the early childhood setting. In I. Doxey (Ed.), *Child care and education: Canadian dimensions* (pp. 178–192). Toronto: Nelson Canada.

Essa, E.L. (1981). An outdoor play area designed for learning. *Day Care and Early Education. 9*(2), 37–42.

Essa, E.L. (1987). The effect of a computer on preschool children's activities. *Early Childhood Research Quarterly, 2,* 377–382.

Essa, E.L. (1990). *Practical guide to solving preschool behavior problems* (2nd ed.). Albany, NY: Delmar.

Essa, E.L., Hilton, J.M., & Murray, C.I. (1990). The relationship of weather and preschool children's behaviour. *Children's Environments Quarterly, 7*(3), 32–36.

Essa, E.L., & Rogers, P.R. (1992). *An early childhood curriculum: From developmental model to application.* Albany, NY: Delmar.

Essa, E., & Young, R. (1994). *Introduction to early childhood education* (1st Canadian ed.). Toronto: ITP Nelson Canada.

Ethics Commission. (1987). Ethics case studies: The working mother. *Young Children, 43*(1), 16–19.

Evans, E.D. (1975). *Contemporary influences in early childhood education* (2nd ed.). New York: Holt, Rinehart & Winston.

Evans, E.D. (1982). Curriculum models and early childhood education. In B. Spodek (Ed.), *Handbook of research in early childhood education* (pp. 107–134). New York: Free Press.

Evans, E.D. (1984). Children's aesthetics. In L.G. Katz (Ed.), *Current topics in early childhood education* (Vol. 5, pp. 73–104). Norwood, NJ: Ablex Publishing.

Faggella, K., & Horowitz, J. (1990). Different child, different style, *Instructor 100*(2), 52.

Faust, V., Weidmann, M., & Wehner, W. (1974). The influence of meteorological factors on children and youths. *Acta Paedopsychiatrica, 40,* 150–156.

Feeney, S. (1988a). Ethics case studies: The aggressive child. *Young Children, 43*(2), 48–51.

Feeney, S. (1988b). Ethics case studies: The divorced parents. *Young Children, 43*(3), 48–49.

Feeney, S., Christensen, D., & Moravcik, E. (1991). *Who am I in the lives of young children?* New York: Merrill.

Feeney, S., & Chun, R. (1985). Effective teachers of young children. *Young Children, 41*(1), 47–52.

Feeney, S., & Kipnis, K. (1985). Professional ethics in early childhood education. *Young Children, 40*(3), 54–56.

Feeney, S., & Moravcik, E. (1987). A thing of beauty: Aesthetic development in young children. *Young Children, 42*(6), 7–15.

Fein, G.G. (1979). Play and the acquisition of symbols. In L.G. Katz (Ed.), *Current topics in early childhood education* (Vol. 2, pp. 195–225). Norwood, NJ: Ablex Publishing.

Fein, G.G. (1982). Pretend play: New perspectives. In J.F. Brown (Ed.), *Curriculum planning for young children* (pp. 22–27). Washington, DC: National Association for the Education of Young Children.

Fein, G.G., & Clarke-Stewart, A. (1973). *Day care in context.* New York: John Wiley.

Fein, G.G., & Fox, N. (1988). Infant day care: A special issue. *Early Childhood Research Quarterly, 3,* 227–234.

Fein, G.G., & Schwartz, P.M. (1982). Developmental theories in early education. In B. Spodek (Ed.), *Handbook of research in early childhood education* (pp. 82–104). New York: Free Press.

Ferber, R. (1985). *Solve your child's sleep problems.* New York: Simon & Schuster.

Fernandez, J.P. (1986). *Child care and corporate productivity.* Lexington, MA: Lexington Books.

Finkelstein, B. (1988). The revolt against selfishness: Women and the dilemmas of professionalism in early childhood education. In B. Spodek, O.N. Saracho, & D.L. Peters (Ed.), *Professionalism and the early childhood practitioner* (pp. 10–28). New York: Teachers College Press, Columbia University.

Flack, M. (1931). *Angus and the cat.* New York: Doubleday.

Flanagan-Rochon, K.F. (1992a). Addendum: Child care in Prince Edward Island, 1988–1990. In A. Pence (Ed.), *Canadian child care in context: Perspectives from the provinces and territories.* Ottawa: Statistics Canada & Health and Welfare Canada.

Flanagan-Rochon, K.F. (1992b). An overview of child care legislation in Prince Edward Island. In A. Pence (Ed.), *Canadian child care in context: Perspectives from the provinces and territories.* Ottawa: Statistics Canada & Health and Welfare Canada.

Flanagan-Rochon, K.F., & Rice, C. (1992). An historical overview of child care in Prince Edward Island. In A. Pence (Ed.), *Canadian child care in context: Perspectives from the provinces and territories.* Ottawa: Statistics Canada & Health and Welfare Canada.

Flaste, R. (1991, April 28). Sidelined by loneliness. *New York Times Magazine,* pp. 14–15, 23–24.

Fleming, W.G. (1971). *Ontario's educative society: Vol. 5. Supporting institutions and services.* Toronto: University of Toronto Press.

Flerx, V.C., Fidler, D.S., & Rogers, R.W. (1976). Sex role stereotypes: Developmental aspects and early intervention. *Child Development, 67,* 998–1007.

Fogel, A. (1991). *Infancy: Infant, family, and society* (2nd ed.). St. Paul, MN: West Publishing.

Forman, G.E., & Kaden, M. (1987). Research on science education for young children. In C. Seefeldt (Ed.), *The early childhood curriculum: A review of current research* (pp. 141–164). New York: Teachers College Press, Columbia University.

Forman, G.E., & Kuschner, D.S. (1977). *The child's construction of knowledge: Piaget for teaching children.* Monterey, CA. Brooks/Cole.

Fowler, W. (1971). *Demonstration program in infant care and education: Final report.* Toronto: Ontario Institute for Studies in Education, University of Toronto.

Fowler, W. (1972). A developmental learning approach to infant care in a group setting. *Merrill-Palmer, 18,* 145–175.

Fowler, W. (1973). *The development of a prototype infant, preschool and child daycare centre in Metropolitan Toronto: Year II Progress Report.* Toronto: Ontario Institute for Studies in Education, University of Toronto.

Fowler, W. (1974, June). *From intuitive to rational humanism: The comparative effects of group and home care on infant development.* Paper presented at the annual meeting of the Canadian Psychological Association, Windsor, Ontario.

Fowler, W. (1978). *Day care and its effects on early development: A study of group and home care in multi-ethnic, working-class families* (Research in Education Series, No. 8). Toronto: Ontario Institute for Studies in Education, University of Toronto.

Fowler, W., & Khan, N. (1974, April). *A follow-up investigation of the late development of infants in enriched group care*. Paper presented at the annual meeting of the American Education Research Association, Chicago.

Frankenburg, W.K., Dodds, J.B., Fandal, A.W., Kajuk, F., & Cohr, M. (1975). *Denver Developmental Screening Test: Revised reference manual*. Denver: LADOCA Foundation.

Frazier, A. (1980). Making a curriculum for children. *Childhood Education, 56,* 258–263.

Friedman, D. (1989, August). A more sophisticated employer response to child care. *Child Care Information Exchange,* pp. 29–31.

Friesen, J. (1992). An overview of child care legislation in Manitoba. In A. Pence (Ed.), *Canadian child care in context: Perspectives from the provinces and territories*. Ottawa: Statistics Canada & Health and Welfare Canada.

Friesen, J., Humphrey, M., & Brockman, L.M. (1992a). Addendum: Child care in Manitoba, 1988–1990. In A. Pence (Ed.), *Canadian child care in context: Perspectives from the provinces and territories*. Ottawa: Statistics Canada & Health and Welfare Canada.

Friesen, J., Humphrey, M., & Brockman, L.M. (1992b). An historical overview of child care in Manitoba. In A. Pence (Ed.), *Canadian child care in context: Perspectives from the provinces and territories*. Ottawa: Statistics Canada & Health and Welfare Canada.

Froschl, M., Colon, L., Rubin, E., & Sprung, B. (1984). *Including all of us: An early childhood curriculum about disability*. New York: Educational Equity Concepts.

Frost, J.L., & Henniger, M.L. (1982). Making playgrounds safe for children and children safe for playgrounds. In J.F. Brown (Ed.), *Curriculum planning for young children* (pp. 48–55). Washington, DC: National Association for the Education of Young Children.

Frost, J.L., & Klein, B.L. (1979). *Children's play and playgrounds*. Boston: Allyn & Bacon.

Frost, J.L., & Wortham, S.C. (1988). The evolution of American playgrounds. *Young Children, 43*(5), 19–28.

Fullum, H. (1992a). Addendum: Child care in Quebec, 1988–1990. In A. Pence (Ed.), *Canadian child care in context: Perspectives from the provinces and territories*. Ottawa: Statistics Canada & Health and Welfare Canada.

Fullum, H. (1992b). An overview of child day care legislation in Quebec. In A. Pence (Ed.), *Canadian child care in context: Perspectives from the provinces and territories*. Ottawa: Statistics Canada & Health and Welfare Canada.

Furman, E. (1982). Helping children cope with death. In J.F. Brown (Ed.), *Curriculum planning for young children* (pp. 238–245). Washington, DC: National Association for the Education of Young Children.

Furman, E. (1987). More protection, fewer directions. *Young Children, 42*(5), 5–7.

Furth, H.G. (1969). *Piaget and knowledge: Theoretical foundations*. Englewood Cliffs, NJ: Prentice-Hall.

Galdone, P. (1973). *The little red hen*. New York: Seabury.

Galinsky, E. (1981). *Between generations: The six stages of parenthood*. New York: Times Books.

Galinsky, E. (1988). Parents and teacher-caregivers: Sources of tension, sources of support. *Young Children, 43*(3), 4–12.

Galinsky, E. (1989). Update on employer-supported child care. *Young Children, 44*(6), 2, 75–77.

Galinsky, E. (1990). Why are some parent/teacher partnerships clouded with difficulties? *Young Children, 45*(5), 2–3, 38–40.

Gallagher, J.M., & Coche, J. (1987). Hothousing: The clinical and educational concerns over pressuring young children. *Early Childhood Research Quarterly, 2,* 203–210.

Gallimore, R., & Tharpe, R. (1990). Teaching mind in society: Teaching, schooling and literate discourse. In L.C. Moll (Ed.), *Vygotsky in education* (pp. 175–205). New York: Cambridge University Press.

Gamble, J. (1992a). An historical overview of child care in New Brunswick. In A. Pence (Ed.), *Canadian child care in context: Perspectives from the provinces and territories.* Ottawa: Statistics Canada & Health and Welfare Canada.

Gamble, J. (1992b). A socio-geographic overview of New Brunswick. In A. Pence (Ed.), *Canadian child care in context: Perspectives from the provinces and territories.* Ottawa: Statistics Canada & Health and Welfare Canada.

Garbarino, J. (1990, June). Child abuse: Why? *The World and I,* pp. 543–553.

Garbarino, J., Dubrow, N., Kostelnyk, & Pardoc. (1992). *Children in danger: Coping with the consequences of community violence.* San Francisco: Jossey-Bass.

Garcia C., Kagan, J., & Reznick, J.S. (1984). Behavioural inhibition in young children. *Child Development, 55,* 1005–1019.

Garcia, E.E. (1982). Bilingualism in early childhood. In J.F. Brown (Ed.), *Curriculum planning for young children* (pp. 82–101). Washington, DC: National Association for the Education of Young Children

Gardner, D. (1949). *Education under eight.* London: Methuen.

Gardner, H. (1982). *Art, mind, and brain: A cognitive approach to creativity.* New York: Basic Books.

Gardner, H. (1983). *Frames of mind.* New York: Basic Books.

Gardner, H. (1989). Learning, Chinese-style. *Psychology Today, 23*(12), 54–56.

Garmezy, N. (1984). Stressors of childhood. In N. Garmezy & M. Rutter (Eds.), *Stress, coping and development in children* (pp. 43–84). New York: McGraw-Hill.

Garn, S.M., & Clark, D.C. (1976). Trends in fatness and the origins of obesity. *Pediatrics, 57,* 443–456.

Gartrell, D. (1987). Punishment or guidance? *Young Children, 42*(3), 55–61.

Gartrell, D. (1995). Misbehaviour or mistaken behaviour? *Young Children* (July), 27–34.

Geller, L.G. (1985). *Word play and language learning for children.* Urbana, IL: National Council of Teachers of English.

Gelman, R., & Gallistel, C.R. (1978). *The child's understanding of number.* Cambridge, MA: Harvard University Press.

Genishi, C. (1982). Observational research methods for early childhood education. In B. Spodek (Ed.), *Handbook of research in early childhood education* (pp. 564–591). New York: Free Press.

Gersten, R. (1986). Response to "Consequences of three preschool curriculum models through age 15." *Early Childhood Research Quarterly, 1,* 293–302.

Gesell, A. (1923). *The preschool child: From the standpoint of public hygiene and education.* Houghton Mifflin.

Gesell, A. (1928). *Infancy and human growth.* New York: Macmillan.

Gestwicki, C. (1987). *Home, school, and community relations: A guide to working with parents.* Albany, NY: Delmar.

Gettman, D. (1987). *Basic Montessori: Learning activities for under-fives.* New York: St. Martin's Press.

Gibson, L. (1989). *Through children's eyes: Literacy learning in the early years.* New York: Teachers College Press, Columbia University.

Gilkeson, E., & Bowman, G. (1976). *The focus is on children: The Bank Street approach to childhood education as enacted in Follow Through.* New York: Bank Street College of Education.

Gilmore, B. (1971). Play: A special behavior. In R. Haber (Ed.), *Current research in motivation* (pp. 343–355). New York: Harper.

Gineshi, C. (1987). Acquiring oral language and communicative competence. In C. Seefeldt (Ed.), *The early childhood curriculum: A review of current research* (pp. 75–106). New York: Teachers College Press, Columbia University.

Ginsburg, H., & Opper, S. (1969). *Piaget's theory of intellectual development: An introduction.* Englewood Cliffs, NJ: Prentice-Hall.

Glassman, M. (1992a). An historical overview of child care in Newfoundland. In A. Pence (Ed.), *Canadian child care in context: Perspectives from the provinces and territories.* Ottawa: Statistics Canada & Health and Welfare Canada.

Glassman, M. (1992b). A socio-geographic overview of Newfoundland. In A. Pence (Ed.), *Canadian child care in context: Perspectives from the provinces and territories.* Ottawa: Statistics Canada & Health and Welfare Canada.

Glazer, J.I. (1986). *Literature for young children* (2nd ed.). Columbus, OH: Merrill.

Gleason, J.B. (1985). Studying language development. In J.B. Gleason (Ed.), *The development of language* (pp. 1–35). Columbus, OH: Merrill.

Goelman, H. (1988). The relationship between structure and process variables in home and day care settings on children's language development. In A.R. Pence (Ed.), *Ecological research with children and families: From concepts to methodology* (pp. 16–34). New York: Teachers College Press, Columbia University.

Goelman, H., & Pence, A. (1990). The Victoria and Vancouver research projects. In Doxey, I. (Ed.), *Child care and education: Canadian dimensions* (pp. 269–277). Toronto: Nelson Canada.

Goffin, S.G. (1987). Cooperative behaviours: They need our support. *Young Children, 42*(2), 75–81.

Goldfarb, W. (1943). The effects of early institutional care on adolescent personality. *Journal of Experimental Education, 12,* 106–129.

Good discipline is, in large part, the result of a fantastic curriculum! (1987). *Young Children, 42*(3), 49.

Goodman, K.S., Smith, E.B., Meredith, R., & Goodman, Y.M. (1987). *Language and thinking in school: A whole-language curriculum* (3rd ed.). New York: Richard C. Owen.

Goodman, Y.M. (1986). Children coming to know literacy. In W.H. Teale & E. Sulzby (Eds.), *Emergent literacy: Writing and reading* (pp. 1–14). Norwood, NJ: Ablex Publishing.

Goodwin, W.L., & Goodwin, L.D. (1982). Measuring young children. In B. Spodek (Ed.), *Handbook of research in early childhood education* (pp. 523–563). New York: Free Press.

Goodz, N.S. (1982). Is before really easier to understand than after? *Child Development, 53,* 822–825.

Gordon, A.M., & Browne, K.W. (1989). *Beginnings and beyond: Foundations in early childhood education* (2nd ed.). Albany, NY: Delmar.

Gordon, A.M., & Browne, K.W. (1993). *Beginnings and beyond: Foundations in early childhood education* (3rd ed.). Albany, NY: Delmar.

Gordon, I. (1967, June). *The young child: A new look.* Paper presented at the conference on The Young Child: Florida's Future, University of Florida.

Gordon, T. (1974). *T.E.T.: Teacher effectiveness training.* New York: Peter H. Wyden.

Gordon, T. (1976). *P.E.T. in action.* New York: Peter H. Wyden.

Gottfried, A. (1984). Home environment and early cognitive development: Integration, meta-analyses, and conclusions. In A. Gottfried (Ed.), *Home environment and early cognitive development.* San Francisco: Academic Press.

Gould, R.L. (1978). *Transformations: Growth and change in adult life.* New York: Simon & Schuster.

Graue, M.E., & Shepard, L.A. (1989). Predictive validity of the Gesell School Readiness Test. *Early Childhood Research Quarterly, 4,* 303–315.

Greenberg, P. (1987). Lucy Sprague Mitchell: A major missing link between early childhood education in the 1980s and progressive education in the 1890s–1930s. *Young Children, 42*(5), 70–84.

Greenberg, P. (1988). Ideas that work with young children: Avoiding me against you discipline. *Young Children 44*(1), 24–29.

Greenleaf, P. (1978). *Children throughout the ages: A history of childhood.* New York: Barnes & Noble.

Greenspan, S., & Greenspan, N.T. (1986). *First feelings: Milestones in the emotional development of your baby and child.* New York: Penguin Books.

Greenwood-Church, M., & Crozier-Smith, D. (1992). A socio-geographic overview of Alberta. In A. Pence (Ed.), *Canadian child care in context: Perspectives from the provinces and territories.* Ottawa: Statistics Canada & Health and Welfare Canada.

Griffin, E.F. (1982). *Island of childhood: Education in the special world of nursery school.* New York: Teachers College Press, Columbia University.

Griffin, S. (1992). Addendum: Child care in British Columbia, 1988–1990. In A. Pence (Ed.), *Canadian child care in context: Perspectives from the provinces and territories* (pp. 87–99). Ottawa: Statistics Canada & Health and Welfare Canada.

Grimsley, R. (1976). Jean Jacques Rousseau. In P. Edwards (Ed.), *The encyclopedia of philosophy* (Vols. 7–8, pp. 218–225). New York: Macmillan and Free Press.

Guilford, J.P. (1962). Creativity: Its measurement and development. In S. Parnes & H. Harding (Eds.), *A sourcebook for creative thinking* (pp. 151–168). New York: Charles Scribner's Sons.

Gunnar, M., Senior, K., & Hartup, W. (1984). Peer presence and the exploratory behavior of eighteen- and thirty-month-old children. *Child Development, 55*, 1103–1109.

Gunsberg, A. (1989). Empowering young abused and neglected children through contingent play. *Childhood Education, 66,* 8–10.

Hakuta, K. (1988). Why bilinguals? In F.S. Kessel (Ed.), *The development of language and language researchers* (pp. 299–318). Hillsdale, NJ: Lawrence Erlbaum.

Hakuta, K., & Garcia, E.E. (1989). Bilingualism and education. *American Psychologist, 44,* 374–379.

Halpern, R. (1987). Major social and demographic trends affecting young families: Implications for early childhood care and education. *Young Children, 42*(6), 34–40.

Hampden-Turner, C. (1981). *Maps of the mind: Charts and concepts of the mind and its labyrinths.* New York: Collier Books.

Harms, T., & Clifford, R. (1980). *Early childhood environment rating scale.* New York: Teachers College Press, Columbia University.

Harms, T., Clifford, R., & Padan-Belkin, E. (1983). *The day care home environment rating scale.* Chapel Hill, NC: Homebased Day Care Training Project.

Harms, T., & Clifford, R.M. (1980). *Day care environment rating scale.* New York: Teachers College Press, Columbia University.

Harms, T., Cryer, D., & Clifford, R. (1990). *Infant/toddler environment rating scale.* New York: Teachers College Press, Columbia University.

Harris, J.D., & Larsen, J.M. (1989). Parent education as a mandatory component of preschool: Effects on middle-class, educationally advantaged parents and children. *Early Childhood Research Quarterly, 4,* 275–287.

Harsh, A. (1987). Teach mathematics with children's literature. *Young Children, 42*(6), 24–27.

Harste, J.C., Short, K.G., & Burke, C. (1988). *Creating classrooms for authors: The reading–writing connection.* Portsmouth, NH: Heinemann Educational Books.

Hartup, W.W. (1983a). Peer interaction and the behavioral development of the individual child. In W. Damon (Ed.), *Social and personality development: Essays on the growth of the child* (pp. 220–233). New York: W.W. Norton.

Hartup, W.W. (1983b). Peer relations. In P.H. Mussen (Ed.), *Handbook of child psychology: Vol. 4. Socialization, personality, and social development* (4th ed., pp. 103–196). New York: John Wiley.

Haskins, R. (1985). Public school aggression among children with varying day care experience. *Child Development, 56,* 698–703.

Haugland, S.W., & Shade, D.D. (1990). *Developmental evaluations of software for young children.* Albany, NY: Delmar.

Hautman, L., Read, M., & Greenwood-Church, M. (1992). An overview of child care legislation in Alberta. In A. Pence (Ed.), *Canadian child care in context: Perspectives from the provinces and territories.* Ottawa: Statistics Canada & Health and Welfare Canada.

Hayward, D., Rothenburg, M., & Beasley, R. (1974). Children's play and urban playground environments: A comparison of traditional, contemporary, and adventure playground types. *Environment and Behaviour, 6*(2), 131–168.

Healy, J.M. (1991, February). Ten reasons why "Sesame Street" is bad news for reading. *The Education Digest,* 63–66.

Helburn, S., Culkin, M.L., Howes, C., Bryant, D., Clifford, R., Cryer, D., Peisner-Feinberg, E., & Kagan, S.L. (1995). *Cost, quality and child care outcomes in child care centers.* Denver: University of Colorado at Denver.

Helfer, R.E. (1987). The developmental basis of child abuse and neglect: An epidemiological approach. In R.E. Helfer & R.S. Kempe (Eds.), *The battered child* (4th ed., pp. 60–80). Chicago: University of Chicago Press.

Hendrick, J. (1986). *Total learning: Curriculum for the young child* (2nd ed.). Columbus, OH: Merrill.

Hendrick, J. (Ed.). (1997). *First steps toward teaching the Reggio way.* Upper Saddle River, NJ. Merrill-Prentice Hall.

Henkens-Matzke, A., & Abbott, D.A. (1990). Game playing: A method for reducing young children's fear of medical procedures. *Early Childhood Research Quarterly, 5,* 19–26.

Herr, J., & Morse, W. (1982). Food for thought: Nutrition education for young children. In J.F. Brown (Ed.), *Curriculum planning for young children* (pp. 151–159). Washington, DC: National Association for the Education of Young Children.

Herrera, J.F., & Wooden, S.L. (1988). Some thoughts about effective parent–school communication. *Young Children, 43*(6), 78–80.

Hess, R.D., & Shipman, V. (1965a). Early blocks to children's learning. *Children, 12,* 189–194.

Hess, R.D., & Shipman, V. (1965b). Early experience and socialization of cognitive modes in children. *Child Development, 36,* 869–886.

Hess, R.D., & Shipman, V. (1968). Maternal influences upon early learning: The cognitive environments of urban pre-school children. In R.D. Hess & R.M. Bear (Eds.), *Early education.* Chicago: Aldine-Atherton.

Hetherington, E.M., Stanley-Hagan, M., & Anderson, E.R. (1989). Marital transitions: A child's perspective. *American Psychologist, 44,* 303–312.

Hills, T.W. (1987). Children in the fast lane: Implications for early childhood policy and practice. *Early Childhood Research Quarterly, 2,* 265–273.

Hilton, J.M., Essa, E.L., & Murray, C.I. (1991). Are families meeting the nonphysical needs of their children? A comparison of single parent, one-earner and two-earner households. *Family Perspectives, 25*(2), 41–56.

Hinde, R.A. (1983). Ethology and child development. In P.H. Mussen (Ed.), *Handbook of child psychology: Vol. 2. Infancy and developmental psychobiology* (4th ed., pp. 27–93). New York: John Wiley.

Hitz, R., & Driscoll, A. (1988). Praise or encouragement? New insights into praise: Implications for early childhood teachers. *Young Children, 44*(5), 6–13.

Hofferth, S.L., & Phillips, D.A. (1987). Child care in the United States, 1970 to 1995. *Journal of Marriage and the Family, 49,* 559–571.

Hoffman, W. (1989). Effects of maternal employment in the two-parent family. *American Psychologist, 44,* 283–292.

Hohmann, M., Banet, B., & Weikart, D.P. (1979). *Young children in action: A manual for preschool educators.* Ypsilanti, MI: High/Scope Press.

Honig, A.S. (1979). *Parent involvement in early childhood education.* Washington, DC: National Association for the Education of Young Children.

Honig, A.S. (1982). Prosocial development in young children. *Young Children, 37*(5), 51–62.

Honig, A.S. (1983). Sex role socialization in early childhood. *Young Children, 38*(6), 57–70.

Honig, A.S. (1985a). Research in review: Compliance, control, and discipline (Pt. 1). *Young Children, 40*(2), 50–58.

Honig, A.S. (1985b). Research in review: Compliance, control, and discipline (Pt. 3). *Young Children, 40*(3), 47–52.

Honig, A.S. (1986a). Stress and coping in children (Pt. 1). *Young Children, 41*(4), 50–63.

Honig, A.S. (1986b). Stress and coping in children (Pt. 2): Interpersonal family relationships. *Young Children, 41*(5), 47–59.

Honig, A.S. (1987). The shy child. *Young Children, 42*(4), 54–64.

Honig, A.S. (1988a). Caring and kindness: Curricular goals for early childhood educators. In G.F. Robertson & M.A. Johnson (Eds.), *Leaders in education: Their views on controversial issues* (pp. 58–70). New York: University Press of America.

Honig, A.S. (1988b). Humor development in children. *Young Children, 43*(4), 60–73.

Honig, A.S. (1990). *Parent involvement in early childhood education.* Washington, DC: National Association for the Education of Young Children.

Honig, A.S. (1993). The Eriksonian approach. In J.L. Roopnarine & J.E. Johnson (Eds.), *Approaches to early childhood education* (2nd ed., pp. 47–70). New York: Merrill.

Hough, R.A., Nurss, J.R., & Wood, D. (1987). Tell me a story: Making opportunities for elaborated language in early childhood classrooms. *Young Children, 43*(1), 6–12.

Howes, C. (1983). Caregiver behavior in center and family day care. *Journal of Applied Developmental Psychology, 4*, 99–107.

Howes, C. (1987). Social competency with peers: Contributions from child care. *Early Childhood Research Quarterly, 2,* 155–167.

Howes, C. (1988). Same- and cross-sex friends: Implications for interaction and social skills. *Early Childhood Research Quarterly, 3*, 21–37.

Howes, C., & Farver, J.A. (1987). Social pretend play in 2-year-olds: Effects of age of partner. *Early Childhood Research Quarterly, 2*, 305–314.

Howes, C., & Hamilton, C.E. (1993). The changing experiences of child care: Changes in teachers and teacher–child relationships and children's social competence with peers. *Early Childhood Research Quarterly, 8*, 15–32.

Howes, C., & Olenick, M. (1986). Family and child care influences on toddlers' compliance. *Child Development, 57*, 202–216.

Huesmann, L.R. (1986). Psychological processes promoting the relation between exposure to media violence and aggressive behaviour by the viewer. *Journal of Social Issues, 42*, 125–139.

Huesmann, L.R., Lagerspetz, K., & Eron, L.D. (1984). Intervening variables in the TV violence–aggression relation: Evidence from two countries. *Developmental Psychology, 20*, 746–775.

Humphrey, J.H., & Humphrey, J.N. (1985). *Controlling stress in children*. Springfield, IL: Charles C. Thomas.

Hunt, J. McV. (1961). *Intelligence and experience*. New York: Ronald Press.

Hunt, J. McV. (1968). Revisiting Montessori. In J.L. Frost (Ed.), *Early childhood education rediscovered* (pp. 102–127). New York: Holt, Rinehart & Winston.

Huston, A.C., Watkins, B.A., & Kunkel, D. (1989). Public policy and children's television. *American Psychologist, 44*, 424–433.

Hymes, J.L. (1981). *Teaching the child under six* (3rd ed.). Columbus, OH: Merrill.

Hyson, M.C. (1986). Lobster on the sidewalk: Understanding and helping children with fears. In J.B. McCracken (Ed.), *Reducing stress in young children's lives* (pp. 2–5). Washington, DC: National Association for the Education of Young Children.

International Reading Association. (1986). Literacy development and pre-first grade: A joint statement of concerns about present practices in pre-first grade reading instruction and recommendations for improvement. *Young Children, 41*(4), 10–13.

Irwin, S., & Canning, P. (1992a). Addendum: Child care in Nova Scotia, 1988–1990. In A. Pence (Ed.), *Canadian child care in context: Perspectives from the provinces and territories*. Ottawa: Statistics Canada & Health and Welfare Canada.

Irwin, S., & Canning, P. (1992b). An historical overview of child care in Nova Scotia. In A. Pence (Ed.), *Canadian child care in context: Perspectives from the provinces and territories*. Ottawa: Statistics Canada & Health and Welfare Canada.

Isaacs, S. (1993). *Intellectual Growth in Young Children*. New York: Schocken.

Ishee, N., & Goldhaber, J. (1990). Story re-enactment: Let the play begin. *Young Children, 45*(3), 70–75.

Izard, C. (1982). *Measuring emotions in infants and children*. New York: Cambridge University Press.

Jalongo, M.R. (1986). Using crisis-oriented books with young children. In J.B. McCracken (Ed.), *Reducing stress in young children's lives* (pp. 41–46). Washington, DC: National Association for the Education of Young Children.

Jalongo, M.R., & Collins, M. (1985). Singing with young children! Folk singing for non-musicians. *Young Children, 40*(2), 17–22.

Javernick, E. (1988). Johnny's not jumping: Can we help obese children? *Young Children, 43*(2), 18–23.

Jenkins, S. (1987). Ethnicity and family support. In S.L. Kagan, D.R. Powell, B. Weissbourd, & E.F. Zigler (Eds.), *America's family support programs: Perspectives and prospects* (pp. 282–294). New Haven, CT: Yale University Press.

Jensen, A.R. (1985a). Compensatory education and the theory of intelligence. *Phi Delta Kappan, 66*, 554–558.

Jensen, M.A. (1985b). Story awareness: A critical skill for early reading. *Young Children, 41*(1), 20–24.

Johnson, J. (1993). Evaluation in early childhood education. In J.L. Roopnarine & J.E. Johnson (Eds.), *Approaches to early childhood education* (2nd ed., pp. 317–336). New York: Merrill.

Johnson, L., & Joe, M.J. (1992). An historical overview of child care in Yukon. In A. Pence (Ed.), *Canadian child care in context: Perspectives from the provinces and territories*. Ottawa: Statistics Canada & Health and Welfare Canada.

Johnston, J.R., & Slobin, D.I. (1979). The development of locative expressions in English, Italian, Serbo-Croatian, and Turkish. *Journal of Child Language, 6*, 529–545.

Jones, C., Marsden, L., & Tepperman, L. (1990). *Lives of their own: The individualization of women's lives.* Toronto: Oxford University Press.

Jones, E., & Prescott, E. (1978). *Dimensions of teaching—Learning environments, II: Focus on day care.* Pasadena, CA: Pacific Oaks College.

Jordan, N.H. (1993). Sexual abuse prevention in early childhood education: A caveat. *Young Children, 48*(6), 76–69.

Jorde-Bloom, P. (1988). *A great place to work: Improving conditions for staff in young children's programs.* Washington, DC: National Association for the Education of Young Children.

Joy, L.A., Kimball, M.M., & Zabrack, M.L. (1986). Television and children's aggressive behavior. In T.M. Williams (Ed.), *The impact of television: A natural experiment in three communities* (pp. 303–360). Orlando, FL: Academic Press.

Kagan, J. (1987). Introduction. In J. Kagan & S. Lamb (Eds.), *The emergence of morality in young children* (pp. ix–xx). Chicago: University of Chicago Press.

Kagan, J., & Reznick, J.S. (1986). Shyness and temperament. In W.H. Jones, J.M. Cheek, & S.R. Briggs (Eds.), *Shyness: Perspectives on research and treatment* (pp. 81–90). New York: Plenum Press.

Kagan, S.L., & Newton, J.W. (1989). For-profit and non-profit child care: Similarities and differences. *Young Children, 44*(6), 4–10.

Kamii, C. (1982). *Number in preschool and kindergarten.* Washington, DC: National Association for the Education of Young Children.

Kamii, C. (1984). Obedience is not enough. *Young Children, 39*(4), 11–14.

Kamii, C. (Ed.). (1990). *Achievement testing in the early grades: The games grown-ups play.* Washington, DC: National Association for the Education of Young Children.

Kamii, C., & DeClark, G. (1985). *Young children reinvent arithmetic: Implications of Piaget's theory.* New York: Teachers College Press, Columbia University.

Kamii, C., & DeVries, R. (1980). *Group games in early childhood.* Washington, DC: National Association for the Education of Young Children.

Kamii, C., & Lee-Katz, L. (1982). Physics in preschool education: A Piagetian approach. In J.F. Brown (Ed.), *Curriculum planning for young children* (pp. 171–176). Washington, DC: National Association for the Education of Young Children.

Kaplan, P. (1991). *A child's odyssey* (2nd ed.). St. Paul, MN: West Publishing.

Karnes, M. (1969). *Research and development project on preschool disadvantaged children.* Washington, DC: U.S. Office of Education.

Karnes, M., & Lee, R.C. (1979). Mainstreaming in the preschool. In L.G. Katz (Ed.), *Current topics in early childhood education* (Vol. 2, pp. 13–42). Norwood, NJ: Ablex Publishing.

Karnes, M., Shwedel, A., & Williams, M. (1983). A comparison of five approaches for educating young children from low-income homes. In The Consortium for Longitudinal Studies (Ed.), *As the twig is bent.* Hillsdale, NJ: Lawrence Erlbaum.

Katz, L.G. (1972). *Teacher–child relationships in day care centres.* (ERIC Document Reproduction Service). No. 046 494.

Katz, L.G. (1977). *Talks with teachers: Reflections on early childhood education.* Washington, DC: National Association for the Education of Young Children.

Katz, L.G. (1980). Mothering and teaching: Some significant distinctions. In L.G. Katz (Ed.), *Current topics in early childhood education* (Vol. 3, pp. 47–63). Norwood, NJ: Ablex Publishing.

Katz, L.G. (1984a). The education of preprimary teachers. In L.G. Katz (Ed.), *Current topics in early childhood education* (Vol. 5, pp. 209–227). Norwood, NJ: Ablex Publishing.

Katz, L.G. (1984b). The professional early childhood teacher. *Young Children, 39*(5), 3–10.

Katz, L.G. (1988). Where is early childhood education as a profession? In B. Spodek, O.N. Saracho, & D.L. Peters (Eds.), *Professionalism and the early childhood practitioner* (pp. 75–83). New York: Teachers College Press, Columbia University.

Katz, L.G. (1989). *Engaging children's minds: The project approach.* Norwood, NJ: Ablex Publishing.

Katz, L.G., & Chard, S. (1993). The project approach. In J. L. Roopnarine & J. E. Johnson (Eds.), *Approaches to early childhood education* (2nd ed., pp. 209–222). New York: Merrill.

Katz, L.G., Evangelou, D., & Hartman, J.A. (1990). *The case for mixed-age grouping in early education.* Washington, DC: National Association for the Education of Young Children.

Katz, P.A. (1982). Children's racial awareness and intergroup attitudes. In L.G. Katz (Ed.), *Current topics in early childhood education* (Vol. 4, pp. 17–54). Norwood, NJ: Ablex Publishing.

Katz, P.A. (1983). Developmental foundations of gender and racial attitudes. In R.L. Leahy (Ed.), *The child's construction of social inequality* (pp. 41–78). New York: Academic Press.

Katz, P.A. (1986). Modification of children's gender-stereotyped behaviour: General issues and research considerations. *Sex Roles, 14*, 591–602.

Keats, E.J. (1967). *Peter's chair.* New York: Harper & Row.

Keele, V.S. (1966). *Individual-time formula: The golden formula for raising happy, secure children.* Unpublished paper.

Kellogg, R. (1969). *Analyzing children's art.* Palo Alto, CA: Mayfield.

Kelly, F.J. (1981). Guiding groups of parents of young children. *Young Children, 37*(1), 28–32.

Kelly, J. (1989). *Early, middle, or late immersion?* Unpublished master's thesis, Brock University, St. Catharines, Ontario.

Kempe, R.S., & Kempe, C.H. (1978). *Child abuse.* Cambridge, MA: Harvard University Press.

Keogh, J., & Sugden, D. (1985). *Movement skill development.* New York: Macmillan.

Kersey, K. (1985). *Helping your child handle stress: The parents' guide to recognizing and solving childhood problems.* New York: Acropolis.

Kessen, W. (1965). *The child.* New York: John Wiley.

Ketchel, J.A. (1986). Helping the young child cope with death. *Day Care and Early Childhood, 14*(2), 24–27.

Kids freed from carpet factories join protest against child labor. (1993, February 16). *The St. Catharines Standard,* p. C10.

Kilpatrick, W.H. (1914). *The Montessori system examined.* Boston: Houghton Mifflin.

Kinsman, C.A., & Berk, L.E. (1982). Joining the block and housekeeping areas. In J.F. Brown (Ed.), *Curriculum planning for young children* (pp. 28–37). Washington, DC: National Association for the Education of Young Children.

Kleckner, K.A., & Engel, R.E. (1988). A child begins school: Relieving anxiety with books. *Young Children, 43*(5), 14–18.

Kohlberg, L. (1966). A cognitive-developmental analysis of children's sex-role concepts and attitudes. In E.E. Maccoby (Ed.), *The development of sex differences* (pp. 82–173). Stanford, CA: Stanford University Press.

Kohlberg, L. (1969). Stages and sequence: The cognitive development approach to socialization. In D.A. Goslin (Ed.), *Handbook of socialization theory and research* (pp. 347–480). Chicago: Rand McNally.

Kontos, S. (1986). What preschool children know about reading and how they learn it. *Young Children, 42*(1), 58–66.

Kopp, C.B. (1982). Antecedents of self-regulation: A developmental perspective. *Developmental Psychology, 18,* 199–214.

Kostelnik, M.J., Whiren, A.P., & Stein, L.C. (1986). Living with He-man. *Young Children, 42,* 3–9.

Kounin, J.S., & Sherman, L.W. (1979). School environments as behaviour settings. *Theory into Practice, 18*(3), 145–151.

Kritchevsky, S., Prescott, E., & Walling, L. (1977). *Planning environments for young children: Physical space.* Washington, DC: National Association for the Education of Young Children.

Krogh, S.L., & Lamme, L.L. (1985). "But what about sharing?" Children's literature and moral development. *Young Children, 40*(4), 48–51.

Kubler-Ross, E. (1969). *On death and dying.* New York: Macmillan.

Kushner, D. (1989). "Put your name on your painting, but ... the blocks go back on the shelves." *Young Children, 45*(1), 49–56.

Kyle, I. (1992a). Addendum: Child care in Ontario, 1988–1990. In A. Pence (Ed.), *Canadian child care in context: Perspectives from the provinces and territories.* Ottawa: Statistics Canada & Health and Welfare Canada.

Kyle, I. (1992b). An historical overview of child care in Ontario. In A. Pence (Ed.), *Canadian child care in context: Perspectives from the provinces and territories.* Ottawa: Statistics Canada & Health and Welfare Canada.

Kyle, I. (1992c). An overview of child care legislation, programs and funding in Ontario. In A. Pence (Ed.), *Canadian child care in context: Perspectives from the provinces and territories.* Ottawa: Statistics Canada & Health and Welfare Canada.

Kyle, I. (1992d). A socio-geographic overview of Ontario. In A. Pence (Ed.), *Canadian child care in context: Perspectives from the provinces and territories.* Ottawa: Statistics Canada & Health and Welfare Canada.

Labov, W. (1970). *The study of nonstandard English.* Urbana, IL: National Council of Teachers of English.

Lally, J.R., Mangione, P.L., & Honig, A.S. (1988). The Syracuse University Family Development Research Program: Long-range impact on an early intervention with low-income children and their families. In D.R. Powell (Ed.), *Emerging directions in parent–child intervention* (pp. 79–104). Norwood, NJ: Ablex Publishing.

Lamb, M.E., & Bornstein, M.H. (1987). *Development in infancy: An introduction.* New York: Random House.

Lambert, W. (1977). The effects of bilingualism of the individual: Cognitive and socio-cultural consequences, In P. Hornby (Ed.), *Bilingualism: Psychological, social and educational implications.* New York: Academic Press.

Langenbach, M., & Neskora, T.W. (1977). *Day care curriculum considerations.* Columbus, OH: Merrill.

Larsen, J.M., & Robinson, C.C. (1989). Later effects of preschool on low-risk children. *Early Childhood Research Quarterly, 4,* 133–144.

Laughing all the way. (1988). *Young Children, 43*(2), 39–41.

Lavatelli, C.S. (1970). *Piaget's theory applied to an early childhood curriculum.* Boston, MA: American Science and Engineering.

Lawton, J.T. (1988). *Introduction to child care and early childhood education.* Glenview, IL: Scott, Foresman.

Lay-Dopyera, M., & Dopyera, J.E. (1987a). Strategies for teaching. In C. Seefeldt (Ed.), *The early childhood curriculum: A review of current research* (pp. 13–33). New York: Teachers College Press, Columbia University.

Lay-Dopyera, M., & Dopyera, J.E. (1987b). *Becoming a teacher of young children* (3rd ed.). New York: Random House.

Lazar, I., & Darlington, R. (1982). Lasting effects of early education: A report from the Consortium for Longitudinal Studies. *Monographs of the Society for Research in Child Development, 47*(2–3, Serial No. 195).

Lee, V.E., Brooks-Gunn, J., Schnur, E., & Liaw, F.R. (1990). Are Head Start effects sustained? A longitudinal followup comparison of disadvantaged children attending Head Start, no preschool and other preschool programs. *Child Development, 61,* 495–507.

Lennenberg, E.H. (1967). *Biological foundations of language.* New York: John Wiley.

Lepper, M.R., Greene, D., & Nisbett, R.E. (1973). Undermining children's intrinsic interest with extrinsic reward: A test of the "over justification" hypothesis. *Journal of Personality and Social Psychology, 28,* 129–137.

Lero, D.S. (1994). In transition: Changing patterns of work, family life, child care ideas. *The Journal of Emotional Well Being in Child Care, 1*(3), 11–14.

LeShan, E.J. (1968) *The conspiracy against children.* New York: Athenaeum.

Levinger, G., & Levinger, A.C. (1986). The temporal course of close relationships: Some thoughts about the development of children's ties. In W.W. Hartup & Z. Rubin (Eds.), *Relationships and development* (pp. 111–133). Hillsdale, NJ: Lawrence Erlbaum.

Levinson, D.J. (1978). *The seasons of a man's life.* New York: Alfred A. Knopf.

Lexmond, T. (1987). Temper tantrums. In A. Thomas & J. Grimes (Eds.), *Children's needs: Psychological perspectives* (pp. 627–633). Washington, DC: National Association of School Psychologists.

Lieberman, A.F. (1994). *The emotional life of the toddler.* New York: The Free Press.

Liebert, R.M., & Sprafkin, J.N. (1988). *The early window: Effects of television on children and youth* (3rd ed.). New York: Pergamon Press.

Lillard, P.P. (1973). *Montessori: A modern approach.* New York: Schocken Books.

Lindauer, S.L.K. (1987). Montessori education for young children. In J.L. Roopnarine & J.E. Johnson (Eds.), *Approaches to early childhood education* (pp. 109–126). New York: Merrill.

Lindauer, S.L.K. (1993). Montessori education for young children. In J. L. Roopnarine & J. E. Johnson (Eds.), *Approaches to early childhood education* (2nd ed.) (pp. 243–260). Columbus, OH: Merrill.

Linderman, C.E. (1979). *Teachables from trashables: Homemade toys that teach.* St. Paul, MN: Toys 'n Things Training and Resource Center.

Lindfors, J.W. (1987). *Children's language and learning* (2nd ed.). Englewood Cliffs, NJ: Prentice-Hall.

Lombardi, J. (1986). Training for public policy and advocacy: An emerging topic in teacher education. *Young Children, 41*(4), 65–69.

Lombardi, J. (1990). Developing a coalition to reach the full cost of quality. In B. Willer (Ed.), *Reaching the full cost of quality in early childhood programs* (pp. 87–96). Washington, DC: National Association for the Education of Young Children.

Lovell, P., & Harms, T. (1985). How can playgrounds be improved?: A rating scale. *Young Children, 40*(3), 3–8.

Lowenfeld, V. (1962). Creativity: Education's stepchild. In S. Parnes & H. Harding (Eds.), *A sourcebook for creative thinking* (pp. 9–17). New York: Charles Scribner's Sons.

Lozoff, B. (1989). Nutrition and behaviour. *American Psychologist, 44*, 231–236.

Lutes, D. (1992). An overview of child care legislation in New Brunswick. In A. Pence (Ed.), *Canadian child care in context: Perspectives from the provinces and territories.* Ottawa: Statistics Canada & Health and Welfare Canada.

Lutes, D., & Gamble, J. (1992). Addendum: Child care in New Brunswick, 1988–1990. In A. Pence (Ed.), *Canadian child care in context: Perspectives from the provinces and territories.* Ottawa: Statistics Canada & Health and Welfare Canada.

Maccoby, E.E. (1990). Gender and relationships. *American Psychologist, 45*, 513–520.

Maccoby, E.E., & Jacklin, C. (1974). *The psychology of sex differences.* Stanford, CA: Stanford University Press.

Maccoby, E.E., & Jacklin, C.N. (1987). Gender segregation in childhood. In H.W. Reese (Ed.), *Advances in child development and behavior* (Vol. 20, pp. 239–288). New York: Academic Press.

Maccoby, E.E., & Martin, J.A. (1983). Socialization in the context of the family: Parent–child interaction. In P.H. Mussen (Series Ed.) & E.M. Hetherington (Vol. Ed.), *Handbook of child psychology: Vol. 4. Socialization, personality, and social development* (4th ed., pp. 1–101). New York: John Wiley.

Machado, J.M. (1985). *Early childhood experiences in language arts* (3rd ed.). Albany, NY: Delmar.

Maier, H.W. (1965). *Three theories of child development.* New York: Harper & Row.

Maier, H.W. (1990). Erikson's developmental theory. In R.M. Thomas (Ed.), *The encyclopedia of human development and education: Theory, research, and studies* (pp. 88–93). New York: Pergamon Press.

Malaguzzi, L. (1993). A bill of three rights in innovations in early education. *The International Reggio Exchange, 2*(1), 9.

Marcotte, R., & Young, R. (1992). *The effects of changing themes on children's play in the drama centre.* Unpublished manuscript, Brock University, St. Catharines, Ontario.

Mardell-Czudnowski, C.D., & Goldenberg, D.S. (1983). *Developmental Indicators for the Assessment of Learning-Revised (DIAL-R).* Edison, NJ: Childcraft Education.

Marshall, H.H. (1989). The development of self-concept. *Young Children, 44*(5), 44–51.

Maslow, A. (1970). *Motivation and personality.* New York: Harper & Row.

Mattingly, M. (1977). Introduction to symposium: Stress and burnout in child care. *Child Care Quarterly, 6,* 127–137.

Mauch, D. (1992a). Addendum: Child care in the Yukon, 1988–1990. In A. Pence (Ed.), *Canadian child care in context: Perspectives from the provinces and territories.* Ottawa: Statistics Canada & Health and Welfare Canada.

Mauch, D. (1992b). An overview of child care legislation in the Yukon. In A. Pence (Ed.), *Canadian child care in context: Perspectives from the provinces and territories.* Ottawa: Statistics Canada & Health and Welfare Canada.

Mauch, D. (1992c). A socio-geographic overview of the Yukon. In A. Pence (Ed.), *Canadian child care in context: Perspectives from the provinces and territories.* Ottawa: Statistics Canada & Health and Welfare Canada.

Mavrogenes, N.A. (1990). Helping parents help their children become literate. *Young Children, 45*(4), 4–9.

Maxim, George (1989). *The very young* (3rd ed.). Columbus, OH: Merrill.

Mayesky, M. (1990). *Creative activities for young children* (4th ed.). Albany, NY: Delmar.

Mayfield, M. (1990). *Work-related child care in Canada.* Ottawa, ON: Labour Canada.

McAfee, O.D. (1985). Circle time: Getting past "two little pumpkins." *Young Children, 40*(6), 24–29.

McCarthy, D. (1972). *Manual for the McCarthy Scales of Children's Abilities.* New York: Psychological Corp.

McCaughey, W.G. (1997). *Multiple intelligences: An introduction to the work of Howard Gardner.* A workshop for adult learners. Brock University, St.Catharines, ON.

McCracken, J.B. (Ed.). (1986). *Reducing stress in young children's lives.* Washington, DC: National Association for the Education of Young Children.

McDonald, D.T., & Ramsey, J.H. (1982). Awakening the artist: Music for young children. In J.F. Brown (Ed.), *Curriculum planning for young children* (pp. 187–193). Washington, DC: National Association for the Education of Young Children.

McDonell, L. (1992). An historical overview of child care in British Columbia. In A. Pence (Ed.), *Canadian child care in context: Perspectives from the provinces and territories.* Ottawa: Statistics Canada & Health and Welfare Canada.

McDonell, L., & Griffin, S. (1992). An overview of child care legislation in British Columbia. In A. Pence (Ed.), *Canadian child care in context: Perspectives from the provinces and territories.* Ottawa: Statistics Canada & Health and Welfare Canada.

McIntosh, A., & Rauhala, A. (February 3, 4, 6–8, 1989). Who's minding the children? *The Globe and Mail.* Toronto, Ontario.

McIntyre, M. (1984). *Early childhood and science.* Washington, DC: National Science Teachers Association.

McLaughlin, B. (1984). *Second-language acquisition in childhood: Preschool children* (Vol. 1, 2nd ed.). Hillsdale, NJ: Lawrence Erlbaum.

McMillan, M. (1919). *The nursery school.* London: J.M. Dent.

McMillan, M. (1930). *The nursery school* (rev. ed.). London: J.M. Dent.

McTear, M. (1985). *Children's conversations.* Oxford, United Kingdom: Basil Blackwell.

McWilliams, M. (1986). *Nutrition for the growing years.* New York: John Wiley.

Mead, M., & Metraux, R. (1993). A new understanding of childhood. In R.H. Wozniak (Ed.), *Worlds of childhood.* New York: Harper Collins College Press.

Meddin, B.J., & Rosen, A.L. (1986). Child abuse and neglect: Prevention and reporting. *Young Children, 41*(4), 26–30.

Medeiros, D.C., Porter, B.J., & Welch, I.D. (1983). *Children under stress.* Englewood Cliffs, NJ: Prentice-Hall.

Meisels, S.J. (1986). Testing four- and five-year-olds: Response to Salzer and to Shepard and Smith. *Educational Leadership, 44*(3), 90–92.

Meisels, S.J., & Sternberg, S. (1989, June). Quality sacrificed in proprietary child care. *Education Week,* p. 36.

Miezitis, S. (1972). The Montessori method: Some recent research. *American Montessori Society Bulletin, 10*(2).

Milkovich, G., & Gomez, L. (1976). Day care and selected employee work behaviours. *Academy of Management Journal, 19,* 111–115.

Miller, C.S. (1984). Building self-control: Discipline for young children. *Young Children, 40*(1), 15–19.

Miller, G.A., & Gildea, P.M. (1987, September). How children learn words. *Scientific American,* pp. 94–99.

Miller, L.B., & Bizzell, R.P. (1983). Long-term effects of four preschool programs: Sixth, seventh, and eighth grade. *Child Development, 54,* 727–741.

Miller, L.B., & Dyer, J.L. (1975). Four preschool programs: Their dimensions and effects. *Monographs of the Society for Research on Child Development* (5–6, Serial No.162).

Mitchell, A., & Modigliani, K. (1989). Young children in public schools?: The only ifs reconsidered. *Young Children, 44*(6), 56–61.

Monighan-Nourot, P. (1990) The legacy of play in American early childhood education. In E. Klugman & S. Smilansky (Eds.), *Children's play and learning* (pp. 59–85). New York: Teachers College Press, Columbia University.

Montessori, M. (1965). *The Montessori method* (A.E. George, Trans.). Cambridge, MA: Robert Bentley. (Original work published 1912)

Montessori, M. (1967). *The absorbent mind* (A. Claremont, Trans.). New York: Holt, Rinehart & Winston.

Moore, R.C., Goltsman, S.M., & Iacofano, D.S. (1987). *Play for all guidelines: Planning, design and management of outdoor play settings for all children.* Berkeley, CA: MIG Communications.

Moore, S.G. (1982). Prosocial behavior in the early years: Parent and peer influences. In B. Spodek (Ed.), *Handbook of research in early childhood education.* New York: Free Press.

Morado, C. (1986). Prekindergarten programs for 4-year-olds. *Young Children, 41*(5), 61–63.

Morgan, E.L. (1989). Talking with parents when concerns come up. *Young Children, 44*(2), 52–56.

Morin, J. (1989). We can force a solution to the staffing crisis. *Young Children, 44*(6), 18–19.

Morrison, G.S. (1984). *Early childhood education today* (3rd ed.). New York: Merrill.

Morrison, G.S. (1988). *Education and development of infants, toddlers, and preschoolers.* Glenview, IL: Scott, Foresman/Little, Brown College Division.

Morrison, G.S. (1991). *Early childhood education today* (5th ed.). New York: Merrill.

Morrow, R.D. (1989). What's in a name? In particular, a Southeast Asian name? *Young Children, 44*(6), 20–23.

Moskowitz, B.A. (1982). The acquisition of language. In *Human communication: Language and its psychobiological bases: Readings from Scientific American* (pp. 121–132). San Francisco: W.H. Freeman.

Mullen, S. (1992). A socio-geographic overview of Prince Edward Island. In A. Pence (Ed.), *Canadian child care in context: Perspectives from the provinces and territories.* Ottawa: Statistics Canada & Health and Welfare Canada.

Munro, J.G. (1986). Movement education: Balance. *Day Care and Early Education, 14*(2), 28–31.

Mussen, P.H., Conger, J.J., Kagan, J., & Huston, A.C. (1990). *Child development and personality* (7th ed.). New York: Harper & Row.

Mussen, P.H., & Eisenberg-Berg, N. (1977). *Roots of caring, sharing, and helping: The development of pro-social behavior in children.* San Francisco: W.H. Freeman.

Myers, B.K., & Maurer, K. (1987). Teaching with less talking: Learning centres in the kindergarten. *Young Children, 42*(5), 20–27.

Myers-Walls, J.A., & Fry-Miller, K.M. (1984). Nuclear war: Helping children overcome fears. *Young Children, 39*(4), 27–32.

NAEYC. (1989a). *Developmentally appropriate practice in early childhood programs serving infants.* Washington, DC: National Association for the Education of Young Children.

NAEYC. (1989b). *Developmentally appropriate practice in early childhood programs serving toddlers.* Washington, DC: National Association for the Education of Young Children.

NAEYC Information Service. (1990). *Employer-assisted child care: A NAEYC resource guide.* Washington, DC: National Association for the Education of Young Children.

NAEYC position statement on developmentally appropriate practice in early childhood education programs service children birth to age 8. (1986). *Young Children, 41*(6), 3.

NAEYC position statement on standardized testing of young children 3 through 8 years of age. (1988). *Young Children, 43*(3), 42–47.

NAEYC. (1993). Position statement on violence in the lives of children. *Young Children 49*(3), 68–77.

Napier-Anderson, L. (1981). *Change: One step at a time.* Toronto: Faculty of Education, University of Toronto.

National Child Care Information Centre, Child Care Programs Division. (1991). *The status of day care in Canada 1990.* Ottawa: Minister of Health and Welfare.

National Child Care Staffing Study. (1989). *Who cares? Child care teachers and the quality of child care in America.* Child Care Employee Project. Oakland, CA: NCCSS.

National Council of Welfare. (1988). *Childcare: A better alternative.* Ottawa: Supply and Services Canada.

National Council of Welfare. (1990). *Women and poverty revisited.* Ottawa: Supply and Services Canada.

National Dairy Council. (1980). *Food ... early choices: A nutrition learning system for early childhood.* Rosemont, IL: National Dairy Council.

National Guide. (1996). *College and University Programs, 1996.* Ottawa: Public Works and Government Services Canada.

Nauta, M.J., & Hewett, K. (1988). Studying complexity: The case of the child and family resource program. In H.B. Weiss & F.H. Jacobs (Eds.), *Evaluating family programs* (pp. 389–405). New York: Aldine de Gruyter.

Neisworth, J., & Buggey, T. (1993). Behavior analysis in early childhood education. In J. L. Roopnarine & J.E. Johnson (Eds.), *Approaches to early childhood education* (2nd ed., pp. 113–136). New York: Merrill.

Neugebauer, R. (1988, January). How's business? Status report No. 4 on for-profit child care. *Child Care Information Exchange*, pp. 29–34.

Neugebauer, R. (1991, January/February). How's business: Status report No. 7 on for-profit child care. *Child Care Information Exchange*, pp. 46–50.

Niagara Early Childhood Mentoring program. (1997). *Information package.* St. Catharines, ON: Early Childhood Community Development Centre.

Norris, D., & Boucher, J. (1980). *Observing children.* Toronto: Board of Education for the City of Toronto.

Northway, M. (1973). Child study in Canada: A casual history. In L. Brockman, J. Whiteley, & J. Zubek (Eds.), *Child development.* Toronto: McClelland & Stewart.

Noyes, D. (1987). Indoor pollutants: Environmental hazards to young children. *Young Children, 42*(6), 57–65.

Nykyforuk, J. (1992a). An historical overview of child care in Saskatchewan. In A. Pence (Ed.), *Canadian child care in context: Perspectives from the provinces and territories.* Ottawa: Statistics Canada & Health and Welfare Canada.

Nykyforuk, J. (1992b). A socio-geographic overview of Saskatchewan. In A. Pence (Ed.), *Canadian child care in context: Perspectives from the provinces and territories.* Ottawa: Statistics Canada & Health and Welfare Canada.

Obler, L.K. (1985). Language through the life-span. In J.B. Gleason (Ed.), *The development of language* (pp. 277–305). Columbus, OH: Merrill.

Oden, S. (1982). Peer relationship development in childhood. In L.G. Katz (Ed.), *Current topics in early childhood education* (Vol. 4, pp. 87–118). Norwood, NJ: Ablex Publishing.

Oken-Wright, P. (1988). Show-and-tell grows up. *Young Children, 43*(2), 52–58.

Orlick, T. (1978a). *The cooperative sports and games book: Challenge without competition.* New York: Pantheon Books.

Orlick, T. (1978b). *Winning through cooperation.* Washington, DC: Acropolis Books.

Orlick, T. (1982). *The second cooperative sports game books.* New York: Pantheon Books.

Owens, R.E. (1984). *Language development: An introduction.* Columbus, OH: Merrill.

Parke, R.D., & Slaby, R.G. (1983). The development of aggression. In P.H. Mussen (Ed.), *Handbook of child psychology: Vol. 4. Socialization, personality, and social development* (4th ed., pp. 547–641). New York: John Wiley.

Parker, J.G., & Gottman, J.M. (1989). Social and emotional development in a relational context. In T.J. Berndt & G.W. Ladd (Eds.), *Peer relationships in child development* (pp. 95–131). New York: John Wiley.

Parten, M.B. (1932). Social participation among preschool children. *Journal of Abnormal and Social Psychology, 27,* 243–269.

Partners in Practice: Successful Canadian Mentoring Programs. (1997). In Niagara Early Childhood Mentoring Program Information Package. Welland, ON: Niagara College of Applied Arts & Technology

Patterson, G.R. (1982). *Coercive family practices.* Eugene, OR: Castalia Press.

Patterson, G.R., DeBaryshe, B.D., & Ramsey, E. (1989). A developmental perspective on antisocial behavior. *American Psychologist, 44,* 329–335.

Patterson, G.R., & Gullion, M.E. (1971). *Living with children: New methods for parents and teachers.* Champaign, IL: Research Press.

Pease, D., & Gleason, J.B. (1985). Gaining meaning: Semantic development. In J.B. Gleason (Ed.), *The development of language* (pp. 103–138). Columbus, OH: Merrill.

Pence, A. (1990). The child care profession in Canada. In I. Doxey (Ed.), *Child care and education: Canadian dimensions* (pp. 87–97). Toronto: Nelson Canada.

Pence, A. (1992). *Canadian child care in context: Perspectives from the provinces and territories* (pp. xiii–xvii). Ottawa: Statistics Canada & Health and Welfare Canada.

Pence, A., & Moss, P. (1994). Towards an inclusionary approach in defining quality in valuing quality. In P. Moss & A. Pence (Eds.), *Early childhood services* (pp. 1–9). New York: Teachers College Press, Columbia University.

Pence, A., Read, M., Lero, D., Goelman, H., & Brockman, L. (1992). An overview of the NCCS data for British Columbia. In A. Pence (Ed.), *Canadian child care in context: Perspectives from the provinces and territories* (pp. 65–86). Ottawa: Statistics Canada & Health and Welfare Canada.

Peters, D.L. (1988). The Child Development Associate credential and the educationally disenfranchised. In B. Spodek, O.N. Saracho, & D.L. Peters (Eds.), *Professionalism and the early childhood practitioner* (pp. 93–104). New York: Teachers College Press, Columbia University.

Peters, D.L., Neisworth, J.T., & Yawkey, T.D. (1985). *Early childhood education: From theory to practice.* Monterey, CA: Brooks/Cole.

Phenice, L., & Hildebrand, L. (1988). Multicultural education: A pathway to global harmony. *Day Care and Early Education, 16(2),* 15–17

Phillips, D.A. (Ed.). (1987). *Quality in child care: What does research tell us?* Washington, DC: National Association for the Education of Young Children.

Phillips, D.A., & Howes, C. (1987). Indicators of quality child care: Review of research. In D.A. Phillips (Ed.), *Quality in child care: What does research tell us?* (pp. 1–20). Washington, DC: National Association for the Education of Young Children.

Phillips, D.A., Scarr, S., & McCartney, K. (1987). Dimensions and effects of child care quality: The Bermuda Study. In D.A. Phillips (Ed.), *Quality in child care: What does research tell us?* (pp. 43–56). Washington, DC: National Association for the Education of Young Children.

Phillips, D.A., & Whitebook, M. (1986). Who are child care workers?: The search for answers. *Young Children, 41*(4), 14–20.

Phyfe-Perkins, E. (1980). Children's behavior in preschool settings: A review of research concerning the influence of the physical environment. In L.G. Katz (Ed.), *Current topics in early childhood education* (Vol. 3, pp. 91–125). Norwood, NJ: Ablex Publishing.

Piaget, J. (1926). *The language and thought of the child.* London: Routledge & Kegan Paul.

Piaget, J. (1932). *The moral judgment of the child.* New York: Harcourt, Brace & World.

Piaget, J. (1951). *Play, dreams, and imitation in childhood.* New York: W.W. Norton.

Piaget, J. (1983). Piaget's theory. In P.H. Mussen (Ed.), *Handbook of child psychology: Vol. 1. History, theory, and methods* (4th ed., pp. 103–128). New York: John Wiley.

Pipes, P.L. (1989a). Between infancy and adolescence. In P.L. Pipes (Ed.), *Nutrition in infancy and childhood* (4th ed., pp. 120–142). St. Louis, MO: C.V. Mosby.

Pipes, P.L. (1989b). Special concerns of dietary intake during infancy and childhood. In P.L. Pipes (Ed.), *Nutrition in infancy and childhood* (4th ed., pp. 268–300). St. Louis, MO: C.V. Mosby.

Plomin, R., & Daniels, D. (1986). Genetics and shyness. In W.H. Jones, J.M. Cheek, & S.R. Briggs (Eds.), *Shyness: Perspectives on research and treatment* (pp. 63–80). New York: Plenum Press.

Poest, C.A., Williams, J.R., Witt, D.D., & Atwood, M.E. (1989). Physical activity patterns of preschool children. *Early Childhood Research Quarterly, 65,* 367–376.

Poest, C.A., Williams, J.R., Witt, D.D., & Atwood, M.E. (1990). Challenge me to move: Large muscle development in young children. *Young Children, 45*(5), 4–10.

Powell, D.R. (1986). Parent education and support programs. *Young Children, 41*(3), 47–53.

Powell, D.R. (1987a). After-school child care. *Young Children, 42*(3), 62–66.

Powell, D.R. (1987b). Day care as a family support system. In S.L. Kagan, D.R. Powell, B. Weissbourd, & E.F. Zigler (Eds.), *America's family support programs: Perspectives and prospects* (pp. 115–132). New Haven, CT: Yale University Press.

Powell, D.R. (1989). *Families and early childhood programs.* Washington, DC: National Association of the Education of Young Children.

Prescott, E. (1987). The environment as organizer of intent in child-care settings. In C.S. Weinstein & T.G. David (Eds.), *Spaces for children: The built environment and child development* (pp. 73–78). New York: Plenum Press.

Price, G.G. (1989). Mathematics in early childhood. *Young Children, 44*(4), 53–58.

Project Head Start Fact Sheet. (1994, January). Washington, DC: Administration on Children, Youth and Families.

Proshansky, H.M., & Fabian, A.K. (1987). The development of place identity in the child. In C.S. Weinstein & T.G. David (Eds.), *Spaces for children: The built environment and child development* (pp. 21-40). New York: Plenum Press.

Provincial and Territorial Child Care Organizations. (1997). Ottawa: Canadian Child Care Federation.

Radomski, M.A. (1986). Professionalization of early childhood educators: How far have we progressed? *Young Children, 41*(4), 20–23.

Ram, B. (1990). *Current demographic analysis: New trends in the family* (Cat. No. 91-535E). Ottawa: Supply and Services Canada.

Ramey, D., Dorvall, B., & Baker-Ward, L. (1983). Group day care and socially disadvantaged families: Effects on the child and the family. In S. Kilmer (Ed.), *Advances in early education and day care* (Vol. 3, pp. 69–132). Greenwich, CT: JAI Press.

Ramsey, P.G. (1982). Multicultural education in early childhood. In J.F. Brown (Ed.), *Curriculum planning for young children* (pp. 131–142). Washington, DC: National Association for the Education of Young Children.

Ramsey, P.G. (1987). *Teaching and learning in a diverse world: Multicultural education for young children*. New York: Teachers College Press, Columbia University.

Randall, V. (1992a). Addendum: Child care in Newfoundland, 1988–1990. In A. Pence (Ed.), *Canadian child care in context: Perspectives from the provinces and territories*. Ottawa: Statistics Canada & Health and Welfare Canada.

Randall, V. (1992b). An overview of child care legislation in Newfoundland. In A. Pence (Ed.), *Canadian child care in context: Perspectives from the provinces and territories*. Ottawa: Statistics Canada & Health and Welfare Canada.

Rarick, G.L. (1982). Descriptive research and process-oriented explanations of the motor development of children. In J.A.S. Kelso & J.E. Clark (Eds.), *The development of movement control and co-ordination* (pp. 275–291). New York: John Wiley.

Read, M. (1992). Addendum: Child care in Alberta, 1988–1990. In A. Pence (Ed.), *Canadian child care in context: Perspectives from the provinces and territories*. Ottawa: Statistics Canada & Health and Welfare Canada.

Read, M., Greenwood-Church, M., Hautman, L., Roche, E., & Bagley, C. (1992). An historical overview of child care in Alberta. In A. Pence (Ed.), *Canadian child care in context: Perspectives from the provinces and territories*. Ottawa: Statistics Canada & Health and Welfare Canada.

Reiber, J.L., & Embry, L.H. (1983). Working and communicating with parents. In E.M. Goetz & K.E. Allen (Eds.), *Early childhood education: Special environmental, policy, and legal considerations* (pp. 152–183). Rockville, MD: Aspen Systems Corp.

Reifel, S. (1984). Block construction: Children's developmental landmarks in representation of space. *Young Children, 40*(1), 61–67.

Reppucci, N.D., & Haugaard, J.J. (1989). Prevention of child sexual abuse: Myth or reality? *American Psychologist, 44,* 1266–1275.

Resnick, L.B. (1989). Developing mathematical knowledge. *American Psychologist, 44,* 162–169.

Rich, S.J. (1985). The writing suitcase. *Young Children, 40*(5), 42–44.

Richarz, A.S. (1980). *Understanding children through observation*. St. Paul, MN: West Publishing.

Riessman, F. (1962). *The culturally deprived child*. New York: Harper & Row.

Risley, T.R., & Baer, D.M. (1973). Operant behavior modification: The deliberate development of behavior. In B.M. Caldwell & H.M. Ricciuti (Eds.), *Review of child development research* (Vol. 3, pp. 283–329). Chicago: University of Chicago Press.

Ritch, A., & Griffin, S. (1992). A socio-geographic overview of British Columbia. In A. Pence (Ed.), *Canadian child care in context: Perspectives from the provinces and territories*. Ottawa: Statistics Canada & Health and Welfare Canada.

Robinson, B.E. (1988). Vanishing breed: Men in child care programs. *Young Children, 43*(6), 54–57.

Rogers, C.S., & Morris, S.S. (1986). Reducing sugar in children's diets: Why? How? *Young Children, 41*(5), 11–16.

Rogers, D.L., Perrin, M.S., & Waller, C.B. (1987). Enhancing the development of language and thought through conversations with young children. *Early Childhood Research Quarterly, 2,* 17–29.

Rogers, D.L., & Ross, D.D. (1986). Encouraging positive social interaction among young children. *Young Children, 41*(3), 12–17.

Rogers, F., & Sharapan, H.B. (1991). Helping parents, teachers, and caregivers deal with children's concerns about war. *Young Children, 46*(3), 12–13.

Roopnarine, J., & Johnson, J. (Eds.). (1993). *Approaches to early childhood education* (2nd ed.). New York: Merrill.

Rothlein, L. (1989). Nutrition tips revisited: On a daily basis, do we implement what we know? *Young Children, 44*(6), 30–36.

Rothman Beach Associates. (1985). A study of work-related day care in Canada. In *Childcare: The employer's role* (pp. 58–138). Ottawa: Status of Women.

Rowland, T., & McGuire, C. (1968). The developmental theory of Jean Piaget. In J.L. Frost (Ed.), *Early childhood education rediscovered* (pp. 145–152). New York: Holt, Rinehart & Winston.

Royce, J.M., Darlington, R.B., Murray, H.W. (1983). Pooled analyses: Findings across studies. In *The Consortium for Longitudinal Studies ... As the twig is bent ... Lasting effects of preschool programs* (pp. 444–459). Hillsdale, NJ: Lawrence Erlbaum Associates.

Rubin, K. (1977). Play behaviors of young children. *Young Children, 32*(6), 16–24.

Rubin, K. (1982). Early play theories revisited: Contributions to contemporary research and theory. In D. Pepler & K. Rubin (Eds.), *The play of children: Current theory and research.* Basel, Switzerland: Karger AG.

Rubin, K., Fein, G., & Vandenberg, B. (1983). Play. In P.H. Mussen (Ed.), *Handbook of child psychology: Vol. 4. Socialization, personality, and social development* (4th ed., pp. 693–774). New York: John Wiley.

Rubin, Z. (1980). *Children's friendships.* Cambridge, MA: Harvard University Press.

Rudick, E., & Nyisztor, D. (1977). *The emerging educator.* Toronto: Nelson Canada.

Ruopp, R., Travers, J., Glantz, F., & Coelen, C. (1979). *Children at the center: Final report of the National Day Care Study.* Cambridge, MA: ABT Associates.

Rutter, M. (1983). Stress, coping, and development: Some issues and some questions. In N. Garmezy & M. Rutter (Eds.), *Stress, coping, and development in children* (pp. 1–41). New York: McGraw-Hill.

Saida, Y., & Miyashita, M. (1979). Development of fine motor skill in children: Manipulation of a pencil in young children aged two to six years old. *Journal of Human Movement Studies, 5,* 104–113.

Saltz, E., Dixon, D., & Johnson, J. (1977). Training disadvantaged preschoolers on various fantasy activities: Effects on cognitive functioning and impulse control. *Child Development, 48,* 367–380.

Saltz, R., & Saltz, E. (1986). Pretend play training and its outcomes. In G. Fein & M. Rivkin (Eds.), *The young child at play* (pp. 155–173). Washington, DC: National Association for the Education of Young Children.

Salvia, J., & Ysseldyke, J. (1991). *Assessment* (5th ed.). Boston: Houghton Mifflin.

Sameroff, A.J. (1983). Developmental systems: Contexts and evolution. In P.H. Mussen (Ed.), *Handbook of child psychology: Vol. 1. History, theory, and methods* (4th ed., pp. 237–294). New York: John Wiley.

Samuels, S.C. (1977). *Enhancing self-concept in early childhood.* New York: Human Sciences Press.

Sarafino, E.P. (1986). *The fears of childhood: A guide to recognizing and reducing fearful states in children.* New York: Human Sciences Press.

Saunders, R., & Bingham-Newman, A.M. (1984). *Piagetian perspectives for preschools: A thinking book for teachers.* Englewood Cliffs, NJ: Prentice-Hall.

Saville-Troike, M. (1982). The development of bilingual and bicultural competence in young children. In L.G. Katz (Ed.), *Current topics in early childhood education* (Vol. 4, pp. 1–16). Norwood, NJ: Ablex Publishing.

Scales, B., Almy, M., Nicolopoulou, A., & Ervin-Tripp, S. (1992a). Defending play in the lives of children. In B. Scales, M. Almy, A. Nicolopoulou, & S. Ervin-Tripp (Eds.), *Play and the social context of development in early care and education* (pp. 15–31). New York: Teachers College Press, Columbia University.

Scales, B., Almy, M., Nicolopoulou, A., & Ervin-Tripp, S. (Eds.). (1992b). *Play and the social context of development in early care and education.* New York: Teachers College Press, Columbia University.

Scarr, S., Phillips, D., & McCartney, K. (1990). Facts, fantasies and the future of child care in the United States. *Psychological Science, 1*(1), 26–35.

Schickedanz, J.A. (1982). The acquisition of written language in young children. In B. Spodek (Ed.), *Handbook of research in early childhood education* (pp. 242–263). New York: Free Press.

Schickedanz, J.A. (1986). *More than ABCs: The early stages of reading and writing.* Washington, DC: National Association for the Education of Young Children.

Schickedanz, J.A., Hansen, K., & Forsyth, P.D. (1990). *Understanding children.* Mountain View, CA: Mayfield.

Schilder, P., & Wechsler, D. (1934). The attitudes of children toward death. *Journal of Genetic Psychology, 45*, 406–451.

Schirrmacher, R. (1986). Talking with young children about their art. *Young Children, 41*(5), 3–10.

Schirrmacher, R. (1990). *Art and creative development for young children.* Albany, NY: Delmar.

Schwarz, S., & Robison, H. (1982). *Designing curriculum for early childhood.* Boston, MA: Allyn & Bacon.

Schweinhart, L.J., Barnes, H.V., & Weikart, D.P. (1993). *Significant benefits: The High/Scope Perry Preschool Study through age 27.* Ypsilanti, MI: High/Scope Press.

Schweinhart, L.J., & Weikart, D.P. (1985). Evidence that good early childhood programs work. *Phi Delta Kappan, 66*, 545–551.

Schweinhart, L.J., & Weikart, D.P. (1993). Changed lives, significant benefits. *High/Scope Resource, 12*(3), 1, 10–14.

Schweinhart, L.J., Weikart, D.P., & Larner, M.B. (1986a). Consequences of three preschool models through age 15. *Early Childhood Research Quarterly, 1,* 15–45.

Schweinhart, L.J., Weikart, D.P., & Larner, M.B. (1986b). Child-initiated activities in early childhood programs may help prevent delinquency. *Early Childhood Research Quarterly, 1,* 303–312.

Sciarra, D.J., & Dorsey, A.G. (1990). *Developing and administering a child care centre* (2nd ed.). Albany, NY: Delmar.

Seaver, J.W., & Cartwright, C.A. (1986). *Child care administration.* Belmont, CA: Wadsworth.

Seefeldt, C. (1987a). The visual arts. In C. Seefeldt (Ed.), *The early childhood curriculum: A review of current research* (pp. 183–211). New York: Teachers College Press, Columbia University.

Seefeldt, C. (Ed.). (1987b). *The early childhood curriculum: A review of current research.* New York: Teachers College Press, Columbia University.

Seefeldt, V. (1984). Physical fitness in preschool and elementary school-aged children. *Journal of Physical Education, Recreation, and Dance, 55*(9), 33–40.

Seefeldt, V., & Haubenstricker, J. (1982). Patterns, phases, or stages: An analytical model for the study of developmental movement. In J.A.S. Kelso & J.E. Clark (Eds.), *The development of movement control and co-ordination* (pp. 309–318). New York: John Wiley.

Seifert, K. (1988). Men in early childhood education. In B. Spodek, O.N. Saracho, & D.L. Peters (Eds.), *Professionalism and the early childhood practitioner* (pp. 105–116). New York: Teachers College Press, Columbia University.

Seifert, K. (1993). Cognitive development in early childhood education. In B. Spodek (Ed.), *Handbook on research on the education of young children* (pp. 9–23). New York: Macmillan.

Seitz, V., Rosenbaum, L.K., & Apfel, N.H. (1985). Effects of family support intervention: A ten-year follow-up. *Child Development, 56,* 376–391.

Selye, H. (Ed.). (1980). *Guide to stress research* (Vol. 1). New York: Van Nostrand Reinhold.

Shapiro, E., & Biber, B. (1972). The education of young children: A developmental–interaction approach. *Teachers College Record, 74,* 55–79.

Shatz, M., & Gelman, R. (1973). The development of communication skills: Modifications in the speech of young children as a function of listener. *Monographs of the Society for Research in Child Development, 38*(5, Serial No. 152).

Sheehy, G. (1976). *Passages: Predictable crises of adult life.* New York: Dutton.

Shefatya, L. (1990). Socioeconomic status and ethnic differences in sociodramatic play: Theoretical and practical implications. In E. Klugman & S. Smilansky (Eds.), *Children's play and learning* (pp. 137–155). New York: Teachers College Press, Columbia University.

Sheldon, A. (1990). "Kings are royaler than queens": Language and socialization. *Young Children, 45*(2), 4–9.

Sheldon, J.B. (1983). Protecting the preschooler and the practitioner: Legal issues in early childhood programs. In E.M. Goetz & K.E. Allen (Eds.), *Early childhood education: Special environmental, policy, and legal considerations* (pp. 307–341). Rockville, MD: Aspen Systems Corp.

Sheppard, W.C. (1973). *Teaching social behavior to young children.* Champaign, IL: Research Press.

Shimoni, R., Baxter, J., & Kugelmass, J. (1992). *Every child is special.* Don Mills, ON: Addison-Wesley.

Sholtys, K.C. (1989). A new language, a new life. *Young Children, 44*(3), 76–77.

Shure, M.B., & Spivak, G. (1978). *Problem solving techniques in childrearing.* San Francisco: Jossey-Bass.

Shweder, R.A., Mahapatra, M., & Miller, J.G. (1987). Culture and moral development. In J. Kagan and S. Lamb (Eds.), *The emergence of morality in young children* (pp. 1–83). Chicago: University of Chicago Press.

Siegel, A.W., & White, S.H. (1982). The child study movement: Early growth and development of the symbolized child. *Advanced Studies in Child Development and Behavior, 17,* 233–285.

Siegler, R.S. (1983). Information processing approaches to development. In P.H. Mussen (Ed.), *Handbook of child psychology: Vol. 1. History, theory, and methods* (4th ed., pp. 103–128). New York: John Wiley.

Siegler, R.S. (1986). *Children's thinking.* Englewood Cliffs, NJ: Prentice-Hall.

Sigel, I.E. (1987). Does hothousing rob children of their childhood? *Early Childhood Research Quarterly, 2,* 211–225.

Silberman, C. (1990). *Crisis in the classroom.* New York: Random House.

Silin, J.G. (1985). Authority as knowledge: A problem of professionalization. *Young Children, 40*(3), 41–46.

Silver, R.A. (1982). Developing cognitive skills through art. In L.G. Katz (Ed.), *Current topics in early childhood education* (Vol. 4, pp. 143–171). Norwood, NJ: Ablex Publishing.

Simons, J.A., & Simons, F.A. (1986). Montessori and regular preschools: A comparison. In L.G. Katz (Ed.), *Current topics in early childhood education* (Vol. 6, pp. 195–223). Norwood, NJ: Ablex Publishing.

Singer, J.L., Singer, D.G., & Rapaczynski, W. (1984, Spring). Family patterns and television viewing as predictors of children's beliefs and aggression. *Journal of Communication,* 73–89.

Skeels, H. (1966). Adult status of children with contrasting early life experiences. *Monographs of the Society for Research in Child Development, 31*(3, Serial No. 105).

Skinner, B.F. (1957). *Verbal behavior.* New York: Appleton-Century-Crofts.

Skinner, B.F. (1969). *Contingencies of reinforcement: A theoretical analysis.* New York: Appleton-Century-Crofts.

Skinner, B.F. (1974). *About behaviorism.* New York: Alfred A. Knopf.

Skinner, L. (1979). *Motor development in the preschool years.* Springfield, IL: Thomas Publishers.

Smilansky, S. (1968). *The effects of sociodramatic play on disadvantaged preschool children.* New York: John Wiley.

Smilansky, S. (1987). *On death: Helping children understand and cope.* New York: Peter Lang.

Smilansky, S. (1990). Sociodramatic play: Its relevance to behavior and achievement in school. In E. Klugman & S. Smilansky (Eds.), *Children's play and learning* (pp. 18–42). New York: Teachers College Press, Columbia University.

Smith, C.A. (1982). *Promoting the social development of young children.* Palo Alto, CA: Mayfield.

Smith, C.A. (1989). *From wonder to wisdom: Using stories to help children grow.* New York: New American Library.

Smith, D. (1991). Here they come: Ready or not! In B. Scales, M. Almy, A. Nicolopoulou, & S. Ervin-Tripp (Eds.), *Play and the social context of development in early care and education* (pp. 51–61). New York: Teachers College Press, Columbia University..

Smith, M.M. (1990). NAEYC annual report. *Young Children, 46*(1), 41–48.

Smith, P.K., & Connolly, K.J. (1980). *The ecology of preschool behaviour.* Cambridge, United Kingdom: Cambridge University Press.

Smith, P.K., & Connolly, K.J. (1981). *The behavioural ecology of the preschool.* Cambridge, United Kingdom: Cambridge University Press.

Smith, R.F. (1982). Early childhood science education: A Piagetian perspective. In J.F. Brown (Ed.), *Curriculum planning for young children* (pp. 143–150). Washington, DC: National Association for the Education of Young Children.

Snow, C.E., & Ninio, A. (1986). The contracts of literacy: What children learn from learning to read books. In W.H. Teale & E. Sulzby (Eds.), *Emergent literacy: Writing and reading* (pp. 116–138). Norwood, NJ: Ablex Publishing.

Sobel, J. (1983). *Everybody wins: Non-competitive games for young children.* New York: Walker.

Soderman, A.K. (1985). Dealing with difficult young children. *Young Children, 40*(5), 15–20.

Spitz, H. (1986). *The raising of intelligence: A selected history of attempts to raise retarded intelligence.* Hillsdale, NJ: Lawrence Erlbaum.

Spitz, R. (1945). Hospitalism.: An inquiry into the genesis of psychiatric conditions in early childhood (Pt. I). *Psychoanalytic Studies of the Child, 1*, 53–74.

Spodek, B. (1985). *Teaching in the early years* (3rd ed.), Englewood Cliffs, NJ: Prentice-Hall.

Spodek, B., Saracho, O., & Lee, R.C. (1984). *Mainstreaming young children.* Belmont, CA: Wadsworth.

Spodek, B., & Saracho, O.N. (1982). The preparation and certification of early childhood personnel. In B. Spodek (Ed.), *Handbook of research in early childhood education.* New York: Free Press.

Spodek, B., & Saracho, O.N. (1994). *Dealing with individual differences in the early childhood classroom.* New York: Longman.

Sponseller, D. (1982). Play and early education. In B. Spodek (Ed.), *Handbook of research in early childhood education* (pp. 215–241). New York: Free Press.

Stapleford, E.M. (1976). *History of the Day Nurseries Branch: A personal record.* Toronto: Ontario Ministry of Community and Social Services.

Statistics Canada. (1985). *Women in Canada.* Ottawa: Statistics Canada.

Statistics Canada. (1991). *Families: Number, type and structure.* Catalogue No. 93-312. Ottawa: Supply and Services Canada.

Statistics Canada. (1993a). *Basic facts on families in Canada, Past and present.* Catalogue No. 89-516. Ottawa: Supply and Services Canada.

Statistics Canada. (1993b). *Labour force activity of women by presence of children.* Ottawa: Statistics Canada.

Stevens, H. (1992). A socio-geographic overview of Manitoba. In A. Pence (Ed.), *Canadian child care in context: Perspectives from the provinces and territories.* Ottawa: Statistics Canada & Health and Welfare Canada.

Stevenson, J. (1990). The cooperative preschool model in Canada. In I. Doxey (Ed.), *Child care and education: Canadian dimensions* (pp. 221–239). Toronto: Nelson Canada.

Stevenson, R.L. (1985). *A child's garden of verse* (M. Forman, Illus.). New York: Delacorte Press.

Stone, J. (1993). Caregiver and teacher language: Responsive or restrictive? *Young Children, 48,* 12–18.

Suggestions for developing positive racial attitudes. (1980). *Interracial Books for Children Bulletin, 11*(3–4), 10–15.

Sutherland, Z., & Arbuthnot, M.H. (1986). *Children and books* (7th ed.). Glenview, IL: Scott, Foresman.

Swick, K.J. (1994). Family involvement: An empowerment perspective. *Dimensions of Early Childhood, 22*(2), 10–13.

Swigger, K.M., & Swigger, B.K. (1984). Social patterns and computer use among preschool children. *AEDS Journal, 17*(3), 35–41.

Sword, J. (1987). Help! I'm selecting children's books. *Day Care and Early Education, 15*(2), 26–28.

Table toys: A creative curriculum for early childhood. (1979). Washington, DC: Creative Associates.

Teale, W.H., & Martinez, M.G. (1988). Getting on the right road to reading: Bringing books and young children together in the classroom. *Young Children, 44*(1), 10–15.

Teale, W.H., & Sulzby, E. (1986). Emergent literacy as a perspective for examining how young children become writers and readers. In W.H. Teale & E. Sulzby (Eds.), *Emergent literacy: Writing and reading* (pp. vii–xxv). Norwood, NJ: Ablex Publishing.

Thomas, A., & Chess, S. (1969). *Temperament and development.* New York: New York University Press.

Thomas, A., Chess, S., & Birch, H.G. (1968). *Temperament and behavior disorders in children.* New York: New York University Press.

Thomas, R.M. (1990a). *The encyclopedia of human development and education: Theory, research, and studies.* New York: Pergamon Press.

Thomas, R.M. (1990b). Basic concepts and applications of Piagetian cognitive development theory. In R.M. Thomas (Ed.), *The encyclopedia of human development and education: Theory, research, and studies* (pp. 53–56). New York: Pergamon Press.

Thomson, C.L., & Ashton-Lilo, J. (1983). A developmental environment for child care programs. In E.M. Goetz & K.E. Allen (Eds.), Early childhood education: Special environmental, policy, and legal considerations (pp. 93–125). Rockville, MD: Aspen Systems Corp.

Thorndike, R., Hagen, E., & Sattler, J. (1985). *Stanford-Binet Intelligence Scale* (4th ed.). Chicago, IL: Riverside.

Thornton, J.R. (1990). Team teaching: A relationship based on trust and communication. *Young Children, 45*(5), 40–43.

Tietze, W. (1987). A structural model for the evaluation of preschool effects. *Early Childhood Research Quarterly, 2,* 133–153.

Tire hazards, woodworking, and crib safety. (1986). *Young Children, 41*(5), 17–18.

Tizard, B., Mortimer, J., & Burchell, B. (1981). *Involving parents in nursery and infant schools.* Ypsilanti, MI: High/Scope Press.

Torrance, E.P. (1963). Adventuring in creativity. *Childhood Education 40,* 79–87.

Townson, M. (1985). Financing child care through the Canada Assistance Plan. In Status of Women, Canada (Ed.), *Financing child care: Current arrangements. A report prepared for the Task Force on Child Care, Series 1.* Ottawa: Status of Women, Canada.

Trahms, C.M. (1989). Factors that shape food patterns in young children. In P.L. Pipes (Ed.), *Nutrition in infancy and childhood* (4th ed., pp. 160–170). St. Louis, MO: C.V. Mosby.

Tribe, C. (1982). *Profile of three theories: Erikson, Maslow, Piaget.* Dubuque, IA: Kendall/Hunt Publishing.

Truemner, T. (1992). An overview of child care legislation in Saskatchewan. In A. Pence (Ed.), *Canadian child care in context: Perspectives from the provinces and territories.* Ottawa: Statistics Canada & Health and Welfare Canada.

Ulich, R. (1947). *Three thousand years of educational wisdom.* Cambridge, MA: Harvard University Press.

Ulich, R. (1967). Johann Heinrich Pestalozzi. In P. Edwards (Ed.), *The encyclopedia of philosophy* (Vols. 5–6, pp. 121–122). New York: Macmillan and Free Press.

U.S. firms join forces to build daycare centres. (1992, July 10). *The Toronto Star,* p. D1.

Van Heerden, J.R. (1984). Early under-nutrition and mental performance. *International Journal of Early Childhood, 16*(1), 10–16.

Vandell, D.L., & Corasaniti, M.A. (1990). Variations in early child care: Do they predict subsequent social, emotional, and cognitive differences? *Early Childhood Research Quarterly, 5,* 555–572.

Vander Ven, K. (1986). "And you have a ways to go": The current status and emerging issues in training for child care practice. In K. Vander Ven & E. Tittnich (Eds.), *Competent caregivers—Competent children: Training and education for child care practice.* New York: Hawthorne Press.

Varga, D. (1997). *Constructing the child: A history of Canadian daycare.* Toronto: Lorimer.

Vygotsky, L.S. (1962). *Thought and language.* New York: John Wiley.

Vygotsky, L.S. (1976). Play and its role in the mental development of the child. In J. Bruner, A. Jolly, & K. Sylva (Eds.), *Play—Its role in development and evolution* (pp. 537–554). Harmondsworth, United Kingdom: Penguin.

Vygotsky, L.S. (1978a). The prehistory of written language. In M. Cole, V. John-Steiner, S. Scribner, & E. Souberman (Eds.), *Mind and society: The development of higher psychological process* (pp. 105–119). Cambridge, MA: Harvard University Press.

Vygotsky, L.S. (1978b). *Mind in society.* Cambridge, MA: Harvard University Press.

Wade, M.G., & Davis, W.E. (1982). Motor skill development in young children: Current views on assessment and programming. In L.G. Katz (Ed.), *Current topics in early childhood education* (Vol. 4, pp. 55–70). Norwood, NY: Ablex Publishing.

Wadsworth, B.J. (1984). Piaget's theory of cognitive and affective development (3rd ed.). New York: Longman.

Walker, D.K., & Crocker, R.W. (1988). Measuring family systems outcomes. In H.B. Weiss & F.H. Jacobs (Eds.), *Evaluating family programs* (pp. 153–176). New York: Aldine de Gruyter.

Wallerstein, J., Corbin, S.B., & Lewis, J.M. (1988). Children of divorce: A ten-year study. In E.M. Hetherington & J. Arasteh (Eds.), *Impact of divorce, single-parenting and step-parenting on children* (pp. 198–214). Hillsdale, NJ: Lawrence Erlbaum.

Wallerstein, J.S. (1983). Children of divorce: Stress and developmental tasks. In N. Garmezy & M. Rutter (Eds.), *Stress, coping, and development in children* (pp. 265–302). New York: McGraw-Hill.

Walton, S. (1989). Katy learns to read and write. *Young Children, 44*(5), 52–57.

Wash, D.P., & Brand, L.E. (1990). Child day care services: An industry at a crossroads. *Monthly Labor Review, 113*(12), 17–24.

Washington, V., & Oyemade, U.J. (1985). Changing family trends: Head Start must respond. *Young Children, 40*(6), 12–18.

Wass, H. (1984). Concepts of death: A developmental perspective. In H. Wass & C.A. Corr (Eds.), *Childhood and death.* New York: Hemisphere Publishing.

Watson, J.B. (1925a). *Behaviorism.* New York: W.W. Norton.

Watson, J.B. (1925b). What the nursery has to say about instincts. In C. Murchison (Ed.), *Psychologies of 1925.* Worcester, MA: Clark University Press.

Watson, J.B. (1928). *Psychological care of infant and child.* New York: W.W. Norton.

Watson, J.B., & Rayner, R. (1920). Conditioned emotional reactions. *Journal of Experimental Psychology, 3,* 1–4.

Weber, E. (1984). *Ideas influencing early childhood education.* New York: Teachers College Press, Columbia University.

Weber, L.E. (1971). *The English infant school and informal education.* Englewood Cliffs, NJ: Prentice-Hall.

Wechsler, D. (1989). *Wechsler Preschool and Primary Scale of Intelligence-Revised.* San Antonio, TX: Psychological Corp.

Wechsler, D. (1991). *Wechsler Intelligence Scale for Children* (3rd ed.). San Antonio, TX: Psychological Corp.

Weikart, D.P., & Schweinhart, L.J. (1987). The High/Scope cognitively oriented curriculum of early education. In J.L. Roopnarine & J.E. Johnson (Eds.), *Approaches to early childhood education* (pp. 253–267). Columbus, OH: Merrill.

Weikart, D.P., & Schweinhart, L.J. (1993). The High/Scope curriculum for early childhood care and education. In J.L. Roopnarine & J.E. Johnson (Eds.), *Approaches to early childhood education* (2nd ed., pp. 195–208). New York: Merrill.

Weinstein, C.S. (1987). Designing preschool classrooms to support development. In C.S. Weinstein & T.G. David (Eds.), *Spaces for children: The built environment and child development* (pp. 159–185). New York: Plenum Press.

Weiss, H. (1987). Family support and education in early childhood programs. In S.L. Kagan, D.R. Powell, B. Weissbourd, & E.F. Zigler (Eds.), *America's family support programs: Perspectives and prospects* (pp. 133–160). New Haven, CT: Yale University Press.

Werner, E.E. (1984). Resilient children. *Young Children, 40*(1), 68–72.

Werner, E.E. (1986). Resilient children. In H.E. Fitzgerald, & M. G. Walraven (Eds.), *Annual editions: Human development.* Sluice Dock, CT: Dushkin.

Werner, P. (1974). Education of selected movement patterns of preschool children. *Perceptual and Motor Skills, 39,* 795–798.

Wertsch, J.V. (1985). *Vygotsky and the social formation of mind.* Cambridge, MA: Harvard University Press.

West, S. (1988). *A study of compliance with the Day Nurseries Act at full-day child care centres in Metropolitan Toronto.* Toronto: Ministry of Community and Social Services.

White, B. (1968). Informal education during the first months of life. In R.D. Hess & R.M. Bear (Eds.), *Early education.* New York: Aldine-Atherton.

White, B. (1975). *The first three years of life.* Toronto: Prentice-Hall.

Whitebook, M. (1986). The teacher shortage: A professional precipice. *Young Children, 41*(3), 10–11.

Whitebook, M., Howes, C., Darrah, R., & Friedman, J. (1982). Caring for the caregiver: Staff burnout in child care. In L.G. Katz (Ed.), *Current topics in early childhood education* (Vol. 4, pp. 211–235). Norwood, NJ: Ablex Publishing.

Whitebook, M., Howes, C., & Phillips, D. (1989). *Who cares? Child care teachers and the quality of care in America: Executive summary, National Child Care Study.* Oakland, CA: Child Care Employee Project.

Whitebook, M., Phillips, D., & Howes, M. (1993). *National Child Care Staffing Study revisited: Four years in the life of centre-based child care.* Oakland, CA: Child Care Employee Project.

Wilderstrom, A.H. (1986). Educating young handicapped children: What can early childhood education contribute? *Childhood Education 63*(2), 78–83.

Willer, B. (1987). Quality or affordability: Trade-offs for early childhood programs? *Young Children, 42*(6), 41–43.

Willer, B. (1990). Estimating the full cost of quality. In B. Willer (Ed.), *Reaching the full cost of quality in early childhood programs* (p. 55–86). Washington, DC: National Association for the Education of Young Children.

Willer, B., & Bredekamp, S. (1993). A new paradigm of early childhood professional development. *Young Children, 48*(4), 64.

Willert, M.K., & Kamii, C. (1985). Reading in kindergarten: Direct vs. indirect teaching. *Young Children, 40*(4), 3–9.

Williams, T.M. (Ed.). 1986 *The impact of television.* Orlando, FL: Academic Press.

Winner, E. (1986). Where pelicans kiss seals. *Psychology Today, 20,* 24–35.

Wolery, M., Holcombe, A., Venn, M.L., Brookfield, J., Huffman, K., Schroeder, C., Martin, C.G., & Fleming, L.A. (1993). Mainstreaming in early childhood programs: Current status and relevant issues. *Young Children 49*(1), 18–88.

Wolf, A.D. (1990). Art postcards—Another aspect of your aesthetics program? *Young Children, 45*(2), 39–43.

Women's Bureau. (1970a). *Women in the labour force: 1970 facts and figures.* Ottawa: Information Canada.

Women's Bureau. (1970b). *Working mothers and their child care arrangements* (Cat. No. L38–2970). Ottawa: Queen's Printer.

Women's Bureau. (1990). *Women in the labour force* (1990–1991 edition). Ottawa: Supply and Services Canada.

Woodrich, D.L. (1984). *Children's psychological testing: A guide for nonpsychologists.* Baltimore, MD: Paul H. Brookes.

Wortham, S.C. (1990). *Tests and measurement in early childhood education.* Columbus, OH: Merrill.

Wright, M. (1983). *Compensatory education in the preschool: A Canadian approach. The University of Western Ontario preschool project.* Ypsilanti, MI: High/Scope Press.

Yarrow, L.J. (1961). Maternal deprivation: Toward an empirical and conceptual re-evaluation. *Psychological Bulletin, 58,* 459–490.

Yarrow, M.R., Scott, P.M., & Waxler, C.Z. (1973). Learning concern for others. *Developmental Psychology, 8,* 240–260.

Young, B. (1994). Custody disputes and pick up authorization. In E. Essa & R. Young (Eds.), *Introduction to early childhood education* (p. 134). Toronto: Nelson Canada.

Young, R. (1981). *Association for Early Childhood Education, Ontario (AECEO) submission to the Minister of Education.* Toronto: AECEO.

Young, R. (1987). *Bringing the "bedtime story" into inner city classrooms.* Toronto: Queen's Park, Ontario Ministry of Education.

Young, R. (1993a). *The acquisition and use of knowledge about the story schema.* Manuscript submitted for publication, Brock University, St. Catharines, Ontario.

Young, R. (1993b). *Child care in Canada: History, regulation, teacher training, scope, and parental needs.* Manuscript submitted for publication. Brock University, St. Catharines, Ontario.

Young, R., & Shattuck, D. (1993). *The communicative competence of inner-city children.* Manuscript submitted for publication, Brock University, St. Catharines, Ontario.

Ziajka, A. (1983). Microcomputers in early childhood education. *Young Children, 38*(5), 61–67.

Ziemer, M. (1987). Science and the early childhood curriculum: One thing leads to another. *Young Children, 42*(6), 44–51.

Zigler, E.F., & Berman, W. (1973). Discerning the future of early childhood intervention. *American Psychologist, 38,* 894–906.

Zigler, E.F., & Freeman, J. (1987). Head Start: A pioneer of family support. In S.L. Kagan, D.R. Powell, B.F. Weissbourd, & E.F. Zigler (Eds.) *Approaches to early childhood education* (2nd ed., pp. 261–273). Columbus, OH: Merrill.

Zimiles, H. (1987). The Bank Street approach. In J.L. Roopnarine & J.E. Johnson (Eds.), *Approaches to early childhood education* (pp. 163–178). Columbus, OH: Merrill.

Zimiles, H. (1982). Psychodynamic theory of development. In B. Spodek (Ed.), *Handbook of research in early childhood education* (pp. 135–153). New York: Free Press.

Zimiles, H. (1993). The Bank Street approach. In J. L. Rospharine & J.E. Johnson (Eds.). *Approaches to early childhood education.* (2nd ed., pp. 261–273). Colombus, OH: Merrill.

Zion, G. (1965). *Harry by the sea.* New York: Harper & Row.

Zlomke, L., & Piersel, W. (1987). Aggression. In A. Thomas & J. Grimes (Eds.), *Children's needs: Psychological perspectives* (pp. 19–26). Washington, DC: National Association of School Psychologists.

Name Index

Subject Index